Trilogy of Three Romanian Jewish Communities: Bacau, Iasi and Podu Iloaiei

By I. Kara

(Itsik Cara Schwartz)
(1906 - 2001)

Original Books Published in Romanian by Hasefer Publishing House, Bucharest

Itzic Svartz-Kara 1939

Published by JewishGen

An Affiliate of the Museum of Jewish Heritage - A Living Memorial to the Holocaust
New York

Trilogy of Three Romanian Jewish Communities: Bacau, Iasi and Podu Iloaiei

First Printing: August 2016, Av 5776

Layout: Alan Roth, Lynn Mercer and K. M. Elias
Cover Design: Jan R. Fine

Published by JewishGen, Inc.
An Affiliate of the Museum of Jewish Heritage
A Living Memorial to the Holocaust
36 Battery Place, New York, NY 10280

"JewishGen, Inc. is not responsible for inaccuracies or omissions in the original work and makes no representations regarding the accuracy of this translation. Digital images of the original book's contents can be seen online at the New York Public Library Web site."

The mission of the JewishGen organization is to produce a translation of the original work and we cannot verify the accuracy of statements or alter facts cited.

Printed in the United States of America by Lightning Source, Inc.

Library of Congress Control Number (LCCN): 2016935547
ISBN: 978-1-939561-39-8 (hard cover: 480 pages, alk. paper)

Front Cover: FedRom (Federation of Jewish Communities of Romania) (2013)

Back Cover: Chana Gelber, Mr. Kara's sister

JewishGen and the Yizkor-Books-in-Print Project

This book has been published by the **Yizkor-Books-in-Print Project,** as part of the **Yizkor Book Project** of **JewishGen, Inc**.

JewishGen, Inc. is a non-profit organization founded in 1987 as a resource for Jewish genealogy. Its website [www.jewishgen.org] serves as an international clearinghouse and resource center to assist individuals who are researching the history of their Jewish families and the places where they lived. JewishGen provides databases, facilitates discussion groups, and coordinates projects relating to Jewish genealogy and the history of the Jewish people. In 2003, JewishGen became an affiliate of the **Museum of Jewish Heritage - A Living Memorial to the Holocaust** in New York.

The **JewishGen Yizkor Book Project** was organized to make more widely known the existence of Yizkor (Memorial) Books written by survivors and former residents of various Jewish communities throughout the world. Later, volunteers connected to the different destroyed communities began cooperating to have these books translated from the original language—usually Hebrew or Yiddish—into English, thus enabling a wider audience to have access to the valuable information contained within them. As each chapter of these books was translated, it was posted on the JewishGen website and made available to the general public.

The **Yizkor-Books-in-Print Project** began in 2011 as an initiative to print and publish Yizkor Books that had been fully translated, so that hard copies would be available for purchase by the descendants of these communities and also by scholars, universities, synagogues, libraries, and museums.

These Yizkor books have been produced almost entirely through the volunteer effort of researchers from around the world, assisted by donations from private individuals. The books are printed and sold at near cost, so as to make them as affordable as possible. Our goal is to make this important genre of Jewish literature and history available in English in book form, so that people can have the personal histories of their ancestral towns on their bookshelves for themselves and for their children and grandchildren.

A list of all published translated Yizkor Books in the project with prices and ordering information can be found at:
http://www.jewishgen.org/Yizkor/ybip.html

Lance Ackerfeld, Yizkor Book Project Manager

Joel Alpert, Yizkor-Book-in-Print Project Coordinator

This book is presented by the
Yizkor Books in Print Project
Project Coordinator: Joel Alpert

Part of the
Yizkor Books Project of JewishGen, Inc.
Project Manager: Lance Ackerfeld

These books have been produced solely through volunteer effort of individuals from around the world. The books are printed and sold at near cost, so as to make them as affordable as possible.

Our goal is to make this history and important genre of Jewish literature available in English in book form so that people can have the near-personal histories of their ancestral towns on their bookshelves for themselves and for their children and grandchildren.

Any donations to the Yizkor Books Project are appreciated.

Please send donations to:
Yizkor Book Project
JewishGen
36 Battery Place
New York, NY 10280

JewishGen, Inc. is an affiliate of the
Museum of Jewish Heritage
A Living Memorial to the Holocaust

Introduction and Acknowledgements

This book consists of the translation of three of works documenting this history of three important Romanian Jewish communities by I. Kara (Itzhak Schwartz), the noted Jewish Romanian intellectual. HaSefer Publishing House in Bucharest Romania originally published these books in Romanian; the translations are presented herein with their permission.

KM Elias supplied the material on Podu Ilonaiei, which we present exactly as he supplied it to JewishGen, Inc., with the exception of the header. We gratefully thank him for his cooperation in the publication of this book.

Yizkor-Books-In-Print is fortunate to have found Yale Strom and Jeffrey Gorney, who both had met the author, I. Kara and have provided descriptions of the author and their meeting with him. Yale Strom's article includes a biography of I. Kara, written by Kara's brother.

Thanks to Harry Green, who coordinated the translation of the Bacau book and his daughter Leslie Erschen who provided scans of many of the the books images.

Thanks also to Robert Sherins (robert.marlene.sherins@verizon.net) and Jeffrey Gorney for providing images of Iasi.

Kara (Itzhak Schwartz)

Born: Oct. 13, 1906 in Podu Iloaiei
Died May 29, 2001, the 2nd day of Shavuot

Obituary for Itic-Svart Kara, May/2001

The following obituary was delivered by Prof. Dr. Silviu Sanie

The passing of Mr. Kara marks our separation from the representative of an elite generation that had among its last gone to join their ancestors from the Iasi community Dr. S. Kaufman and Prof. S. Friedenthal. It was a *heder* generation for which Yiddish was truly a maternal language. A generation for which life had prepared a road full of obstacles they were the actors and the witnesses of some great catastrophes for the Jewish community.

Itic Svart was born almost 95 years ago in Podu Iloaiei, in a large family where faith and customs were highly respected.

The Svart family gave three personalities to the Jewish culture – Simha, Iulian and Itic – a sculptor, a writer – actor and one who was to manifest interest in many fields.

I. Svart graduated from The Faculty of French Language, but has also been a professor of Yiddish language and he followed this second calling for a longer time and it brought him great satisfactions.

These are some of the Yiddishist's accomplishments:

In 1948, he published a Yiddish language grammar. Within the short period of time when Salom Alechem's language was allowed to affirm itself in schools, his work proved to be most useful.

As the literary secretary of the Jewish State Theatre of Iasi, he translated from several languages into Yiddish and worked hard to improve the quality of the Yiddish language spoken by the actors. He loved the theatre and this is maybe the only area where his brother Iulian had an advantage – he was also an actor.

However, Yiddish is the language of many of Mr. Kara's writings. Certainly, he could have said as Mircea Eliade did about the Romanian language that it is “the language of his dreams”. In Cernauti, he found himself in the proximity of several poets like Itic Manger (who later came to Iasi) and Eliezer Steinberg, in the very core of the cultural life of the “small Vienna”, in the period between the two WW. The writer brought to the public facts and events that he wrote about in the Yiddish papers in Vilna, Warsaw, New York, etc. He coordinated some volumes of the paper “Bucarester Shriftn”. The prose writer wrote many stories, some of them with autobiographic content. He later gathered them in the 1976 printed volume "A Moldavis Ingl" ("A Boy from Moldavia") and, in 1987, "Iurn fon Hofmung" ("Hope Years").

The man who traveled the world all the way to the Soviet Far East where Svart became Kara, the French professor who also spoke Russian and English continued to be the same "Moldavis ingl", but accomplishing many. He received awards from the Israeli Yiddish specialists and FCER's "J. Pineles" award.

The man who started his journey from a *stetl* has also been a folklorist, carefully recording some of the things he felt would disappear together with the world that gave them birth. Proverbs, sayings, children's holiday wishings and many more.

He had a call for history. Like Iacob Psantir in the XIX-th century, I. Kara knew that he had to save for the history the documents and moments of the communities' lives; he also published different testimonies that some considered of minor importance, but he understood their significance. He permanently improved the method, the style as well as the critical apparatus of his works. His writings touched issues from the cultural and socio – economical life. Historiography will remember him as the author of the monographs on Bacau, Podu Iloaiei, that was also published in German by the great humanist E. R. Wiehn, and "Contributions to the History of the Jewish Community of Iasi". He published in museum and academic institutes' magazines.

He published, together with Dr. Stela Cheptea, "Medieval Hebrew Inscriptions (aprox. 300) in Iasi" which was awarded by the Romanian Academy. He was a bibliophile. A scholar.

An unostentatious believer, but possessing extensive knowledge from his childhood and adolescence years (as described in his books), Mr. Kara was one of the main counselors of the Iasi community. He discretely guided the cultural activities, he possessed the skill, the patience and the understanding needed to be a *malomad* and to prepare those who trained to put *tefilim*, he conducted the Seder on Pesach, etc.

He was at the same time one of the main men who attended the *sil.*

He could talk to people of all ages and professions. He also knew, together with the missed Mss. Tili, how to be a pleasant host.

He was a man with an ever strong will to gather knowledge, quickly to adapt to all kinds of situations and places – from Podu Iloaiei. Iasi and Cernauti to the Soviet Far East and Berlin, as a soldier, professor, literary secretary, librarian, community activist and, above all, a writer and a historian. A full life that spread over almost an entire century.

The man we are saying good – bye now to was a complex and important personality, a representative symbol of the Iasi community.

FOREWORD

The genesis of this trilogy occurred when a good friend, Dorothy Klepper, told me that her family came from Iasi, Romania and that she was looking for information about the town of her ancestors. We found that the Yizkor book for the town had been published and also translated on the Yizkor Books project. I also discovered that the author, I. Kara, had also written books on the towns of Bacau and Podu Iloaiei and so decided to combine them into a trilogy of the three Romanian towns by I. Kara. We obtained permission from the Hasefer Publishing House in Bucharest to publish the translations. KM Elias was generously provided the formatted material on Podu Iloaiei, making the assembly of the book much easier. At the IAJGS International Conference on Jewish Genealogy in Boston in 2013, Yale Strom gave a talk on I. Kara, whom he had met, so I asked him to provide any material to enrich the book. I hope the reader finds this material of this remarkable scholar of value and interest.

Joel Alpert, Coordinator of the Yizkor Books in Print Project

January 2016

Map of Romania with the three towns indicated

Geopolitical Information:

Bacau

Bacău, Romania: 46°34' N, 26°54' E

Alternate names for the town are: Alternate names: Bacău [Romanian], Bakou [Yiddish], Barchau [German], Bákó [Hungarian], Baków [Polish], Bacovia [Latvian]

	Town	District	Province	Country
Before WWI (c. 1900):	Bacău	Bacău	Moldavia	Romania
Between the wars (c. 1930):	Bacău	Bacău	Moldavia	Romania
After WWII (c. 1950):	Bacău			Romania
Today (c. 2000):	Bacău			Romania

Jewish Population in 1900: 7,924 (in 1896)

Nearby Jewish Communities:

- Mileştii de Sus 10 miles SE
- Dămieneşti 12 miles NNE
- Buhuşi 14 miles NW
- Izvoru Berheciului 15 miles E
- Răcăciuni 17 miles SSE
- Plopana 17 miles ENE
- Moineşti 21 miles WSW
- Pungeşti 23 miles ENE
- Tazlău 23 miles WNW
- Tîrgu Ocna 24 miles SW
- Roman 24 miles N
- Dofteana 25 miles SW
- Băceşti 25 miles NE
- Ocheni 25 miles SE
- Roznov 26 miles NW
- Căiuţi 27 miles S
- Budeşti 27 miles NNW
- Bozienii de Sus 29 miles NNW

Iasi

Iaşi, Romania: 47°10' N, 27°36' E

Alternate names: Iaşi [Romanian], Yas [Yiddish], Jassy [German, Polish], Jászvásár [Hungarian], Iassy [Russian], Iasy [Ukranian], Yaş [Turkish], Yassy, Yassi, Yashi, Jasi, Socola, Socol, Podgoria, Păcureţ, Păcurari, Munteni, Ilasi, Galata, Copou-Târg, Copou

	Town	District	Province	Country
Before WWI (c. 1900):	Iaşi	Iaşi	Moldavia	Romania
Between the wars (c. 1930):	Iaşi	Iaşi	Moldavia	Romania
After WWII (c. 1950):	Iaşi			Romania
Today (c. 2000):	Iaşi			Romania

Jewish Population in 1900: 39,441 (1899), 33,135 (1941)

Nearby Jewish Communities:

- Sculení 10 miles N
- Ungheni, Moldova 10 miles ENE
- Sculeni, Moldova 10 miles N
- Covasna 16 miles SE
- Podu Iloaiei 16 miles WNW
- Pîrliţa, Moldova 16 miles NE
- Lucăceni, Moldova 20 miles N
- Sîrca 20 miles WNW
- Răducăneni 22 miles SE
- Codăeşti 22 miles SSE
- Corneşti, Moldova 23 miles ENE
- Negreşti 24 miles SSW
- Bivolari 26 miles NNW
- Băceşti 28 miles SW
- Nisporeni, Moldova 28 miles ESE
- Făleşti, Moldova 28 miles N
- Târgu Frumos 28 miles W
- Vărzăreşti, Moldova 29 miles E

Podu Iloaiei

Podu Iloaiei, Romania: 47°13' N, 27°16' E

Alternate names: Podu Iloaiei [Romanian], Podeloy [Yiddish], Podu Iloaie, Podulloae, Podul-Iloaiei, Podul-Iloaei, Podu Iloaei, Podul-Leloaei

	Town	District	Province	Country
Before WWI (c. 1900):	Podu Iloaiei	Iaşi	Moldavia	Romania
Between the wars (c. 1930):	Podu Iloaiei	Iaşi	Moldavia	Romania
After WWII (c. 1950):	Podu Iloaiei			Romania
Today (c. 2000):	Podu Iloaiei			Romania

Jewish Population in 1900: 1,962 (in 1899), 1,601 (in 1930)

Nearby Jewish Communities:

- Sîrca 4 miles WNW
- Târgu Frumos 13 miles W
- Iaşi 16 miles ESE
- Sculení 18 miles ENE
- Sculeni, Moldova 19 miles ENE
- Lucăceni, Moldova 22 miles NE
- Hîrlău 23 miles NW
- Bivolari 23 miles NNE
- Paşcani 25 miles W
- Băceşti 25 miles S
- Ungheni, Moldova 26 miles E
- Roman 26 miles SW
- Negreşti 28 miles SSE
- Frumuşica 28 miles NW
- Lespezi 28 miles WNW
- Pîrliţa, Moldova 29 miles ENE
- Heci 30 miles WNW
- Storeşti 30 miles NW

Notes to the Reader:

Within the text the reader may note "{34}" standing ahead of a paragraph. This indicates that the material translated below was on page 34 of the original book. However, when a paragraph was split between two pages in the original book, the marker is placed in this book after the end of the paragraph for ease of reading.

Also please note that all references within the text of the book to page numbers, refer to the page numbers of the original Yizkor Book.

A list of this book and all books available in the Yizkor-Book-In-Print Project along with prices is available at:

http://www.jewishgen.org/Yizkor/ybip.html

Table of Contents

Memories of a Jewish Ethnographer

By Yale Strom

Intrigued by Iasi's Yiddish theatre history, I traveled there the first time in 1981 (Romania was an important destination on a year-long ethno-musicological trek throughout the East Bloc). My first impressions of Iasi were, quite frankly, disheartening. There were people in long lines waiting to buy bread and long queues in front of various farm wagons for carrots, cabbage and potatoes. Potholes and garbage was strewn about in most of the streets. The electric trams and buses were in a terrible state of disrepair, with doors hanging off the hinges and broken windows; and the few private modes of transportation were trucks that belched thick, black smoke from their broken exhaust pipes. I also noticed a large number of Roma in the city, wearing their distinctive colorful clothes, scarves and hats. Many had horse carts filled with bedding, children and food. They all looked impoverished. At my hotel, there was no hot water, no heat in the rooms and my bed sheets looked as though they had not been cleaned for some time.

The only creatures that seemed to be thriving in the city were the multitudes of stray dogs. Most looked pitifully hungry and mangy, and were scared of human contact. I'd throw pieces of bread to several of them, which of course made me their friend. As I walked they warily followed me from a distance.

The produce stores had very little that looked fresh, and the canned goods, judging by the layers of dust on them, had been there for months. I satisfied my hunger with *langos* – greasy fried Hungarian flatbread with *brinza* (briny sheep's milk cheese), which were sold at kiosks on the street corners. It was hard to imagine the Romania that Yiddish singer-composer Aaron Lebedeff (1873-1960) was writing about in his nostalgic hit Yiddish song "Romania, Romania" in 1925. That anthem to the delights and beauty of Romania included the verse: "Oh, Romania, Romania, was a land so beautiful, so fine..." Alas no longer. To top it off, Romania, more than any other country on my trek, was pervaded by a distinct paranoia, fear and suspicion. It took little time to realize that my movements were being closely monitored by the notorious *Securitate* (secret police) - they first questioned me as I checked into my hotel. Although I am not an especially paranoid person, once in Romania, I started to look over my shoulder a little more, becoming more conscious of my movements. I still had six weeks to go of this precarious Kafkaesque existence. I could hardly have anticipated how much I would grow to love Iasi and the rest of Romania.

I hit the mother lode for my *klezmer* research when I came to Iasi and met Itsik Schwartz (as he spelled it in Romanian, *Svart*), the foremost historian and folklorist of Jewish culture in all of Romania and the world.

Dr. Simon Kaufman (at the time the *rosh kahal* – head of the Jewish community), who worked at the *kehile* offices, introduced me to Schwartz at the kosher canteen when I told him why I had come to Iasi.

Schwartz – or simply "Cara" (his pen name) as everyone in the Jewish community called him – came to the cantina every day to eat his lunch and bring lunch home for his wife Cili, who didn't go out much during the wintertime. He appeared to be in his mid-seventies, about five foot six, with a distinctive pointed nose and graying hair that fell haphazardly over the nape of his neck. On the day I met him, he wore a long black wool coat over his thin, boney frame. He carried a kind of lunchbox made from four aluminum containers, each one smaller than the other, and designed to fit inside of each other. They were held in place by a metal brace, which formed the handle.

He sat down to eat while the waitress took his lunch container to the kitchen to fill it for his wife. Mr. Kaufman came over and said something to Cara in Romanian, Cara nodded his head twice, turned to me while eating his kugel, and in perfect English said: "Please, please sit down. I understand you are a vegetarian *klezmer*. Do you sing Yiddish songs about vegetables?

Cili and Itsik Cara Schwartz (Iasi, Romania, 1994)

Cili and Itsik Cara Schwartz and Yale Strom (Iasi, Romania, 1996)

I laughed and sat down across from this skinny man who ate as if there were no tomorrow (two qualities I shared). He asked me how long I was staying in Iasi. I told him at least two weeks, if not more. He said he would meet me here at the kosher canteen in two days and tell me of the rich history of *klezmer* music in Iasi and its environs. Just before we said goodbye I asked him why Cara was his pen name. He explained it meant 'black' in Turkish. Since his last name Schwartz meant black in Yiddish, and Moldavia had been a Turkish vassal state, Cara was an appropriate pen name. At the front door of the canteen he turned back to me and asked in Yiddish: *"Zingstu vu a zeyg oder a shperel"?* (Do you sing like a saw or a sparrow?) He laughed and quickly walked with a hitch across the street before I could ask him to translate. This was my introduction to Itsik "Cara" Schwartz, the S. Ansky of Moldavia.

Itsik "Cara" Schwartz was born in Podu Iloaiei, a small town just 17 miles west of Iasi, on Oct. 13, 1906. He was the oldest of three boys and one sister. His brothers were Simcha and Julian. Simcha was involved in theatre as a writer. He worked in the *Hakl Bakl* theatre in Paris (1945-56) and became a well-known sculptor in Romania. Julian was an actor and writer and wrote many essays and several books on Yiddish folk songs, Yiddish literature and Jewish culture in Romania. And then there was Cara. His community activity in Iasi began in 1924 with his involvement in the "*Kultur –Lige.*" (Culture League). Cara's sister was the only European exile, moving to Toronto after the war.

Julian, Cara's brother, recalls: "I was working in a library and he gave lectures on literature. I was three and a half years younger than him and I remember he used to read a lot on various subject matters, for example, *belles lettres*, politics, novels and dramas. He would read so quickly as if swallowing the pages of the book.

I had the opportunity to be in the same literary circle as my brother as a guest with his students. It was held in at a family holiday home. And when I came in he asked who I was? He acted the part of this well-known scholar of literature with all of his jokes, stories and humor that was part of his personality.

Early on my brother had an interest in Yiddish theatre and began his professional career acting as well as writing. Once in 1922 there was a play Itsik Cara translated called: "The Siege of Tulchin" which was presented in Podolia (Tulchyn, Ukraine) and starred Gedalia Vestheler and Itsik Cara, both from Iasi. It was the beginning of winter and I traveled along this cold somewhat snowy way from Iasi to Podolia. I arrived from Iasi just before the start of the performance in the large auditorium in the Romanian Jewish School. I was a bit tired from the difficult travel that was more than twenty kilometers away. My brother was pleased to see me.

In 1926 he began his pedagogical activity at what was then called "The Romanian Yiddish Folks-School" in Iasi. In 1928 he went to Cernauti, in Bukowina (today Chernitvtsi, Ukraine) to celebrate and honor the "Czernowitzer Yiddish Language Conference" as a delegate from the Iasi "*Kultur-Lige.*" A year later he traveled to back Cernauti where he was a teacher in the professional Jewish School Number 4. Then in the summer time he traveled to the summer colonies where he was a founder of this school the "Yiddish Linguists Seminar" Finally in 1934 Itsik Cara finished studying at the faculty of Romanian Philology and Philosophy in Cernauti.

His name was often seen in many different Yiddish journals and newspapers like: the Bucharest paper "Undzer Veyg, (Our Way)" "Di Vokh, (The Week)" "Shoybn, (Window Pane)" the Szigheter Paper "Oysgang, (Exit)" and the Czernowitzer Bleter, (Czernowitzer Pages)" therefore I must say he is one of the foremost critics of Yiddish literature like Yankl Yakir, and Benyomin Tushnitsky. These people and Itsik Cara gave to the outside world an impression that Jewish culture in Romania was of a high stature. Thus this was the first epoch of I. Cara's life from 1924-1944. Then as he matured he did a major scientific research about the Czernowitzer burial society from burial society's archives (Pinkas) from 1768 for the YIVO Bleter No. 5 in 1939. And in the same year he catalogued all the (Pinkas') Jewish archives in all of Romania. He also helped edited many Yiddish stories from such writers as: Leyb Druker, Meyer Kharets, Wolf Tambur, Hersh Leyb, and Eliezer Shteynberg. At this time he began to travel to some of the smaller villages Moldavia visiting Jewish families and conducting ethnographic research. There he collected Yiddish folk stories, Yiddish expressions, Yiddish songs, and was curious to know about everyday life for these Jews. Itsik Cara was meticulous in taking excellent notes and asking insightful questions. All of this research was done in the *mame-loshn*, (mother-tongue) Yiddish.

From 1936 to 1944 – a long eight years I did not see my brother until he came home from the Front. He fought in the Soviet army against the Hitler desecrators. He was then 38 years old. He was older, exhausted and his hair was thinner and grayer. You could see the signs of his suffering. However he was full of hope and courage. During the evacuation all the soldiers slept on the bare ground. His life often hung like a hair just pulled out and floating in the air.

Life during the war was difficult especially through the bombings. He was like a wanderer in the desert during these difficult times among these wild animals. He once came upon a Jewish man who was learned and studied all the time who was starving. He tried to help him with some food but suddenly the Nazi fiends started shooting. The old Jew was immediately killed and luckily Itsik Cara was only wounded and was taken to a field hospital where eventually he healed. No sooner had he healed then he went willingly back to the army fighting on the front. In the middle of this hell Cara wrote songs that were filled with optimism. I would have to say that through fire and storms "This I believe – *Ani Maamin*" Cara.

He married the well-known Lycee professor of history Dr. Herzog's daughter Ana in 1942. She had worked in a children's home in Bacau. After the war encouraged by his wife he began his work on the history of the Jews of Romania. Then harsh living conditions after the war, little food and heat during the winters, disease all around proved difficult for Ana. She soon became very ill and died from a terrible sickness in 1947. He was all alone and found comfort only in his work.

In 1946 Itsik Cara published in the YIVO Bleter vol. 27 where he wrote a short interesting piece about an unknown song from Avram Goldfaden that he found in town's archives. It was printed in Bacau in a pamphlet in Romanian called '*Marturii din Veacuri*' (The evidence of generations). Soon he opened the "Friends of Jewish Scientific Research Institute in Iasi." This was heady work and the first of its kind in Romania. A number of the members of the institute were members from Romania as well as outside of its borders. Their research was published in "*Varshever Bleter* (Warsaw Pages) for History," "YIVO *Bleter*," and *Yidishe Kultur*," in New York in the *Bukareshter Tsyatshriftn* (periodicals), and which was issued by the Romanian academy. They were busy for two years researching all of the thousands of Jewish communities in Romania.

Itsik Cara was a good essayist and theatre critic and began to get the attention of his fellow critics. He never merited any criticisms and compliments. From his accurate voice came only restorative words. He had no tolerance and compulsion to just criticize.

Then there was a period when we were both busy in our lives we did not see each other for a while. Then on one mild winter day with the sun touching the snow that had fallen on the Bucharest streets the night before, I found myself in the State archives. I was researching material about *klezmers* and Yiddish theatre of the past. Suddenly there was Itsik Cara sent officially from Iasi to the same archives. He was now the secretary of literature in the new Romanian Yiddish State Theatre. And thus a second epoch began in Itsik Cara's life.

Itsik Cara continued to do his ethnographic research and write about his findings. One of his monumental research projects he wrote about was on the history of Yiddish theatre in Romania. Itsik Cara was also very aware that if Yiddish theatre was to continue on for more generations the Jewish youth had to be inspired to attend the performances and to read the plays and he began to mobilize the children to come to the performances of "Children's Section" in the Iasi Yiddish State Theatre. Itsik Cara now was the literature secretary in the Yiddish theatre where he translated plays and wrote the theatre programs in Yiddish. Every Yiddish program had to be prepared for the theatre performances and all of the local social events. Then in 1948 the Federation of Jewish Communities printed for the teacher courses throughout the country a book on Yiddish grammar by Itsik Cara. He understood what good would it be if the Jewish youth did not understand Yiddish? How could they then appreciate Yiddish theatre and literature?

In that same year Itsik Cara he also helped to present three new works in both State Yiddish theatres (Iasi and Bucharest) they were: "*Gibe Gime*" by Goldfaden, "The Magical Tailor" by Sholem Aleichem and "Hershl of Ostropol" by Moshe Gershonzon and more than thirty other texts were by himself or in conjunction with someone else.

In all his years working at the Yiddish theatres he translated nearly 53 plays for the theatre from Russian, Romanian and French and also wrote reviews of each performance. You should understand that his fruitful activities stimulated him to write more articles and essays and only enriched the director and pedagogue from the Iasi Yiddish theatre, the famous personality of Jewish culture Iza Shapiro. At the same time Itsik Cara printed some new material on the history of Yiddish theatre in Romania in the *Yivo – Bleter.*

Every year I have visited my brother at his apartment located in one of the blockhouses in the central part of Iasi. In his study we have had many discussions. Sitting by the open window I can see the city center of Iasi covered in mosaics. A spring breeze blows in through the window and the music from the radio floods the room where we are talking. On the table is some tea and Cili's cherry cheese kugl.

Itsik Cara owns a rich library of Judaica: religious books and objects, old Yiddish printed material, Iasi publications, bibliophile rarities, etc. In the second room hanging in the walls are paintings from his friend Artur Kolnik, Shlomo Lerner, V. Dobryin and Izu Sherf.

Our conversation was about the different work he was doing. It was his intention to create a monumental work about the development of the historical Jewish community in Romania and their aspirations and struggles. The emphasis was the economic and cultural history. His research and writing kept him busy through the 1960's. In 1962 he stopped working full time for the State Yiddish Theatres in Iasi and in Bucharest. Then the third epoch began with his new creativities.

There is so much to describe to you from the vast number of essays my brother wrote dealing with the Jewish history in Romania I will mention only a few: "*Khasidism* and the Enlightenment in Romania," A Brief Look at the Social Movement of the History of Yiddish Culture in the last 150 years in Romania, The Social Economic Structure of the Romanian Jews and Their Dealings with the Theatre Studio Fidelio, Jewish Guilds in Romania in the 18th and 19th centuries, and Jewish Business Correspondence in Moldavia. All of this was very informative to me. He finally published two volumes about the history of the Jews in Romania, the first volume covering their lives through 1848 and the second volume from 1848 to 1917. Both volumes were printed in Romanian and Yiddish. For the sake of not writing more about his publications let me just say his bibliography numbers 418 titles dealing with Yiddish culture and Jewish history and a considerable number pertinent articles on the Romanian culture and history."

The section you just read came from Julian Schwartz's book "Portraits and Essays" (1979). Cara gave me a copy of this book on our first meeting in his apartment, which I vividly remember. Cara's apartment was often the first stop for any one doing some kind of Jewish research, since he lived only a few blocks away from the train station. Cara remained prolific through the 1980's and 1990's, writing the monographs of the Jewish communities in Podu Iloaie, Bacau and Iasi that were published by the Hasefer Publishing House in Bucharest Romania. He also twice received literary awards in Israel, and he received the Hurmuzachi history Award of the Romanian Academy for 1991.

Before I close this short essay on Itsik Cara Schwartz, I want to tell to short stories that will give you essential insight into Cara's *mentshlekayt* and scholarly prowess. In 1993, while again conducting ethnographic research in Romania, I visited Cara's apartment at the same time a film crew was there. They were shooting a documentary film about the Jewish life that had existed before the Holocaust and what existed today, and Cara was one of the "talking heads." At the same time, some guests from France were visiting. While all of the film preparation was taking place, Cara was holding conversations with the film crew in Russian, French with his visitors, Hebrew with one of his French guests, English with me and Yiddish with his wife. He never missed a beat and was as animated as ever.

Then, in early spring 1996, I traveled with my future wife to Romania. Her paternal side of the family was from Iasi and Targu Frumos, so I knew she had to meet Cara. We all sat down in Cara's and Cili's living room, still as filled with books, records, paintings, photos, art

And *tsotskes*. Cili only spoke Yiddish, so I translated for my wife. After a conversation about Jewish life in Targu Frumos, looking at some books to see if we could find any mention of my wife's grandparents, Cili invited Elizabeth into the kitchen while she made some simple sugar cookies. This was a real treat, watching Cili measure with her fingers, a pinch here and a handful there while regaling us with stories of her childhood. Cara was the obvious scholar known to the world, but Cili in her own right knew so much about Jewish life before and after the Holocaust in Moldavia as well. After putting the cookies into the oven to bake, we once again retired to the living room, this time to listen to Cili reminisce and sing Jewish melodies she remembered from her childhood. After a while my wife (who has a very sensitive nose) smelled something burning in the kitchen and sure enough most of the *gebeks* (simple sugar cookies) were burnt. We ate them anyhow, washed down with delicious sour cherry juice. It couldn't have been more delicious.

I will always be grateful to Itsik Cara Schwartz for helping me with my ethnographic research, introducing me to some great *klezmer* musicians in Iasi and just being the wonderful teacher he was. He was truly a *bal-toyve* (benefactor) of Yiddish culture.

Itsik Cara Schwartz and Yale Strom (Iasi, Romania)

Yale Strom is an ethnographer who has focused the last 30 years of his research among the Jewish and Roma communities of Eastern Europe. His research has resulted in 14 books. 15 recordings and 9 documentary films, 4 plays and many photograph exhibitions throughout the world. He is a professor and artist-in-residence in the Jewish Studies Program at San Diego State University.

Meeting I. Kara

By Jeffrey Gorney

In autumn of 1994 I visited Romania for the first time, accompanied by my mother. Ours was a genealogical quest, and a personal contact from New York City arranged for us to visit the city of Iasi. where my grandparents came from. That was where I met Itic Kara, recalled in my recent memoir, MYSTERIOUS PLACES (Friesen Press), about travel and genealogical research in Romania....

"We arrive at the Great Synagogue in Iasi on Rosh Hashanah. There was once in Iasi a great Jewish presence. At the outbreak of World War II, about 150,00 people lived here, one quarter of whom were Jews. Today only several hundred remain, mostly the elderly or those who have been left behind.

. Of the approximately 127 synagogues that lined the avenues of this city prior to World War II, only The Great Synagogue survives. It is also the oldest, "built in 1570," a sign on the stucco façade advises, then "rebuilt in 1670 after an earthquake." Contrary to its imposing name the Great Synagogue is simple in scale and inviting in presence. On its silvery domed roof A Star of David shimmers like a glimmer in God's eye.

In front of the curled wrought iron gate, a few men and women mill about, and we are shortly showered with greeting. "They knew you were coming," says our contact in Romania. "They were waiting."

Once again, as on our cross-Romania train trip, we are accidental celebrities. Luisa asks my mother to deliver a message to her cousin in Queens. Radu tells us his son has opened a computer supply store in Iasi. Miriam says her biggest regret is not moving to Israel with her children. "Fate is odd," she goes on, saying her son is leaving Israel for a job in Germany, a plum career move.

We are certain my mother's fluency in Yiddish will come in handy. "You speak Yiddish?" says Titi, a stocky middle-aged woman in a pale green suit. "Oh my God," she burbles on, "No one under sixty speaks Yiddish. Oh, my God." A pregnant pause. "Do you speak French?"

"Yiddish? It disappeared," says old Malvina. "Young people, they got *famisht mit de goyim*, literally mixed-up with the non-Jews, undoubtedly the most colorful euphemism ever coined for assimilation. Malvina thinks for a long minute, and then looks deep into my mother's eyes. "You speak French?"

And so it goes, proof of the saying "Old Romanians never die, they just go to Paris." The French connection is even more apparent once we enter the synagogue. Grand chandeliers and sophisticated décor sparkle in ornate defiance of the temple's simple extrerior, Cases of polished wood and glass showcase antique and fine-looking plates, menorahs, candlesticks, and prayer books.

After services, outside the temple, people swarm around us and everyone has something to say. Titi suggests we visit the Botanica Gradina, part of the Copou Park, which is where my Uncle Viktor once ran a beer garden. Alma tells us she is sure she is related to us, she can see it in our eyes, she says, and to prove the point, she pulls out a picture of her grandson who bears no resemblance to anyone.

But the best of the bunch is Itic Kara. A popular lecturer and senior academic, the continental Kara wears a beret, as did many of the men in the synagogue. Elderly but spry, he speaks animatedly about his latest project; a book on the overlooked role of Jews in Romanian arts and letters in the early part the 20th century....

"Most of Romania's great writers and artists were Jews,' he says, "but they often changed their names to hide their Jewish identities." He cites Tristan Tsara and Marcel Yanku as examples. "So we have not gotten the credit we deserve for our very big contributions"

We talk and talk and before saying goodbye, I comment on surname. "Kara is such a beautiful sounding name," I say.

"It's not my real name," he answers. "What you might call aprofessional name."

"What is your real name?"

"Schwartz.

Itic Svartz-Kara, as he was officially known, gifted me with a picture of himself, taken decades earlier when he was a young Romanian soldier. His generous nature and passion for honoring Jewish life in Iasi and Romania at large was evident even in our brief meeting.

###

I. KARA
JEWISH COMMUNITY IN BACAU

EPITROPIA COMUNITATIL ISRAEL
No. 421
Bucharest 1995

Editura
Hasefer

Bratianu
The Jewish Community in Bacau by I.Kara

Federation of Jewish Communities in Romania and Centrul Pentru

This book has been accomplished with the help of the Jewish Community in Bacau through Iosif Antoniu, Iosca Brill, Iosif Leibu, Carol Isac, Gheza Lovingher, Carol Marcusohn, Hary Rotman, Arion Simhas, Ernest Simon.

Some of the documents related to the history of Jewish people in Bacau have been submitted by Professor Dumitru Zaharia.

The material in this book has been put together by C. Litman.

This book has been written with the material help of DITA and MUNDI, in memory of their parents EVELINA and ITIC BRAUNSTEIN.

We wish to express our gratitude for their support to the following sources:

- States' Archives, offices Bacau and Iasi
- The Central Archive of the History of Jewish People – Jerusalem (Israel)
- The A.C.M.E.O.R. Archive– Tel-Aviv (Israel)

This English translation is credited to Ruth Blanch, Toronto, Canada; Dana Melnic, Toronto, Canada; Daniela Cornestan, Iasi, Romania; Leslie Erschen, Cape Coral, FL; and Harry Green, N. Ft. Myers, FL.

Editor Paul Litman

Graphics and pictures ... Valeriu Giodac

Table of Contents

FOREWORD

The publishing house "HASEFER" proposed the writing of a second volume of the collection the book "THE JEWISH COMMUNITY IN ...."

The first volume of the collection describes the life of Jewish people in PODUL ILOAIEI. This volume describes the life of another Jewish community, the one from the town of Bacau.

These books are very important to preserve the history of the Jewish people from the past and the small towns they lived in.

This work contains information regarding the location, the traditional style of living and governing organisations of the Jewish population who lived in the city situated on the banks of the river Bistrita. Jewish people had lived there ever since the XVIIth century, and their fate was often common with that of the Romanian population.

The Jews in Bacau were present at all the important events in the history of Romania. They were amongst the ones fighting for a modern society, for the unification of all the Romanian provinces and for independence of the country.

In the first World War they fought for the ideals of the whole nation, and their graves stand as proof.

As you read this book you will find a very comprehensive story describing everyday life of the Jewish population, active in every aspect of the economic, cultural and spiritual life.

We acknowledge the valuable contribution of all who assisted the respected historian I.Svart-Kara in gathering the documents necessary for writing this book, but especially the expertise of Dr.I.Svart-Kara in culling from archived documents, information that has developed an authentic image of a world that existed, and which has left behind proof of a substantial presence in all aspects of life.

We hope that this historical work which will reference more monographs, will enrich the knowledge about the Jewish communities in Romania, thus supporting an unbiased portrayal of the Jewish community and will contribute to bringing everyone together.

I have said this before and have also written about it many times: knowledge brings people together while ignorance sets them apart!

Prof. N. Cajal
15 February 1995

A. DEMOGRAPHIC EVOLUTION OF JEWISH POPULATION IN BACAU.
THE PARTICIPATION IN THE ECONOMIC LIFE AND ASPECTS OF RELATIONS WITH THE ROMANIAN POPULATION

I. The Jewish presence in Bacau in the XVIIIth century.

"Bacau, like all the other medieval towns in Moldova, had its beginnings in an ancient rural setting, protected by forests and waters, at the junction of rivers Siret and Bistrita. Long before the actual development of the feudal state of Moldova, this rural setting became more important than the neighbouring villages, due to its location [...] which enabled the population to develop a more active commercial life. This was the place where peasants from all neighbouring towns came to sell their products and to buy some of the necessities of their everyday lives. Mountain people and prairie people met here. It was a place of both passing through and rest for the merchants and carriers who used the transcontinental road that was parallel to the river Siret [...]. The earliest documented mention about Bacau is found in the commercial literature from 1408 written by Alexander the Good to the merchants of Liov [...]. In this document and in the following ones, Bacau is mentioned as a commercial and trade center. The continuous development of the economic life made it possible for Bacau to become the residence of some feudal lords [...]"[1].

The historians mention that Bacau existed since the XVth century as an important customs point on the road which transversed Moldova along the river Siret. "Until the second part of the XVIth century, the town progressed in development, but the Turkish economic monopoly [...] stagnated the economic prosperity of Bacau. In the XVIIth century the economic development of Bacau as well as almost all other Moldavian towns slowed down." [2].

Around the beginning of the XVIIIth century, Bacau became "a small town residing as an oasis on the river Bistrita"[3]. At the time, the town was located in the path of the Turkish and Russian armies, which were fighting on Moldavian ground. The destruction caused by uninterrupted battles was so great that in 1770, the Austrian Frank Joseph Sulzer declared that "Bacau is a big town, which is now empty" [4].

There is evidence that at the beginning of the XVIIIth century a Jewish population existed along side the native population, sharing the hardships of the times. The first to describe the existence of the Jewish population was Iacob Psantir, an avid researcher of Jewish history in Romania. In a book published in 1871, he mentioned: "The Jews must have lived in Bacau 200 years ago since I have found a tomb stone at the cemetery belonging to a Jewish person dated 167 years ago. Therefore, the Jews must have been here 30-40 years. Before this date in order to bury their dead. In this cemetery there are many other tomb stones which cannot be read, since for some the letters are erased by time, while others are buried so deep that I could not dig them up to read. However, the one that I did find and could read has marvellous and legible letters, but somehow was never mentioned in any registry."[5]. The cemetery he's referring to is the one found on the former Cremenei Street. Mr.I.Kara researched this location in 1936 and 1946 and found the tombstone mentioned by Mr.Psantir. He copied the inscription from the stone and published the text in a work where he underlines that this stone dated 1703 couldn't be the oldest one in Bacau, but it bears witness to the fact that at the beginning of the XVIIIth century there existed a Jewish population of numerical significance[6]. The inscription from this tombstone (currently displayed in Bucharest at the Historical Museum of Jewish Communities) reads: "This important man, honourable Aharon, son of departed Josef, died on the 29th of Ijar, buried on the 15th Sivan year 5464" [7]

1. Dumitru Zaharia, Emilia Chiriacescu, Guide to the States Archives, Bacau County, Bucharest, 1979, p. 37.
2. Ibid
3. Dimitrie Cantemir, The Description of Moldavia, Bucharest, 1936
4. F. J. Sulzer, *Geschichte des Transalpinischen Daziens*, 1781, vol. I, p. 219
5. Iacob Psantir, *Sefer divrei haiamim Ieartot Rumenie* – History Book for the Romanian Counties – Iasi, Bidfus H. Goldner, 1871, p. 23-24.
6. Itic Svart (I. Kara), *Testimonies from earlier times*, Bacau, 1947, p. 5 – 10.
7. *Sources and Testimonies regarding Jews in Romania* (I.M.E.R.), vol. II/1, 1988, doc. no. 11, p.10

It is still a mystery why so many days had passed between the death and the burial of Aharon, knowing that in the Jewish tradition it is disrespectful for the dead to wait that long before burying him. After careful consideration, Mr.Kara decided that he had to have died somewhere where there wasn't a Jewish cemetery, and he was buried there temporarily, but later exhumed and transported to Bacau for his final resting-place [8].

Regardless of what the reason was for this decision, what we are interested in is the fact that around the 1700's in Bacau there was a Jewish population and that they had their own cemetery.

However, the question remains with regards to whether the Jewish population in Bacau had existed before the XVIIIth Century. It is appropriate now to mention the existence of an 1887 monograph, edited by the president of the Jewish community of the time, A.D. Birnberg, requested by the historical society "Iuliu Barasch". In this monograph regarding the history of the Jewish society in Bacau which has remained in its original form, Birnberg writes the following: "Our parents have told us that before the present cemetery, there existed an old cemetery that was abandoned because of the plague. The position of the old cemetery is given in two versions. Some say that it was situated under a hill where the Precista Church was, while others believe it was under the hill called Izvoarele" [9].

This implies that the Jewish population in Bacau dates back far before the 1700's. Unfortunately many other elements, which would validate Birnberg's claim are missing. Therefore we don't know whether in 1699, under the reign of the king

Ioan Antohi, the Jew named Lazar was living in Bacau or just came there to solve a monetary conflict he had with a landlady of Gherghel Dumitrasco [10].

There is however, a lot of information attesting to the existence of a local Jewish community in Bacau before the 1800's. There are documents that show that in 1742, the ruler of Moldavia, Constantin Mavrocordat, ordered the sheriff of the county of Bacau to assist the Jews Avram and Boroh in establishing themselves in Bacau. It is worth mentioning "The Defence Book" (probably meaning passport) given to these two Jews which said "I give this book to protect you two Jewish men, Avram and Boroh against anybody who tries to infringe upon your land by horse or carriage. I give them permission to establish themselves in Bacau." In addition, in 1742, the same ruler asked the mayor of Putna to order his employees not to collect taxes from the remaining family of Boroh who lived there[13]. In the cemetery on Cremenei Rd., Mr. I. Kara found a stone dated 1763 with an inscription, which he later translated and published. "[...] the rabbi from Sepetovca, our teacher, Rabbi Ischer Dov, the son of our teacher, the late Rabbi Iehuda Leib. He died in 2 Adar in 5524 by the Jewish calendar (1723). May his soul rest in peace in eternity" [14].

A document dated January 1766, which represents the book of customs from Movilau mentions Moses the Jew from Bacau who paid 25 Grosi for merchandise brought in from abroad. The Jew seems to be "the drunken wolf from Bacau" who doubled as a horse trader, bringing into the
country a horse for which he paid 75 Grosi [15].
From documents dated from the eighth decade of the century we find information regarding the number of Jews living in Bacau at the time. This document represents the census of the Moldavia population done between 1772-1774 when Moldavia supported the Tsar's army against the Turks - a war that ended with a peace treaty at Kuciuk-kainardji. The results of this census completed by the employees of the ruler of Moldavia, were preserved in a Muscovite archive, and were published in Kishinev [16]. The information referring to Bacau, indicated only 69 houses in the community, out of which there were 5 Jewish merchants: Hersh, Avram, Leibu, Marcu, and David[17]. All this information was possible only in communities of at least 20-30 Jewish families.[18] The oldest record in the book of Hevra Kedosa dates to 5534(1774) but the anagram of the title page gives the number 5531 meaning 1770. The Hevra Kedosa book contains a lot of information from the XVIIIth century, especially 1785, 1792, 1797 etc. In an English work ("Yivo Annual", X, 1955 p313) I. Kara reproduced some of those writings. Here is an example from 1798 "Today there was a new member elected to the Hevra Kedosa, the illustrious Zeev Wolf, the son of Ithak Segal. During the first three years he will not have voting rights, and will be very humble. Hol Hamoed Sucot 5558 in the orthodox community of Bacau". Another example is from the spring of 1799: "Today, Monday, the first day of Hol Hamoed Pesach, 5559, we the voters of Hevra Kedosa from Bacau, appoint Manase, the son of Mordehai, as treasurer of the society and Shalom, the son of Iehuda as his assistant, and loyal (neeman) to the society."

8. I. Voledi-Vardi, *The town on the banks of Bistrita river*, vol. I, Tel-Aviv, 1988, p. 14

9. A.D. Birnberg, *The Antiquity of Jews in Bacau*, The Central Archives for the History of the Jewish People, R.M./269, Jerusalem
10. Gh. Ghibanescu, *Sources and Testimonies XIV, XLI*, p. 27-28 and I.M.E.R., vol. II/I, doc. no. LXXV, p. 233-234.
11. I.M.E.R., vol. II/1, doc. no. 169, p.144
12. N. Iorga, *Studies and documents regarding the history of Jews in Romania*
13. I.M.E.R., vol II/1, doc. no. 190, p. 157
14. I. Svart, op. Cit., p. 9
15. I.M.E.R., vol. II/2, Bucharest, 1990, doc. no. 49, p. 60 and *The registry of Customs in Moldavia 1765*, from "Ioan Neculce Bulletin", II/1922, p. 192-272
16. P.G. Dimitriev, *Moldavia in the Feudal Era*, vol. VII, *The Census of the Moldavian People between 1772 –1774.*
17. I.M.E.R. , vol. II/2, doc. no. 84, p. 122

There is another document from the XVIIIth century, dated July 23rd, 1794 which states: "We, the citizens, together with Tanasie, the Judge of the city of Bacau, signed this document prepared by the Jew Leib the lawyer, certifying that the house in the alley behind the Jewish school belongs to Leib the lawyer by decreeing that six meters in front and ten meters in the back is all his. To enforce this document we put our names and fingerprints today 1794, 23rd of July. Me, the Judge Tanasie,; me, Andronic; me Iacob Mocanu; me, Ion Crasmar; me, Ionita Falca; me, Stefan Barana; me, Albul; me, Anton Aflori; me, Iuje; me, Mihai Toma; me, Gheorghe Verce; me Mihai Colta. I wrote on their behalf Alexandru Rusu(?)"[19]

This document is significant in a few ways. First, it signifies that the Jews in Bacau could get approval from the local administration of that time for building houses. It also gives the name of the lawyer representing the Jews in Bacau as Leib. Therefore, it proves that the Jewish community of Bacau was organised, being represented by a lawyer recognised by the local authorities. Finally, it proves that the Jews of Bacau had a "Jewish school" - therefore a house of worship, a synagogue. It was probably of wooden construction, because as mentioned by Dimitrie Cantemir in "Description of Moldova" the laws of the time gave permission to the Jews to have only wooden Synagogues far away from Churches. [20]

We are therefore justified in our belief that towards the end of the XVIIIth century, the Jewish community in Bacau were of a significant number and that more and more Jews were coming to establish themselves there. In fact, during that period, the nobility as well as the ruler of Moldavia were creating advantageous conditions for foreign merchants and tradesmen, many of them Jews, to come and establish themselves in the region. The nobility was interested in populating the villages and small towns emptied by the wars, in order to have the natural richness of the land restored. The rulers encouraged the establishment of merchants and tradesmen in these cities since they constituted an important source of revenue. This process continued in the first few decades of the following century.

In this spirit, the July 23rd document regarding Bacau, ordered by Ioan Sandu Sturza becomes important. This document strengthens the privileges of the citizens and also contains laws meant to attract the foreign merchants and tradesmen of any nationality, some of them Jewish. The Document gave them permission not only to establish themselves in Bacau, but also to own land and to obtain wood for construction from the adjacent forest[21]. It was a judicial act that favoured the development of new economic relations, specifically the economy of trading and had important consequences: growth of the population, expansion of the borough, and the involvement of the new social categories of citizens in the administration of the city. Information regarding the number of Jews in Bacau at the end of the XVIIIth century is obtained from a fiscal document dated 1803, called "Condica Liuzilor" – The Registry of the contributors, which mentions 58 Jews as contributors. We presume that there were at least 58 families of Jews meaning that at that time the Jewish population was circa 230-250 people. A similar number, 232 Jews in 1803 is also mentioned in a different source [22].

18. I. Svart, literary works, p. 11-18
19. States Archives of Iasi, Tr. 381, work 398, brief 104, file 21 and I.M.E.R., vol. II/2, doc. no. 285, p. 413
20. *Yearbook for the Jewish Community,* year XIV, Bucharest, 1890-1891, p.212
21. *Towns and boroughs of Moldavia,* 1960, series A, vol. II, no. 59

II. Information Regarding Jews in Bacau until the Mid XIXth century

Starting in the XIXth century, the sources of documentation regarding Jews in Bacau become more numerous. There are also statistical documents which show that, among other things, the movement of the Jewish population and the role they played in the economic life of the town.

In this historical time, we witness in Moldova the destruction of the feudal system structure through the replacement of the agricultural and forestry with those of the trade economy. The production and distribution of goods gained more and more importance. However, during the first few decades of the century, the size of this process was quite small in Bacau. We come across that from the monograph of the city of Bacau at the beginning of the XIXth century: "In 1820, the city was in its infancy and consisted of very few houses" [23].

In fact, the census of the city of Bacau from 1820 mentions the existence of only 22 houses owned by the Nobility, and a population of only 1000 people in total[24]. Out of the 138 tax payers, there were 55 families of Jews which had an official paper called a Hrisov given by the treasury where they were paying taxes. It is probable that these 55 families consisted of about 200-250 people, meaning that the Jews represented a fifth of the total population. In one of his works, Verax mentions as well a number of 55 families of Jews in Bacau for the year 1820 [25].

The census also mentions the presence in Bacau of persons who were originally from other countries but had retained their original citizenship to benefit from fiscal advantages. It is possible that there were also Jews among them, however few in number since "the census of foreign citizens in Moldavia" from 1824-25 shows that only 57 foreign citizens existed in Bacau at that time; even in

1828, the number of foreign citizens in the county of Bacau did not get larger than 87 people, out of which only 12 resided in the city of Bacau[26].

A more comprehensive statistical data shows up in the next decade. Although some sources[27] note that in 1830 the Jewish population consisted of 220 "souls", there are facts that prove a growth process of the Jewish population had already started.

The treaty of Adrianopol signed in 1828 at the end of the Russian/Turk wars, and which eliminated the Turkish monopoly over the economy of the Romanian Provinces, brought new methods in governing the public affairs. In this sense, according to the stipulations of the Organic Rule, a census had been completed in Moldova every seven years beginning from 1831. The mapping results from the censuses aren't just of a fiscal nature, but give us an appreciation of the demographic evolution of the population.

The researchers contended that the data obtained in that period have a lot of imperfections with an error margin of up to 25%. That explains the necessity of the authorities to improve their methods. Hence, "The Administrative Manual of Moldova" published on April 4th 1839 (vol. I, p. 514) has rules regarding the methods of the census. As relating to the Jews, their census had to be done in tandem with two representatives of the Higher Church (in Iasi) and in the suburbs together with the official government representatives. The heads of the trade guilds had to certify the existence of the tradesmen belonging to their guild, and to submit it to the census registry. Article 23 of this manual, provided that each Jew registered will receive an identity paper valid for one year showing all vital information about them.

Despite the shortcomings of the statistical information, the results obtained through the census showed continual growth of the Jewish population in Bacau.

22. Eugene Tatomir, Contributions To The Study of Jews As Productive Element in the National Economy, Bucharest, 1937, p. 22

23. Costache Radu, Bacau between 1850-1900, 1900, p.5

24. State Archives Iasi, Tr. 166, work 184, Registry 10, p 211-220

25. Verax, La Roumanie et les Juifs – Romania and Jewish People, Bucharest, published by Socec, 1903, p. 8

26. Stela Maries, The Foreign Subjects in Moldavia between 1781-1862, Iasi, 1985, appendix VIII.

27 Eugen Tatomir, literary works, p. 22

The census from 1831 was redone in 1832. "The Statistical Extract" completed in Bacau for the year 1832[28] indicated a total population of 2,903 people. There were 519 Jews, out of which 112 men, 109 women, 126 boys, 111 girls, 51 male servants, and 10 female servants. The Jews represented at this point 13.5% of the total population of the city. In Bacau there were 614 houses.

As can be observed, in the third decade of the century, the total population of Bacau had tripled and the number of Jews had doubled. However, in the socio-economic life of the city there still existed a large feudal system. Almost 400 of the borough's people were sdervants who were owned by the Nobility, and the Church diocese that consisted of 70 people. Furthermore, out of 1843 citizens that made up "the middle class with their families and servants", a large portion was involved in the legal administration of the city. There had existed even from that time different social classes for the production and distribution of merchandise, involved either in commercial activity or as tradesmen and workers in the twelve "factories" mentioned in the census (windmills, candle making, tanneries, etc) and also the eight smith trader shops, and printing press. Verax indicates the following numbers for the year 1831[29]: out of the 2,584 Christians (412 families) there were 110 families of merchants and tradesmen; the Jewish population of 519 souls represented 68 families, who depended on commerce and the trades.

An example of this is shown in the report of the Jewish merchants and tradesmen of Bacau in a document dated 1836:

6 butchers,
30 store keepers,
1 copper maker,
4 silver workers,
3 jewellers,
1 tool and dye maker,
1 bucket maker,
1 pot maker,
1 butcher,
2 milliners,
2 tavern keepers,
2 cobblers,
21 tailors,
1 cantor,
1 teacher,
1 rides operator,
1 stable boy,
1 stone mason,
1 wine maker,
1 glass blower,
1 safar,
1 cap maker,
2 cigarette vendors,
1 velnicer,
and 3 unemployed [30]

Seven years after the first census, in 1838, the town's population was 3,132 and the number of Jews was 1740[31], representing 55% of the total population. The growth of the population (including the Jewish population) shows that Bacau had developed into a centre of production and merchandise trade. Accordingly, new administrative changes were taking place as well. In 1831 the town's guardianship had been founded under the Ministry of the Interior. The appointment of the guardians reflected the growing importance of the new social forces: in 1840, 8 nobles, 8 merchants, and 8 farmers were appointed as guardians. The new economic relations required people with some education. In 1839 the first public elementary school opened. The city was expanding with all its suburbs being developed, amongst which was Leca, where the poor Jewish population and the Gypsies lived.

The following census from 1845 shows this demographic situation: 408 Christian families, 435 Jewish families, some of which were part of the 70 families of foreign subjects. Hence, at this time the proportion of the Jewish families surpasses that of the rest of the population. The census of that year also shows that in Bacau the number of Jewish merchants and tradesmen was 354[32]. One of the community books, which showed all the taxes incurred by the people of Moldova, indicates that the 338 Jewish merchants and tradesmen from Bacau had paid taxes to the government in the amount of $18,315 lei for the year 1845[33].

In 1854, 3,812 Jews lived in Bacau. Although towards the middle of the XIXth century the administration insisted that people renounce their foreign citizenship, (which assured them of economic advantages) we find that in Bacau there still were 31 Jews with foreign citizenship. Among them, 5 were tradesmen: 2 tailors, 1 bucket maker, 1 stone mason, and 1 cobbler [34]. Also in 1854, it is noted that recruits for the army had been required also from the Jewish population from Bacau - 1 recruit for every 70 families[35]. In that same year, the Jewish Merchants Guild had 365 names. In this Guild there were butchers, bakers, vendors, cobblers and other tradesmen with the exception of tailors, boot makers, and milliners who had their own Guilds [36].

28. The States Archives – Iasi, Tr. 644, work 708, no. 107, file 13
Verax, *Literary Works*, p. 372-373
The States Archives – Iasi, Tr. 696, work 372, no. 1, file 554
Eugen Tatomir, literary works, p. 22
Leonid Boicu, *Studies, historical magazine*, no. 3/1963, p. 256-287
The States Archives – Iasi, Tr. 166, work 154, registry 10, P. 211-220, brief 1 558, p. 26-27
Ibid – State Archive of Moldavia, no. 1 778, p. 21
Ibid – Tr. 1772, work 2020, no. 7 984 from May 2nd 1854
Ibid, no 31 984 from May 5th 1854

In one of the lists of all Jews of Bacau sent to Yashi in 1858, there were 817 families and 36 widows, a total of 853 families[37]. According to "The Official Monitor of Moldavia" number 89-1858 in Bacau there were 868 Jewish merchants and qualified tradesmen. The number of Jews in Bacau that year was 3,711, representing 41% of the total population.

Therefore, in the first half the XIXth century, the number of Jewish people living in Bacau grew continuously. There were numerous factors that contributed to this growth. First, there was an increase in the birth rate, (births surpassing deaths). Moreover, the economic and political influx facilitated by the rulers of the time also contributed to the population growth in the period. Yet another factor was the migration of Jewish population from the Nordic border regions of Moldavia towards the south. Furthermore, many of the Jews who had lived previously in the neighbouring villages established themselves in the town whenever they could find better living conditions. In addition there was the migration of Jews from Poland, and Russia forced by the continuous hardships in their country that looked for new places in Moldavia.

Let's view for a moment the physical aspect of Bacau in the mid XIXth century, after the previous decades, when it had expanded and its population increased. We will reproduce here the characterisation of Bacau in those years, given in a monograph: "Bacau was a conglomerate of small wooden houses covered in moss. There were only two main streets (the Royal Street and the main street), other than that, maybe 3 or 4 small districts named after wealthy citizens, merchants, and for poor people some unpaved streets. The town's guardianship, the courthouse, and the police were functioning out of rented houses. The lighting on the streets was primitive: great distances between poles with small lanterns with a candle inside.

The town's water came out of wells, and the garbage was spread on the banks of the Bistrita River. The overcrowding of the houses facilitated fires, like the one that happened in 1853 which destroyed hundreds of houses."[38]

What were the occupations of the Jews of Bacau in the first half of the XIXth century? By and large, a great number participated in commerce and trades, however of small magnitude since their activity is only partially reflected in the archives' papers. To fill in the gaps, we have to use the information we gather from their descendants.

The Jewish merchants sold the products specific to the region (grain, wood, animal products, oil, and other derivatives of these) and brought from other parts products that the local population needed.

Ever since the end of the XVIIIth century there were Jews involved in the trade (and later on the industrialisation) of wood gathered from the extensive forests in the region. A document from 1775 reports "the Sum Received by Hersului Baiesu for lumber" shows us that Jews were directly involved in the export of lumber, which was taken down by barges to Galati [39].

Another occupation, which appealed to many Jews, was the grain trade and other agricultural produce specific to the region. A document from 1805 describes the corn trade between Solomon the Jew and Constantin Nistor from Margineni [40]. In April 1830, Herscu the son of Meier and Marcu the son of Lupu (supervisors) bought 100 sacks of corn flour from the flour maker, Constantin Ciudeu [41]. In 1834 Lupu Boroh bought fruits in the amount of $11,000 lei from the villagers of Dealul Nou [42]. On July 11th 1844, Iancu Baltar the Jew bought from Alecu Ioachim 100 kg of corn (as per L. Saineanu a kilo represented 430 litres of grain) and in 1845 a Jew bought 23 haystacks [43]. In 1805, the Jew Aron bought 223 caskets of wine [44], and he had monetary problems with Vasile son of Gheorghe. In 1842 Avram Hanguil the Jew from Bacau was fighting in court with I. Cofman for 66 caskets of wine [45].

The Archives of Bacau, Bacau City Hall, brief 38/1858, p. 36
38. Costache Radu, *Literary works*, p. 6
39. The Archives of Bacau, doc. II/98 (cat. I, 236)
40. Ibid, IV/194 (cat. I, 506)
41. F.C.E.R. Archive, Bucaharest, IV, a, 111
42. *The Bulletin,* Official Paper, no. 23/1834, p. 257
43. State Archives of Iasi, fond Bacau City Hall, brief 1560/1845
44. State Archives of Bacau, Col. Doc. IV/117 (cat. 1480)
State Archives of Iasi, Bacau Court, Inv. 776, Tr. 764, work 873, no. 9. brief 34

As can be seen, by the end of the XVIIIth century and throughout the XIXth century, the trade with grain, including its export had become the most important occupation of the Jews of Bacau (see also "The year 1848 in the Romanian Counties" VOL II Bucharest 1904 pg. 201).

In memory of the Brill family, who lived in Bacau until after the Second World War, a memorial of their ancestor - Hersel Brill the German - had been preserved. At the end of the XVIIIth century, in the summers, he used to build caravans of barges to float grain and flour to Galati. During the winters he used to organize caravans of wagons transporting grain, flour and venison to Leipzig bringing in return groceries. He had come to Tg. Neamt in Bucovina in 1774 and had moved to Bacau since that was the origin of the barges on the Bistrita; he was buried in Bacau in 1846. His sons continued their father's trade, and while the older son, Itic Leib became a grain merchant, a younger one, Marcu traded in alcoholic beverages; in the winters he used to organise caravans of sleds on which he transported animal pelts and grains to Galati, for export; from there the sleds brought back cotton, manufactured and imported products which he sold to other merchants. In 1838 Marcu Brill, founded in Bacau on the street Mihai Viteazul the first store with cotton articles with a branch in Tg-Ocna, run by Zisu Foscaneau, which served the population of the Trotus River valley. Another son, Strul was trading in salt and agricultural produce.

One of the studies regarding the extraction of salt at Luncani mentioned that around the year 1828 a lot of merchants from Bacau, among them Zisu, had traded salt both from the salt mines of Ocna and from Luncani[46].

Another occupation, which appealed to Jews, was the cattle trade. On August 13th 1805 a Jew from Bacau had bought from a rich woman by the name of Catinca a herd of cows for the sum of $17,000 lei[47].

Another trade with diversified products such as cheese, horilca, etc. is mentioned in "the financial dealing between Bercu I. Marcu and Meeru" [48]. Both in 1832 and 1846 there were some Jews who traded oil products that came from the region. In 1846 they sold in Yashi 76 wagons of crude oil[49].

As mentioned in a document from 1805, there were a lot of Jews involved in the commerce of finished goods[50]. Another document dated 1833 informs us of the sale of 540 meters of cotton fabric[51]. Verax mentions that in 1831 in Bacau, a Jew was selling groceries, two others were selling tobacco, and another one knitted goods [52]. Avram Igner, Zisu Focsaner, and others traded groceries in the first half of the XIXth century.

The 1830 census regarding "markets, kiosks, and other commercial buildings" in Bacau indicates that Itic the Jew had a butchery and Bercu was a hat merchant[53]. It is also mentioned that out of 55 taverns that existed in the town, there was the "basement of Lupu Boroh" with 6 caskets, the one of Itic the Jew with four caskets, and the tavern of Sandu Bacal. The census also mentions the names of other Jews involved in other trades: cotton merchants, grocers and other tradesmen. In 1846 the first glassware store was founded in Bacau and it belonged to Bainglas.

Some Jews owned inns. One document mentions an inn bought from Marioara Mortun by Mendel Pascal and Pinkas Idelstein[54]. On the October 26, 1842 the innkeeper Iancu Falticineanu rented a house from a rich woman signing the following contract "I, the Jewish undersigned Iancu Falticineanu, know that I have rented the houses from Madame Efrasinia Popovici, in the town of Bacau for a year starting from October 19th 1842 till the year 1843 for the sum of $420 lei[55]." We get more information with regards to the trades the Jews participated in from papers from 1831[56]. The trade was done in partnership with either only Jews or between

Jews and Christians - for example, the partnership between Avram, son of Bercu, with the Priest Simion.

States Archives, *125 Years of Activity*, Bucharest 1957, p. 424
47. State Archives of Bacau, Col. Doc. V, no. 15
48. Ibid, VII/183 (cat. I, 1086)
49. C.M. Boicu, *Contributions to the History of Romanian Oil*, Bucharest, 1971, p. 157
50. State Archives of Bacau, Col. Doc. IV, no. 114
51. State Archives of Iasi, Bacau City Hall, 1833
52. Verax, *Literary Works*, table LXV
State Archives of Iasi, Literary Brief D/55, p. 51-54
54. State Archives of Bacau, 1852, p. 35

Some Jews in Bacau were employed by different government offices, that collected taxes either locally or for the entire region. The City Council was responsible for administering local taxes but would often auction off the various duties to the highest bidder. In 1832 Zisu contracted to collect all the taxes for wagons, and oil trade in the area and his competitor was Lupu Boroh [58]. Also in the year 1832 Haim Fosaneanu contracted the taxes for lumber[59]. In 1835 Herscu was in charge of all the fields that belonged to the ruler of the region [60]. Many of these contracts would end up in court since one of the sides would not respect the contract. Another supervisor in Bacau was Itic Leiba, who contracted all the taxes imposed on hard liquor for three years starting January 1843 for the amount of $12, 700 lei annually. Later, L. Carniol took over the charge for hard liquor, for which he made his own seal. On September 23, 1843 the ministry of the interior made the following announcement with regards to "the tax of the scales" in Bacau: Hercu Avram is in charge of taxes over all scales, over all the merchants in Bacau, and he will be paying $3000 lei per year while he is in charge" [61]. For the next three years, in 1853, Mathos the son of Lupu Boroh, took over the duties of the taxes imposed on import/export in Bacau[62]. Many supervisory jobs were done in partnership by Jewish or non Jewish people; for example, in 1845 there was a partnership between Iosif Railer and Constantin Alecu[63] or previously the one between Moisa David and the High Steward Gheorghe Neculai[64].

We can get a fairly good idea about the magnitude of Jewish merchants activity in Bacau reached at that time from some documents in the archive, which describe the buying and selling process of both houses and the land used for construction. For example in 1857 the Jew Alter Braunstein, bought for $6300 lei a kiosk/store with "two rooms in the back of it, all under the same roof" [65]. In that same year, Avram Hertanul bought from Dumitru Mateiu a house lot, witnessed by Iosub Kaufman[66]. In 1856, another kiosk was sold for $200 gold coins[67]. Sometimes there were conflicts; for example in 1835, the merchants from the market had filed a lawsuit against Avram the Jew for four kiosks in Bacau[68].

These exchanges sometimes took place between Jews only: in 1846, Alter the son of Itic, and Iosup the son of Aron, sold a lot to Iosif Ciubotarul, and in 1855, Mathos the son of Zisu sold a kiosk to Herman Firidioarul[69]; after two years he sold the kiosk to Itic son of Strul and his wife Brana Leia[70]. At other times, a Jew was the seller of the house while a Christian was the buyer: In 1818, Isac the Jew sold a house with a fenced lot to Ion Rana for $350 lei. The seller signed in Yiddish. This is the content of the contract[71]: "I, Isac the Jew, together with my wife and son, who will sign here in the city of Bacau, that we have indeed given the papers to Mr. Ion Rana, also of Bacau, of our own free will, stating that we sold him a house with the fenced lot, with all the trees inside the fence, as per the measurements written in the purchasing documents, for the amount of $350 lei which we received in hand. He is the sole proprietor of this property with his descendants forever, and nobody from my family can contest that. This is our signature, August 22nd 1818(three Yiddish Signatures) upon receiving I witnessed and signed Andrei Diaconul. Another witness, Captain Ion Voicu. The judge Dumitru Andrei witnessed signatures from both sides."

55. B.A.R., C.C – 167. See also Manascu Cotter in *Mozaic Cult Magazine*, no. 311/1973
56. State Archives of Bacau, Col. Doc.packet 11/98 and *The Romanian Bee*, Iasi, no.39/1832
57. *The Official Moldavia Bulletin*, Sep. 13, 1833, p. 101
58. C.M. Boicu, *Literary Works*, p. 324
59. State Archives of Iasi, Bacau City Hall, brief 178/1845
60. Ibid, Bacau Court House, letter J, Tr. 346, work 372, no. 186, from Jan. 2nd 1835
61. Ibid, brief 10301, file 115, 117, 121
62. *The Bulletin*, Offical Paper, 1853, p. 267
63. State Archives of Iasi, Bacau City Hall, brief 178/845
64. Ibid, Bacau Court House, Inv. 276, Tr. 580, work 63, no. 32, letter J, brief 2701
65. *The Bulletin*, Offical Paper, Iasi, no. 35 May 6th 1857
66. State Archives of Bacau, Col. Doc.packet X/6 (cat. II, 1419)
67. Ibid, packet X/162 (cat. II, 1400)
68. State Archives of Iasi, Bacau Court House, Tr. 2086, work 232, no.71, brief 110
69. State Archives of Bacau, Col. Doc.packet IX/162 (cat. II, 1400)
70. State Archives of Bacau, Col. Doc.packet X/2 (cat. II, 1480)
71. Ibid, packet V, no. 141, (cat. I, 664)

Sometimes they exchanged lots: in 1851 Anastase Frone exchanged lots with tradesmen Mendel Pascal and Penihus Edelstein[72]. At other times, more complicated operations took place: Hagi Constatin Calin sold a plot in 1858 to Bercu Pistiner[73], who after two years sold a part of this plot to Moise the son of Aron[74] and the rest to Moise son of Cisar, who sold it to Usar Bir Ciobotaru[75].

Some of the tradesmen who had reached a better financial situation also engaged in this kind of transactions. They were another category of Jews who helped shape the development of economic life at that time.

At the end of the XVIIIth century and during the first half of the XIXth century, many Jewish tradesmen contributed to the manufacture and exchange of material goods. A.D. Birnberg mentions in his monograph that the elder generation remembered the tailors Sloime, Slits, and Kiva, who lived at the end of the XVIIIth century. In a census table from 1831, Verax mentions[76] the following categories of Jewish tradesmen in Bacau; 1 tinkerer, 1 silver smith, 1 barber, 11 tailors, 1 butcher, 1 brick maker, 2 bucket repairmen, 21 boot makers, 4 furriers, 2 candle makers, 1 milliner, 2 bread makers, 2 glass blowers, and 4 saddle makers. A document from

1846 mentions other trades the Jewish people were involved in: tool and dye makers, bucket maker, stone masons, scale makers, wagon drivers; compared to 1831 the number of tailors had doubled[77].

The existing documents in archives show that a lot of Jewish tradesmen were engaged in garment manufacturing, hence the tailors became some of the most respected people in town. A.D. Birnberg's Monograph mentions the names of many of them from the middle of the century: Avram Oger, Haim Louz, Moise Leib the son of Iancu, Peiseh Leib, Ioel Itic, Hers Tolber, Ioel Vulechiser, Buium Catis, Bercu Pistiner, Zisu Goldstein, Sloime Bernstein, and Sapse. "The document of forever sold" from 1846 refers to "a lot of land of two yards in the back of the house of Iosif Itic the tailor." In 1847 Avram Croitoru sold a house for $3400 lei [78]. There is also the lot purchased by the tailor Bercu Pistiner in 1856. The number of tailors had become so large that in 1815 they opened their own synagogue on Taverna Street, founded by Moise Leib son of Iancu [79]. Their guild, founded in 1832, was one of the most important guilds of the time, as noted by I. Kara in "Yivo-bleter", volume 45, 1975, p. 96.

We obtained the books of this guild, which shows that they took care of the trade, the guild members' day to day co-existence, and enforcing the religious laws as well as the moral and ethical rules of the guild. This guild book was published in the book of I. Voledi-Vardi "Kehilat Bacau" Tel Aviv, 1990(pg. 225); Lucian Zeev Herscovici did the translation in Hebrew. The rules of the guild outlined that the tailors must stop working before Sabbath and Holy days, and also in the days of Hol Hamoed, during Passover, and Succoth. There was also a stipulation that required members to collect money for charity. The guild's leader had great authority but also very precise responsibilities: he had to personally collect the membership and apprentice fees (article 5). Just like in any other guild, any new member had to pay a registration fee as well as pay for a dinner or luncheon for all guild members (articles 14-18). The guild's leader was the one who settled arguments between members. Tailors who did not belong to the guild or came from a different city could not practice the trade (articles 12, 13, 25). If members engaged in arguments/quarrels, they had to pay fines (article 23). Some of the members of the guild did not renounce their foreign citizenships (it protected them from abuse by local authorities); that explains why part of the fines collected for breaking the rules went to the Austrian Consulate. Article 24 of the guild rules described the organisation of production. Many of the notes in the guild book show in detail the activity of the guild (Appendix II).

72. Ibid, packet LV, 9 (cat. II, 1269)
73. Ibid, packet IX, no. 155
74. Ibid, packet X, no. 123
75. Ibid, packet X/123 (cat. II, 1629)
76. Verax, *Literary Works*, p. 376-377
77. State Archives of Iasi, States Secretary of Moldavia, no. 1778, f. 21
78. *The Bulletin*, Offical Paper, Iasi, 1847, p. 464
79. Marius Mircu, *The Tailor from the Back*, Tel-Aviv, 1988, p. 462

Another category of workers was the one of Cap and winter hat makers. A.D. Birnberg reminds us of a famous hat maker by the name of Haim Weinrauch. In 1834, Itic the hat maker, owed $600 lei to Ilie the Silver smith [80]. In 1853, Smil the cap maker was in litigation for $2000 lei [81]. The defendants were Hersh Stringher, and Elie the Silver smith.

The boot makers in Bacau also were numerous.A.D. Birnberg's Monography mentions some of their names: Volf, Elie, Smil, Hers Volf Cutis and User Bir Abramovici. In 1837, Strule Chiubotarul (Shoemaker) and the Jew Rahmil[82] were on trial for a house in Bacau. In 1847 the boot maker Marcu, son of Meyer borrowed $100 golden coins putting up as collateral his houses in Bacau[83]. In 1851 the boot makers had formed their own guild while the cobblers had their own synagogue. Buium Vianer, Burah God, and Aba Thalpalar were Moccasin makers.

In constructions there were carpenters, bricklayers, and glassmakers. At the time, carpenter Peisah Leib, son of Avram made two kiosks for Zamfira Bacal [84] while Volf Vesler - furniture maker - founded the Borough Parincea. The glassmakers made windows for households [85]. One of those tradesmen, Meyer Leib, a talented sculptor, had sculpted the altar for a synagogue, which burned down in 1853.

Other trades practices at the time included: water wagon and carriage drivers, saddle makers, carriage painters, bakers, and pita makers. The names of some Metal Workers and Silver smiths are mentioned in different legal documents of the time. In 1835, Itic the Silver smith and Itic Cofman were on trial for 2.6 kg of silver (2 ocale, oca=1.291 grams) [86], as were the tax collectors Pinkus and Mandel against Zalman Argintaru (the Silver smith) for some silver jewellery in 1846 [87]. The grocer, Marcu the Jew also found himself in court against the Bucket makers Peret and Iancu for some copper in 1835 [88]. The first oil lamps were made at that time by Vigder Sleifer. One of his sons, Shale Vigderescu was a smith foreman.

There were other tradesmen such as barrel makers, musicians, and writers (Mihel Fone or Burah Sraiber etc.). A document signed in Hebrew dated 1848, shows that the undersigned had effectively delivered two barrels he had made, which were sold by two other people [89]. One of the Musicians who deserves recognition for spreading the Romanian Folk Music was Avram Volf Lemes, the conductor of a folk Jewish Gypsy band.

Some historians, although hostile towards Jews, had to acknowledge the large number of Jewish tradesmen at the time. In 1849, out of all the taxpayers, 351 were Jewish merchants and tradesmen[90].

In fact, in many cases, their profession had become their last name: Croitoru (Tailor), Ciubotaru (Shoe maker), Argintaru (Silver smith), Caciularu (Hat maker), Sepcaru (Cap maker) etc.

During those times, the Jewish population found its niche in the life of the larger community since the relations between them and the Romanians were generally peaceful. I have mentioned before that Jews and non-Jews had formed partnerships, some of them even between priests or lower aristocracy. From a judiciary standpoint, in this era, the Jewish community was considered as a separate religious entity. "The Jewish guild" (or "The Jewish nation) as it had been called, had its leaders elected by its people, and was being recognised by the Romanian authorities as a separate entity. Some of the rabbis, Shohets and cantors functioning at the time were paid either by the community or by the members of the already numerous synagogues. It was in these synagogues where they organized religious elementary schools (heiders) as well as some higher learning schools. To support the schools, in 1837, they formed an organisation named "Talmud Torah". The community had its own cemetery on Cremenei Street, for which the "Sacred Society – Hevra Kedosa"was responsible both with its up keeping as well as ensuring that religious rules of burial were followed.

80. State Archives of Iasi, brief 583/1843
81. Ibid, brief 154, March 23rd 1853
82. State Archives of Iasi, Bacau Court House, Tr. 371, work 462, letter J, brief 1973, no. 46
83. *The Bulletin*, Offical Paper, no. 41/1847, p. 226
84. Ibid, 1841, p. 202
85. State Archives of Iasi, Bacau City Hall, letter J, brief 297, Oct. 7th 1835
86. *The Bulletin*, Offical Paper, 1835, p. 609
87. State Archives of Iasi, Bacau City Hall, brief 113/1846
88. State Archives of Iasi, Bacau City Hall, brief 135, May 2nd 1832
89. State Archives of Bacau, 1848, packet IX, no. 3000
90. M. Soutzo, *Notions sur la Moldavie*, 1849, p. 22

Some of the trade guilds had organised themselves (such as the Tailor's guild – Poalei Tedek). They also initiated organisations for social assistance such as Ghemilat Hasadim. "The Jewish Guild", represented by the their own elected leaders, was in permanent contact with the authorities, and intervened only in special cases, eventually impelling the Jewish population to gradually adapt to the evolution of the Moldavian society. For example: Both the general tendency of the era as well as Jewish tradition recommended that all litigations should be settled within the Jewish Nation or Guild, in front of the Rabbi, or other members of the guild chosen by the litigants.

The weak organisation of both the judicial and law enforcement systems of the time justified this practice. However, there are numerous documents in the archives showing that many Jews were abandoning this practice and were adapting to the rules followed by the general population. During this time there had been many trials in the local court in Bacau. On March 24, 1837, Mariam Beila was in litigation with her husband Lupu Volf over her dowry[91]; again in 1838 she was in the court for the estate matters of her brother who had passed away [92]. In 1841 Buna Ruhla, Haim Focsaneanu's wife was in litigation for her daughter's dowry contract, against the wife of Iancu Ehrlich [93]. On May 6th 1841, Alter Ruhla, Peste Alb's (White Fish) wife was in litigation with her husband for some money. There were many similar litigations[94].

Sometimes prejudice took over and created conflicts between the Romanian and Jewish population. In one of his works, written in Yiddish, Iacob Psantir describes an event that took place in Bacau in 1824. According to Psantir, in the story, the woman uses one of the oldest prejudices against Jews - accusing them of ritual murder [95]. Psantir had been told this story by the old Tvi Hers Caizer, the son of the hero from the story, and it was confirmed by the elders Hers Teper, and David Iancu son of Rhamil. Later, Lazar Schein (later named Lazar Saineanu) used and completed this source of information and published the essay “Ritual Sacrifice Indictment in Bacau” in his work called “The Blood Letting Slander and its History in Romania” [96] in 1824. In the same year, a similar event took place in Bacau. A woman sold her four-year-old daughter to some Turk merchants, but being afraid of public scrutiny, she let out a rumour that her daughter had disappeared and that the Jewish community should be searched since they were the ones needing blood for Passover. About two days prior to this, the new Shohet who was temporarily dwelling in the house of one of the community’s members, wasn’t feeling well, so he called the doctor and donated some blood; the basin with the blood was discarded in the back yard behind his residence. Meanwhile, the local police being alarmed by the mother’s cries for her daughter, went to search the Jewish quarters house by house until they reached the Shohet’s quarters, and found the discarded blood and vessel in the backyard. Taking the vessel as proof of the girl’s murder, they arrested the owner of the house, his wife, and children; they tortured them but could not get them to confess to the crime, but rather, all they got was the truth that the doctor confirmed.

However, when they were looking for the Shohet, he had disappeared and the police could not free the arrested people without his testimony. The non-Jewish population lost patience, and started torturing, and robbing the whole Jewish community. While the entire Jewish community lived in fear, a German windmill owner, travelling outside the city, happened to be in the Tavern where the Turks left the little girl. Knowing the situation was getting out of hand and recognising the little girl, he returned her back to the police in Bacau. The Jews were set free, and the Shohet who was wondering through the mountains out of fear for his life, returned to the community.

91. State Archives of Iasi, Bacau Court House, Tr. 341, work 462, brief 1989
92. Ibid, Inv. 59, brief 2504, Jan. 18th 1838
93. Ibid, Inv. 276, Tr. 769, work 873, Letter J, no. 8, brief 3591, Oct. 27, 1841
94. State Archives of Iasi, Bacau Court House, Tr. 731, work 320, brief 3517
95. I. Psantir, *Lecorot haiehudim be Rumania (Regarding The History of Jewish People in Romania)*, Lemberg, 1873, p. 142
96. *Yearbook for Jewish People*, year V, Bucharest, 1881-1882, p. 69-70

Having gone through such dramatic moments, the Jews in Bacau continued to work and adapt to the life of the society and became helpful to all those around. A significant manifestation of this aspect is shown in a document addressed to the City Hall on May 28th 1847: “the Jewish nation of this city” asks for the City Hall’s approval to open a hospital which would “beautify the city, and be a monument to the population of this region.” The hospital will be maintained by the Jewish nation, and it would be supported financially by the taxes imposed on the Hard liquor bought and sold by Jews as follows: one penny for the buyer and seller, six pennies for each casket of wine which the local Jewish tavern would negotiate, 20 pennies per wagon of products brought in from Galati, 20 pennies for each wagon with small items, 30 pennies for each wagon with groceries which the local grocers would bring in and sell around." The authorities had approved the hospital, but within the Jewish guild there were financial problems regarding the Rabbi and Shohet's salaries, and so the guild was divided. Hence, the hospital could not be founded anymore. However, on October 22nd 1848 [97], a part of the community petitioned the higher court with another request, signed by 92 members, asking permission to bring in another Rabbi and Shohet. The opening of the Jewish hospital occurred in the second half the XIXth century. The Biographical note published in "The Yearbook for Jews" of 1888-89 relating to Leiba Herscovici shows the attitude that some enlightened Jews had with regards to division. Leiba Herscovici was a Hebrew translator in the courthouse of Bacau, who had bought back from the Turks in 1821 some Christian servants and also recovered some religious artefacts for the church; he also helped finance the revolutionary movement of 1848.

Once again A.D. Birnberg's Monograph is the source for information with regards to some of the customs and clothing worn by Jews of Bacau during that period: "The Jews wore country outfits: shirts, pants, and wide belts over the usual Jewish attire. They wore boots or high shoes. On their heads they wore "Cavuc", some kind of cap/hat made out of satin. The wealthier Jews wore colourful handkerchiefs instead of wide belts. During the winter they wore long sheepskin coats of different lenghts. The Jewish women dressed like peasant women but instead of the Catrinta (apron from Romanian folk attire) they wore full skirts. Usually, the masses would gather on Saturday afternoon, for a dance called the Hora (a popular Romanian dance where the participants held hands dancing in an enclosed circle). The kids played with walnuts "ochinca" and bobetes".

III. The Jewish Community In Bacau In The Second Half Of The XIXth Century And The Beginning Of The XXxth Century.

During this period when the Romanian boroughs were experiencing significant development into a modern society, Bacau had also developed tremendously. Its geographical positioning (on the road connecting the North and the South counties of Romania), as well as its rich natural resources favoured the economic development of the city. The commercial, trading and manufacturing activities had all intensified, resulting in the appearance of many new factories. All of this sped up the urbanization process, attracting more people from the villages that surrounded Bacau, since there was an abundance of work places. The social categories interested in the modern development of the economy became more influential. The city expanded, new streets and suburbs were being built, and the population increased dramatically. The new administrative rules imposed on the process of modernising the city also contributed to its development. A new law passed in 1864 appointed the mayor's office as the administrative leader of the city, the first Mayor was Gheorghe Negel, who started the development process that was amplified in the following decades. As part of the urbanization, many streets were paved and widened as the sanitation process of the city began. It was at this time that new administrative buildings were being built: new schools, post office, city hospital, public park, and later the administrative palace, the high school, train station, and other buildings all facilitating the progress in different areas of technology. As in the rest of the country, the negative influence of the electoral system improperly managed (the vote based on censuses) as well as the lack of agricultural reform necessary to the peasants, stagnated the progress into the next era. Furthermore, during this period, the Jewish persecution was still in place. They had no political rights even though they had the same financial obligations as the rest of the population.

97. Manascu Cotter, in *Mozaic Cult Magazine*, no. 311/1973

Let's take a look at what the documents show with regards to the demographic evolution of the Jewish population in Bacau, and the place it occupied in the economic life of the city during that period.

In 1866, the number of Jews in Bacau was 3771[98], around 41% of the total population. Information referring to the year 1880 shows the following numbers: There were 3912 families in the city for a total of 12, 675 people, out of which 1821 were Jewish families totalling 6122 people[99], around 48% of the total population. The occupations of the heads of the Jewish families were as follows: 350 tradesmen, 442 merchants, 120 professional people and 409 manual labourers and people without a profession. The professional people were either leaders of the religious community (rabbis, shohets, cantors), teachers from the Jewish schools, administration employees or commissioned intermediaries working in connection with the Government.

Among the existing documents in the archive AC.M.E.O.R. from Tel Aviv, we find a directory of Jewish tradesmen, produced by the Jewish community in Bacau in 1884. It underlines the various specialities, over 42, in which the Jewish tradesmen worked.

We find similar numbers in a census from 1890[100], showing that Jews represented almost half the population of the city. The newspaper, "Egalitatea" (Equality) estimated that in 1896 the number of Jewish families in Bacau was 1659 totalling 7924 people. The professional structure was as follows: tradesmen - 635 men and 82 women; apprentices - 410 men and 492 women; manufacturers - 12; wagon drivers - 60; builders - 54; labourers - 86 men and 8 women; servants - 14 men and 51 women; merchants - 432; sales people - 402; tavern keepers - 118; bookies - 5; agents - 7; couriers - 55; entrepreneurs - 7; doctors - 6; dentist -1; lawyer - 1 [101]. An official document from 1896-1897 indicated there were 1721 families of Jews totalling 8209 poeple (1529 men, 1788 women, 2596 boys, 2296 girls) and as professions: 569 merchants, 598 tradesmen, and 1224 other professions[102].

In 1899, out of a total population of 16,378 people, 7,850 were registered as Jews, meaning 47% [103] of the population. Similar statistical information appeared in published works in the beginning of the XXth century [104].

The role of the Jewish population in the commercial activity of the town is emphasized in the statistical information of the time. The document mentioned above in reference to 1896-97, which indicates the presence of 569 tradesmen of different specialities, points out the variety of stores run by Jews:

> Accessories shop (*Galanterie-a shop selling scarves, gloves, intimate lingerie)* - 11, shoe stores - 3, lipscanii - 29 (*Lipscanie-a shop selling merchandise brought over from Leiptzig)* lingerie - 2, book stores - 5, convenience stores- 57, textiles - 1, porcelain - 6, furniture - 3, groceries - 63, paint supplies - 8, pottery - 4, leather goods store - 7, oil merchants - 9, smiths - 14, coat makers - 7, hoteliers - 8, chicken sellers - 7, fish sellers - 10, tobacco shop - 3, glass stores - 8, saddle makers - 8, cobblers - 3, and tavern keepers 128.

It is unusual that this list does not include the grain sellers, who occupied a very important place in Bacau's trades. In the same census, marked as "different professions", we find other Jewish commercial activities: pastry chefs, coffee storeowners, milkmen, butchers, commissioners, couriers, etc.

In order to portray a more comprehensive image of the Jewish influence in the commercial life, let's mention the names of some of the most remarkable people of Bacau. The Brills continued to be some of the most prominent names in the grains trade. Among the leaders of this trade were owners of large silos such as Shae Cofler, Pinhas Edelstein, Berl Malai, Mordehai Ber, and later the brothers Iacobsohn, Isac Avram, Dikman, Avram Gutman, Weissbuch, as well as many others. Not by chance, the greatest and most important Synagogue in Bacau was and continued to be the grain merchants' synagogue. Some grain merchants even had printed official postcards with their name and qualifications (for example Iacob Berkovici). A remarkable figure in this field was Moise Klein, originally from Poland, who in a very short time, became the most important grain merchant on the Bacau-Piatra Street. His son, Buium was the owner of the largest silos on the bank of the canal where all the windmills and watermills existed, later called the Filderman Watermill. Another important grain merchant was Aron Schuler, known for his philanthropic activities – among other things the hospital he founded named "Mina and Aron Schuler Hospital". In 1914 he founded the agricultural society named "The First Seed". Some merchants were interested in the export of grain. A.C.M.E.O.R. archives in Israel hold remnants of business correspondence from 1899 between David Reisel, from Bacau and international grain merchant M-Z-Chrisoveloni from Braila.

98. State Archives of Bacau, brief 19/1866, p. 64 - verso
99. State Archives of Iasi, Bacau City Hall, brief 14/1880, p. 70, 84
100. Ortansa Racovita, *Geographical Dictionary of Bacau County*, 1895
101. *Equality*, no. 34, Aug. 30th 1896

102. State Archives of Bacau, Bacau City Hall, brief 68/1898, p. 1-7
103. *Statistical Yearbook of Romania, 1912*, p. 15 and Verax, *Literary Works*, p. 35-37
104. N. Colescu, *Statistics of Trades*, Bucharest, 1901, p. 104-104 and *Industrial Inquiry of 1901-1902*, Bucharest, vol. I, p. 126 127, table XXIV

One of the trades that had strongly influenced the economic development of Bacau and all of Moldova was the iron trade. In his monograph, GR. Grigorovici mentions the largest iron merchant in Moldova was Faivis Klein, whose business was one of the oldest in Bacau and who provided the rails for the railroad. The author also emphasizes his great philanthropic work[105]. There were other Jews who participated in the iron commerce such as David Haran, Kahane, and others.

The Jews were also present in the lumber business, as well as construction materials, both very important to the development of the town.

Many Jews had grocery stores in Bacau and in the surrounding areas. Let us mention the brothers Hirschenbein, who provided groceries to many towns throughout Moldova and the surrounding villages of Bacau.

The first library in Bacau was founded in 1860 by Herman Margulies.

The Jewish people were also involved in manufacturing leather goods, for which the brothers Leibu and Iosef Brill were renowned having founded the first factory of this kind.

Many Jewish merchants owned small ware shops (sewing articles, buttons, threads), some were involved with fisheries, groceries while others owned taverns, and inns; moreover, others had food chains, farm supply stores selling reins for horses, plows, bricks, and all kinds of household products, their stores being lined up along Strada Mare (Great Street), Strada Leca, as well as the streets leading to the main neighbouring towns such as Piatra, Roman and Focsani.

Jewish merchants also lent their great personal characteristics to the trade: innovative spirit, open mindedness, and diversification, engaging in multiple trade sectors, and capital rotation (charging cheaper prices in order to increase the volume of sales). While some were interested in doing import/export as a diversification, others had learned how to invest their profits in a more evolved form of capitalisation (industrial, and banking).

The statistics from the end of the XIXth century indicate that over 20% of the Jewish population from Bacau had worked in trade shops as either owners or apprentices. N. Colescu left us a representation of all trades in which the Jews from Bacau were involved. Here is his list: 3 silver smiths, 6 barbers and hairdressers, 6 furriers, 2 tool and dye makers, 5 candy makers, 5 cheese makers, 18 bread makers, 2 cotton gin owners, 1 hat maker, 2 bucket makers, 5 watch makers, 3 saddle makers, 97 boot makers, 2 pastry chefs, 5 bagel makers, 91 tailors, 13 restaurateurs, 16 belt makers, 60 dress makers, 11 coachmen, 2 carpenters, 2 iron makers, 2 rope makers, 6 window installers, 4 jewellers, 5 lock smiths, 1 lumberjack, 1 candle maker, 14 butchers, 16 couturiers, 1 montor adjuster, 1 milliner, 3 shoe makers, 2 brush makers, 1 polisher, 1 wood sculptor, 5 steel workers, 2 tabacco makers, 17 crate makers, 7 furniture makers, 14 roofers, 12 printing press operators, 2 umbrella makers, 2 barrel makers, 5 masons, and 3 painters [106].

It is quite remarkable the diversity of trades that people specialized in. Some of the trades, which had not been mentioned in the prior century were: lock smiths, montor (installers), steelworkers, umbrella makers, jewellers, pastry chefs and watchmakers. This proves that Jewish tradesmen were keeping abreast of the evolutions of the period, and diversified their specialities accordingly to satisfy the new necessities. Strangely enough is that in the long list provided by N-

105 Gr. Grigorovici, *Bacau, Yesterday and Today*, 1933, p. 140
106. N. Colescu, *Literary Works*, p. 102-104

Colescu we don't find some trades that many Jews were working in such as: oven makers, wagon drivers, and drivers for different means of transportation. The wagon drivers were so numerous that in 1885 they formed a union. Since 1875 the wagon drivers also had their own synagogue. Some of them became quite wealthy. One of the documents attesting to their financial well being is the Will left in 1879 by Smil Ber, son of Nahman Tudic. The Will comprised not only stipulations with regards to the wealth and properties of the estate but also indicated that "half of my place at the wagon drivers synagogue, which I have purchased in partnership with Moise son of Herscu, as well as half of the Torah can not be sold or given away, not even by my wife or descendants and will remain forever as a prayer place in the memory of my soul [107].

Another profession worth mentioning is that of a sifter of grain, a trade linked to the existence in Bacau of a large number of grain merchants. Moise Lupovici was a sifter before the 1900s.

The list mentioned above also shows that many Jewish tradesmen continued to practice the traditional professions related to clothing, and shoe making. There were so many tailors that in 1875, they founded a second synagogue called "The Synagogue of the Young Tailors." Also there were a large number of shoe makers/repairers.

The large number of tradesmen and their need to look out for their own interests gave rise to their own union – "The Union of Various Tradesmen" on April 24th, 1881; after many years, the union had reached such a high level that in 1915 that it was recognised officially as a moral and judicial entity [108].

The multitude of tradesmen who worked in constructions (bricklayers, masons, painter, carpenters, roofers, stove makers, etc.) unified in 1885 into a mutual help association named "Aghidas Haborinim", which lasted till the beginning of the Second World War.

The Jewish tradesmen introduced new methods of work, which increased production. The print-setter M. Margulies, who had been in business since 1880 brought to Bacau in 1882 the first automated printing press with Latin and Hebrew letters, following in 1883 by the M. Haber, D. Rosenberg, A. Goldsmit, I. Copel and N. Auslander. The photo shops wanted to keep abreast with the new technology as well and they were making color photos since 1877-78 (the stores of Max Agatstein, Segal, etc.).

The tradesmen numbers continued to increase after the beginning of the new century. As such, in 1903, there already existed in town 654 Jewish *patentari* (workers that applied a heat treatment to metals to facilitate their processing), representing approximately 2/3 of all tradesmen in Bacau [109]. In 1910, the Jewish *patentari* represented almost half of all *patentari* in Bacau County [110]. This is even more remarkable, considering the tough restrictions imposed by the Profession Organizing Law from 1902, which assimilated the Jewish merchants with the foreign ones. These restrictions, as many other anti-Semitic actions of the time had forced many Jews both in Bacau and other towns to leave the country, between 1899-1904. Furthermore, such anti-Semitic manifestations that took place in the 1912 elections for tradesmen corporations; the Jewish press strongly combated the affirmations according to which the Jewish owners did not accept Christian apprentices.

The first factories were founded in Bacau in the second half of the XIXth century and it's fair to say that the Jewish people were the pioneers in this area. Naturally, they had started this industrial activity using the plentiful natural resources of the area: grains and other agricultural products, cattle, forests, oil etc. Many of the factories they built were initially simple workshops and only through perseverance were they able to develp them into top performing units of the field.

During those times tanneries, leather goods manufacturing and shoe making experienced the most intense and continuous development. The main factors contributing to this development were that the region favoured cattle raising and that the river Bistrita was so close by. The Brill brothers, Leibu and Iosif (part of the tradesmen with the same name) were the first ones to found tanneries. In the tannery on Flower Street, near Bistrita they brought over as foreman a Hungarian – Iosca, and a German – Carol Lahman. Unfortunately the tannery was destroyed not much later by flood. As a result they decided to open another tannery on Leca Steet which they moved subsequently to Tanners Street, on the other side of Bistrita river. This new factory, later renovated by the family descendants (Ch.S. Brill, Sahna Brill and Aron Davidshon) functioned for many decades till 1948, when the communists took over the property.

107. State Archives of Bacau, Bacau City Hall, brief 6/1932, file 344, 344/v, 345, 345/v
The Equality, Dec. 4th 1915
Verax, *Literary Works*, p. 302
The Statistical Yearbook of Romania, 1912, Bucharest, p. 309

Since there was no leather goods factory in a "Russian system" – "iuft", the same two brothers brought over to Bacau David Iuftaru in 1850, who founded such a factory on the north side of the town. This is mentioned in Gr. Grigorovici's monograph (Literary Works, p.199)

The Unification of the Romanian Principalities and later the Agrarian Reform in 1864 favoured the development of this industrial area. In 1876, Samuel Filderman, initially a show salesman, also founded a tannery in north part of the city. The production process was rudimentary, his former employees saying that in the beginning, the owner himself would gather bird residues and oak barks using them as tannin. However, this primitive factory evolved in the decades to come into the glorious complex “S. Filderman Enterprises”. The documents in archives indicate that in 1884 the tannery was organized as a factory, being listed in 1890 in the Industrial business registry. Although many of archived documents got lost, the important phases of the development and technical modernization of the complex can still be reconstituted. Aside from the tannery, S. Filderman bought from Paul Kisten a leather-manufacturing factory, already in existence since 1892. In 1908, Dr. H. Perlbergher founded in Bacau a leather-manufacturing factory, where he produced for the first time black and coloured leather by using a chromium leather tanning process. Filderman’s factory, which at the time could only offer regular leather, had also been modernized with machinery and leather specialists brought over from abroad. In 1908, the two businessmen merged founding the “First Chromium Processed Fine Leather Factory in Romania as well as Systematic Tannery in Bacau” [111].

During the first world war, Filderman Enterprises were the only factories in the country supplying the army with leather manufactured goods and soles, producing for the first time boots, harness and furred goods [112].

On Fabricilor Street (Street of factories) there were many other tanneries owned by Jewsih people: Herman Abramovici (tannery founded in 1900), Weiss, Zelter, Froiche Grinberg. Moreover, many other leather-manufacturing factories were founded at the time, amongst which were L. Klein’s in 1880 and H. Pfeferman’s in 1875.

Another industrial area that the Bacau Jews were very active in was the milling trade. The mills in Bacau benefited from the grains and corn from the Eastern part of the county, centralized in Plopana, a center economically tied to the town. In the second half of the XIXth century, Brill Nemteanu (The German) founded the first systematic mill. At the time, there was also a much smaller mill belonging to Natan David, an agent of the Fighel brother’s mill. In 1904, Herman Brociner founded a mill, which was later taken over by Calmanovici and his sons who modernized it.

The development of the textile industry in Buhusi facilitated the expansion of this industrial area in Bacau as well. The oldest textile factory was Singher’s Thick Cloth Factory, founded in 1908; in the beginning, it would produce country folks thick cloth, later specializing in superior quality cloth. Another textile factory of the time was A. Isvoranu’s Thick Cloth Factory, founded in 1898 initially in Tg. Neamt, later relocated to Bacau. “Gloria” - The Ribbon and Cloth Factory founded by Leon Grad in 1913 was to become the most important factory in the country in the textile industry. In 1907, S. Oringher started a factory to make quilts and mattresses. Other examples of textile factories: Thick Clothing Factory of Leon and Moritz Gros, Housewifes’ Factory H. Schulemschon (founded in 1913), Quilt Factory S. Marcusohn (founded 1915).

The existence of vast forests in Bacau as well as the rafting done on the Bistrita through Bacau, allowed a rapid development of the wood industry, in which many Jewish entrepreneurs got involved. In 1916, Strul Kendler created a lumber mill factory, while in 1918 the timber factory “Bicazul” (founded in 1913) was taken over by I. Feldher. Other factories in this industry belonged to D. Goldenberg and sons[113].

Dumitru Zaharia, Emilia Chiriacescu, *Literary Works*, The Leather-goods Industry, brief 93
Dumitru Zaharia, Emilia Chiriacescu, *Literary Works*, The Leather-goods Industry, brief 93, p. 139-140
Ibid, *The Wood Industry*, brief 189

In the food industry, the oldest, though primitive establishments were "velnite" (primitive system for making alcohol and brandy). In 1834 Zisu Focsaner and Dumitrache Florea created such a factory where they made brandy with some workers they brought over from Galitia. In 1892, in Margineni-Bacau, Ellenberger had a rubbing-alcohol factory which was later taken over by Blum-Fainaru. The first brewery in Bacau, founded in 1867 was taken over in 1919 by Orzis Herscovici. Then, in 1884 there was a carbonated-water factory owned by J. Ellenbogen and in 1900 the one belonging to Tecuceanu.

In the metallurgical industry, the most active factories were Herscu Svart's Foundry and The Metal Enterprises of Moise Svart. However, the most important unit was the Foundry Davidovici & Sons, founded in 1918[114], although a modest factory in its beginnings it expanded greatly after the First World War.

There were other industrial enterprises initiated by the Jews. In 1870, Moscovici's brick factory was founded. Then, in 1892 and 1919, Bercu Gros and Ellenberger set up soap factories; candle factories – A. Hercovici 1892, I. Hechlingher 1893, M. Faclior 1895; dye-houses and chemical Laundromat's – Iulius Ilovici in 1910. In 1887, Blum Fainaru's oil refinery started functioning in Margineni-Bacau.

Many of these industrial units were quite modest, only few of them ever making it to the top; however all have contributed to the active economic life of the town, providing various goods as well as creating work places for the town's population. As such, the number of Jewish workers increased, mostly in the textile industry, in tanneries and leather manufacturing factories, mills and printing houses. Many of them lived on Leca District and around the tanneries on Fabricilior Street (Factories' Street), others on Bacau-Piatra Street, most of them working in the neighbouring factories.

During this period, some Jews were active in the banking and financial industry. As early as the first few decades of the XIXth century there were Jews lending money. There is one named Zeilic mentioned as a creditor first in 1828 and then in 1832[115]. In 1845, great amounts are mentioned, when the moneylender Pinhas was in litigation with Avram Volf for 2,500 lei[116]. In 1862, two moneylenders, Mahal & Mendel also owned a coffee shop [117]. In 1864, Moise Vertisntein borrowed from Bercu Berinstein 400 lei for 3 months [118].

In 1912, a Credit Union named "Hope" was set up in Bacau, with a starting capital of 20,000 lei; it was the "first Jewish financial institution in Bacau" [119]. "The Credit Bank" – a credit union serving especially the Jewish tradesmen – was active in 1919 [120], its director being Ludvig Goldstein.

Starting in the second half of the XIXth century, the Jews just like the rest of the country manifested their desire of changing their living conditions. Becoming more aware of what was useful for the Jewish community and influenced by the enlightening ideas of the Hascala movement, more Jews than ever were interested in studying the country's language, adapting to the modern culture, in supporting those forces seeking the progress of the Romanian Society. They wanted to actively participate in the maintenance as well as spiritual life of the town they lived in, to be part of the life of the entire country as citizens with the same rights and obligations as any other residents. On December 29th 1864, the Jewish community leaders wrote a thank-you letter to the ruler Al. I. Cuza, for his plans of granting citizenship to all Jews[121]. Expressing their gratitude for his projects, they added: Rest assured your Majesty, that the Romanian Jew will be worthy of the future you have in store for him, you will find him to be a good man as well as a loyal aide for your Majesty", signed by the Romanian - Jewish representatives in Bacau: S. Alterescu, Alter Zilberhert, Mendel Pascal, and David Orenstein.

State Archives of Bacau, Commerce and Industry Chamber, brief 21/1934, p. 199
State Archives of Iasi, Bacau City Hall, brief 156/1832
116. Ibid, brief 177/1845
117. State Archives of Bacau, Commerce and Industry Chamber, packet X/123 (category II, 1629)
118. Ibid, packet X/147 (cat. II, 1656)
119. *Equality*, no. 20, July 1912, p. 226
120. *Argus*, Feb. 13th 1920
The Romanian Academy Library , Archive Al. I. Cuza, Manuscripts, Folder 16, "Letter".

In Israel's Central Archives for the History of Jewish People, we find among others, a minutes report from a meeting on July 8th 1868, in which the Jewish Community leaders of Bacau, Moinesti, Tg. Ocna and Parincea participated. The main objective of the meeting was to discuss the Appeal of the Central Committee in Bucharest regarding "a monetary subscription to buy firearms". Unanimously, the participants decided to honour this appeal, which would "raise the national prestige" since "the objective of equipping the country's army is to win Europe's respect and more important that of our neighbours". Signing this appeal on behalf of Bacau was the president of the committee Mendel Pascal and a series of members, among which were Itig Igner, Avram Balter, Leib Focsaner, Mono Hirsenbain, Leon Caufman and others.

However, the hopes and dreams of the Jews were opposed on many occasions by reactionary forces comprised especially by those who had come to power after taking down Al. I. Cuza (the first ruler of the United Romanian Principalities). The Governors (Liberal Party and other parties) considered that Jews were foreign people, even if they were born and raised in Romania, not citizens of any other country benefiting from its protection or even though they had satisfied the military status. At the time many laws were passed, which restricted Jews' rights as well as many administrative measures against them. Some of these governors were even encouraging local Anti-Semitic excesses.

In the spring of 1868, the government under I. Bratianu passed through Parliament a discriminatory law, which banned Jews from living and working in rural areas. The anti-Semitic Mayor of Bacau County, Leca took advantage of this law and launched a barbaric action of driving away all Jews in the county's villages. Tens of families were driven away being able to take with them only a small part of their possessions. The remaining belongings were robbed. Many Jews were beaten and tortured, some of the most unfathomable events took place: a pregnant woman being taken out of bed, a woman with two children left in the woods in the middle of the night and others. The press tried to inform the population about these barbaric acts, but the Mayor would deny their existence; he would say that these were isolated cases, initiated by some villagers. In the same time, in Bacau, the so-called "National Guard" would act in the same anti-Semitic manner, closing off synagogues and destroying the Jewish cemetery [122]. Since the internal authorities dismissed their protests, the Jews had to alert the International public to these atrocities. On April 9th 1868, they sent a letter to baron Rotschild in Vienna, describing how: "hundreds of Jewish families in Bacau have been driven away barbarically from their residence at the order of the Mayor, with total disregard for losses, sorrow and needs." After indicating that all this had been reported to the authorities in Bucharest, the letter mentioned: "Our complaints are being disregarded while the situation gets worse day by day and the danger increases progressively. Thousands of people are suffering in horrid condition. We plead to your Excellency to intervene and save them" [123]. The letter was signed by the Jewish Community Committee in Bacau, Moldavia. The Western Jewish press vigorously exposed the Government's position, which persecuted Jews through "legal" and administrative manners encouraging local "arbitrariness". In Paris, the paper "Halevanon" (subtitled "Le Libanon, journal hebreu") published Karpel Lippe's letter, dated May 6th 1868, in which the Government's attitude and "arbitrariness" were described in fact, as well as the fact that the Austro-Hungarian Consul in Iasi, Wahlfort had attested the existing reality. The author of the letter, a medicine student, later becomes a renowned physician in Iasi, as well as an important militant in the fight for Jewish rights and Zionism. Both the foreign press and the Western Diplomatic Corps had been informed of the situation. On May 9th 1866, the Conservatory Party's leader, P.P. Carp, interrogated the Government with regards to the events in Bacau; I. Bratianu was forced to promise that the ones responsible for these actions would be prosecuted and stated that the town's defence would be taken over by the army. In a subsequent letter published in "Le Libanon" on May 20, 1868, no. 20, K. Lippe indicated the the ruler Carol had visited Bacau and finding out about what had taken place, ordered Mayor Leca's dismissal and disarming the National Guard. However, the Anti-Jewish atmosphere was continued by the local police chief, Zaharia Moldovan and by professor Movileanu. The Jewish leaders in Bacau had to address the Ministry of Internal Affairs with a petition signed by 30 people, which described this anti-Semitic disorder. In his monograph, the former Mayor of Bacau, Costache Radu also mentioned the outrageous actions of Zaharia Moldovan.

123. Newspaper *The Present* (Bacau), March 27, 1868, p.1

124. *The Archives of Vienna,* P.A. XXXVIII, Karton 178, Consulates 1868, Bucharest, 1 – V.

The following years also witnessed hostile actions against Jews, as exemplified by a physician who refused admitting in the hospital a Jewish Teacher who was sick, even though the City Hall had approved his admission [125].

However, the truly enlightened people of the time were far from exhibiting these attitudes. The painter Nicolae Grigorescu who lived at the time in Bacau shared a great friendship with the Grimberg family, whose descendants later became renowned for their talents (painters, artists, scientists). Iosif Haim Grinberg had been the principal of the first Modernized Jewish School in Romanian in Bacau between 1863 and 1865.

The Jews of Bacau also gave their support to the Independence War in 1877. Some of the ones who participated were: Leibovici Avram, Abramovici Haim, Marcu Iancu, Avram Smilovici, Cazacu Moise, Herscu Zaharia and Avram Moise. In the old community cemetery lies Haim Grinberg, veteran of this war. Among the front line war participants were Artur Ehrilch who, as a non-commissioned officer, received many war decorations and later became chief of troops. The country's first Jewish Newspaper "Prezentul" written in Romanian published a vivid propaganda supporting the War. Its publisher was A. L. Lobel, a great liberal who had been nicknamed "the iron head". The editor in chief was a student Iacob Rosenzweig, who was later known as physician and community activist Sotec-Lenteanu. Aside from the mobilizing articles "Presentul" also published the actual activities in support of the army: donations of clothing, footwear, food and money. Here is an example of what was collected for the army: 54 Jews donated 2065 bread loafs and money varying from 10 bani (pennies) to 150 lei [126].

Unfortunately, even after the war ended the Government anti-Semitic attitude continued. The Jews were refused citizenship, being granted only individually after a very complicated procedure. In the whole country, only a total of 95 Jews had been granted citizenship by 1900. In Bacau, only 5 people received their citizenship: Avram Focsaner, Tule Welt, and Adolf Meisels – all tradesmen as well as the lawyer Herman Grimberg and Lieb H Focsaner - landlord. Moreover, the Government kept on implementing measures against foreigners, which really targeted the Jews. They were banned from owning land, taking part in elections, and discriminated against in public functions, state education or in the army. At any point they could be discharged as happened to prominent people like M. Gaster, H. Tiktin, Lazar Saineanu etc or to newspaper editors. The most affected by these measures were the Jews living in villages, the tradesmen as well as the craftsmen. Enforcing the above-mentioned orders, the mayors of these rural localities forced Jews to leave the villages. We find in Jerusalem, in the Central Archives of the History of Jewish People an order from April 15, 1894 of Mayor Puscasu addressed to Iosub Mendel from Bahnaseni, Bacau county that stipulated: "According to the order given by Assistant Mayor no. 1363 and Mayor 2586, you are asked to leave the village immediately" and on top of it all the Mayor had the nerve to "politely" add: "You'll receive my considerations!"

Jews were also banned from owning smoke-shops; even the tavern keepers had to have Romanian citizenship. The Jewish merchants were required to register in and pay dues to various corporations, but could not be elected as chairmen; on the contrary they were obstructed from even participating in electing the leadership. The corporation had to have at least 50% of its members as Romanians, but in Bacau for a long time, the Jewish merchants predominated in numbers. Furthermore the Jews were not admitted in public auctions, and the Romanian craftsmen could not use Jews to complete their work. The directors of any bank, trading exchange, the commissioned salespeople or buyers had to be Romanian.

In Bacau, the situation was worsened by the activities of some of the local anti-Semitic forces. The leader of these events was Radu Porumbaru, the managing director for the paper company "Letea".

125. Costache Radu, *Literary Works*, p. 102
126. The Newspaper *The Present*, March 11, 1876
127. Ibid, May 8, 1877

Not only that he would not hire Jews, but he also would organize extreme anti-Semitic acts – beatings, material destructions as well as an anti Jewish attitude, recommending their drowning in Bistrita. His horrendous activities took place for years under the approving eyes of the authorities, even though the media would always make public his fanatic behaviour. In his book "The Town on Bistrita", Voledi-Vardi has a chapter suggestively called "Porumbaru's Catapults". Here, he gave proof of actual cases, describing in detail how Porumbaru had built these catapults and how his people would throw stone shells over the Jewish district Leca and over the funeral convoys that passed through Sarata street on their way to the cemetery. These horrific acts have all been "branded " in a brochure published in Leipzig in German by Elias Schwarzfeld, the renowned fighter for the Jewish cause: "Radu Porumbar und seine Grauelthaten in der Papierfabrik zu Bacau in Rumanien". (Radu Porumbar and his Atrocities in the Paper Factory in Bacau, Romania).

Of similar magnitude was the terrorist conduct of two police officers: I. Talianu and I. Georgescu against Jews in 1896 [127]. Moreover, in that same year, the Jewish school was closed for two months on the order Ministry of Internal Affairs, since the Community did not hire two teachers imposed by them; it is also important to mention the authorities' hostile attitude regarding the appointment of a brilliant professor, L. Torceanu in the Jewish Junior High School in Bacau.

Financial troubles, being discriminated against as well as all the abuses suffered at the hands of authority workers, all explain why so many Jews chose to emigrate. By August 1882, almost 20 families of Jewish tradesmen, totalling 131 people left the country [128]. The same problem existed in 1886 [129] and in 1889, 40 youngsters were enrolled in English & German language courses, their ultimate goal being emigration [130]; in 1900-1901, approximately 400 Jews emigrated from Bacau. This was one aspect of the legendary "pedestrian emigration" (in Yiddish known as the Fusgeyers), also caused by the great economic crisis of the end of the century. The Jewish people were also attracted by baron Hirsch' colonization attempt in

Argentina. At the same time, the Jews in Bacau were more and more absorbed by the Zionist movement and ideas and emigrating to Eretz Israel. In 1882, together with some Jews from Moinesti, the first group immigrated to the Holy Land. Another group left to Eretz Israel in 1892. The Jewish participation played a great role in the Zionist movement and in the colonization efforts of Israel and as such we have dedicated a special chapter for it in this monograph.

Far from adopting the hostile attitude of the authorities, the majority of Romanians in town shared great relationships with the Jewish population. Among the ones accompanying the Jews on their emigration endeavours were many Romanians who, until then had shared the hurdles of the times. The sensible, honest Romanians knew there was no reason for mutual hate. In the Central Archives for the History of Jews we find a letter from the Mayor of Bacau to physicians in the Hospital "Pavel and Ana Cristea" in which he wrote: "We respectfully ask you to admit in your hospital the old vaccinating physician Iancu Apfelberg, who has throughout times served both the community and the county of Bacau, give him the best care you are capable of." The Romanian residents from the neighbouring areas of Leca street disapproved of the barbaric anti-Semitic acts and many times tried to jump in and help the victims. Major Piersiceanu made a public protest in front of the City Hall regarding the fact that no measures had been taken to stop the horrendous acts of Radu Porumbaru. Meanwhile, the Jews had found ways to show their devotion to the country as well as for the care of their community. It is significant that Faivis Klien left in his will a considerable amount of money for the City Hall, which financed the construction of a new wing for the town's hospital.

In the period under discussion, more and more Jews in Bacau realized that they had to fight the backwards process which the authorities enforced upon them, advocate their civil and political rights, as well as modernizing Jewish life. In his collaboration with "The Historical Society 'Dr. Iului

127 *Equality*, Aug. 9th 1986
128 *Brotherhood*, Aug. 20th 1882
129 *Fraternity*, Nov. 7th 1886
130 *Equality*, Nov. 5th 1899

Barasch'", A.D. Birnber sent them various documents, which echoed Jews' life in Bacau as well as his monograph regarding Jewish roots in Bacau. Together with Iosif Bernstein, he initiated a financial support action for the "Jewish Yearbook", an organization advocating progress. Rosenzweig, Faivis Klein, Haim Grimberg and others.

Other progressive press associations were supported in a similar manner. The list of supporters published in this Yearbook (year III, 1879-1880, p. 136) mentions among others Daniel Daniel, Volf Clejan, Manase Balter. In another list compiled by student Isac Brinberg were mentioned Iacob in 1890, the section "Patria" (Native Country), part of the General Association of Jewish People was set up, led by Dr. Fischler. The Association had offices in Bucharest, Barlad, Braila and Iasi and was led by Dr. Adolf Weinberg (who later changed his name to A. Vianu – he was the father of the famous writer and philosopher Tudor Vianu). The museum "The Community History of Jews in Bacau between 1703 - 1944" holds the membership card to "Patria" of Ignatz Gutman issued in 1890. In 1907, the president of the Bacau section (later called "Dreptatea" i.e. Fairness) was A. Silberscher. In that same year, Dr. L. Ghelerter, member in the Central Council of the Association held a conference in Bacau, encouraging Jews to legally fight for their political rights [131]. This association later produced in 1911 the Union of Native Jews. Through public meetings and other propaganda, the local members of the association persuaded Jews to support the country's interests, fight discrimination against Jews as well as the anti-Semitic organizations, which manifested themselves in various aspects: high school students disturbing a Jewish theatre act, public disturbance at the elections of Tradesmen Corporation in 1912 [132]; minimizing the Jewish contribution to the Balkan War in 1913 and their registration to the national fleet [133].

Jews like H. Rozenberg have promoted the Workers Campaign hoping that by materializing the Socialist Principle they would absolve humankind of all its sufferings. Dr. H. Aroneanu who adhered to the same beliefs was the leader of "The Working Romanians" group in Bacau in 1905.

The War for Romania's Unification in 1916-1918 required great sacrifices both from the Jews of Bacau as well as from the entire population. A great series of documents and tomb stones stand as proof of the blood contributions made by the Jews of Bacau. There are no statistics with respect to the actual number of the Jews in Bacau fighting on the front lines or any regarding the victims of this war. The only document mentioning any numbers is the brochure named "Soldiers from Bacau's Heroes Cemetery, who died in the Unification War 1916-1918, identified by their official documents" – published by Bacau City Hall [134]. It mentioned the names of 35 Jews buried in the Heroes Cemetery near the shooting range. Here are some of their names as buried with a grave number:

355 – Zalingher Itic,
356 – Bercu Leibu,
357 – Miosa Moscovici,
358 – Solomon Itic,
360 – Orenstein Herscu,
361 – Isac V. Hirschenbaum,
362 – Cahana Casian,
363 – Idel David Friedman,
364 – Leibu Moisa,
365 – Ioina Itic,
366 – Klaimberg M. Aizic,
367 – Herscovici Leibu,
369 – Schoper Peisah,
370 – Moscovici Leib,
371 – Chitac Smil,
372 – Zilberman Sloim,
373 – Adil Balol,
374 – David Crostic,
376 – Froim Zeilig,
379 – Zlate Marcu,
380 – Bernfeld Herman,
381 – Iulius Iosif,
382 – Polac Isac, 3
83 – Smil Leibu,
384 – Schinderman Solomon.

Destroyed by weather throughout time, these grave stones are illegible and thus many names cannot be deciphered anymore. However, many of the war victims were buried in other cemeteries as well. Thus, the Old Jewish Cemetery holds the burial places of soldiers: Herscu Leon, Iosif Brener, Ernest Segal, Physician Aron Schwartz, while in the New Cemetery is buried Major Iancu Feldman decorated for his courageous acts with a medal named "Manhood and Loyalty", 2nd class. One of Bacau's newspapers "Dreptatea" published the names of other Jews who died in this war: private Mendel Svart, sub captain Herman Buium, sergeant Samuel Aron, captain Lazar Davidescu and private Leibu Smil. Another journal "The Prayer", published by Alex Manolescu, dedicated to the "Red Cross heroes who died for their country, 1916-1920" [135] listed more names of the Jewish heroes of Bacau. As mentioned by A. L. Iosif in "Mosaic Cult Magazine" no. 678/1983, many more war victims were buried in the cemetery "near the Postei street corner, in the great field where the yearly fairs were held. During the First World War, there was a hospital called "Lazaret" where all people infected with typhoid fever and cholera were brought." The author cites Gr. Grigorovici: "here lie all heroes from all ranks and all armies, both Jews and Christians who died of typhoid fever as civilians. They were buried in communal graves, soldiers, civilians, men, women, Christians, Jews." As a consequence, in 1923 when there was a debate regarding measures to be taken for honouring the victims' memory, the Jewish community pledged to care for the heroes' cemetery "Lazaret" [136].

131. *Equality*, July 18th 1897
132. *Equality*, June 29th 1912, p. 201
133. *The Jewish Courier*, Feb. 8th 1913
134. State Archives of Bacau, Bacau City Hall, brief 42/1933
135. State Archives of Bacau, Bacau City Hall, Jewish Common foundation, brief 6/1941 (extract from the bulletin "The Union of Reserve Officers", no. 9-12, 1940)

Another Bacau Jew who sacrificed for the country in the First World War was Zalman Herman Kornhauser. Born in Bacau in 1881, he was married to the daughter of Simion Recu, a veteran from the Independence War. Kornhauser had moved to Targoviste where he was working as an electrician. During the war, he was arrested by the German army for helping the Romanian soldiers from the prisoner camp. As a sign of recognition, in 1931 he was offered post-mortem the medal "War Military Virtue", 2nd class.

The war years did not spare Jews from the hostile manifestation of the backward population. Speakers of Yiddish (language containing many words of German origin) were driven away and sometimes beaten. This caused instances when Jewish soldiers were charged as German spies and therefore signed over to the Military Court where they were executed. Sadly, later on it was discovered that these accusations had no real basis and thus they had fallen victims of prejudice and ignorance [137].

IV. Bacau's Jews In The Inter-War Period.

During these two decades, so important for Romania's history, occurred a number of events, which shaped Jewish history in this part of Europe. While at the beginning of the century there were 7850 Jews in Bacau representing 47% of the total population, in 1927, according to a memo edited by the Bacau's Rabbi agency, there were already 10205 Jews in 2041 families [138]. Another document, found in the Archive of the Jewish Community mentioned for the year 1928 - 9600 Jews in 2400 families [138]. The 1930 official census confirms the number of Jews living in Bacau – 9593, representing 30.8% of the total population. In 1939, according to another archived document there were 2636 Jewish families totalling 8883 people [140]. Thus, we notice variations in the numbers of Jews living in Bacau, reflecting on one hand the decrease in birth rate as a result of city life and on the other hand the influence of emigration towards Western Europe and the United States (in 1927-1928 alone 2924 Jews left Romania). Although the number of Jews living in Bacau was still large, it decreased in comparison to the city's total population since many people from the neighbouring villages were attracted to the economic development the city had experienced.

The statistical data of this period do not include references with respect to the socio-professional structure of the Jewish population in Bacau, and thus does not reflect the dynamics of its evolution. There are not even materials to statistically represent the working sectors of the Jews in Bacau. For 1930, the percentages regarding Jews, mentioned in the Census must have been generally valid: 36.5% Jews were active in trades (possibly owners and tradesmen), 28.1% in various industries (owners, workers, technicians), 6.3% in agriculture, 5% in public institutions, 3.5% in banking, 3% mining and transportation. Even though we lack statistical data for the period, it is known that the inter-war years intensified the Jewish social layering process, which had already started at the end of the XIXth century. The social layers of the Jewish population in Bacau were comprised of a few important manufacturers, merchants and bankers who desired to integrate themselves in the leading structures of the Romanian society; another small category of wealthy small business owners, many middle and lower class workers (tradesmen, technicians and professionals); and last but not least many salaried Jewish workers (industrial workers and various office workers). This layering process greatly influenced the organization and attitude of the Jewish population with respect to various problems of their social life.

136. State Archives of Bacau, Bacau City Hall, Jewish Common foundation, brief 8/1923, p. 8
137. *The Jewish Courier*, Aug. 8th 1920
138. State Archives of Bacau, Jewish Common foundation, brief 5/1927, p. 48, 49, 49/v
139. State Archives of Bacau, Jewish Common foundation, brief 3/1940, p. 75
140. State Archives of Bacau, Jewish Common foundation, brief 19/1939, p. 44, 45

The only existing statistics are the unofficial ones published in 1943 by the Central office of Jews in Romania [141], from which we can conclude that before the Second World War, there were 1,038 owners (commerce and industry), 2,219 tradesmen and workers, 999 public officials, 115 professionals, 120 teachers and clergy, and 152 others.

Let us try and make a connection between these statistics and what is known about the Jews' role in the economic and social life of the city of that time. During the years between the two world wars, the Jews in Bacau played an important role in merchandise transportation. A picture of the Jewish commerce of the time showed "the traveller who came into Bacau through one of the city borders, Piatra-Neamt, Focsani or Roman, would face a picturesque scenery. On each side of the streets Bacau-Piatra, Bacau-Focsani and Calea Marasesti, and continuing on Strada Mare, Bulevardul Carol, strada Stefan cel Mare, Hala Pietei Centrale there were stores with various products, cosmetics, iron works, textiles, farmer equipment, grains, bricks, horse gear, clothing, book stores, coffee shops, furniture store, bakeries, winery, lumber yards, green grocers, butchers, gas stations, tanneries etc. Each store had its own sign indicating the speciality and the army division in which the owner had served during the war [...] [142]"

Clearly, we cannot enumerate systematically all the Jewish commerce owners in Bacau of that time. We must limit ourselves in mentioning randomly the names and events, which for some reason have remained in the memory of the people in Bacau.

The grain commerce continued to be the most important occupation of many Jews at the time. Aside from those mentioned prior to the First World War, we must mention the name of Isac Reizel and I. Herscovici. The important role that Jews played in the grain commerce is reflected by the fact that in 1933, the president of the grain owners association, Oboru, was Avram Simon.

Of equal importance was the role of Jews in the cattle commerce. With respect to this trade we found that: "at the slaughter house, both in the days of market as well as during the yearly fairs, the most important transactions were those for working and slaughter cattle, which were transported in great numbers to Craiova and towards the Danube to Galati, Braila, and Calarasi [143]". A great farmer and exporter of cattle was Lazar Haber or Iancu Iancovici (called "the shepherd") who had high quality sheep and breeding cattle.

In the iron industry, we have to mention Moritz Merdler and Jacques Klein, who took over the store from Faivis Klein and held it until the middle of the fourth decade of the century. We must also mention Iancu Iakerkaner and the brothers Cohn.

Iancu Kendler and the Goldenberg brothers were engaged in the lumber commerce, while Manascu Goldstein, B. Weissman, H. Alterescu and others were in involved the construction materials business (paint, bricks and others).

In the commerce of colonial products (tea, coffee) there were– not in the order of importance -aside from brothers Hirschenbein (import and wholesale), the brothers Fighel, Hary Solomon, Natan Isac, Lupu Isac, Aron Kreuer, Strul Schwartz, etc.

The brothers Kitner, Bahman, and I.Rozenberg owned bookstores -some of which were still open after the Second World War.

In the commerce branch of Bridal gowns and accessories, Gr.Grigorovici mentioned M.Hirschenbein and H.Horovitz, Grinberg (the Elegant Bride), the store for wool textiles Sache Moscovici, the store"Mona Lisa", D.Leventer, storekeepers S.Bernstein, Fritz Lupovici, Leizer Grimberg, (Ceho-Romana), Pincu Gloter and others. There were others Jews who manufactured and sold various products: Haim and Iancu Brill (cotton), Moritz and Heinrich Aroneanu, brothers Horn (hats), Pascal Lazarovici (silk and clothing) N.Seidman (furs), and others who sold threads, socks, leather articles, shoes, musical instruments, chemical products and paints. Jews were also active in the fish market - Balau, Balan, bakeries - A.Pais, Schwartz, groceries - brothers Leibovici, M.Blank, confectionery among which was the famous Abramovici, butchershop - Smil Klein, H.Herscu, J.Rechler, gas stations - Fillip Schweiger, Blum, Fainaru, wine stores, etc.

141. The Jewish Central in Romania, Statistical Breviaryof the Jewish Population, 1943
142. I. Voledi, Literary Works, p. 238
143. Gr. Grigorovici, Literary Works, p. 149

Many Jews owned bars, restaurants and inns. Some of the famous names were "Mielul alb" (The White Lamb), "Consumul general" (General Consumption), "Micul Consum" (Small Consumption), "La Balena" (The Whale's), "Pui de Lup" (Wolf Cubs).

Rubin Waksman and Haim Stopler were in the scrap iron business.

Many drugstores opened in Bacau were founded or run by Jewish people: for example, A.Averbuch, I.Nahmansohn, Golesteanu, Rozenzweig, L.Rintzler, and S.Fainaru.

The important role that Jews played in diverse business areas is also illustrated by the fact that at various times they were elected to run numerous Business Public Institutions. As such in 1920, the leaders of the Commerce Chambers were 4 Jews and 6 Christians[144]. Some were awarded the distinction "commercial and industrial merit[145]". At the helm of the Chamber of Commerce were, at different times, Ozias Herscovici, Aurel Negrescu, and Iosif Feldher. The president of the commercial council was, for a long period, Herman Kisler.

Evidently, we are unable to present in these pages a scientific evaluation of the significant role played by the Jews in Bacau in merchandise transportation. Such an estimate can only result from a thorough study. All we can mention is that there was a great number of Jewish tradesmen, considering both the large and small Jewish stores in an area where the Jewish population was predominant, such as Strada Mare, Leca borough, Bacau-Piatra street, and other major Jewish areas. Their personal characteristics influenced positively the economic development of the town: innovative spirit, accelerating methods of rotating the capital, conscientious acceptance of trade risk. The import/export practice brought by many merchants from Bacau also produced a great influence on the national economy; another phenomenon worth mentioning is the evolutionary use of capital (banks and development of industrial venues)-discussed here as well.

Let's discuss the different trades the Jews of Bacau were involved in in the inter-war years. First, let's discuss the auto shops, the most renowned being Herman's and Strulica Schwartz's, as well as Marcu Steinberg's and Ekstein Deju's.

Benis David had an electrical bobbins shop; other people were electricians, with or without their own shop.

There were a great number of tinker shops, amongst which we need to mention the ones owned by Lazar Digot and Volf Marcovici. Zeider and Zilberman were well-known window makers. The house painter N.Inger represented an example of good work and honesty. Pizam's sharpening shop and Iriham Antler's ropemaking shop were also well known in the town.

The watchmakers Leon and Artur Solomon executed the finest and most precise work, and were renowned in the whole town for their honesty and loyalty. Other Jewish tradesmen were S.Steinstein, A.Gutman, Zeigherman and Leon Zilberstein, jewellers I.S.Segal and Bernat Goldrin, and photographers Agatstein, Segal, Strulescu.

L.Tukerman and David Segal had carving shops, while A.Ghelber and Smil Moscovici owned wool-combing shops. The paint shops of the town were those of I.Ilovici, Avner Idelovici and Nuhamovici; B.Baranceanu, David Vataru, and Iosef Rozenfeld owned laundromats and die-houses.

There were a great number of tailor shops. Lets mention only the fine ones: "La Vienezu", H.Schwartz, G.Iusen, Sloime Rozenfeld, Micu, Lupu Saler, as well as the shops of Alter Ghersin, I.German, Aron Grinberg, Moise Kraus, Pincu Schwartz, Haim Gutman, and many others, who had numerous workers and apprentices, both Jews and Christians.

Lora David and Carolina Moscovici owned designer boutiques while Paula Schwartz, Fani Aronsohn, Pescaru and Gheiman Nuta were women's tailors, fashion designers and lingerie makers.

144. State Archives of Bacau, City Hall foundation, brief 32/1936, p. 19-21.
145. *The* Morning, Aug. 2nd, 1929

Itic Blumenfeld, Avram Ghelberg, Isac Atlas, Iosif Braunstein, Cusmaru Ilie and others were furriers (men) while N. Gheiman made fur coats for women [146].

There were also numerous shoe makers/repair shops – Hofman Avram's, Leizer Moise's, H. Lovingher's, M. Leibu's. The most talented ones were the leather-boot makers – Bercu Leibovici, Leon Leobovici, Lovingher Gheza and many others.

Avram Hausfater owned a belt-shop while, N. Ghersin built luggage cases. The tanneries of the time were owned by Leibovici brothers, Gustav Clemer, Max Wechsler, Morit Schild. The Rotman brothers' tapestry shop was appreciated for the high quality of the work.

Leon Rapaport owned a dowry-case making shop, along with many other smaller carpenters: Minter, H. Zisman, Calman Croitoru, Avram Moscovici etc. J. Romascanu and M. Pescaru were painters of logo signs, while David Rozenberg, A. Goldsmit and H. Copel had printing shops on King Ferdinand Street and General Grigorescu Street respectively [147].

Among Jews there were also many butchers and gut makers, some with businesses and others who were working for the slaughterhouse. Moreover, most of the carriage drivers were Jewish. Some had exclusivity for certain services: E. Braunstein for weddings, Wolf Iser for funeral convoys as well as Lipa Goldstein. After 1920, A. Goldenberg owned an automobile, which was used to transport people from Bacau to various other cities within the county.

There were also many Jewish barbers and hairdressers in Bacau: Moritz's salon (in the centre of the city), others spread throughout the neighbourhoods: Haim & I. Cioara's, Leon Parah's, Leizer Avram's and H. Cojocaru's.

The large number of tradesmen is reflected by the organization of synagogues based on trade: the one belonging to the tanners, bricklayers, young and old tailors, carriage drivers, shoe makers, furriers etc.

It is obvious that the Jewish tradesmen were active in all kinds of trades, even those considered as more difficult, requiring great physical effort. Thus, they fulfilled many of the country's economical needs, demonstrating an innovative spirit and striving to produce high quality work. They played an important role in the development and modernizing process of the economy as well as in the urbanization process of the town.

However, although the town was developing greatly, many Jewish merchants led a difficult life. Most of the poor merchants and almost all carriage drivers lived on Leca Street. This was the Jews' street, with very tiny houses, all linked and crowded along half a mile. Starting from Bistrita River, the other end represented the downtown, in Plaza Florescu. The street had a modest aspect, but it had a pictorial view. Here were most of the synagogues, especially the ones belonging to the tradesmen. There was a bakery, a coffe/tea shop and of course a few bars where the clientele were mostly tradesmen. One of them was called "La Calul balan" (White Horse).

During the inter-war years, the Jewish Industrial activity in Bacau was remarkable, the most famous conglomerate being the Filderman Enterprises. After 1922's fire, which destroyed most of the leather factory, the owners rebuilt it and took various measures of expansion and development reorganizing its energy system. During this time, the collective society "Filderman Enterprises" founded new sectors and factories in many fields. In 1939, they consisted of two factories, one for thick cloth and one for civilian and military footwear (founded in 1931), a horse gear section (founded in 1936), a systematic mill and a hydro plant. Through these new factories, the complex was able to offer various elaborate products. The factories were also an important supplier for the army. During the Second World War, the Antonescu regime had militarised these factories using them to their full capacity. In 1943, the leather factory had 554 workers, of which 154 were unskilled labourers. In 1934, the Filderman Mill (founded in 1923), ranked as one of the most systematic mills in the country, employed 52 people. Nearby, the Filderman Association built one of the largest and most modern bakeries, "Sanitas". The Thick Cloth factory had at some point 450 workers. In 1944, the eviction notices as well as the damages created by the German troops had destroyed most of these factories; those that remained were taken over by the Government in the Nationalization process in 1948

146. State Archives of Bacau, the foundation for Industry and Trade Chambers, brief 2/1934, p. 371-373
147. State Archives of Bacau, City Hall foundation, brief 32/1936, p. 19-21.
148. Dumitru Zaharia, Emilia Chiriacescu *Literary Works*, p. 144

In the leather industry there were other factories, those of L. & L.C. Klein's (still functioning in 1941), Brill & Davidsohn's, Ettinger's, Hercovici's as well as the shoe-making factory of Moise Zalman [149]. In the textile industry, Isvoranu's factory was in 1944 the largest in the country employing 547 people. The second largest was Filderman's Thick Cloth Factory while the third one with 255 workers was "Bacau" (former J. Singer), which in 1921 had been approved to benefit from the Industrial Law [150]. There were other factories at the time: the ribbon and cloth factory – "Gloria" – Leon Grad, the knitted goods factory "Lanarie" owned by I. Isersohn, founded in 1923, the handkerchief and bandanna factory – "Camelia" founded by I. Milcovici in 1923, the stockings/socks factory "Idealul" founded in 1926 by I. Nahmansohn which in 1941 had 44 workers.

In the milling industry, the mill taken over by H. Calmanovici & Sons was modernized after a fire in 1926, functioning till after the Second World War; in 1930, it had 30 salaried workers [151]. The Mills "Aurora" property of the Schuller brothers had 27 workers. The smaller mills belonged to Iacob Rubin, Smil Moscovici, Manase Lazarovici and Avram Aberman [152]. Furthermore, in the food industry, there was Ozias Katz' distillery – "Bistrita", L. Adelstein's – "Saturn", A. Stramwasser's Candy factory, L. Haber & Ciuga Segal's Vegetable Oil Factory and Lupu Klein's Carbonated Acid Factory.

Among the forestry enterprises were: in 1918 Iosif Feldher founded a Timber factory – "Bicazul", later transformed in "Forestiera de Nord" S.A. (inc.), which had 97 workers in 1944. Calmanovici's Timber Factory had 200 workers [153]. Other factories in this field were D. Z. Goldenberg & Sons with 20 workers and "Lemncom" owned by J. Ellenbogen.

In the metallurgical sector, the most important was Davidovici & Sons foundry, created in 1918 [154]. Initially in 1925, it had only 25 workers; it developed gradually, through technical investments and by increasing its number of workers fivefold.

Another important unit was Blum-Fainaru's Oil Refinery, which aside from diesel and paraffin produced gasoline for the aviation and automobile industries [155].

It is beyond the scope of this book to describe all the factories founded and managed by Jewish people. However, it is clear that hundreds of Jewish and Romanian workers and technicians worked in these factories.

The Jewish workers from the textile industry, tanneries and leather factories, mills and printing organizations lived mostly on Leca Street and the neighbouring areas (near the tanneries on Factories Street) as well as in the Bacau-Piatra area, all districts of poor people.

Furthermore, the economic life of Bacau was also enhanced by some of the banks founded by Jewish people. In 1919, the Credit Bank was founded as a Credit Union for the tradesmen. S. Filderman was the Central Bank's chairman of the administrative council while Aurel Negrescu was director; in 1924 the bank doubled its social capital [156]. Ozias Hersovici also owned a bank. The other banking institutions that Jews were employed in were Marmorsch-Blank branch in Bacau, Small Credit Bank and The Romanian Commercial Bank.

The talented journalist Marius Mircu had the unique idea of publishing a list of all the households that existed during the interwar period on Main Street and on the central part of the Bacau-Piatra Street. Thus he painted a very authentic picture of all the trades of people living in these areas, among which were many Jews. The picture is significant for the Jewish socio-professional structure as well as for the social psychology of the era. We list here some of the existing businesses from this part of the city: The Jewish Teashop, Herman Schwartz' Viennese Tailor shop, the Moritz' Salon, acupuncture salons, the "Consumption" bar/restaurant, Herman Isac's Fine Restaurant, the renowned Old Grunberg – for yeast; "Voaleta Bacaului" – Milca Marcusohn, the resturant "Sorbona" – Taica Gutman, and the bars "The Fair Scale", "The Riders' Junction", "The White Horse" etc.

149. State Archives of Bacau, the foundation for Industry and Trade Chambers, brief 21/1934, p. 200-202 and Gr. Grigorovici, *Literary Works*, p. 208
150. Ibid, City Hall Foundation, brief 27/1921
151. Dumitru Zaharia, Emilia Chiriacescu *Literary Works*, The Food Industry, brief 193
152. State Archives of Bacau, the foundation for Industry and Trade Chambers, brief 21/1934, p. 150-169
153. Dumitru Zaharia, Emilia Chiriacescu *Literary Works*, The Wood Industry, p. 181
154. State Archives of Bacau, the foundation for Industry and Trade Chambers, brief 21/1934, p. 199
155. Gr. Grigorovici, *Literary Works*, p. 120
156. *The Official Monitor*, Feb. 2nd 1926

A similar list of the households in Leca Street would have been as noteworthy. Unfortunately, we must rely only on the memories of those who spent their childhood on the street where many tradesmen, office workers, merchants and industrial workers lived. This was the street of the poverty-stricken Jews. Its residents spoke both Romanian and Yiddish and even though they were not very religious people, they were closer to the Jewish tradition than many of the wealthy Jews who lived in other parts of the city. Leca Street was the centre of Jewish gatherings during the Purim, when it would be become animated by the fiddlers' music. It would also become full of life in the fall holidays, when even the rich would go to Bistrita to wash off their sins by doing the "Tasleh"; you could see them throwing away in the river…the dust from their pockets. On Leca Street, there were also sidewalk artists who would bring with them the songs of all Jewish areas. This is where the big muscled porters and carriage-drivers would organize the "defence" when it was known that Cuza's supporters or the "green shirts" intended to "visit" the Jews. Without being an actual ghetto it was the street that conferred them protection, a street where many Jewish and Zionist Organizations had their headquarters.

However, from time to time, there would be trouble on Leca Street, among which was the memorable fire, which immortalized Bacau in the famous quartet:

In Bacau, in Bacau
In a suburb
A great, great mess
Cropped up…

The challenging life of this large number of simple people, poverty-stricken but always hopeful for a brighter future has been reflected in the works of Marcel Marcian, Mihail sabin, Al. Simion and Al. Sever. As early as the end of the First World War, the Jews realized that they had to continue fighting to obtain their civil and political rights, equal to the rest of the population. The Native Jews Union, later named The Romanian Jews Union had resumed its activity in Bacau. In 1918, the local office of the Union organized a solicitor's office committee for citizenship having 6 members, led by physician A. Brill [157]. The Jews welcomed the late government approval for Jewish naturalization as well as the proclamation of the new Constitution. The Jews enlisted themselves on the naturalization lists, while the Jewish community followed closely the judicial process by which the citizenship was conferred.

Alongside its leaders, the entire Jewish community of Bacau took part in expressing their joy regarding the unification of the country under a democratic process. However, they soon noticed that the anti-Semitic forces were opposing the democratic progression. Such anti-Jewish events, for which both high-school and university students were trained, took place in Bacau in 1922 [158]. During the same time, manifestos against the New Constitution were being dispersed. In 1923, also part of the anti-Semitic movement, they disturbed a show organized by some Jewish students, breaking windows and destroying some Jewish houses and stores [159].

Many more such chauvinistic acts took place in Bacau in the inter-war decades. In 1925, the Jews passing by the Public Garden were disrespected and beaten up[160], while in 1927 some groups armed with clubs destroyed many Jewish districts[161] and spread a hatred document called "The Manifesto of the Christian National Romanian Worker's Group" [162]. Grigore Urziceanu, a fascist writer published many articles full of hatred, mocking the Jews who fought and died in the country's Unification War [163].

The impoverished Jews held the memory of Dr. Aroneanu who had been savagely killed in police dungeons for advocating social-democratic ideas. In the Leca district, one could hear the now famous song:

157. RJU's Bulletin, year 1, no. 1, Sept. 1st 1918, p.2
158. State Archives of Bacau, the Jewish Common foundation, brief 23/1922, p. 98-99
159. Ibid, brief 9/1923, p.99
160. *The Equality*, October 2nd 1925
161. *The Jewish Courier*, April 3rd, 1927
162. State Archives of Bacau, the Jewish Common foundation, brief 8/1927, p. 12
163. *Fraternity*, (governing body for the Christian students of Bacau), July 1st 1929.

"The sad children are looking up and down
Wondering where their father has been taken
He's not coming back, not on this ground
Since Major Polter, crazy dog
Has killed Dr. Aroneanu..."

The large Romanian population, preoccupied with its everyday living were estranged from the chauvinistic attitudes. In 1930, when Solo Brucar, one of the town prestigious lawyers died, stores were closed and the courthouse delayed its trials, while all his colleagues went to the funeral.

The direction promoted by the Romanian Jews Union (RJU), also shared by the leaders of the community in Bacau, was that Jews had to fight for obeying the laws, working in the democratic parties. They had been accepted in various parties, however without playing any important role. It is well known that the political parties of the time, instead of intensifying the democratic process, were promoting a "blind" policy by tolerating various antidemocratic, chauvinistic and retrograde movements. Common sense forced these parties to allow Jews to be part of the democratic life, but they only admitted this to the local authorities.

Some of the proficient Jews had enlisted on the Communal Election Party Lists; as such in 1926, there were 6 Jews enlisted on the National Labourers Party list[164]. Although the discrimination against Jews was quite visible, the RJU persisted in its attitude, even more so making it a priority in the Community Leadership elections. Its advocating position was also made public in the 1926 conference, led by the industrialist Ozias Herscovici, the president of Bacau's community as well as the Community's Councillor. The lawyer Eugen Manas was also part of the Community Council [165] and together with Herscovici got re-elected in 1928. The County's Council was made up of I. L. Ianovici, L. Iosup – lawyer and A. I. Israilovici [166]. In 1930, ten Jews were elected as members of the Community Council: Iosif Feldher, Herman Kisler, Avram Simon, Ozias Herscovici, Dr. A. Brill and others [167].

The community leaders in Bacau were encouraging the Jewish population to show their dedication for the country. As such, on "National Days" (May 10th, Heroes Day, and Unification Day) the Jews were called to take part in the public referendums. Should the city's administration call on its people, the Jews were encouraged to participate. As a result, in 1928 around Christmas, when City Hall had made a request to help the poor, many Jewish business made important donations: F. Klein's business, The Commercial Club through C. Braynstein and I. Iancovici, L. & L.O. Klien etc [168]. As a sign of solidarity to the town's population, in 1933 the Jewish community was involved in collecting money for rebuilding the town of Marasesti, which prompted the City Hall to show their gratitude [169]. Furthermore, in 1939, when the campaign for lending equipment was launched, the Jews thought they should be the first to honour it [170]. During the same year, due to a great drought, the Rabbi's Office instituted a day to fast and pray for rain [171].

The numerous journalists from the local newspapers have also worked on bringing together the Jewish and Christian communities. Advocating fair resolution of the town's issues, they promoted a spirit of order, legality and responsibility, thus trying to create a lobby group favouring democracy and progress. Bernard Klein was vice-president of the Newspapers Association of Bacau; Paul Kissler-Bistriceanu – editor-in-chief of "Bacau's Newspaper"; Emil Mititelu – director of "Bacau's Tribune", Roland Kaufman – editor of the weekly magazine "Bacau's Issues" and then of "The Hour". The most important local newspaper was "Bacaul", which for many years was edited by M. Margulius Maragrit, I. Voldei and M. Zilberstein; a permanent columnist for this newspaper was Hary Rabinsohn. Lupu Glasman and Marius Mircu, a renowned columnist were correspondents for the central press.

164. *The Equality*, February 26th 1926
165. Ibid, April 9th 1926
166. *The Equality*, August 27th 1926
167. *The Universe*, July 6th 1930
168. State Archives of Bacau, fond City Hall, brief 12/1928, p.39, 65, 67
169. Ibid, the Jewish Common foundation, brief 4/1937, p. 79
170. Ibid, the Jewish Common foundation, brief 25/1934, p. 5
171. Ibid, the Jewish Common foundation, brief 8/1934, p. 25

It is worth mentioning here a phenomenon specific for Bacau of those times, which affected both the Romanian and Jewish population alike. We are talking about the great fires, which arose for some unknown reason quite frequently, destroying many households, usually the less fortunate ones. Bacau was famous for its great many fires and this became obvious in the folk songs the children were singing: "Popovici's mill is burning and the firemen in Bacau have made it even worse." The writer Marius Marcu echoed this calamity in his works in a typical Jewish humour, emphasizing the "Great Fire of 1926".

In the years following 1930, internationally, the ascension of the aggressive fascist troupes became a threatening force. Nationally, the activities of right-wing extremists amplified.

Many Jews started to see they were facing tough times ahead, when the Jewish population may itself be brutalized by fascists. In an attempt to prevent the threatening dangers lying ahead, some Jews, especially the workers, joined illegal leftist associations, taking part in factory strikes (for example, Lovingher Herman, Zisu Weingarten, Ioinovici Serena etc). Many were arrested, sentenced to many tough years in prison and later sent to prison camps (Steinbach Iosif, Leibu M. Volf, Seinstein Mali, Zisu Solomon and others). Six Jews from Bacau went as volunteers to Spain, taking part in the civil war along side the anti-Fascist forces.

To be truthful, we must mention that, although they shared RJU's attitude, which favoured their status, the prosperous leaders of the Jewish community felt the precarious attitude of this organization; they recognized its insufficiencies in front of the strengthening anti-Jewish movement. Many of them would manifest their approval of the Zionist Cult, especially in front of the Central Organizations. As far as the Jewish masses were concerned, the Zionist Movement was their only hope in creating a Jewish territory on their ancestors' land. Numerous youngsters enrolled in various Zionist organisations and began diverse Zionist spiritual & ideological preparation activities. Some of them reached Palestine, thus becoming the pioneers of creating the future Israel.

Translation:

"Here lies the great man, honoured Aharon, the son of the late Iosif, who passed away on Jan 29, buried on 12 Sivan 5464, May his soul rest in peace."

Funeral Stone

Found in the old cemetery in Bacau and laid at the Jewish Community Federation Museum in Bucharest – confirming Jewish origins in Bacau as early as 300 years ago

5752-5464 = 288 years

[5464 was 1704]

The Museum "The History of the Jewish Community in Bacau, 1703-1944

Vechimea Evreilor în Băcău

Așezat lângă râul Bistrița, orașul Bacău pare a avea o vechime considerabilă. Istoria nu ne dă în mod precis nici originea numelui Bacău și nici data fundării orașului. Tradițiunea cea mai răspândită prin popor [illegible] în asta privință, este că cel d'intâi, care s'a așezat p'aici, a fost un Ungur cu numele de Bacut, și că data fundării este anterioară anului 1500. Unii bătrâni spun chiar că ar fi auzit de la părinții lor, că biserica Precista este fundată de Ștefan cel Mare, care cu ocaziunea trecerii sale prin această localitate, găsind aici creștini ortodocși fără biserică, le-a zidit el cea d'intâi biserică.

Primii locuitori ai acestui oraș au fost catolici; după dânșii au venit Românii și apoi Evrei, Bulgari, Greci, Armeni, Sârbi, etc. Și astăzi încă dintre creștini cei mai vechi sunt Ungurii. (?)

Data fixă a stabilirii Evreilor în acest oraș, nu se poate preciza, dar că a existat aici o comunitate veche, se constată din cartea I a descrierei d-lui Psantir, care a cercetat inscripțiunile [illegible] de pe mormintele vechi ale cimitirului actual. Părinții însă ne-au povestit, că înainte de cimitirul actual, a existat un cimitir vechiu, părăsit din cauza [illegible] ciumei. În privința situațiunii vechiului cimitir sunt două versiuni: unii spun, că ar fi fost așezat sub dealul bisericii Precista, iar alții cred că a fost sub dealul Izvoarele pe lângă fabrica de hârtie. Din

First page of A. D. Birnberg's monograph "The Jewish Origins in Bacau"

The Central Archives for the History of the Jewish People

L. Carniol's Seal – Brandy Making – year 1856

The Museum "The History of the Jewish Community in Bacau, 1703-1944

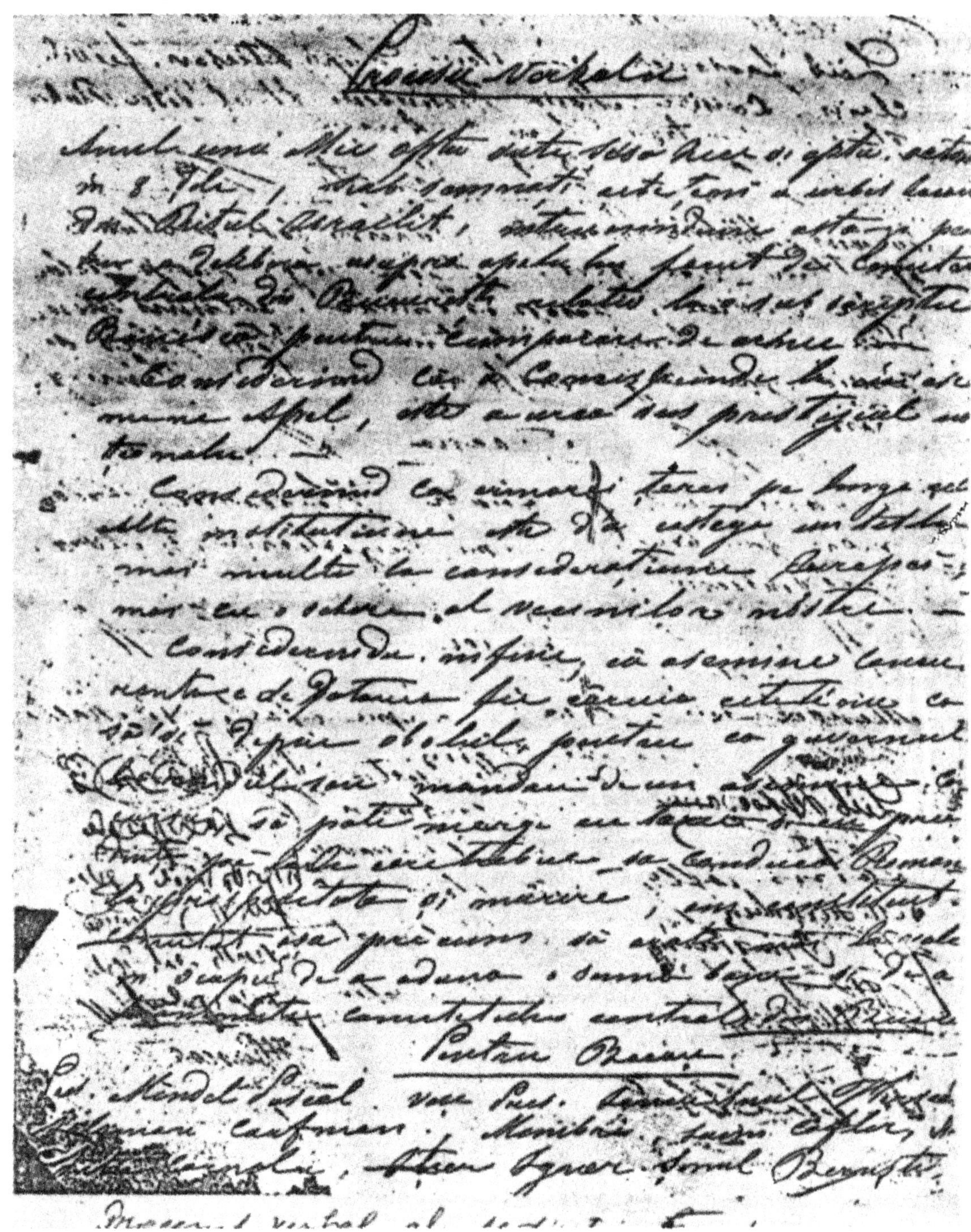

The Minutes Report of the Community Leader's Meeting from Bacau, Tg. Ocna and Parincea from July 8th 1898, for appointing the country's enarming

The Central Archives for the History of the Jewish People

Arthur Ehrlich, erou al războiului din 1877

rthur Ehrlich și cei trei feciori ai săi, în uniformă

Arthur Ehrlich, Hero of the 1877 War
(Arthur Ehrlich and his three sons in uniform)

The Museum "The History of the Jewish Community in Bacau, 1703-1944

Inscriptions on a funeral stone

H. Haimberg
Veteran of the 1877 war
Deceased May 10, 1915
69 years old

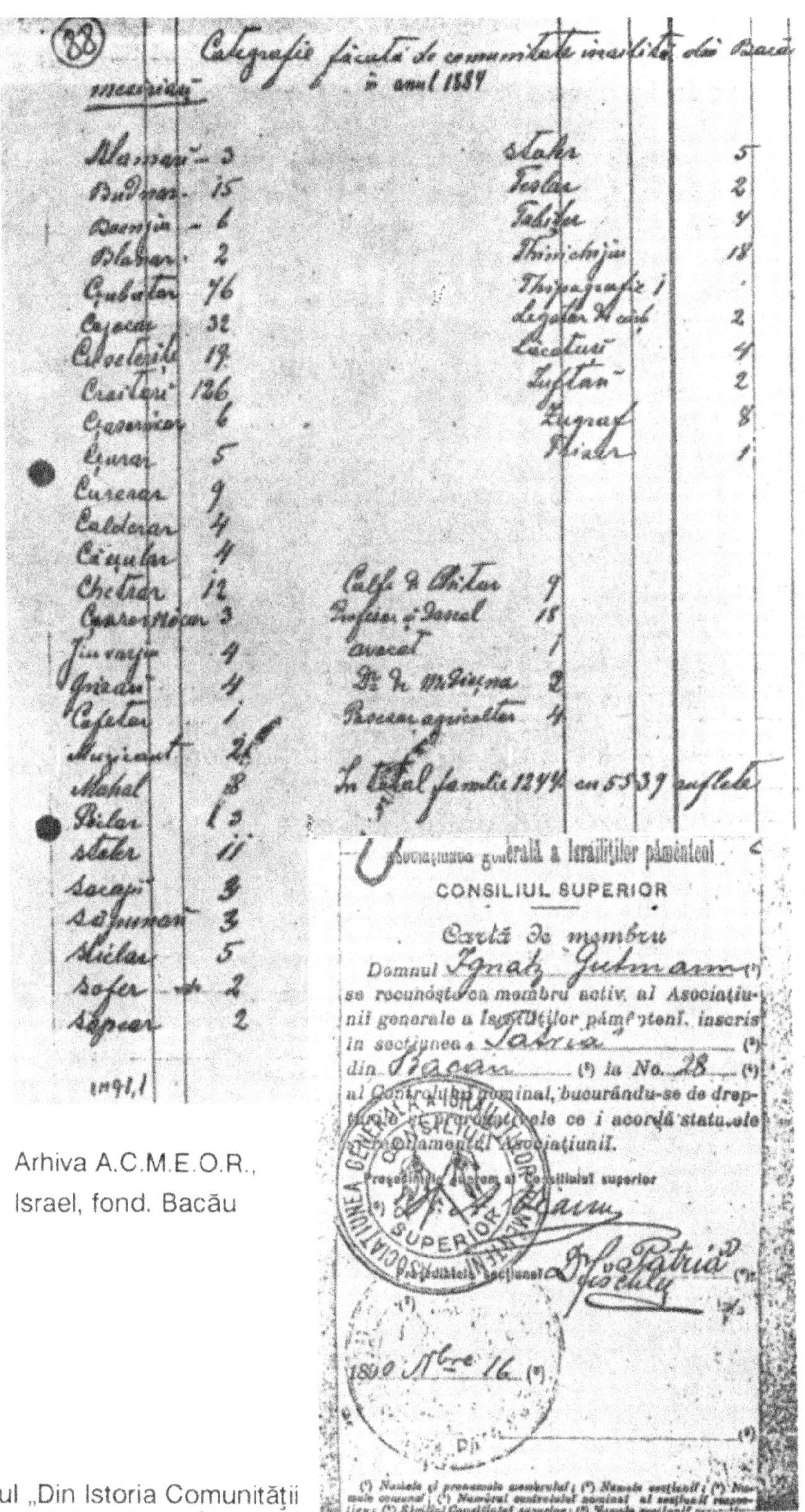

(88) Catagrafie făcută de comunitatea israelită din Bacău în anul 1884

meseriași

In total familii 1244 cu 5539 suflete

Asociațiunea generală a Israeliților pământeni

CONSILIUL SUPERIOR

Cartă de membru

Domnul Ignatz Gutmann (¹) se recunoaște ca membru activ, al Asociațiunii generale a Israeliților pământeni, inscris in secțiunea „Patria" (²) din Bacau (³) la No. 28 (⁴) al Controlului nominal, bucurându-se de drepturile și prerogativele ce i acordă statutele și regulamentul Asociațiunii.

Președintele Comitetului Consiliului superior

Președintele secțiunei

1890 Nbre 16 (⁵)

Arhiva A.C.M.E.O.R., Israel, fond. Bacău

ul „Din Istoria Comunităţii

Photo of the philanthropist Flaivus Klein

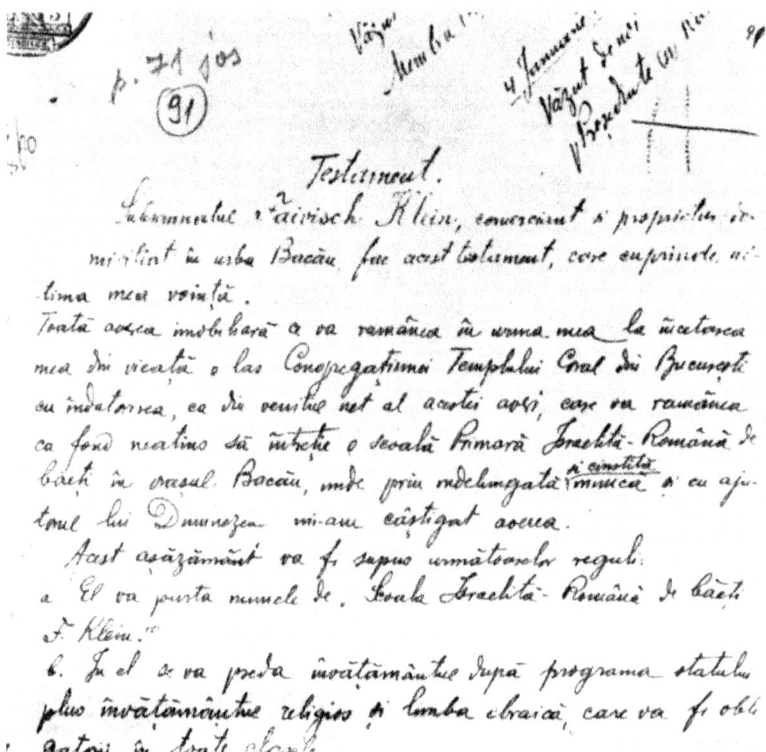

p. 71 jos

(91)

Testament.

Subsemnatul Faivisch Klein, comerciant și proprietar domiciliat în urbea Bacău, fac acest testament, care cuprinde ultima mea voință.

Toată averea imobiliară ce va rămânea în urma mea la încetarea mea din viață o las Congregațiunei Templului Coral din București cu îndatorirea, ca din venitul net al acestei averi, care va rămânea ca fond neatins să întreție o școală Primară Israelită-Română de băeți în orașul Bacău, unde prin îndelungata și cinstita muncă și cu ajutorul lui Dumnezeu mi-am câștigat averea.

Acest așezământ va fi supus următoarelor reguli:

a. El va purta numele de „Școala Israelită-Română de băeți F. Klein."

b. În el se va preda învățământul după programa statului plus învățământul religios și limba ebraică, care va fi obligatoriu în toate clasele.

The undersigned Faivisch Kelin, owner in Bacau, let this testament represent my last wishes. All my properties shall be given after I am no longer alive to the Congregation of the Coral Temple in Bucharest, with the obligation to maintain them and from their income also maintain a boy school in bacau where, through hard work and with God's will I have earned my fortune. The property shall be under the following restrictions:

a The school will take the name "The Jewish Romanian Boy School F. Klein"

b. The teachings will be done according to the state's program and in addition religious and Hebrew teachings, which will be mandatory in all classes."

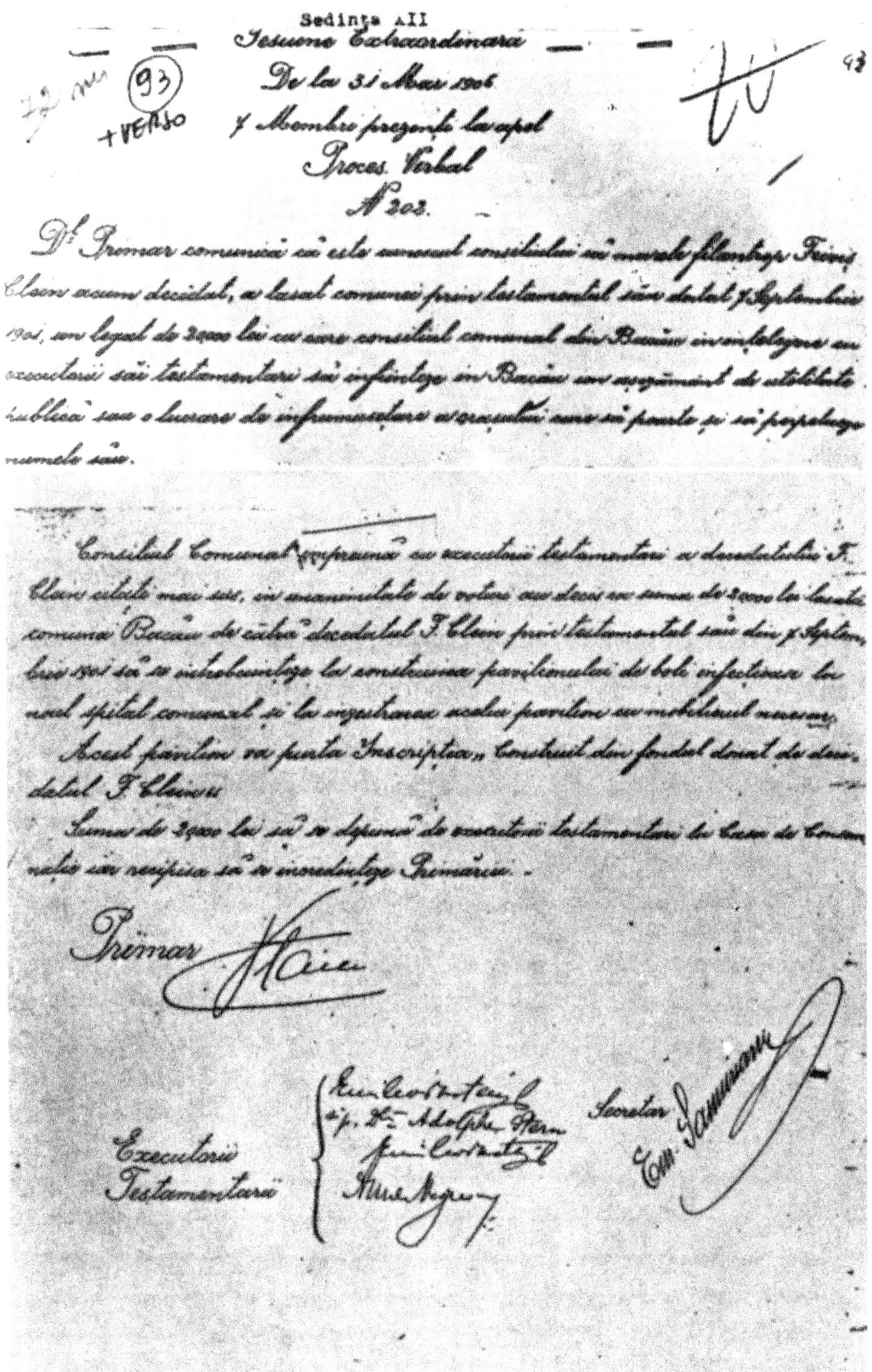

Sedinta a II

Sesiune Extraordinara

De la 31 Mai 1906

7 Membri prezenţi la apel

Proces Verbal

№ 203.

D-l Primar comunică că este cunoscut consiliului că marele filantrop Feiş Clein acum decedat, a lasat comunei prin testamentul său datat 7 Septembrie 1901, un legat de 2000 lei cu care consiliul comunal din Bacău in înţelegere cu executorii săi testamentari să înfiinţeze in Bacău un aşezământ de utilitate publică sau o lucrare de înfrumuseţare a oraşului care să poarte şi să perpetueze numele său.

Consiliul Comunal împreună cu executorii testamentari ai decedatului F. Clein citaţi mai sus, cu unanimitate de voturi au decis ca suma de 2000 lei lăsată comunei Bacău de către decedatul F. Clein prin testamentul său din 7 Septembrie 1901 să se întrebuinţeze la construirea pavilionului de boli infecţioase la noul spital comunal şi la înzestrarea acelui pavilion cu mobilierul necesar.

Acest pavilion va purta inscripţia „Construit din fondul donat de decedatul F. Clein“.

Suma de 2000 lei să se depună de executorii testamentari la Casa de Consemnaţiuni iar recipisa să se încredinţeze Primăriei.

Primar

Executorii Testamentari

Secretar

Extracts from F. Klein's will

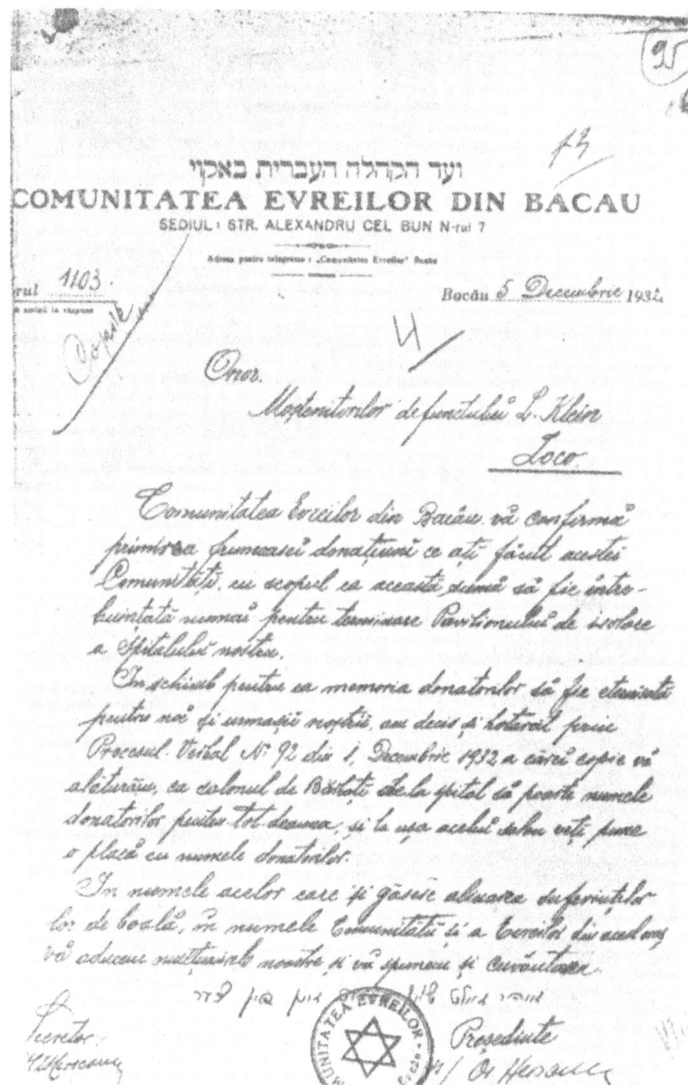

ועד הקהלה העברית באקוי

COMUNITATEA EVREILOR DIN BACAU

SEDIUL: STR. ALEXANDRU CEL BUN N-rul 7

N-rul 1103.

Bacău 5 Decembrie 1932

Onor.

Moștenitorilor defunctului L. Klein

Loco

Comunitatea Evreilor din Bacău vă confirmă primirea frumoasei donațiuni ce ați făcut acestei Comunități, cu scopul ca această sumă să fie întrebuințată numai pentru terminarea Pavilionului de izolare a Spitalului nostru.

În schimb pentru ca memoria donatorilor să fie eternizată pentru noi și urmașii noștri, am decis și hotărât prin Procesul Verbal № 92 din 1 Decembrie 1932 a cărui copie vă alăturăm, ca salonul de Bărbați de la spital să poarte numele donatorilor pentru totdeauna, și la ușa acelui salon veți pune o placă cu numele donatorilor.

În numele acelor care își găsesc alinarea suferințelor lor de boală, în numele Comunității și a Evreilor din acel oraș vă aducem mulțumirile noastre și vă spunem și [illegible].

Secretar [illegible] Președinte [illegible]

Extracts from F. Klein's will

The JEWISH COMMUNITY OF BACAU

Bacau, December 5, 1932

To the Heirs of F. Klein's estatate:

The Jewish Community of Bacau will confirm receiving the donations made to this community, with the purpose that this money be used for finishing the Isolation Pavilion of our Hospital. In the memory of those who made donations we propose that one of the hospital's wings people to be named after them. In the memory of those who find comfort for their illnesses and in the name of the community and of the Jewish people, we express our gratitude.

Signed by President

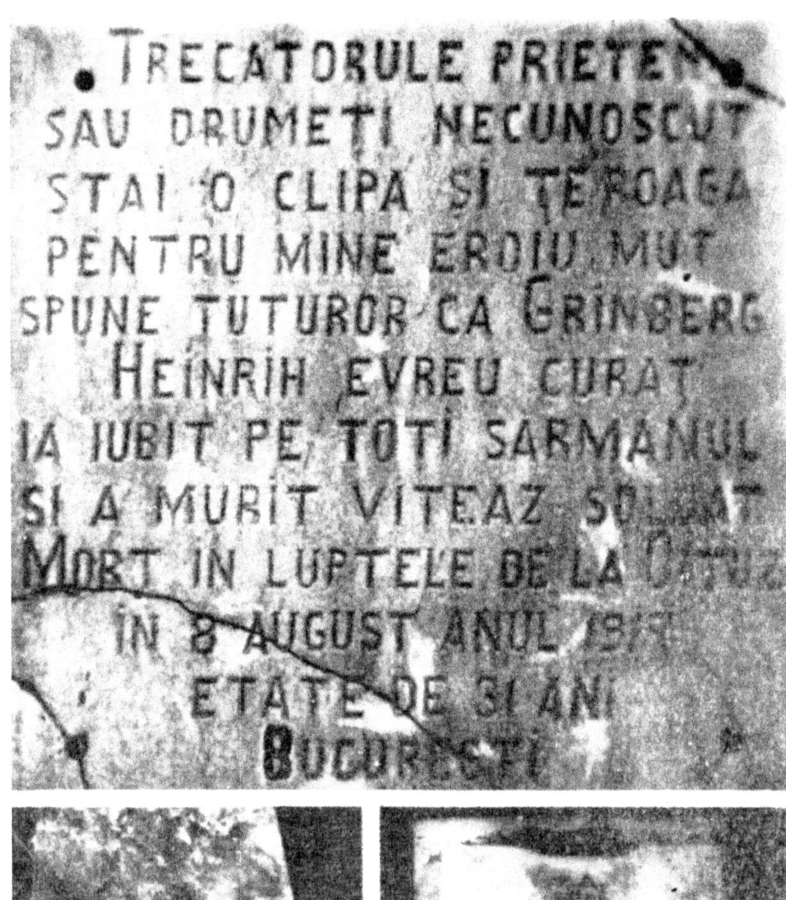

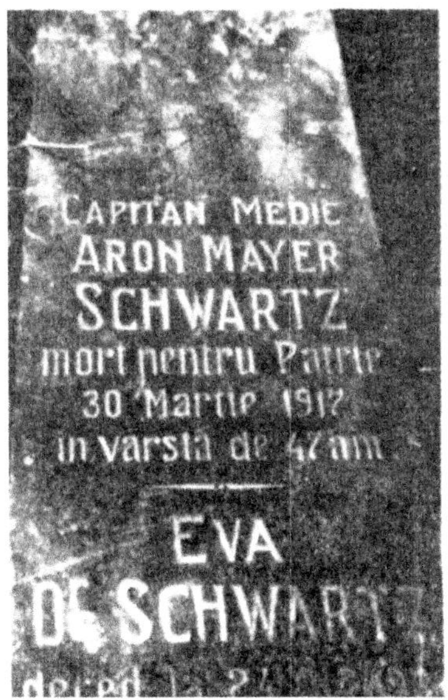

TOP: You friendly passerby or you unknown traveler, take a moment and pray for me, mute hero. Tell everyone that Grinberg Heinrih, honest Jew, loved everybody poor him and died as a courageous soldier. He died in the fight from Untuz on August 8, 1917. He was 31 yars old. Bucharest.

BOTTOM: Captain Aron Mayer Schwartz – died for the country on March 30, 1917 – 42 years old

Ornamentation on a funeral stone, 5608 (1848)

REGATUL ROMANIEI

MINISTERUL DE RESB

BREVET

Din Ordinul

Majestatei Sale Regele Carol I

Şeful suprem al Armatei

... Altar de la

Cercul de recrutare Bacau ... medalia

Avântul Ţării pentru că a luat parte în campania din anul 1913.

In numele Ministrului de Resbel

Comandant Cercului

The Museum "The History of the Jewish Community in Bacau, 1703-1944

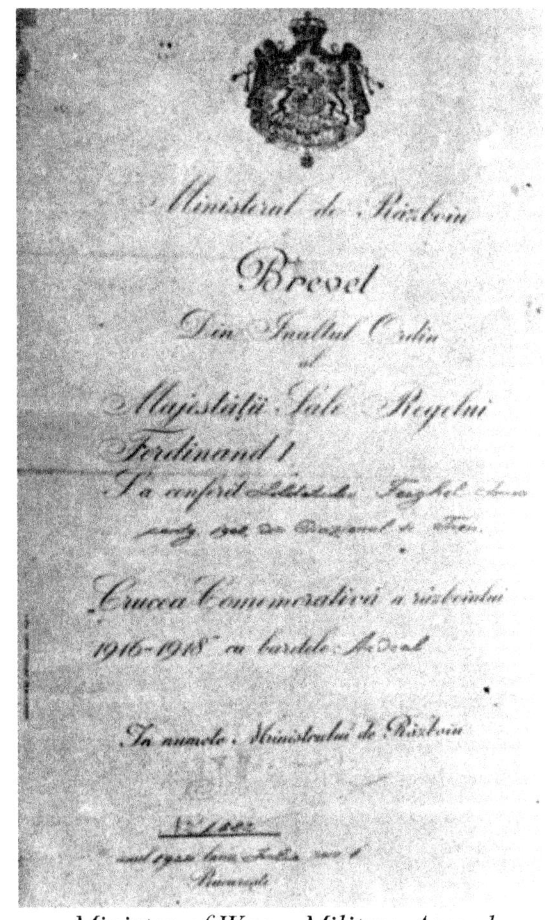

Ministerul de Războiu

Brevet

Din Înaltul Ordin

al

Majestăţii Sale Regelui

Ferdinand I

S'a conferit [illegible]

[illegible]

Crucea Comemorativă a războiului

1916-1918 cu baretele [illegible]

În numele Ministerului de Războiu

[illegible]

Ministry of War – Military Award

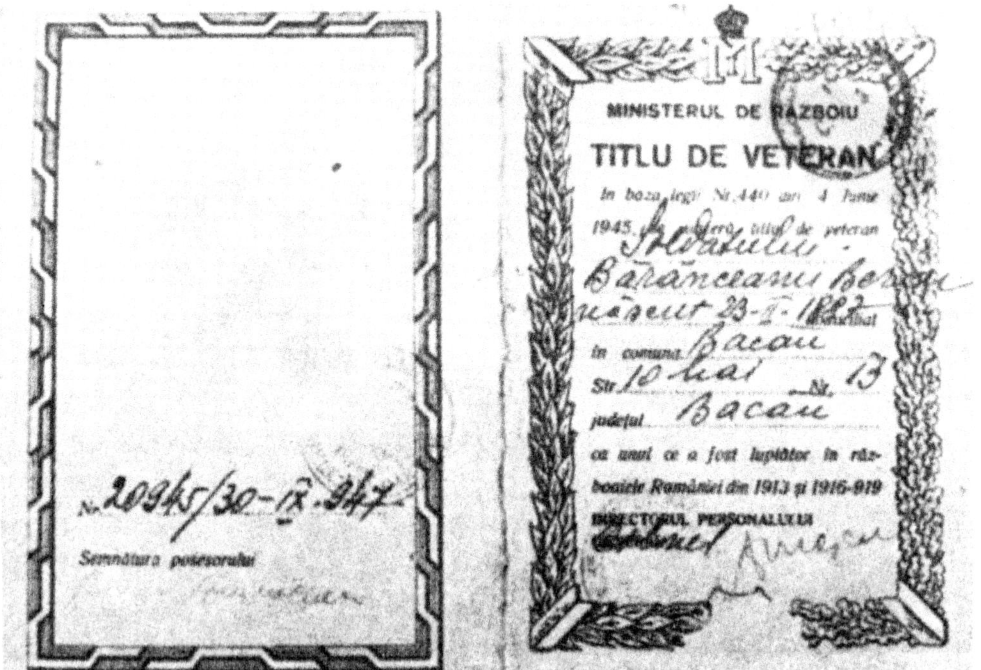

Nr. 20945/30-IX-947

Semnătura posesorului

MINISTERUL DE RAZBOIU

TITLU DE VETERAN

In baza legii Nr. 440 din 4 Iunie 1945, se acordă titlul de veteran Soldatului Barănceanu născut 23-II-1887 domiciliat în comuna Bacau Str. 10 Mai Nr. 13 judeţul Bacau ca unul ce a fost luptător în războaiele României din 1913 şi 1916-919

DIRECTORUL PERSONALULUI

Given to soldier Baranceanu born on February 23, 1887 in Bacau, address 10 May Street No13 Bacau in recognization of his efforts as a fighter in Romania's wars from 1913 and 1916-1919. Signed by the staff director Military Awards.

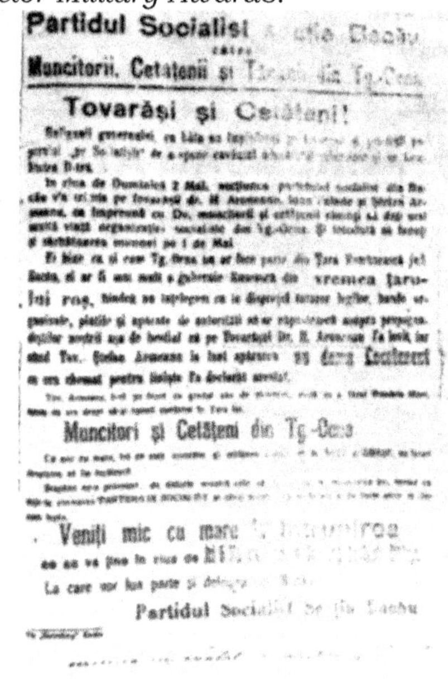

Partidul Socialist

către

Muncitorii, Cetăţenii şi

Tovarăşi şi Cetăţeni!

Muncitori şi Cetăţeni din Tg.-Ocna

Veniţi mic cu mare

Partidul Socialist

Doctor H. Aroneanu l88l-1920.
Died as a martyr in trying to accomplish the workers' claims. Dec.2

B. The Jewish Community of Bacau Throughout the Years

1. Historic Evolution of the Jewish Community

During the years of the feudal system, the Jews in Moldova were organized in the "Jewish Guild", which ensured them a religious autonomy, but also corresponded to the interests of the princely Treasury and those of the local authorities. Indeed, the guild had the obligation to gather the tributes and taxes that the Jews owed and transfer them to the "account" of the Treasury or of the local authorities; they had to inform the Jews about the decisions made by the reign or by the regional sub-prefects and to make sure they respected these decisions. At a local level, the community chiefs, who were elected by the Jewish population and confirmed by the Reign, fulfilled these tasks. In 1828, the Chief-Rabbi of Moldova, Hahambasa Saim, Iehosua Naftulovici, received the right from the Ruler to name the chiefs of all the Jewish communities in Moldova.

At Bacau, the first chief who was historically certified was Leiba, who got permission from the townsmen of Bacau to build a house.

According to A. D. Birnberg's narration, after many decades, the old men of the town remembered that, in 1809, there were "Motel's father", who was called "old Aron" and "Iona Beer's father". In 1830, Herscu san Meier and Marcu san Lupu, who traded in corn, were community chiefs.

Although, after the Treaty of Adrianopol, the Organic Regulation provided the elimination of the ethnical and religious guilds, the Jewish guild was maintained for a while, as the Treasury could not collect the tributes directly from the Jewish population. The guild continued to collect sums of money by means of the "taxes on ritual slaughtering of cattle and poultry" (gabela). From the cash collected for the ritual slaughtering, the guild paid the tribute of the Jewish population. But, out of this amount, they also had to make payment to the worship servers (Rabbi, Hahami), the expenses for religious education (Talmud Tora), for social assistance, etc. Therefore, taxing was a problem for the community leaders, and often times a difficult problem to solve.

In his monograph, A. D. Birnberg showed that, in the first decades of the 19th century, wealthy Jews named the leaders of the community in Bacau. During the reign of Ionita Sandu, a certain Aron san Motel named who ever he wanted to lead the community.

The community chiefs had problems with tax collection, as we can see in a document from 1832[172]. In 1834/1836, Volf (the Wolf) Rosenberg was the community chief. (A document from the Archives of 1835[178] mentions the wife of

[172] State Archives of Iasi, Prefecture of Bacau, Tr. 84, op. 1009, file 252.
[173] "Bulletin", official paper, 1835, p. 435.

"the Wolf, Chief of Bacau"). This chief had conflicts with the "Sudit" Jews (a category of the inhabitants under foreign jurisdiction), who did not want to take part in the expenses and the taxes paid by the "Raiele" Jews, that is the Jews who were "obedient to the land". A complaint of the Sudit Jews, dated January 12th, 1834, shows that Volf Rosenberg, Chief of the Raiele Jews, oppressed them[179]. The Sudits claimed that, after the entry of the Russian army, they paid four times the taxes paid by the Raiele Jews. "Volf, the Chief, having made an understanding with the Prefecture, encouraged the Raiele to hold taxes for all the Jews, that is 8 coins for the slaughtering of a poultry and for three pounds of meat. If they did not obey, "they were not given meat". Claiming that they "starved" because they were not given meat, the Sudits asked for "the Sword Bearer Sion to leave them alone and to be given meat, and not to be obliged to pay taxes". Signed: Marcu Pauker, Nisan Pauker, Ilie Cofler, Pinhas san Lupu, Yeiling Barladeanu, Yeiling san Cune, Itic Leiba, Avram Vechsler, Smil Kindler, Iosif Burman, Iontu Cofler, Marcu Zingher, and Moise Leiba.

Taxes were levied every year – another source of conflicts. In 1845, the Jewish community of Bacau made a complaint that the tenant of the taxes hadn't paid the taxes of the community to the Treasury, as provided in the leasing contract of the taxes[175].

The leaders of the community had to face material difficulties, as well as other problems. In 1836, the Jews asked for permission to "rebuild two synagogues made of wood which are in ruins". Based on this request, the Prefecture of Bacau analyzed the documents, according to which these two synagogues had been built, controlling the distance they at which they find themselves from the church. Here is what the report of the prefecture claimed: "...the holy Christian church has been built for 140 years, and there is no other proof than two documents from 1790 and another one from 1794, of some citizens, showing that they gave to a certain Iancu, Jewish commander, and to a certain Leibu, a piece of land next to the Jewish school, without being clear neither in copy nor at the Prefecture what the distance is between these places and the school in order to make any notice"[176]. After this report, there was an order to move the synagogues. As a consequence, the Jews submitted, on July 13th, 1836, the following complaint: "We, the Jewish people from the town of Bacau, following with honor the order of the Big Chancellery and Ministry of Foreign Affairs from July 3rd, 1836, no. 109, where we are ordered that, having been given by the townsmen the place three years ago, we had built the school at the cost of 1500 ROL, we cannot afford to move it, and first of all the school has been built on that location since the beginning of the town"[177]. The following people signed in Hebrew letters: Iosef from Bacau, Smuel Kendler, Todros, son of Pinhas, Abraham Iunger, Iehuda Toref (that is sealer, engraver – *n.n.*), Moise Ithac from Bacau, Moise Leib, son of Iosef, Mordehai Hendler. Subsequently, on September 23rd, 1836, "the community of the town of Bacau"

---

179 State Archives of Iasi, Tr. 1764, op. 2013, no. 265, p. 314.

175 *Idem*, Inv., State Secretariat of Moldova, 1866, no. 1300.

agreed to the rebuilding of a synagogue; actually, the approval came from a further authority, from the Department of Inner Affairs, on the condition that the new synagogue should be rebuilt "in the same yard"[178].

In 1837, the leaders of the Jews in Bacau had difficult financial problems again[179] and in September 1839, the Jews from Bacau were on trial with the Sword Bearer Telman Lazar, for the "demolition of their school", that is of their old synagogue[180].

On June 7th, 1845, Leibu Buium made a contract with the leaders of the Jewish people from Bacau for the lease of a "Jewish public bath", an institution of urgent necessity from the ritual point of view, and which ensured a certain income to the community[181]. In 1855, the Jews in Bacau obtained from the Treasury a barren piece of land so they built themselves a synagogue on it: they paid annual long lease[182].

In that period, the administration of the cemetery, the ritual of the burial, as well as certain community problems were handled by the sacred fraternity ("Hevra Kedosa"), which had been founded since the end of the previous century. There were several philanthropic associations ("Ghemilat Hasadim", created in 1836), aiming to find solutions for different financial and community problems, or to support the religious education ("Talmud Tora" Association, founded in 1837).

The last chief of the Jews from Bacau who is historically certified was Lupu Burah. But Iancu from the Ward also seems to have been a chief, as he is introduced in Gr. Grigorovici's Monograph as the President of the Jewish community in 1848. He is the one who initiated the creation of a Jewish hospital; therefore, he was mentioned in the report of the Schuler hospital from 1940.

However, the middle of the 19th century is the moment when the documents of the Archives no longer talk about the "Chiefs of the community", but about the "Community", about the "Guardians of the Community" or about the "Community Committee". Here is what A. D. Birnberg said in his monograph: "Under the reign of Prince Cuza, the old 'Jewish community' was recognized as a 'community' with a legal status". During the decade 1850-1860, when decisive events took place in the Romanian Principalities, events that marked the transition of the Romanian society towards a modern state, the new administrative organization and the new fiscal laws caused changes in the functions and activities of the Jewish authorities. As they no longer had the obligation to collect and deposit the sums owed by the Jewish population as taxes, or the obligation to keep the record of the registrar's office, the community authorities had the opportunity to focus more on the organization of the inner life of the community, on the problems of worshipping, of education, of social assistance. The administrative authorities no longer had the

[176] *Idem*, Tr. 361, op. 392, no. 114, p.30.
[177] *Idem*, Tr. 361, op. 392, no. 167, penultimate page not numbered
[178] *Idem*, Tr. 361, op. 392, file 104, p. 11
[179] *Idem*, Prefecture of Bacau, file 95/1837
[180] *Idem*, Tr. 940-0, p. 1082, file 159
[181] *Idem*, Tr. 1318, op. XIII, 1491, file 154
[182] State Archives of Bacau, Neamt Monastery, file 611, no. 104, package 11/1855.

right to interfere in the organization of the inner life of the Community, which thus received more autonomy. In 1851, the Community of Bacau had the benefit of a "spatial seal", given to the Jewish leaders[183], and on March 15th, 1857, by the address no. 899, the Ministry of Cults granted "the Jewish cult" its patronage and legalized its statute[184]. In order to be able to handle its expenses, the Community leadership still resorted to the salt tax, which they used to lease; thus, in 1860, we see Moise Vaisam on trial with Moise Copelovici, his associate in holding the tax[185]. But the Community leadership did not have the means to impose on the community members its decisions related to the salt tax, the organization and the use of the income of different institutions (synagogues, cemetery, etc.). All these issues would be sources of dissatisfaction and conflicts.

In 1864, the leadership of the Community in Bacau expressed its gratitude to Prince Cuza for his projects of emancipating the Jews. The telegram sent to the Prince was signed by: S. Alterescu, Alter Zilberherz, Mendel Pascal, and David Orenstein.

In the same year, 1864, the Community leadership created a budget which reflected the preoccupations that the Committee had at that time. Initially, the budget included costs of 1153.29 ducats. The Rabbis' wages were of 920 ROL. Of the five chiefs responsible for the ritual cuttings (circumscions), one of them received 48 ROL, another one 62 ROL, and the other three 45 ROL each. A psalm reader was also paid for. The hospital costs, which had four beds, were 168 ROL. Aids for poor children – 37 ROL. 74 ROL were spent to help ill and needy people. For the school (the first modern primary school, created in 1863), the costs were of 270 ROL (the wages of four teachers and a maid, the rent, the winter wood). The budget mentioned the way the necessary amount for all these goals would be obtained: 1205 ROL were to be received from the 12 coin tax; 125 ROL – of bath lease. 222 more ducats had to be collected to build the synagogue "behind the one which was burnt"[186]. One can notice that the community income did not include amounts coming from burials, and the expenses did not mention sums for the maintenance of the cemetery. We can draw the conclusion that, at that time, a "Hevra Kedosa" (Sacred Society) handled these problems, as it was independent from the community authorities.

In 1866, the Jewish leaders replied to the request of the City Hall: "...their cult includes 6 persons: one Rabbi, 5 chiefs responsible for the ritual cuttings, all of them natives, 14 worshippers; there is no modern synagogue or choral temples in this town, but simple schools (houses of prayer) and one worshipper is designated for every school". At the same time, it was mentioned that no religious contract had been signed, "but mere guardians, with prior designation from the Committee, as

---

[183] *Idem*, Jewish Community, package 3, file 36, p.13.
[184] State Archives of Iasi, personal fond. Svart-Kara, Box 4, no. 2.
[185] *Idem*, Law Court of Bacau, Tr. 1636, file 24.
[186] State Archives of Bacau, City Hall of Bacau, no. 51, 1864, p. 34.

you know, whom the Community with no documents elects". It was signed: "Jewish Leadership of Bacau"[187].

In 1868, when Prefect Leca organized the banishment of the Jews in the villages of the county, the Community authorities addressed the Government, asking for measures to be taken in order to stop the abuses. Noticing that the request was not considered the Community leadership asked Baron Rotschild from Vienna to intervene and stop the arbitrary deeds. The following people signed on behalf of the Committee: Iosef Carl Mano, Loeb Grünberg, Moses Birnberg, C. Balstein, R. Wolf.

Still in 1868, the Committee of the Community from Bacau, together with the ones from Moinesti, Tg. Ocna and Parincea, organized themselves to take action to raise money subscriptions in order to buy guns for the country (the minutes of that meeting is in Jerusalem, at the Central Archives for the History of the Jewish People).

The 1877-78 War of Independence was the opportunity for the Community leadership to take action and support the battle for independence, by collecting money, food and drugs for the army.

During the post-war period, people of the community manifested their dissatisfaction towards their leaders. In his monograph, A. D. Birnberg considers that the cause of the conflicts within the community was the difference of opinion between the traditional elements and those that were more opened to modernity. But these were mixed with personal pride and with the tendency towards independence of leaders of certain community institutions (Sacra, synagogues, etc.). It can also be the issue of an unwise administration, as the conclusion can be drawn from a complaint submitted to the City Hall of Bacau in 1880. From this complaint we find out that "between 1873 and 1880, the community guardians cashed around 3 thousand ducats every year from taxes, plus the income from the public bath and the cemetery of 500 ducats, and they gave nothing to the hospital. Between 1877-78, they cashed an extra tax in order to pay the Government 1500 ducats. Only 1200 francs were given. They gave no justification whatsoever for the money". (A request is made for their investigation)[188]. A reaction to this complaint may have been the publishing by the Committee of an "Account of income and expenses from May 22nd 1878 to March 15th 1880", with the note that there are "supporting documents"[189].

One reason that caused the weakness of the community leaders was the fact that they were not representative enough, as they were elected only by the delegations of the synagogues. According to certain sources, the elective system was changed at a certain moment, but the old formula was effective soon afterwards.

---

[187] *Idem*, file 24/5, 1886, p.24.

[188] *Idem*, City Hall of Bacau, file 45/1880, p. 1, 4.

[189] The original is at the Central Archives for the History of the Jewish People, Jerusalem, R. M./77.

In 1884, the Community leadership took the initiative to draft an inventory of the craftsmen in town (the original inventory is at the Central Archives for the History of the Jewish People).

In 1888, the Community leadership was reorganized, including among its members David Orenstein, L. Focsaneanu, Flaivis Klein, H. Grünberg and A. D. Birnberg (who became President)[190]. The Committee took a set of measures to improve the material condition. The Community took the salt tax and leased it to Ch. Bruker, for the amount of 2830 ROL every month, thus ensuring financial means to sustain the worshipping institutions, the social assistance and the education. The tax official was to collect 10 coins for every kilo of meat. A committee was held responsible to control and develop a report related to Talmud Tora, which was attended by many poor children[191].

On March 23rd, 1888, the building from Alex. cel Bun Street, which is still the Community office, was bought from Dimitrie Rosetti-Tetcanu[192].

Here is its financial situation, according to the report of the balance for the year 1890, presented by A. D. Birnberg: the income was of 93,295 ROL, coming mainly from the salt tax and real estate rents. In order to increase the income, they organized collections, balls and other actions, which benefited from the collaboration of D. Marcovici, C.Cofler, I. A. Calman, M. Orenstein, M. Balter and others. The expenses were 33,251 ROL. The report mentioned the good performance of the hospital, which now had 14-15 beds and had taken care of 160 patients; the hospital director was Dr. Marcovici, assisted by Dr. Fr. Müller, Ed. Baroni, N. Mancas and C. Fischler. The classes at Talmud Tora had been subsidized with 3897 ROL and 8420 ROL had been given to the poor[193].

The new committee, which was elected in 1894, was led by A. Balter, and it included the following people: Is. Z. Giuvaergiu, I. L. Hertanu, Artur Ehrlich (veteran from 1877), Ozias Feldman, Nuta Ernst, Herman Isac, Filip Grünberg, F. Davidescu and Israel Kraus. By their efforts, the hospital building was rebuilt, after a fire, that now included 20 beds, and was still being administered by Dr. Marcovici. The Jewish-Romanian primary school, having M. Braunstein-Mibasan as Principle, included now 400 pupils, and it was supported "in excellent conditions" by a school committee made of Faivis Klein, A. Bittman, Saul Hertanu, I. M. Horovitz and Iosef Balter. At that time, the philanthropist Faivis Klein built, on Vasile Alecsandri Street, a new bath, a construction that cost 100,000 ROL and which he donated to the Community. In 1895, its budget provided an income, 63,736 ROL (out of the salt tax and the rent for two buildings), and expenses the same amount (28,332 ROL for school, 7000 ROL for hospital, 9750 ROL for worshipping, 2400 ROL for wood for the poor, etc.)[194]. The Community leadership at that time got support in the activity of a community association: "Fraterna",

---

[190] Jewish Magazine, year II, issue 4, February 15, 1888.

[191] *Idem*, no. 14, July 15 1889.

[192] State Archives of Bacau, Jewish Community, file 14-1923, f. 6, 6-s.

[193] "Egalitatea", no. 11, March 15th 1891.

[194] State Archives of Bacau, City Hall of Bacau, file 61/1895, p.2, 5, 5/v, 6, 6/v and 7.

"Handicraftsmen's Union", "Aghidas Haboinim" ("Constructors' Association"), "Marpe Lenefes" ("Healers of the Soul"), "The United Brothers".
In 1897, the Community income was 37,000 ROL, and 6600 ROL was spent for the hospital, 11,000 ROL for the school, 4000 ROL for worshipping, and 10,000 ROL were given to the poor[195]. The great interest in the hospital is explained by the fact that the Jewish students were received with difficulty in the public schools, and the Jewish patients could not fulfil their ritual prescriptions related to food in the public hospitals.

At the end of the 19th century, the Community faced new problems related to the salt tax. At the beginning of the year 1898, after a sustained action, which involved A. D. Birnberg, D. Orenstein, L. Focsaneanu, Faivis Klein and N. Grünberg, the Committee assumed the tax, in order to fulfil the needs of the school and those for social assistance[196]. Disputes followed related to the amount of the tax (10 or 20 coins), so that the school, the hospital and the social assistance activities had to suffer from lack of funds. A donation (3200 ROL) from I. Isic was supposed to bring about a certain improvement[197]. Unfortunately, at that time there was a serious economic crisis, a disastrous one for a great part of the Jewish population, and this fact – as well as the anti-Semitic actions – caused a wave of massive emigrations, sometimes in very difficult conditions – "pedestrian emigrants" also known as the "foosgeyers"..

"Following the example of the youth in other cities, on March 3rd, 1900, the first group of 120 persons was created, which, under the leadership of F. Braunstein, set off for Hamburg, where they embarked towards America. Before leaving Bacau, the 'pedestrians' or the 'travelers', as they called that current of emigration by foot, took a vow in the Synagogue of the Corn Dealers, after which they gave a theatrical production in order to collect the money for the way. The group was dressed in blue uniforms, with white caps. They were also wearing peasant sandals.

On June 13th, another group, including 110 young people, left the town, with the intention to emigrate to Canada. The group was called 'The New Life' and it was led by schoolmaster B. Friedman. On July 7th and July 14th, five other groups left for Roman, Pascani, Burdujeni and, from there, through Poland, to Hamburg.

The total number gathered more than 400 young people, boys and girls, even grown-ups, who left Bacau. They joined other thousands of Jews from other cities, who marked their place in history as members of the "pedestrians' movement"[198].

The situation within the Community, at the beginning of the new century, was confusing. Various articles in "The Jewish People" newspaper give the impression that there were actually two distinct committees at that time, each of them having a Rabbi and a part of the Community institutions. Wealthy people, who wanted a quick integration with the Romanian bourgeoisie and who merely

[195] "Egalitatea, issue 24, June 20 1897.
[196] "The Jewish Magazine", issue 4, February 6 1898.
[197] "Macabeul", issue 8, January 6 1901.
[198] I. Voledi-Vardi, *op. Cit.*, p. 27.

considered the social assistance issues from a philanthropic point of view, controlled one of the leaderships. The opposed leadership, which was more popular and more traditionalist, represented the Jews with moderate or small income. They believed that the administration of the income coming from different sources (salt tax, cemetery, synagogue) had to be conducted by the community leadership, that the self-administration of different community institutions had to stop, so that the Community committee can grant the necessary amounts for social assistance, which could no longer depend on the philanthropists' kindness.

One can not underestimate the importance of the philanthropic actions. They gave the community an opportunity to accomplish many of its plans. Thus, at the beginning of the 20th century, after the death of the well-known wealthy man Faivis Klein, the Community was given a very large donation from his final will and testament, iuncluding a fund for the maintenance of the primary school for boys, and an amount to buy the building of the school, another amount for the maintenance of the primary school for girls, etc. It should that in the same will, there was a provision for a donation of 20,000 ROL towards the City Hall of Bacau, for the establishment for the public an amount was used to build the infectious disease ward within the communal hospital, according to the decision from May 31st, 1906 of the Communal Council). Of similar importance was the ;ast will and testament from 1914 of Marcu Braunstein, for the maintenance of the Jewish hospital[199].

In 1909, the Community Committee could nor dispose of the income coming from the salt tax, and it had to obtain larger funds especially from donations; that is why Rabbi Moise Blanc made an appeal to the population to gather around the committee[200]. He repeated this appeal in 1911[201]. In 1912, there were big difficulties in the social assistance issues, a reason for which Rabbi Betalel Safran conducted a philanthropic society[202].

During the First World War, and the years afterwards, the Community leadership had to face new problems, beside the usual ones. We should mention the fact that they knew how to take position towards the political events which interested the Jews in the country and worldwide. In this respect, we mention the satisfaction manifested by telegrams at the coronation of the first monarch of the unified Romania and at the adoption of the new Constitution of the country, which was considered a document that brought the "solution for the Jewish issue in a sense of justice and according to the general interests of the country"[203].

In the same respect, we mention the public manifestation organized in order to hail the decision of the League of Nations related to the support given to a national shelter for Jews, in Palestine[204]. But they also needed solutions for actual problems of great importance. The successive laws of naturalization demanded

[199] State Archives of Bacau, Jewish Community, file 27/1923, p. 6, 6/v, 7 and 22/1924, p. 1-13.
[200] "The Jewish People, issue 19, July 20 1909."
[201] *Idem*, issue 8, June 8 1911.
[202] "Egalitatea", issue 47, September 28 1912.
[203] State Archives of Bacau, Jewish Community, files 5/1922, p. 18, 66-69.
[204] *Idem*, Jewish Community, files 21/1922, p. 39.

great efforts from the Community, in order to convince the entire Jewish population in town fill in the legal forms to obtain citizenship. A complex action of convincing was developed, including the activity of spreading posters in the Jewish neighborhoods[205]. At the same time, there was a need to intensify the actions of supporting the orphanage created for the 30-40 orphans from the war, and for assistance to dress the poor students, who became more numerous after the war. Additionally, the Community leadership had to organize the support given to the Jewish refugees from the Ukraine, passing through Bacau. It was then when they also had to give real answers to the numerous requests for help coming from other places, as it was the Appeal of the Central Committee for the support of the Jewish hungry orphans in Ukraine, and the calls for help coming from other communities, especially from areas that had been haunted by the war. All these, in a very unfriendly environment, maintained by all the anti-Semitic actions which took place in the town and then in the county[206]; among other issues, these circles asked for the rejection of the Constitution that granted political rights to the Jews.

In the following decade, the activity of the Jewish Community interested not only the Jewish population, but also several political parties, aiming to achieve their own electoral goals, and who wanted that members of their parties (Liberal, Averesacn or National-Peasant) should lead the Community. Actually, the Union of the Romanian Jews also considered that it would be useful for the Jews to be a part of different political parties, acting from within in order to maintain and strengthen democracy. This stimulated the introduction of political methods in the activity of the community leadership. In addition there was the mentality embraced by certain Jewish leaders who considered the community issues from a philanthropic point of view and who saw nothing wrong in the fact that different institutions of the community were independently led by the Community, sometimes by people with the same mentality, driven, not only once, by personal pride and ambitions. This state of affairs was opposed to by those who wanted the Community affairs to be the responsibility of the Community Committee only, whether an issue of worshipping, of confessional or secular education, of social assistance, etc. In this respect, traditional elements within the community took action, representing the middle class and the poor class of the population, as well as Zionist leaders, especially from Zionist religious organizations. The disputes for the leading positions have been largely invoked in testimonies that were published by the community activists Abrahami Lica Gutman and Mayer Eibschitz. From these testimonies, one can see the negative influence that political borrowings had on the Community affairs, as well as the unrest which was reflected in frequent resignations, intermarry commissions and elections[207].

Despite all this agitation to establish successive leaderships, they managed to have some results for important community issues. In 1927, after a fire that destroyed many Jewish households, the Community leadership launched an appeal,

---

[205] *Idem*, Jewish Community, files 1/1923, p. 12/v, 16-24, 35.
[206] *Idem*, Jewish Community, files 23/1922, p. 65. 65/v.
[207] *Idem*, Jewish Community, files 16/1926, 2/1932, 5/1934, 7/1934.

asking for support from the Jews throughout the entire country; the appeal had an echo. As it had been helped by others, in its turn, the Community from Bacau also helped the needy; for example, to support the Jews from Basarabia, who were starving because of the drought[208], as well as the Jews from Borsa and Balaceana, victims of anti-Semites' aggression and of the fires the latter caused[209].

No sooner than in 1932, was the Jewish Community acknowledged as a legal person of public rights[210]. In the same year, the Community published a statute and a regulation for the election of their representatives. In November the same year, there were the elections for the Community leadership. These elections were democratic, meaning that the electors were all the members of the community who were of age, and not just the delegates of the synagogues. Ozias Herscovivi, Dr. L. Tecuceanu, Iosif Feldher, Dr. H. Saler, L. Leneter and others[211] were elected. The elected committee tried to improve the leadership's prestige, to bring back all the rightful goods back to the Community patrimony, and they took action to get income from the cemetery, the baths, from subscriptions and donations. On one hand, there is the remarkable introduction of the subscription system for the community members, and on the other hand, the fact that a whole range of philanthropists supported the Community throughout the years by donating goods or buildings. Such donations have been made by: the Schuller brothers, Marcu Braunstein, Benedict and Berta Rehler, Seina and Lupu Ochs, and Aurel Negrescu.

In June 1934, there were new elections for the leading Committee. Dr. Lazar Tecuceanu led the newly elected committee, which seemed to be oriented more towards the preservation of the traditional values. The new leadership had to face difficult financial problems as well. A statement made in 1935 related to the income of the Community showed difficulties to get this income from the cemetery, as well as the allowances for the schools, which were expected from the F. Klein Foundation[212].

In the years to come, when, as it is known, there would be an increasing threat against the Jews, the Community leadership reflected very well the confusion in which the population lived. There was a time with successive resignations, suspensions, intermarry commissions, despite the difficult problems that the Community had to face.

In 1939, the committee had Lawyer David Ionas as its President and Herman Kisler and Hascal Istric as Vice-presidents. Then the task of the committee was the sore issue of the legal assistance for the Jews who had their Romanian citizenship withdrawn by application of the racist law promoted by Goga-Cuza Government. We should also mention here the action that took place in 1939 to help the Jewish refugees from Poland, a country which had been invaded by Hitler's army. The Jewish Community from Bacau organized a "Committee to assist the

---

[208] *Idem*, Jewish Community, file 3/1929, p. 5, 39.
[209] *Idem*, Jewish Community, files 15/1930, p. 48/84.
[210] *Idem*, Jewish Community, file 5/1932, p. 12, 132.
[211] "The Jewish Courier", issue 30, November 20 1932.
[212] State Archives of Bacau, Jewish Community, file 12/1935, p. 23, 23/v, 24.

Polish refugees". Here is – partially – the activity of this Committee, reflected in a document elaborated on October 24th 1939:

"On September 20th, this year, 290 refugees arrived successfuly, stopping in our town, people belonging to different social classes: engineers, doctors, lawyers, manufacturers, traders, clerks, handicraftsmen and of other profession. Their families (wives and children) accompanied some of them.

A special committee was created to assist these people sharing the same religion, we managed to provide them housing and shelter, food, and clothes, and, to a significant number, the necessary cash for every day expenses.

Since the day of their arrival in our town, after a temporary stay of 10-12 days and 20 days, some of them continued their journey to other towns and 28 refugees were directed by the local authorities towards Pucioasa, where a home was established for them.

Currently, there are 147 Polish Jewish refugees in Bacau, according to the nominal list which we submitted at your request. In order to cover the cost for their maintenance, the support committee in Bacau has managed to collect the amount of 121,853 […]

[…] Our action, under the aegis of the Community, has been conducted by a special committee, which, in the meeting of the 23rd, designated the following persons to continue the actions of supporting the refugees:

President: Dr. H. Perlbergher
Secretary: Mrs. Coca A. Isvoreanu
Financial administration: Mrs. Bianca Dr. Sarf
Mrs. Coca A. Isvoreanu
Mr. Jean Singher
Mr. Iacob Elenboghen

Clothing Commission: Mrs. Rasel Dr. Perlbergher
Mrs. Sofica Dr. Sabath
Mrs. Rena Filderman
Mr. Dr. H. Perlbergher

Quartering Commission: Mrs. Sidonia Simsensohn
Mrs. Bianca Grinberg
Mr. Hascal Istric
Mr. Iacob Elenboghen

Commission for the connection with and assistance with the authorities and information:
Mr. Dr. H. Perlbergher
Mr. Eng. I. Filderman
Mr. Herman Kisler

Commission for distribution: Mrs. Rasel Dr. Perlbergher
Mrs. Sofica Dr. Sabath
Mr. Osias Herscovici
Mr. I. Elenboghen

The Committee is assisted by a Commission which has been designated by the refugees in the town, whose task is to provide the Committee with data and information"[213].

During the war, the leading Committee of the Community was still conducted by Lawyer Ionas. But, when Antonescu's dictatorship prohibited the activity of the Jewish communities and created the Central of the Jews, as a body which could apply its orders, the authorities no longer considered the elected leadership of the Community, usually addressing to the county office of the Central, led by the manufacturer Misu Grad.

After the fall of Antonescu's dictatorship, in 1944, when the community activity became legal again, the Jewish population had to face – beside the general problems of the entire population of the country – a set of problems caused by the consequences of the racist legislation, related to reintegration, and to bringing the Community back to life. But soon afterwards, the Community activity had to face the influence of the Jewish Democratic Committee, which – on the line of the administrative atheism promoted by the Communist Party – actually aimed to abolish any form of organization owned by the Jewish population and especially of the religious institutions. In these circumstances, despite the obstacles, there was an increasingly strong wave of people who were leaving for Israel, as the number of members of the Jewish Community got smaller and smaller.

Only after the self-dissolution of the Jewish Democratic Committee and when the activities of the Federation of the Jewish Communities in Romania, led by Chief Rabbi Dr. Moses Rosen, became more obvious, did the leadership of the local community get bigger opportunities of action. But the work of those who took turns as leaders (M. Schaler, D. Vataru, M. Tenker, M. Hausfater, I. Wenger, A. Gutman, A. Aizerman, I. Brill and M. Cojocaru) who tried to organize the community activity in different fields, had to face the problems brought about by the new, permanently changing circumstances – that is: the massive leaving for Israel and the increasingly judicious use of the aids given by "Joint". Due to the work of the community leaders and their collaborators, there were remarkable achievements in the social assistance work (aids for the assisted, ritual restaurant, consulting room), in the activity of the synagogues, in the traditional education (classes of Talmud Tora), in maintenance of the cemeteries and in the cultural activity. There were five cycles of conferences, choir, organization of traditional feasts, especially Hanuka, library, and recently the organization of the Museum "History of the Jewish Community in Bacau", 1703 – 1944, for which important contributions came from L. Iosif, C. Marcusohn, B. Bercovici and S. Mendel.

These activities continue to take place, although there are only a few hundred Jews left in Bacau, most of them old people. They still feel connected to the Jewish tradition and they want this tradition to be continued by the few young people who can still be found in the town, some of them trying to connect their destiny to the one of their ancestors' country, Eretz Israel.

---

[213] *Idem*, Jewish Community, files 20/1939, p. 131-133.

2. Community Preoccupations and Institutions

a. *Cemeteries. The Sacred Society*

The cemetery has always been one of the first institutions created by any Jewish Community, including at least several dozens of families. Small communities could use the cemetery of a bigger community near by, until the number of Jews belonging to that particular settlement increased.

In an article entitled "The Jewish Cemeteries in Bacau", which was published in "The Magazine of the Mosaic Cult", issue 671/1989, A. L. Iosif listed four Jewish cemeteries in the town of Bacau. Two of them, The Heroes' Cemetery and the "Lazaret" Cemetery are actually cemeteries where there have been buried – beside Christian soldiers – Jewish soldiers who died on the front during the War for Reunification from 1916-1918 or who died from contagious disease during the war.

There are two really Jewish cemeteries, that is cemeteries where only Jews are buried, and which are maintained by the Jewish Community: the so-called Old cemetery and the New Cemetery.

The Old cemetery, from the old Cremene Street, was already there in the 18th century. In this cemetery was found the tombstone dated 1703, which was probably not the oldest one. Here are some inscriptions from funeral stones from the 19th century:

"Here rests an important woman, Haia, daughter of Natan, who died on 17 Kislev year [5]578" (November 24th, 1817).

"Here rests an important woman, Haia, daughter of Ithac, who died on 3 Tamuz [5]581" (July 3rd, 1821).

"Here rests a rightful man of integrity, the honoured Tvi, son of Mr. Ioel, who died on 15 Adar [5]582" (March 7th, 1822).

"Here rests an important woman, Mrs. Mariese, daughter of Zeev Segal the learned man, who died on 2 Svat [5]583" (January 15th, 1823).

"Here rests an important woman, Mrs. Haia Sara, daughter of Mr. Ioel, who died on 18 Menahem Av [5]584" (Agust 12th, 1824).

Participants at the War for Independence from 1877 and at the War for the Reunification of the country were buried here.

The tomb of Faivis Klein the philanthropist is here too; there are also two little houses with the graves of the members of several Rabbi families who shepherded in the town.

But is this the oldest cemetery in Bacau? Let us remember the versions known at the time of A. D. Birnberg, according to which there used to be other Jewish cemeteries in Bacau, (...) giving us the right to consider them the fruit of folks' imagination. They can be traces, in the collective memory, of some realities of the remote past.

Coming back to the cemetery from Cremenei Street, we should also mention some data that have been registered in the archive documents. In 1865, its thorn fence was replaced with a wood one. In 1885, the chapel at the entrance was built; in its wall, the funeral stone from 1703 was fixed, and it remained there until it was taken to Bucharest, after the World War II, at the History Museum of the Jewish Communities in Romania. In 1937, a concrete fence surrounded the land of the Old Cemetery[214].

In 1912, the Old Cemetery proved to be too small. Then a piece of land was bought from the City Hall for a new cemetery, which was opened in 1917, after it had been surrounded too in 1915[215]. In 1919, an appeal was made to the Jewish population to make contributions to build a practicable road towards the new cemetery[216]. Many personalities who played a part in different walks of the Jewish Life from Bacau are buried here. In the fall of 1940, during the persecution from the Iron Guard, the City Hall despotically confiscated a part of the graveyard for agriculture[217]. The New Cemetery is the one which the small Jewish community of Bacau still use.

Who took care of the maintenance of the cemeteries and of the funeral rituals? In the past, the complicated Jewish funeral ritual did not have to be solemnized by a clergyman or by professional undertakers, but on the contrary, by religious and important people who formed funeral fraternity, called "Hevra Kedosa", meaning "The Sacred Society" (with the modern short version "Sacra"). Even though it did not have a fixed written organization, the funeral fraternity did exist, it was active, it administrated the cemetery and had an income from selling pieces of land, from funeral taxes and donations.

In Bacau, such a fraternity had been created since the last decades of the 18th century. It had a register (List, Pincas) and its own statutes; all this even before the leading body of the Community had a functioning statute. The phenomenon is explained by the fact that the existence of a cemetery and the certainty of the respect given to the funeral ritual had priority before any other problems of the community life.

What information do we have about the "Hevra Kedosa" fraternity in Bacau? In his monograph, written in 1887, A. D. Birnberg notes that the oldest document of the Jewish community in Bacau is the Pincas of the Sacred Association from 1771. He shows that the following people were written in this pincas, among the persons registered as "gabaim" (chiefs): David san Itic, Suher Beer san Sloime, Manase Leib, Marcu Ionita san Peret, Lupu san Itic, David san Itic, Aron Volf, Burah san Hosea Zelig. It is mentioned here that "only in 1829 was Lupu Burah elected gabai, who was followed by Hers Kindes, Moche' s father [...] (who subscribes today as Moche Braunstein) [...] who functioned until the dissolution of the society. We do not know anything about the persons who are registered as the first leaders of this Association and about their help [...]. As we can draw a conclusion even from the rules provided for in the Pincas, the gabaims

[214] *Idem*, Jewish Community, file 15/1937, p.1.
[215] *Idem*, Jewish Community, file 24/1922, p. 2, 2/v
[216] *Idem*, Jewish Community, file 24/1922, p. 11.
[217] *Idem*, Jewish Community, file 6/1941, p. 68.

were elected from the oldest members, and they had to be native inhabitants of Bacau". As this is all the information given by A. D. Birnberg about "Hevra Kedosa", we understand that, at a certain moment in the 19th century, it was dissolved, and it no longer existed when the author wrote his monograph. Unfortunately, he did not write who took care of the cemetery maintenance and of the funeral ritual in his time.

We come across new information about this "Hevra Kedosa" and about its Pincas in an answer sent in 1928 by the leadership of the Community in Bacau to a questionnaire received from Manfred Reifer, a researcher from Cernauti. Here is what was included in this answer: "This Pincas comprises a preface, then different reports on religious topics, a regulation of the society, articles [...]. It is shown how and when the elections take place, the role of the society, the gabaims' s role. There are 3 pages missing, the beginning of a will, then there are receive minutes". It also mentioned that "this document is very important and is artistically written", that it had been written by David, son of Iehiel Mihal and that the Society had "a previously arranged schedule as well as aspects related not only to the funeral ritual, but also issues of social assistance"[218].

I. Kara offered more complete information about this "Hevra Kedosa", about its list and its statutes. In 1939, he could analyze and copy the register of the fraternity, which was owned at that time by I. Carniol, who had inherited it from a grandfather, member of the Society leadership. The register was beautifully bound in leather and its dimensions were of 35/22 cm. Based on this research, Kara published the first article in the "Veltspigl" magazine of Bucharest (issue 13, from March 1940), where he showed, among other things, that the oldest entry in this register is from 1774, but the anagram of the title page "Hagoel mimavet" ("The death Deliverer") mentions the number 1771. (The title page of this pinkas has been photographically reproduced in "Pinkas Hakehilot Romania", vol. I, Jerusalem, 1970, p. 11). Kara also shows that the first 13 pages the statutes of the fraternity were written – calligraphically, in the Rasi alphabet – as traditional considerations about death and about the importance of the funeral ritual. Then there were pieces of news from the life and activity of the fraternity. The register included hundreds of member names. The author mentioned that, unlike the similar fraternity from Roman, this was where, in 1833, a decision was made that the fraternity leadership should include, beside the chief (gabai), other persons as well: a president (ros), a vice-president, a censor (ros hesbon). David, son of Iehiel Mihal, who had also written the registers of "Hevra Kedosa" from Roman and Telenesti, wrote the register. Kara analyzed this pinkas in other personal[219] or collective[220] papers.

What is the conclusion from this research? First of all, that "Hevra Kedosa" was not a company of "funeral furnishers", as we could imagine nowadays. On the contrary, it had many of the Community previous duties: it took care not only of funerals and the cemetery, but also of ill people (bicur holim), of the poor, of the

[218] *Idem*, Jewish Community, file 12/1928, p. 1, 2, 2/v, 3, 3/v, 4.
[219] I. Kara, *op. cit.*, p. 11-18.
[220] I. Voledi-Vardi, *op. cit.*, p. 14-16.

bath, of the synagogues, etc. Therefore, the fraternity members were important people of the Community.

From the fraternity statutes, which are in an alphabetic order (see Appendix I), we find out many interesting details from the life of the Society, but also about the social life of the Jews from Bacau in the 18th and 19th centuries.

Candidates to the to the position of full member of the fraternity had to spend three years on probation (sames). After this period, they paid an admission tax ("berbanta") and they offered a feast to the entire fraternity. Initially, all the members of the fraternity had fulfilled the funeral ritual; then this ritual became the duty of certain candidates, who were paid by the members.

Those who belonged to the fraternity had to live in peace; they were forbidden to bring conflicts before the official judges; they took part in three feasts every year, which were organized in the synagogue (de Pesah, de Savuot and de Sucot); they had the obligation to behave appropriately ("they must not throw the hat on the ground").

Here is how the leadership of the fraternity was elected: the names of the "society members" were written on notes and put inside a urn ("kalfe"). The first three names coming out of the urn represented the electors ("borerim"). They designated the chief of the fraternity, his assistant ("bimcom"), the "believer" ("neeman") and the censor ("ros hesbon").

The chief established the prices for the pieces of land, the funeral tax and the tax for the construction of the tombstone, the tax for the admission in the fraternity and different fines. He was the one who kept the funds and the register of the fraternity, he presided at the meetings, the funeral ceremonial and the funeral feasts; he was the one to judge the misunderstandings among the members, he considered the opinion of the general meeting of the fraternity, which took place on a regular basis.

Before digging the grave for a deceased, if his family didn't have money, they made a pawning to the chief, which had to be redeemed within one year, and after this term the pawning could be sold in an auction. The fines for different violations of the statute provisions, between 5 and 15 coins, were shared among the chief and the members of the fraternity. Another detail about this register, which is worth mentioning, is the fact that there was a special artistic interest, both by the beautiful calligraphy of the writings, and by the traditional ornaments of the page borders.

Notes have been kept in the register about receiving members, elections, accounting, trials, fines, for the years 1774-1831, a total number of 55 entries; we can suppose that some others may have got lost. It seems that sometimes the members of the fraternity did not follow the chief's orders and conflicts broke out. In 1832, the candidates ("samesim") pledged to follow the chief, but conflicts occurred repeatedly.

We do not know the date when "Hevra Kedosa" dissolved, nor de we know how the cemetery and the funeral ritual were taken care of during the following period. Analyzing the balances of the community leaderships from different years, we notice that there were times when the community leadership provided in its budget income from funerals and expenses for the maintenance of the cemetery, which means that there was no autonomous sacred society at that time. At other times, on the contrary, the community budgets had no such provisions, therefore, we understand that the activity of "Hevra Kedosa" had an independent leadership and administration.

We should mention here that, in 1947, I. Kara found and analyzed, at Iesaia Ghersei, from Bacau, a register dated 1869 and entitled "Pincas menahavura risona avur refuat haholim ve halviat hamet" ("The first fraternity for the help of the ill people and for participation in funerals"). Both the title page and some of the initials in the text were written in red and in bronze. The dimensions of the manuscript: 34/22 cm. The first 47 sheets of the register were not written. On pages 48-57, there were opinions about the importance of the help given to ill people and of the funeral ritual. Then there were the statutes, which were dated 1907 though, being drafted by Hanoh Henih Safran (son of Rabbi Betalel Zeev Safran), written by Ithac Kaufman (Leon I. Kaufman) and approved by Rabbi Safran's signature and seal. One hundred and twent one (121) names of fraternity members were mentioned next. As we can tell from this, this association was not a substitute for "Hevra Kedosa", but an association with a philanthropic character, meant to help those in need, in cases of sickness or death. The title of the register did not show any concern for the administration of the cemetery and of its income.

Documents show that, in 1901, there was a "Sacred Society", autonomous from the community leadership. The appeal made in 1919, which called the population to make contributions for the road towards the new cemetery, was signed by the Sacred Society, not by the community leadership. It seems that, in 1922, there were attempts to improve the existing relations, so that the administration of the cemetery and its income to be made by the Community leadership. A meeting of the population was organized for this purpose[221]. But this settlement did not last too long or it offered no satisfaction. As it can be seen from the evocation of the community life published by the traditionalist Zionist Mayer Eibschitz, in 1931, the cemetery leadership was under the direct supervision of the Community President, a member of a "historic" party. This one, says the author, had a very partial attitude: "the pieces of land in the front of the cemetery were kept for the rich and for those who had adopted their political opinions; peripherical places were meant for apolitical intellectuals, traders, clerks and handicraftsmen". In the article about the cemeteries, A. L. Iosif wrote: "Dr. Tecuceanu established the normal right that the poor could also be buried in the new cemetery (they had been buried only in the old cemetery before that)".

At the Central Archives for the History of the Jewish People in Jerusalem, there is the Convention signed, on March 1st, 1933 by the president of the "Sacred Society" (Samuel Filderman) and by the president of the Community leadership (Ozias Herscovici), and it stipulated the fact that the administration and leadership of the cemetery were the task of the Community, including the "Hevra Kedosa" Department, as a special department. (We underline that this document mentions that "Sacra" functioned based on the statute in 1901). Thus the Conventioned

[221] State Archives of Bacau, Jewish Community, file 23/1922, p. 14, 16.

consented with the statute provisions of the Community in Bacau, published in 1932[222]. The settlement, which was provided by this statute, was valid for the entire period to come.

b. *The Bath. Securing the ritual nourishment*

The public bath was an absolutely necessary institution in every Jewish community, not only from a hygienic point of view, but also from a ritualistic one (ritual baths at least once a week for men and once a month for women in "micva" – the life water basin, permanently refreshed). At Bacau, the public bath is certified in documents since the 18th century. In his monograph, A. D. Birnberg writes: "The old men say that, in Bacau, in 1800, there was a steam bath belonging to the Community and another one of Ioina Beer, which he had inherited from his father". The Community had income from the bath, leasing it; documents mention the leasing of the "Jewish public bath" in 1845. On February 26th, 1854, the tenant of the bath was complaining to the Prefecture that the Russian army had occupied the "public bath"[223]. In 1864, the bath was leased for 125 ROL per year[224]. In 1877-78, the income from the bath, together with the one from the cemetery, was of 500 ducats[225]. In 1882, it was mentioned that the public bath functioned, after it had been renovated in 1871[226].

Actually, there were more Jewish baths, probably with inappropriate draining systems, as, in 1892, the authorities invoked this reason when they decided to close the public bath in Leca Street and the ones in Pavel and Ana Cristea Street[227].

Obviously, these public baths were rather primitive: an arch in the ground, a big oven and about three ranges of benches for the steam baths; baths in tubs were taken in two small rooms; the public baths also had a water system, which was always refreshing from the springs that were their sources – this was the "micva", where the ritual baths were taken.

Seen from the perspective of our days, these baths were rudimentary. The image of the bath man, walking in the small Jewish streets, wearing a pole with straws and cloths on top, and crying "budaran, budaran" ("time for the bath, time for the bath…"), seems a picturesque weirdness to us. However, at that time, the Jewish community provided to the people means, even though rudimentary ones, to secure a minimum hygiene of the body.

In 1894, the philanthropist Faivis Klein built, on V. Alecsandri Street, a systematic bath, which he donated to the community. Afterwards he built another bath, on Post Street, for the poor to use. The Jewish baths were available to the entire population, being used by the military units in town as well.

---

[222] *Idem*, Jewish Community, file 1/1938, p. 11, 12.
[223] *Idem*, City Hall of Bacau, file 38-1854, p. 1.
[224] *Idem*, file 51/1864, p. 34.
[225] *Idem*, file 45/1880, p. 1, 4.
[226] "Fraternitatea", 1882, p. 319.
[227] State Archives of Bacau, Jewish Community, file 24/1892, p. 4. 5. 19, 19/v, 24.

In 1925, the committee of the F. Klein Foundation organized an auction to lease the central bath and "the small bath" in the Post Street[228]. After a decade, "the small bath" would be available to the City Hall for 10 years, with no rent[229].

In 1940, the central bath was expropriated and taken over by the City Hall. But the legal bodies decided that this measure was illegal[230]. Even the National Center for Becoming a Romanian had to reject the repeated requests of the City Hall to be granted patrimony over this settlement which had been taken by the Iron Guards.

After the war, the public bath was again the property of the Jewish Community, and it functioned until the demolitions ordered by the new plan for the systematization of the town.

*

Throughout its entire existence, the Jewish community from Bacau took care of the ritual cutting (Kosher) of cattle and poultry. A. D. Birnberg's monograph mentions the names of the first hahams (butchers), whom the old men remembered as having functioned in the first half of the 19th century (Faivis, Haim Zeling, Ilie Elie, then Hanina and Hoisie), as well as the names of several hahams from the second half of the same century (Aron Hers, Nahman, etc.). In 1864, there were five active hahams. The numerous archive documents mention hahams' employment, their wages, the responsibilities they took in order to respect the religious rules, as well as their understandings with the administrative bodies about selling the meat.

Among the hahams who were active between the two wars, there were I. Marant, H. I. Sehter, Haim Tukerman, Buium Clejan, etc. In 1926, the Community built a slaughterhouse for poultry in the yard of the central bath.

Among the measures taken against the Jews during Antonescu's dictatorship, we should mention the interdiction of the ritual slaughtering[231]. Here is what the published material said related to this interdiction:

"We, the Mayor of the city of Bacau;

Considering the decision of the Sate Secretariat of the Agriculture and Estate Department, no. 12502, published in the Official Gazette, issue 162 from July 15th, 1942, we dispose:

Art. 1 – Beginning with the date of this published material, the animal and poultry ritual slaughtering is forbidden, both for public consummation and for the private one, even though with prior numbness.

Mayor, M. Vagunescu, retired Lt. Col.".

The issue was no. 34 from July 18th, 1942.

During the years after the war, when the last Rabbis from Bacau left for Israel, the spiritual leadership of the community was left especially to the hahams and the psalm readers for a long time, until it was their turn to leave; but up to

---

228 *Idem*, Jewish Community, file 12/1925, p. 11.

229 *Idem*, City Hall of Bacau, file 47/1934, p. 3, 3/v, 4, 5, 7.

230 *Idem*, City Hall of Bacau, file 7/1943, p. 35-35/v.

231 *Idem*, City Hall of Bacau, file 21/1942, p.66.

present the ritual (Kosher) nourishment is provided for by regular slaughtering and distribution of beef; at Bacau there is one of the eleven ritual restaurants in the country. The poor Jews are regularly given food secured by the concern of "Joint".

*

Another issue of permanent concern for the community leadership was that of baking the unleavened bread for Pesah. The Jewish community from Bacau pays a lot of attention and appreciation to the celebration of the Jews' exit from the Egyptian slavery. At the same time, making the unleavened bread was another source of income for the needy population. The community leadership intervened to forbid the baking of the unleavened bread by private businessmen or bringing it from another locality[232]. Even during the last war, the Community struggled to get the quantity of flour that was necessary to bake the unleavened bread.

Many archive documents confirm the fact that, during the persecution, the Community used to send traditional unleavened bread to the Jews in prison too. The unleavened bread factory functioned even after the Second World War for a short time; as the number of Jews decreased in Alia, the factory no longer justified its activity. But the unleavened bread is still provided for by the help of F.C.E.R., from abroad.

c. *Synagogues. Cult staff. Religious education*

Throughout the years, many synagogues have been founded in Bacau. Some of them belonged to certain professions or communities, others were built out of devoutness or out of the wish to relate the family name to the one of a cult house. Let's not forget that a Jewish prayer house could be a modest building, with few rooms. The officials (hazan) were very numerous and there was never a lack of believers, willing to build such a house. In some synagogues, "heider" classes were held (elementary religious schools). Usually, the synagogues were not only prayer houses, but also places for religious study, of religious initiation. Meetings for community interests were held in the synagogues too. Concerning all these aspects, there is the illustrating evocation made by A. D. Birnberg in his monograph.

Let's mention first of all some of the synagogues that functioned in the first half of the 19th century. The prayer house entitled "The Big Synagogue" was near St. Nicholas Church; a fire destroyed it in 1853. A wealthy tailor, named Moise Leib ben Iacov, founded the tailors' Synagogue in 1815. This synagogue had a wine cellar next to it, and wood was bought for poor families from its income; another fire destroyed it too, also in 1853. The Habad Synagogue was founded in 1841, in a time when this branch of the Hasidic movement was very popular among the Jewish communities of Moldova. Here are other synagogues from that period: Volf Burau

---

[232] *Idem*, Jewish Community, file 8/1930, p. 18 and file 2/1932, p. 5.

Synagogue, the Furriers' Synagogue, the Tanners' Synagogue, Alter Ioines Synagogue, etc. Iedidia Hazen, Berl Hazen, Velvel Bendl and Iosef Burd are mentioned as officials of that time. The number of synagogues increased in the second half of the 19th century. There were 14 synagogues in 1864. There were 21 synagogues around the year 1890; many of them were very modest, such as the synagogues Froim Aizic, Alter Leibl, Itic Leib Bril, the Lipscans' Synagogue, etc., others were better arranged, such as the Young Tailors' Synagogue, the Cabmen's Synagogue, the Shoemakers' Synagogue, the Masons' Synagogue, the synagogues Rabi Israel, "Sion Brotherhood", Snapic, Maria and Saim Cofler ("Mariesche") and especially the Corn Dealers' Synagogue This last synagogue, which was founded around the middle of the century, has been destroyed many times by fires, so frequent in Bacau, and it has been rebuilt several times, eventually as a temple; people called it "Popsoinikes" (the Corn Dealers' Synagogue). Here are some of the well-known officials of that time: Rabi Israel, Solomon Rapner, Iser san Aizic. After the First World War, there were 22 synagogues[233]. Some of the old prayer houses had disappeared, some new houses had been founded (synagogues Weissman, Safran, Blanc, David Herscovici, Calmanovici, "The Palestine", Filderman, etc.). During the inter-war period, between 23 and 26 synagogues functioned, some of them disappearing, others newly founded (synagogues Rabin Warman, Rabin Landman, Avram Simon[234]). Here are some names of officials of that time: Iosef Magulius, Pavda, Idel Orenstein, Aizic Jucovschi, etc. In 1939, there were 25 synagogues[235].

The synagogues were maintained from the member' subscriptions and donations, as well as from the selling of arm chairs (lecterns), especially on important holy days. Here are the contents of the "ownership document" of the lectern at one of these synagogues ("The Palestine"):

"We, the undersigned Ioil Weissbuch, Haim Neuman, Elias Siegler and Sulim Schächter, residing in the town of Bacau, as guardians of the synagogue from 6 Prince Neagoe Street, in this town, donated for a prayer house by Mr. Michel san Mendel, a donation for which we are named Guardians and authorized representatives by the donation document authenticated by the Law Court of Bacau, registered with no. 517 from May 1896.

According to the regulation of the synagogue, we mandate Mr. Iancu Bercovici to own lectern no. 8, in part SPIGL I, together with Mr. Avram Bercovici, his father, and with Mr. Marcu san Aron, on the condition to comply with all the provisions of the synagogue, to contribute to all the expenses, to watch over the good order and respect owed to a house of prayer [...]. November 20th, 1896".

As we can see, synagogues had a certain autonomy, the guardians administrated the funds, paid the wages to their own Rabbis, to the psalm readers and the other servants; they were supported by the community leadership only when there were problems with the public administration.

---

[233] *Idem*, Jewish Community, file 20/1922, p. 57.

[234] *Idem*, Jewish Community, file 6/1934, p. 3/v

[235] *Idem*, Jewish Community, file 5/1939, p. 13-14/v.

Here is an example of the way in which synagogues were organized: at the Corn Dealers' Synagogue (temple), there was a Pincas of their own, which regulated the members' rights and duties. The synagogue leadership was elected every year. Those who had the right to vote were the believers who had been members for two years and who had paid their subscription. The believers who had been members of the synagogue for four years could be elected as leaders. The leadership had the right to judge the litigation among believers. The expenses for the maintenance of the synagogue had to be approved by a collective that was especially designated for this goal. Another remarkable thing was the artistic ornamentation of the register. Beside the Pincas, there was also a minutes register for the period 1920-1937. The synagogue was self-financed from subscriptions and donations. The excess income was not donated to the community. The victims of the disaster in Buhusi received aid from this income in 1927 (Appendix VI).

During the war, the majority of the synagogues had many functioning difficulties. They hardly got the approval to perform the daily or the occasional prayers[236]. Some of them were arbitrarily evicted and used by the authorities for other goals. This is what happened to "Rebeca and Ozias Herscovici" Synagogue, the only one existing in the neighbourhood beyond the iron bridge[237]. Here are some other examples: on August 9th, 1941, the guardians of "Maria Cofler" Synagogue, on 8 Winter's Street, addressed to the president of the Community, asking him to intervene to the proper authorities so that "our synagogue, which is left for the Jews in this town to say their religious prayers, should be let free".

The demolitions made after the war affected even more buildings where synagogues had been functioning. The Corn Dealers' Temple is the only one left upright, and "A. Rosen Synagogue", near the office of the Community, is used for daily prayers; it is named after gaon Avram Arie Rosen, father of the much mourned Chief Rabbi Moses Rosen.

*

The first Rabbi whom the people of Bacau remembered was Ithac Botosaner, who had served for 55 years (1803-1858). He was known as a very educated man, who knew how to settle different civil and religious conflicts, and imposed the principles from "Sulhan Aruh" to be strictly respected. It seems his authority went beyond the believers (some of them considered him a "miracle maker"), even among authorities. He was a very temperate man, but also a very charitable person. When he got ill, he was given a daian, Moise Marcu, to help him. Rabbi Ithac Botosaner was mentioned in a trial for a house land, in 1834[238].

Since the middle of the 19th century, Rabbi Rahmune Derbaremdiker is mentioned, who, judging by his name, must have come from a famous family of

---

[236] *Idem*, Jewish Community, file 21/1940, p. 127, 133, 143.
[237] *Idem*, Jewish Community, file 21/1940, p. 152,
[238] State Archives of Iasi, Prefecture of Bacau, letter P, file 489.

Hasidic Rabbis. He is thought to have served at Bacau between 1825 and 1846, contributing to the spread of the Hasidism.

A document from 1859 shows that three Rabbis were exempted from recruitment; they were probably synagogue Rabbis[239].

After Ithac Botosaner, one of his students served in Bacau, Rabbi Alter Ioines, who had also been brought from Botosani. He was also very well instructed in the religious literature, and he was known as a righteous man, loved by the believers. He served until 1873. He left to his successors a paper entitled "Divrei Moise" ("Moses' Words"), which was subsequently published by his sons.

Rabbi Alter Löbel, son of Haim Leib, from Botosani succeeded him. Characterized by A. D. Birnberg as a man of integrity and with no prejudice, he also had a wide rabbinical culture. In 1887, he disposed of the right to issue certificates of graduation from classes of religion to the Jewish students[240]. He is mentioned in the paper entitled "Sefer Divrei Haim" ("The Book of Life"), written by his son Iehuda Löbel, and published in Roman in 1891.

The great spread of Hasidism among the Jews from Bacau, made the tailors' community hire, in 1885, Rabbi Israel, from the dynasty of Israel Rijner, from Sadagura. He served as a hazan. In 1887, a synagogue named after him was built on Leca Street.

Rabbi Betalel Tva Safran was a representative image; well-known as a Talmudist, born in 1851, he was hired in Bacau in 1905. He had an intense activity as Prime-Rabbi until 1929, when he died. In 1931, his bones were taken to Israel. He drafted the paper "Seelot Utesuvot ha-Rabaz" ("Rabbis' Questions and Answers"), Talmudic commentaries that were published in Warsaw in 1930, accompanied by the notes of his son, Henoh Henih Safran.

A learned man, who was also very active both in the community life and in the Zionist movement, was Rabbi Mose Blanc. Born in Botosani, in 1850, he was hired in Bacau in 1902. He served until 1944, when he died.

Rabbi Tvi Landman also served in Bacau; he is the author of remarkable papers such as "Sefer matoca snat haoved" ("Sweet is the road of the hard worker").

Rabbi Dr. Alex. Safran has been serving in Bacau since 1934. In 1939, when he was only 29, he was elected Chief Rabbi of the Jews in Romania. Currently, he is a Great Rabbi of Geneva, and a professor of Jewish studies at the University in this city. He is considered a great authority in the study of Cabala.

Among the Rabbis who served during the Second World War in Bacau, there were Iom-Tov Dermer, Pinhas Ghinsberg, Varman, Bahman, beside the numerous Rabbis in synagogues. The last Rabbi in Bacau was the Talmudist M. Marilus, who served here between 1950 and 1961, after which he was called as prime-Rabbi to Bucharest, where he died in 1986; his bones were taken to Israel. He published commented fragments from the works of the Rabbis in Romania in "The Magazine of the Mosaic Cult".

---

[239] *Idem*, Tr. 1772, op. 2020, no. 31984, from May 2 1859.

[240] "Unirea", year I, issue 205, October 16 1887.

*

The concern for children's education – which is characteristic to all the Jewish communities – has been a permanent one within the community of Bacau, too. During the first decades of the 19th century, education was merely religious, confessional, being developed in the so-called "heider", where the teacher ("melamed"), who was usually paid by the parents, guided the children in the study of basic religious texts. Children learned how to read and speak in Hebrew, the language of the Bible, they were taught the religious norms, they discovered the meaning of the prayers, which was explained and commented in Yiddish, the current language used by the Jews in Moldova in every day life. In order to support the good functioning of these elementary schools, and to make sure that poor children got the necessary education as well, the "Talmud Tora" association was founded, in 1837, beside the Community, and from this association we still have the register with its functioning statutes (Appendix IV). The members of the association checked the heider classes, reported the way in which they activated and, in the same time, they watched over correct relationships among teachers, and between teachers and their assistants (belfers).

A. D. Birnberg, who wanted the past of the community in Bacau to be known by generations to come, sent to "'Iuliu Barasch' Historic Society" the Pincas of the association (written in Hebrew by Aser David Mordehai, from Hotim), and the statutes of the association, translated in Romanian by Lazar Casvan. In 1946, all these were in M. Scwarzfeld's archive from Bucharest, and now they are at the Central Archives for the History of the Jewish People from Jerusalem (R. M./269).

We do not know the activity length of this association, whose initial goal was the functioning of 13 confessional classes. However, it is certain that the support that the Community gave to the Talmud Tora activity was consistent throughout the 19th century, and it was continued in the next century, until today; this is proven by many documents in the Community archives. There has been a constant supervision of the elementary confessional classes, by means of the cult staff. The community Rabbis checked the heiders, which used to function within the synagogues. Thus, in 1934, there were 6 Talmud Tora classes, including 150 children[241]. The teachers that are remembered by the people from Bacau were Saie Hersel, Solomon, Bloh, Mehel, Pinhas, a.s.o. Not even during the difficult years of persecution did the material support of the Community stop for these classes[242]. The "Talmud Tora" classes and the choir, existed even after the last war, due to the F.C.E.R. guidance, have continued and they continue the tradition of the Jewish education.

Every year, appropriate holidays schedules were established (Hanuca, Hamisa Asar Bisvat, Purim, Pesah), under the guidance of Professor L. Iosif.

Many students who were educated at Talmud Tora left for the Holy Country.

---

[241] State Archives of Bacau, Jewish Community, file 27/1934.

[242] *Idem*, Jewish Community, file 27/1941, p. 5-24.

Beside these elementary forms of education, we should mention that there have also been developed in Bacau the possibilities to study the Talmud; for example, in 1851, there was founded "Hevra Misnaiot", an association for the study of the Talmudic "Misna" texts.

d. Social and sanitary assistance

The help for the needy – an old tradition of the Jewish population – was reflected in Bacau in the actions of the community leaderships, of the synagogue believers and of the community associations. (Some of them had a philanthropic character, other were associations of mutual help). Around the middle of the 19th century, a small night shelter for the poor ("hekdes") was founded beside the Furriers' Synagogue.

"Ghemilat Hasadim" ("Social Assistance") Association had the character of a mutual help society, being founded in the fourth decade of the 19th century. There is little information about the activity of this association. Nevertheless, a manuscript from 1836 has been kept, including the Pincas and the statutes of the association, written by Aser David ben Mordehai, and having beautiful ornamentation (Appendix III). As we can see from the statute, the association had circulating funds from the weekly subscriptions of its members and from donations on special occasions (wedding, circumcision, and holidays). Loans were given from this fund to the members of the association who needed them, in exchange of a pawning they had to give. The first chief (gabai) of the association was Iosef ben Meir.

"Fraterna" Society also had the character of mutual help, which was founded in 1879 and was permanently active for 62 years, until 1941.

"Materna", an association of the Jewish women to assist poor women lately confined and to look after the suckling, had a philanthropic character. In 1934, they founded a maternity, in a place donated by the Community.

Successive community leaderships tried to contribute to fulfilling the traditional obligation of helping those who suffer. In all the balances submitted by the community leadership throughout the years, there are expenses meant to help the poor, under different forms: distributing wood, unleavened bread, monthly allowances or regular amounts of money, free drugs, rent allowances, meals for the poor children, aids for the Jewish prisoners, etc. since 1926, the Community supported by grants the alms-house for old people founded in Calea Oituz, which included several dozens of old poor Jews; the alms-house was administrated by the Association for the alms-house[243].

The support from "Joint" has been and still is of considerable importance for the actions of social assistance.

Social assistance became a priority during the war.

*

---

[243] *Idem*, Jewish Community, file 1/1939, p. 85.

The necessity of a hospital for the Jewish population, in parallel with the development of public medical assistance in Moldova in the 19th century, imposed for several reasons. First of all, because of the insufficient number of beds in public hospitals. There was also the problem of the ritual nourishment and of the specific prayers. There also general conditions of the environment and, not seldom, the discrimination from a part of the medical staff.

The first attempts to found a Jewish hospital dated from January 25th 1848. The document file was entitled "The Jewish Hospital that I Want to Found in this Town"[244].

In 1862, the Guardianship of the Jewish Community from Bacau informed the Prefecture that the hospital is founded "with the money left by late Pincas Edelstein, and, partly, with the income from the salt tax that the Jewish inhabitants impose themselves for meat"[245]. These data also result from a statement submitted to the City Hall in 1901[246]. A piece of land was bought to build the hospital, and the purchasing deed was registered at the Law Court[247]; doctor I. Meiseles donated 100 ducats for the acquisition of the land. In 1864, the amount of 168 ROL was spent for the maintenance of the hospital, which had at the beginning 4 beds[248]. In the next year, they collected the sum of 8034 ROL and 22 coins[249].

The hospital maintenance had many difficulties to face. An appeal in Yiddish, launched in 1884, required the population's support for the hospital. In 1890, the unit had 12 beds and it had taken care of 160 patients; the doctor of the hospital was Dr. E. Marcovici, helped by three other doctors. Documents from the archives of the City Hall show that, in 1893, the Jewish hospital, administrated by two ephors, had been functioning with 12 beds and had been treating 113 patients, for which they needed 1007 ROL and 85 coins[250]. A newspaper article informs us that, in 1894, the hospital was rebuilt, as a fire had affected it. It also shows that Dr. Tr. Hilariu offered his services for free, thus money could be saved in order to help the Jews who had been chased away from villages[251]. In 1896, Dr. Marcovici gave free consultations to the patients of the hospital, which now had 20 beds. In 1908, although it no longer had income from the salt tax, the community secured the activity of the hospital, where 233 patients were hospitalized; out-patient consultations and free medication were also provided[252]. Around the First World War, a set of misunderstandings led to the closing of the hospital. At that time, Dr. Ozias Brucar, who was very popular among the poor Jews, was noticed from the medical staff.

---

[244] State Archives of Iasi, Prefecture of Bacau, Tr. 1318, op. 15, XVI, 1491.
[245] State Archives of Bacau, City Hall of Bacau, file 78, no. 1901.
[246] *Idem*, City Hall of Bacau, file 79/1901, p. 1-2.
[247] *Idem*, Jewish Community, file 22/1926, p. 11-12.
[248] P. Pruteanu, *Contributions to the history of the hospitals in Moldova*, Bucharest, 1959, p. 29.
[249] State Archives of Bacau, file39/1866, p. 45-46.
[250] *Idem*, City Hall of Bacau, file 101/1893, p. 4-7.
[251] "Egalitatea", issue 7, October 1st 1894.
[252] "The Jewish People", issues 2-3, January 23rd, 1909.

After the brothers Schuler's donation of 150,000 ROL, in 1915, to complete the funds to re-open the hospital, the latter was restored under the name "Aizic and Anette Hospital"[253]. In 1923, a fence surrounded the land on which the hospital had been built. Throughout the years, the maintenance of the unit was made possible by means of the donations and the collected amounts, the students' shows, sports festivals, etc.[254]. Among the donors, we should mention Ilie Blumental (deceased in 1924), who left his entire fortune to the hospital.

The appreciation related to Schuler hospital is obvious, if we follow the actions developed throughout the years for its support. In 1925, Marcel Vogel deposited 11,800 ROL at he Community pay-office, an amount that had been collected by the late I. Vogel for the use of the hospital. In the same year, Leon Iacob donated 11,020 ROL on behalf of his aunt, Hava Klepper, for acquisition of surgical instruments. Still in 1925, the Opera Company conducted by S. Friedman gave a performance for the benefit of the hospital. The performance given by a "group of students and dilettantes" had the same goal. In 1932, the heirs of the late F. Klein donated an amount of money to finish the isolation ward of the hospital[255]. Here are the doctors who were activated in different periods: I. Marcusohn, M. Saler, I. Creter, A. Brill and S. Schwartz. Patients were hospitalized no matter what their religion was[256]. The City Hall subsidized the hospital too. Since 1937, the hospital had an autonomous leadership – provided by the "Fraterna" Society – and a number of doctors (Eckstein, E. Iticovici, A. Klein, I. R. Rotenberg, S. Sabat, M. Saler, I. Sarf, M. Sontag, H. Suler, L. Tecuceanu, M. Zerner). In 1940, the |Jewish Hospital ceased its activity, the building being used to accommodate the Jewish refugees from Poland and Basarabia. During the war, the Jewish hospital was taken over by the German army. At that time, the maternity was still functioning, as the Community leadership had given to the "Materna" Association the building at 9 Alex. cel Bun Street, in 1934[257].

e. Education

The economic-social changes which took place in Moldova during the second half of the 19th century, had a considerable influence on the mentality and the behaviour of the Jewish population. There was an increasing and developing influence of the enlightening movement named "Hascala", which had militants ("maskilim") who wanted the Jews to adapt to the new conditions of the historical evolution. The more and more complex relationships that the Jews had with the Romanian population and with the public administration also had a decisive influence towards the same direction. That is why, in Bacau, as well as in other urban centers, there was a need to educate children in the language of the country

---

[253] "Egalitatea", November 20th 1915.
[254] State Archives of Bacau, Jewish Community, file 9/1924, 4, 5/1925, 92/1926, 4 and 9/1929.
[255] *Idem*, Jewish Community, file, 1932, p. 73.
[256] *Idem*, Jewish Community, file 8/1923, p. 14-16.
[257] *Idem*, Jewish Community, file 7/1934, p. 126.

and in the modern spirit. It would have been normal if this education had happened in public schools, but, the discrimination that the Jewish students had to face, made the admission of the Jews' children in public schools even more difficult, as they had to pay school taxes. In some cases, there was an obvious conservative spirit of the parents, afraid their children might be estranged from the Jewish tradition by attending public schools. For these reasons, and wishing students to know the ancient traditions, the Community began to create the "Jewish-Romanian" schools, having the same training schedule as the public schools, but there were the Jewish language and the Mosaic religion as additional objects.

The first attempt to found a primary Jewish school in Bacau is dated in 1863 to1865, when such a school functioned, being conducted by teacher Iosif Haim Grimberg (father of the painter N. Vermont). An attempt to reactivate the school in 1868-1869 failed. Between 1869 and 1871, Mauriciu Schwarty (known for his pedagogical activity in Iasi and for the textbooks that he had published) administrated a Community supported primary school in Bacau. After he had left the town, the school ceased its activity, until 1873. At that time, the "Zion" section, which had been recently created, founded a primary school for the Jewish children with 250 students, which functioned until 1879, with the support of the Community.

The school could not function for the following period, because of the financial difficulties, although M. Hirschenbein had granted an interest-free loan for the school budget[258]. The parents who wanted to have their children educated made efforts to include them in public schools; for instance, in the school year 1878/1879, from the total of 833 students, 150 of them were Jews. The Jewish-Romanian primary school for boys was re-opened by the Community in 1890, on Bacau-Piatra Street. After three years, thanks to the final will and testament of F. Klein, the school was moved to a building on Sachelarie Street (on the place donated by S. Z. Giuvaergiu) and began to be named the "F. Klein School", a name which was kept for decades to come. In 1896, the school had 370 students.

In 1893, the Jewish Women's Reunion founded a primary school for girls, named the "Cultura" School, for which O. Brucar, the doctor to be, made an important contribution. The school had four classes, with 150 students.

Although the traditional Talmud Tora continued to exist, the thousands of children who came and left the desks of the two primary Jewish-Romanian schools throughout the decades received a modern education here, appropriate for the time, and the necessary Jewish traditional knowledge as well. Therefore, the school committees tried to develop harmonious school programmes, excluding the excessive attitudes adopted at different times, either with conservative elements, or with assimilating elements[259].

Although many times they had to face great difficulties (inappropriate places, grants that were not always enough), although the successive community leaderships did not make constant efforts to give material support to the schools, the achieved results were good. The schools had the benefit of a well-instructed and

---

[258] "Fraternity", August 3rd, 1884.

[259] State Archives of Bacau, Jewish Community, file 2/1896, p. 383 and file 5/1923, p. 66/67.

devoted didactic body. Thus, at "F. Klein" School activated, since the beginning of the century, Isidor Augenstrif, V. Holländer, M. Braunstein-Mibasan, Lazar Casvan (the last two were well-known scholars) and others, and, during the between-war period, H. Maier, Isac Sehter, sami Iticovici, Ozias Rozenberg, Vasile Irimescu and others. At "Cultura" School, which was administrated at first by teacher Catz, Roza Goldstein, Jeanette H. Maier, Eti Lepner, Aspasia Hilariu, Paula Zaharia and others activated here. Roza Grimberg (named Roza Ghita after her marriage to the Zionist Moise Ghita, the brother of Dr. Zeiling, a man of culture from Moinesti). In 1930, Jeanette and Herscu Maier, received the "Work Reward" order, class I, for the didactic activity they had performed for decades[260].

The Community, which did not always have the necessary funds (especially during the First World War, as well as in 1933), awarded different grants to the schools, looked after the poor students, providing food and clothes for them[261]. The Community established for years a school restaurant, and it monitored the good functioning of the schools in general.

The material difficulties faced by the Community influenced the activity of the schools. For example, in 1898, the boys' school, which had 500 students, opened with after a long delay, for lack of funds. In the same year, the girls' school was menaced to be evicted because it hadn't paid the rent, which "Alinarea" (the Caress), the Young Ladies Society, finally managed to pay.

At the same time, a relatively large number of Jewish children were studying at public schools. Thus, there were 201 Jewish students in these schools in 1892-1893, and 518 in 1896-1897. During the between-war period, too, the Jewish children studied in public schools, as the Community provided classes of Mosaic religion for them.

Ever since the end of the 19th century, older children began to attend secondary schools. In 1885-1886, 35 Jewish children were registered at the secondary school, the next year 30, and in 1896-1897 23. Of course, discriminations were present here, as well. as in 1910-1914, the Jews' registration in secondary schools was forbidden, and thus the Community had to provide parallel classes.

During the between-war period, the number of secondary school students increased. For instance, in 1924-1925, there were 228 Jewish pupils at the secondary school[262]. The Community provided them the Mosaic religion class with Rabbi B. Safran and Rabbi M. Blanc, and with teacher I. Iticovici[263].

In this chapter about education, we must also mention the kindergartens that functioned in Bacau. Ever since 1899, Haia Strul founded a kindergarten[264]. In 1925, the Community founded a kindergarten, which functioned for all the years to come[265].

Education became a big problem during the years of persecution.

---

[260] "The Jewish Courier", April 6th, 1930.
[261] "Egalitatea", December 25th 1915.
[262] State Archives of Bacau, Jewish Community, file 18-1924, p.5
[263] *Idem*, Jewish Community, file 5/1934
[264] *Idem*, City Hall of Bacau, 1899, p. 1, 1/v.
[265] *Idem*, Jewish Community, file 44/1942.

p. 117

ACCOUNT

Of income and costs of the Jewish Community in the City of Bacau, between May 22nd, 1878 and March 15th, 1880.

No.	SOURCE OF INCOME	ROL	Coins	No.	TYPES OF COSTS	ROL	Coins
1	Surplus of the income from the accounts of May 22nd 1877	1,582	80	1	Costs of hospital repairing according to the account	2,244	20
2	From the contractor of the Salt tax for 17 months and a third after the contract	49,48 6	66	2	Idem repairing of the public bath	2,277	25
3	Idem production of the Salt tax on the day of its dissolution	134	65	3	Salary of the Cult servants for 17 months and a third of 735 fr. 15 coins per month	12,742	55
4	From the contractor of the public bath, with a guarantee of 360 new ROL	3,228	20	4	Monthly sums distributed to the poor by 2 members	4,938	
5	Surplus from the income of the cemetery	123	80	5	Hospital maintenance for 14 months	9,338	
6	Donation for the hospital from Mr. Iancu Klein	24		6	Salary for the teachers of Romanian, German and Hebrew	18,331	10
7	Idem for the school	60		7	Rent for the school building for 13 months, 195 ducats	2,297	72
8	Idem donation for the school from Mr. Strul Klancu	36		8	Different stationery and maintenance costs for the school	1,211	85
9	For the grass at the hospital in the summer of 1879	24		9	For the wood given to the poor in the winter 1878-1879	300	14
	Total of income	54,70 0	11	10	Grant for every ... in the yard of the Synagogue Cathedral	200	
				11	Donations for the poor directly form the Committee House according to the account	816	
	Summing up Sum of costs is of 54,977 – 42 Sum of income is of 54,700 – 11			12	Costs for Thodums and national celebrations	57	91
	There is a deficit of 277 – 31			13	To complete the salary for Rabbi Lebel and Rabbi Levi	212	40
							30
					Total costs	54,977	42

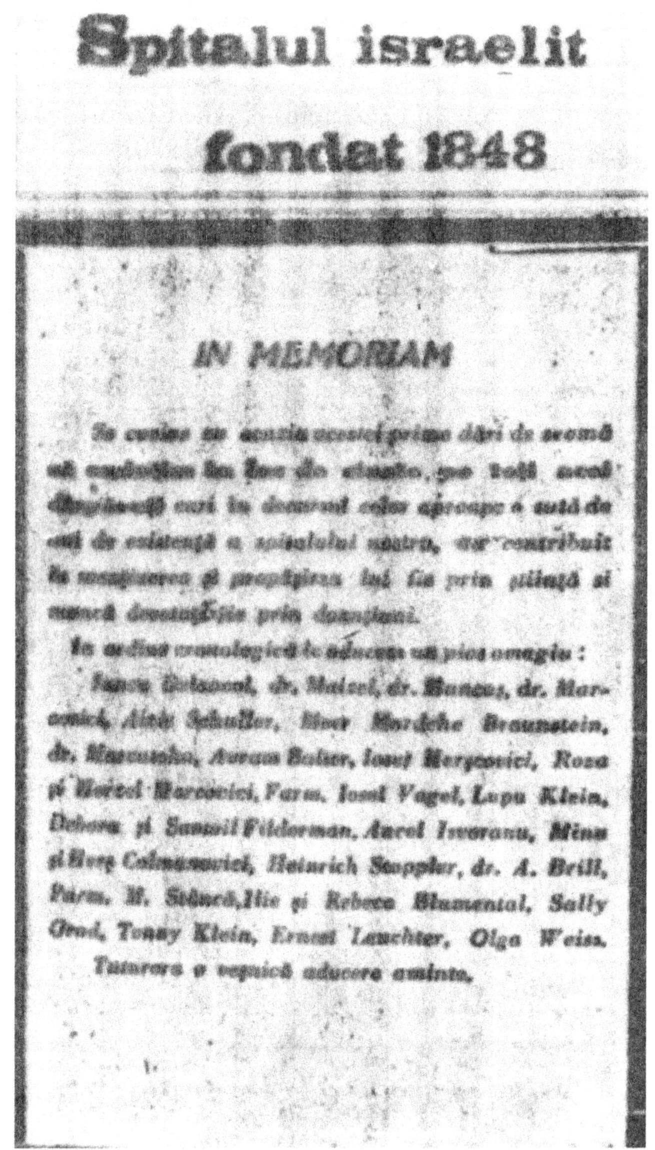

Spitalul israelit

fondat 1848

IN MEMORIAM

Se cuvine [illegible] dări de seamă [illegible] acei [illegible] aproape o sută de ani de existență a spitalului nostru, au contribuit la [illegible] lui fie prin știință și muncă [illegible] prin donațiuni.

In ordine cronologică le aducem un pios omagiu:

[illegible], dr. [illegible], dr. [illegible], dr. Mar[illegible], [illegible] Schuller, [illegible] Mordche Braunstein, dr. [illegible], Avram [illegible], Iosef Herscovici, Roza și [illegible] Marcovici, Farm. Iosif Vogel, Lupu Klein, Debora și Samoil Filderman, Aurel [illegible], Mina și Herș [illegible], Heinrich Stoppler, dr. A. Brill, Farm. M. [illegible], Ilie și Rebeca Blumental, Sally Grad, Tonny Klein, Ernest Leuchter, Olga Weiss.

Tuturora o veșnică aducere aminte.

The Jewish Hospital
Founded 1848

In Memoriam

Paying homage to various members of the Jewish Community.

The museum "From the history of the Jewish People Living in Bacau" 1703- 1944

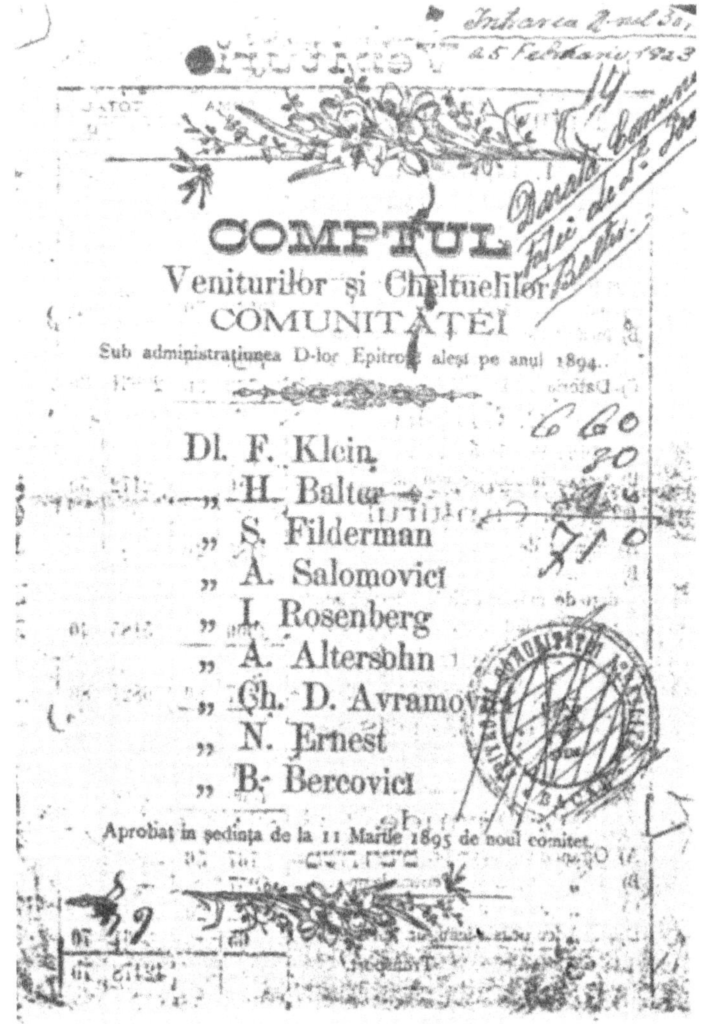

COMPTUL
Veniturilor și Cheltuelilor
COMUNITĂȚEI
Sub administrațiunea D-lor Epitropi aleși pe anul 1894.

Dl. F. Klein
„ H. Balter
„ S. Filderman
„ A. Salomovici
„ I. Rosenberg
„ A. Altersohn
„ Ch. D. Avramovici
„ N. Ernest
„ B. Bercovici

Aprobat în ședința de la 11 Martie 1895 de noul comitet.

Balance Sheet for the Community, under the administration of the guardians elected for the year 1894. Approved by the new committee on March 11, 1895.

The Archives of Bacau County, the Jewish Community of Bacau, brief 31/1922, file 14-19

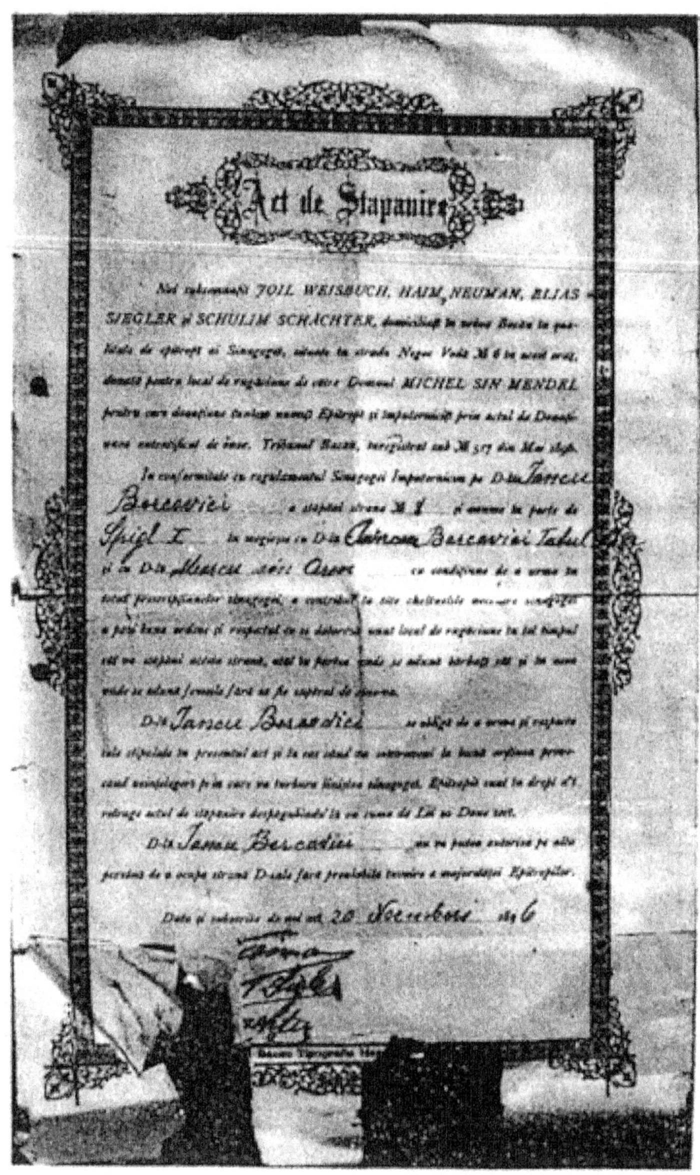

Act de Stapanire

Ownership certificate, through which a lectern from one of the Synagogues in Bacau is being donated to Mr. Iancu Borcovici for reading scripture lessons in the synagogue. Dated November 26, 1896 by the guardians of the Synagogue.

The museum "From the history of the Jewish People Living in Bacau" 1703- 1944

Page 120

Sinagoga Cerealiştilor
SINAGOGA CEREALIŞTILOR
BACAU
Act de Stăpânire
SINAGOGA CEREALIŞTILOR DIN BACAU

A)

B)

C)

A) Corn dealers' synagogue

B) The Golden book of the Corn dealers' synagogue

C)Ownership Certificate of the Corn dealers' synagogue from Bacau, which stipulates the ownership of lectern no. 16 from the ground floor of the synagogue by Mr. Iosif Aranevici, dated October 26, 1927.

The museum "From the history of the Jewish People Living in Bacau" 1703- 1944

Page 121

SOCIETATEA „SACRA" ISRAELITĂ
— DIN BACĂU —

APEL

Către populaţia evreiască a oraşului Bacău!

Ştiţi cu toţii că încă înainte de războiu, Societatea „Sacra" a cumpărat lângă oraş un teren destinat pentru un nou cimitir evreiesc, cel vechi fiind pe atunci mai în întregime complectat. Mulţimea deceselor din timpul războiului a grăbit şi mai mult utilizarea noului cimitir, cel vechi trebuind să fie definitiv închis.

Dar acest nou cimitir e cam departe de oraş şi drumul până acolo este cu desăvârşire impracticabil. Nici vara nu se poate merge măcar cu trăsura la cimitir din cauza mulţimei hopurilor, gropilor şi podeţilor stricate. Când vine, însă, anotimpul ploios, străbaterea distanţei dela bariera oraşului până la cimitir este un adevărat chin.

Noroaie care ţin mai până la mijlocul verei, băltoace adânci că nici carul funebru nu poate trece prin ele, lipsa de şanţuri laterale pentru scurgerea apei etc. pus pe cei mai mulţi în imposibilitate de a-şi îndeplini, cum trebue datoria la procesiunile funerare. Ori câtă bunăvoinţă ar avea cineva pentru îndeplinirea acestei datorii, este peste puterile unui om să străbată fie pe jos, fie cu trăsura, drumul până la cimitir pe o zi de toamnă sau iarnă. Nu o singură dată s'a întâmplat ca, din această cauză, carul funebru să ajungă la cimitir fără să fi urmat măcar de cei zece oameni trebuincioşi la rostirea rugăciunei obligatoare.

Aceiaşi împrejurare face ca îngrijirea mormintelor de către familiile respective şi vizitarea acestor morminte, potrivit datinelor noastre religioase, să fie foarte anevoioasă.

In această situaţiune, Societatea „Sacra" s'a văzut nevoită să ia asupra ei facerea unei şosele practicabile, începând dela bariera oraşului până la cimitir.

Planul şi devizele au şi fost făcute iar lucrarea s'a dat prin licitaţie publică, pentru executare.

Facerea acestei şosele este legată însă, cu cheltueli foarte mari. Aceste cheltueli se ridică la peste 60.000 lei.

Situaţia financiară a Societăţii „Sacra" este, însă acum foarte precară, cea mai mare parte din fondurile ei fiind epuizate în cumpărarea terenului, îngrădirea lui — distrusă şi ea în timpul războiului — precum şi în suportarea cheltuelilor de înmormântare, din nenorocire atât de numeroase în anii din urmă.

In această situaţiune critică, Societatea „Sacra" apelează la generozitatea publicului evreiesc local. Ea va trimite în curând comisiuni care se vor prezenta fiecărui coreligionar spre a-i cere obolul pentru realizarea scopului mai sus arătat.

Publicul evreiesc din localitate, în generozitatea lui fără margini, a dat pentru orice scopuri, a dat la oricine i-a cerut, a dat din toată inima. Nu se poate dar ca apelul nostru la acest public să n'aibă ecoul dorit.

Cu drept cuvânt s'a spus că gradul de civilizaţie al unui popor se măsoară şi după cultul ce are pentru morţii săi. Poporul evreu a avut din tot-deauna acest cult. Venerarea memoriei celor morţi a fost pentru el nu numai o datorie de pietate religioasă, dar şi o pildă dată generaţiilor viitoare, de cum trebue să cinstească aducerea aminte acelor dispăruţi pentru vecie.

Răspunzând la chemarea noastră, veţi dovedi astfel că posedaţi şi acum acest cult şi tot-odată vă veţi face o datorie de conştiinţă către voi înşivă, ca oameni şi ca evrei.

Daţi dar din toată inima ca să putem duce la bun sfârşit lucrarea începută.

Comitetul Societăţei „Sacra"
din Bacău

Bacău, Septembrie 1919

Tip. Avr. Gold[illegible] Bacău
Cenzurat 18/VIII 1919

Appeal made by the Sacred Jewish Society of Bacau to the Jewish population of Bacau, through which they are being asked to contribute financially to build a better road from the town of Bacau to the existing cemetery located in the outskirts of the city. At the time it was almost impossible to use the existing road, already destroyed by the war and full of bumps, especially in the rainy season. Dated September 1919.

Bacau State Archives, foundation "The Jewish Community of Bacau", brief 24/1942, file 16

Page 122

Epitropia Comunităței Israelite din Bacău

ועד הקהלה העברית באקוי

EVREI!

Numai câteva zile mai sunt pentru îndeplinirea formalităților de încetățenire.

Joi, 28 Iunie a. c., expiră termenul pentru încetățenire și acest termen fiind acordat prin Constituție, orice prelungire a lui este cu desăvârșire exclusă.

Grăbiți-vă dar a vă folosi de puținele zile în care se mai primesc declarațiunile de încetățenire.

Este în joc situația voastră și viitorul copiilor voștri!

Comunitatea vă stă la dispoziție cu sfaturi și vă face toate formalitățile în mod absolut gratuit.

Președinte, **Osias Herscovici**

Secretar, H. L. HERȘCOVICI

No. 20 din 22 Iunie 1923.

Arh. St. Bacău, fond. Comunitatea Israelită Bacău, dos. 1/1923, f. 35

Comunitatea Evreilor din Bacău

ועד הקהלה העברית באקוי

9/

COMUNICAT

Se aduce la cunoștința publicului evreesc că după intervenția făcută de noi, am obținut dela Onor. Ministerul Cultelor aprobarea și viza statutului nostru și prin adresa No. 9353|848 din 25 Ianuarie 1932 ne face cunoscut că Comunitatea noastră a devenit persoană juridică de drept public.

Președ. Comunit. Israelite Bacău

Osias Herșcovici

Arh. St. Bacău, fond. Comunitatea Israelită Bacău, dos. 6/1932, f. 12—13

a)
TRUSTEESHIP OF THE JEWISH COMMUNITY OF BACAU

JEWS!

There are only a few days left to accomplish the naturalization formalities.
Thursday, June the 28th, the current year, the term for naturalization expires. As this term is granted by the Constitution, any extension of it is absolutely excluded.
Hurry then to use the few days left for submitting the naturalization declarations.
You are responsible about your situation and your children's future!
In this respect, the community is ready to give you advice and also provides all the naturalization formalities for free.

President, Osias Hersovici

Secretary, H.L. HERSCOVICI

No. 20 dated June 22nd 1923

b)
THE JEWISH COMMUNITY OF BACAU

ANNOUNCEMENT

We hereby inform the Jewish public that following the intervention made by us, we obtained the approval and visas for our statute from the Honourable Ministry of Religions. By the address no. 9353/848 dated January 25th, 1932, we are informed that our Community became a juridical person of public right.

The President of the Jewish Community of Bacau

Osias Herscovici

Bacau State Archives, foundation "The Jewish Community of Bacau", brief 5/1932, file 12-13

C. ASSOCIATIONS OF MUTUAL SUPPORT AND OTHER SOCIETIES FOUNDED BY THE JEWS

JEWISH COMMUNITY OF BACAU

Bucharest, 1995

Solidarity, mutual help, unification of forces to achieve common goals, all these represent an old tradition in the Jewish communities. In time, many associations of this kind developed their activity in Bacau. The typical element for these associations was the mutual help when needed (illness, material difficulties, death, etc.). This kind of a mutual help association was "Ghemilat Hasadim" Association, which was founded in the fourth decade of the 19th century, and which we mentioned in the chapter for social assistance.

"Fraterna" Society had the same character, which was founded in 1879. According to the statutes, its goal was the mutual help of the members in case of illness, material difficulties, death of a relative or the impossibility to find a job. Additionally, the society could get involved in social actions as well: aids for the poor, support for community institutions, etc. In 1898, J. Herscovici conducted the executive committee of "Fraterna"; the minutes of the elections in that year has been kept; some of the participants signed it in Hebrew (they probably didn't know how to write in Romanian)[266]. The stamp that the society used has the following inscription in Romanian and in Hebrew: "The First Society to Heal the sick and Care for the dead". As aids for community actions, we mention that, during 1888-1900, "Fraterna" was involved in supporting the hospital as well as the Jewish schools. The leadership of "Fraterna" from 1925 included Iancu Baratz, Leon Iacob, David Rozemberg and others[267]. During the following years, wealthy Jews were members of the society such as: Ozias Klein, Iosif Feldher, Zisu Calmanovici, Leon Grad, Avram Isvoranu, etc. Throughout the years, the society also distributed aid to the poor, helped certain students with scholarships. "Fraterna" also had a synagogue of its own. In 1941, when it was dissolved, there was a capital of more than 150,000 ROL that was invested in public programs (different categories of value notes)[268].

"Aghidas Haboinim", an association that was founded in 1885, shared the same character of mutual help of societies. According to its title, people with smaller income were involved this time: handicraftsmen from the branch of constructions (masons, stone hewers, carpenters, tinkers, plasterers), perhaps traders of construction materials as well. The summons to a gathering of this society for March 28th, 1898, signed by

---

[266] *Idem*, Jewish Community, file 6/1938, p. 80.
[267] *Idem*, Jewish Community, file 22/1925, p. 1, 2, 3.
[268] *Idem*, Jewish Community, file 22/1940.

Simsen Volsohn, as President, and Filip Grünberg, as Secretary, has been kept. The text of the summons is in German, but in Hebrew letters. The round stamp put on this summons included a text in three languages: on the outside circle, in Romanian – "Society of Handicraftsmen to Heal the Sick and Guide (to the cemetery)"; in the middle, in German, with Hebrew letters – "Kranken und Leichen Verein Bauarbeiter"; in the inside circle, in Romanian – "Founded on August 18th, 1855"; the center is occupied by the title of the society, in Hebrew – "Agudat Haboinim" (in local pronunciation, "Aghidas Haboinim"). The Society continued its activity, with interruptions, until 1941, when the racist legislation dissolved it. In 1909, it had 60 members and a capital of 3000 ROL. In 1912, its President was M. Moscovici. In 1924, it included 189 members. Having as its main concern the help for its members, the society (which in some documents was named "Aghidas Haboinim Fraternity") accumulated a capital of more than 85,000 ROL, partly in cash, partly in value notes[269]. As the archive documents show us, during the between-wars period, it settled the litigation among its members, and sustained relationships with the National Union of Handicraftsmen and Workers in Greater Romania; moreover, it was familiar with the community problems (especially with the school functioning) and had close contacts with the Zionist movement.

"Marpe Lenefes" was another society of mutual help, founded in 1893. In 1922, Lupu Itic Mandel was its President; in 1941M Sami Kaufman and Marcu Mendelovici were its representatives. When the racist legislation dissolved it, the society had a capital of 100,000 ROL (collected from subscriptions and donations).

"Tamaduirea" (" The Healing") Society ("Bikir Hoilim") activated since 1925, which also had as a goal the mutual help of its members. In 1941, Avram Iosefsohn led it, and it had a capital of 32,000 ROL.

Other societies of mutual help were "Providenta" ("Providence") and "Aghidas Aham" (The Harmony) societies, both of them founded in 1923[270], as well as "The Union of Different Handicraftsmen", present within the Community since the end of the 19th century; in 1895-1896, this group took the initiative of founding an alms-house for old people, for which they collected 2,000 ROL[271].

Let us also mention the fact that, on the tombstones of the deceased who had been members of these associations, this fact was also mentioned; in the cemetery from Bacau, there are many such tombstones.

Beside all these organizations, which (although they were involved in certain social actions) had as their main concern the help for their own members, many circles and associations, having as sole concern the philanthropic, the charitable goal, also developed their activity in Bacau. In this field, we mention the actions conducted to help the confined women, in 1887, and to distribute wood to the needy, in 1892[272]. In 1891, "Malbis Arunim" ("Dressing the Naked") Society was founded. Two years later, it had 13 supporting members. It gave clothes to 36 poor students from Talmud Tora,

---

[269] *Idem*, Jewish Community, file 22/1940.
[270] *Idem*, Jewish Community, file 4/1923.
[271] "Egalitatea", January 26th, 1896.
[272] *Idem*, February 7th 1892.

with the intention to open a vocational school for these children[273] The "Caress" Society for Young Ladies supported the "Culture" Girls' School.

In 1912, out of Rabbi Betalel Safran's initiative, a social assistance society was founded.

Every year, different circles initiated winter actions to collect clothes and shoes for the poor children. "Caritas" Society of Educated Women developed such an action in 1915; 90 children took benefit from this action[274]. "Humanitas", the local section of Bnai Brith lodge, which had been founded in 1926, under the presidency of the well-known manufacturer Dr. H. Perlbergher, had similar initiatives. There are actions dated from the same period, meant to help the victims of a big fire, which had destroyed 500 households, most of them Jewish houses[275].

In 1929, out of the initiative of A. Isvoranu, the manufacturer, an alms-house for old people was founded. The Community offered a building in Calea Oituz Street, the Association for old people's alms-house was created, which collected funds from donations and subscriptions (among other sources, from the Community and from the City Hall) and administrated (with rather important material difficulties) this institution where several dozens of old people lived the last days of their lives. The place continued its activity until 1949, with interruptions during the war, when its office was taken over.

We must underline the extremely efficient activity of "Materna" Society, the Jewish women's association to help the poor confined women and look after the infants. As we have shown, in 1934, this society created a maternity in a place that had been donated by the Community (on Alexander the Good Street), and maintained this very important place for many years with no interruptions[276].

*

Other community organizations developed their activity in Bacau, but in other fields than the ones indicated so far. It is known that, during the inter-war period, the Jewish University students had many difficulties (registration in faculties, means of maintenance, procuring and sending to Iasi the corpses that the medical students needed for dissection, etc.). In order to solve some of these problems, the Jewish Students Circle was founded in 1922, which – by means of cultural actions developed in time – tried to collect funds for the poor students. The Community helped them by grants and by giving them the bodies of deceased men, whom no one claimed[277].

"Nitvat Am" ("The Ways of the People"), founded in 1869, was a society with cultural goals. On the same shore, "Culture" Society, founded in 1918, developed its activity, founding a very active library ("Raza" library), which had about 10,000 volumes, and organizing many conferences and cultural affairs, until 1941; within this frame, Felix Aderca, the writer gave lectures about the "Silbermann" novel, by Jacques

---

[273] *Idem*, February 5th, 1893.
[274] *Idem*, December 25th 1915.
[275] "The Jewish Courier", May 23rd, 1926.
[276] State Archives of Bacau, Jewish Community, file 7/1934.
[277] *Idem*, Jewish Community, file 9/1925, 14/1926, 4/1928.

de Lacretelle. "Avoda" ("the Work") Society took actions on the cultural side since 1926. The Cultural Association of the Jewish Women (A.C.F.E.), as well.

Thanks to the cultural initiatives of the Jews in Bacau, the "Mizmor" ("Song") Society was created in 1909, for musical education, and (after the Second Worls War) the dramatic circle in Yiddish, conducted by actor Lazar Cornaciu.

In the sports field, the "Macabi" association was active, as a result of the unification of several sports associations[278].

---

[278] "Our Rebirth", February 6th 1926.

Page 129

This page is a handwritten Yiddish doument with an offical-like stamp dated 1862.

The Central Archives for the History of the Jewish People, Jeruslem, R.M./792

Page 130

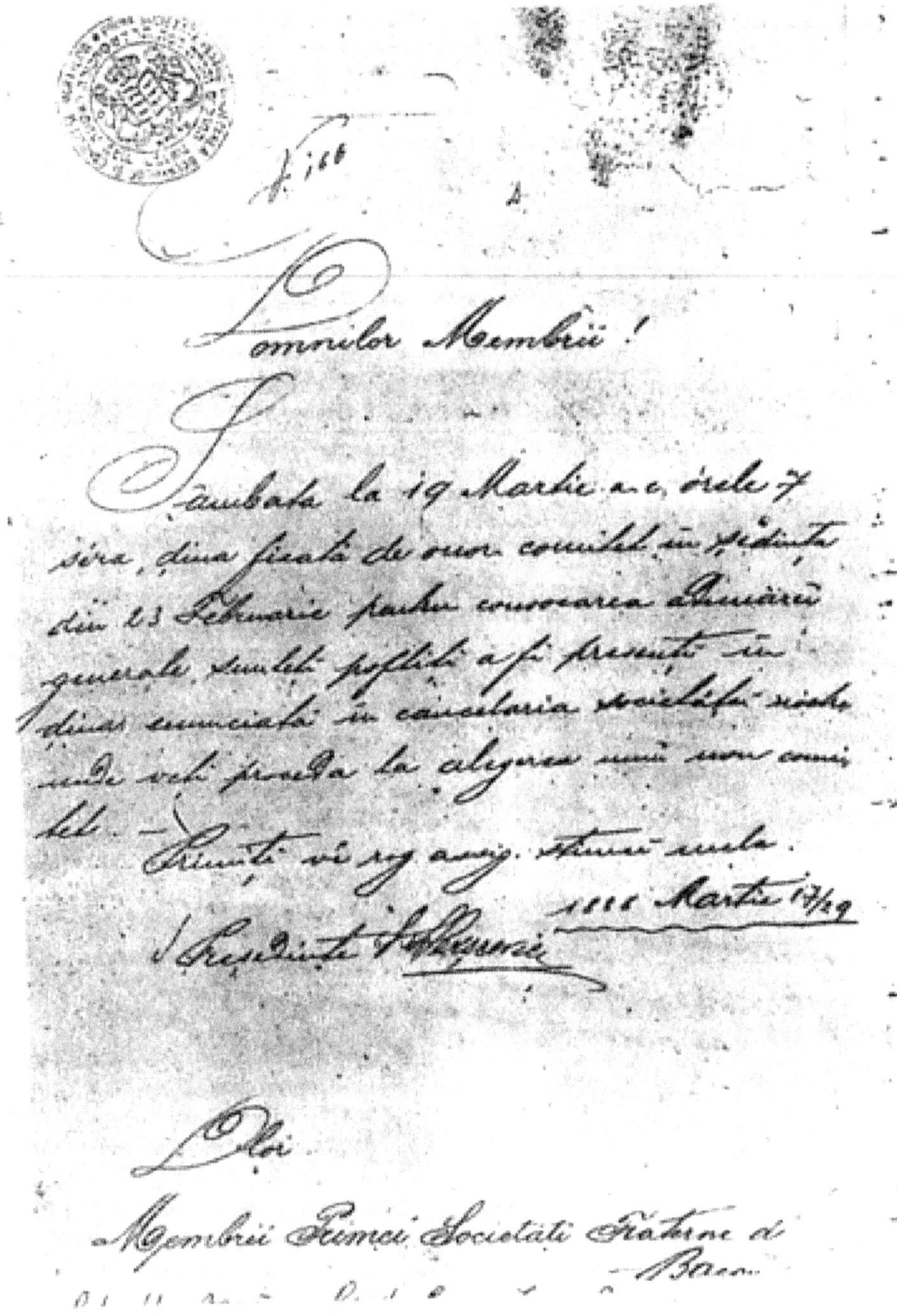

Domnilor Membrii!

Sâmbata la 19 Martie a.c. orele 7 sera, dina fixata de noul comitet în şedinţa din 23 Februarie pentru convocarea Adunării generale, sunteti poftiti a fi prezenti în dina enunciata în cancelaria societăţii, unde veti proceda la alegerea unui nou comitet. — Primiti vă rog asig. stimei noastre.

1866 Martie 17/29

Presedinte [illegible]

Dlor Membrii Primei Societati Fraterne de Bacau

Dear Members,
Saturday, March 19th 1866, at 7 PM, as appointed by the honorary committee on February 23rd, you are invited in the office of the Jewish Society for electing a new committee. Signed by the president of the society, on March 17, 1886.
Bacau State Archives, foundation "The Jewish Community of Bacau"

Page 131

STATUTELE

PRIMEI SOCIETAŢI FILANTROPICE

A DIFERIŢILOR MESERIAŞI ISRAELITI

„AGHIDAS-HABOINIM"

PENTRU VINDECAREA BOLNAVILOR

ŞI CONDUCEREA CELOR INCETAŢI DIN VIAŢĂ.

FONDATĂ IN BACAU LA 12 APRILIE 1891.

EDIŢIA II-a

סטאטוט דעם

ערשטען פילאנטראפישען פעראיינ'ס

יודישער פערשיעדענען האנדווערקער

„אגודת הבונים"

פיר

היילונג דער קראנקען אונד בעגלייטונג דער אבלעבענדען.

געגרינדעט אין באקוי אם 12 אפריל 1891

— צווייטע אויפלאגע —

The Statues of the first Charitable Society of the various Jewish Tradesmen "Aghidas Haboinim" for curing the sick and leading the ones not among us any longer. Founded on April 12, 1891 in Bacau.

The Library Center for the Historical Study of the Jewish in Romania. No. 1090, the second cover page of the book.

Page 132

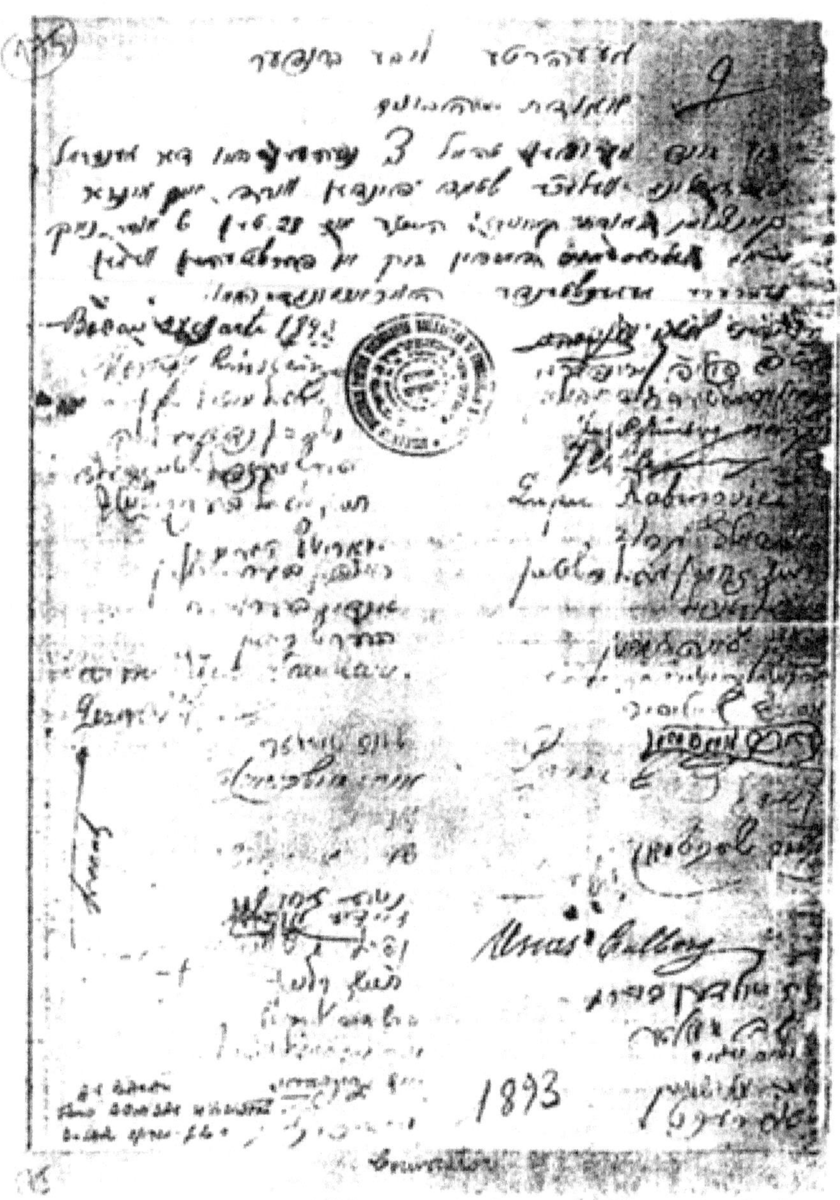

Convocator

„Societatea meseriaşi pentru vindecarea bolnavilor şi conducerea morţilor"
Invitaţie la o adunare generală la 28 martie 1893

Arh. St. Bacău, fond. Aghidas Haboinim, dos. 2/1920, f. 9

Invitation by "The Charitable Society of the various Jewish Tradesmen "Aghidas Haboinim" for curing the sick and leading the ones not among us any longer" to a general meeting on March 28th 1893.

The State Archives of Bacau, Aghidas Haboinim, brief 2/1920, file 9

Page 133

Societatea „PROVIDENȚA" (SPRIJIN ȘI AJUTOR) Bacău

Domnule Membru,

Statutele societății noastre sunt gata alcătuite, examinate și studiate de comitetul administrativ, care le-a aprobat cu mici modificări.

După multă muncă, ce comisiunea de redactare a depus cu alcătuirea acestui statut, a izbutit a-i da o formă clară, care va da organizației noastre o îndrumare sigură și de progres, ca să corespundă exact scopului pentru care societatea a fost înființată.

Nu este deajuns însă ca statutul să fie bine alcătuit, ci este nevoe ca fiecare să înțelegem rostul nostru în societate și să ne supunem cu sfințenie fiecărui articol din statut, ferindu-ne de a cădea în păcatele celor-lalte societăți similare, unde statutele nu sunt de cât o ficțiune și păpușărie.

Nu este de ajuns ca acei cari conduc o societate să fie buni conducători, ci e nevoe ca toți membri cari compun organizația să-i urmeze, din dragoste și devotament, iar nu din frica de amenzi.

Trebue dar ca fie-care să cunoască bine prescripțiunile statutare, ca să fie feriți de a se abate de la ele, de cât în cazuri de forță majoră.

Vă invităm deci, a lua parte negreșit, la

Adunarea Generală Extraordinară

în ziua de Duminică 11 Noembrie cr. ora 2 p. m. fix, în localul din Str. Vasile Alexandri (Școala de fete Cultura) pentru

votarea Statutului

când veți putea avea și posibilitatea de a lua cunoștință de drepturile și datoriile ce aveți ca membru în societate.

Nu e îngăduit nimănu-i să lipsească de la această adunare care are menirea să rezolve o chestiune care atinge însuși existența și organizația societății, și în caz de absență vom aplica amenda cuvenită.

Președinte, LITMAN SCHWARTZ

Secretar, Avr. Goldsmith

"PROVIDENCE" SOCIETY (FOR SUPPORT AND HELP) BACAU

Dear Member,

The statutes of our society are already prepared, examined and studied by the administrative committee which approved them without any modifications.

After many hours of hard work, the issuing committee has been able to steer the organization in a clear direction, corresponding exactly with the purpose on the basis of which the society was established.

It is not enough for the statute to be just well done; there is a certain need for each of us to understand the role we play in the society and to respectfully obey every article of the statute, avoiding to be trapped in the sins of the other similar societies, where such statues are regarded as a real fiction.

It is not enough for those leading us to be good leaders, but rather that all members who compose this society to follow the leaders with love and devotion, and not only because they are scared by penalties.

Therefore, everybody should know very well the provisions of the statutes such that no one can be tempted to disobey them, except in rare circumstances.

As such, we invite you to attend the ***Extraordinary General Meeting***

On Sunday, November 11th , at 2:00 p.m, in the building located on Vasile Alecsandri str. (Girls Cultural School) in order to

v o t e t he s t a t u t e

where you will have the opportunity to learn about the rights and duties you have as a member of the society.

Nobody is allowed to miss this meeting which is meant to solve matters that comprise the existence and organization of the society itself. In case you are absent, you will receive the afferent penalty.

President,
LITMAN SCHWARTZ

Secretary, Lawyer Goldsmith

Bacau State Archives, foundation "The Jewish Community of Bacau", brief 4/1923, file 93

Page 134

(177) 055%

1924, Aprilie 30

Bacau 29 Aprilie

Societatea
Agihidas Ahim
(Armonia)

No 8

8

Domnule Presedinte

Cu Onoare aducem la Cunoştinţa Comunităţii, Ca in Ziua de 30 [illegible]
1923, miam Constituit, o Societa[te]
pentru ajutorarea reciproc in
Caz de boala, şi deces.
Denumirea societăţii Aghidas Ahi[m]
(Armonia)
Sediul societăţii str. [illegible] No [illegible]
in present societate se Compune
din 60 membrii, presedinte a fost
Ales D-lui Haim Avram,

Primiţi stima şi Consideratiunile noastre [illegible]

Presedinte
Haim Avram

Secretar
[illegible]

(Armonia)

D-sale Domnului Presedinte al Comunităţii
Israelite Bacau

"Agihidas Ahum" Society
(The Harmony)
Mr. President,

Honorably, we inform you that on November the 30-th 1923, we constituted a society for mutual help in case of illness and/or death.

The name of the society is Agihidas Ahum (The Harmony).

The society will have its residence on Negoi Voda str. No. 4.

Presently, the society has 60 members, Mr. Haim Avram being elected as president.

Please accept my best regards and full consideration.

President,
Haim Avram

Secretary,
L. Gurberg

To his honour. Mr. President....................

The museum "From the history of the Jewish People Living in Bacau" 1703- 1944

Page 135

"Providenta" Society Bacau

Funeral stone for Leibu Aizig, deceased on July 3rd 1826. age 70.

The museum "From the history of the Jewish People Living in Bacau" 1703- 1944

Page 136

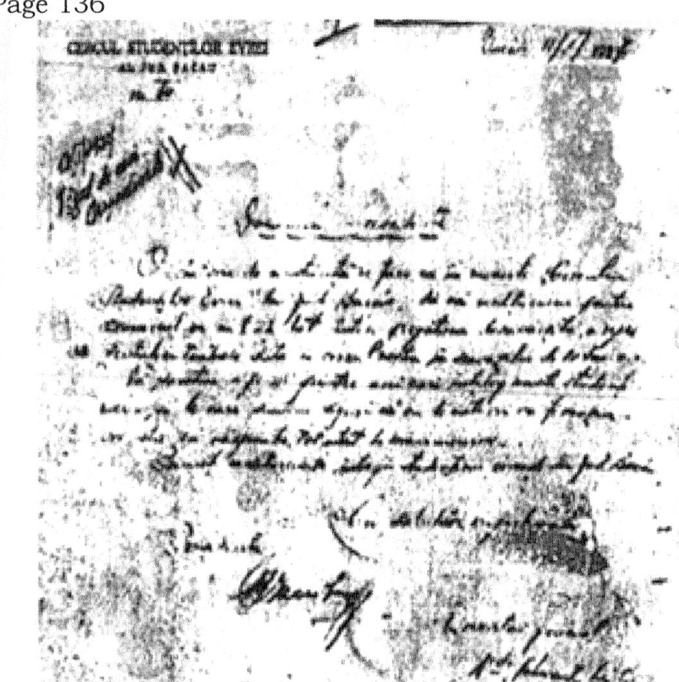

Arh. St. Bacău, fond. Comunitatea Israelită Bacău, dos.3/1927, f. 4

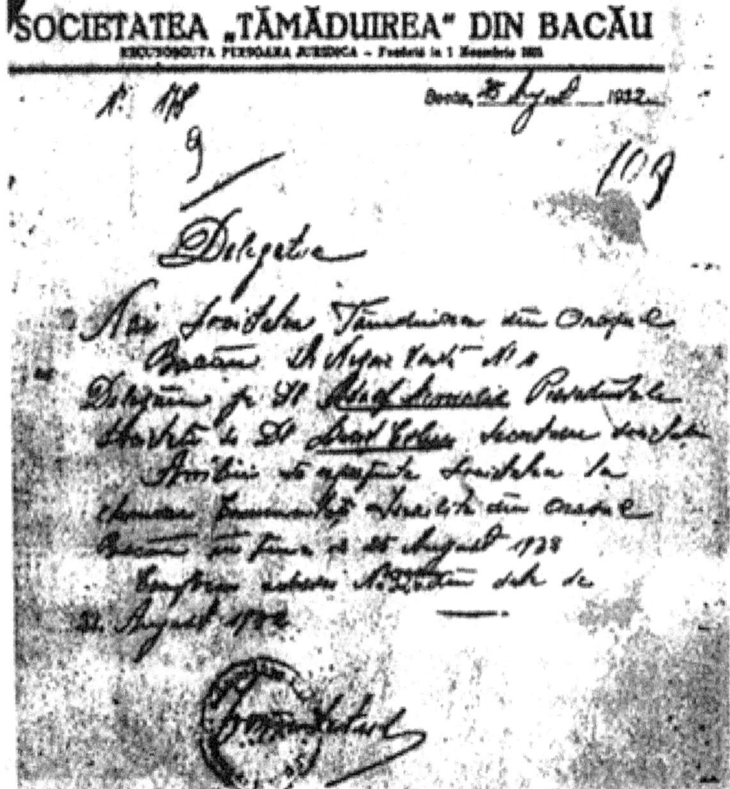

SOCIETATEA „TĂMĂDUIREA" DIN BACĂU

The founding letter proposing the name for The Jewish Student Association of Bacau.
The Healing (Tamaduirea) Society of Bacau – recognized as a business since November 1st 1881

Letter assigning power of attorney to two Jewish men to set up the Society as requested by the Jewish community of Bacau on August 25, 1932.

The museum "From the history of the Jewish People Living in Bacau" 1703- 1944.

D. THE ZIONIST MOVEMENT

JEWISH COMMUNITY OF BACAU

Bucharest, 1995

The ideas spread by Tvi Hers Kaliser ever since 1873, and promoted by "Hoveve Zion" related to the emigration and colonization in Eretz Israel, began to take root in Bacau around the year 1880. In the first Zionist conference, in Focsani, Avram Balter and Israel Groper from Bacau took part (together with David Bucsester and Mendel Grimberg from Moinesti). In 1881, the section of the movement entitled "Colonization of Eretz Israel" was founded in Bacau. Here is how the appeal in Yiddish of the "Committee of the circle for the colonization of Eretz Israel by agricultural work", spread during the summer of 1881, began:

"To our brothers in faith, sons of Israel from Bacau.

You all know the necessity to support the holy purpose of colonization in Eretz Israel. We make an appeal to every one, depending on their wealth, to make a contribution for the holy purpose, the Eretz colonization, and we will publish in newspapers all these donations with the donor's name. Thanks to such actions we will set off singing for Zion" [...][279].

The appeal had huge echo. By donations or by monthly contributions, the Jews from Bacau were among the top communities who supported the movement. In 1882, a number of families from Bacau, beside the ones from Moinesti (conducted by David Schub), decided to leave for Eretz. An eye witness, Iosef Brüll from Bacau, evoked, in "The Protector" newspaper from August 18th, 1882, the touching moments he had witnessed: the crowd of Jews and Romanian who had accompanied those who were leaving at the station, the encouraging words said by Talmudist E. A. Teller, by the medicine student I. Rosenweig and by Y. M. Hass, the rounds of applause which broke at the moment they set off[280]. Together with those from Moinesti, three men from Bacau founded the "Ros Pina" colony, and other eight men were among the founders of the "Zichron Iaacov" colony (Kibbutzes, probably). In order to collect the necessary funds for those who were leaving, the Jewish community increased the meat tax.

These first groups' departure increased the wish of the others as well. A group conducted by A. Balter and A. Groper was created, aiming to found a colony under the name of "Neuschatz". This attempt failed, and those who had arrived in Eretz Israel joined the one from "Ros Pina" and from "Zichron Iaacov". The Aaronsohn family must be especially mentioned as a member of this group, as this family gave many remarkable personalities to the Jewish people.

---

[279] I. Voledi-Vardi, *op. cit.*, p. 24.
[280] *Idem*, p. 23-26.

In 1892, there was a section entitled "Hoveve Zion" ("Those Who Love Zion") in Bacau, which included about 100 members. Here is the text that can be read on one of its stamp, in Romanian and in Hebrew: "Jewish Society for Advantages in Palestine, Bacau, July, 1892". In the center of the stamp there are two shaking hands, in sign of unification. Seven families left for Eretz from Bacau that year, and eight families the next year[281]. Among the pioneers of the "Hovene Zion" movement there was Bercu Vigderescu, one of the people who founded "The first society of the Jewish farmers in Palestine" in 1899. He had been the leader of a Jewish reading club, having M. Focsaner as President, and teachers L. Casvan and M. Braunstein-Mibasan among its members[282].

Another man from Bacau who got to the Holy Country in that age was Brill, who founded a large farm at Ioknan, near Haifa.

A feminine section, named "Bnot Zion", was founded within "Hoveve Zion"; the two sections together included 400 members. They founded a Zionist library, they organized public conferences, literary soirées, and they financially helped the colonies in Eretz[283]. The youth founded a "Reading Club of the Jewish Youth"[284]. Ever since that time, at the beginning of the 20th century, animated by the Hovevean-Zionist ideas, Iosif Iticovici began his activity, and, during the decades to come, he would have special merits for his efforts to make many generations of children acquire elements of Hebrew.

At the beginning of the new century, there were certain trends among the Zionists in Bacau, which also existed in the Zionist movement around the world. The trends of the political Zionism also appeared. In 1902, there was a section "Max Nordau", which organized one of Horia Carp's conferences, and a "Calman Schulman" section, which founded a reading club and collected money for the Jewish National Fund (F.N.E.). Since 1907, the "Tikvat Zion" section ("The Hope of Zion") began its activity, and, for many years, it performed hard work of Zionist education and propaganda in conferences, reading clubs, by activating the Zionist library and by organizing Hebrew classes[285]. Money for F.N.E. was also collected.

In 1912, the Zionist leader Nahum Socolov was invited to Bacau, as he published the Hebrew newspaper "Hatefira" ("The Aurora") in Warsaw. He found an organized Zionist center in Bacau: men within the "Tikvat Zion" circle (led by Volf Iser, I. Glasman and Isac Avram), women within the "Iulia Dr. Herzl" circle (led by Frida Rothenberg, by sisters Davidovici and by Vatarescu). Dr. I. Niemirower, from Iasi (who would become Chief-Rabbi of Romania), was one of the lecturers who were invited to Bacau.

After the war between 1916-1918, and then during the inter-war period, the Zionist movement had a strong activity in Bacau. We find it reflected in the texts

---

281 "The Jewish Courier", March 21st 1926.

282 "Egalitatea", January 21st, 1894.

283 "The Voice of the Zion", June 5th, 1899, and January 22nd, 1900.

284 "The Sunrise", October 15th, 1899, p. 8.

285 "Egalitatea", March 2nd and August 17th 1912.

with numerous informative data that were published by Abrahami Lica Gutman Mayer Eibschitz and by Dr. I. R. Rotenberg.

The great meeting where the Balfour Declaration was welcome, and where the speech of the experienced Zionist militant, Frida Rothenberg, made a special impression, represented an important moment in the development of the movement.

The ideological diversity of the Zionists increased during the inter-war period. A lively debate took place in Bacau on January 19th 1920, "between the Zionists and the Zionist crowds", as was reported by a press correspondent[286]. The general increase of the movement is reflected by the fact that the 16th Congress of the Zionists in Romania was held in Bacau in 1927: materials related to this Congress are kept in the A.C.M.E.O.R. Archives (618/50).

On the practical side, we mention the remarkable activity of the members of the Centrist Zionist Organization, made of traders and manufacturers involved in the Community leadership; usually, they were members of U.E.R. and even of the Romanian political parties, but, at the same time, they gave their children a Hebrew education, and they took active part in collecting money for the Jewish national funds. Isac Avram must be mentioned among the centrists, as he conducted the local organization till after the war, being helped by Davidovici, Iosif Iticovici and Eli Rapaport. The Organization also published the "Bulletin of the Jewish National Fund".

M. Eibschitz, V. Iser, Balter and Weissbuch led the Mizrahists. They militated within the Community against the assimilating tendencies and for the teaching of Jewish subjects in schools. After the Second World War, the Mizrahists' youth organization, "Bnei Akiba", was founded.

Teachers Mrdler and Rabin, Eng. Zinger and Lawyer Ionas militated within "Renasterea" ("The Rebirth") literary circle, which supported the Jewish Party.

An important part of the young people, especially those with an intellectual training, adopted the "Hasomer Hatair" movement, as they were attracted by its socialist ideas. The organization from Bacau was founded around 1923, having the secondary school pupil Itic Braunstein as madrih (instructor). (The sponsors of this book are Itic Braunstein's children). Many Halutims left for Israel from "Hasomer Hatair", and we mention Alfred Avram, Bernanrd Rabinovici, Leon Haran, Haim Svart, etc. As it is known, several members of "Hasomer" were arrested during the war, and some of these people were from Bacau (Moise Ghitler, Buium Carol and Izu Suler). Sara Avram-Rotenberg developed a vivid activity within this organization, a person who – because of this – had a lot to suffer during both Antonescu's regime and the Communist one. Doctors S. Sabat, A. Klein, I. R. Rotenberg, and brothers Iser and Blanc must be mentioned among the mature people with a leftist Zionist orientation. In 1924, "Hanoar Hationi" (The Circle of the Zionist Youth) was founded by the young centrist Zionists, led by Mayer and Hana Zeilicovici. The group from Bacau laid the basis of other sections in the rest of the country and even abroad, by halutz Slomo Rotenberg, native from Bacau. In 1932, the center for the entire country moved to Bucharest (being led by Har-Zaav,

---

286 "Mantuirea" ("The Salvation"), January 29th 1920.

Ciubotaru, Frenkel), while the local group continued its activity, being led by F. Goldenberg, Lica Gutman, then by Polsi Reisel, Margulius, etc. The organization developed an activity of education and propaganda, therefore they invited Hebrew writers Bistritki and Slonski for lectures, and they published the "Moledet" ("The Country") magazine. Among the mature militants in this direction, we mention Zighi Drimer, and, among the Halitzims, N. Enghelberg, I. Steinbock, Hari Iacobsohn, Haim Reizel, etc.

"Gordonia" activated during the last years of the war and after the war, when they founded their own working youth organization "Dror Habonim". Militants: RicaTecuceanu, Gloter, Sasa Smelter, Dudu Gutman and others.

Some Zionists, dissatisfied with the working methods of the Zionist Executive, grouped themselves in a revisionist organization in Bacau, led by Dr. Martin Resu, Sami Iekerkaner, etc. They invited the revisionist leader Jabotinski to lecture at Bacau. The youth organization "Betar" was another source of halutzims, especially within the Illegal Alliance.

In 1924, a local section of the Cultural Association of the Jewish Women (A.C.F.E. - WIZO) was founded, which developed a sustained Zionist and cultural activity. With their helped, several young women left for the agricultural school "Aianot", in Israel, then becoming kibutznics (for instance, Marica Marcus, Clara Haran, a.s.o.). A.C.F.E. collected money for the Zionist funds, they supported a kindergarten[287], as well as the cultural center that founded the "Raza" library. We should mention here that the Zionist activity among the youth also considered their practical training for the pioneer life. A conclusion may be drawn from one of Dr. S. Sabat's reports, which is kept in the A.C.M.E.O.R. archives, that, throughout the years, 6 "snifs" of "ahsara" (training by work) functioned in Bacau before the war: 3 of "Hasomer Hatair", 1 of "Bnei Avoda", 1 – "Gordocia" and 1 – "Hanoar Hationi". After the war, 4 snifs of ahsara functioned. From all these halitzims left, especially for kibutz Dalia, Barcai and Manghen. Another material from the same archives shows that "Betar" organized a mosava (camp for agricultural training) at Doftana.

[287] "News from the Jewish World", October 2nd, 1930.

Page 144

Efraim Fişel AARONSON cu familia, originari din Bacău. AARON AARONSON, botanist renumit, SARA, sora, ZWI, fratele şi FIŞEL, tatăl, fondatori ai organizaţiei de spionaj „NILI", au înlesnit englezilor cucerirea Palestinei în războiul din 1917.

אפרים פישל אהרונסון ומשפחתו מ־בקאו BACAU (רומניה).
אהרון אהרונסון, שרה, צבי ואביהם היו בין המיסדים של ארגון
הריגול „נילי" אשר הקל לצבא הבריטי לכבוש את א"י בשנת 1917.

OCT. - DECEMBRIE 1975 BULETIN No. 13/III

A.C.M.E.O.R א.ק.מ.או.ר.
האגוד העולמי לתרבות
ליהודים יוצאי רומניה בישראל
ת"א, רש"י 39, טל. 03-284074

Efraim Fisei AARONSON with his family, native from Bacau. AARON AARONSON, a famous botanist, SARA, his sister, ZWI, his brother and FISEL, his father, founders of the spying organization "NILI". They facilitated the Brittish army to conquer Palestine in the 1917 war.

October – December 1975 Bulletin, No. 13/III

The A.C.M.E.O.R. Archives, Israel, foundation Bacau.

Page 145

Organizaţia Sionistă
Bacău
No 122

Bacău 28 Iunie 1920 (12 Tamuz)

Onor
Societatea [illegible]
Loco

Domnule Preşedinte,

Odată cu prezenta avem onoare a vă înainta în copie o circulară a Comitetului Central din Bucureşti, de al cărei cuprins vă rugăm a lua cunoştinţă.-

[illegible] fiind împrejurările că ziua de 6 Iulie [illegible] ziua pentru întregul popor evreu, cu care ocazie se vor organiza [illegible] [illegible] şi [illegible] [illegible] D.C.R. [illegible] datoria fiecărui evreu [illegible] national.-

[illegible] un [illegible] cu toate organizaţiile şi societăţile din localitate [illegible] parte în [illegible].-

Vă invităm deci să [illegible] şi a lua dispoziţiuni [illegible] de [illegible] 6 Iulie ora 5 p.m. [illegible] societăţii [illegible] în localul Societăţii pentru [illegible] Israel unde la ora [illegible] [illegible].-

[illegible] dispoziţiuni, ca de la ora 6 toate prăvăliile, cafenelele etc. să fie închise.-

[illegible] speranţă că [illegible] de evreu [illegible] al unui popor renăscut, vă veţi [illegible] la îndeplinire, în măsura cea mai largă posibilă, invitaţiunea noastră, pentru a fi astfel la înălţimea solemnului moment.- Primiţi fraternele noastre salutări

Cu dor în Zion
[illegible]

[illegible]

Letter addressed to the president of the Jewish Agihidas Ahum Association by the Zionist Organization, in which they are asking him to ensure orderliness and full cooperation of the association's members to the meeting on July 6th as well as to close all Jewish stores and coffee shops by 6 pm on that day.
Signed by the president of the Zionist organization on June 28th 1920 in Bacau.

The Archives of Bacau County, Agihidas Ahum foundation, brief 2/1920, p. 69.

Page 146

COMUNITATEA ISRAELITA BACAU

ועד הקהלה העברית באקי

Frați Evrei!

Trăim cea mai frumoasă clipă din viața noastră ca popor.

Liga Națiunilor a ratificat mandatul Palestinei.

Pentru sărbătorirea acestui strălucit moment istoric, veniți la grandioasa

DEMONSTRAȚIE NAȚIONALĂ

organizată de mișcarea Sionistă

care are loc

Duminică 30 Iulie st. n. 1922, ora 4 p. m.

în Scoala Israelito-Română de băeți „F. Klein"

Veniți în număr cât mai mare!

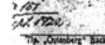

Președintele Comunității
OSIAS HERSCOVICI

Tip. „Gutenberg" Bacău

THE JEWISH COMMUNITY OF BACAU

JEWISH BROTHERS!

We live the most beautiful moment of our life as a nation.

The Nations League ratified the mandate of Palestine.

In order to celebrate this marvelous historical moment come to the magnificent

N A T I O N A L
D E M O N S T R A T I O N

organized by the Zionist movement, taking place on Sunday, July 30th 1922, at 4 p.m.
at the " F. Klein " Boys' Jewish-Romanian School

Come in a large number to this demonstration!

President of the Community,
OSIAS HERSCOVICI

The museum "From the history of the Jewish People Living in Bacau" 1703- 1944

Page 147

Federaţiunea Zioniştilor din România
Secţia „TIKWAS-ZION" Bacău

No. 15

Iubiţi Coreligionari

Astăzi Luni 15 Februarie a. c. ora 8 seara fix, cunoscutul şi mult talentatul conferinţiar

Dr. Niemerower

din Iaşi va da în localul secţiunei noastre (cassa Arabin)

Referatul asupra Congresului al IX-lea din Hamburg

în care scop facem un călduros apel către toţi coreligionarii noştrii, fără deosebire de sex, să vină în număr cât se poate de mare, dat fiind însămnătatea acestui referat.

Cu salut zionist
COMITETUL

Intrarea 50 b. de persoană

The Romanian Zionists Federation
"TIKWAS-ZION" Section, Bacau

Issue 15

Dear Coreligionists,

Today, February 15th of the current year, at 8 PM sharp, the well known and talented lecturer Dr. Niemerower from Iasi, will present in the office of our section (The Arabin house)

The Report regarding the IXth Congress from Hamburg.
Considering the above mentioned, we invite all our coreligionists, without any sex discrimination, to come to the conference in a large number, as this report has an important value.

With Zionist greetings,
The Committee

The cover fee: 5o bani

The A.C.M.E.O.R. Archives, Israel, foundation Bacau.

Page 148

ANUL I MOLEDET No. 6

APARE ODATĂ PE LUNĂ

REDACȚIA ȘI ADMINISTRAȚIA: STRADA ȘTEFAN CEL MARE No. 50, BACĂU

ABONAMENTE: IN ȚARĂ LEI [illegible] ANUAL; IN STRĂINĂTATE LEI [illegible]

TAMUZ - AV 5691

Atelierele „Gutenberg". D. [illegible]

Cover page of the monthly Moledet magazine, 1st year of publication, Issue No. 6, published by the "Guttenberg" Publishing house. The yearly subscription fee is 250 lei nationally and 500 lei abroad.

File belonging to the Library of the Romanian Academy

Page 149

28 AUGUST 1935 ANUL I No. 6

BULETINUL
Fondului Național Evreesc

REDACȚIA ȘI ADMINISTRAȚIA

קימת לישראל

Congresul al XIX-lea

A. ȘARAGA-LORIAH

Excerpt from the newspaper "The National Jewish Foundation Bulletin"

The XIXth Congress

On August 29th 1897, for the first time the Zionist movement met in Bacau. The paper discusses various Jewish artists and writers, mentioning that a few days before the Jewish artist Saraga Logan had died.

File belonging to the Library of the Romanian Academy

E. THE JEWS FROM BACAU DURING THE YEARS OF WRATH OF THE WAR AND THE RACIST LAWS. THE COMMUNITY FROM BACAU AFTER THE WAR.

THE JEWISH COMMUNITY FROM BACAU

Bucharest, 1995

May 16th, 1939. The leadership of the Jewish Community from Bacau, was addressing Dr. W. Filderman, asking for guidance in a serious matter. Applying the legislation regarding the Jews' citizenship, which the Goga-Cuza Government had promulgated in 1938, the Law Court of Bacau had decided that about 2000 of the Jewish inhabitants of the city are no longer Romanian citizens. The factories in the city had received dispositions to dismiss the Jews who were in this situation; thus, only from one textile company (Isvoranu factory), 150 Jews were announced that they would be fired[288]. For instance, Golda Leder, the widow of a cashier of the charitable societies, asked the Community for money so she could make an appeal to the sentence of the Law Court; thus, her daughter would be fired[289]. At the end of the year 1939, the Chamber of Commerce and Industry announced the names of dozens of Jewish firms, which had been erased from the commercial register because of loss of citizenship; for example, Hascal Rotenstein, Aron M. Blumer, Leon Reiyel, User Vechsler, Herman Hoffman and many others were in this situation[290]

It was the beginning of the nightmare, lived, from now on, not only by a small group of Jews, but by the entire Jewish population in the country. The Jews from Bacau saw some of the faces of this nightmare in the autumn of 1939; they saw the despair of several hundreds of Jews who had managed to escape Hitler's army in Poland, and were now passing through Bacau, hoping to find a haven, as far away from the fascist wrath as possible[291]. The Jewish Community from Bacau considered their duty to support them, and they did everything they could for them. But the Community had to face other difficult problems too.

The local anti-Semitic elements began to be present. The Jewish journalists were fired. Cuza's followers, Urziceanu-Antoniu, conducted the bar of lawyers, teachers like Stoian, Klug, Popescu, Focsa did not hide their anti-Semitic feelings in the secondary school.

There were an increasing number of poor people who needed material help; more and more families were left without any means of subsistence, because – among many other things – able men had been called up in different military units, at

[288] State Archives of Bacau, Jewish Community, file 5/1939, p. 8, 8/v.

[289] *Idem*, "Fraterna" Society, file 3/1900, p. 178.

[290] *Idem*, Jewish Community, file 4/1939, p. 53, 54/v.

[291] *Idem*, Jewish Community, file 26/1939, p. 131-134, 150, 152.

the country border[292]. Moreover, there had been launched the appeal to subscribe for army equipment, and the Community leadership had asked the Jews to do their duty in this respect[293].

Not after along time – only a few months after – a whole range of destroying blows started to come upon the Jews. In July 1940, as a consequence of the Soviet ultimatum, Romania had to give up Basarabia and Northern Bucovina. Terrified, the Jews from Bacau learned about the pogrom in Dorohoi, where Emil Aroneanu, a Jew from Bacau, had been killed, while serving the Romanian army; and also about the Jews who had been shot in other localities in Northern Moldova or who had been thrown out of the wagons, while the trains were in motion.

Soon after, the new racist laws of Gigurtu Government were published and applied. Jews holding positions in the public administration (teachers, doctors, jurists, etc.) were fired; even Malca Iancu David, holding the "important" position of operator at Parincea was fired[294]. Jews were forbidden to trade at the countryside, even the tobacconists in the city owned by the Jews, even if they were invalids, widows and orphans from the war. The Jewish children of school age learned they no longer had access to public schools, and the Community leadership had to struggle to get the permission to organize classrooms in improvised rooms, instead of "F. Klein" and "Culture" schools (which had been occupied by the army). The Jews were taken out of the army to be used for mandatory labor.

Only one month after all these, the country leadership was taken over by General Antonescu, who proclaimed Romania as a national Iron Army State. The iron army terror was unleashed in Bacau and in the whole country.

The iron army commander I. Panzaru was designated for the position of controller at the Population Compartment of the Police Department in Bacau: his duty was to make sure there was no illegal change in the Jews' juridical situation: "Prefecture of Bacau County, October 22nd, 1940. To the Mayor of Bacau City. Motivated by the order of the Minister of Inner Affairs. General Police Inspectorate, no. 73309/940, which informs us that a large number of Jews intend to choose Romania or stay illegally in the country, and to develop a serious check of all the Jews included in this category, and forbid any illegal change in their juridical situation, we are honoured to ask you, in agreement with the Iron Army Commander, to name an iron army soldier for the position of controller at the population office within the police department in this city. (undersigned) Prefect (undecipherable). Signature of City Hall representative: Comrade Panzaru is designated by the City Hall"[295].

Offended and brutalized in all circumstances, the Jewish population in the city no longer had either safe living, or the safety of their belongings. The iron army authorities confiscated Jewish settlements, they took over the central bath, which belonged to the Community, and a big part of the grave yard.

---

[292] *Idem*, Jewish Community, file 23/1939, p. 1-6.

[293] *Idem*, Jewish Community, file 4/1939, p. 51.

[294] *Idem*, City Hall of Bacau, file 159/1939.

[295] *Idem*, City Hall of Bacau, file 27/1940, p. 239.

On May 19th 1941, the Community in Bacau wrote: "Most honoured Union of Jewish Communities in the Old Kingdom. We inform you that, in the autumn of 1940, the agronomist from the City Hall of Bacau and several clerks entered the Jewish cemetery with no forms whatsoever, they had the graveyard ploughed and seeded [...]"[296].

The iron guards started the action of "making Romanian" the staff of the private companies; protégés of those who had know taken over the local administration leadership were now replacing the fired Jews.

Then they learned about the iron army rebellion, about the pogrom in the Capital, where Aurel User had been killed as well.

Having defeated the iron army rebellion in January 1941, General Antonescu began to apply his policy regarding the Jews, a methodical policy, which was meant to destroy them. They started by confiscating the radios. In March-April, they began to expropriate the Jews' urban real estates. More than 1200 buildings were expropriated in Bacau[297]. Jews were called up for mandatory labor, and they were sent in detachments to remote localities. At the same time, there was a methodical propaganda action to stirring the population against the Jews. The Community leadership in Bacau was accused in the press for not having disowned the so-called aggressive actions against the Romanian troops, when they retreated from Basarabia. Severe interdictions were obstacles related to the Jews' circulation, to their contacts in groups including more than several persons. Before the beginning of the war, Jews who had been evacuated from near-border localities, as precaution, passed through the station in Bacau towards the camps in Caracal, Slatina and Turnu-Severin.

When the war began, the Jews in Bacau, trapped within so many interdictions, didn't learn too soon about the massacres in Iasi and about the "death trains", which had passed through the station in Bacau, too. However, they felt the increasing harshness of their living conditions ever since the first days of July 1941. On July 4th, they displayed the announcement according to which all the Jews had to wear the discreditable "yellow star". The chief of the police department, sub-inspector I. Cuptor, signed the order. Within a few days, they began to apply the order (no. 817 from July 3rd) by which 4-5000 Jews from Tg-Ocna, Moinesti and from the villages of the county were evicted from their homes and forced to come to Bacau, bringing along only a very small part of their belongings. The administrative bodies strictly respected the orders they had received (for example, order no. 4467 from June 28th), and gave no support whatsoever to the evacuees. Helped only by the relatives they had in Bacau and by the Community leadership, they could find rooms for shelter; it was the beginning of the very difficult problem of finding means to subsist. Thus, a considerably large number of people who had been brutally deprived from everything they struggled to have, added to the poor already existing in the city[298]. The Jewish population in Bacau had increased in a short while with more than 4000 people. From 9000 Jews, the number before the war, 13,038 Jews were

[296] *Idem*, Jewish Community, file 6/1941, p. 68.
[297] *Idem*, City Hall of Bacau, file 20/1942.
[298] *Idem*, City Hall of Bacau, file 13/1941, p. 66, 67.

registered in 1942, compared to a total population of 31,578 persons[299]. But the anti-Jewish measures didn't stop here. Leaders of the Community were taken as hostages in "Rabi Israel" and "Corn Dealers" synagogues, under the threat that they would be shot if the Jews dared to perform actions of rebellion or sabotage; only in 1942 was the hostages order abrogated.

The Jewish political prisoners, some of whom were native from Bacau or from other localities in the county, were transported to Transnistria – to Vapniarca and other camps.

Sisters Rena and Stela Marcusohn and the Pipergals died after deportation, according to the official documents.

At the same time, the City Hall ordered the Community leadership to provide, every day, about 200 Jews, whom they could use for the maintenance of the city[300]. They were used foe the works performed at the channel of the hydraulic plant, at city cleaning (under the supervision of the street sweepers employed by the City Hall), at the barracks of the military units or for the German Commandment in the city.

In autumn, the Government issued the decrees according to which all Jews, with no exceptions (therefore, including those in the labor detachments), are obliged to give the army items of clothing and shoes (jackets, coats, laundry, bed sheets, boots, etc.). The Community was held responsible for the execution of this measure. Despite all the efforts they made and all the material support that the Community tried to give to the poorer Jews, more than 3000 of the Jews who registered in Bacau at that time couldn't provide the quantities they had to give. Many of them didn't have the money to compensate for the value of these items. These Jews were declared offenders and involved in lawsuits; archives include evidence that more than 100 Jews from Bacau were sentenced by law courts to harsh penalties (years of imprisonment) and huge fines[301].

In the following years, the application of the systematic measures continued and worsened, helping Antonescu's regime to physically and spiritually destroy the Jewish people. The Jews in Bacau experienced the effects of these measures, which emphasized their poverty, their disqualification, the aggravation of the conditions in which they lived. There was a considerable increase in the number of the Jews who were sent to mandatory labor in remote detachments (Ucea de Jos-Fagaras, Suraia-Putna, Parliti-Basarabia), as well as in the number of the handicraftsmen who were distributed to mandatory labor at C.F.R. (Railway Company) and military units (harness workshop in Focsani, tailors workshop in Rm. Sarat, etc.). After months of work in harsh conditions, many of the Jews in the detachments found themselves in the situation of not having anything left to wear and addressed desperate appeals to the Community to help them.

---

[299] Jewish World Congress, *Jewish Settlements in Romania – Statistic Memento*, Bucharest, 1947, p. 43.

[300] State Archives of Bacau, Jewish Community, file 36/1941.

[301] *Idem*, Jewish Community, file 57/1941, p. 1-117.

In the same time, many other Jews, who were available to the City Hall, were asked to perform all sorts of humiliating works for the town utility[302].

Here is the reproduction of a document which exists at the branch of State Archives in Bacau, illustrating the harsh situation of those who had been called for mandatory labor: "The Community of the Jews in Focsani. 1942, October 18. Most honoured Community of the Jews in Bacau. We are honoured to inform you the following: Today the Jews Finkelstein Sloim, contingent 1935, 69 Leca Street, and Finkelstein Meilich, contingent 1933, 159 Stefan cel Mare Street, came at the office of our Community, both of them from Suraia mandatory labor detachment, native from your city, completely naked. Almost everyone in this detachment is in the same situation of terrible poverty [...]. Please do everything in your power to send without delay the necessary clothes and shoes... President, Dr. H. Copelovici, Secretary, S. Baron"[303].

General Antonescu's order was applied, according to which, beside the mandatory labor, every Jew had to perform community service for ten years or pay money in exchange.

Beside the restrictions for doctors (the interdiction to see Christian patients, the obligation to have firms and headers with the inscription "Jewish Doctor"), some doctors were called to work for several months in sanitary units from Transnistria.

Here are some of those who were taken for mandatory labor in Transnistria: Dr. S. Sabath, from Bacau, Dr. C. Litman (evacuee from Moinesti) and Dr. M. Bernstein (evacuee from Tg.-Ocna). Four decades later, Dr. S. Sabath, established in Israel, remembered: "I left for Transnistria with a big wish to help – if possible – as many unhappy Jews as I could, and I managed – by a series of fortunate circumstances – to save from death a relatively large number of Jews, who had been destined to a one way road. I had been in the ghetto for 4 months"[304].

According to Community statistics, about 2500 Jews performed different categories of mandatory labor[305]. Repeated laws and orders forced the Jews to pay important sums of money: the reunification loan, the exceptional subscription, fines for the smallest violations of the interdictions, all sorts of taxes for the exemption from some labor category, etc. Thus, a Community report showed that, until January 20th 1942, the Jews from Bacau paid about 19 million ROL for the reunification loan, and they would deposit the same amount once again during the next days[306]. In the same time, all sorts of measures forbade sending money, food or clothes to those who were in the outside detachments or to those deported in Transnistria. The Jewish population from Bacau was forbidden to procure the necessary food supplies, not only because they were always poorer, but also because repeated orders of the City Hall (which were displayed even during the first half of the year 1944) included severe interdictions for Jews: they could buy food only from certain places and at

---

[302] *Idem*, City Hall of Bacau, file 30/1942, p. 18 and file 44/1942, p. 13-16.
[303] *Idem*, Jewish Community, file 12/1942, p. 50.
[304] I. Voledi-Vardi, *op. cit.*, p. 120.
[305] State Archives of Bacau, Jewish Community, file 12/1942, p. 58.
[306] *Idem*, Jewish Community, file 4-1942, p. 9.

certain hours, they were not allowed any contacts with the rural population, the rationalized food quotas sugar, oil and even bread) were much smaller for Jews than for the rest of the population[307].

Here are some fragments from the orders, which were displayed by the City Hall and Prefecture of Bacau during Antonescu's regime: The sugar ratio for May 1942: 500 grams per person for Christians and 200 grams for Jews (Disposition no. 18/4.VI.1942). The oil ratio for June 1942: 350 grams per person for Christians and 150 grams for Jews (Disposition no. 38/7.VIII.1942). The Jewish population will get their bread ratio after 10 a.m. (Disposition no. 39/10.VIII.1942). The bread ratio for Christians is of 250 grams per person, for Jews 150 grams per person (Disposition no. 1276/29.I.1943). Three bakeries were established for the Jews (Disposition no. 3499/3.III.1943). The price of bread is 17 ROL/loaf for Christians and 33 ROL/loaf for Jews (Disposition no. 9096/10.VI.1943). The rural population is forbidden to enter Jewish houses in order to sell food. Jews are allowed to buy supplies only from markets and stores, only after 10 a.m. (Disposition no. 31841/17.VI.1944), etc., etc.

Other restrictive measures were imposed to the Jews beside all these: for example, the special regime of rents that the Jews owed, living in buildings which had been expropriated from them (the Jews had to pay bigger rents than the rest of the population), the Jewish pharmacies were closed, evictions of Jews from buildings that were turned into public property[308]. Often it happened that Community buildings were abusively occupied (synagogues turned into warehouses, a building from Calea Oituz was turned into the contagious disease ward, etc.). The authorities continued to impose the "making Romanian" process to the enterprise staff. Thus, there was a continuous deterioration of the Jews' living conditions, large groups had always poorer sanitary conditions, many of them were undernourished fell prey to disease. One way or another, about 6500 Jews had become dependent on the aids that the Community could no longer provide. The systematic census of the Jewish population, which was ordered in 1942, was felt by the Jews from Bacau as a prelude to the application of the programme of massive deportation to Transnistria, and of sending the Jews from Bacau in ghettos, a programme that was increasingly more spoken of (it was given up only because of the changes in the front situation).

There were also Jews from Bacau who tried everything to get to Israel, thinking that they would escape the terrible conditions in which they had been brought. Embarking themselves on the "Struma" ship, in 1942, they died, drowned with the ship: Mircea Grünberg, Rubin Iehuda, Tvi Reicher, as well as Arnold Gartenberg and his wife (native from Moinesti), Iticovici with his wife and a niece (native from Tg.-Ocna).

Herbert Reichert, 18 years old (from 4 Stefan cel Mare Street) and Herscovici Iosif, 16 years old (from 7 Precista Street), from Bacau, were among the 315 Jews who died during the sinking of "Mefkure" ship[309].

---

[307] *Idem*, City Hall of Bacau, file 20/1943, p. 25, andfile 11/1944, p. 11, 43.

[308] *Idem*, City Hall of Bacau, file 3/1943, p. 198, file 7/1943, p. 80, 82, 84 and file 34/1944, p. 65.

[309] Zionist Central Archive in Jerusalem, file L 15/295, B. cf. Albert Finkelstein, *Mefkure Tragedy*, p. 183-184.

The registered figures are significant for the disastrous social consequences of the restrictive measures imposed by Antonescu's regime against the Jews, as they show, for the Jewish population in Bacau, a decrease in birth rate from 15.1% in 1938 to 5.6% in 1942, and an increase of mortality from 10.9% in 1938 to 18.7% in 1942[310].

Despite all these difficult conditions, the community from Bacau found resources to limit, as much as possible, the effects of the measures aimed at its physical and spiritual degradation. The Community supported the activity of a canteen, where many young people volunteered to work, and where 7-800 poor people got a meal every day (people from the C.F.R. Site, from the Technical Service of the City Hall and, especially families of those taken to the outside detachments).

The old people alms-house, where about 40 persons lived, received permanent aids. The Community had to collect and spend large amounts of money for these activitites, and to help the poor with wood, drugs, unleavened bread for Pesah, money for those who had trials, for not having given the clothes asked by the Government, winter aids, clothes for those in the detachments and even for those who had been deported to Transnistria, etc.

The youth, students of the Jewish primary schools and secondary school, helped by their teachers, organized a shelter for poor children, within synagogues.

The permanent aggravation of the Jews' material conditions imposed increasingly worsened financial tasks to the Community. In 1943, it had to spend 16,157,992 ROL for social assistance, twice more than the amount spent in 1942. When orphans were repatriated from Transnistria, the Community made a special effort to accommodate and look after the 21 children who had been brought to Bacau. Many Jews' actions of fraternal solidarity made an important contribution: those who had some material possibilities donated money; Community employees gave their salary for one day; the students of the Jewish primary schools and secondary school offered the little money they had. The Rabbi Office organized the education of these children in the Jewish spirit.

"The entire education of these children from an intellectual, religious and ritual point of view is an absolute necessity for them, as the future of these young people is their settling in Eretz, where they must come trained and educated in this spirit", wrote Prime-Rabbi M. Blanc at that time[311].

There were constant actions in the sanitary field, where all the doctors volunteered (including those who had come with the evicted Jews from the county). Distributed on neighborhoods, they guided the population to avoid contagious disease (especially typhoid, which had appeared, as well as exanthemum typhus). The Community clinic provided about 1000 free consultations every month. The maternity developed its activity, and a small ward for patients suffering from inner illness was added to it.

---

[310] State Archives of Bacau, Jewish Community, file 1/1943, p. 195, 225.

[311] *Idem*, Jewish Community, file 5/1944, p. 228, file 20/1944, p. 4, 31, 32 and file 9/1944, p. 28.

There were also important efforts related in education, in circumstances where the Jewish children didn't have access to public education. The orphanage was supported to function in "Marieskes" Synagogue, then in "Rabi Israel" Synagogue. There was no interruption in the courses for boys and girls within primary education, although in totally inappropriate conditions. A mixed theoretic secondary school and a commercial secondary school were founded, where, beside the analytic programme in the public schools, there were the additional subjects like Hebrew, history of the Jews, and cultural conferences were held; the students who had attended these secondary schools could take the exam in public schools in the autumn of 1944, therefore not only did they prove to be a center of spiritual resistance against Fascism, but also a step of life training. Although teaching was also performed by non-professionals, the results were many times exceptional. Famous people like the learned mathematician Solomon Marcus or the opera singer Blanche Adelstein were educated in these schools.

Children of pre-school age were not neglected. Two kindergartens were founded, and skillfully managed by Olga Iser and A. Solomon, with the material contribution of the A.C.F.E. Society.

Here is the number of students from the Community schools[312]:

Year	*Talmud Tora*	*Primary Schools*	*Secondary Schools*	*Total*
1940	20	518	291	829
1941	100	728	328	1156
1942	130	761	317	1208
1943	140	761	317	1218

Here are the teachers: A. Wagner, M. Hirssohn, M. Herscu, E. Smeltzer, C. Zaharia, M. Zaharia, Z. Drimer, H. Iticovici, A. L. Iosif, I. Idelovici-Voledi, H. Simion, L. Haber, J. Hirssohn, J. Koffler, E. Mititelu, A. Lazarovici, E. Lupovici, S. Marcusohn, R. Marcusohn, I. Grinberg, G. Avram, F. Leopold, S. Smil, M. Lespeyeanu, M. Grunvald, E. Colenberg, S. Leibu, M. Aronovici, A. Schapira, P. Gutman, N. Vaserman, S. Knoll, E. Schwartz, I. Abramovici, H. Haimsohn, F. Marcu, I. Ilian, B. Stein, L. Videnfeld.

There were also attempts to start a vocational school, as well as a music school. However, they managed to organize an orchestra of classical and rhythmical music, which gave concerts, and contributed at shows where the youth manifested their hope for better days and their trust in a less sinister future for the Jews (for instance the show in 1943 performed by the secondary school students). The attempts to reopen the "Raza" library failed, as the front drawing near forbade any activity in this direction.

Many papers, such as those published by I. Voledi-Vardi, mentioned memories about the actions of spiritual resistance that had involved many young people: "The City upon Bistrita" and "Students without Uniform", which were published in Israel.

---

[312] *Pinkas Hakehilot Romania*, vol. I, Jerusalem, 1970, p. 14-15.

*

The end of the war found the Jews in Bacau in a state of physical exhaustion, because of all the interdictions that had been imposed to them, and in a situation of economic disorganization, with about 2000 people trying to find means of subsistence (more than 700 workers and handicraftsmen and more than 550 clerks who were unemployed, as well as more than 600 ex-employers, whom had been deprived of their belongings). It was a community that had been profoundly marked by the brutalities and the constraints they had been enduring for so many years, a community that doubted, in its majority, the possibility to take life anew. During the first years after the war, there were enough Jews from Bacau who participated in the wave of emigration for Eretz Israel, especially as soon as the existence of the independent Jewish State was proclaimed. Those who didn't leave then, tried to reintegrate in the economic life of the country and rebuild a spiritual life, based on the old Jewish traditions. In this respect, it is worth mentioning the fact that, in 1945, the Community from Bacau organized a practical agriculture school at Margineni[313], that the organization of an industrial general school was being aimed at, and that, until 1948, the kindergarten, the Jewish schools and the Talmud Tora classes continued their activity.

We must also remember that, in 1946, the branch from Bacau of O.S.E. (the Sanitary Jewish Organization for mother and child protection) founded the "Sip of Milk" center at the maternity, where there was free distribution of the milk necessary for small children[314], Dr. S. Sabath being the one who initiated this action.

During the period to come, when the Stalinist policy was promoted in Romania in all the fields, and when the Zionist movement was presented as an agency of imperialism, the Jewish population from Bacau was also confronted with the pressures from the Jewish Democratic Committee, which actually aimed to dissolve the Jewish religious institutions and suppress everything related to the Jewish tradition. At the same time, it was more and more obvious to the Jews that the "democratic" slogans of the totalitarian regime were actually hiding the methodical action of marginalizing the Jews, so that, in Bacau too, there were many people who, despite all risks involved (especially losing their positions), submitted applications to leave for Israel.

Only after the Jewish Democratic Committee had been "self- dissolved" and there was an obvious action from the Federation of the Jewish Communities in Romania, led by Chief Rabbi dr. Moses Rosen, was there an organized activity both in the field of social assistance and in the direction of revitalizing the Jewish traditions. And, when the members of the Government accepted (of course, not from "ideological" reasons) to re-open the gates for emigration, the majority of the Jews in Bacau joined the several hundred thousand Jews who had left Romania, making their contribution to the strengthening of Israel, the reborn country of the Jewish people.

---

[313] State Archives of Bacau, Jewish Community, file 1/1945.

[314] *Idem*, Jewish Community, file 1/1946, p. 3, 4.

Page 165

RECENSĂMÂNTUL PENTRU LOCUITORII AVÂND SÂNGE EVREESC

ADEVERINȚA Nr.

S'A PRIMIT DE NOI, COMPLETATĂ, FOAIA DE RECENSĂMÂNT

A DECLARANTULUI

DOMICILIAT ÎN Bacău STR.

Nr. SEMNATĂ DE:

LA Bacău LA DATA DE

Muzeul „Din Istoria Comunității Evreilor Băcăuani, 1703—1944"

POLIȚIA ORAȘULUI BACĂU

157

ANUNȚ

In 48 ore, orice evreu și evreică, vor purta pe piept în partea stângă, steaua evreiască (două triunghiuri suprapuse) din postav galben, a căror laturi vor fi de 6 cm. fiecare, afară de cei îmbrăcați militari în serviciul armatei.

Cei ce nu se vor conforma, după această dată, vor fi arestați și predați organelor polițienești și comandaturii militare.

4 IULIE 1941.

Șeful Poliției,
Subinspector I. CUFTOR

The Central Archive of Jewish people in Romania

Census info for population having Jewish blood

Confirmation paper of receiving the census information with regards to the Jewish population in Bacau.

POLICE OF BACAU

ANNOUNCEMENT

Within 48 hours, every Jewish man or woman, except the persons dressed in military uniform, serving in the army, will wear on the left side of the chest the Jewish star, two superposed triangles with sides of 6 cm made of yellow cloth.

Those who do not obey this regulation after the period specified above, will be arrested and handed over to the police authorities and military commendatory.

July 4th, 1941

Chief of the Police,
Sub inspector I. CUPTOR

The Bacau State Archives, Bacau City Hall, brief ***21/1942, file 1***

Page 166

Nr. 4174 TELEGRAMA

CENZURAT == COMUNITATEA ISRAELITA BACAU

LK 148 SIBIU 2349-60-26-11-30=

TRIMITETZI URGENT IN CONTUL COMUNITATZII IZRAELITE SIBIU PRIN VIRAMENTE LA BANCA ROMANEASCA SUMA DE LEI UNASUTA CINCIZECI MII PENTRU INTRETZINEREA DETASAMENTULUI DE EVREI DIN BACAU AFLATORI LA VOILA FAGARAS COMPLECT LIPSITZI DE MIJLOACE - SUMA ACEASTA O VOM RETOURNA LA PRIMIREA LEFEI CE SE VA FACE LA SFARSITUL CONF ORD DIRETZIEI CFR MEDICUL DETASAMENTULUI DR BERENSTEIN

Arh. St. Bacău, fond. Comunitatea Israelită Bacău, dos. 6/1941, f. 187

Publicație

Nr. 688 -- 23 Ianuarie 1942

Urmare publicației Nr. 161 din 9 Ianuar 1942;

Se aduce la cunoștința cetățenilor că cota de ulei pe luna Ianuarie 1942, se vinde numai pe baza cartelelor Ministerului Economiei Naționale (bonul Nr. 1), la prețul de lei 84 litrul.

Din cantitatea de 10.000 kg. ulei repartizată oficial acestui oraș, revine pentru populația stabilă câte 200 gr. de persoană iar evreilor evacuați în acest oraș câte 100 gr. de persoană.

Pentru internate, cămine, cantine, restaurante etc., uleiul se distribuie pe bază de tablouri dela magazinele Oancea și „Trotușul".

Prezenta publicație, va sta afișată vizibil în toate magazinele comercianților.

Primăria Orașului Bacău
Serviciul Economic

PUBLICATION

Nr. 688 - January 23-rd 1942

Following the publication no. 161 dated January the 9-th 1942;

We hereby inform the citizens that the oil ratio for the month of January 1942, will be sold on the basis of cards issued by the Ministry of National Economy (ticket no. 1). The price is of 84 ROL for one liter.

From the quantity of 10 000 kg oil officially distributed to this town, 200 g for each person is due to the people living here permanently. In the same time, for the Jews who have been evacuated to this town we owe 100 g oil for each.

For the boarding houses, hostels, canteens, restaurants, etc. oil is distributed based on the schemes from "Oancea" and "Trotusul" stores.

The present publication will be displayed in order to be clearly seen in all traders' shops.

The Town Hall of Bacau
The Economic Department

The State Archives of Bacau, The Jewish Community foundation

Page 167

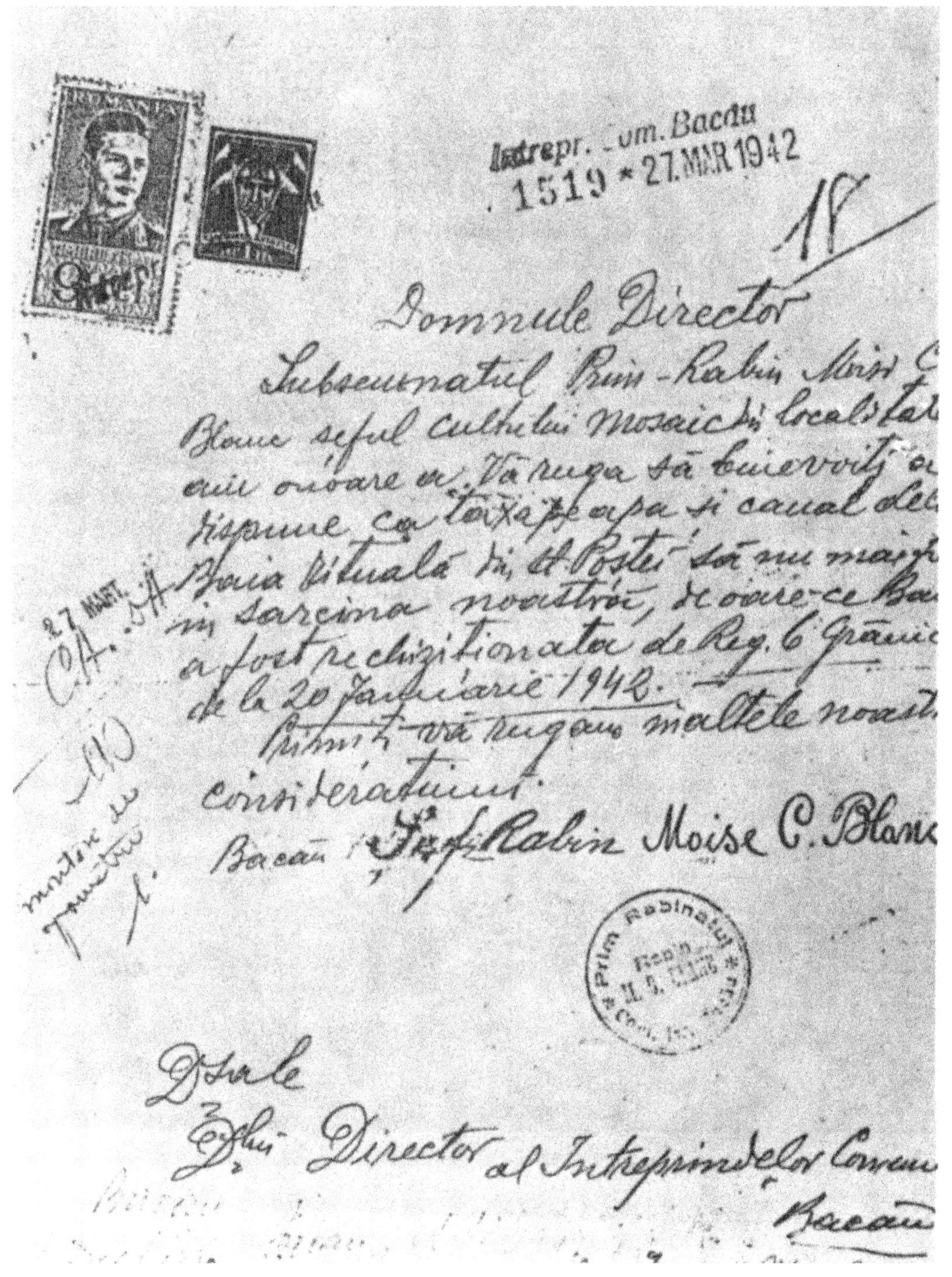

Intrepr. Com. Bacău
1519 * 27 MAR 1942

18

Domnule Director

Subsemnatul Prim-Rabin Moise C. Blanc şeful cultului mosaic din localitate cu onoare vă rugăm să binevoiţi a dispune ca taxa pe apa şi canal dela Baia Rituală din str. Poştei să nu mai fie în sarcina noastră, deoarece Baia a fost rechiziţionată de Reg. 6 Grăniceri dela 20 Ianuarie 1942.

Primiţi vă rugăm înaltele noastre consideraţiuni.

Bacău Prim-Rabin Moise C. Blanc

Prim Rabinatul

D-sale
Domnului Director al Intreprinderilor Comunale
Bacău

Mr. Director,

The undersigned, First Rabbi Moise Blana, chief of the Mosaic Cult from Bacau, please allow me to ask you kindly to absolve us of the responsibility of collecting the tax on the water from the Ritual Bath, since the Bath has been bought off by Region 6 as of January 20, 1942.

Please accept our great considerations.

Bacau,

Chief Rabbi Moise C. Blana

Stamped on March 27, 1942

Next letter is addressed to the Director of the town's factories.

The State Archives of Bacau, The Jewish Community foundation

Page 168

(215) 05796

România

100

MINISTERUL AFACERILOR INTERNE

PRIMARIA ORAŞULUI BACAU

Către
Ministerul Afacerilor Interne
Direcţia Administraţiei Locale

BUCUREŞTI

3267

Răspuns ordinului circular No.46.714 din 4 Martie 1942, avem onoarea a raporta următoarele:

În localitate sunt expropriate peste 1200 imobile evreeşti, din care se vor putea împroprietări credem aproape toţi îndreptăţiţii români, demobilizaţi la vremea lor, şi conform normelor ce se vor stabili pentru asemenea împroprietăriri.-

Totuşi în afară de aceste imobile se vor putea împroprietării şi construcţii cel puţin încă 200-250 gospodării pe teren comunal anume destinat prin procese şi decizii definitive a căror aplicare nu poate fi împiedecată de situaţiunea creiată prin schimbarea-fără drept a distincţiunei acestui teren, despre care tratează raportul nostru No. 3133/941 de aici anexat în copie, certificat şi aşteptăm fie ordine de urmare, fie momentul potrivit pentru sesizarea eventual direct sau incidental a Justiţiei.-

Anexăm şi răspuns la chestionarul ordonat.-

Primar,

Secretar General,

MINISTRY OF INTERNAL AFFAIRS

BACAU TOWNHALL

To :

Ministry of Internal Affairs

Direction of Local Administration

BUCHAREST

As a result of the circular order H.4G.714 from March 4, 1942, we are honoured to report the following:

In Bacau, there over 1200 Jewish buildings which have been expropriated. We believe that these buildings can be given in the possession of all Romanians with full rights, who have been demobilized in their time, according to norms which will be established for this process.

Moreover, with the exception of these buildings, it is also possible to give in possession buildings for at least 200-250 houses currently located on the communal land, specifically designated for this purpose by processes and definitive decisions. Their application cannot be stopped by the situation recently created of changing the destination of this land without right of distinction. Our report no.85331941 addresses this issue and it is enclosed in a copy, certified and waiting either for an order to be executed or for the right moment when the Justice Department will intervene directly or incidentally.

Please find attached a copy of the requested questionnaire.

Mayor,

General Secretary,

The Bacau State Archives, Bacau City Hall, brief 20/1942, file 100

Page 169

12 Mai 1942

DOMNULE PREFECT,

Subsemnatul, Av. D. Jonas Președinte le Comunității Evreilor din Bacău, cu onoare supun cunoștiinței Domniei Voastre, următoarele:

Comunitatea noastră are sub îngrijirea sa o cantină pentru săraci, unde mănâncă zilnic un număr de peste 800 de suflete.-

Pentru aprovizionarea acestei cantine, este absolut necesară deplasarea delegatului cantinei în fiecare dimineață la piață și băcănii.-

Cum prin Ordonanța D-voastră Nr. 12088 din 6 Mai 1942, este cu desăvârșire oprită aprovizionarea populațiunei evreești până la ora 10, oră după care nu se mai găsește aproape nimic în piață sau în orice caz timpul fiind prea scurt nu se mai poate face aprovizionări, cu onoare vă rugăm să bine voiți a aproba și a dispune să se dea o autorizație specială delegatului nostru Dl. Tauber Zalman intendentul cantinei, în baza căreia să poată avea acces în piață și magazine de coloniale - cu obligațiunea expresă ca totul ce cumpără, să fie numai pentru cantina săracilor evrei a Comunității.-

Fără de aceasta, ar însemna închiderea cantinei - rămânând în neagră mizerie, un număr destul de apreciabil de oameni săraci - cari nu au altă posibilitate de a-și întreține viața.-

Primiți, vă rugăm, Domnule Prefect, deosebita noastră considerațiune,

Președinte,

Av. D. Jonas

Secretar,

Mr. Prefect

The undersigned, Lawyer D. Ionas, President of the Jews Community of Bacau, with much respect I submit to your attention the following:

Our community takes care of a canteen for poor people where 800 people eat daily.

In order to supply the needed food, it is absolutely necessary for the canteen's delegate to go each morning at the market and groceries stores.

Due to the fact that by your order no. 12088 dated May 6, 1942 it is completely forbidden for the Jewish population to do any shopping until 10 o'clock, an hour when almost nothing can be found on the market, or in any case, it is quite late to buy one's stock. Therefore, please kindly approve and dispose the issuing of a special authorization for our delegate Mr. Tauber Zalman, the canteen's administrator, based on which, he may go to the market and groceries stores, with the special obligation that everything he buys is designated only for the Jewish poor people of our Community.

Without this authorization the canteen will have to be closed. Therefore, a large number of poor people having no other possibility to support themselves will be abandoned in the worst misery of life.

Please receive, Mr. Prefect, the expression of our special consideration.

President,

Lawyer
D. Jonas

The museum "From the history of the Jewish People Living in Bacau" 1703-1944

Page 170

PRIMARIA ORAŞULUI BACAU

PUBLICAŢIE

Nr. 34 din 18 Iulie 1942

Noi, Primarul Oraşului Bacău:

Având în vedere Deciziunea Secretariatului de Stat al Departamentului Agriculturii şi Domeniilor Nr. 12.502, publicată în Monit. Of. Nr. 162 din 15 Iulie 194

DISPUNEM:

Art. 1.- Cu începere dela publicarea prezentei publicaţii, se interzice tăierea rituală a animalelor şi păsărilor de curte, atât pentru consumul public cât şi cel particular, fie chiar cu o ameţire prealabilă.

Art. 2.- Autorităţile comunale şi poliţieneşti vor lua măsuri pentru respectarea dispoziţiunilor prevăzute în Deciz. Nr. 12.50(mai sus menţionată, anulând totodată autorizaţiile date hahamilor, conform art. 72 din Regulamentul pentru abatorii.

Art. 3.- Nerespectarea dispoziţiunilor prevăzute în Deciziunea sus menţionată, constitue o contravenţie şi se poate pedepsi conformitate cu art. 8 din Legea pentru protecţia animalelor.

Domnii Ofiţeri şi Agenţi ai Poliţiei Generale a Statului, Organele Servidului Sanitar-Veterinar, precum şi Poliţia Comunală, sunt însărcinate cu aducerea la îndeplinire a prezentei publicaţii.

Primar, M. Văgăunescu
Lt.-Colonel în retr.

TOWN HALL OF BACAU

PUBLICATION
No. 34 from July 18th, 1942

We, the Mayor of the Town of Bacau,
Considering the Decision of the State Secretariat of the Agriculture and Estate Department, no. 12.502, published in the Official Gazette issue 162 from July 13th, 194

DISPOSE:
ART. 1.- Starting with the date of issuance of this publication, we forbid the ritual slaughtering of cattle and poultry, for both public and private consumption, even with prior dizziness.
Art. 2- The community and police authorities will take measures to ensure compliance of the provisions in the above-mentioned Decision no. 12.502, canceling the previously given authorizations, according to Art. 72 from the Slaughter Houses Regulations.
Art. 3- The violation of the provisions in the above-mentioned Decision represents a major offence, and it can be punished according to Art. 8 of the Law for Animal Protection.
Officers and Agents of the State General Police Department, Bodies of the Sanitary-Veterinary Service, as well as the Community Police, have the duty to fulfill this act.

Mayor, M. Vagaunescu
Retired Lt.-Colonel

State Archives of Bacau, Jewish Community in Bacau, file 25/1942, p. 125

Page 171

COMUNITATEA EVREILOR
DIN BACĂU
TELEFON

No. 1616

Dtu. 19

43

Domnilor Colegi,

Am împărțit orașul în 14 sectoare ca fiecare medic să aibe sectorul cât mai mic.

I-iul pe listă va da consultații la domiciliul bolnavilor iar al doilea se va ocupa cu partea sanitară a sectorului, vizitând sectorul în mod amănunțit odată pe săptămână.- Peste 30 zile primul se va ocupa cu partea sanitară iar al doilea va da consultații la domiciliul bolnavilor.

Înțelegem perfect de bine că dela corpul medical se cer sacrificii mari în comparație cu colegii creștini, dar timpurile excepționale în care trăim ne cer acest sacrificiu și sperăm că nimeni din Dv. n'are să refuze ajutorul lui unui evreu în suferință.-

Dealtfel acest lucru s'a făcut și în celelalte orașe.

Cu toată stima

Dr. Lasarev
Șeful Serviciului Sanitar al Comunității

1) Străzile Leca până la Opanez și Cantemir, inclusiv Rahovei, Postul Grandea
D-nii Dri. Grinberg și Măgură

Totodată pentru consultații Mihai Viteazul, Dobrogei, Clotilda Gl. Averescu și 10 Mai.-

2) Leca dela Opanez până la No 117, Plevnei stânga fără soț și Petru Rareș
D-nii D-ri Rotenberg și Schuler

3) Leca dela No 117 până la Florilor, str. Zorilor inclusiv Plevnei dreapta cu soț
D-nii Dri Davidsoan și Segal

4) Leca dela Florilor până la Bistrița plus str. Fabricilor
D-nii D-ri Bernștein s. Zerner

5) Precista, Cremenei, Miron Costin
D-nii Dri Valdștein și Litman

6) Mircea, Florilor, Aprodul Purice, Aurel Vlaicu, Vasile Conta Iulia Hașdeu și Grănicerul Niculcea
D-nii Dri Ițicovici și Sontag

7) Buna Vestire, Valea Albă, Edisohn, Andrei Mureșanu, Pavel și Ana Cristea
D-nii Dri Crețu și Schvartz

8) Basarabiei, Platon, Trec. Palosanu, Bul. Carol până la pod
D-nii Dri Friedman și Rosman

9) Ioniță Sturza, General Averescu, Busuioc, Cal Oituz, Vultur, Lepescu și Cristoveanu
D-nii D-ri Sarf și Eckștein

10) Regina Maria, Decebal, Banca Națională, 15 August, Horia Cloșca și Crișan, Ardealului, Apolodor
D-nii Dri Dulbergher și Regu

The Jewish Community of Bacau, July 22, 1942

Dear Colleagues,

We have divided the town into 14 sectors such that each physician will have a smaller area of population to attend to.

The first physician on the list will make house calls attending to the sick population, while the second one will ensure the health and sanitary procedures are followed as required, visiting almost every family once a week. The following month, the roles will alternate and so each physician will be making house calls every two months. We understand that we are asking for a lot of sacrifices from the medical personnel in comparison with their conational counterparts, however given the difficult times we are going through, we hope that no one will refuse to help any sick Jewish person. In fact, this took place in almost every other city.

Best regards,

Dr. Lasarov,

Chief of the Sanitary Committee of the Jewish Community

1 – 10 names the doctors assigned to the various streets of the town.

State Archives of Bacau, Jewish Community in Bacau, file 12/1943, file 55

Page 172

No. 1979

1942 Luna August Ziua 9

REG. 5 PIONIERI

Detaşamentul de Indiguiri

către

Comunitatea Evreilor

Bacău

Cu onoare vă rugăm binevoiţi a lua urgente măsuri de a trimite efecte de îmbrăcăminte necesare evreilor săraci aflaţi la munca obligatorie pe acest sector întrucât au rămas complect dezbrăcaţi; şi neavând mijloace proprii de a-şi procura singuri îmbrăcămintea necesară, —

Rugându-vă să binevoiţi a ne comunica urgent rezultatul.

Cdtul Detaşamentului de Indiguiri

Reg. 5 Pionieri — Detaşamentul de Indiguiri

No. 1979 from August 9th, 1942
REGIMENT 5 PIONEERS
Damming Detachment
To the Jewish Community of Bacau

Honorably, we ask you to take urgent measures and send the supplies of clothes and shoes to the poor Jews who perform mandatory labor on this site, as they are left completely naked, since they don't have the means to procure the necessary clothes for themselves. Please send us the confirmation urgently.

Commander of the Damming Detachment, signed and stamped

State Archives of Bacau, Jewish Community in Bacau, file 12/1942, p. 82

Page 173

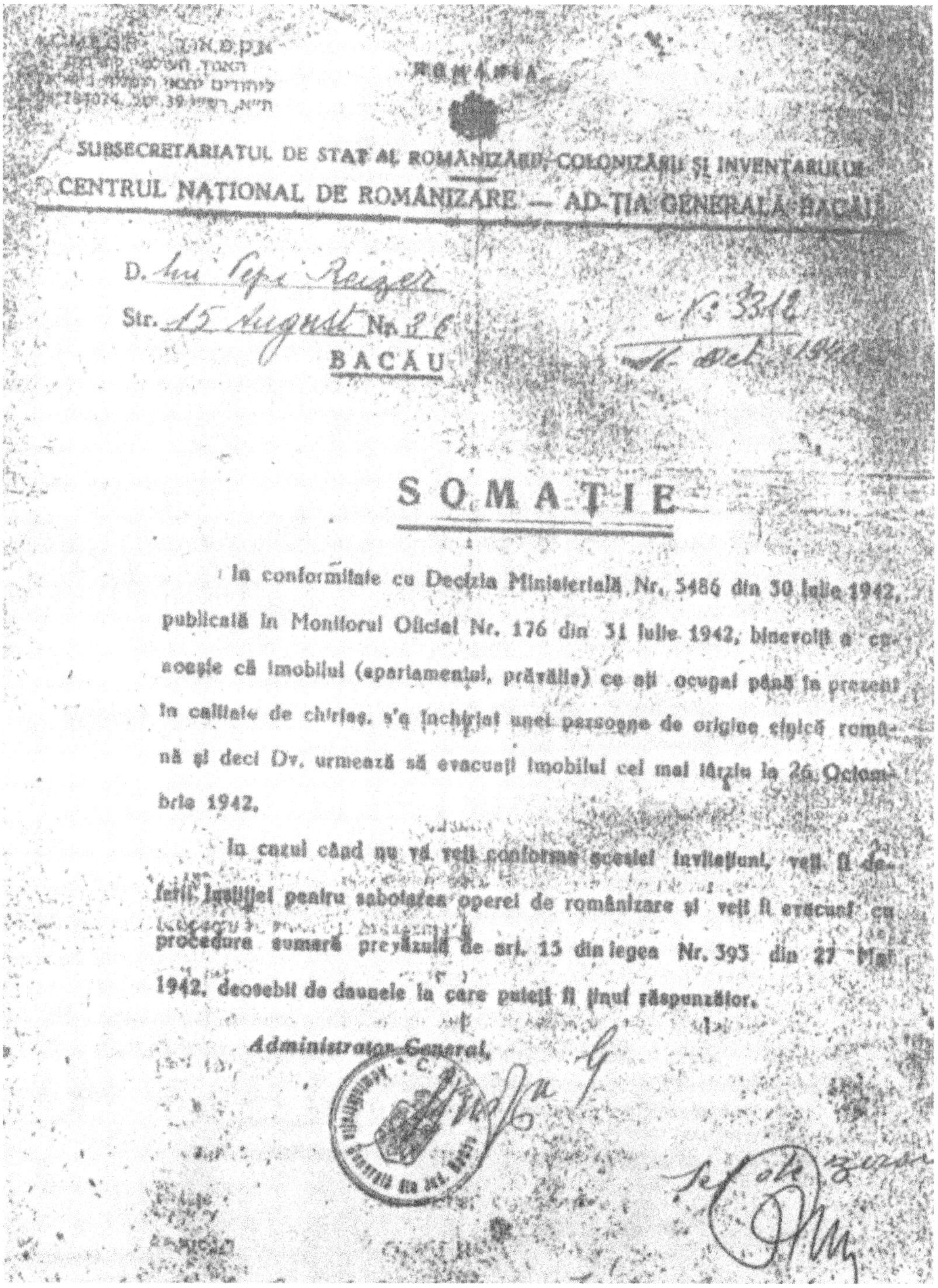

ROMÂNIA

SUBSECRETARIATUL DE STAT AL ROMÂNIZĂRII, COLONIZĂRII ŞI INVENTARULUI
CENTRUL NAŢIONAL DE ROMÂNIZARE — AD-ŢIA GENERALĂ BACĂU

D. lui Pepi Reizer
Str. 15 August Nr. 26
BACĂU

Nr. 3312
[illegible] Oct. 1942

SOMAŢIE

În conformitate cu Decizia Ministerială Nr. 5486 din 30 Iulie 1942, publicată în Monitorul Oficial Nr. 176 din 31 Iulie 1942, binevoiţi a cunoaşte că imobilul (apartamentul, prăvălia) ce aţi ocupat până în prezent în calitate de chiriaş, s'a închiriat unei persoane de origine etnică română şi deci Dv. urmează să evacuaţi imobilul cel mai târziu la 26 Octombrie 1942.

În cazul când nu vă veţi conforma acestei invitaţiuni, veţi fi deferiţi Justiţiei pentru sabotarea operei de românizare şi veţi fi evacuaţi cu procedura sumară prevăzută de art. 15 din legea Nr. 393 din 27 Mai 1942, deosebit de daunele la care puteţi fi ţinut răspunzător.

Administrator General,

STATE SUB-SECRETARIAT FOR THE "ROMANIZARE" PROCESS (I.E. A PROCESS BY WHICH ROMANIANS ARE ENTITLED TO LAND & PROPERTY), COLONIZING AND CENSUS INFORMATION - GENERAL DEPARTMENT BACAU

To Mr. Pepi Reiger
15 August Street, No. 26 No. 3312 from October 1942

SUMMONS

According to the Ministerial Decision no. 5486 from July 30th, 1942, published in the Official Gazette issue 176 from July 31st, 1942, please acknowledge the fact that the building (apartment, shop), which you have rented so far, has been leased to a person of Romanian ethnic origin, therefore you will have to evict the building on October 26th, 1942, the latest.
If you do not comply with this invitation, you will be referred to the Justice Department, for having sabotaged the "Romanizare" process, and you will be evicted according to the provisions of Art. 15 of Law no. 393 from May 27th, 1942, depending on the damage for which you will be held responsible.

General Administrator,
Signed and stamped

A.C.M.E.O.R. Archives, Israel, Bacau

Page 174

ROMANIA

Prefectura Judeţului Bacău

ORDONANTA No. 1097

7 Noembrie 1942

Noi, Lt. Colonel Constantin Ionescu, Prefectul Judeţului Bacău.

Având în vedere, nevoile împiedicării propagandei pe care o fac unii evrei în contactul ce au cu sătenii; şi pentru stârpirea comerţului ilicit şi clandestin.

Pe baza dispoziţiunilor art. 7 din Decretul Lege No. 3219-940 şi art. 100 din LEGEA ADMINISTRATIVA,

ORDONAM:

Art. 1. Se interzice cu desăvârşire accesul sătenilor, în locuinţele şi curţile evreeşti, fie pentru vinderea de alimente, sau pentru orice alte motive.

Se va institui o atentă supraveghere asupra contactului evreilor cu sătenii, atât pe pieţe, străzi, cât şi în magazine.

Art. 2. Se interzice cu desăvârşire evreilor, de a face pe intermediarii, atât în ceace priveşte comerţul cu vite, cereale, cât şi alte ramuri de comerţ.

Art. 3. Comercianţii şi meseriaşii evrei, trebuie să stea în sediile comerţului sau meseriilor, în timpul exercitării acestor profesiuni fiind interzis a circula, sau a staţiona pe străzi, pieţe etc., pentru acaparare de clienţi.

Art. 4. Nici un evreu nu va putea intra în târgul de vite Bacău, decât numai măcelarii autorizaţi, având formele legale, spre a face cumpărăturile de vite pentru abator, în vederea aprovizionării populaţiei cu carne de vită, posedând autorizaţie specială eliberată de Prefectură, Oficiul Economic Judeţean, precum şi carnet de intrare în târg, eliberat de Camera de Comerţ şi Industrie Bacău.

Art. 5. Contravenienţii la DISPOZIŢIUNILE PREZENTEI ORDONANŢE, pe lângă celelalte sancţiuni, vor fi internaţi imediat în lagăre de muncă în cazurile prevăzute de legile speciale.

Se menţin ordonanţele anterioare date în legătură cu dispoziţiunile sus menţionate.

Art. 6. Toţi ofiţerii de poliţie Judiciară şi Administrativă, vor supraveghia executarea prezentei ordonanţe, şi vor dresa acte contra celor vinovaţi.

Dată în cabinetul nostru astăzi 7 Noembrie 1942.

Prefect,

Lt. Colonel C. S. IONESCU

Şeful serviciului Administrativ,

N. Vlahuţă

ROMANIA

Bacau County Prefecture

Decree No. 1097

We, Lt. Col. Constantin Ionescu, the Prefect of Bacau County

Given the numerous attempts made by some Jewish people in sabotaging the propaganda and in order to stop illegal & dishonest trade, on the basis of Art. 7, law No. 3229-940, and art 100 of the Administrative Law, we are ordering the following:

Art. 1 It is strictly forbidden for any Romanian person to enter any Jewish house, either for selling groceries or for any other reason.
Art. 2 It is strictly forbidden for any Jew to participate either as a middle person or directly in the commerce with cattle, grains or any other goods.
Art. 3 It is strictly forbidden for any Jewish tradesmen or professionals to walk around on or to station themselves on the streets for the purpose of acquiring clients; they will have to stay within the limits of their shops while exercising their profession.
Art. 4 No Jew will be allowed to enter the market, except authorized butchers, having in their possession the legal forms allowing them to shop for the slaughter houses they work for.
Art. 5 Those not obeying the present order will be immediately sent to concentration camps, according to the current legislature.
Art. 6 All Judicial & Administrative police officers will ensure the present order will be adhered to and will punish the ones disobeying it.
Dated today November 7th 1942 in our office.

Signed
Lt. Col. C.S. Ionescu & N. Vlahuta

State Archives of Bacau, Jewish Community in Bacau, file 20/1942, p. 106

Page 175

Învăţători care au predat elevilor din cursul primar, în sinagogi, în timpul războiului

Rândul de jos:
Lespezeanu (Feferman)
M. Grünvald
E. Colenberg

Rândul al doilea:
I. Grinberg
Haimolă
E. Lupovici
S. Leibu
A. Lazarovici
L. Volfshaut
L. Friedman

Rândul de sus:
S. Vasserman
F. Leopold
L. Iosif
S. Şmil

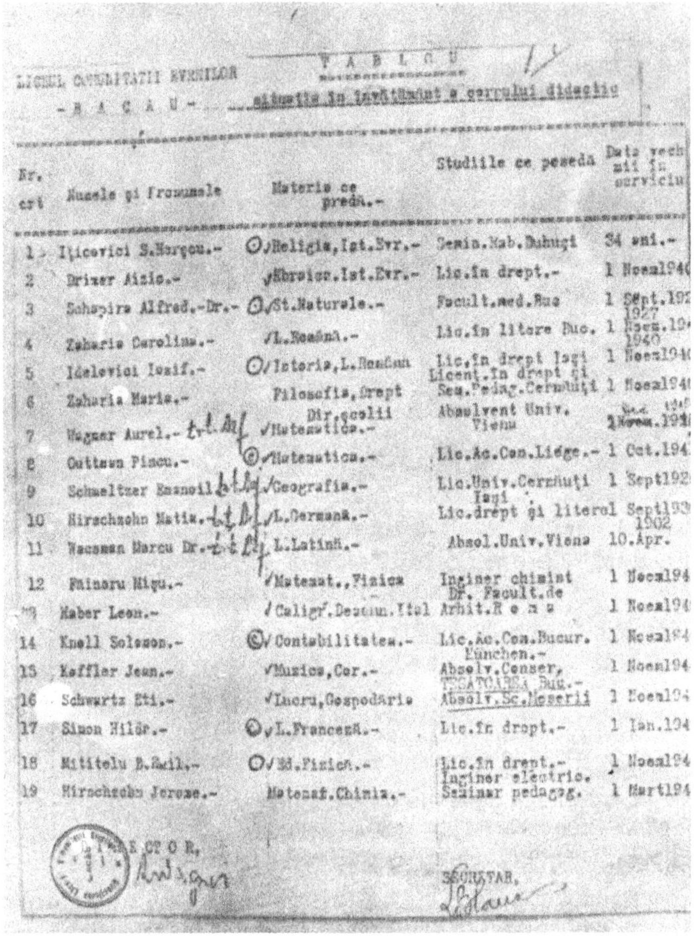

LICEUL COMUNITATII EVREILOR — BACAU — TABLOU situatia in învățământ a corpului didactic

Nr. crt	Numele și Pronumele	Materia ce predă	Studiile ce posedă	Data vechimii în serviciu
1	Iţicovici S.Horşcu.-	Religia, Ist.Evr.-	Semin.Rab.Bucureşti	34 ani.-
2	Driser Aizic.-	Ebraica. Ist.Evr.-	Lic.în drept.-	1 Noem1940
3	Schapira Alfred.-Dr.-	St.Naturale.-	Facult.med.Buc	1 Sept.1927
4	Zaharia Carolina.-	L.Română.-	Lic.în litere Buc.	1 Ocm.1940
5	Idelevici Iosif.-	Istoria, L.Română	Lic.în drept Iaşi	1 Noem1940
6	Zaharia Maria.-	Filosofia, Drept	Licenţ.în drept şi Sem.Pedag.Cernăuţi	1 Noem1940
7	Wagner Aurel.-	Dir.școlii Matematica.-	Absolvent Univ. Viena	1 Noem.1940
8	Guttman Pincu.-	Matematica.-	Lic.Ac.Com.Liège.-	1 Oct.194[illegible]
9	Schmeltzer Emanoil	Geografia.-	Lic.Univ.Cernăuţi	1 Sept192[illegible]
10	Hirschsohn Natia.-	L.Germană.-	Iaşi Lic.drept şi literel	Sept193[illegible]
11	Wacsman Marcu Dr.-	L.Latină.-	Absol.Univ.Viena	1902 10.Apr.
12	Fainaru Mișu.-	Matemat., Fizica	Inginer chimist	1 Noem194[illegible]
13	Haber Leon.-	Caligr.Desemn.[illegible]	Dr. Facult.de Arhit.Roma	1 Noem194[illegible]
14	Knell Solomon.-	Contabilitatea.-	Lic.Ac.Com.Bucur.	1 Noem194[illegible]
15	Kaffler Jean.-	Muzica, Cor.-	München.- Absolv.Conser,	1 Noem194[illegible]
16	Schwartz Eti.-	Lucru, Gospodăria	[illegible] Buc.- Absolv.Sc.Meserii	1 Noem194[illegible]
17	Simon Hilda.-	L.Franceză.-	Lic.în drept.-	1 Ian.194[illegible]
18	Mititelu B.Emil.-	Ed.Fizică.-	Lic.în drept.-	1 Noem194[illegible]
19	Hirschsohn Jerome.-	Matemat.Chimia.-	Inginer electric. Seminar pedagog.	1 Mart194[illegible]

DIRECTOR, SECRETAR,

The Jewish Community High school
The Teaching Staff

No.	Name	Courses taught	Academic Credentia
1	Iticevici, Harscu	Religion, History	Rabbi
2	Driser, Aitic	Jewish History & Hebrew	Law Degree
3	Sohapira, Alfred	Natural Science	Medicine Fac/Buc
4	Zaharia, Carolina	Romanian	B.A. Lit & Lang.
5	Idelevici, Iosif	History, Romanian	Law Degree, Iasi
6	Zaharia, Maria	Philosophy, Law	Teaching College, Ce
7	Wagner, Aurel	Mathematics	Vienna University
8	Cutnann, Pincu	Mathematics	Liege University
9	Schneltzer, Emanoil	Geography	Iasi University
10	Hirschezohn, Natia	German Lang.	Law degree, Lit. & La
11	Waceman, Marcu Dr.	Latin Lang.	Vienna University
12	Fainaru, Misu	Mathematics, Physics	Dr. Chemist Eng.
13	Haber, Leon	Drawing & Fine Arts	Fac. Of Architecture
14	Knell, Solemon	Accounting	Munchen University
15	Kaffler, Jean	Music	Conservatory, Buc
16	Schwartz, Eti	Home Economics	Tradesmen School
17	Sinon, Hilda	French Lang	Law Degree
18	Mititelu, B. Buil	Phys. Ed	Law Degree, Electric Eng.
19	Hirschezohn, Jeroze	Mathematics, Chemistry	Teaching College

Principal,
Maria Zaharia

The museum "From the history of the Jewish People Living in Bacau" 1703- 1944

Page 177

Corespondență din lagărul de exterminare de la Auschwitz

Envelope sent from the concentration camp in Auschwitz by Muyel Brill to Leon Brill in Bacau in 1943 with a German stamp

The museum "From the history of the Jewish People Living in Bacau" 1703- 1944

Page 178

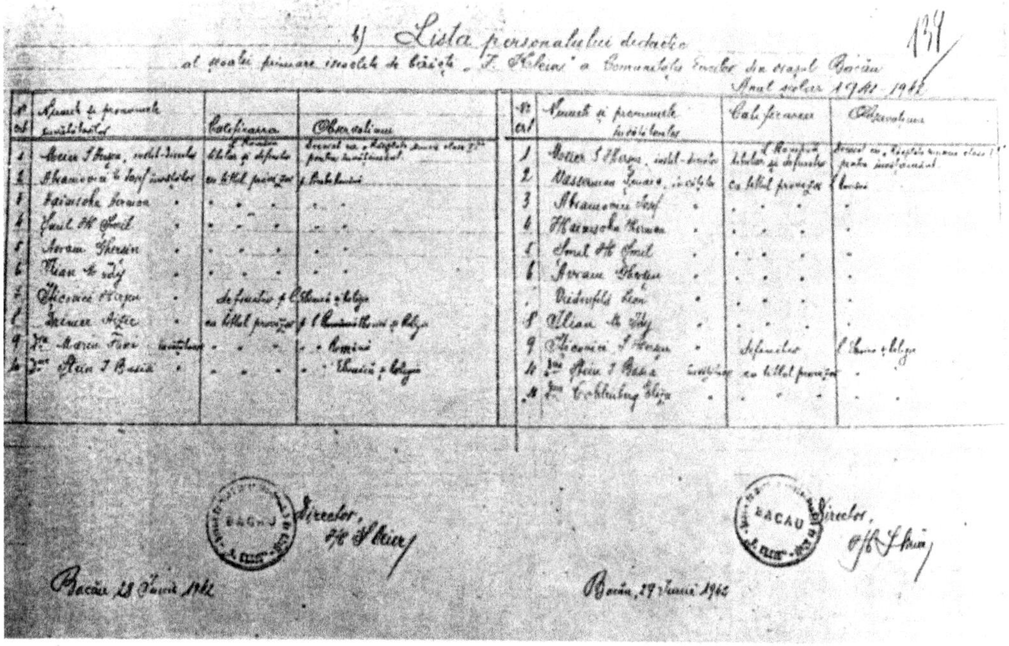

List with the names of the teaching staff of the Jewish Elementary Boy School F. Klein of the Jewish Community of Bacau, academic year 1941 – 1942

Dated June 29, 1942 Bacau

The museum "From the history of the Jewish People Living in Bacau" 1703- 1944

Page 179

SALA COMUNITĂŢII

Mai 1943

SE REPREZINTĂ

„HALOIMES - MELODY“

FANTEZIE HUMORISTICO-MUZICALĂ

— în 2 acte şi prolog (30 tablouri). —

de N. KANNER

SUB PATRONAJUL D-LUI MIŞU GRAD
preşedintele Oficiului Jud. Bacău

PROGRAM

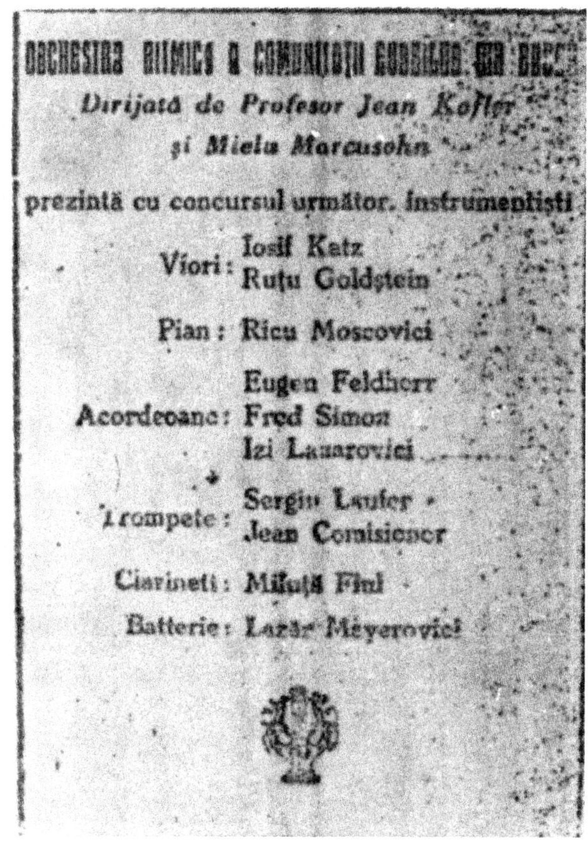

Dirijată de Profesor Jean Koffler
şi Miela Marcusohn

prezintă cu concursul următor. instrumentişti

Viori: Iosif Katz, Ruţu Goldştein

Pian: Ricu Moscovici

Acordeoane: Eugen Feldherr, Fred Simon, Izi Lazarovici

Trompete: Sergiu Laufer, Jean Comisioner

Clarinetti: Miluţă Fini

Batterie: Lazăr Meyerovici

Community Auditorium

May 1943

Presents

"Haloimes – Melody"

Humouristic-musical fantasy in 2 acts & prologue

By N. Kanner

Under the patronage of Mr. Mise Grad, honorary president of Bacau County

Schedule

The Jewish Community Orchestra in Bacau, led by Professor Jean Koffler & Mirela Marcusohn presents the following instrumentists:

Violin: Iosif Katz, Rutu Goldstein
Piano: Ricu Moscovici
Accordion: Fred Simon, Eugen Feldherr, Izi Lazarovici
Trumpet: Sergiu Laufer, Jean Coralsicor
Clarinet: Miuta the son
Drums: Lazar Mayerovici

Page 180 & 181

Tabel

de corespondență colectivă adresată de Evrei din lagărul Grosulovo familiilor lor din orașul Bacău.

Correspondence table with writings by Jews in the concentration camp Grosulovo to their families. 32 Jews had written to their families. At the bottom, there is a stamp which states that the writings have been censored and checked by authorities.

The museum "From the history of the Jewish People Living in Bacau" 1703-1944

Page intentionally left empty

Page 182

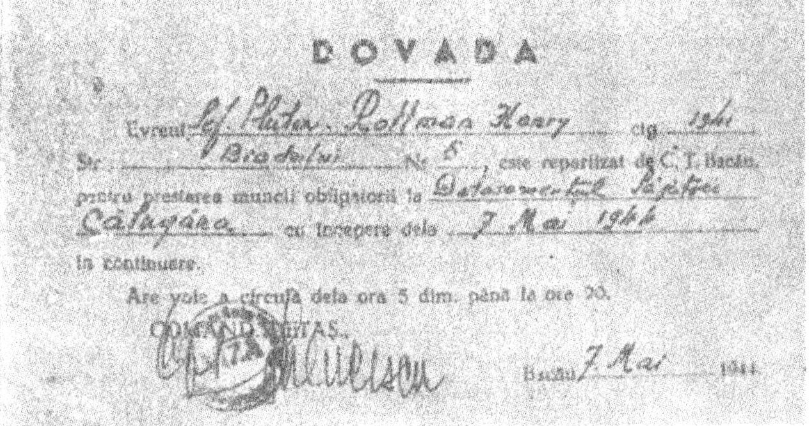

DOVADA

Evreul Sf. Plutar Rollman Harry clasa 1941
Str. Bradului Nr. 6, este repartizat de C. T. Bacău, pentru prestarea muncii obligatorii la Detaşamentul Săpători Călugăra cu începere dela 7 Mai 1944 în continuare.

Are voie a circula dela ora 5 dim. până la ora 20.

COMANDANTUL CERCULUI TERITORIAL,

Bacău 7 Mai 1944

Comunicat

43

In conformitate cu ordinul M. U. „Baricada" Nr. 33 din 7 Mai 1944

Se pune în vedere tuturor evreilor ce au vârsta 18-50 ani (ambele inclusiv) din oraşul Bacău că sunt obligaţi a se prezenta negreşit în Curtea Cercului Teritorial Bacău în ziua de 11 Mai 1944, orele 7,30 precis (la ora 9.30 vor fi trecuţi în revistă de un delegat al M.U.)

In afară de evreii aflaţi disponibili se vor prezenta şi următoarele categorii, cari până în prezent au fost scutiţi a se prezenta:

1. Cei scutiţi cu carnete eliberate de Împuternicitul Guvernului sau Marele Stat Major, dela orice întreprindere sau [illegible] din acest oraş.

2. Inapţii provizoriu, inapţii definitiv, clasaţi cu munca manuală uşoară şi muncă intelectuală.

3. Toţi titraţii academici, precum medici, farmacişti, avocaţi, contabili, technicieni, de toate categoriile, desenatori etc.

4. Cei veniţi după rata altor Cercuri Teritoriale.

5. Cei aflaţi în prezent în custodiu sau concediu medical.

6. Evreii cari în prezent sunt disponibili, desconcentraţi recent.

7. Evreii încadraţi la Apărarea Pasivă...

8) Evreii dela Rampa C. F. R. precum şi cei [illegible] repartizaţi în plus la instituţii şi [illegible], prefectură, primărie, Comitetul de Patronaj, etc.)

9. Evreii [illegible] Cercul Teritorial Bacău şi Regt. [illegible]

Nu se vor mai prezenta evreii repartizaţi la muncă în ziua de 7 Mai 1944.

Toţi acei evrei ce nu se vor prezenta de bună voie la acest apel, vor fi [illegible] şi condamnaţi de Serviciul Pretorei [illegible]

Cercul Teritorial Bacău

MAI 1944

Authorization Paper

The Jewish Sergeant Rottman Henry (from year 1941) located on Str. Bradului No. 5 is re-assigned for mandatory work on regiment Laptari Calugara starting on May 7th 1944. Furthermore, he is allowed to walk on the streets from 5 AM till 8 PM.

Signed by commander on May 7th 1944 in Bacau.

Announcement

In accordance with the "Baricada" order No. 33 issued on May 7th 1944, all Jewish people between the ages of 18-50 from Bacau are to present themselves to the Bacau Communal Court on May 11th 1944, at 7:30 am for a census reading.

The museum "From the history of the Jewish People Living in Bacau" 1703- 1944

F. ASPECTS OF THE SPIRITUAL LIFE
THE JEWISH COMMUNITY FROM BACAU
Bucharest, 1995

The Jews were bilingual in Bacau. They spoke – of course – Romanian. However, there was not one family – of poor or wealthy people – where Yiddish, the common language of the Jews from Eastern Europe, was not spoken.

Of course, every child acquired at heider (the orthodox school) elements of Hebrew, the language of the Biblical texts: the alphabet, reading the prayers and other religious texts, writing in Jewish letters, basic norms of the Jewish religion. A more profound knowledge of Hebrew was acquired only by those - relatively few – students who studied in iesivot, places for the systematic study of the Bible and of Talmud. The Jewish population used Hebrew only at religious services, which took place in synagogues, or on the occasion of other ritual events. Otherwise, what the ordinary Jews (especially women) knew from Hebrew were the Hebrew words and expressions, which had become a part of the Yiddish linguistic thesaurus throughout the centuries. Yiddish was an essential means of communication, beside the one used with the Romanian population. People used Yiddish, speaking and writing, in all the circumstances of every day life, beginning with family life, continuing with the relations within different preoccupations, and even in the spiritual life, in a considerable measure. Yiddish was used for different notes and calculations, engagement, marriage and divorce documents, private or commercial correspondence. Beside Hebrew, Yiddish was used in the registers of the Jewish handicraftsmen communities and of other fraternities. The sermons, the occasional speeches, the greeting were made in Yiddish. In order to understand the meaning of the prayers, Yiddish translations were used; there were also special prayers in this language ("Tehines"). There was a very popular Yiddish compilation of the Biblical texts ("taicihimes"). Of course, the oral folk creation was also produced in Yiddish.

The Jews from Bacau started to use Romanian gradually, as they increased their relations with the majority population. As it had become currently spoken, Romanian got to be used in writing as well, after the development of modern primary education system.

*

Let us analyze a bit the Yiddish folk creation of the Jews in Bacau. We can say that it played an important part in their life; it included stories, anecdotes, and especially proverbs and sayings. The Yiddish folklore from Bacau enjoyed the attention from collectors and researchers only in the 20th century. I. Kara, who published folkloric material ever since 1923, collected poems, stories and anecdotes from Bacau. They say that the Hasidic tzadik Rabi Mihel Dorohoianu came "on tour" to Bacau. A fruit trader, named Haim Rubinstein, came to him complaining that he had too many fruit and no buyers. The tzadik told him to be patient. Winter passed too, but the plums were still unsold. Then the trader wired the tzadik the following text: "Purim has passed, I haven't sold my plums, what is to be done?"[315]. Dr. Israel Fuhrman, who lived in Bacau between 1946 and 1965, collected many proverbs and sayings from this place, which he included in a remarkable work with folkloric material from Romania[316]. He disposed the material in alphabetic order. Only at the last five letters of the alphabet were there 47 proverbs and sayings collected in this city. Here are some examples, with an attempt of translation and adaptation: "Andere taitn andere laitn", meaning "Other times, other people" or "People change with the circumstances"; "Me darf tisteln a times steindlah", meaning "We make a stone compote" – in other words, something impossible to achieve; "Tures ghein avechi in naie angstn kimen un", "Troubles are going, necessities are coming".

*

The creations of those popular troubadours, known as "badheni", were closely related to folklore. At the same time, authors, composers, actors and, sometimes, editors of their own productions, they wrote poems and songs with educational contents, they improvised programs closely related to the realities of the age, and performed them in different circumstances (weddings, baptisms, Purim celebrations, etc.); all these had a special echo among ordinary people.

The most famous representative of this category of creators, Velvl Zbarjer Ehrenkrantz (subsequently considered as a forerunner of the Yiddish Theater and to whom great Itic Manger, decades later, paid his respects in a poetic creation a great sensibility), came in 1860-1870, to present his programmes in Bacau too. He also had a friend here, A. Meisel, known for his activity as a doctor, and for his taking part in community actions, where he manifested his opinions as a militant of Hasacala.

A typical modern representative of this category of popular troubadours was Lipa Rudich (Lipa Radescu, as he undersigned sometimes), native from Bacau. He was an author of poems and songs as well, a fan of the theater (perhaps a prompter too), interpreting his own creation, sometimes with a satirical nuance.

He had the life of a Bohemian, which took him to Bucharest and to other towns of the country, even abroad, to Constantinopol (where, apparently, he also got married). In 1882, he published "Col Rina", a collection of songs, written in Yiddish. And a play, having the title in Romanian "Father's Will" or "The Knave", and which had 5-6 characters. In 1884, he continued to publish songs, but the material success was a weak one. Then he wrote and published texts for amateurs who played Purim theater ("Pirempsil"). His work, entitled "Lipoles Verk", which included 15 songs,

---

[315] I. Kara, in collection "Bukarester Sriftn", vol. 5, 1972, p. 173.

[316] Dr. Israel Fuhrman, in "Sprichverter in Rednsartn ghezamit in Rumenie", Tel-Aviv, 1960, issues 1350, 1362, 1380.

was published at Bacau at Azriel Margulies' printing house; the cost of a copy was of 50 coins.

In 1886, he was planning to publish a weekly magazine, "Die Tukunft" ("The Future"), registering subscribers for it; the magazine was published, entitled "A mesimet in der mispuhe" ("A Renegade in the Family"). Lipa Rudich's songs, such as "The Thief after Death" or "It's a Shame" (the monologue of a tailor's apprentice), are filled by the type of humor similar to the one in "The Testament" of François Villon, whom Lipa obviously did not know. Lipa Rudich had a premature death, when he was only 40. Here is the note on his modest tombstone in Bacau: "Year [5]658. In the memory of a learned man, late Lipa Meier, son of Tvi, deceased on 8 Menahem Av and buried on the Fast day. May his soul be included in the connection of the eternal life". In 1948, one of his sisters still lived in Bacau, holding the position of "firzugern" at the synagogue (meaning she was a lecturer for those women who were not well familiarized with the prayers). She still had some manuscripts left from her brother, and was able to reproduce some of his songs.

Here are, in approximate translation, fragments from the song "The Thief after Death", which we have found at Lipa Rudich's sister. The song begins with the lyrics:

"My mother told me that in my childhood I proved to be mean,
She used to say I was possessed by devils,
As I was gamboling, singing, dancing, jumping,
I made my parents' life a living hell"

After he has talked about how he had learned to steal as a child, and mentions, in a humorist way, different situations when he proved his skill of stealing, the thief – now on the death bed – concludes:

"And now there is no use for you, death, to believe that everything comes to an end. If it is true that Heaven includes wealthy people sitting on golden chairs, Then you should know that no locks could stop me. I will enter Heaven and pick everyone's pocket".

V. Isac published memorable words about Lipa Radescu[317], as he mentions the following quatrain, which legend attributes to him:

"We are all mortals,
This I have always said;
But I am sorry that the odds
Chose that I should die as well..."

The other troubadour mentioned in the article was another picturesque figure: Eliahu Margulies.

In 1895, he published the brochure "Zamlung fin ale naiste in senste folcsider aroisgheghebnfin Eliahu Margulies". (Its translation would be: "A Collection of the Latest and Most Beautiful Folk Songs, edited by Eliahu Margulies"). The author (who entitled himself "Mnemonic physiognomist") published here a set of poems,

---

[317] V. Isac, *Two Troubadours*, in "The Magazine of the Mosaic Cult", issue 119/1965.

which had been dedicated to him in Hebrew, Yiddish, Romanian and Latin; one of them was signed by A. Goldfaden. The booklet also included a portrait of Margulies, as well as advertisements, one for his "art", others for his "sponsors". In 1895, Eliahu Margulies also published the brochure entitled "Teater lider in folcslider" ("Songs from the theater and folk songs"), sold for 15 coins per copy[318].

*

Printer H. Margulies published between 1894 and 1899 Jewish calendars (Iuah). In every calendar, he published in Yiddish one or more moralizing poems, in the tradition of the bards "badhunim"[319]. In 1898, he also published the Yiddish version of the statute of the Mutual Help Society "Aghidas Haboinim".

Iacov D. Rozenweig showed a special attachment to the Yiddish culture, as he was the one who had published – as a secondary school student – A. I. Lobel's nespaper "The Present" at Bacau in 1876-1878. As he knew Yiddish very well, he published later on, under the name of Sotec-Leteanu, "Micol Rina", a collection from Velvl Zbarjer's texts, drafting linguistic studies and elaborating original concepts in this field.

Volf Iser from Bacau also used Yiddish in his works beside Hebrew. He began to write poaems since he had been 15. Although the majority of his productions were in Hebrew, in 1930, he published at Bacau (at Goldsmit printing house) the paper "Reflecsn iber idn in idntum" ("Thought about the Jews and Judiaism"), in Yiddish, and a year later, a booklet including poems in Yiddish.

In 1946, several Jewish writers, repatriated from Northern Bucovina, settled in Bacau. While they lived here, they participated in the cultural activity in Yiddish, both by means of conferences, and by spreading the literature in this language. Hers Segal, a teacher of mathematics, distinguished supporter of the Yiddish culture, took notes with the folklore of the deported people from Transnistria, and with the confessions of the orphans from the deportation camps; then he published them in Israel, where he eventually settled.

Mr. A. Klein made a remarkable contribution to the knowledge of the modern Yiddish literature by publishing in 1947, at Bacau, his valuable translation in Romanian of Eliezer Steinbarg's fables. As he also left for Israel, he continued his activity as a writer and a translator there.

The Jews from Bacau had always manifested their attachment to the Yiddish culture, by the interest with which they welcomed, during the inter-war period, the tours of important Yiddish theater companies (Mali Picon, Kaminska, Vilna, Alexandru Moisi). Local amateur troupes (students and athletes) also gave performances. Saraga Lorian, an actor and a lyricist, remembered for his unforgettable role of Zeilig Sor from Ronetti Roman's play "Manasse", was greatly appreciated by the Jewish and Romanian audience.

---

[318] "Folksblat", Bucharest, issue 108, August 1895.

[319] Itic Svart, *Confessions from old times*, Bacau, p. 37.

*

We have shown in another part that some Rabbis from Bacau gave their contribution by works in the development of the Hebrew traditional culture. There were also lay learned men, such as Volf Iser and Mayer Eibschitz, who published works in Hebrew. However we shall analyze the contribution to the promotion of Hebrew language by certain Jewish teachers, who worked in Bacau and who were "maskili" (followers of the rationalistic trend Hascala).

During 1869-1871, M. Schwartz administered the Jewish-Romanian primary school from Bacau. Born in Breslaw (Wroclaw), he immigrated to Romania, quickly learned to speak Romanian and managed to publish a set of school textbooks, for both the Jewish schools and public schools (arithmetic and reading textbooks). W. Schwarzfeld published information about the life of this teacher[320]. His first Hebrew textbook was entitled "Imrot tehorot lehadrin ialdei bnei Israel badereh haemuna..." and the Romanian title was "Clean words or sentences from the Bible to be used for teaching religion to the Jewish youth from the United Principalities. Collected and corrected according to the Jewish text by M. Svarti, the Inspector of the Jewish-Romanian schools from Iasi". The textbook was published in 1862. In 1863, Schwartz published another textbook, which was meant to replace the traditional system of learning the Pentateuh (Torah), by means of the folk language. It was entitled "Biblical history, adapted from the original text by M. Svartiu, inspector and religion teacher of the Jewish-Romanian schools from Iasi". Another textbook of M. Schwartz, entitled "Mesilat halimud Vehakeria", with a German subtitle "Erstes Hebraeisches Lehrund Lesebuch" ("The First Hebrew Textbook for Learning and Reading"), was published in 1873 and it was supposed to replace the educational system in the orthodox schools. Starting from the maskilic prejudice according to which Hebrew was "bad" German, the author wanted to teach the Jewish children good German, by translations from Hebrew texts. The book also included elements of religious education, as well as issues of Hebrew grammar.

In 1895, a book of popularizing the history of the Jewish people, "Sefer Divrei haemet", was published in Bacau. Its author was M. Braunstein, whose pen name was Mibasan. Born in Iasi in 1858, he worked in the Jewish primary schools, in Bacau and other localities, and he was the co-founder of "'Dr. Iuliu Barasch' Historical Society". He published "The History of the Jews for the use of the Jewish schools in the country" ("Samitca" Printing House from Craiova), translations from Hebrew, "Hamore" ("The Teacher") textbooks of Hebrew.

In 1897, "Sefer more ivrit", by Mose Orenstein, was published in Bacau, an instructional textbook for the first two primary classes. The same Mose Orenstein edited at Bacau the Hebrew magazine "Lahoren".

Lazar (Eliezer) Casvan (the son of the well-known Rabbi Avner Casvan), born in 1852 and who was a teacher at the Jewish school in Bacau for a while, is the author of a grammar book of Hebrew, entitled "Sefer tora sefat ever". The book was

---

[320] "Year book for the Jews", year XII, 1889-1890, p. 34-35.

published in Bucharest, in 1895, as it was edited by the Society for Jewish-Romanian instructional books.

The information related to "pre-inscribers" gives us a certain image of the interest regarding the Yiddish and Hebrew cultures among the Jewish people. There had been a habit that the authors of works in Hebrew and Yiddish (Biblical and Talmudic comments, panegyric comments, rabbinic responses, occasional works, etc.) should visit different communities and enroll people in a list of subscribers for the works which were to be published, with payment in advance. Of course, only a part of the subscribers were really interested in the contents of the papers, which sometimes surpassed the level of their knowledge; but their gesture was an efficient support for the authors, who thus had dozens of subscribers. A very valuable book, published in 1985, shows that there were many such "pre-inscribers" in the communities from Bacau and in the whole county.

*

As the Jews in Bacau began to use Romanian, an increasing number of Jews developed their activity in the intellectual field, using this language. We mention here "The Present" newspaper, created by A. L. Löbel in 1876, and which, until 1878, approached issues of both general and Hebrew interest. Personalities such as A. S. Gold, Elias Scwarzfeld, Rabbi Taubes (from Barlad), B. Labin (from Botosani) and I. H. Flor (from Dorohoi) collaborated for "The Present". Under Löbel's supervision and M. Scwarzfeld's editorship, the "Calendar for the Jews" was printed at Bacau in 1877, where (with the collaboration of L. and M. Brociner, of Richard Torceanu and Dr. Karpel Lippe) studies of Jewish folklore were published, as well as translations from universal literature and original stories,

Actually the press in Romanian became increasingly used by many Jewish intellectuals from Bacau, who thus contributed to the creation of a climate favorable to culture in the city. In his monograph, Gr. Grigorovici enumerates, among the leaders of the press in Bacau, Bernard Klein (who was the vice-president of the Press Association in the city), Paul Kissler-Bistriceanu (chief-editor of the weekly publication "Gazette of Bacau"), Roland Kaufman (who edited the "Trend of Bacau" and then daily paper "The Hour"), M. Margulius-Margarit (who ran the newspaper "The City of Bacau") and Lupu Glasman (correspondent of the newspaper "The World"). In the book "Special Delegate", this list is completed with other journalists who had a notable activity in Bacau: Emil Mititelu, H. Rabinson and I. Voledi.

Let's also mention other contributions of the Jews to the local cultural life.

Gr. Grigorovici notes that Daniil Klein was the President of the Cultural League for a while.

In 1915, the magazine "New Horizons" was published in Bacau, as a result of the commune activity of three men of culture: the poet G. Bacovia, Ion Iordachescu and Smil Kraus; all three of them published poetry and prose here, using a pen name.

During the inter-war period, the Association of the Jewish Students, as well as other Jewish cultural circles invited famous writers for lectures in the city: Gala Galaction, N. D. Cocea, Gh. Marinescu, Felix Aderca and others.

The "Raza" library, with the thousands of books it included and the conferences organized there, was a center of culture for the entire population. Those Jews, who functioned as teachers at the public secondary school, attracted entire generations of students to them and culture. The Jewish actors Lori Cambos and Misu Rozeanu, who successfully played at the Theater in Bacau, created a cultural environment.

*

Many Jews started from Bacau, and tried to do something in different fields of the spiritual life of Romania. It would be difficult to name all those who left their marks in thess fields: scientists, actors, writers, literary critics, musicians, etc. Time will tell who represent authentic cultural values. We only limit ourselves to mention several prestigious names here, who were related to the city on the Bistrita river: painter N. Vermont, mathematicians Solomon Marcus and Alfred Haimovici, actor N. Stroe...

*

We close this chapter with fragments from a text that we owe to Carol Isac and which describes the Jews' life in Bacau as reflected in literature and arts:

"The impressions created after the contact of some remarkable artists with the Jewish inhabitants of Bacau, underlines, beyond their professions, their spiritual restlessness, their passion for books and for the philosophical dispute. Painter Nicolae Grigorescu owes his Jewish portraits, which was characterized by the artistic critic George Oprescu as an important element of his work, to his visit in Bacau, in July 1874[...]

The canvas entitled 'Pub from Bacau', 'Rabbi', 'A Jew from Moldova', 'Old Jew', shows faces where we can see wisdom, but also suffering for all the great pains of the world, the tragedy and the triumph of a poor life, based, however, on spiritual harmony. 'A Jew from Moldova' includes realistic elements in its compositional structure, an emphasized human verisimilar, marking the sublime concord between external existence and inner life [...]

The poet George Bacovia, for whom living among Jews, all being citizens of Bacau, was an absolutely normal thing, notes the tragedy of being separated from the native land of 'Ebreia' (a poem which was initially published in 'The Cultural Athenaeum', issue 2, 1927), by the eulogy brought to the sensitiveness of those 'swallowed up by America', but who 'don't forget their country'. The poet's identification with the destiny of Ebreia is according to the resistance to a destiny that fights the normal wishes of a human being, 'Ebreia / as we miss our country, / You die in tears, looking across the ocean, / I cry in the old continent'. Allusions to the Jewish co-citizens, whom the poet appreciated a lot, also appear in his prose, but not in an emphasized manner; it is defiantly the proof of the lack of difference in destiny and suffering of all people – a poetic creed, which influenced the entire work of the poetic genius in Bacau.

Other Descriptions of the Jewish inhabitants are included in D. D. Patrascanu's prose; there are observations related to their traditions and everyday life, but with no exotic emphasis. The writer includes the life of the native people in a cosmos of somewhat stereotypical everyday life, shifting between major worries and troubles and small joys. The Jews participate to this only with some distinctive color, which actually belongs, according to the poet, in their integrity, to this place just like the other inhabitants […]

The prose writer Marius Mircu reflected the Jewish community in his volumes 'Special delegate' (1974), 'The Tailor in Back' (1979) and 'I was Born a Reporter' (1981). There is the opinion of the reporter who is interested, by the nature of his profession, in everything and everyone. According to M. Mircu, the city of Bacau in the first half of the 20th century had a flourishing Jewish community, with no inferiority complex. His narrations are according to the real documents he makes reference to, and to the memory of the contemporaries; there seems to have been no field of activity in which the Jews were not included. They were among the great manufacturers and among the obscure intermediaries, involved in suspicious business related to intended fires.

Marcel Marcian's prose is even more aware of the characteristic nuances of the Jewish community. 'Tell you' (1977) and 'And as I Was Telling You' (1980) are the delight of the reader who wants to learn more details or to find himself in the specific atmosphere that the writer evokes. It is a world of subtle pictoresque, not at all ostracized in its own laws, which makes all the joy of his writings; just like the other writers evoked hereby – Jews or not – there is an emphasis on the unit of existence with the entire population; a ghetto, even if it is only a spiritual one, is a notion which is rejected or avoided from the very beginning.

However, in Alexandru Sever's prose, the Jews' everyday rituals are more emphasized. In the story volume 'Memory of Pain' (1986) there are such aspects of relationships that are only left in the memory of those who have lived them. 'The Sadchen from Bacau' reminds all of the wedding practices from remote times from a nostalgic-ironic perspective.

There are other evocations of the Jewish community from Bacau in other sporadic or occasional writings, such as those related to the activity of the Jewish secondary school, which functioned here during the years of the racist persecution, writings that are subjective and, of course, incomplete concerning specifically the Jewish physiognomy of the community".

*

This monograph about Bacau can be continued, as related to many other aspects of the past. Unfortunately, there will be no page about the future. In the city on the Bistrita river, "the Jewish world" is a notion, which is about to disappear…

Page 196

CALENDAR
PENTRU
ISRAELIȚI
PE ANUL
5638
(1877–1878)
Editor: A. L. LÖBEL
ANUL I
BACAU
1877.

שיחת־אחים
SICHATH-ACHIM
WOLF ISSER

Prima Societate „FRATERNA" pentru ajutorarea
in cas de lipsă, boló și deces
Fondată la 27 Ianuare 1879 15 שבט תרלט

No. 59

Bilet de Intrare
LA

Concertul lyrico-vocal

dat de renumitul violonist și cantor B. HELSINGER cu concursul câtor-va tineri pentru fondarea sinagogeĭ

„THEODOR HERZL"

Localul, data și specificarea bucăților alese se vor anunța printr'un avis special.

COMITETUL

Loc Reservat 1 leu.

a) *Calendar for Jewish People for the year 5638 (1877-1878), by A.L. Lobel*

b) *Jewish Document*

c) *Entry Ticket issued by the "First Society '**FRATERNA**' for helping the ones affected by sickness & death. Founded on January 27th 1879 to a Concert given by the renowned violin player and singer B. HELSINGER to support the foundation of "Theodor Herzl" synagogue. The date, place and a schedule of the concert will be published at a later date in a special announcement. For a reserved space – 1 Leu. June 20th 1904*

Page 197

SINAGOGA „THEODOR HERZL" BACĂU

APEL.

Pentru a eternisa numele acestui mare bărbat al lui Israel, cea mai veche societate a acestui oraş înfiinţează o sinagogă în memoria lui şi face un apel călduros pentru a i se da bine-voitorul Dv. concurs.

Numele şi numărul biletelor cumpărate de fie-care se vor da publicităţii şi vor fi înscrise pe tabloul comemorativ, ce va fi păstrat pentru tot-de-auna în acest locaş sfânt.

Cu profund respect
COMITETUL

Bacău, 1 August 1904.

Iosef Brail
Fabrica de apă gazoasă
BACĂU

Arh. St. Bacău, fond. Comunitatea Israelită Bacău, dos. 4/1923, f. 1 f/v

"THEODORE HERZL" SYNAGOGUE BACAU

APPEAL

With the purpose of making the name of this great man of Israel everlasting, the oldest society of this town builds a synagogue in his memory. Therefore, the society appeals warmly to you in order to kindly support this project.

The name and number of tickets bought by each person will be made public and written on the commemorative picture preserved forever in this holly place.

With deep respect,
The Committee

Bacau, August the 1st 1904

a) *Book cover "Poems in Hebrew & Yiddish" by Wolf Isser, published in Bacau in January 1931*

b) *Another book cover "Fables" by Ezer Steinbarg, translated from Yiddish by A. Clain, Bacau 1931*

The museum "From the history of the Jewish People Living in Bacau" 1703- 1944

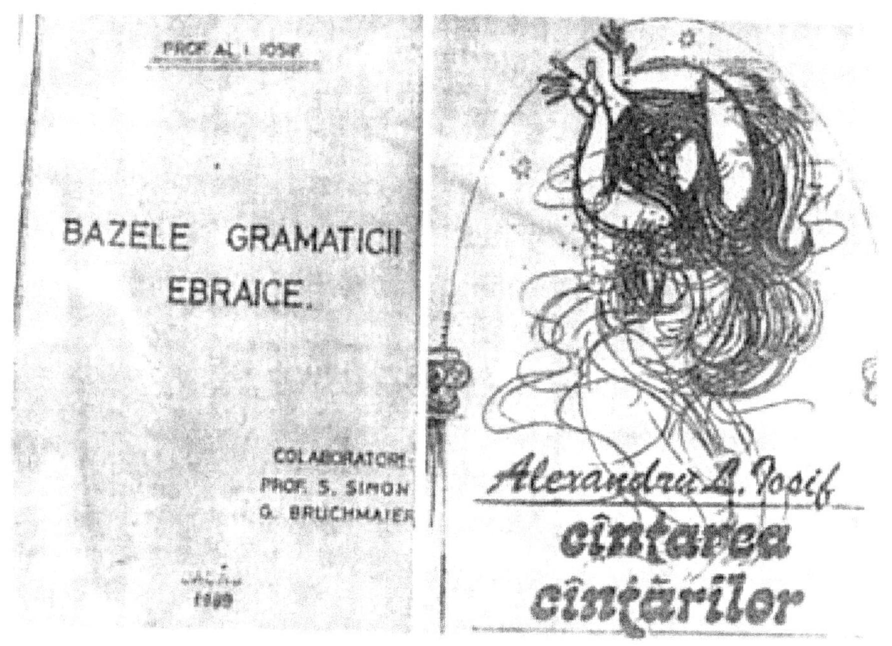

Muzeul „Din Istoria Comunității Evreilor Băcăuani, 1703—1944

FEDERAȚIA COMUNITĂȚILOR EVREIEȘTI
DIN ROMÂNIA
COMUNITATEA EVREILOR BACĂU

Ghid
al MUZEULUI
"Din istoria Comunității Evreilor băcăuani
1703 - 1944"

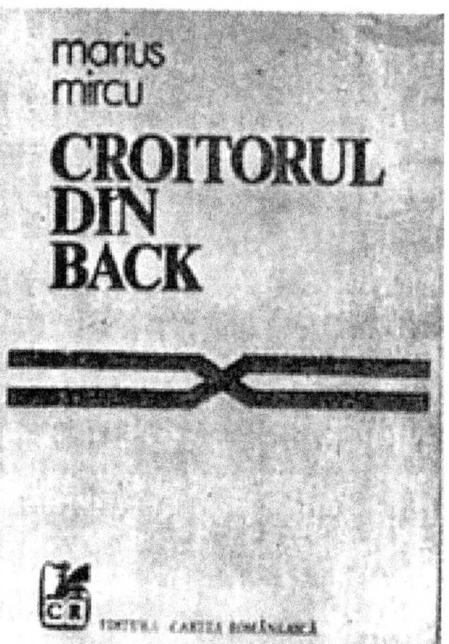

a) Professor Al.L.Iosif

THE BASIS OF HEBRAIC GRAMMAR

In collaboration with: Prof. S. SIMON & G. BRUCHMAIER, 1989

b) ALEXANDRU L. IOSIF

THE SONG OF SONGS

The museum "From the history of the Jewish People Living in Bacau" 1703-1944

c) THE FEDERATION OF JEWISH COMMUNITY IN ROMANIA

THE JEWISH COMMUNITY OF BACAU
11 Alexandru cel Bun str.

GUIDE
OF THE MUSEUM
"From the history of the Jewish People Living in Bacau". 1703 -1944

d) marius mircu

The Tailor of Back

Printed by Cartea Românească (The Romanian Book)

Page 199

Solomon Marcus in a passionate discussion with Yehudi Menuhin.
The Mosaic Cult Magazine, no 800, March 16, 1995

Lori Cambos and Misu Rozeanu and Rozina Cambos respectively,
Jewish actors on the stage of State Theatre of Bacau.

The museum "From the history of the Jewish People
Living in Bacau" 1703- 1944

Appendix I
THE STATUTE OF "HEVRA KEDOSA" FUNERAL FRATERNITY FROM BACAU

From the register (Pincas) dated in the year [5] 531 (1771)

a.
b. The members of the fraternity have to comply with all their duties and avoid conflicts among them.

1. In case of death, the chief will personally go to show the place of the grave.
2. All the members of the fraternity have to obey the chief. Those who do not, are fined and they will apologize to the chief. An "usher" who uses the tools of the fraternity for other pirposes will be punished with "Malcut", 39 whips.
3. The chief will have a double vote.
4. Admission of new members is only made in (Hol Hamoed) Pesah, Savuot, Sucot. Those who want to be replaced at their duties can pay a "samas" to replace them. The new emtries will pay "barbanta" (the admission fee) of three coins and he will offer a guardian to the entire fraternity. 6. Every year, only one member of the fraternity will be admitted. Ushers can be admitted in any number.
5. A member of the fraternity cannot enter (the premises) during the funeral ritual, not even to give help. Those who violate the rule will be fined.
6. If a member gets sick, two people will be sent, and they will take turns in sleeping in the room of the sick person. The Samas (the candidate) who is still a child has someone else to replace him. The chief cannot be contradicted.
7. The chief will start the funeral ritual. Those members who refuse to perform the ritual will pay a fine of three coins.
8. Those who begin the ritual before the chief does, either at washing, or at digging the grave, will be fined with 15 coins.
9. The fraternity tools are kept in the synagogue. Their use without the chief's approval is fined with 15 coins. The chief can borrow them in exchange of a guarantee. Any broken tool will be repaired with the fraternity funds.
10. Those who enter the premises without a coat will be fined with 10 coins, as the fraternity must be respected.
11. Before starting to dig the grave, the relatives will deposit the object of guarantee, which will be kept by the chief. It will not be

returned before "slosim" (30 days from the funeral). The chief and the fraternity can postpone paying for the piece of land. When payment is not made, the guaranteed object cannot be sold within one year. The chief will pay the damage if it is stolen.

12. On Simhat Tora, the chief will give candles to all the members of the fraternity.
13. The fraternity will organize a common feast for Pesat, Savuot, Succot. If the chief doesn't want to do this from the fraternity funds, expenses will be made out of the "Charity box". If there are no funds, the members will contribute with 20 coins. If the chief does not agree to the feast, especially to the one on Simhat Tora, he can be dismissed.
14. All the members of the fraternity will be called to the Tora by the chief, in the order of the signatures as recorded in the register, three times a year: on Iom Kipur, "Col habhor" and "Ase taase".
15. All the events of the year will be recorded in the register: minor offences, admission of new members, violations of the statutes. Every Hol Hamoed (Sucot) the register will be handed to the new chief.
16. All the collected amounts, including the ones from Iom Kipur' Eve will be deposited to the chief. He can give money to the street beggars or in other ways.
17. Elections will be made on Hol Hamoed Pesah. If they don't take place within a few days, the old chief maintains his position for another year.
18. An important man can be admitted with no probation (3 years as an usher). He will give a feast where he serves personally.
19. Ushers must listen to any member of the fraternity. They cannot sit on the same bench with the members and they have to greet first. Ushers will wear modest clothes (at meetings) and will wait on the members, bringing the wine, etc. At the feasts, they eat after the members have finished.
20. They announce the proposals, which are accepted only with a majority of votes.
21. Statutes cannot be modified.
22. At meetings, the members are seated in the order of their signatures in the register, one at the right of the chief, another at his left. Any member can give up his seat to another member.
23. An important man can be admitted with no probation.
24. Before being recorded in the register, the new member gives wine to all the members of the fraternity, 10 coins to the ushers, and 15 coins to the secretary.

25. The chief has priority in the funeral ritual; he can give up this role to another member.
26. Those who speak about other issues during the meetings will be fined with 10 coins.
27. Those who want to eat or drink during a funeral have to do this outside the cemetery.
28. The grave cannot be marked with wood, stone, etc., without prior consent of the chief. Offenders will be fined.
29. Ushers will get 3 coins at a relative's death and 15 coins from others.
30. "Matieva" (tombstone) cannot be put up within one year of mourning.
31. The right to vote is obtained after 3 years of probation.
32. It is forbidden to take off the hat inside the premises and at the cemetery. Fine – 10 coins.
33. There will be silence and appropriate behavior during the meetings.
34. When a child is registered, the admission fee will be paid. He will sign in the register only after his marriage.
35. If a member, who is more than 12, dies, the shops will be closed till after the funeral. Fine – 15 coins.
36. At the commemorations of the dead, at first the chief's dead relatives will be mentioned, then the members', in the order of the register.
37. A Cohen can also be admitted as a member of the fraternity.
38. The tailors and the other handicraftsmen, who are members of the fraternity, will not work till the funeral of a member. Fine – 10 coins.
39. At meetings, the right to speak will be asked from the chief. People will speak standing. Only the old and the ill can speak while sitting down.
40. If the chief is not in town, he can designate a deputy, who will have the same authority like him.
41. The electors (borerim) elect the chief for 3 years. If they elect one of them, a new consultation takes place (notes with the names of all the members are put in an urn, and 3 names are extracted, becoming "electors").
42. If a member of the fraternity dies, he is asked for forgiveness after he has been lowered in the grave, and "his farewell from the living" has been proclaimed. His name is erased from the register.

Appendix II

REGISTER OF "POALEI TEDEK" JEWISH TAILORS' GUILD, BACAU, 1832

A. D. Birnberg sent a copy of this register to 'Dr. Iuliu Barasch' Historical Society from Bucharest, in 1887. The text was translated in Romanian by Lazar (Eliezer) Casvan, and then revised by M. Goldenkron. The translation is clumsy. We reproduce the translation, modernizing the orthography.

(Preamble). The great merit of the handicraft is explained by the words of our scholars in many places. Here is what we find in Talmud: "Braver is the one who earns a living with their hands than the one who fears God, as it is written about the one fearing God: 'Happy is the one fearing God' etc., while, about the one who earns a living with their hands, it is written: 'If you eat from the work of your hands, you will be happy and well'. And our scholars also said: 'Man should always learn a handicraft, which is easy and clean'. What does it mean an easy and clean handicraft? Rabbi Iehuda says: 'The sewer's needle', and by 'clean' they mean 'clean from theft and concurrence', as our scholars noticed related to the verse: 'And Bileam raised his eyes and saw Israel doing his activities'. And what did he see? He saw that the entries of the tents are not placed one in front of the other, so that they cannot look into each other's tent. What the scholars wanted to show by this was that no man should crave for his neighbor's belongings, he should not harm him, he should not cheat and make concurrence to him, as they explained the verse: 'Everyone from his work', they emphasized the words FROM HIS WORK and not from his neighbor's work, as no one touched what had been decided as belonging to the other. Then they said: 'There is no handicraftsman who disappears from this world without people needing him. Happy is the one with a noble handicraft, pity the one with a degraded handicraft. However, there is no handicraft without poverty and richness, as everything is depending on men's merits. Man should pray the one who has richness and wealth, to give him luck in what he does with his hands. Amen."

The statutes begin at page 4.

And these are the statutes and the regulations of the POALEI TEDEK society.

Art. I. All members, on the eves of Saturdays and holidays, must add to the holiness of the day, by ceasing their work, from lunchtime.

Art. II. No member must work during the days of Hol Hamoed (semi-holidays) and those who violate this rule will be punished for the community use as the chief (gabai) considers suitable. And will pay a ducat to the Austrian consul, and his signature will be marked in the register, with no forgiveness.

Art. III. Every member must give the chief as tedaka the amount of 5 coins every week, and Heaven will give more to those who give more.

Art. IV. Any journeyman tailor who works at a member of the society will give tedaka (charity) too, no less than 2 coins per week.

Art. V. The chief must go with the box every Friday, to collect money the money from the members.

Art. VI. Every Iom Kipur's eve, the chief and two other people from the society must sit with the pot in the synagogue and collect the tedaka from the members of the society.

Art. VII. A member of the society whose parents have died, or who will be a godfather, must pay 18 coins.

Art. VIII. When someone from the society has a wedding or a baptism, he must pay 18 coins to the society.

Art. IX. When a journeyman tailor gets married, he must pay 18 coins 4 times.

Art. X. A member must be stopped from creating concurrence to his neighbor, that is when someone has made marks on a material, no matter its quality, the other must not take this material in his hands. And the one who violates, this payment for the performed work will be given to the one who started it; beside all this, he will be punished as the chief considers appropriate.

Art. XI. If a member hires a journeyman tailor for a year, then another one cannot hire him too. The journeyman tailor must work at the initial master or leave the town.

Art. XII. He who is not in the society is not entitled for anything belonging to the society, and someone from another town cannot work inside this city, but only to sign as members in Pinkas, with the consent of all the society members, and even if he is a member of the society, he must give the chief 10 coins, as tedaka, every week before the first year, and then he will be equal with the other members.

Art. XIII. A citizen from here who is not allowed to enter the society cannot work inside this city, not even alone, without a journeyman tailor, as it is the rule in this country.

Art. XIV. Elections must be made on Hol-Hamoed Pesah, and three electors (borerim) must be chosen, who will name the chief. If they want to name the chief without the electors, and the chief would be the one whose name is taken out from the urn, they can do this as well. The money of the society is given to the one who will be the chief.

Art. XV. When elections take place, the previous chief will present the records of the society.

Art. XVI. Those who want to be accepted in the society will pay the sum required by the chief and the majority of the society, and give a feast.

Art. XVII. If someone from the society is trialed, the issue is judged by the chief, and no other person; he, together with the chief of the Sacred Society (Hevra Kedosa) will analyze the matter, and nobody but them is allowed to say his opinion related to the society.

Art. XVIII. When someone wants to introduce his son in the society, the consent of the chief and the members is needed, he must pay a karbovetz and give a feast.

Art. XIX. When elections are due, and the members do not come to the meeting, then the old chief keeps his position for another year.

Art. XX. The chief must supervise all these provisions, and if he violates them, he will be fined with 18 ROL, and he will be dismissed from his position.

Art. XXI. Every Simhat Tora, the chief gives a feast, and all the members go to the synagogue with lit candles, following the Sacred Society.

Art. XXII. When the chief gives the feast, everyone must contribute with 20 coins for the feast expenses, even those who don't want to come to the feast.

Art. XXIII. When the society is gathered, and they are all together, no one will raise their voice and argue, and the one who starts the dispute will be fined with one ducat for the Sacred Society and one ducat for our society, as they must sit in love, union and peace

Art. XXIV. Those who make "gensca" (this is the name for women clothes), are not allowed to make "nemtesc" (men clothes) too, and those who work men clothes should not work women clothes, either by themselves or by some of their tenants, and those who violate this rule will pay a fine, as imposed by the chief of the Sacred Society, the chief of our society and one of the community leaders.

Art. XXV. If a tailor comes from another town, making clothes either for men or for women, no one in the society can take him to work in association, but only in pieces (stuckarbeturer) can he work with him; and it is also forbidden to go to that person whenever necessary and give him any order, either for men or women clothes; and when this provision is violated, he will be fined as the chief of the Sacred Society, our chief and a community leader consider appropriate, and their decision will be accepted without objections, and without any other trial before our law court or the authorities'.

The entire statute above is written in Rasi; and now I get to the other writings and signatures in the Pinkas (translator's note).

May God's grace be on the hands that undersign here, in order to sustain the statutes provided in the Pinkas of the "Poalei Tedek" society, pledging to support and strengthen them by our word and powers.

APPENDIX III
THE REGISTER OF THE "GHEMILAT HASADIM" ASSOCIATION OF MUTUAL HELP LOCATED IN BACAU – YEAR [5] 596

(1836)

The title sheet: Pure pinkas(register) of the Association "Ghemilat Hasadim"who gathered together and associated with the purpose of a very good deed, the one of helping, here, in the holy community of Bacău. Hereinafter are explained the statutes and indications which were made with enforcement. All members of the association established and accepted both for their own use and for their descendents' use that these statutes should be preserved and accomplished in their whole validity. The statutes that are exposed in the above mentioned register and also their memory should be never forgotten. Help us God in favouring us to return in Sion in songs and glory.

I, the writer and ornamentation making person, the humble Aşer David, the son of the deceased Mordehal from the holly community Hotin. In the year of {....) {5}596.

The year is indicated by a biblical quotation. Three points having a triangle shape mark some letters. The ciphered value of these letters indicates "596" (the "5" – th millennium is understood by itself). Up, on the left side, all letters are bearing a signature "David, the son of Ierahmiel".

The calligrapher of this register is also the author of the register of the "Talmuda Tora" Association in Bacău, 1837 (I.K.)

THE STATUTES

0. These are the statutes (tekandt) made with the whole "Ghemilat Hasadim" Association consent.
1. Each member of the association is obliged to give at least three pennies, each week. The one giving more than that will be rewarded by Holiness.
2. The member, who does not pay his due within 6 months, will be excluded from the association and his signature will be cut from the register without any mercy.
3. All association members are obliged to gather for elections each year, specifically in the second day of the Hol-Hamad Pesah.
4. Each week, the chief will go with the box in order to gather the dues from the association's members.

5. The chief is enabled to give loans up to 10 ROL without any approval from the association. He can not lend more than 10 ROL without the association's approval. In case he lends a bigger amount, he will pay from his own money, without any objection.
6. The chief will lend money only in exchange of a good pawn (deposit) and versus a good mortgage. The lending period will not exceed 6 months. After this period passes, the pawn will be sold. The will be three arbiters, elected among the members of the association. The pawn should bear a double value compared to the lent amount.
7. When elections are held, the chief will respond in front of the members.
8. Each eve of Iom Kipur, the chief will be present at the synagogue, when incomes from the members are encashed and donations are collected.
9. Each member of the association, at the circumcision ceremony of his boy or at the marriage of one of his children will make a donation of 60 pennies.
10. Each member of the brotherhood who will be "sandik" (co-officiator) or Godfather at a circumcision ceremony will make a deposit of 18 pennies at the association's pay office.
11. The donations from the Saturday before pericope's "Mişpatim" as well as from the second day of the Hol-Hamond Pasah, belong to the association.
12. The one who wants to become a member of the association will pay an admission fee (bărbânţa- I.K) and will offer a party.
13. In the first three years, the new member will not have the right to vote. After this period, he will be equal to the other members of the association.
14. The chief will organize a party each Simhat Torah. Each member will make a donation of 20 pennies and no money are taken from the association founds. In the same time, the members will go with the lighted candles to the synagogue, following the funeral association "Hevra Kedoşa".
15. If no elections are held at the established time, the chief will be in his position one more year.
16. Even though the association is informed, the chief cannot lend more than 50 ROL to the same person and the lending period will not exceed 30 days.
17. Illegible.
18. It is forbidden to tear sheets from the register. In case the register is finished, it will be preserved carefully, and a new register is made,

19. Even though there are funds amounting more than 1000 ROL in the pay office, no bigger amounts will be lent, except when buying Sefer Torah or Talmud.
20. There will be elected for the committee only reliable persons (Anaşim betuhim al haemet).
21. In case the chief leaves for travel, he will inform the censor ("roe heşbon").
22. The pinkas will be held at the chief's residence. The one who takes it out will be penalized
23. ....excluded from the Torah call.
24. The chief may receive new members having the consent of 4 important members of the association.
25. The chief must know the statute very well.
26. When receiving cash, the chief will have the debtor's list and will not let any penny from the debt.

I translated the first 15 articles towards the incomplete copy that was obtained in conformity with the original that can be found now at the Institute "Yivo New-York". The next ones were resumed in 1947, in Bucharest, when I had the copy sent in 1887 by Bimberg from Bacău to the "Historical Society "Iuliu Barasch"(I.K.)

Appendix IV
THE STATUTES FROM THE "TALMUD TORA "ASSOCIATION, BACĂU, 1837

1. Each member of the association will pay a due of 5 pennies each week.
2. The person who does not pay the due within a 6 months period will be excluded from the association.
3. Each Hol – Hamed of Pesah (semi-celebration of Pesah) the chief (gabal) will be elected. The chief will take over the association's money immediately.
4. Each Thursday, the chief will go personally to the members' houses in order to encash the due.
5. At the general meetings for elections, the chief will report the financial statements of accounts.
6. The chief will daily control the education in heider (the confessional school) and at the Talmud Torah (the same for the poor children). The chief will control if the children wear ţiţit [fimbre} on Saturdays, as well.
7. At meetings, the chief will report about the educational situation in schools.
8. On Iom Kipur eve, the chief and 2 members will sit at the donation table and will encash donations for Talmud Torah.
9. Each new employed melamed [teacher] will give to the association one and a half sorcovăţ, and each belfer [teacher's assistant] will give one sorcovăţ.
10. During the semester, one melamed is not allowed to register the pupil of another melemed.
11. It is not permitted for a melamed to accept a child whose parents did not pay the previous melamed.
12. When a melamed gets the payment, he will give 10 % from the amount for theTalmud Torah.
13. The chief will judge the eventual misunderstandings between melamed and belfer.
14. When a circumcision or a wedding takes place, every association member will give 60 pennies for the association.
15. Each Godfather will make a donation of 18 pennies.

16. When a new member is accepted in the association, he will give bărbânţa [acceptance tax] and will offer a feast for the association's members.
17. The donations made with the occasion of pericope's "Vaicra" reading belong to the association.
18. The chief who is not obeying the statutes will be penalized with 18 lei [18 is a ciphered value of the letters Het and Iod that are equal to 18].
19. If no elections take place, the old chief will keep his position for another year.
20. When Simhat Torah takes place, the association will organize a feast. Each member will give 20 pennies. At the procession, the associates will walk with lighted candles after "Hevra Kedoşa" funeral brotherhood.
21. When a child starts to learn humaş [Pentateuch] with translation in Yidish, his father, even though he is an association member will make a donation of 18 pennies.
22. When a member has iurţat [commemoration of a deceased person in the family] he will give the association 18 pennies.
23. The statutes will be read daily in the synagogue.
24. Each sandek [coofficiator at the circumcision ceremony] will make a donation of one sorcovăţ to the association.

Appendix V
BOOKS PRINTED IN BACĂU

1. In 1882 Lipales Verk [...] (idish) “Contains 18 songs that were sung and applauded everywhere in the theatres...” Bacău, Iehezkiel Margulies printing house (V).
2. 1882. Der practişer araber [Lessons for Arab language for those who will dwell in Eretz Israel- I.K.] by Isaac Naiştain, Bacău, 40 p.
3. 1 895. Teater in folcslider” [Songs for the theater and folksongs – I.K.], Bacău, printed by Eliahu Margulies (V).
4. Der Album[Yidish] “ a beautiful work for the families” composed by Lipa M. Rădescu, Bacău, “ Progresul” printing house , 1896, 64 p in 16.
5. 1896. Hespad Mar [ebr.] Necrology in the memory of the Hasidic Rabin Itzhak ben Ahalom Fridman. Author: Iaacoov Mordehai, Bacau, “ Progresul” printing house, 16 pages.
6. 1896. Sefer Divrei Haemet [The book of the words of the truth – I.K] by M. Braunstein Mibaşan, Bacau, 1896 (V).
7. 1897. Sefer Musar Ivrit (ebr.)[The Book of the Hebraic Moral- I.K) by Moshe Orenştein, Bacau, “Progresul” printing house, 40 pages with translation in Romanian (V).
8. 1898. Statute [.....] (idish) ‘The statute of the first philanthropic association of different Jewish craftsmen ‘Agudas Haboinim” for curing the sick people and for participation at the funeral of the deceased members”. Established in Bacau in April the 12-th 1891, the second edition, Bacau. Iehezhiel Margulies printing house, 1898, 62 pages, type 200x 165 mm.
9. 1900. Teuda Eliahu (Jewish).

Periodical printings

I.HAHOLEH (ebr) paper of Moshe Orenştein, Bacau. 1900.
II. LUAH [Calendar] for the year of 5654(1893-1894) Bacau. Eliahu Margulies printing house .
III. LUAH [.....] for the year 5655 (1894-95), ibid.
IV. LUAH [.....] for the year 5656 (1895-96), ibid.
V. LUAH [.....] for the year 5657 (1896-97), ibid.
This luah appeared subsequently, as well.

- I.Kara, Hebraic Printer in Romania until 1900, in “Kyriat Sefer” vol. 41, no.2/1987, page 339 -340

Appendix VI
TEMPLE OF CEREAL DEALERS IN BACĂU

This modern temple located on Ştefan cel Mare str. No. 29, was built on a piece of land bought by parishioners in 1899.The buying document is signed by Zisu, son of Herş Zalmanovici, Isaac Avram, Leon Davidovici and Josef Marcus. In 1937 another piece of land was bought with 31,361 lei. After the fire from 1927, it was rebuilt and enlarged. Other repairs were made in 1974 and 1986.

According to the documentary materials, the temple's activity, the committee elections and the budget can be observed. Once, the number of parishioners was 310. In 1935, there were given 186 pews or arm chairs. The committee was elected in a democratic way. In 1920, the committee was composed of the following persons: Herş Calmanovici, Josef Aronovici, Isaac Avram.In 1937, the leaders were as follows: Rabin Vacsman, Moise Mendel and Iancu Volf. The incomes were provided by selling pews, dues, rents, and donations. In 1925, the Rabin S. Hoerer was employed for 10 years. In 1929, on the temple's land a new poultry abattoirs was built. During the persecution, 50 prisoners were housed in there. The poorest of them were fed from the temple's founds. The decrease of the Jewish population has the effect of transforming the temple into a museum.

Appendix VII
IMAGES OF FORMER BACĂU

In the work "The town laying on Bistriţa Bacău" belonging to the well known Bacău's writer, who left for Israel, I. Voledi- Vardi (Tel- Aviv, 1989, vol 2, page 187-195), Marius Micu, the infamous writer, journalist, easiest, published a list of the inhabitants dwelling on the two main streets of Bacău in the period between the World's Wars: Bacău – Piatra str., down-town and the Main Street.The information, even though it is not quite complete, has real value because it helps the social-cultural knowledge of the Jewish people living in Bacău. It starts from Sf. Nicolae market from the house of dr. O.Brucăr and passes the public garden. It follows: 1. Hotel "Europa" director Golf. 2. Modiste Tauber 3. Jewish teahouse. 4. The shoemaker Vasile Baciu (former socialist with doctor Aroneanu). 5. The office of iron casting Blaşca brothers. 6. Furniture Caufman. 7. Gherman Lady's tailor shop. 8. Bookshop Solomon Kitner. 9. Photo Adele. 10. Dye house DUCO of Idelovici. 11. Ghidale Mendelsohn.Taphouse 12. Empty land for Circus. 13. Hotel Central, transformed into the Main Post Office. 14. Special food Kalusian. 15. Grocer's shop Marian. 16. Bookshop and printing house M.Haber. 17. Barber's shop Tunaru. 18. Newspaper shop. 19. The tailor's shop Iancu Schwartz. 20. "La consum" pub restaurant, luxury restaurant Herman Isac. 21. The apothecia Marin Malhasovici. 22. Tailor shop haberdashers Schwartz. 23. Miclescu's Sweet shop, and then, 24. Ionescu's Sweet shop. 25. Lottery. 26. "Lux Cinema. 27. Goldschmidt Printing house. 28." Viennese Tailor shop", Herman Schwartz. 29. "Bursa" Café, Ţiperman. 30. D. Pascal Salami shop.. 31. Autotechnics Al. Bramovici. 32. "Regal" Hotel. 33. Town Hall . 34. Administrative Palace. 35. Jean Singer house. 36. Lawyer Mircea Cancicov (finance minister). These were the buildings on the right side. On the left side, starting from St. Nicolas Cathedral: 1. Steinbock Pub. 2.Şaler son Lady's tailor shop. 3. Jean Avram printing house. 4. I. Creţu shoemaker. 5. Ruckenstein, modiste. 6. The shoemaker of Moişe de Bubes (bearded). 7. Church singer Alter Hais. 8. "Mode's progress" tailorshop and cloth manufactory, Alter Gherşen Marcus. 9. Carolina Marcovici, modiste. 10. Dentist I. Ordnung. 11. Lawyer Mititelu. 12. Barber's shop Frantz Buzătescu. 13. Watch shop Zegherman. 14. Furniture Vigder. 15. Cohnţs pub. 16. The Bank of Bacău. 17. Bookshop Margulies. 18. Tailor shop Gutman Haim Bercu. 19. Zeller, musical devices. 20. Iţic Mendel Café. 21. "New life "pub, Sorin Cunea. 22. Aron Grinberg tailor shop. 23. Print shop and bookshop "Gutenberg", D. Rosenberg. 24. Moritz barber's shop, ping glasses and leeches. 25. Andrei Vraşti Bookbindery. 26. Bachman's bookshop. 27. The branch of Marmorosch- Blank Bank. 28. Goldring – jewelleries. 29. Hazu – bookshop. 30. "Oituzul" Bank 31. Alexandru Gheorghiu sweet shop, luxurious. 32. Vogel apothecia. 33. Constantin Drăgan Pub. 34. Max photo. 35. Dr. Cervinschi 36. Dentist Ehrlich. 37. " Naţionala " Insurance , Kendler. 38. Osias Herşcovici Bank. 39. Hamugea, café. 40. C. Drăgan pub. 41. Weinberg photo. 42. Office for documents copying. 43. Tobacconist's shop. 44. Central Bank, Filderman. 45. Rabin Landman

Synagogue. 46. Lawyer Mihai Văgăunescu. 47. Lawyer Grigore Mârza 48. Doctor Şapira. 49. "Ateneu "Hall. 50. Police. 51. Firemen headquarters.

MAIN STREET. Starting from St. Nicolas Market , on the right side : 1. Steinbock pub. 2. Furnishings for tailing work Max Blitz. 3. Gheorghiu barber's shop. 5. Dye house " At the Carpathians mountains", Heinrich Avram. 6. " Sorbona" pub. 7. Dye house " At the camel" , Sigler. 8. Bank of Small Credits of Jewish craftsmen. 9. Factory and shoe shop Constantin Iordănescu. 10. Wool, Alterson sisters. 11. Furniture and tapestry work, Zeidel Loewensohn. 12. „ Traian „Hotel and restaurant. 13. Workshop for priests clothes Rosental. 14. Chemical cleaning Rosenberg. 15. S. Craus Tailor shop. 16. Bernard Goldring watches shop. 17. Moise Kraus tailor shop.18. Furrier's shop Zeidman. 19. Skin dressing shop Herş Abramovici. 20. Moş Grinberg, yeast. 21. Copel printing house. 22. Valeria D. Ionescu, lady' s tailor shop. 23. Saddler's shop Hausfather, named Haim Aron Rimer. 24. Grocery „ At the little wolf, Hari Solomon (Haim Aron) . 25. Passmanterie „ At Rusu" , Goldberg. 26. „ At the golden globe" , wools, silks, Gloter. 27. I. Gherman tailor shop. 28. Gutman's grocery. 29. Silks „ At the ant' , Fritz Lupovici. 30. Silks and wools at Şuler. 31. Shirts " At Ancora', Leibovici. 32. Brand's watch shop. 33. Shoe shop "At the country's brand" , Zeilicovici. 34. Haberdasher's, parfumes, Haim Loebel. 35. Ready made clothes " At Luna Park" , Goldenberg. 36. Leon Solomon jewelry and watch shop.37. Furnishings for shoe making Stopler. 38. "At Mona Lisa" , manufacturer, haberdasher's , David Leventer. 39. A. Iacubovici tailor shop. 40. Brul, furnishing for tailor shops. 41. Woven texture " At the Mascote" , Rubinştein. 42. Woven texture Bernard Lazarovici . 43. Shoe shop "At the Romanian crown" , Mrs. Weissman. 44. Manufacturer "Galia" , Pascal Lazarovici. 45. Woven texture, Sache Moscovici. 46. Whole house of the factory "Găină Brothers" . 47. Woven texture, Pincu Gloter. 48. Ready made clothes, Grunberg and sons. 49. Smith's shop. B. Iakerkaner. 50. Clothes "At the Prince Ferdinand" , Solomon Leizer. 51. "At Luvru's", silks , Sami Kaufman. 52. Hunting arms, Lazarovici. 53. Hats, Heinrich Aroneanu. 54. Braşovenie, Solomon Posmantirer. 55. Shoe shop , Meir Weissman. 56. Woven texture, Bernştein. 57. Şnapic. 58. Small ware shop "At the golden mill", Medelovici and Bercovici. 59. Grocery, Fighel brothers. 60. Cohn bakery. 61. Gh. Forescu's drugstore. On the left side : 62. Aron Krauter grocery. 63. Furrier's shop Ghelman. 64. Alter Gherşin tailorshop. 65. Glass shop Beinglass. 66. Mihăilescu bakery. 67. H. L. Herşcovici tailor shop. 68. Smithţs shop "At the bell", Faiviş Rothenberg. 69. Glass shop Silberstein . 70. Glass shop Zeiden. 72. Apothecia Iliescu. 72. Smith's shop , Zisman. 73. „At the socks' spring" , Leibovici brothers. 74. „At Fortuna" , Rabinovici. 75. „Au Bon Gout", Rabinovici. 76. The shop of the sock's factory Nachmansohn. 77. , "Czech- Romanian" ready made clothes, Grunberg. 78. "Bacău's veil", Milica Marcusohn. 79. Galantery Akerman. 80. The representation of the „ Hercules" factory. 81. The shop of the waving factory, Iţicson brothers. 82. "Elita" woven texture, Herman Leventer. 83. "Manufacturer's spring" , I. Leventer. 84. Cottonery Leia Moscovici. 85. Dye shop "Amphora" .86. The shop of the Factory of casinci "Gloria",Leon Grad. 87. Branch of the shop Luca P. Niculescu,

Bucharest. 88. Braşovenie, Ion Jaliu. 89. The cottonery of Bigman brothers. 90. Fine hats.Finkelstein. 91.Cotton Yarn Brul. 92. "At the elegant bride", Grunberg. 93. Cottonery "At the white lamb", Weinberg. 94. Ready made clothes "At Napoleon" ,Zisman 95. Kleinerman cottonery. 96. Cotton "At the golden star", Leia [....] 97. Cottonery "At the peacock", Iţic Aron. 98. Linen, Zalman Şvab. 99. Small ware shop, passmanterie, Abramovici and Iasir. 100. Skin dressing shop articles. 101. Linen „At the Rose". 102. Linen Grunberg. 103. "At Vidra" , Horn brothers, hats and furs. 104. Furnishing for the tailor shop, Nuham Cleper. 105. Cotton yarns, moş Lazarie. 106. Small ware shop Saie Grunberg. 107. "Colţei" watch shop , Arthur Solomon. 108. Apothecia Stâncă (Ştein).

EPILOGUE

Dear reader, if you had the patience and interest to read this book up to this point, please do not close it yet....

We must share a history with you : true in its whole......

More than eight years ago, the Centre for Studying the Jews' History concluded that, besides the documents volumes (I.M.E.R.) it would be fit to pay attention to the day by day life of Jews, belonging to the different communities living in Romania. And therefore, a monograph started.

When we presented our intentions to the country's communities, we received – among first works- a research of the professor Iosif Leibu , named " Data regarding the Jews Community of Bacău.

Considering that this work is a precious initiative, our centre obtained, with the support of that time's president of the community, Mr. Lawyer I.Brill, the agreement of a collective potential co laboratories. Therefore we reached the conclusion that it was possible to bring additional information to Mr. Prof. I. Leibu.

This was the way the collective of persons presented on the second page of this book appeared.

This way we could make a larger work, organized on chapters having a specific theme. In order to make a solid work, we appealed to the large experience and the full energy of the historian of Jewish people from Moldavia, Mr. I.Kara, respectively.

The local archives had been seriously researched with much competence by Mr. C. Marcusohn; in the same time we got a large number of documents from the Israelian archives.

Therefore, we could gather rich material, a new organization and completeness of the work followed afterwards.

It is clear that such a work is difficult to be realized and what is important, it can be realized through a collective work.

In this respect, we hope the work will be appreciated.

A good thought for the sponsors, young people living in Israel who wanted to honor their parents, their country and their town where they can find their own roots.

Editorial staff,

Bucharest, May 1995.

Other books by I. Kara

Naje Jidise Dichtung-A Collection of Modern Hebraic Poems, Crnauti, 1934
Testimonies from Centuries Ago, Bacau, 1947 (Yiddish)
The Grammar of the Yiddish Language, Bucharest, 1948 (Yiddish)
A Moldavis Ingl. – A Boy in moldavia, Bucharest, Knterion, 1976
Inghe Lum – The Youth Years, Bucharest, 1989 (Yiddish)
Lum fin hoftenung – The Hope Years. Bucharest, 1986 (Yiddish)
The Jewish Community of Podu Ilioaiei, Bucharest, 1990
Hebraic Inscriptions, Iasi, The Romanian Academy Publishing house, Iasi Branch, 1994
Numerous articles published in the national media and abroad.

172 State Archives of Iasi, Prefecture of Bacau, Tr. 84, op. 1009, file 252.
173 "Bulletin", official paper, 1835, p. 435.
179 State Archives of Iasi, Tr. 1764, op. 2013, no. 265, p. 314.
175 Idem, Inv., State Secretariat of Moldova, 1866, no. 1300.
176 Idem, Tr. 361, op. 392, no. 114, p.30.
177 Idem, Tr. 361, op. 392, no. 167, penultimate page not numbered
178 Idem, Tr. 361, op. 392, file 104, p. 11
179 Idem, Prefecture of Bacau, file 95/1837
180 Idem, Tr. 940-0, p. 1082, file 159
181 Idem, Tr. 1318, op. XIII, 1491, file 154
182 State Archives of Bacau, Neamt Monastery, file 611, no. 104, package 11/1855.
183 Idem, Jewish Community, package 3, file 36, p.13.
184 State Archives of Iasi, personal fond. Svart-Kara, Box 4, no. 2.
185 Idem, Law Court of Bacau, Tr. 1636, file 24.
186 State Archives of Bacau, City Hall of Bacau, no. 51, 1864, p. 34.
187 Idem, file 24/5, 1886, p.24.
188 Idem, City Hall of Bacau, file 45/1880, p. 1, 4.
189 The original is at the Central Archives for the History of the Jewish People, Jerusalem, R. M./77.
190 Jewish Magazine, year II, issue 4, February 15, 1888.
191 Idem, no. 14, July 15 1889.
192 State Archives of Bacau, Jewish Community, file 14-1923, f. 6, 6-s.
193 "Egalitatea", no. 11, March 15th 1891.
194 State Archives of Bacau, City Hall of Bacau, file 61/1895, p.2, 5, 5/v, 6, 6/v and 7.
195 "Egalitatea, issue 24, June 20 1897.
196 "The Jewish Magazine", issue 4, February 6 1898.
197 "Macabeul", issue 8, January 6 1901.
198 I. Voledi-Vardi, op. Cit., p. 27.
199 State Archives of Bacau, Jewish Community, file 27/1923, p. 6, 6/v, 7 and 22/1924, p. 1-13.
200 "The Jewish People, issue 19, July 20 1909."
201 Idem, issue 8, June 8 1911.
202 "Egalitatea", issue 47, September 28 1912.
203 State Archives of Bacau, Jewish Community, files 5/1922, p. 18, 66-69.
204 Idem, Jewish Community, files 21/1922, p. 39.
205 Idem, Jewish Community, files 1/1923, p. 12/v, 16-24, 35.
206 Idem, Jewish Community, files 23/1922, p. 65. 65/v.
207 Idem, Jewish Community, files 16/1926, 2/1932, 5/1934, 7/1934.
208 Idem, Jewish Community, file 3/1929, p. 5, 39.
209 Idem, Jewish Community, files 15/1930, p. 48/84.
210 Idem, Jewish Community, file 5/1932, p. 12, 132.
211 "The Jewish Courier", issue 30, November 20 1932.

212 State Archives of Bacau, Jewish Community, file 12/1935, p. 23, 23/v, 24.
213 Idem, Jewish Community, files 20/1939, p. 131-133.
214 Idem, Jewish Community, file 15/1937, p.1.
215 Idem, Jewish Community, file 24/1922, p. 2, 2/v
216 Idem, Jewish Community, file 24/1922, p. 11.
217 Idem, Jewish Community, file 6/1941, p. 68.
218 Idem, Jewish Community, file 12/1928, p. 1, 2, 2/v, 3, 3/v, 4.
219 I. Kara, op. cit., p. 11-18.
220 I. Voledi-Vardi, op. cit., p. 14-16.
221 State Archives of Bacau, Jewish Community, file 23/1922, p. 14, 16.
222 Idem, Jewish Community, file 1/1938, p. 11, 12.
223 Idem, City Hall of Bacau, file 38-1854, p. 1.
224 Idem, file 51/1864, p. 34.
225 Idem, file 45/1880, p. 1, 4.
226 "Fraternitatea", 1882, p. 319.
227 State Archives of Bacau, Jewish Community, file 24/1892, p. 4. 5. 19, 19/v, 24.
228 Idem, Jewish Community, file 12/1925, p. 11.
229 Idem, City Hall of Bacau, file 47/1934, p. 3, 3/v, 4, 5, 7.
230 Idem, City Hall of Bacau, file 7/1943, p. 35-35/v.
231 Idem, City Hall of Bacau, file 21/1942, p.66.
232 Idem, Jewish Community, file 8/1930, p. 18 and file 2/1932, p. 5.
233 Idem, Jewish Community, file 20/1922, p. 57.
234 Idem, Jewish Community, file 6/1934, p. 3/v
235 Idem, Jewish Community, file 5/1939, p. 13-14/v.
236 Idem, Jewish Community, file 21/1940, p. 127, 133, 143.
237 Idem, Jewish Community, file 21/1940, p. 152,
238 State Archives of Iasi, Prefecture of Bacau, letter P, file 489.
239 Idem, Tr. 1772, op. 2020, no. 31984, from May 2 1859.
240 "Unirea", year I, issue 205, October 16 1887.
241 State Archives of Bacau, Jewish Community, file 27/1934.
242 Idem, Jewish Community, file 27/1941, p. 5-24.
243 Idem, Jewish Community, file 1/1939, p. 85.
244 State Archives of Iasi, Prefecture of Bacau, Tr. 1318, op. 15, XVI, 1491.
245 State Archives of Bacau, City Hall of Bacau, file 78, no. 1901.
246 Idem, City Hall of Bacau, file 79/1901, p. 1-2.
247 Idem, Jewish Community, file 22/1926, p. 11-12.
248 P. Pruteanu, Contributions to the history of the hospitals in Moldova, Bucharest, 1959, p. 29.
249 State Archives of Bacau, file39/1866, p. 45-46.
250 Idem, City Hall of Bacau, file 101/1893, p. 4-7.
251 "Egalitatea", issue 7, October 1st 1894.
252 "The Jewish People", issues 2-3, January 23rd, 1909.
253 "Egalitatea", November 20th 1915.

254 State Archives of Bacau, Jewish Community, file 9/1924, 4, 5/1925, 92/1926, 4 and 9/1929.
255 Idem, Jewish Community, file, 1932, p. 73.
256 Idem, Jewish Community, file 8/1923, p. 14-16.
257 Idem, Jewish Community, file 7/1934, p. 126.
258 "Fraternity", August 3rd, 1884.
259 State Archives of Bacau, Jewish Community, file 2/1896, p. 383 and file 5/1923, p. 66/67.
260 "The Jewish Courier", April 6th, 1930.
261 "Egalitatea", December 25th 1915.
262 State Archives of Bacau, Jewish Community, file 18-1924, p.5
263 Idem, Jewish Community, file 5/1934
264 Idem, City Hall of Bacau, 1899, p. 1, 1/v.
265 Idem, Jewish Community, file 44/1942.
266 Idem, Jewish Community, file 6/1938, p. 80.
267 Idem, Jewish Community, file 22/1925, p. 1, 2, 3.
268 Idem, Jewish Community, file 22/1940.
269 Idem, Jewish Community, file 22/1940.
270 Idem, Jewish Community, file 4/1923.
271 "Egalitatea", January 26th, 1896.
272 Idem, February 7th 1892.
273 Idem, February 5th, 1893.
274 Idem, December 25th 1915.
275 "The Jewish Courier", May 23rd, 1926.
276 State Archives of Bacau, Jewish Community, file 7/1934.
277 Idem, Jewish Community, file 9/1925, 14/1926, 4/1928.
278 "Our Rebirth", February 6th 1926.
279 I. Voledi-Vardi, op. cit., p. 24.
280 Idem, p. 23-26.
281 "The Jewish Courier", March 21st 1926.
282 "Egalitatea", January 21st, 1894.
283 "The Voice of the Zion", June 5th, 1899, and January 22nd, 1900.
284 "The Sunrise", October 15th, 1899, p. 8.
285 "Egalitatea", March 2nd and August 17th 1912.
286 "Mantuirea" ("The Salvation"), January 29th 1920.
287 "News from the Jewish World", October 2nd, 1930.
288 State Archives of Bacau, Jewish Community, file 5/1939, p. 8, 8/v.
289 Idem, "Fraterna" Society, file 3/1900, p. 178.
290 Idem, Jewish Community, file 4/1939, p. 53, 54/v.
291 Idem, Jewish Community, file 26/1939, p. 131-134, 150, 152.
292 Idem, Jewish Community, file 23/1939, p. 1-6.
293 Idem, Jewish Community, file 4/1939, p. 51.
294 Idem, City Hall of Bacau, file 159/1939.
295 Idem, City Hall of Bacau, file 27/1940, p. 239.

296 Idem, Jewish Community, file 6/1941, p. 68.
297 Idem, City Hall of Bacau, file 20/1942.
298 Idem, City Hall of Bacau, file 13/1941, p. 66, 67.
299 Jewish World Congress, Jewish Settlements in Romania-Statistic Memento,Bucharest,1947, p. 43.
300 State Archives of Bacau, Jewish Community, file 36/1941.
301 Idem, Jewish Community, file 57/1941, p. 1-117.
302 Idem, City Hall of Bacau, file 30/1942, p. 18 and file 44/1942, p. 13-16.
303 Idem, Jewish Community, file 12/1942, p. 50.
304 I. Voledi-Vardi, op. cit., p. 120.
305 State Archives of Bacau, Jewish Community, file 12/1942, p. 58.
306 Idem, Jewish Community, file 4-1942, p. 9.
307 Idem, City Hall of Bacau, file 20/1943, p. 25, andfile 11/1944, p. 11, 43.
308 Idem, City Hall of Bacau, file 3/1943, p. 198, file 7/1943, p. 80, 82, 84 and file 34/1944, p. 65.
309 Zionist Central Archive in Jerusalem, file L 15/295, B. cf. Albert Finkelstein, Mefkure Tragedy, p. 183-184.
310 State Archives of Bacau, Jewish Community, file 1/1943, p. 195, 225.
311 Idem, Jewish Community, file 5/1944, p. 228, file 20/1944, p. 4, 31, 32 and file 9/1944, p. 28.
312 Pinkas Hakehilot Romania, vol. I, Jerusalem, 1970, p. 14-15.
313 State Archives of Bacau, Jewish Community, file 1/1945.
314 Idem, Jewish Community, file 1/1946, p. 3, 4.
315 I. Kara, in collection "Bukarester Sriftn", vol. 5, 1972, p. 173.
316 Dr. Israel Fuhrman, in "Sprichverter in Rednsartn ghezamit in Rumenie", Tel-Aviv, 1960, issues 1350, 1362, 1380.
317 V. Isac, Two Troubadours, in "The Magazine of the Mosaic Cult", issue 119/1965.
318 "Folksblat", Bucharest, issue 108, August 1895.
319 Itic Svart, Confessions from old times, Bacau, p. 37.
320 "Year book for the Jews", year XII, 1889-1890, p. 34

Jewish Community of Bacau

Jewish Community of Bacau

Contributions to the History of the Jewish the Community of Iasi

By I. Kara

Introduction by Prof. Mihail M. Cernea

**Original Book in Romanian Published by
Hasefer Edition, Bucharest 1997**

Translated by
Alma Barozzi
Marcel Bratu
Avi Klammer
Rony Shaham
Susanna Vendel

Title Page of Original Romanian Book

I. Kara

CONTRIBUȚII LA ISTORIA OBȘTII EVREILOR DIN IAȘI

Cuvânt înainte de
prof. MIHAIL M. CERNEA

București, 1997

Translation of the Title Page of Original Romanian Book

I. Kara

Contributions to the History of the Jewish the Community of Iasi

Introduction by
Prof. Mihail M. Cernea

Hasefer Edition

Bucharest 1997

Jewish Community of Iasi

Cover: Adrian Yonescu
Editor: Paula Litman

Ha'Sefer Edition of the Federation of the Jewish Communities of Romania, Bucharest, 1997

Jewish Community of Iasi

Iasi -5

The edition of this book has appeared with the support of
Prof. Mihail M. Cernea

The printing was made by S.C. ROMACARTEXIM S.A.
Tel: 211.30.16 Fax 211.27.52
Bucharest

TABLE OF CONTENTS

[Note: Page Numbers the original Romanian Book Page Numbers]

This Book Translated by
Alma Barozzi
Marcel Bratu
Avi Klammer
Rony Shaham
Susanna Vendel

{7-10}

PROLOGUE

Hasefer Publishing Company presents the third monograph from a series dedicated by the distinguished historian and man of letters Itic Svart-Kara to some Jewish communities in Moldova.

The two previous works in this series by the same author – the excellent volume about the little-known Community from Podu-Iloaiei (1990) and the substantial monograph dedicated to the Community in Bacau (1995) – each represent an essential contribution to the demographic, economic, and cultural history of the Jewish community in Romania.

The present volume, a new step in this series, is dedicated to the most numerous and most important Jewish community in Romania – the one in Iasi. It offers the reader a far superior synthesis, both in documentary richness and in sociological perspective, to any previously published writings about this community. Together, these three works converge into a larger panorama of the history of Jewish communities on Romanian soil, of the place of these communities in the general history of the Jews in the Diaspora, as well as their specific role in the local history of the formation of modern Romania. For the contribution made by these three works, in particular by the present one, we must pay respectful homage to their author, the eminent writer Itic Svart-Kara.

I asked the author why he wrote this work and how he perceives its purpose. He answered: "It is a subjective moment. Since 1940 I have published approximately 35 works, large or concise, concerning the Jewish population of Iasi, to which I am profoundly attached. I feel the urge to shed light on those four centuries of history of the Jewish Community in the ancient capital of Moldova, as a citadel of the Jewish spirituality in Romania and as an objective source of historic truth." And indeed, the author has achieved both his objective and subjective goals.

The author's activity as a scientist, researcher and writer is recognized and appreciated internationally today, in several continents and many countries, where his studies and articles have been and continue to be translated, published and reviewed. In itself, the author's work exemplifies a basic idea of his writings regarding the history of the Romanian Jews: namely, that the cultural activities of the members of this community contributes simultaneously to the Jewish culture as well as to the Romanian culture. As a matter of fact, the Romanian Academy has recently recognized and publicly honored the contribution of Professor Svart-Kara, conferring, in 1996, a high distinction – the Hurmuzaki Prize – upon the work "Inscriptions from the Medieval and

Modern Romanian Epochs: The City of Iasi" - <<Hebrew Inscriptions>>, prepared by Svart-Kara in collaboration with Stela Cheptea. The work, published by the Iasi branch of the Romanian Academy, the European History and Civilization Center, contains the Romanian translation of about 300 Hebrew inscriptions on headstones from two Jewish cemeteries in Iasi – Ciurchi and Pacurari – and from two synagogues in Iasi – the Great Synagogue and the Tailors' Synagogue. The majority of the unpublished records of headstone inscriptions came from Kara's personal collection, the fruit of many years of tireless investigations.

The antiquity and the significance of some headstones erected in memoriam of important figures of the Iasi Community had attracted the early attention of several men of culture, who were aware of the importance of such historical artifacts – among them I. Psantir, N. Beldiceanu and others.

Invited by the author and by the Hasefer Publishing House to write – as a son of Iasi and a sociologist – an introduction to the present volume, I read the work of Professor Kara with arising surprise and admiration. I am convinced that many future readers will experience, in their turn, the same surprise finding, for the first time, about fruitful facts and hardly known events. I spent the first 13 years of my life in Iasi, have since cherished the city of my childhood, and I love it for its extraordinary cultural history. But even though I knew a few facts about the Jewish community of Iasi, only when reading the current book did I realize the multiple dimensions that this community gradually acquired, attested in documents as early as the 15th century, especially in the 19th century and the first part of the 20th century.

For instance, in demographic respect, data from 1831 and 1859 censuses indicate more than 17,000 and 31,000 Jewish inhabitants lived in Iasi, approximately half of the total population. In its turn, The Great Geographic

Dictionary of Romania (vol. 4, 1901) gives the information that in 1899 Iasi had 59,427 inhabitants, of which 33,140 were Jewish.

The Jewish handicraftsmen stimulated the organization of the guilds, an important moment in the transition from medieval economy to incipient capitalism. The author offers what may be the most complete list – including the brick layers, the carters, the bakers, the tailors, the harness makers, the carpenters, the hatters guilds and others (in total 23 guilds documented in 1863, the predecessors of small and middle industries, to be developed in the following decades). So we learn how the economic structure of the Jewish community of Iasi reflected the denial of their access to public positions and to civil service (for example post office, railroads) and their concentration in handicrafts and commerce.

The current monograph contains vast, informative material on the cultural life of this community, on religious institutions, on internal tensions, on numerous newspapers and periodicals that appeared and disappeared throughout the ages, and on the discrimination and persecutions suffered for decades.

Ardently written, with emphasis on documented data, figures, names and facts, without digressions, the work offers the reader the most significant product of the micro monograph: the image of the daily life, the life of a community that no longer exists today.

We can talk about a reconstructive sociology or about an open window to a barely known past. Undoubtedly other works on that community will be written and published in the future, as an inseparable part of what was called "the sweet town of Iasi." Certainly, the image built in this book is and will remain a precious gift from the author to its readers.

Prof. MIHAIL M. CERNEA
Corresponding Member of
The Romanian Acade

{11-12}

A Few Words and Point of View from the Author

The present contribution to the history of the Jewish community of Iasi is one of the results of my works regarding the history of the Jewish population in the Romanian Countries. I started to publish such works in 1938 (in Warsaw), I continued in Vilna (1939) and in Bucharest (1940). My works appeared in professional magazines, in the Yiddish and Romanian press, but also in English (New York), French (Brussels, Paris), Hebrew (Jerusalem) etc.

For the present work I strived to bring into relief previous works, but particularly studies and materials little or not at all known, especially in Hebrew, Yiddish, Aramaic and Judeo-Spanish. The exposition strives to be accessible to any reader. The scientific apparatus brings the essential; the references are made to a bibliography mentioned on page 101.

A considerable part of my works is dedicated to the discovery, study, revaluation and publication of new or too little known historical sources. I published guild and brotherhood registers, correspondence, official and private documents, headstone inscriptions, excerpts from the press of the era, travel notes, biographies and autobiographies, historical bibliography, literary and artistic folklore, etc. In the last five years I published in a volume two monographs on the Jewish communities of Podu Iloaiei and Bacau and a volume of Hebrew inscriptions from Iasi (with the collaboration of the researcher Stela Cheptea), as well as articles in the press. The historic materials are also included in the three Yiddish volumes published by the Kriterion Publishing House of Bucharest (1976, 1980, 1987).

The history of the minorities is an integral part of the history of the common Homeland: all the citizens of the country are an organic part of the Romanian reality, without denying their specific ethnicity.

I. K.

{13-28}

BEGINNINGS

The first Jewish settlements in Iasi date to the period between the end of the 15th century and the middle of the 16th century. The Academic C. C. Giurescu[1] considers the Jewish population to have established itself at the same time as the Armenian population, having common interests in the field of commerce.

The relative rarity of documents and testimonies regarding the city life in Moldova, within its historic boundaries, may explain the rarity of data related to the Iasi Jews of the time. The void is partially filled by some Hebrew documents. For the 16th century there is a travel account from 1619, which confirms the leadership of the Jews of Iasi to a Rabbi Arroyo, for a period of 40 years, beginning in about 1580. Nothing indicates that he was the first to occupy the Iasi Rabbinic seat. As a matter of fact the frequent passages through Iasi of some Jewish merchants from the Balkans, during the reign of Stefan cel Mare [Stephan the Great], in front of whom they sought justice in their disputes with their Moldovan carters, implies the presence of a Jewish population which had to have at least a kosher slaughterer, a synagogue, and a ritual bath. The historian Dr. M. A. Halevy confirmed the existence of Rabbi Arroyo from a preface written by Shmuel Askenazi to a book written by Slomo Delmedigo.[2] As a matter of fact the date of the oldest headstone, 1610, found in the cemetery located in Ciurchi and still existing in 1943, when the cemetery was destroyed, also proves the existence of a Jewish community and its religious institutions as early as the 16th century. It is possible that this headstone was not the oldest.

Rabbinic consultations preserved from the 17th century concerned Jews who lived in Iasi prior to 1605.[3] The accounts of some foreign travelers, like Paolo Bennicio from Malta[4] (1632) supplements the little we know about the Jews of Iasi in that period.

The peasant revolt in Ukraine, led by Bogdan Chmielnicki, between 1648 and 1649, against the Polish Catholic landowners and the Jews, quickly degenerated into a monstrous pogrom with 150,000 innocent victims. Some Ukrainian Jews saved their lives escaping to Moldavia, between the Dniester and the Carpathian Range. Timush, the son of Bogdan, came to court Ruxanda, the daughter of Vasile Lupu, on which occasion many Iasi Jews were killed or robbed in a pogrom.

The land for the Great Synagogue of Targu Cucului (still existing today - 1997) was bought in 1657. The purchase documents were signed by the brother-in-law of the "doctor" Moise, a practitioner appreciated by the entire population. In 1662 this doctor bought several houses in Iasi (on Ulita Strimba).[5] The Synagogue was inaugurated in 1670 under the pastorate of the famous scholar Rabbi Natan Nata Hanover. The ritual slaughter house was documented in 1685 and 1686 according to the documents mentioned as numbers 165, 168 and 170 in the above-mentioned collection.

The Jewish population increased continuously during the 17th Century, with no possibility of exact evaluations, since precise data concerning the entire population of the Moldavian capital are missing.

The organization of the community during that period

In the specific way of traditional living of the Jews, the complicated and demanding religious rituals stipulated that even the smallest Jewish settlement of 16-20 families, if there was no bigger community in the vicinity, must organize its own, adequate institutions: a prayer house, a ritual bath, a religious leader who should also be a cantor, a seminary teacher, a cemetery, and some charity associations. They had to have some occupations related to the Halacha, the religious code: bakers, butchers and shoemakers. At the end of the 16th century and the following years the presence of a scholar rabbi and of a community leadership required recognition by the authorities.

This is confirmed by documents from 1620 and 1666. The Prof. N. Grigoras wrote: "Since the majority of the Armenian population and later on the Jewish one, lived in cities and were involved especially in crafts and trade, the Armenian and Jewish guilds had a predominant economic character and their organizations resembled those of the local craftsmen and dealers..."[6]

The purpose of these guilds was.... "to defend their own economic interests and their linguistic and religious privileges."[7] Consequently the Jewish guild was the community representation with the authorities. The rights and the obligations of the guild were established by a decree. This kind of royal document dated 1622 can be found in the archives of Dr. M. A. Halevy.

Gheorghe Gibanescu mentioned in two lines a decree given to the Jews of Iasi by Ilias Alexandru Voivode in 1666.

The pastorate of renown Rabbis such as Natan Nata Hanover, Petahia Lyda and in particular the great Rabbi "....the teacher Arie Leib, son of our teacher Rabbi Shmuel, blessed be the memory of the righteous, died on 7 Nissan 5438," i.e. on 30 March 1671, confirmed the existence of a stable, organized community.[8] The existence of the Jewish cemetery in the Ciurchi quarter of Iasi implies the presence of a burial society – Hevra Kadisha – which was not a guild of undertakers, but a benevolent association of prominent members of the community which undertook the mitzvah, the supreme charity, and the funeral ceremony. We have information on some of these volunteer pious men, entitled "aluf," which translates as "leader, champion, chief." Here we mention some of them: Naftali Hirt, son of Itzchak Rozes of Lvov, deceased in August 1676, Baruch, son of Moshe, deceased in December 1677.

The cultural life of that time is primarily illustrated by the presence of prominent personalities, Rabbis who gathered around them a group of people that engaged in studies and debates of biblical, talmudic or cabalistic subjects. These groups did not reach the quality or quantity of the great European communities but had a significant role in preserving traditions and in developing ideological debates. An Arroyo - kabalist, scholar, physician and philosopher - could not live four decades in a backward spiritual environment. Rabbi Natan Nata Hanover, famous as historian, lexicographer and mystic, was born in Krakow about 1620. In "Ieven Metzulah" he brings an eyewitness account of the Khmelnitzky slaughters. He held Rabbinic office in Iasi between 1652 and 1670. He was killed in Poland during a pogrom. In Iasi he wrote the lexicographic work "Safa Berura" ("Clear Language") and the collection of mystical prayers "Sha'arey Zion," which has often been republished. (One edition was published in Iasi in 1843 by the Gheorghe Asachi printing house.) Also important is the Rabbinate of the Great Rabbi Arie ben Shmuel. Also to be mentioned are the names of several scholars entitled "more horaya" (teacher of the Law), perhaps heads of a "yeshiva" - institute of advanced religious studies, like Meir ben Moshe, deceased in April 1661, the young scholar Iacov Copl, son of the scholar Meshulam Feivish, deceased in April 1681. Other scholars are mentioned on the tombstones of close relatives. That proves the existence of an authentic spiritual environment.

As to the cultural aspect of the people, let's not forget that all Jewish children learned to read the Hebrew prayers and translated them into Yiddish, at least the Pentateuch and its commentaries. Many of them also studied the popular Talmudic dissertation "Pirkei Avot," in daily speech called "Peirik," along with the traditional Book of Esther ("Megilah") for Purim, Haggada for Pesach, and the "Ecclesiastes" ("Cohelet"), Ruth, Eikha and some stories about the Prophets. Writing of Hebrew characters was less common, especially among women. However, no commerce or practice of certain professions can be imagined without the study of elements of calculation.

The enlightening sermons of the rabbis or of some of the professional traveling preachers completed the spiritual landscape of the common people up to the beginning of the 18th century.

In the following years, as books became cheaper, they became more accessible to larger groups of the population.

In the rabbinical texts of the 17th century we find a lot of information regarding the commerce of Moldavian Jews - that is to say Jews from Iasi – with Poland and Turkey as well as news about the Jewish craftsmen.

Another source that is worth mentioning is the old Jewish cemetery in the Ciurchi neighborhood of Iasi that is mentioned by the Moldavian chronicler of 1711. This cemetery was used until 1881, when the cemetery in Pacurari was established. In 1943 – after the destruction of the old cemetery – 23,700 corpses were dug out, indicating the economic and cultural development of the Jews of Iasi. The preserved inscriptions indicate some of the occupations of the Jews of Iasi in the 17th century. Commerce was a main occupation: It is mentioned that a Jew from Iasi bought 800 fur caps from Liov (Lvov). There are many examples; Iasi was exporting raw materials (including skins) and importing manufactured products. The need for the development of certain handicrafts was necessary and the Jews responded to that need to a certain extent.

The demographic and historic development during the 18th century and the beginning of the 19th century

Statistics provide important data regarding the population of Iasi in general and its Jews in particular. According to Gh. Ghibanescu[9] there were approximately 1,353 houses in Iasi – 65 belonging to Jews, 30 owned by converts and 33 owned by Christians married to Jewish women. These are figures for the year 1755. The same source also mentioned the professions of some Jews: Shmil the silversmith, Moisei the cantor, Isac Hahambasha, the administrative leader of the community and two other famous rabbis. There was Marco – former leader, Samson – old clothes dealer, converted, Ioan the cap maker, converted, David the goldsmith, Neculai, converted, servant at the Metropolitan Church. At that time the total population of Iasi was growing. The Register of taxable subjects of 1803 lists 367 Jews "that pay for the whole month."

Verax[10] calculated the number of Jews in Iasi: In 1803 – 2420 people; in 1820 – 4,396 heads of families; in 1831- 17,570 people. From other sources we find that in Iasi in 1808 there were 432 Jewish "Raia" families with 1,822 members (ed. note: inhabitants of the Romanian territories compelled to pay taxes) and 142 Jewish "Sudit" families (582 people) (ed. note: settled foreigners who were exempt from taxes) of Russian and German origin. In 1821 Iasi had 4,654 Jewish tax payers.

"The Census of the inhabitants of Moldavia in 1831" served as the baseline document for all subsequent censuses and is also of great value for the history of the Jews. At the turn of the 19th century the economic role of the Jews of Iasi, both in commerce across the borders and as small shopkeepers, was a positive one, as they were considered "indigenous subjects," paid high taxes and were "merchants and publicans" – according to Dimitrie Cantemir (he also noted the fact that the Jews could only have wooden synagogues).

In 1711, when Dimitrie Cantemir was forced to retreat from Russia, the disorder created by the war caused a lot of damage to the Iasi economy, also affecting the small Jewish community. In addition to that, the Tatar invasions, the famine and epidemics – all during the third reign of Mihai Racovita – brought suffering and instability. Moreover, the greedy Greek Prince Mihai Racovita staged, during Passover of 1716, an alleged ritual killing. Consequently he tortured the alleged guilty persons and extorted a huge ransom from the Jews of Iasi.

These abuses contributed to his banishment.

Constantin Mavrocordat, who ruled in Moldavia intermittently between 1739 and 1749, was just slightly more moderate. However, he introduced some discriminatory measures too, for example forbidding Jews from having Christian servants younger than 30 years old.

The Jewish community of Iasi continued to suffer in the following years. It is a known fact that Ioan Mavrocordat robbed the Jewish families and Matei Ghica (1750-1756) adopted discriminatory measures. The great fire of 1779 destroyed the street Ulita Mare where many Jews were living. During Alexandru Mavrocordat's reign (1782-1792) many Jews were banished from their villages and settled in Iasi, creating big problems for the citizens of Iasi.

The events in a disintegrating Poland brought Jewish refugees to Iasi among other places. Some of them could profit from the "protection" imposed upon Moldavia and Muntenia by Russia, Austria, Prussia and later by England, France, etc. This protection favored the "sudits," (foreign subjects) in relation to the native inhabitants, Jews included. The sudits of all religions were exempt from paying taxes and their respective consulates defended them from administrative abuses. Over time many Christian merchants, boyars and clergymen acquired the status of sudit. Some of the Jewish sudits came into conflict with the local Jews, so they tried to build their own organization. The conflict escalated after 1796.

The Jewish population was plundered and killed by the eterists (ed. note: members of Eteria – revolutionary Greek movement of 1821). Mihai Sutu took measures to stop these crimes, defending the entire population of Iasi, including the Jews.

The beginnings of the Moldavian economic modernization imposed the development of local and foreign commerce, small and medium-sized industry, transport, and services. All of this deeply involved the Jewish population, especially in the towns. The Organic Regulations of 1831 legislated new economic and social tendencies, a legislation that would influence the development of the Jewish community.

The Jewish guild of Iasi continued to represent the Jewish population in front of the authorities and undertook the organization and the communal activities of the Jewish community of Iasi and of its institutions. The ancient charters, granted by the Moldavian princes to the Jews of Iasi, confirmed the freedom of commerce and of the trades. The guild was governed by elected leaders and was autonomous in solving its internal problems. The high official was entitled "Rosh Medina." By agreements with the Treasury of the Department of Finance, the guild paid the collective tax of all the Jews, which it would then recover from the tax on kosher meat and similar fees. In view of the deficiencies of the state apparatus, the authorities were interested in having active Jewish community organizations that could make sure of the tax collection.

The ancient charters are only partially known, but complete texts from the 18th century were preserved in totality: The charter granted by Prince Grigore Ghica on May 21, 1741, confirms the existence of ancient charters. It determined that the elected high officials of the Jews will collect the "crupca" ("tacsia, gabela," i.e. tax on the ritual meat), a tax that had to be paid by all Jews, "being for the benefit of all."[11]

At that time "the leaders of the guild" and "together with the whole guild" decided to oppose any outside involvement or other abuses in the election of their own leaders. In a meeting at the Great Synagogue they decided to restore the old custom of electing a single high official, with no right to a tax exemption.[12]

The original document was written in Hebrew and signed by the leaders of the Jewish community and the representatives of the economic guilds of the Jewish artisans and merchants. Here are their names in Romanian transcription of the time: Ursul (= Berl, Bercu), Minas (= Manes), Leiba, Iosif sin Ursul (Iosif ben Dov). Following is a list of the most important persons of the community: Marcu, son-in-law of Iaacov, Lazar, son-in-law of Solomon, Leiba Hotinceanu, Leiba, son-in-law of Ursu, Cerbul (= Hers), son of Moise, another Cerbu, brother of Boroh (= Burah), Lupul Moisei (= Volv, Velvl), Smil, son of Naftule, Leiba, son of Minas, Minas, son-in-law of Leiba, David..., Biniamin..., Iancul......, Avram the tailor, Cerbul, Novac (= Noiah?), Minas from Coroca[13]. In these documents is also mentioned a certain Meier, leader of the Jews.[14] Around 1777 the community was made responsible for the crimes committed by its members: A certain Calmen Cascaval, mentally ill, injured some inhabitants of Iasi. The guild was sentenced to pay for the medical treatment and the material damage. The Court permitted the sale, by the community, of a house owned by Calman, in order to recover its expenses.[15]

The funeral inscriptions give us information about the names of some of the leaders of the Jewish guild from Iasi. High Official Shalom, son of the teacher of the Law, Meir, deceased on 25 Tishri 5489 (October 1728)[16]. The great historian Shmerl ben Shlomo died in Av 5493 (July 1773). High official Josef, son of the Rabbi Ischar Ber, died on 6 Adar 5518 (March 1758)[18]. The leader Tsvi, son of Moshe, died on 2 Shevat 5529 (January 1769). He is mentioned under the Romanized name Cerbu in a document of 1741.[19] Another high official with the same name, son of Simon, died on 26 Elul 5529 (September 1769).[20] A high leader is mentioned on the graves of his sons in 1770.[21] The high official Henemia Segal died on 13 Sivan 5530 (May 1770).[22] The rich and learned high official, the appreciated Shimon ben Baruch, died on 27 Iyar 5532 (May 1772).[23] Another high official, famous for his erudition and charity, Shlomo ben Aziel, died on 4 Adar 5587 (March 1827).[24] These few bits of information can serve as references in establishing the date of some documents.

"Hahambasa"

During the pro-Turkish regime, community life of the Jews of Iasi became more complicated by the naming of a Chief Rabbi, ordered by Constantinople, who bore the Turkish title of the Bash-haham from the Ottoman. "Haham," meaning "wise man" in Hebrew, famous erudite, person able to decide in religious matters, was used as the title for the Chief Rabbi. Prior to that, the election of a religious chief by the representatives of the community was based on the erudition, ethical personality and personal prestige of the person. The pro-Turkish regime had improperly broadened the administrative and organizational competence of the elected person and interfered in establishing the income, the tax exemption and the privileges of the new religious leader, the "haham basha."

According to an unverifiable tradition, the first person named to this post was Rabbi Naftali ben Itzhak who, having cured some high-level Turkish dignitaries of a serious illness, was rewarded with this newly created position in 1724. He died in Constantinople without having exercised his duties. The first documented haham basha was his son, Yeshaya. He was followed by his son, Betzalel, Bezal in Romanian documents, who died on 25 Heshvan 5504 (November 1743). His son, Itzhak, Isac in the Romanian documents, occupied the post of administrator and deputy to his father in Muntenia, and then replaced his father in his post upon his death. In 1754 he had a house in

Targul de Sus on Podu Hagioaiei in Iasi. His appointment was confirmed the same year.

The same Itzhak was given jurisdiction over the Jews of Muntenia. He names as his representative his brother, Yeshaya, who dies in Bucharest in 1765.

After the death of Itzhak, the guild of the Jews of Iasi tried to eliminate the monopoly of the Naftulovici family over the seat of the haham basha, and it succeeded in naming to the vacated post an erudite and venerated rabbi, Mordehai ben Moshe Haim. Alexandru Ghica Voivode appointed "... Marco the Jew ... who is a scholar and knows the law according to their religion and customs...." He exempted him from taxation and he allowed him certain incomes: "... for his position as haham he can earn from weddings, engagements, divorces and from the Jews according to their customs...." He would also collect one leu from every head of household, would adjudicate disputes among Jews with the right of appeal to the Vel Camaras, the superior court for the Jews. Every year three representatives of the guild would be elected.[25]

After Mordehai's death, the position was held by Naftali, which he held until he died in 1808. Through the act of 1793, Naftulea [Naftali] was named haham basha over the whole of Moldova. In the year 1786, he received an order from the Sultan's "High-Chair" to prepare an inventory of a certain dowry, following a specific inheritance. On 17 May 1789 the administration of the Russian occupation reconfirmed him as haham basha. His son Avram took over from 1809 until his death, 12 Shevat 5573 (January 13, 1813). The position was then taken over by his youngest son, Yaakov, who was under the tutelage of his uncle Yeshaya, Shaim in Romanian documents. Yeshaya then succeeded in being named to the position of haham basha, which he held until September 14, 1834, when the post was eliminated by law. Shaim died on 8 Iyar 5600 (May 11, 1840).

Shaim often surpassed his judicial duties, since he oversaw inheritance proceedings, made legalized translations of Hebrew documents, controlled the taxation budget, kept community records, and obtained tax dispensations for his relatives. He became the feudal representative of highest authority of the Jewish population in an era that promoted the modernization of every aspect of life in the Romanian principalities.

The elimination of the position of haham basha unfortunately produced a crisis in the leadership of the Jewish community of Iasi, just when the Jewish population of the capital of Moldova was undergoing some complex quantitative and qualitative changes.[26]

Economic Life in the 18th Century
and the Beginning of the 19th Century

The contribution of the Jews of Iasi to the development of commerce and trade was very important. "Trade of wine and brandy has been almost exclusively Jewish since the 17th century."[27] "The other merchandise that filled the small Jewish shops was: tobacco, cotton, iron, rice, ropes, copper, boots, pots, salt – peasant household objects."[28] Later trade developed with the large Galician center of Brody. Some Jews of Brody settled in Iasi and built their own synagogue. G. Zane remarked, "Even before the 18th century, a determining role in the commerce of Moldova has been attributed to the Jews, or at least of Iasi."[29]

Some foreign travelers, such as the Hungarian Mikes Kelemen in 1739 and the Greek Katsaitis Marcos Antonios in 1742, attest to the Jewish importance in the commerce of Iasi. The Jewish merchants of Iasi dealt with the export and import of merchandise. Their importance grew after the peace treaty of Kuciuk Kainardji of 1774, when the Turkish monopoly over the Romanian commerce decreased.

Let us take a detailed look at the occupations of the Jews of Iasi. In 1777 there are the shops of the Jewish silversmiths Iosef and Moise. In 1793 "the Bear," the Jew from the town of Tirgul de Sus "the Upper Market," took over a brewery in Podu Ros with "... a few houses paying 350 lei." It was to be inherited by his son Leib in 1817.

The Jewish bakers and pretzel makers knew how to respect certain ritualistic stipulations. There is a Jewish pretzel maker in 1774, according to information in the documents of that time.

Jewish haymakers had their own guild in 1820. By 1831 the number had grown to 59.

Bricklayers had their own synagogue in the 19th century (in 1838, on a street later named the Functionarilor (Clerks') Street).

Jewish watchmakers were held in high esteem. In 1763 there was an Aron, famous in the trade. In 1764 a watchmaker came from Ham Tatar. In 1762 a Jew Danila worked for Boyars (nobility). In 1794, the shop of the watchmaker Moise from Ulita Mare (Big Street) was valued at 375 lei.

Some carriage makers were also known, among whom an Aron Subar was working in 1798.

The Jewish hatters were especially sought after in the population of the city. In 1777 the master Vigder worked for the family of the boyar Iancu Canta. The Samaria Jew "... works for the manor-house and receives 3,800 lei." The guild membership was strengthened in 1796, when it opened its ranks to tailors.

There were many shoemakers in Iasi in the beginning of the 19th century. They had their own guild, and their leadership (Pinkas) was strengthened on Tuesday 5 Av 5569 (July 18, 1809) by the renowned Iasi Rabbis Apter Rav and Zvolever Rav. The statutes set the rules for relationships among masters, apprentices, piece workers and other workers. There were rules governing different aspects of family life and respect for rituals. There were rules for electing the leadership of the guild, disciplinary measures to be taken against infractions, and dates were set for communal festivals. The guild's synagogue was still functioning in 1829. In 1831 there were in Iasi four Jewish master shoemakers and 145 Jewish bootmakers (for peasants and modest workers).

The Jewish tailors guild still existed in the year 1797, being united with the hatters. Its register was renewed in 1814.

"Doftors," or rather popular doctors, also existed in small communities. Certain dignitaries had Jewish learned doctors. In 1774 a doctor Iosap was registered. A Jewish woman doctor practiced in 1798. In 1803 Doctor Meier was remembered; in 1820 – Doctor Avram. Zelig Rosenkrantz was known in Iasi in 1824 and it was known that he came from Galicia some 10 years earlier. He was 27 years old, he dressed traditionally and he was considered a "Jew doctor." In 1832 a "Doctor Perit" leased the Scolbalteni Estate. Soon thereafter cadres of Jewish doctors with superior medical schooling appeared and contributed to the development of the medical school of Iasi.

In 1845 there were many Jewish barrel-makers and coopers. Their number rose to 62. As early as 1737 Cerbul the Jew was exempt from paying taxes because he made barrels for members of the nobility.

In 1774 there was a lantern maker named Avram. Jewish masters worked on lamp-posts to light the streets of Iasi in the next century.

Jewish butchers strictly adhered to all ritual laws. They were bound by tenant's taxes, to the demands of the haham and to some abusive measures of the local authorities.

The role of Jewish musicians (fiddlers) is recognized in Romanian folklore music. In 1741 a Solomon Tambalaru complained that two horses were stolen from him. Supposedly his troupe was traveling with the carriage through the country. Their guild also had its own synagogue.

Jewish seal engravers were renowned. An Iancu Pecetaru also worked on crafting pieces of precision mechanics.

Jewish stonecutters were not lacking either; in 1704 there was mention of a Jew who worked at Repedea, the quarry.

Under the name of glass-man were merchants and/or glaziers who went to people's homes to install glass. In 1774 there were four Jewish glass-men in Iasi. In 1778 a glass-man named Isac sold 66 glass panes to a certain boyer, which of course, he also installed.

Jews also play an important role in the transportation of merchandise. In 1820 "for ordinary needs one still goes ... to the Jewish carriages, real stage-coaches that travel from Iasi to Galati."[30] In the year 1845, in Iasi, there were 79 "Jewish waggoners, carriage drivers and coachmen."[31] In 1828 a French traveler figured that in order to travel from Iasi to Leipzig it was more comfortable to use the Jewish carriages than to wait by the Danube for the ship from Vienna.[32]

The role of Jewish artisans in the development of small industries of the time is well known. Some produced alcoholic drinks. Jews were accused because the spirits produced in the distilleries encouraged alcoholism and decreased their import. As early as 1737, Grigore Ghica exempted the Jew Cerbul from Iasi, the son of the doorkeeper, from paying taxes "because he made vodka for the nobles."

Jews were pioneers in the paper industry of Hirlau and in the production of gunpowder; they were the first to manage steam mills and mechanical workshops. They were also first to create the modern organization of credit, insurance companies, postal service, etc.

{29-39}

MOMENTS FROM THE MODERN ERA
The Interim Years 1831-1869

The dissolution of the Ottoman monopoly over Moldavian commerce – beginning in the year 1774 and formally ending with the peace pact at Adrianopol in 1828, led to a modernized economy, a stronger relationship between cities and towns and contributed to the progress of existing urban settlements and the founding of new localities. In the county of Iasi new settlements were created – Podu Iloaiei (1818), Bivolari (1834), Sculeni, Poieni – all with an overwhelming Jewish population. The Jewish population in older cities also grew: Hirlau, Targul Frumos and, naturally, Iasi. The census of 1831 confirms that there were 17,570 Jews, the one of 1838 – 29,052, and in the year of the Union, 1859, there were 31,015 Jews living in Iasi.

This demographic growth occurred in the backdrop of the general demographic growth of the localities, although there were grave and frequent discriminatory measures taken by the ruling lords, such as Mihai Sturza, known for his pecuniary greed. Some social strata – the small mushrooming Christian bourgeoisie, anchored in various occupations – also applied certain pressures. Civil servants demonstrated hostile attitudes, abuses, and acts of corruption. Their real aim was usually to extort money from the Jewish merchant or craftsman. The vagrant law, for example, caused expulsions of many "vagrant hobos" – who in fact were clerks or craftsmen, with their own homes inherited from their parents. The abuse was redeemed through corruption.

The romanticist participants to the Movement of 1848 had on their program "the gradual emancipation of the Moldavian Jewry." Regardless of their intentions, this remained a simple case of wishful thinking and never became a reality, as concluded by the French historian, Prof. Carol Iancu.

The Organization of the Community

The dissolution of the "Jewish guild" demanded a new form of organization. When the new city councils were created, Jews were able to participate in their leadership. After some time, the mushrooming bourgeoisie got rid of "foreign" competitors and, of course, the foreign citizens. The system of collecting taxes from every resident gradually lessened the interest of the authorities in the organization of the Jewish community. Neither was the Jewish population of Iasi able to escape the inertia. The Jewish foreign subjects, being exempt of paying taxes before the changes, tried to organize their own taxing union, with their own haham; however, the new fiscal rules of the treasury forced them to pay the general tax like everyone else.

In 1824 Marco Marcovici and Volf Moscovici were leaders of the native Jews. Solomon Rozenstein was the leader of "Camara gospod" (the financial department). A document of 1826 was signed by Moise sin Eliezer, leader in Iasi. On September 16, 1830 the authorities offered the leadership of the community to some of their prominent persons: Zisu Caufman, Hascal Botosaneanul, Leiba Asler, Nahman Botosaneanul, and Leiba Carniol. In 1831 the Jewish guild, headed by Iancu sin Leiba, informed the treasury that it could not pay, at that time, the debt of 4,000 gold coins from past years, since the occupying Russian army charged them large sums of money.

In 1831 the banker Michel Daniel was charged with forming a leadership committee of the community. He tried to attract the famous Iancu Leiba and other respected members of the community. But most of them declined the offer for personal reasons.

The economic and administrative modernization raised many problems for the Jewish population. Several Jewish leaders, influenced by the rationalistic ideas of the haskala (enlightenment), agreed in 1849 to form a committee of leadership of the Jewish community of Iasi. The overseers were: the banker Israel Haim Daniel, his son Michel, the pioneer of modern credit in Moldova, Leiba Cana, great merchant and banker, prominent merchants such as Isac Wexler, Naftuli Caufman, Solomon Herman, Moise Hers Cahana, Simon Saraga, Simon Leib Schwarz and the famous banker and businessman Leibis Mayorhoffer. In spite of the new leadership stability was not achieved. The situation got worse due to the unstable economic and legislative situation in the second half of the 19th century.

An article in the Hebrew newspaper *Hamagid* from Lyk[33] mentions that after 1829 the Jewish community of Iasi was to be governed by leaders confirmed for 3 years by the country's Government. These leaders had almost unlimited authority. They were even permitted to decide civil cases among Jews.

An analysis of the existing historical information of this period leads to the conclusion that the situation of the Jews of Iasi was more favorable than that of the Jews of Galicia, which perhaps explains the demographic development, as well as the abundant information contained in the documents of the time and in pages of Romanian literature.

The Jewish community had the obligation to organize its own institutions. The meeting of the leaders of 6 March 1855 decided that the elections for the community's committee would be done through the 23 leaders of the Jewish economic guilds. Twenty-two – representatives of the community would be added to help them – appointed by the local authorities. The election would take place every two years at the community's headquarters. The elected leaders would be recognized by an official document.

Later on the budget of the community's Administration would have to be approved by the Administrative Council of Moldavia.

The elected leaders didn't manage the financial difficulties and their activity stagnated. The elections took place every two years in spite of the stagnation. There are minutes preserved from the elections of 1861 and 1863. The elected leaders would appoint the administrators of the schools and institutions, follow their activities, check the finance of the community, and have the right to introduce new taxes...

The years went by and the activity of the community oscillated because the elected officials were not prepared to work permanently for the well-being of the community. We can say that after 1866 the management of the community was inoperative.

The Sudits

A few decades after 1774 – "sudits" (foreign subjects), mainly Russians, but also Austrians, Prussians, later French and English, living in Moldavia, presented difficult problems to the country – while Jewish "sudits" increased the difficulties of the Jewish community. Having certain privileges – a result of the Kuciuk-Kaindargi peace – tax exemptions, consular jurisdiction, the "sudits" were at times in a situation more favorable than the natives.

In 1820-1821 there were 1451 Christian and 484 Jewish foreign subjects living in Moldavia.

The Jewish Sudits used their privileges in contact with the Jewish Community.

Thus, in 1796 Jewish Russian subjects refused to pay the increased ritual meat tax. A compromise was finally reached. Frequent confrontations took place, but ultimately the Sudits integrated themselves within the general organization of the entire Jewish population of Iasi.[34]

The Economic Life

After 1831 the Jews of Iasi continued their intense modernization of the economic activity. "The technique of the Jewish commerce is intended to bring in the clients... The Romanian shopkeeper waits for the customer to enter his shop, according to the traditional method, conducting a quiet life with many parties." The Jewish commerce was innovative and encountered "...hostility from the traditionalists. The Jews strive to increase their current clientele and for the development of a new one by stopping and tempting those that pass nearby and by lowering prices."[35]

"The Jewish merchants are disciplined and cautious and they put new products on sale, for example rabbit skins."[36]

As for tradesmen, we mention Gheorghe Asachi's finding that the graduates of the Trade School in Iasi, which was intended to encourage trading amongst the non-Jews, did not turn to the trades, but instead took low paying employment.

Some demographic data helps us to better grasp the economic structure of the Jews of Iasi in the studied period. In 1832 - from the total population of Iasi of 48,314, the Jews numbered 17,032 - as noted by E. Negruzzi in the study *Populatie si societate* ("Population and Society") vol. I, published in Cluj in 1972.

In 1844, there were 6,168 Jews listed in the census, namely: 2,073 merchants, 2,219 tradesmen, 860 journeymen and servants. Other professions were: kosher butchers - 5, teachers - 30, rabbi - 1, clerk - 1, cantors – 6, rabbi assistant – 1, grave diggers – 4, secretary – 1.[37]

In 1851, 1,169 Jewish merchants and 1,430 tradesmen of various professions were active in Iasi. Journeymen and servants were only 606.[38]

The Jewish economic guilds continued to exist as professional unions, defending the interests of the guild members. In 1885 there were 23 Jewish guilds in Iasi, namely: brass workers and bricklayers, grocers, coopers, butchers (their leader was M. Rozenstein), innkeepers, tailors (leader: Iosap sin Markovici). There were also harness makers, saddlers, carters, bakers, musicians, hatters (leader Fishl), shoemakers (Hevra Sandlers), street vendors, carpenters (leader Aron), fur and cap makers, upholsterers, old-clothes dealers, money changers, house painters and five leaders with no guild mentioned.

In 1845 more than 2073 Jews were involved in 11 different fields of commerce, "overrepresented in some of them."[39]

The contribution of the Iasi Jews to the modernization of Moldavia was not political but of an economical nature, evidently efficient and noted by the researchers of the specified historical period.

The Cultural Life

In the first half of the 19th century the cultural life was dominated by two important trends: the Hassidism, the popular one, and the Haskala, the enlightened one, specific to the Jews of Southeast and Eastern Europe.

The Hassidic Movement

An ancient local tradition indicates that the Baal Shem Tov, the father of the Hassidic Movement, might have been born on Moldavian territory, in the north of Bucovina. In reality he was born in Galicia near the border with Bucovina. It is very possible that during his wanderings in the Carpathians he might have reached the surroundings of the town of Piatra Neamt. However, it is definitely known that the Hassidic movement became popular in Moldavia, especially in Iasi, around 1775. Here the "tzadik" Arie Leibish Volcinsker was rabbi for some time, then departed for the Holy Land and left his son Iosef Ioshke as rabbi.

Between 1805 and 1813 the Rabbinical leadership of the Iasi community was held by "the famous Apter Rav," Rabbi Avraham Iohoshua Heshl (1756-1825), nicknamed "Ohev Israel" (The Lover of Israel) – after the title of his main work. He kept in touch with the Iasi Community even after his not so voluntary departure. His influence competed for a while with that of the Hassidic Movement BABAD.

It is intriguing that the above mentioned movement – which promoted the intensive study along with the profound, authentic religious way of life and the picturesque popular behavior – could find an interest in the Jewish masses of Moldavia, which were characterized by their piety and observance of ritual regulations. Later the BABAD movement established roots in the whole of Moldavia – where synagogues appeared bearing the name of the movement, or HABOD in the local Yiddish phonetics. The adherents of the movement were called "habotnics," hence the appearance in the Romanian language of the word *habotnic*, meaning pious or fanatic.

In 1813 the famous Tzadiks (venerated Hassidic Rabbis) Levi Itzchak Bardichever, his son Itzchak from Pikow, Rabbi Chaim from Moghilev, also known as Reb Chaim Czernowitzer, met at a rabbinic wedding in Iasi. The later also held rabbinic office in Botosani. On Friday night they worshiped in the ancient Sinagoga Mare (Great Synagogue, inaugurated as such in 1670). Here 2000 Hassidim gathered to meet them, denoting the importance of the meeting.

Another great Rabbi, Zvolever Rav, held office in Iasi until 1831. A synagogue on Cucu Street was named after him and continued to exist until 1944, when it was bombed. Between 1837 and 1853 Litiner Rav, whom the people called "Baal Nes" (miracle maker), held office in Iasi.

The Iasi Community was of a great importance in the Principalities. That can be seen in the documents which mention the visit to Iasi of the tzadik Israel Rujiner, the founder of the Sadagura center. He was hosted by the banker Michel Daniel and thousands of Jews came from Moldavia to Iasi to receive his blessing. It is known that the followers of Israel Rujiner founded Hassidic communities in Stefanesti, Buhusi, Adjud and Galati.

The importance of the Moldavian Hassidic movement is also seen in the domain of typography. Between 1842 and 1843 a number of Hassidic books in Hebrew and Yiddish were printed at Gheorghe Asachi's printing house "Albina."

Since the import of religious books was profitable, it lasted for awhile. Later, a group of Jewish leaders formed a partnership with Gheorghe Asachi, providing him with types and specialized typesetters. After awhile T. Codreanu's printing house also printed prayer books in Hebrew.

Haskala

The rationalistic, reforming, secularizing movement of the Jewish enlightment, the Haskala, appears in a restricted circle in the second third of the 19th century. It was founded in Germany by Moses Mendelssohn. It had its beginnings in the 18th century. In Germany Haskala led to assimilation or baptism, a reform that was brought about by economic and cultural modernization.

Haskala spread into Central and Eastern Europe, the Habsburg Empire, Poland, Ukraine, the Romanian states, etc.

In the areas we are dealing with, Haskala stressed the importance of knowing the German language, perfecting the reading and writing of the Romanian language, and the establishment of Jewish primary schools. These schools offered the study of Torah and Jewish prayer, as well as secular studies following the curricula of Romanian schools. In Iasi the watchmaker Uhrman was a *maskil* (supporter of the Haskala).

In 1847 some reformers tried to wear European suits ("German clothes"), but throngs of the pious demonstrated against them. These reformers (Finckelstein) were also the pioneers of the first modern schools, which, along with traditional studies, taught the curriculum of modern Romanian schools.

Jewish school reform in Iasi would have to wait another decade to score its first success. Even the attempt of a newspaper in Yiddish and Romanian did not last for more than eleven issues.

Beniamin Schwarzfeld (1822-1896) played an important role in the creation of modern Jewish schools. Father of the well-known historians and journalists Moses, Wilhelm, and Dr. Elias Schwarzfeld, he was a scholar and an inspiring force in the cultural development of the Jewish population of Iasi.

Moritz Schwartz contributed greatly to the area of teaching. He was a school headmaster and inspector, as well as the author of many teaching manuals that were used in state-run schools. The troubadour Velvl Zbarjer-Ehrenkranz was also well known. Originally from Galicia, he was an author, composer and interpreter in Yiddish and Hebrew. He was a popular rhapsodist who performed at weddings and family gatherings, holidays, and at restaurants and summer gardens in Jewish neighborhoods.

Zbarjer also satirized aspects of Hassidism of questionable authenticity in tzaddikism, the abuses of the wealthy, and immoral behavior. He was much appreciated in Iasi – he was in fact a precursor of Avram Goldfaden, the creator of the professional, permanent, modern, educational Yiddish theater. The creation of modern Yiddish theater was an important moment for the world Yiddish culture of the 19th century. It should be noted that Yiddish theater began in the "Pomul Verde" [The Green Tree] summer garden, which became famous in the history of the city of Iasi.

In the domain of learning, the publication of two Hebrew books is to be noted. The first, in a moderate rationalist spirit was "Darca shel Tora" ("The Way of the Torah") by Zvi Mendel Pineles of Galati (1806-1871). It was published in Iasi in 1864 by the Hersh Goldner Printing House. The banker and scholar from Iasi, Moshe Waldberg (1829-1901), future father-in-law of the great linguist H. Tiktin, reacted along traditional lines to this publication with his own polemic work "Cakh hi darca shel Tora" ("This Is the Way of Torah").

The development of the city of Iasi paved the way for the Jewish population towards modern culture, and a more intense and efficient enlightenment. In 1855 we see a Romanian primer printed especially for Jews by Mihail Vitlimescu, a converted Jew. A similar primer was printed in 1862 by Gusti's printing shop.

The Finkelstein enlighteners succeeded in maintaining a modern primary school in Iasi in the years 1853-1857, despite some pressure from the traditionalists, who predominated Jewish community life. The inspiring presence of Wilhelm Schwarzfeld, deceased prematurely, resulted in two Jewish schools, one in Tg. (Tirgul) Cucului, the other on Ulita Mare (the Big

Street). The tendency toward the modernization of education is even more evident. In 1861 the Jews of the Pacurari district asked to have a modern school built. In 1864-1866 three such schools existed in a different district, in Podu Ros. In spite of the many difficulties, elementary education, modeled after Romanian public schools, became more widespread. Schools would become more numerous, the subject matter more diversified – all of this contributing to a widening scope of knowledge for Jewish students.

It should be noted that some maskilim from Galicia, residing in Iasi, also published in the Hebrew press of Central and Eastern Europe. Numerous letters, written in Iasi, constitute today a rich source of historical information. Despite some modernistic elements found in them, social and religious problems were dealt with along traditional lines.

{40-64}

Walking Through the Centuries

The history of Romania in the period 1859-1918 took a decisive path towards a modern economy, within the framework of European democracy and stability. The unresolved problem of the peasantry, deficiencies in the electoral system, remnants of a xenophobic mentality ably used in political life, brought about difficult times in the development of the Jewish community. The politics of Romanian governments justified the conclusion of a modern-day researcher, Leon Volovici: "...After 1880 anti-Semitism in Romania becomes a current social and political phenomenon... For foreign observers, Romanian society gives the impression, from here on, of a generalized anti-Semitic environment..."[40]

According to the Great Geographic Dictionary of Romania (vol. 4, 1901, p. 25), in 1899 the city of Iasi had a population of 59,427 inhabitants, of whom 33,141 were "Israelites." Two thirds of the Jewish population worked in commerce and trades (tailors, shoemakers, bricklayers, carpenters, blacksmiths...). In the industrial domain Jews owned several factories – one umbrella factory, one cardboard factory, two soda factories, one chair factory, several for manufacturing candles and soap, one beer factory, two steam flour mills, and several horse-driven flour mills.

The development of the Jewish community was reflected in its demographic growth. According to the last census of the 19th century the Jewish population in Iasi numbered 39,441 people, almost 51% of the total population. By 1910 the number had decreased to 35,000, due to years of economic crisis, discriminatory laws, and emigration.

Demographic growth after 1866 was not only the result of natural progression. The Jews that had been driven out of villages went to Iasi, where the misery of these pillaged refugees could be somewhat alleviated with the help of the urban Jewish community, which was somewhat better off. Even after the Treaty of Berlin (1878), which strongly recommended, although inefficiently, the emancipation of Jews, the anti-Jewish politics continued and even intensified, underlining the above-mentioned process.

Economic congresses organized by xenophobic nationalists aimed to destroy the Jewish commerce – not through lawful competition, but rather through abusive measures. In 1890-1892 stronger measures were taken against Jewish tradesmen. Nevertheless, in 1906, 3048 Jewish artisans worked alongside 2150 Romanians and 1125 foreign citizens. There were 3404 Jewish merchants and 836 Orthodox Christian merchants. In 1909

Jews were 77% of the total craftsmen of Iasi, a strong indication of the Jewish contribution to the development of the city.

The governments were neglecting the "Jew town," affecting its general development. Anti-Semitic turmoil was promoted by some university professors – from the time of S. Barnutiu (1806-1864), and to an even greater extent by the philosopher Vasile Conta (1846-1889), whose works were published by the well-known editors and printers of that time – the brothers Saraga. Only Titu Maiorescu did not involve himself with university pogromism, despite the fact that the majority of the Junimists (ed. note: members of the cultural, literary and political movement of the second half of the 19th century, arising from the "Junimea," "The Youth," society of Iasi), with the exception of P. P. Carp, were active anti-Semites.

Between 1890 and 1899, student demonstrations took place inaugurating the "glorious" decades of anti-Semitic brutality in institutions of higher learning. It is known that in this period even Nicolae Iorga was associated with A. C. Cuza; later N. Iorga denounced Cuza's methods.

In the beginning of the 1920s the University of Iasi became a turbulent, devastating center of anti-Semitism. Extremists formed the "Iron Guard," a source of many assaults. It is not surprising that in this atmosphere, the humiliating, absurd medieval type oath named "more judaico" was not abolished until 1911. Anti-Semitic activity is also seen during the war of 1916-1918 (World War I), even though 22,000 Jews served until the end.

The Community Organization

After the abolition of the tax on kosher meat, in 1863, the community organization lacked stability. A central leadership was no longer chosen for the community of Iasi. Some institutions became autonomous, although they were not recognized by the authorities, thus not legalized. The only legal Jewish institution, which was entitled to possess sums of money and income from donations and even lands, was the Jewish Community. These rights were based on old charters. An item from the Iasian newspaper *Progressul* (Progress) of February 23, 1866[41] informs that "The trusteeship of the hospital and of the Israelite community of Iasi invites a bid for the tax on kosher wine that is brought into the city; guarantee: 100 galbeni (gold coins)." The announcement is repeated twice. The lease began on September 1, 1866.

The Community encountered many difficulties when purchasing the land for the Pacurari Cemetery, because it was located on territory belonging to the rural community of Tg. Copou, where Jews were not allowed to own land. The cemetery land was purchased in the name of the Israelite Hospital.

The leadership of the Community was held by the printer Hers Goldner, devoted community activist, and Wolf Wasserman. They succeeded in buying the land for the cemetery for 40,000 lei.

The Israelite Hospital became a top-ranking institution in the life of the Jewish community. In 1903 it sent its new charter to the Ministry of the Interior for approval... In 1916 Moritz Wachtel, the trustee of the hospital, was in fact the president of the Jewish Community of Iasi.

In 1914 the tax on kosher meat was reinstated, with the resulting income going to the hospital and the community. After the Law of Worship of 1923 the hospital became a community institution. (In 1891 the hospital had seceded from the community because of the disputes between the Hahams.) Its leadership represented the Jews of Iasi until 1919, when the representatives of all synagogues and Jewish institutions convened to name a provisionary counsel. The new statutes of the community were approved at a general assembly.

The abolition of the Hahambasha post did not necessarily signify the end of the influence of the Iasi Rabbinate. The changing times called for people who understood the necessity of adopting suitable measures in line with the new economic, socio-political, and cultural situation of the entire country. Unfortunately, the majority of the rabbis of Iasi, overwhelmed by personal problems, did not contribute sufficiently to the consolidation of community institutions. There were some noteworthy exceptions.

The learned rabbi Iosef ben Menachem Landa, who held office in the years 1837-1853, was the author of the collection of rabbinical thought *Birhat Iosef*, printed in Lvov in the year 5628 (1869). He was the inspiring force behind rabbinical studies in Iasi.

Another erudite and prolific author was Aharon M. Taubes, who was rabbi in the years 1837-1852. Of great significance was his collection of thought (Sheelot u Teshuvot) *Carnei Roam*.

Then there was Shmuel Shmelke Taubes, rabbi in 1852-1865, author of the popular book *Haiei Olam*. His brother, Iacov Taubes, was rabbi in 1868-1890 in the Podu Ros district. He was followed by the son of Shmuel Shmelke, Uri Feivel Shraga Taubes. They were both Chief Rabbis of Iasi. The latter was rabbi for four decades and published *Uri veieishi* – rabbinic thought (Lvov, 1887).

Ieshaia Shor, a partisan of strict ritual practice, lived over 100 years and published numerous theological writings. Remarkable among them is a cabalistic commentary on the Pentateuch.

Among the supporters of the Habad movement was Rabbi Berl Rabinovici Berlader, who died in Iasi in 1914.

Among the more modern rabbis were Armand Levy from Alsace, well-known rabbi of Temple Neuschotz, as well as the eminent man of culture and thought, Dr. Iaacov Nemirower – who was Chief Rabbi of Romania between the two World Wars, senator and the true leader of the Romanian Judaism.

The calligrapher Shmuel Laivand, deceased 23 Kislev 5641 (1880), left behind a treatise on the subtleties of sacred Hebrew calligraphy, a mystical Hassidic commentary.

In 1915 the rabbi of the Iasi community was Dr. Meir Thenen – who was also known for his religious publications.

Other rabbis of this period were Meir Gotesman, deceased in the winter of 1916, and Dov Ber Rabinovici, also known as Folticener Rebe (rabbi of Folticeni), deceased January 1, 1865.

The descendants of the tzaddik Bardicever distinguished themselves through their moral stand and their extensive knowledge. Israel Gutman (1820-1894) is the author of the book *Beit Israel*, published in Iasi in 1910. His son, Shalom, continued the religious work of his father. In turn, Shalom's sons, Israel and Menahem, were rabbis in Iasi after WWII, until they made aliya.

The Jewish educational institutions

The development of the economic life in Romania required of Jews a better knowledge in writing and reading, natural sciences, history and geography. The Governments were striking against the Jewish "competition" through discriminating laws and orders to hinder the efforts of the shopkeepers and artisans to survive this difficult period.

The instability of the organization inside the Jewish community was also contributing to the gravity of the situation – but the Jews of Iasi still participated in the development of the city and of the localities in the neighbourhood of Iasi. There was a noticeable progression in the organization of social, cultural and public institutions.

"The Jewish school was one of these institutions that turned more and more to the track of modernization. It had to include in its program the subjects approved for the public education system by the respective Ministry. The religious education was taught in 1895 in 46 Talmud Toras. New schools were required to continue the traditional religious teaching as well."

The School of Tg. Cucului, famous in the cultural life of Iasi, later called "Junimea," continued even after 1864-1866. Between 1870 and 1875 they bought a suitable building for 2,000 gold coins. The building was improved in 1896 with the support of the Society I. C. A., a philanthropic society from Paris. This society had an important role in the improvement of Jewish education in Romania – during many decades.

The School for girls belonging to the "Congregation of the Israelite Women Society" – founded in 1867 by the same Parisian society – had a curriculum quite similar to the Romanian public schools. Supported by the wives of affluent Jews – the school imposed itself into the spiritual life of the city. It is known that Fanny Neuschatz made a donation of 1,000 gold coins, money used to renovate the school. In 1890 the Rabbi Dr. Nemirover and Dr. Carpel Lippe were leaders of a commercial business school. The teachers were: Scherzer, Nesker, Geiger, Weisselberg, and Brandmark.

In the same year was founded the Society "Cultura." The provisional steering committee had Leon Daniel as president and Dr. Haiman Tiktin, the great Romanian philosopher, as vice-president, and N. Weisengrun, famous supporter of the Jewish school, as secretary.

In October 1894 the Committee reported that 6 months after the founding of the school there were 600 students in 5 sections of the 1st grade class, 4 sections of the 2nd grade class and one section each of the 3rd and 4th grade classes. There were 6 Romanian and 7 Jewish teachers. On Saturday the students went to the Synagogue. Hebrew was taught with translation to Romanian, not to Yiddish as it usually was before. The poor students received their Romanian and Hebrew manuals for free.

The School No.1, located at 15 Strada Alba, had 230 students. The School No.2 (15 Palat Street) had 155 students. In the 1st grade class were 47 girls and 34 boys.

The schools of the society "Cultura" were still functioning even in the pre-war conditions of 1940, demonstrating a long and prestigious activity. To help the budget of the schools, the Jews of Iasi organized fundraising balls.

There were also other known schools in Iasi. For example in 1915, the school "Steaua" (The Star) was founded by the lodge "Bnei Brit." The higher grade religious schools were functioning as a continuation of the elementary schools named above.

In 1909 Talmud Tora was closed down by the authorities because it didn't teach the students in Romanian. The measure was taken in spite of the fact that the children were also going to a Romanian elementary school – as required by the Law of the Education.

A Jewish high school was founded by "Moritz Wachtel" during this period. In 1913/1914 the high school had 140 students: the next year 197. It is important to note that all these students passed the examination for entry into a Romanian public school. The building of this school was renovated in 1918; the following years the curriculum was improved. The compulsory study of the Hebrew and Jewish History were introduced in 1920. The school became very well known.

After WWI the Jews obtained the right to become Romanian citizens and were allowed to attend the public schools; the Jewish schools could also issue certificates recognized by the authorities. This new situation had a large influence on the structure and number of schools.

At the beginning of the 20th century the Jewish schools were fighting to survive. In 1903, a committee of intellectuals, Rabbi Dr. Nemirower, Dr. Steuerman-Rodion, engineer, Finklestein, Dr. Blumenfeld, and lawyer Con-Dracsaneanu, supported the society "Cultura" and its schools.

The school "Junimea" No. 2 was threatened with being closed down because the building was not adequate. Other Jewish schools were in danger of being closed, however they continued to exist under very difficult conditions until after WWI, when they became officially recognized.

The Economic Life

The economic status of the Jews from Iasi was concentrated in crafts, commerce, industry, transportation, insurance and credit, because they couldn't have a public job. Also they were not allowed to work in State industry (Railroads, Post Offices, State Education). Some of these serious problems were solved by massive emigration, especially after 1900.

The official demographic data were contested many times. The population of Iasi in 1871 was estimated by "Curierul de Yassi"[42] to include 36,000 Christians and 39,000 Jews. In 1876 others estimated that in Iasi there were 30,000 Christians and 46,000 Jews, figures evidently biased. The author of the article from the above mentioned newspaper indicated that the large number of young marriages, a higher birth rate, a higher degree of hygiene, and a small number of alcoholics, were factors in the large number of Jews.

But the fundamental problem was the economic status of the Jewish population in relation to the growing Christian population of the town. There were anti-Semitic movements and discriminatory legislation against the Jews – measures that led to unfair competition.

In the last decades of the 19th century, economists, politicians, and prominent citizens from Iasi, insisted upon the modernization of the handicrafts and the creation of a national industry. Mainly, a food industry and handicraft branches like: furniture manufacture, clothes manufacture, industry for metallic items, and tools for domestic use. The oil industry started to develop. The results are seen in the "Ancheta Industriala" (Industrial Investigator) in 1901-1902. The 1906 Exhibition - at the 40th anniversary of the King Carol I – shows the country's developments in the mentioned industries. At this exhibition Jewish craftsmen also participated. Some products received prizes. However the economic status of the Jews from Iasi remained precarious.

Sometimes, emigration was the solution. Between 1899-1914 more than 62,813 Jews emigrated. The beginning of the intense emigration started in 1881-1882, when the first Jewish Emigration Society was founded.

In the mean time, the Romanian Authorities made up special registers for the Jewish emigrants who left Romania for America.

In 1887 a law against the peddlers destroyed the businesses of 5,000 Jewish families and emigration increased. On 5 Aug 1884 a 2nd group of 2,022 Jewish emigrants left Iasi, most of them craftsmen. In 1889 the 3rd group of 1,393 left the town. In 1900 the number increased to 6,683 and in 1914 to almost 7,000.

A dramatic episode occurred in 1900-1901, when the Jews started to emigrate by foot, a hopeless action with unbelievable results. This dramatic episode started in Barlad, where the poor Jews walked toward the border with Transylvania. They had only a few wagons with luggage. In some villages the peasants helped them. This movement became known by artistic manifestation like amateur shows and distribution of leaflets, written in Yiddish and Romanian. In this way, Jews from all the corners of Romania walked to Hamburg, where Jewish philanthropic organizations helped them reach America.

The emigrants from Iasi spread 4 kinds of leaflets:

1. JEWISH BROTHERS (goodbye), May 1900;
2. THE TRAVELERS FROM IASI, in Yiddish, 30 May 1900;
3. THE WANDERERS SOCIETY Lev Echod, July 1900;
4. THE JEWISH CRAFTSMEN APPEAL (354 family heads and 1,500 family members) June 1902.

To better understand the gravity of this situation, we mention that in this period, the number of the Jewish craftsmen was 4.5 fold higher than the other nationalities in Romania. In Moldavia, the Jews represented 90% of the total craftsmen; tailors, ironsmiths, slightly less being shoemakers, in transportation, commission, watchmakers, dairy products, hatters, greengroceries, masons and stove makers[43]. In the former Iasi district (judet), 75% of the merchants were Jews. This was illustrated on the Stefan cel Mare Street in 1890, based upon a list written by Rudolf Sutu[44]. Starting from the Gh. Asachi monument toward the center of the city there were:

1. The haberdashery shop Schwan;
2. The house of Albert Daniel;
3. The old firm of manufacturing Lupu Carniol;
4. The shop Berman;
5. La ville de Bucarest. The textile shop of the brothers Polinger, who had a subsidiary in Piata Unirii;
6. The Cahane textile shop (still existing in 1930);
7. The jeweller Iosefsohn;
8. The Neuschatz bank (still existing in 1930);
9. The second-hand bookshop Cuperman;
10. The Daniel bookstore (later he moved to the City Hall street;
11. The brothers Schwartz – in the Braunstein houses;
12. The haberdashery Cornfeld, in Piata Unirii;
13. Photo Weiss, street Lapusneanu;
14. The jeweller Guillaume Nahowski;
15. The Tiktin houses (near Banu Church) – with the Music shop Hirsch and Finke;
16. The wine storehouse Mos Berl;
17. The bakers Itic Ber and Albert Moscovici

Naturalization

In the period 1870-1916 one important challenge was, aside from economic ones, the civil and political emancipation of Jews born and raised in the country, Jews who had completed military service, some of them in the war of 1916. The status of "foreigners not subject to any foreign state" had to be resolved.

The lack of civil rights had a negative influence on the economic life and was humiliating from the social, cultural, national and political points of view. The Jewish intellectual circles had started the struggle for emancipation early. They brought proof of the length of time the Jewish population had lived in Iasi, indicated the role of the Jews in the economic development and underlined their own tendency for assimilation, which, for some, did not exclude baptism.

The most active of these groups was "The General Association of Native Israelites" from Bucharest, people who had completed their military service.

Branches were founded all over the country. Through the press and public debates, a large popularization of the need for Jewish emancipation was achieved, despite the government's harshening of the laws and measures concerning the situation of the Jewish population.

The fever of assimilation remained limited to a small circle, but it would indirectly and involuntarily contribute to the intensification of the consciousness of ethnic and social belonging.

Zionist ideas existed in Iasi as early as the 19th century. The influence of Dr. Karpel Lippe is known starting in 1860 until 1913. In 1878 B. Schwartzfeld, M. Braustein-Mibashan, and N. Frenkel promoted the Hebrew culture and language. Around 1880 an E. Frankel was known to be active on a national level.

In the year 1882 the first committee of "The Association for Eretz Israel" was elected in Iasi, with a membership of 3,000. Its president was Dr. Karpel Lippe, who in 1897 opened the first Zionist Congress in Basel (Switzerland). In 1899 there were several Zionist organizations in Iasi: "Mevasereth Zion," "Nachom Zion," "Ezrath Zion," "Bnoth Zion" (a feminist organization).

In 1900 other groups became active: "Max Nordau," "Shivath Zion," "Dr. Gaster," "Dr. Nemirower." In 1910 all of the sections merged. A "Poalei Zion" organization also appeared which resonated with the ranks of the working class.

B. Ellman wrote[45]: "Romania is the only country in which the old philanthropic and colonizing Zionism has signed a fraternal and durable pact with the new political Herzelian Zionism, fighting side by side for the good of the movement."

In 1906, the enlightenment association "Teynbehalle" was created, supported by Rabbi Dr. Nemirower, Dr. Nacht, A. L. Zissu, Moti Rabinovici, I. Gropper and I. Botoshansky. Jewish literary experts from abroad, such as Shalom Aleichem and M. Sokolov, lectured at some literary meetings. In time lectures in Yiddish were also given.

Socialist ideas also penetrated among the Jewish masses. In 1887 the group "Lumina" was founded, having its own press organ. The magazine resurfaced in 1895.

The Jewish social democracy also addressed the rights of the small Jewish bourgeoisie. Following the model of the Bund party in Russia, *Der Veker* was being published in Iasi to support the struggle of political ideas. *Der Veker* reappeared in 1916 – edited by M. Isac Moscovici, a socialist and community activist. Moreover, the Yiddish and Hebrew press of Iasi reflected the social and public life of the local Jewish community.

The emergence of the Jewish press in Iasi was tied to a moderate internal Jewish reform and to the efforts for emancipation. The events of 1877-1878 were also contributing factors.

In the last quarter of the 19th century, the creation of modern Jewish schools and the growing command of literary Romanian language favor the creation and development of a Romanian language Jewish press. In the beginning, the Yiddish and Romanian language press covered news and current ideas. Following the example of the famous Yiddish newspaper with the Hebrew title *Hajoetz* (the Advisor), published in the years 1874-1913, Iasi created in 1882 the *Naie Yiddishe Zeitung* (the New Yiddish Newspaper), printed by the N. Frenkel printing house, no.10 Primariei St. In the same year, the Hersh Goldner printing house printed *Der RumenisherIisraelit* – a newspaper that was particularly treating the problem of emigration to Eretz Israel.

The same problem was found in *Der Yiddisher Folksfreund* (the Friend of the Jewish People) (1887), a newspaper that competed with *Der Folksfreund* – edited by M. Braunstein (Mibashan). Unfortunately, the latter produced only three issues.

In 1895 *Di Yiddishe Post* was published. Many articles were dedicated to the "Chovevei Zion" movement. In 1896 *Di Hofnung* was published.

Special attention has to be given to the social-democrat periodical *Der Veker*. The editors Max Wecsler, Dr. Litman Ghelerter and Leon Gheler, well-known personalities of the time, were not familiar with literary Yiddish. In the beginning they wrote the articles in Romanian, leaving the translation in the hands of the popular teacher and rhapsodist Zeidl Helman. Later they began to write in Yiddish, leaving Helman the task of correcting and improving the style. An organ of the Social-Democrat group, the periodical *Lumina* appeared between May 1, 1896 and September 27, 1897. The 400 subscribers were not paying their subscription fees regularly, therefore the Marxist oriented weekly ceased to be issued for financial reasons. Twenty years later, we witness the reemergence of this periodical under the editorship of N. Isac Moscovici.

Der Yiddisher Geist, created by Gershon Cohn, with a pronounced Zionist orientation, was short-lived, as were many of the periodicals mentioned thus far. The attempt to publish a daily Zionist paper titled *Die Yiddishe Zunkunft* was also unsuccessful. Only a few issues were published.....

Hamevasser, Z. Helman's modest magazine, was published in 1903. The same year, *Ticvei Israel*, a Zionist propaganda publication, was published both in Yiddish and Romanian. In 1907, *Die Yiddishe Zunkunft* – the third periodical with the same name – was published in Iasi, under the leadership of the popular orator Ira Kreish. *Der Yiddisher Geist* was published between the years 1898-1901. The newspaper *Talpiot*, edited by G. Rockeach between 1898 and 1899 also deserves to be mentioned. Among these publications the *Licht* magazine, which appeared in 1915, holds a distinct position as the voice of the first modern Yiddish literature group in Romania.

The Romanian Language Jewish press reflected the vital preoccupations of the Jewish population in the land. *Vocea Aparatorului* (1872-1873) was militating for the emancipation of the Jews and tried to fight with energy the anti-Semitic accents existing in local newspapers like *Trompeta Carpatilor* and *Curierul de Yassi*. The first literary creations in Romanian of several young Jews appear in its columns: the high school student Elias Schwartzfeld, the law student Goldenthal (who was studying in Brussels), the university student I. Brociner (who was studying in Berlin), the university student M. Brociner (from Leipzig) as well as B. Labin from Botosani.

The five issues of the assimilationist *Ecoul Tinerimii* (the Echo of the Youth), which was disconnected from Jewish reality, did not find support and had to be discontinued.

The periodical *Lumina*, voice of the Israelite youth, was a very important publication. It was written and edited mostly by Stefan Stanca (Stein), a brilliant personality of the intelligentsia of the time. The magazine focused on several fundamental issues: the economic situation, the inertia of community activists, and the elitism of the leadership of the Jewish community. The five issues of the magazine were not well received by the rest of the Jewish press in the country and received a lot of criticism.

In August of 1889 the young publicist Max Caufman began the publication of the newspaper *Propasirea* (The Progress), which also appeared in 1891. He criticized the activities of the community and popularized in his articles the history of the Jews and the current problems of Judaism. Assimilationist tendencies, especially those propagated by certain elements from Bucharest (who had at their disposal a newspaper such as *Asimilarea*), were combated through the articles of Dr. K. Lippe.

Between July 1, 1895 and January 1896, Socialist groups – which parted ways with ex-colleagues that had become liberal – published the magazine *Lumina*, which addressed the working class in general. Issues of relevance to Jewish life, such as naturalization, history, and workers' ideology were also addressed. *Lumina* was published for two years and earned itself a place of distinction in the history of the press of Iasi.

Jewish publications in Romanian during this period had a strong Zionist emphasis. *Rasaritul* (Sunrise) was the voice of the Central Zionist Committee in 1889. *Darabana* (The Drum) espoused the anti-Jewish activities.

Rasaritul was edited by Dr. Steuerman-Rodion, who lent it a high professional standard. It featured articles referring to the acceptance of the (Christian) Orthodox religion and even the baptism of certain prominent local personalities like L. Shaineanu and H. Tiktin. The paper was published for two years and contributed to debate and the knowledge of the important issues of the time.

The Jewish press of Iasi, however, was unable to survive for a prolonged period of time. The Bucharest centralism and the scarcity of financial resources silenced the Jewish press of Iasi by 1918.

The Theatre

A permanent professional theater created by Avram Goldfaden, spoken in Yiddish, the language of the Jewish population of Moldavia, enjoyed great success in the city of its birth. The Jews of Iasi were known to be great lovers of the theater – which blended the pleasant with the practical.

After 1880 one can discern a certain American influence over traditional theatrical concepts. The repertoire changed, there were new actors, and stage music took on a different quality.

The repertoire included Viennese operettas (such as "Pericola" – in 1900) and plays on topics of current events (like Horovitz's play about peddlers who were barred from practicing their profession). Successful plays, such as Jules Verne's *Around the World in Eighty Days,* and *The Two Orphans* – a tearjerker, were also staged in the Romanian theatres.

A. Goldfaden's tour through Romania (1892-1893) was a very special event for the Yiddish repertoire. Various well-known plays were staged, some of which were written by this famous playwright. In 1894 "The Life in New York" was played.

During this time the Yiddish theater repertoire also included plays by Carmen Sylva, the queen of Romania (such as "Master Manole"). Plays by Shakespeare, Gutzkov, I. Gordin, and Lidin were also present on the theater's billboards.

Despite these successes, an actor's life was a difficult one. The theatre could not pass an "artisan" period and achieve a significant material well being. There were, however, some significant events: Clara Young – on tour from America, had a tremendous success and received a great welcome from the people of the city.

With the passing of years, the example set by the Yiddish theater of Iasi brought about the appearance of similar theaters in Bucharest, especially during the period of the German occupation of the capital.

The Literature

In spite of the fact that the city of Iasi had an outstanding literary life in the Romanian language, the literature in Yiddish is of modest proportions. Zeidl Helman (1848? – 1938), of the *Lumina* magazine, was active in Iasi after his return from America. He became a popular writer, actor, singer, composer and performer of his own songs and sketches. We know that he was also a cantor, teacher and editor of some publications; he also translated numerous works. In 1903 he helped to issue the publication *Hamevaser* in Iasi – where he published verses of biblical inspiration. He also published flyers, on the occasion of various events. Among those we can cite: *Iontev Bleter, Kitvei Hazman.* Some of his plays were performed on stages. Helman, through his entire activity, was a picturesque figure in the Jewish Iasi.

Israel Orenstein (Iampol, Poland 1862 – Iasi 1905) published pamphlets targeting the leadership of the Iasi (Jewish) community.

Alongside those two there were other writers, journalists and pamphlet writers illustrative of that period. History has preserved a few names: Moise Birnbaum published verses between 1888 and 1911. His known volume is *Poezii* (Poems) (published in 1893). Haim Zeilig Drucker published, among other works, the historic novel *Der alter vald-bavoiner* (The old forest-dweller). M. N. Litinski (1855-1900) was the editor of the Iasi magazine *Shabes oibst* (Sabbath fruits). In 1907 Leivi Segal edited the magazine *Di rihtike idishe tzucunft* (The real Jewish future).

Also interesting to mention is the fact that before WWI verses and prose from Iasi were published in the Yiddish press of some European countries, countries – showing the quality of this poetry on one hand and on the other hand demonstrating the fact that Iasi writers, modest as they may have been, were trying to make a name outside their country.

The *Licht* epoch constituted the first modern literary Yiddish trend in Romania. It started in Iasi in 1914.

The cultural organization "Toynbeehalle," founded at the beginning of the century, was active in Iasi, offering lectures and literary programs on

Jewish and non-Jewish subjects. Gradually, the circle of participants grew, lectures in Yiddish and popular songs were presented. Beside the renowned lecturers Rabbi Dr. Nemirower, Dr. Karpel Lippe and A. L. Zissu, the youngsters Iacob Groper, S. Lazar (Lascar Saraga), Moti Rabinovici, the student Efraim Valdman, and Mates Fridman collaborated. B. Fundoianu, G. Spina, Brunea-Fox wrote memories about "Toynbeehalle".

Youngsters, who valued the language of the people, edited in the autumn of 1914 the first issue of the planned monthly magazine *Licht* ("The Light"). It was the first platform of an authentic Yiddish literature in Romania. The inspiration for the magazine came from the student Efraim Valdman, devoted to the literary movement, gifted and tireless. He died on the battlefield in WWI.

Moti Rabinovici – who "distinguished" himself after moving towards secularity – was an analytical person, a good organizer and a gifted orator. He remained in the memory of his contemporaries as a remarkable community activist.

Aharon Matatiahu Fridman, the son and presumed heir of the Chassidic Rabbi of Adjud, had a stormy and tragic destiny. After a period of deep social unrest, he became a rationalistic intellectual, without denying the traditional values. His life in his rabbinical family and the early marriage to a girl from the religious medium were in tragic conflict with his philosophical concepts. His studies, published in the *Licht* magazine, are interesting and profound. He died of the flu in 1917, at the age of 25, and his death was a big loss for the modern Jewish culture in Romania.

The Musical Life

The Jewish musicians played an important role in the artistic life of Iasi, whether as preservers of the Yiddish and Romanian musical folklore or as performers and composers. Especially remarkable was the Lemesh family. Zeiling Itzic Lemesh was in 1846 already a member of the Iasi National Theatre orchestra. His son Milo conducted a folk music band that played Moldavian folk music in Bessarabia and was therefore banned from singing in the Moldavian areas across the Prut River. He conducted the Jewish theatre orchestra in 1878 and 1882. He also composed pieces of his own.

H. Lemesh was active between 1892 and 1895. Berl Lemesh was member of the Iasi National Theatre orchestra with Avran Volf Lemesh. Another family of musicians was the Bughici family. They also distinguished themselves as composers. In the third generation, Avram Bughici, of the third generation, sang at the Iasi Jewish State Theatre until 1960, when he was eighty years old.

Berl Segal, who later distinguished himself as a conductor, made his debut in 1914. He lived from 1897 to 1958 and worked as conductor of the Jewish State Theatre orchestra until his death. His father, nicknamed Livik (because he was left handed), lived between 1868 and 1927 and was a close collaborator of A. Goldfaden. The musical tradition of this family continues in our days through Iosif Sava, the son of Berl Segal.

An important place in the field of music is occupied by Ch(aim) I(srael) Bernstein, born in Falciu in 1875. He was music teacher at the Iasi Military Secondary School for 20 years. He conducted the National Theatre orchestra and composed over 100 romances, songs, marches and theatrical music pieces. He was known and popular during that period but died in 1929, forgotten and poor.

The Iasi musical life knows other forms of artistic manifestations. There were mixed ethnic folk bands, which performed on various occasions (family feasts, festivals, Purim); an orchestra of the Jewish theatre also existed.

Personalities

The Jewish community life has brought about the appearance of some distinct personalities in Iasi, people who distinguished themselves in very different domains and entered the city awareness. We content ourselves in this chapter with a brief, incomplete list which can be continued and improved. In any case, the activity of these personalities will be described in a future chapter showing their contribution to the development of Iasi.

For a more didactic treatment we will try to compose an alphabetically arranged list.

The BROCINER family – we mention Iosef B. Brociner, born in Iasi in 1846, deceased in Galati in 1919. He was the author of some fundamental works regarding the history of the Jews in Romania, used as an argument for their right to emancipation. He published *Cestiunea israelitilor romani* (The Romanian Israelites Question) in 1910 and *Chestiunea evreiasca* (The Jewish Question) in 1911. Marco Brociner was born in Iasi in 1852 and died in Vienna in 1942. He was a jurist, graduate in German philology, and journalist. Colonel Mauriciu Brociner fought in the War of Independence. He also had activities at the Royal Palace.

Journalist Max Caufman – DAN died in Iasi in 1944 at the age of 90. He was very appreciated in his profession.

Carol (Haim) DRIMER, son of a Rabbi, born in 1899 in the district of Hertza, was killed in the Iasi pogrom (1941). He had an extensive traditional and universal cultural education. He mastered several languages. He published numerous articles on Jewish subjects, some of them contentious. Some of the articles referred to Jewish writers from Iasi and the German literature in Romania; he was passionate about the local cultural activities and remained in the memories of his acquaintances as a distinct intellectual. The volumes of *Studii si critice* (Studies and criticisms) (Iasi, 1923-1928) revealed a distinguished analysis of the literary phenomena, which he also treated with the passion of a missionary.

The writer with the pseudonym JOSEPHUS FLAVIUS was active around WWII until not long ago.

The poet Enric FURTUNA (Dr. Peckelman), born in 1881 in Botosani, died in Tel Aviv in 1964. He made his debut in Iasi with the anthology *Versuri si proza* (Verses and prose) (1914) – followed by the volume *De pe stanca* (From the rock) (1922) and by *Privelisti si impresii* (Views and impressions) (1926). He also translated Bialik, Groper, and Birnbaum.

GIORDANO (the pseudonym of Berman Goldner) – 1861-1929. Epigramist and lampooner, he published the volume *Epigrame* (Epigrams) (1893) and *Stihuri si Epigrame* (Verses and epigrams) (1925).

The brothers Jean and Alfred HEFTER lived during the period 1887-1979. They were dedicated to journalism and critique. They are also known as editors of some periodicals.

Karpel LIPPE (Natan Petahia L.), descendant of Rashi, distinguished himself as a physician, specialist in Middle East and as a Zionist activist. He was an important personality in all the domains of the Jewish life and spirituality. Arriving in Iasi as a youngster (1860), he was active here until 1913. He died in Vienna at the age of 83. He published in German a series of works about the Talmud and the Bible. In other works, he fought against the anti-Semitic libels and distortions of the epoch.

O NEUSCHOTZ DE JASSY was an original poet who wrote in French, contributing to the knowledge of the national literature. He published several prose volumes in German. He was born in Iasi in 1889.

Eugen RELGIS lived between 1895 and 1978. He was a distinguished personality in literature as well as politics. He was known as essayist and novelist. He was an “inspiring person” for the movement “Umanitarismul” (The Humanitarianism), fighting for peace and understanding between nations.

C. SATEANU (Carol Schonfeld) lived between 1878 and 1940. He was a journalist at the local liberal newspaper *Miscarea* (The Movement) for over four decades. He was a supporter of the arts and culture in Iasi. He made his debut in literature in 1903 with the volume *Viforul* (The Snowstorm). Many of his works of history and literary critique are known. He translated from Shalom Aleichem.

SCRUTATOR, the pseudonym of Dr. Clement Blumenfeld of Iasi, was editor of the Iasi newspaper *Opinia* (The Opinion). He frequently published on literary and theatric in other newspapers as well. He was naturalized in 1905.

A(DOLF, AVRAM) STEUERMAN-RODION lived between 1872 and 1918. Physician by profession, he is also known as poet, essayist, cultural animator, supporter of the Iasi school and journalist. His literary activity is found in the volumes: *Saracie* (Poverty) (1903), *O toamna la Paris* (An autumn in Paris) (1897), *Lirice* (Poetry) (1899), and *Spini* (Thorns) (1915). The following volumes were published posthumously: *Frontul Rosu* (The red battlefield) (1920), *Cartea baiatului meu* (My boy's book) (1920), *Indreptari* (Corrections) (1930). He put his name on numerous volumes of translations from German and French, put together anthologies and wrote critical studies.

Adrian VEREA (Max Vecsler), the physician of the Iasi Opera, is also known as a poet and playwright. He was born in Botosani in 1878. He made his debut in 1914 with the volume of verses *Sa nu-ti faci idoli* (Thou shalt not make idols for yourself). In 1917 his *Iasii* was published. He published a lot in the local press.

Moritz WACHTEL is known as an important manufacturer and banker with wide financial knowledge. He was an animator of the Jewish communitarian life. He died in 1929 at the age of 68.

Dr. YGREC (Glicsman) made a name for himself through his articles in the local press. He had columns of literary critique, but also tackled other themes. He died in 1938.

{65-88}

THE GREAT TURNING POINT

In Romanian modern and contemporary history, the period that begins with the outbreak of World War I, in the summer of 1914, would lead to the great turning point - the realization of the secular dream of the Great Union, the birth of the Great Romania. Those who lived in those times, even as adolescents, cannot forget them. Even the tragic events of World War II, including the racist regime, cannot erase the memory of those events that affected the entire population of the country, and aroused feelings of hope and faith in the future.

The period of active neutrality (1914-1916) marked years of a special financial and economic conjuncture for the trade and export of food, fuel, and certain raw materials.

Then Romania entered the war on the side of the Allies: France, England and ... the Russia of Nicholas II. The first phase of the war was catastrophic, with great suffering for the entire population of the country of Moldavia, and of Iasi. The withdrawal brought to Iasi not only the central authorities, including the Royal Court, but also many refugees, with or without purpose. The crises of housing, food, fuel, and medicine were aggravated by the typhoid fever epidemic. The suffering of the families of soldiers and news about those fallen in the line of duty intensified the state of distress of the population. In the background of these events, the Jewish population experienced some good and some bad times.

Some of the vexing measures taken by the authorities were supportive of the anti-Semitic movement. It was forbidden to speak Yiddish, and the notion that Jews might be collaborating with the Germans was being circulated. Some synagogues had been confiscated and turned into hospitals. The legal status as Romanian non-citizens, the grave economic situation, the increased cost of living, and the decreased income of the community weighed heavily on the Jewish population. And yet, they held on to the hope that Jews might become citizens and anti-discrimination laws might disappear, that they might be able to emigrate freely, and that there might be improved conditions for commerce, trade, and a cultural life.

Universal suffrage, agrarian reform, the democratization of social relations saved the entire population of the country and justified the sacrifices made.

The joys of peace, of the reunification of Romania, and of all great hopes were in opposition to everyday realities.

"Great Romania meant a new social system and a new political system..., the passage from an undemocratic liberalism to a liberal democracy... 'radical reforms' took place... these reforms naturally upset the social equilibrium; on the basis of universal suffrage trivial political elements were elevated ... In 1930 Romania had over 10 million inhabitants, ... Jews made up 4% of the total population, the Magyars 7.9% and the Germans 4.4%."[47]

The researcher Leon Volovici painted a wider picture: "From the second half of the last century antagonism toward Jews was promoted and theorized by an important direction of Romanian nationalism. After 1930 this position is projected into the center of political and intellectual life, and it becomes a litmus test of the ideological orientation of every intellectual involved in any of the options of the time: fascism, communism, democracy. The exacerbation of anti-Semitism contributed, along with other social and political factors, to the discrediting and the weakening of democracy and of parliamentary life."[48]

In 1937 the great Romanian diplomat Nicolae Titulescu wrote to J. Tharaud about the state of anti-Semitism in the country: "This problem is poisoning us. Where would these anti-Semites want to send the Jews to get rid of them? I hope they don't intend to throw them all in the sea or to send them to you. I must confess that I don't understand these furious anti-Semites. I live surrounded by Jews and am very happy about that. They are affable, intelligent, and active. Those whom I have worked with have always proven to be very loyal..."[49]

Far from being a marginal phenomenon or the expression of the juvenile exuberance of an imaginary "Latin Quarter," students' agitations, manipulated from backstage, had the effect of terrorizing the Jewish population of Iasi and of the entire country, a sort of unique kind of apartheid, camouflaged by a constitution that is democratic in appearance only. The students and agitators traveled by railroad for free under the pretext of anti-Bolshevik demonstrations. In 1922, some White Russians, whom escaped from Bolshevik Russia, also took part in anti-Jewish activities. The old Russian pogromist tradition!

In Iasi, the students prevented their Jewish colleagues from attending classes. Jewish female students were chased out of their dorms in the middle of the night.

The H. Goldner printing house, an important agent in disseminating Romanian culture and printing newspapers to which Jewish journalists contributed, was destroyed. It was forbidden to present on the stage of the

National Theater plays by certain well-known playwrights, by reason of their ethnic Jewish origin. Hitlerism to the letter...

The picture of the suffering of the Jewish population of that period incorporated other elements. In the beginning of 1920 there was a movement called "The League for the Protection of the Christian Population," led by Prof. A. C. Cuza, the renowned C. Sumuleanu, Ion Zelea Codreanu, General Tarnowski, and others. It is known that in August 1923 there was great devastation of Jewish houses and stores, as well as measures against Jewish students: beatings, humiliations, demonstrations. C. Z. Codreanu succeeded in assassinating Manciu, the prefect of police in Iasi. A lawsuit was staged and the assassin was acquitted. He became a national hero; in fact he was the pioneer of subsequent legionary crimes, among others. In 1928 a synagogue in the Pacurari district was destroyed. Admission of Jewish students to state universities was halted; in 1929 there was something called "numerus nullus", effectively a quota of zero for Jewish students.

All these lead the Jewish community to take a series of measures. In 1920 a Jewish student hostel with 120 spots was created, as well as a cafeteria with about 300 tables. In 1922 Jewish merchants closed their stores in protest of student hooliganism. The press of the time recorded other manifestations of the resistance of the Jewish population in face of all these acts of discrimination.

The Jewish population suffered economically as well. There were trade restrictions and some stores were boycotted. Craftsmen had to adjust to a reduced sphere of influence, which had an effect on the national economy. The masses were reduced to a state of poverty. Consequently, in the district Socola, known for the poverty of its inhabitants, a cafeteria for 400 destitute Jews was created.

Even the Ministry of Justice and the Orthodox clergy supported xenophobia. The following years of the Goga-Cuza government constituted the first peak of extremist nationalism. The Iasi Legal Association, led by Ionel Teodoreanu, the idyllic romantic writer in whose prose we find Jewish characters, decided not to receive Jewish members for a period of ten years, even though there were Jewish lawyers of utmost professionalism.

For the time being, the "Romanization" contemplated by Al. Vaida-Voivode, former democrat from the Ardeal region, grew in scope. In 1938 the issue of Jewish citizenship – a cause of abuses, corruption, and high-handedness – was revised.

The royal dictatorship flirted with the Iron Guard, then took anti-Semitism seriously with tragic consequences that are known and about which much has been written lately. One small step separated the royal dictatorship from the racist regime. The premises were the pogrom of Iasi, deportations, and forced labor.

The Organization of the Community

In the years 1916-1919, a group of representatives from the synagogues carried out, with some small limitations, their role of leaders of the Community. In the summer of 1919 a commission for the reconstruction of the Community was convened... The statute of the new committee was approved by the Ministry of Worship in accordance with the Law of Worship. Democratic elections took place, but not until 1930. Aside from the leadership committee, a series of sections were created for the purpose of improving the style of leadership and to extend the sphere of activities. Closer attention was paid to the problems of education, social assistance, and culture.

In 1937 the budget of the Community was 7 million lei, a sum that proved to be insufficient. Some institutions of the Community asked to become autonomous, in order to achieve greater mobility and better organization.

In 1939, the president of the Community was the great industrialist Ilie Mendelson, assisted by 25 other members of the "representation." The sections were led as follows:

1. The cultural section was led by the engineer Ghetl Buhman, originally from Podu Iloaiei. The members of the committee were doctors, pharmacists, and lawyers.
2. The president of the socio-economic section was Dr. D. Fruhling.
3. The president of the section of worship was S. Petrusca.

There was an atmosphere of willingness around the Community with respect to the improvement of the social status of the Jewish population. The Community receives important donations of cash, property, etc. The heirs of I. L. Rosenstein donated one million lei for the construction of an industrial school. Important donations were also made by the families Smil Waldman, Bercovici, and others.

The rabbinate was reorganized; every rabbi or haham needed the approval of the Community, in order to stop certain abuses, fraud, and quarrels. In 1939 there were ten active rabbis in Iasi, some with their own synagogues. The official rabbi of the Community was Dr. Joseph Safran. The hahams were employed and paid by the Community with money resulting from the taxes levied on the slaughtering of meat according to ritual religious practice.

Cattle were slaughtered at the city slaughterhouse. For poultry there were modest ritual slaughterhouses in several Jewish neighborhoods.

The synagogues were autonomous but their activity was observed by the Community. 112 Iasi synagogues were listed in the work of H. Gherner and B. Wachtel *Evreii ieseni in documente si fapte* (The Jews of Iasi in documents and facts) (Iasi, 1939). In 1944 Avram Hahamu, president of the Community noted 142 synagogues, without naming them. Corroborating the first list with data from the Iasi Community records, with press news and with documents from the State Archives in Iasi, a list which is close to reality can be constructed. For easier reference the synagogues are arranged in alphabetical order. Since some synagogues did not have a name, only their address is indicated. Hebrew names are given in Sephardic phonetics; Yiddish ones are given in local pronounciation. We remind the reader that the *synagogues list* compiled from the above-mentioned sources reflects the situation of 1939:

1. Azilul de Batrani (Old Persons Home), 20 Crucii Street. In 1892 it was also an association for elementary studies of the Talmud, "Chevra Mishnaiot." In 1947 its register was in the possession of Rabbi Roller of Buhusi. The ornamental graphic work on its cover had a great artistic value. The synagogue was also named "Beit Israel."
2. Babad, also known as Herman Rosenstein, 65 Ghica Voda Street.
3. Babad, also known as Moise Idel Vecsler, Marzescu Street. "Babad" was the name of a special Hassidic movement which had many followers in Moldavia.
4. Baalshem, 24 Broscariei Street. Israel Baalshemtov was the founder of the Hassidic movement. In 1849 a house in the Brosteni slums was bought for the foundation of a synagogue with the same name.
5. Balter, 12 Apelor Street. It also had a "Chevra Mishnaiot," a "Bikkur Cholim," and a "Leviat Hamet," a brotherhood for assistance to the sick and for participation in funeral ceremonies.
6. Hana Berarita (Chana the Beer House keeper), also known as Meir Simha, 52 Cucu Street. This synagogue was functioning in 1862 and was active until 1939. A new synagogue by the same name existed before 1912 - under the management of Rabbi I. Askenazi.
7. Moise Bercovici, also known as David Shoil, 79 Socola Street.
8. Beit Hamidrash (The House of Prayers), 19 (25) Socola Street.
9. Boccegii (Musicians), 6 Calaina Street. Mentioned in various documents dating from 1831 to 1865.
10. Broder, 72 Smardan Street. Mentioned in documents as existing and functioning in 1860, 1887, and 1892.
11. Buhusher Clouz, 70 Socola Street. A "Shos" association - for indepth studies of the Talmud - was active in this synagogue in 1877.
12. Butnari (Coopers), also known as Torat Chaim (= The Teaching of Life), 35 Cuza Voda Street.

13. Calarasher Rebe, Aqueduct Street.
14. "Dinspre Calcaina" ("Towards Calcaina") synagogue, mentioned in a document dated 1798.
15. Caldarari (Braziers), 2 Semnului Street. Idel Braunstein donated this synagogue in 1920. In this synagogue was the brotherhood "Ner Tamid" (Eternal Light).
16. Cantarski, 87 I. C. Bratianu Street. A donation by Meir Canter in 1825. Renovated by the congregation after a serious fire. The altar graphics ("Keviti") date from 1848. The synagogue had traditional murals of great beauty.
17. Caramidari (Brick Makers or Sellers), also known as Haim Taitler, 9 Morilor Street. It is mentioned in documents from 1833, 1841, and 1844.
18. Alter Catemberg, 82-84 C. Negri Street. The building was donated by Catemberg to the Community in 1897.
19. Naftule Caufman, 39 Rosetti Street.
20. Ceprezari (Shmuclers - Gimp Makers), 50B Procopie Street. An 1869 document mentions this synagogue.
21. Cherestegii (Lumberjacks), 6 Trantomir Street.
22. Cizmar (Shoemakers), also known as Finkelstein, 16 Cizmariei Street. Founded by Avram Cizmar, aka Finkelstein, in 1871. However, it was also there in 1829.
23. Cojocari (Furriers), Sinagogilor Street. The building was bought in 1847 by Iosub Leiba sin Iancu with 100 1/2 gold coins.
24. Cotiugari (Carters), 34-36 Ipsilanti Street.
25. Cotiugari, 2 Semnului Street (?). From another source, 60 Broscari Street.
26. Covrigari (Pretzel Makers), 56 Socola Street (or 160 Melcului Street?)
27. Crasmari (Publicans), 7 Ticlaul de Jos Street.
28. Croitori (Tailors), 1 Sinagogilor Street. Renovated in 1824 following a fire in 1822. Belonged to the Tg. Cucului tailors' guild ("Poalei Tsedek"). It was founded with this name in 1847. The building was converted to a different use in 1978.
29. Croitori, 30 Sf. Teodor Street. Renovated in 1907. Rabbi Dr. S. Rabinovici and the cantor S. Solomon were officiating here in 1914.
30. Croitori, 12 Broscariei Street.
31. Croitorii tineri (Young Tailors), 8 Basota Street. The building was converted to a different use after 1970.
32. Cusmari (Fur Hatters), Pantelimon slums. The synagogue was in existence in 1849 and belonged to the respective guild. A list compiled in 1939 does not mention it anymore.
33. Daniel (The Heirs), 8 Rosetti Street.
34. Ilie David, 84 Lautari Street. The building was bought in 1902.
35. Dulbergher, 26 Aqueduct Street. Documented as established before 1883.

36. Zalmina Feighelis, 3 Sinagogilor Street. Z. Feighelis was a leader of the community about 1840-1860.
37. Ghitl Fichner, also known as Tichler. 71 (or 79) Sf. Lazar Street.
38. Reb Haimke Focsaner. The street is unknown. It is known that it was built before 1824 and renovated in 1924.
39. Tipre Goldstein, 11 Crucii Street.
40. Goldstein, also known as Mordhe reb Ioskes, 12 Nemteasca Street.
41. Gutman (Lazar Rapaport), 8 Hagi Lupu Street. The building was bought by Rabbi Gutman in 1912.
42. Heller (Lupu Pascal), 115 Nicolina Street.
43. Herscovici, 8 Armeana Street.
44. Haim Hoffman, 7 Sinagogilor Street. The building was bought in 1880.
45. Reb Iancole (Katz), 40 Aron Voda Street.
46. Reb Ihil, 39 Armeneasca Street.
47. Reb Ioinole, 20 Arapului Street. Beside the synagogue there was a Hevrat Mishnaiot.
48. Iosek reb Mordhes, see no. 40.
49. Jurist (Beit Slomo), 3 Gh. Lascar Street.
50. Juratori, Juratori Street.
51. Kahana, 30 Stefan cel Mare Street. Founded in 1864 by banker Leib Kahane. The building was converted to a different use after the 1960's (?).
52. Katz, see no. 45.
53. Litiner, 8 Pomir Street. Documented as existing in 1847. Rabbi Litiner was commissioned by Moise Ghersen Packer.
54. Lumanarari (Candle Makers), 33 Sarariei Street. The building was bought in 1907.
55. Macelari (Butchers), 3 Aron Voda Street.
56. Reb Meirl, 8 Pomir Street.
57. Meirkes, 3 Stinca Street.
58. Sloime Mendels, 4 Mlastinei Street. In 1856 it had a "Hevra Mishnaiot" – whose register could still be studied until 1955.
59. Menike, 7 Sinagogilot Street.
60. Merari (Apple Merchants), 17 Labirint Street. The building was bought in 1866 with 400 gold coins.
61. Moisa sin Haim, 7 Broscariei Street.
62. Muzicanti (Lautari –Fiddlers), 37 Pantelimon Street. It existed before 1844. The synagogue register was dated starting in 1853. For another "Muzicantii" synagogue – see no. 9.
63. Nahman Botosaner, 39 Bucsinescu Street. In 1830 a "Hevrat Mishnaiot" is mentioned. The founder, Nahman, died in 1849. The synagogue was still existing in 1960.
64. Tempel Iacob Neuscholtz, "Beit Hadash." Built in 1865, it was a modern building in the city center. It was bombed in 1944 and had to be demolished when the neighborhood was reorganized.
65. Packer, also known as reb Saikes, 60 C. Negri Street.

66. "Pe Ulita pescariei jidovesti" ("On the Jewish Fish Shop Alley") synagogue. Existed in 1852.
67. Pietrari (Masons), also known as David Rabinovici, 2 Taietoarei Street.
68. Pietrari, 33 Rufeni Street. Established in 1853. Courses of Talmud Torah were held within its premises.
69. Pietrari, 11 Sipote Street.
70. Pietrari, 24 Ipsilante Street. Existed in 1886. It is possible for the expression "pietrari" to be the "literary form" of the Moldavian "chetrar" = mason or bricklayer. Formerly the city of Iasi had many Jewish masons.
71. Podu Albinet, 26 Marfa Street.
72. Poporenilor (Teasatura – The Fabric), 3 Tutora Street.
73. Rubin Rabinovici, also known as Scoala Unita (The United School), 160 Bratianu Street. David Rabinovici, see note at no. 68.
74. Iacob Raises, 28 (or 86) C. Negri Street. Existed and is mentioned before 1928. Lazar Rapaport, see note at no. 41.
75. Ratsi Iacob (Beit Iacob) Goldenberg, 86 C. Negri Street.
76. Eli Meir Reichemberg, Panaite Stoica Street. The building was donated to the community by the philanthropist Reichemberg in 1860.
77. Rabin Raines, 66 C. Negri Street.
78. Retiv ahava, 118 Nicolina Street.
79. Roite Sil (The Red Synagogue) or Descalecatoare, 43 Nicolina Street. It was still functioning after WWII.
80. Michel Rosiesiva, 12 Sinagogilor Street.
81. Sadagura (Tverski) (Risiser rebe), 11 C. Roseti Street.
82. Salhana, 35 Salhana Street.
83. Sararie, Sararie Street ... Built in 1864 by Saim Horenstein and the Jewish Community. Under the synagogue there are basements rented as dwellings. The rent made up an income for the synagogue. It is a brick building and it has a fence.
84. Sarata. Building built in 1816, next to the Jewish bath.
85. Lupu Schwarz, 90 Socola Street.
86. Solomonica, 31 Stefan cel Mare Street.
87. Spitalul israelit (The Israelite Hospital), 43 Elena Doamna Street.
88. Stoleri (Carpenters), 62 Arapului Street.
89. Stoleri, 44 Cuza Voda Street.
90. Strul Aron, 24 Pacurari Street. The building was converted to a different use after 1975.
91. Piata Sturza, 13 Sarariei Street. Sinagoga Mare din Pacurari (The Great Synagogue of Pacurari – In the 19th century the term SCOALA [School] was meant to denote a more important synagogue. The present list mentions several places of worship named SINAGOGA MARE). See Strul Aron Synagogue, no. 90. Purchasing documents from 1852 exist; a contract from 1855 was preserved; the documents mention it functioning in 1898 as well.

92. Sinagoga Mare pe Podu Lung (The Great Synagogue on Podu Lung). Existed even before 1865 – according to a preserved stamp.
93. Sinagoga Mare din Podu Ros (The Great Synagogue of Podu Ros), founded by Rabbi Iehosua Hesil, also known as Apter Rav. He held rabbinic office in Iasi between 1803 and 1811 and signed the purchasing document of an armchair, a fact mentioned by I. Kara in an article in R. C. M. (Revista Cultului Mozaic, The Mosaic Cult Revue – the organ of the Romanian Jewish Community) of July 15, 1974. The purchase certificate was resigned two years later by the Zvolver Rabbi, who held office in Iasi between 1803 and 1837. The synagogue was renovated in 1864. The building was demolished due to the reorganization of the city.
94. Sinagoga "Scoala" Mare (The Great "School" Synagogue), 43 Smardan Street.
95. Sinagoga Mare din Tg. Cucului (The Great Synagogue of Tirgul Cucului), 1 Sinagogilor Street. At the present the oldest synagogue in Romania. The Great Synagogue, preserved to this day, was built in the late Baroque, Polish style on land bought in 1657. The structure is brick and stone. Rabbi Natan Nata Hanover (who held office in Iasi as well) insisted that the synagogue construction be completed by 1670. The current structure dates from 1762, when the building was renovated, as shown by the inscription on the outside on the southern wall. It was renovated after a fire in 1822. It was also renovated in the interwar period, a dome being added. After WWII additional repairs were made. A small museum of the Iasi Community operates beside the synagogue.
   Sinagoga reb Saikes, see note no. 65 (Packer).
96. Smuses, 61 Nicorita Street. Scoala unita (The United School), see note no. 74.
97. Stefanester Clouz, opposite the "Sinagoga Mare din Tg. Cucului", 8 Elena Doamna Street. Established in 1907. The building, furniture, and religious objects were funded by the donations of the Hassidim.
98. Lupu Tailer, 3 Fundcal Nitescu. The land was donated by the couple Avram and Mara Finkelstein in 1875.
99. Taietorii de lemne (Woodcutters), 6 Brudea Street.
100. Talmud (!), 3 Micsunele Street.
101. Talmud Tora, 8 Sipote Street.
102. Tapiteri (Upholsterers), Rapa Galbena.
103. Lazar Tapiter, 127 Elisabeta Boulevard.
104. Rabi Taubes, 5 Cucu Street.
105. Telali (Old Clothes Dealers), 37 Aqueduct Street.
106. Toiras Moise, 12 Pacurari Road.
107. The synagogue of 70 Toma Cozma Street.

    Tverski, see note no. 82.
    Tikers, see note no. 37.

108. Sinagoga din Ulita Teatrului vechi (The synagogue in the Old Theatre street), cited in documents from 1830 and 1851.
109. Faibis Wahrman, 51 Sf. Lazar Street.
110. Sinagoga "La zid" ("At the Wall" Synagogue). Donated by the congregation members Alter Meir Leib and Azriel Hers. The synagogue belonged to the Community.
111. Ziberari, 13 Blondelor Street.
112. Zidarilor (Builders') (Sraibman), 28 Arapului Street.
113. Zisu Herman. 10 Labirint Street. Functioned until 1979 when it was demolished due to the reorganization of the area.
114. Zugravi (House Painters), in the Muntenimea da Mijloc slums. The construction lot was bought in 1856.
115. Zvolver vechi (Old Zvolver), 16 Horia Street.
116. Zvolver, (?) Cucu Street. This synagogue was known as a center of Talmudic studies. The congregation members were engaged in 24-hour studies, the synagogue being open 24 hours a day.

Information on the other 24 synagogues which operated in Iasi was not found. However, the figure of 140 worship houses was confirmed in 1944 by the President of the Jewish Community.

The Bombings during WWII, emigration, and the urban reorganization of the city in the last 20 years caused the large majority of the synagogues to disappear... Along with the buildings some of the furniture and religious books disappeared, despite some measures taken by the Community.

In 1975 there were 4 synagogues in Iasi: two of them are still functioning and the Community makes efforts to keep them going.

The Jewish Educational System

The period between the two world wars began with great hopes for the Jewish population. Naturalization and the free access, with full rights as citizens, to all the Romanian state schools at all grade levels, should have raised the general level of culture, instruction, and education. At the same time, the Jewish school system of the period prior to 1920 should have disappeared. Reality, however, was different. It is true that aside from the "Wachtel" Gymnasium there were no other middle schools. In Iasi the primary schools from earlier times were functioning normally, ensuring an adequate education for Jewish children.

In 1939 there were 13 Jewish schools in Iasi. One of them, Yeshiva "Beit Aharon," prepared religious educators (30-100 students from 1927). The students from this school were boarders. Beside biblical and Talmudic studies, the students covered the high school subjects, on which they were tested privately. The school also offered vocational instruction; the students were prepared for a variety of trades. Whoever could not become a rabbi, a haham, or a cantor could become a good tradesman or an artisan with a superior religious education. Such cases were frequent in Maramures... Rosh-Yeshiva, the director, was Rabbi I. Wahrman.

The school system contained different levels. The kindergarten that was at the primary school "Junimea" no. 1 had 30 registered children. It appears that it was established in 1936. The primary school "Cultura," on Marzescu Street, had about 150 students. This excellent faculty was renowned in Iasi. The primary school "Junimea" no. 1, on Sarariei Street, bore the name of "Moritz and Beti Wachtel" and was attended by fewer students than the other schools. It also owned a bath, used by the students' parents as well. There was also a cafeteria for the students. The school "Junimea" no. 2, on Palat Street, had its own building from as early as 1908. Due to a lack of funds, the school became part of the Community, which guaranteed its budget.

To meet the requirement for a better preparation for the vocations, the "Complementary School ORT" (a continuation of the four primary grades) organized tailoring courses for its female students as early as 1920. Especially praiseworthy are the efforts of school committee president M. Isac Moscovici, headmaster Haim Haimovici, and teacher Sara Smucler. One hundred and fifty female students were registered. The old girls' school of the "Assembly of Israelite Women" also offered a complementary course and vocational education (tailoring). There were 220 students registered in that program. The primary and vocational school "David Herzenberg," of the philanthropic society "Steaua" (The Star), established in 1900, had 300 students. The primary subject was ladies' tailoring. The school had its own building and was subsidized by the Community. The primary school for girls "Dr. Stern" was supported by the Bnei Brit Lodge and subsidized by the Community. Among the members of the school committee were Dr. H. Solomonovici and the lawyer Jacques Pineles. One hundred and thirty students attended the school.

The persistence of the traditionalist educational convictions maintained four confessional schools (Talmud Tora). The school on Aron Voda Street had its own building and canteen and constantly offered clothing to its needy students. This school had 250 boys.

Talmud Tora from the Pacurari district was established in 1932. It also owned the building for its 150 students. Talmud Tora from the Podu Ros district initiated into Judaism the children enrolled in the four primary grades. It provided them with free books, writing materials and food. Talmud Tora on Rufeni Street offered only religious studies to students enrolled in other institutions. It was the most traditional form of education in Iasi and it had 250 students in attendance – compared to 220 in the school in Podu Ros.

Social and Medical Assistance

In the period between the two world wars the precarious economic situation of a considerable segment of the Jewish population of Iasi led to the creation of institutions of social assistance that coordinated their activities in such a way as to allow the continuation of life as it was known prior to WW I. In Iasi there were several such institutions that became known for their large-scale permanent activities. Among them are the following:

The asylum for the elderly, located at 5 Sf. Constantin Street, established in 1892, withstood the war of 1916-1918. It was rebuilt after a serious fire and housed 150 persons. The bath and the synagogue, located on the premises, could be used by the inhabitants of the district. In 1975 the nursing home still exists as an institution of the municipality of Iasi. The night care home opened in 1922. It also served the Christian population and was subsidized by the Community.

The mutual aid society "Caritas Humanitas," established in 1901, had more than 1,000 members in 1939. It owned its building.

"Ezrat Aniim" (Assistance to the poor) was started in 1927; it offered assistance to the indigent and helped them find employment.

"Hahnasat Cala" was established in 1922 and helped needy young women with the marriage process. The effectiveness of this institution was limited by its modest available resources.

Another charity, "Iubirea de oameni" (Love of Man), was legalized in 1928. It operated in its own building beginning in 1938. That year the clinic gave 1150 free medical consultations.

The "Neuschotz" orphanage, known during the last decades, continued to exist under good conditions. The orphanage was founded in 1920 for Jewish war orphans and was also subsidized by I.O.V.R., a national organization that offered pensions and financial assistance to all war invalids, orphans, and widows. The orphanage housed 95 children. In 1936 it was taken over by the Community and operated in the building on Marzescu Street, which is still in existence.

One of the excellent social assistance institutions was the school canteen "Amalia and Isac Ghelter." The building on Elena Doamna Street offered a good working environment for the school canteen, ensuring warm meals for 500 children. In time the canteen also served meals to adults. The dining room could be rented out for weddings and parties; the income increased the budget of this popular institution.

The "Weinreich" foundation was active since 1934. It offered help, providing firewood, to some needy families.

The Israelite Hospital, more than one hundred years old, also served other communities in Moldavia. Being a legal entity, it could receive both direct and bequeathed donations. In 1939 it owned 35 buildings that were rented out. The income was used for maintenance and hospital expenses. The hospital also owned 11 buildings occupied by Jewish institutions and by donors. The hospital received 2200 patients per year and performed about 650 operations. It also had a shelter for old persons. The medical staff was composed of 15 very distinguished doctors who were also renown outside the Jewish population.

The Israelite maternity hospital expanded with time and treated more than 400 women per year. Both the hospital and the maternity are presently still functioning in the same buildings as state institutions.

Community Life

As a consequence of the naturalization of the Jews, the old organization "Uniunea Evreilor Pamanteni" ("The Native Jews Union"), active since the first decade of the century, changed its name to "Uniunea Evreilor Romani" ("The Romanian Jews Union"). It conducted an intense activity until the new law of collective naturalization simplified the formalities of obtaining citizenship.

No national Jewish party was formed in Moldavia and the Jewish population voted for various parties, particularly in the local elections, achieving at times a vice-president or a counselor seat in the local bodies.

The central role in the Jewish community life in Iasi was occupied by the Zionist organizations. The Zionist activity was mainly agitation, propaganda and fundraising. There were also Hebrew learning courses, Jewish history courses and cultural societies. All these influenced the curricula of the Jewish schools.

There were known student organizations in Iasi. Some owned libraries with books in Romanian, Yiddish, Hebrew and foreign languages.

The social activities of these organizations gave birth to a movement of national identification and promoted various social concerns.

The Balfour Declaration triggered hopes of national resurgence and of emigration under favorable material and moral conditions. In 1922 the short-lived weekly *Rasaritul* (The East) was published in Iasi. In 1929, the farm "Hechalutz" ("The Pioneer") was founded in the neighborhood of Pacurari on a lot owned by the Israelite Hospital. Here hundreds of youngsters underwent Hachshara (ed. note: training for agricultural work in Eretz Israel) – until 1940. In 1940 the racist legislation "nationalized" the land and the inventory and drove away the youth who aspired towards an agricultural way of life.

In 1925, the Zionist Students Organization was founded, thus increasing the number of Zionist organizations in Iasi. It owned a library, a canteen and a hostel, all established with the help of the Jewish population of Romania.

The Jews of Bessarabian origin founded an organization called "Achuza," which also had a library and was engaged in social assistance activities. Among the young activists remarkable in the inter-war period were, I. L. Burstin, Beno Kusanski, Carol Eisenfeld-Barzilai, Grimberg-Moldovan, and Comarovschi. They supported the renewed activity of the old cultural center "Toynbehalle."

"Achva" ("Brotherhood"), another cultural society was founded in 1932. It organized lectures on Judaic subjects. Its library "H. N. Bialik" was appreciated for the number of books held. It also sustained a vast social assistance activity.

The "Hametiv" ("The Benefactor") association – led by Carol Drimer – sustained a remarkable cultural activity, organizing lectures and putting together a lending library.

The Zionist students had organized themselves in various cultural societies, among which "Chashmonea" was remarkable. The "left wing" university and lyceum students founded an organization "Cultur Lige" ["Culture League"], which through lectures in Yiddish, library and press attracted young Jewish workers and apprentices from the neighborhood. This society held its activities in the building of the "Junimea" ("The Youth") No. 2 School between 1925 and 1930.

The "Ronetti Roman" group was another institution which popularized the Judaic values. The "Morris Rosenfeld" group was active in the Jewish neighborhood of Tg. Cucului. In 1924 the author of these lines attended a lecture of the great poet Itzic Manger on the importance of the Yiddish language. The group "Steuermann-Rodion" had a short-lived activity in about 1930.

Shortly after 1918 the Jewish socialist activity was renewed; the Yiddish language library "Der Veker" ("The Worker") was founded. There were lectures, literary meetings and cultural events attended by many people and mentioned in the newspapers of the time.

Besides the cultural activities, the Jewish community of Iasi organized sports, music and theatre events. The "Maccabi" organization began its activity in about 1919. In 1922 its headquarters were at the "Cultura" School where it organized all kinds of cultural events. It set up an orchestra and later a brass band. Another Jewish sports organization was named "Hakoach." It functioned as an independent organization for some time and then merged with "Maccabi." This organization also prepared the athletic instructors for the Jewish schools of Iasi.

Yiddish and Hebrew Literature

After WWI, Greater Romania incorporated a vast minority population from the provinces. The Jewish population doubled. Its economic, cultural and political potential grew. The intellectual situation of the population improved. Access to learning created sufficient channels for the rising of an intelligentsia which meant a lot for Romania. Jews in the new provinces, especially those in Bessarabia, Bucovina and even in Maramures, were to a great extent both consumers and creators of Hebrew and Yiddish culture, both secular and religious. The Jews from the old provinces of Romania were more traditionalists, thus being more authentic creators of Jewish folklore.

The tradition of the *Licht* magazine was surpassed by the work of Itzik Manger, a poet who made his debut in Iasi. He was born in Cernauti (Czernowitz) and moved with his family to Iasi in 1916. His debut verses, dated 1918, revealed a great authentic author. Iasi, Moldavia, and Romania are all described in some literary works of the young Manger. The volume *Stern ofn dah* (Bucharest, 1920) is illustrative of this trend. In his wanderings (Bucharest, Czernowitz, Warsaw, Paris, London, New York, Tel Aviv) he did not forget the Iasi of his adolescence, the Iasi of his first conferences, the young public who came to listen to him, to get acquainted with his profound, original works of great esthetic value. An entire artistic production of major inspiration, the Poet's Charm, of numerous essays, poems, and plays has evolved from these beginnings.

Haim Rabinzon, son of a rabbi, born in 1914, made his debut in Iasi, with poems in Hebrew and in Yiddish. He distinguished himself through Judaic subjects. Leib Drucker (1902-1941) published a volume of verses *27 lider*, during the years some of his plays were played in the Jewish theatre. Strul Braunstein, poet for hire, published the volumes of verses *Moldeve main heim* (1938) and *Ih eifen breit di toiren* (1939). He died of tuberculosis before obtaining official recognition.

The brothers Simha, Itsic and Iulian Schwarz distinguished themselves in the Yiddish language cultural activity. Later they were active in Czernowitz, Paris and Buenos Aires (Simha); Czernowitz, Bacau, and Iasi (Itsic); and Bucharest (Iulian). The storyteller Ghedale Vestler (who later immigrated to Israel) may also be cited, as well as the cultural figures Haim Haimovici and Itsic Mendel.

The troubled inter-war period could not put a stop to the creative spirit of the Iasi Jews, who withstood the tragic persecutions of the Holocaust era. The Jewish population had its own cultural life in the cultural Iasi of those times. We must not overlook the preservation of some folkloric traditions – songs, skits, poems – which blended the secular with the religious and kept alive the Jewish spirituality.

{89-92}

TOWARD THE END OF THE CENTURY AND THE MILLENIUM

My town, Iasi, during WWII and the terrible Jewish persecutions, the years of serious events and unbelievable sufferings are too close in my memory and I don't have the perspective necessary to objectively describe the historical events which took place. There are many objective books describing this period from which the reader can form a personal opinion of these times. Such works appeared in Romania and Israel. Scientific meetings were organized in recent years in order to review the events and still there are many facts which need an objective explanation.

In 1940 in Iasi there was a rise in tension against the Jews, with an anti-Semitic offensive organized by criminal elements. It happened in the town where Mihail Sadoveanu and so many intellectuals showed an understanding and a special affection for the minority population!

These anti-Semite manifestations became an awful terror against the Jews, manifested by a terrible carnage known as "the Iasi Pogrom" and the "Train of death" in between 29 June and 2 July 1941. Over 10,000 Jews died during these terrible tortures.

The Jewish population, which remained in Iasi during the war, suffered the rigors of the war along with the entire population. But the Jews also due to humiliations, anti-racial laws, economic and social degradation. The men were made to perform "forced labor," called "Patriotic labor," for the "good of the community." In these labor camps they were often treated inhumanely, without food, clothing or medical assistance. From this impoverished population, socially humiliated and without any rights, the authorities had the impudence to ask for money "contributions," food and clothes.

The Jews from Iasi resisted with dignity all the attempts of being humiliated. They maintained a limited commerce and handicraft. They founded schools of all grades. In synagogues they organized literary meetings and musical events. The intellectuals of the community tried to maintain a dignified spirit among the people, to encourage them for daily survival.

In the Jewish Almanac 5704-1944 (page 190) it is mentioned that in Iasi the Community and the district office of the Jewish Center had the same leadership: President Avram Hahamu and Secretary Dr. Fisher. After 15 October 1944 Dr. Ionel Fruhling was elected President.

In Iasi, after the pogrom, there were 34,000 Jews, a large number in comparison to other centers. The majority of the Jewish people expected economic help from the Jewish Community because many families were very poor. Over 4,000 men were in labor camps. During the war years the Community budget was over 100 million Lei. As winter approached, the poor people received clothes, shoes, food, and firewood. The Community maintained the Jewish institutions: the orphanage, the nursing home, the Israelite Hospital, the "Ghelerter" Hospital, the Red Bridge Dispensary, the primary and secondary schools. Avram Hahamu, the Community President, distributed clothes, shoes, food and money in the labor camps. In the same *Almanac* (pages 201-202) it is written that 5 million Lei were required to help the poor population.

The Community was able to supply legal assistance to the poor Jews, as a result of the large number of Jewish lawyers in Iasi.

To preserve the Jewish spirituality and traditions in the schools that were created, the Hebrew language was a mandatory subject. This tradition persisted for many years. The city of Iasi was recognized among the important centers of the country for the Jewish traditions.

The good organization of the Community and the initiatives taken in the social, humanitarian and cultural domains were due to the devotion of a large number of intellectuals and leaders of the Jewish people, including: Nacht, Pinchas, Duff, Ilie Mendelsohn, Haim Ghelberg and Solomonovici....

The events which occurred after 23 August 1944, the abolishment of the racist legislation, and the partial restitution of property, was a beginning for the Jews to obtain equality in rights with the Romanian population. But the most important issue was the possibility to immigrate to Israel (especially after the creation of the state). This movement of Jews from Romania brought important changes in demography, in keeping up the cultural monuments and in the Jewish Community itself. In 1995 there were in Iasi only 600 Jews, most of them elderly.

The activity of the "Jewish Democratic Committee" was the founding of an elementary school (temporary), where Yiddish was taught, a Jewish Theater (December 1949- February 1963) led by an eminent Director, Iso Schapira, and other elements of Judaic culture maintained and developed over long periods of time. Also, these institutions popularized classical culture and created artists, musicians, and writers. Especially in the 1950's and 1960's, the cultural houses succeeded in organizing conferences, cultural meetings, and musical concerts.

With the help of the Romanian Chief Rabbi, Dr. Moses Rosen, the Great Synagogue of Tirgul Cucului was renovated, the Pacurari cemetery was repaired, some religious libraries were preserved, which existed next to the synagogues that were destroyed (the synagogues were demolished due to some public utilities changes) and a religious life for the small Jewish community was maintained.

Significant achievements also existed in the social assistance field: the existence of a ritual restaurant, the creation of a Medical Clinic, and donations of money, clothes and food for the poor people. These realizations were made possible with the extensive help of the World Organization, "Joint."

Alongside the Community courses in Talmud Tora, a youth choir (which also traveled abroad), series of lectures on religious, historic and cultural subjects, and a community museum were established. These are some elements that mark the existence of a modest Iasi Community that faces the new century and a millennium with dignity.

{93-98}

JEWISH FOLKLORE AND POPULAR ARTS IN IASI

The literary, musical and theatrical folklore in Yiddish, created or propagated by the Jews of Iasi, as well as the entire Jewish population of the country (especially in Moldavia, between the Carpathians and the Dniester, in Bukovina, in Maramures and in the Northern Ardeal, but also in Bucharest and other important centers), has its roots in Central and Eastern Europe. The researchers had identified a series of original characteristics. Between 1924 and 1939, the author of this book collected and published important pages of this folklore, including that from Iasi. A song, written in 1924, deplored the fate of the detainees in the Pacurari prison:

In Rumeinie, in Ios
Of a voil beconter gos
Steit dus Criminol
Dortn leibn dezertorn
Di fraihait hobn zei farlorn
In dem Criminol.

(In Romania, in Iasi
On a known street
Stands this prison
Where the deserters live
They have foregone their freedom
In this prison)

The themes of this folklore were addressed to the young and old, to the daily events and problems, in an artistic style.

For instance this beautiful lullaby:

Inter dem kinds vighiole
Steit a golden tighiole
Dus tighiole iz ghefurn bondlen
Rojinkes and mondlen....

(Under the kids cradle
Stands a golden goat
This goat went shopping
Raisins and almonds)

The last words of the song were:

Toire iz di beste shoire
(the Bible is the best buy)

Children were playing, reciting, and singing "Dadaistic," texts that came from unknown places and times:

A zin mit a reighn
Di cole iz gheleighn
Vus hot zi ghegat
A inghiole
Hot men es gherifn Mendole
Hotmen es bagruben in a kendole
Hot es gheheisen Moisole
Hotmen es bagruben in a coisole

(A son in rain
and the bride was lying
What did she have
A boy
(If) they call it Mendole
They buried it in a pitcher
(If) its name was Moisole
They buried in a basket)

..

The children also knew the following play-on-words:

Endza, dendza, viha-vaha ponda knaba
Givn, pivn, han a pudle....trosk
Eih bob dih arusghelost.

(Endza, dendza, viha-vaha ponda knaba
Givn, pivn, han a pudle....trosk
Eih bob dih arusghelost.
I let you out)

As in any folklore, the family life is very important. In the Yiddish folklore, unrequited love or disappointment is a frequent theme:

Eih vein kikn in veinen
Of dan seinen portret
In of di folse reidoleh
Vus di est ti mir gheret!

(I will look and cry

At your beautiful portrait
And (at) the false words
That you heard about me)

In prose, there are stories and fairytales which interweave the real with the fiction, transmitted from generation to generation.[50] Very interesting are the stories about the Great Synagogue.

The element of "satire" is represented by typical jokes. Here is an example:

A daughter-in-law is complaining about her mother-in-law and says: ghei eih pavole/ Zugt zi az hbin moale/ Ghei eih gib/ zugt zi az eih teras di sih. (If I walk slowly/she says that I am too soft/ if I walk quickly/ she says that I am ripping the shoes).

The folkloric theater was especially loved during holidays. For instance, during Purim, around 1895, in the Podu Ros district, a group of amateurs, ignoring the tradition, the role of Esther, from the Esther Purim Play based on the Book of Esther from the Bible, was played by a girl with a beautiful canary voice and not by a boy. The group was led by Moise Lipoveanu (the last name being the name of the street where Moise lived). Also some old orthodox Russian carriage drivers were members of this artistic group. The girl who played the role of Esther became a primadonna of the Yiddish Theater of Iasi. It is known that the Jewish Theater was a propagandist of the Jewish folklore.

The popular Arts and the handicrafts, deserve special mention. The artists in Iasi worked to create exquisite religious and lay objects.

The author of this book together with Dr. Paul Petrescu, Dr. Irina Cajal-Marin (now both in USA) and H. Culea from Bucharest, did a study of the stone carvers[51] (mateive sleigher). This work will be published to reconsider this art which existed in Iasi for hundreds of years.

Synagogue architecture is interesting, both at the Great Synagogue of Targu Cucului, built in 1670, and at the Great Synagogue of Podu Ros, which was built in 1805. The murals, painted along traditional themes – Jerusalem, the illustration of the psalm "On the Shores of Babylon," the Twelve Tribes, the zodiac – belonged to some Jewish masters who sometimes also worked for nearby Orthodox churches.

Wood sculpting, around the Ark (Aron Hakodesh), at the altar (Amud) and the furniture, was the work of "wood carvers." These bold artists followed a tradition in the Iasian furniture industry that continued even after WWII.

Candlesticks, chandeliers, brass items from the Amud, some Hanukah lamps, appliqués, and other Jewish ritual items, were made by renowned master craftsmen from Iasi who also worked in churches and noblemen's homes. "Keters," Torah crowns, "Tas," breast plates, "Yads," pointers, etc., were crafted by silversmiths, goldsmiths, and Jewish jewelers, who worked for the royal court, as well as for churches and noblemen's homes.

Kiddush cups, etrog boxes, "adas" (spice boxes for Shabbat), "hanukiot," etc., made with filigree, silver, or silver plated, were used in Jewish homes for religious celebrations. There were also the candlesticks, silverware, and jewelry. We remember the engraver Iancu Pecetaru, the grandfather of the poet Veronica Porumbacu, who created many ritual and secular objects.

The objects used by the royal court as well as the "parohet," the predela which covered the Ark that contained the Torah Scrolls, and "Aron Hakodesh," the wedding canopy, were the creations of these handicraftsmen, admired by the entire community.

Tallit and tefillin bags and prayer shawls for their husbands and fiancées were made by young girls and wives. There were cushions and tablecloths, present in every Jewish household, even the most modest ones. The embroideries used specific motifs, such as birds, animals, flowers, abstract figures, Oriental style knitting – found in graphic works as well as wooden and stone sculptures. Mateivas, the funeral stones made by master stone carvers, are real works of art.

Ink drawings in synagogues: pictures for the "sefira," for the month of Adar, covers for registers (Pinkas), "seviti" from the prayer alter, Remembrance plaques, calligraphed prayers, are true works of art that show the remarkable talent of the artists.

Artistic craftsmanship added beauty to daily life... Popular Jewish music and dance deserve competent and adequate study, so that we may acquire a true image of what has been for centuries the life of the Jewish population of Iasi.

{99-100}

NOTES

1. GIURESCU, C. C. *Targuri sau orase si cetati moldovene* (Moldavian small towns or cities and citadels). Bucharest, p.55.
2. DELMEDIGO, SLOMO. *Matzref lahohma* (Crucible of Wisdom). 2nd edition, Odessa, 1865. p.7.
3. *Izvoare si marturii referitoare la evreii din Romania* (Sources and testimonies regarding the Jews of Romania). Vol. 1, Bucharest, Hasefer Publishing, 1986, document nos. 55, 73, 97, 100, 116, 121, 134, 141, 150.
4. *Ibid,* p. 127.
5. *Íbid,* no. 141, 150; see The State Archives Bucharest, file Neamt Monastery, LXXX/3, and Trei Ierarhi Monastery Register, mss 579, files 1v, 3v
6. GRIGORAS, N. *Institutii feudale din Moldova* (Feudal Institutions in Moldavia). Bucharest, Academy Publishing, 1971, p. 40.
7. *Ibid,* p. 401.
8. KARA, I., CHEPTEA, Stela. *Inscriptii ebraice* (Hebrew Inscriptions). Iasi, 1994, inscription no. 34.
9. GHIBANESCU, Gh. *Catastiful Iasilor* (The Iasi Register). *1755,* Iasi, 1921.
10. VERAX. *La Roumanie et les Juifs* (Romania and the Jews). Bucharest, 1903, p. 42-47.
11. *Izvoare si marturii...*(Sources and testimonies...) Vol. 2, no. 117, p. 103.
12. *Ibid,* no. 121, p. 108.
13. *Ibid,* no. 57.
14. *Ibid,* vol. 2/II, p. 60, 61.
15. *Ibid,* no. 97, p. 143-144.
16. KARA, I., CHEPTEA, Stela, *cited work,* inscription no. 64.
17. *Ibid,* no. 67
18. *Ibid,* no. 75
19. *Ibid,* no. 78
20. *Ibid,* no. 79
21. *Ibid,* no. 82, p. 83.
22. *Ibid,* no. 85
23. *Ibid,* no. 184
24. *Ibid,* no. 184
25. *Revista T. Codrescu* (T. Codrescu Review), 1, no. 2, May 1916, p. 118-120
26. KARA, I., in the magazine “Bleter for geszichte,” Warsaw, 1900, vol. 12, p. 151-169.
27. HALEVY, M.A. *Comunitatea evreilor din Iasi si Bucuresti* (The Jewish Community of Iasi and Bucharest), Vol. 1, Bucharest, 1931, p. 75-77.

28. *Ibid*, p. 76.
29. ZANE, G. *Economia de schimb in Principatele Romane* (The Barter Economy in the Romanian Principalities), Bucharest, 1970, p. 330.
30. IORGA, N. *Istoria industriilor romanesti...*(The History of the Romanian Industries...), p. 33.
31. PLATON, Gh. In *Populatie si societate* (Population and Society), vol. 1, Cluj, 1972, Table XVII.
32. *Buletinul Comisiei istorice a Romaniei* (The Bulletin of the Historical Commission of Romania), no. 9, 1930, p. 182.
33. Dated July 6, 1859, p. 5.
34. MANES, S. In: *Anuarul Institutului de Istorie si arheologie "A. D. Xenopol"* (Yearbook of the History and Archeology Institute "A. D. Xenopol"), Iasi, t. VI, 1969, p.
35. ZANE, G. *Economia de schimb...*(The Barter Economy...), p. 45.
36. *Ibid*, p.145.
37. PLATON, Gh., *cited work*, p. 328-329
38. *Ibid*, p. 147.
39. PLATON, Gh. *Geneza revolutiei romane de la 1848* (The Genesis of the Romanian Revolution of 1848), Iasi, 1980, p. 129.
40. VOLOVICI, Leon, *Ideologie nationalista si "problema evreiasca" in Romania anilor '30* (The Nationalistic Ideology and the "Jewish Problem" in Romania of the 30s), Bucharest, 1995, p. 36-37.
41. The newspaper *"Progresul"*, Iasi, Feb. 23, 1966, p. 4.
42. June 6, 1876.
43. REPIN, *Die Juden in Rumaenie* (The Jews in Romania), Berlin, 1908, p. 28.
44. SUTU, Rudolf, *Iasii de odiniora* (Iasi in the past), Iasi, 1928, p. 137 and on
45. *Almanahul ziarului "Rasaritul" pe anul 1899-1900* (The Almanac of the newspaper "Rasaritul" for 1899-1900), Iasi, p. 87.
46. GEORGESCU, Vlad, *Istoria Romanilor* (The History of the Romanians), 3rd Edition, Bucharest, Humanitas, 1992, p. 221.
47. *Ibid*, p. 203.
48. VOLOVICI, Leon, *cited work*, p. 20.
49. LAUNAY, J. de, *Titulesco et l'Europe* (Titulesco and Europe), Paris, 1976.
50. *Revista Cultului Mozaic* (The Mosaic Cult Review), Bucharest, no. 129, Dec. 15th, 1965, p. 5.
51. The collection *"Bucurester Sriften"*, Bucharest, vol. 2, 1979, p. 107-125.

{101-103}

SELECTIVE BIBLIOGRAPHY

(Note: Only those works essential to the present work are mentioned. Most are in Romanian, but works in other languages were also selected. The author preferred recent studies and editions, which are easily accessible.)

The Annals of the Dr. Iuliu Barasch Historical Society, Bucharest, vol. 1 - 1887; vol. 2 - 1888; vol 3. - 1889.

Year Book for Israelites, vol. 5 - 19. Bucharest, 1890 (Editor: M. Schwarzfeld).

The Mosaic Cult Review. Bucharest, 1957 - 1995.

Sinai. Iasi, 1920 - 1927. (Editor: Dr. M. A. Halevy)

Sinai. Yearbook. Bucharest, vol. 1 - 1920; Vol. 2 - 1929; vol. 3 - 1931.

*
* *

ALMONI, P. Epoca "Licht" (The "Licht" Era). Bucharest. No year.
BADARAU, Dan and CAPROSU, Ioan. Iasii vechilor zidiri (The old buildings of Iasi), Iasi, Junimea Publishing, 1970.

Bechol nafshacha. (With all your heart and soul). Work dedicated to the Iasi school teacher Hana Eisenstein. Tel Aviv, 1988.

BERCOVICI, Israel. O suta de ani de teatru evreiesc in Romania, (One hundred years of Jewish theatre in Romania), 1876 - 1976. Bucharest, 1982.
BOGDAN, N.A. Orasul Iasi (The City of Iasi), Iasi, 1914.

CIHODARU, C., PLATON, Gh. Istoria orasului Iasi (The History of the City of Iasi), Vol. 1. Iasi, Junimea Publishing, 1980.

GHERNER, H., WACHTEL, B. Evreii ieseni in documente si fapte (The Jews of Iasi in documents and deeds), Iasi, 1939.

GIURESCU, C. C. Istoria Bucurestilor (The History of Bucharest). Bucharest, 1966.

HALEVY, M. A. Comunitatile evreiesti din Iasi si Bucuresti (The Jewish Communities of Iasi and Bucharest) Vol. 1. Pana la 1821 (Until 1821). Bucharest, 1931.

IANCU, Cornel, Les Juifs en Roumanie (The Jews in Romania). 1913 - 1918. Montpellier, 1993.

Izvoare si marturii privitoare la evreii din Romania (Sources and testimonies regarding the Jews of Romania). Bucharest, Hasefer, 1986-1993. Vol. 1. 1986; vol. II/I.

IORGA, N. Istoria evreiilor in Tarile Romane (The History of the Jews in the Romanian Countries). Bucharest, 1913.

KARA, I. Istoria evreilor in Tarile Romane (The History of the Jews in the Romanian Countries). Iasi, 1995. In manuscript; The Yiddish translation of the summaries of the first five chapters was published in the annual collections BUCARESTER SRIFTN; vol. 1, p. 121-132; vol. 3, p. 97-104; vol. 4, p. 160-172; vol. 5, p. 57-66; vol. 6, p. 150-158. The volumes were published in Bucharest in the years 1978, 1980, 1981, 1982, 1983.

KARA, I. Obstae evreiasca din Podul Iloaiei (The Jewish Community of Podul Iloaiei). Bucharest, Hasefer, 1990.

KARA, I., CHEPTEA, Stela. Inscriptii ebraice (Hebrew Inscriptions). Iasi, 1994.
Martiriul evreilor din Romania. Documente si marturii (The Martyrdom of the Jews of Romania. Documents and Testimonies). 1940-1944, Bucharest, 1991.
MASSOF, Ioan. Stradania a cinci generatii. Monografia familiei Saraga. (The Endeavour of Five Generations. The Monograph of the Sharaga Family.). Bucharest, 1941.

Pinkas Hakehilot. Romania. Vol. 1, Jerusalem, 1970, p. 141-176.

PODOLEANU, Georgeta. Iasii in arta plastica (Iasi in the Plastic Art). Iasi, 1974. (Catalog of exposition with numerous reproductions)

PODOLEANU, S. Istoria presei evreiesti din Romania (The History of the Jewish Press in Romania). Vol. 1, 1857-1900. Bucharest, 1938.

PODOLEANU, S. 60 de scriitori romani de origine evreiasca (60 Romanian writers of Jewish origins). Vol. 1-2. Bucharest, no year.

ROSENBAUM, L. Documente si note privitoare la istoria evreilor in Tarile Romane (Documents and note regarding the history of the Jews in the Romanian Countries), Vol 1-2. Bucharest, 1947.

SAFERMAN, Simion. Dr. W. Filderman. 50 de ani de istorie a evreiilor din Romania (50 years of history of the Jews in Romania). Tel Aviv, 1989. (In Hebrew)

SUTU, Rudolf. Iasii de odinioara (Iasi in the past). Vol. 1-2, Iasi, 1923, 1928.
TAMBUR, Volf. Presa idis in Romania {The Yiddish Press in Romania). Bucharest, 1977.

VERAX. La Roumanie et les Juifs {Romania and the Jews). Bucharest, 1903.

VOLOVICI, Leon. Ideologia nationalista si "problema evreiasca" in Romania anilor '30 (The Nationalistic Ideology and the "Jewish Problem" in Romania during the 30s). Bucharest, 1995.

{105-111}

CONTRIBUTIONS TO THE HISTORY OF JEWS IN IASI
(Original Summary in English)

I. Kara

The presence of a Jewish population in Iasi as early as the 15th century is a fact, according to prominent historians such as C. C. Giurescu. An organized Jewish community must have lived there in the 16th century since Rabbi Shlomo d'Arroyo, a famous scholarly Talmudist, mystic, philosopher, and physician was reported as functioning there about 1580.

A total of 24,576 tombstones dating from the period 1610-1681 could still be seen in the old cemetery of Iasi's Churki neighborhood in 1941. Princely charters from the 17th century regulating the rights and obligations of the Jews' guild as the community was designated, have been reported by researchers. Dr. M. A. HaLevy used to possess such a document dating from 1620, while Gheorghe Chibanescu once summarized a similar writ from 1666. Jews were thereby granted economic and religious freedom; they had rabbis, Hakhams, synagogues, and were under protection of the authorities. The elder, or *staroste*, of the guild handed the duties of all local Jews in bulk to the treasury. These were collected in the form of taxes on Kosher meat, and sometimes also on liquor, yeast, etc.

Moldavian chronicles tell about a pogrom by hoodlums of Timush Chmielnicki who had come to marry Ruxanda, daughter of Voivode Basil the Wolf. Reports on the peasants uprising and pogrom led by hetman Bogdan Chmielnicki were provided by Rabbi Nathan Hanover, a famous philosopher, historian and physician, who served in Iasi in ca. 1657-1670. The Great Synagogue in Targu Cucului neighborhood, which was still standing in 1995, was erected by him in 1659-1670. There had been only wooden synagogues in town before that.

The demographic, social and economic structure of the Jewish community in Iasi can be assessed from Hebrew sources such as: rabbinical response, tombstones, various registers of the Hevra Kadisha (burial society), economic guilds, charities, and cultural associations. Foreign travelers such as C. Magni in 1687 provided some accounts, while further information on the period to 1800 can be found in three volumes of documents recently published by the History Center of the Federation of Romanian Jewish Communities. Monographs and various historical studies offer further valuable data.

Many historical sources reveal the growth in numbers and economic strength of the Jews in Iasi. Their bustling activity in commerce, various trades, transportation, and services was underscored by both foreign travelers and local historians, who did not fail to mention that Jews were shamelessly exploited by voivodes such as Michael Racovita who squeezed them for money on blood charges in 1726.

In 1756, Jews totaled over 400 out of an overall population of 7000. The fact that prominent rabbis such as Petachio Lyda functioned in town in ca. 1715 and the creation of a *hakham-bashi* office in ca. 1729 imply a rather significant community. The Naftulovicis constituted something like a dynasty of *hakham-bashis*. Naftali, who was first appointed, never functioned, but his son, Yeshaya, put in a vigorous performance in office, which he then handed down to Bezalel, his son. When 'Bezal' (as Moldavian documents would call him) died, the job went to his son. Yitzhak, whose financial, administrative and even political claims brought him in conflict with the elder of the Jewish guild. After Yitzhak's death, Mordecai, a scholarly rabbi, briefly held office (1777) but was soon dead and the post returned to the family by the appointment of Neftali, Bezalel's son. He was followed in 1809 by an underage son, with his uncle Yeshaya as guardian. This son soon grew old enough to take over the job, which he held until 1834.

The Hevra Kadisha, which had run the local cemetery from the very beginning, gradually took up further community tasks. Documents first mention the society in 1610 when the Churki cemetery was also first reported. A register, including charters, meeting reports and various entries on the Hevra's activity, was renewed in the 18th century.

A community organization known as the "Jews' guild" – there also was and "Armenians' guild" at the same time – was in existence in the 17th century when seven of its leading members are reported. Russian records mentioned 171 Jewish families living in Iasi out of a total of 574 in 1774. Jews were involved in mostly every branch of commerce, moneylending, transport, and especially handicrafts. They supplied the voivode's court, the church, the boyars and, of course, the Jewish population. They were particularly famed as silversmiths, brass workers, jewelers, bakers, tailors, bootmakers, hatters, carpenters, bricklayers, watchmakers, upholsterers, mechanics, etc., and had set up their own professional guilds as early as the 18th century. They often impressed foreign travelers as energetic craftsmen and merchants.

Historical demography is the basic instrument for investigating population evolution. Iasi counted 2420 Jewish taxpayers in 1805, but the figure appears incomplete since, in 1820, 4926 Jewish family heads were recorded. The 1831 census found 1570 Jewish families, while seven years later documents tell of 29,562 'souls'. The number rose to 31,015 in 1859, then dropped to 19,941 in 1890. The local Jewish population continued to decline, with many emigrating or moving away as a result of economic and social troubles in the years 1890-1910.

After 1866, community structures ran into difficulties. Central governments neglected the community, discriminatory laws and regulation hurt the economic and social life of the Jews. Community leaders grew unable to cope with an increasing number of problems and could not strike a balance between needs and means, or between aspirations and achievements. In economic life, it was only through dedicated work, initiative, innovation, persistence, sobriety, and adaptability that Jews succeeded in fighting off a crisis arising from hostile legislation and local authority abuse.

Biblical and Talmudic studies stimulated spiritual life throughout the Jewish population, irrespective of social categories. Ethical standards remained high thanks to a thorough observance of rituals and a sense of sharing the same fate, reflected in a high degree of civic awareness.

Hasidism, the mystic and popular reform movement, founded by Rabbi Israel Baal Shem-Tov, spread rapidly in the first decades of the 19th century. In 1800-1850, largely with the support of banker Michel Daniel, Hasidism was quite pervasive amid the local Jewry. Daniel's descendants, particularly R. Israel Rujiner, settled at Sadagura, and founded Hasidic centers at Stefanesti, Buhusi, and Adjud.

Opposed to Hasidism was the Haskalah, a rationalist, modernizing movement, which developed in Germany in the 18th century with the support of Moses Mendelssohn. Its followers, or *mashkilim*, advocated a reform of traditional education to meet contemporary needs and an improved knowledge of both Hebrew and the local language. They also urged their coreligionists to drop traditional garments as well as some customs, rites and forms of worship. Stiff traditionalism had hardly a more scorching for than Velvl Zbarjer Ehrenkranz, a balladist – author, composer, performer, and publisher of his own songs. He used to sing them everywhere – at weddings, family reunions, gatherings, or even in pubs and cafes. His volumes contained both the original Yiddish lyrics and a Hebrew version, also of his own making. Some rationalists were eventually assimilated, converted even. Such is the case of lawyer Alexandru Veinberg, father, of the reputed literary critic Tudor Vianu. Others such as Haiman, Tiktin, Lazar Saineanu converted for the sake of their professional careers. Some trends toward a cultural assimilation without recanting Judaism were promptly discouraged by chauvinism on the rise.

Modern, professional Yiddish theater took a special place in the spiritual life of the community. Born at the Green Tree Garden in Iasi, in 1876, it swiftly spread across Europe and America and wherever Yiddish speakers lived. Drawing on Jewish folklore, recasting ancient Judaic wisdom, improving acting skills and theatrical techniques, it attracted a numerous audience. Its repertoire successfully blended motifs from secular world culture and others from the national-religious tradition, which brightened the Jewish hearts oppressed by their bitter lot.

A Jewish press in Yiddish, Romanian and Hebrew developed over the next decades. Socialist and Zionist organizations emerged on the political scene; trade unions, mutual help associations and charities sprouted up.

While the living standards of Iasi Jews declined against a backdrop of internal economic recession, the drive for emancipation gathered momentum and manifested itself in various forms. Jewish-Romanian primary schools were founded, traditional education was improved, and increasingly more Jews of different backgrounds were attracted to the study of Romanian language and culture. In spite of legal discrimination, growing numbers of Jews attended secondary schools and higher education, and soon enough a Jewish intelligentsia took shape that would make a significant contribution to Romanian culture. In 1915, the first group – *Licht* – of modern Yiddish literature was set up.

The interwar years, 1918-1940, were an extremely dynamic period. The uneven development of Romanian democracy, A. C. Cuza's nefarious anti-Semitic activity, marked by hooliganic outbursts, his manipulation of the academic youth, the Iron Guard – all these convulsed the Jewish population of Iasi. Against the background of a Greater Romania rocked by great structural changes, faced with the growth of industry, commerce and trades, then with the economic depression starting in 1929, hit by racial discrimination (*numerus valachicus, numerus nullus*), the population was sharply pauperized. Young Jews eager to study or improve their economic status were fighting an uphill battle. Various Zionist organisations were active at the time and a specific Romanian-language press expanded. Writers such as B. Fundoianu, Enric Furtuna, I. Ludo, Eugen Relgis, C. Sateanu, Carol Drimer, M. A. Halevy, and the Hefter brothers, as well as groups such as *Tribuna evreiasca* maintained creative links with the community in Iasi.

Distinguished local leaders, including I. Mendelssohn, Moses Duff, I. M. Moscovici, G. Buhman, Dr. Fuhling, and others, were dedicating their efforts to the prosperity of Jewish institutions and an ever increasing prestige of the community.

The city of Iasi witnessed a wide range of political and social trends. Unfortunately, racial terrorism set in among them culminating in the savage pogrom of June 1941, in which more than ten thousand local Jews were killed.

After the terrible years of racial persecution, the new political regime gave rise to fresh hopes for a better life. But soon enough craftsmen, businessmen and merchants saw their properties nationalized and their status lowered. Short-lived demagogic measures – schools, Yiddish literature, a state theater – gave way to a grim, impoverished society, which clearly revealed the nature and prospects of the new totalitarianism. Mass emigration to Israel ensued, often associated with bare destitution and threats from the secret police.

Nevertheless, a small Jewish community is still alive and active in Iasi, working in every field, supporting continuity, promoting the lofty values of Jewish culture, observing the traditions of their forefathers, and making every effort in their might to defend their identity in these times of change.

The following images were not contained in the original book on Iasi, but are included here to enhance the material.

Great Synagogue of Iasi, courtesy of Jeffrey Gorney

Aerial View of Iasi, courtesy of Jeffrey Gorney

Memorial to the Victims of the Iasi Pogrom in 1941, courtesy of Jeffrey Gorney

Plaque Memorial to the Victims of the Iasi Pogrom 1941, courtesy of Jeffrey Gorney

Iasi Synagogue, courtesy of Robert Sherins

Iasi Synagogue, courtesy of Robert Sherins

S. Goldenberg's home, courtesy of Robert Sherins

City Hall, courtesy of Robert Sherins

View from the Jewish Cemetery, courtesy of Robert Sherins

The Jewish Community in
PODU ILOAIEI

Pages from the History of a Moldavian Shtetl

By Itzik Schwartz-Kara

English Edition
Translated, annotated and supplemented with additional material
by Nathan P. Abramowitz and associates.

Table of Contents

1 Preface by KM Elias, Aug/2006

Until five years ago I knew nothing about Podu Iloaiei, the Romanian town in which my great grandparents lived before coming to Canada in 1906. However my posting on JewishGen caught the attention of another JewishGener in NY, Catherine Richter. She later discovered a German book in the New York public library titled "Juden in Podu Iloaiei" (call# PXM 00-1458), which is the translation of an earlier Romanian book, titled "Obstea Evreiasca Din Podu Iloaiei" by Itic Svart Kara. I found the Romanian version in the central public library here in Toronto. (There are only about 30 books in the Romanian section and amongst them was this one, about a small Jewish shtetle in Moldavia. Imagine that!). Kara's book was originally published in Iasi in 1925 and republished in 1990 in Bucharest by Hasefer Publishing House.

The book contains a number of censuses, from which I gathered the following:

- The Jewish community dates back at least to the early 1800's.
- By 1898 there were 723 Jewish households in the town.
- In 1907 many left for America. (That year there were widespread anti-Jewish disburbances across Moldavia).
- By 1910 only 1,895 Jews remained, comprising 68% of the population.

To my amazement, the very first entry in the 1898 census was that of my great grandparents.

A few weeks later Catherine heard about another JewishGen member, Nat Abramowitz, who was working on a translation of the book. It turns out that Mr. Abramowitz (whose father came from Podu Iloaiei) had the book translated a few years earlier by a Romanian acquaitance.

Eventually through Nat and other sources on JewishGen, I learned a little about the author of the book. Itic Svart Kara was born in Podu Iloaiei circa 1906 and lived there until his twenties. He was a very educated man - he spoke some 7 languages and was well respected in the Romanian Academy of Sciences. He was considered the foremost authority on the history of Moldavian Jewry, having written dozens of books on a number of Yiddish Stetlach, one of them being Podu Iloaiei.

And to my surprise Mr. Kara, age 93, was still living in Iasi, near Podu Iloaiei. After writing a few letters that were not answered I called him in March 2001, but his poor hearing made communication impossible. A few weeks later a Romanian researcher interviewed Mr. Kara on my behalf and was able to obtain some more information on my family. He told me that Kara would have answered my letters had he not been confined to his apartment in a wheel chair, not being able to visit the post office to mail a letter. The researcher would not accept any payment for the service, explaining that he knew Mr. Kara for many years and it was a pleasure visiting with him and would not consider profiting from Kara's treasure of information!

At about the same time I came in contact with Toronto filmmaker, Simcha Jacobovici (Deadly Currents, The 12 Tribes, etc, etc), whose mother was born in Podu Iloaiei. It turns out that Simcha had been in Romania earlier that year doing work on a new documentary on the Struma and while there he interviewed Kara for a future project on the Jews of Romania.

A few weeks later we received some sad news from Romania that Mr. Kara had passed away on May 29, 2001, the 2nd day of Shavuot.

As it turns out Mr. Kara had a sister living here in Toronto and while visiting the Shiva house, I was shown the video of Simcha's interview with Mr. Kara. I was very surprised. Despite his age and frailty, Mr. Kara was still quite clear and lucid. So I felt quite bad that we were not able to communicate together on the phone a few months earlier.

And now back to the book on Podu Iloaiei... Having developed a very warm feeling for Mr. Kara, I wanted to see this book as well as his others published in English for everyone's benefit. Unfortunately the tanslation commissioned by Nat Abramowitz was difficult to read as Kara wrote in an academic style and referred to sources written in archaic Romanian which do not lend themselves to a literal translation.

So I persuaded Nat that we get the book translated over again. The plan was to make the book available on JewishGen as a free download, providing we could obtain permission from the original publishers in Romania. We hired a Romanian translator here in Toronto and Catherine did the editing. After working on this project for about a year the translation was completed in August 2002. Although Nat was very pleased to have it finished he was rather frustrated that permission from the publisher had still not been obtained. He made it very clear to me that the book should not be distributed to anyone unless the copyright issue is first resolved.

A few weeks later I received an email with some very sad news. Nat Abramowitz had passed away.

Recently Nat's wife Lucille contacted me, enquiring about the project. She was very surprised when told that the book had not yet made available to JewishGen because we did not have the publisher's permission. She was under the impression that permission had been obtained and a few days later she sent me a letter from Hasefer to that affect.

Now began the work of preparing the book for publication. My initial idea was to make it available as a PDF file on JewishGen, however I've since learned that the JewishGen standard is HTML. As such I've made a number of changes to the style in order to accommodate the JewishGen volunteers who have converted our MS Word document to HTML.

I have also made a number of additions and changes to the original book, which will be described in the next chapter.

I am most grateful to the following individuals who invested much time and effort in seeing this project through:

Nathan Abramowitz z"l	project sponser and organizer (see bio below)
Johanna Danciu	translation of Romanian
Dan Jumara	clarification of certain historical matters and Romanian words
Eugen Hriscu	translation of Romanian
Rosechelle Lipchitz	glossaries
Howard Markus	glossaries
Dana Melnic	translation of Romanian
Catherine Richter	Editor
Simcha Simchovitch [B-1]	translation of Yiddish poems

A number of books have been written about specific shtetlach in Eastern Europe. Most of these were written by Holocaust survivors and describe shtetl life during the first half of the 20th century.

This book is rather unusual in that it was written by a historian. It's an indepth study of the Jewish community and its origins. Kara uses original sources including government documents, court proceedings and census records from the 19th century.

I hope that those with roots in Podu Iloaiei find delight in this book and that it will serve as an important resource for those studying the history of the Jewish communities of Moldavia.

KM Elias
Toronto, Canada
August, 2006

[1] [KME] Simcha Simchovitch is a well-known, Toronto-based Yiddish poet.

1.1 *Pictures of the Book*

1.1.1 Book Cover and Illustration of Bridge

The cover of the book bears an intriguing wood-cut drawing of a river with a small bridge. Standing nearby is an old Jew, beard and *shtramle*, together with a woman, presumably his wife, in front of what appears to be their home. This picture refers back to the very origins of Podu Iloaiei.

Kara tells us in the first chapter that "Podu Iloaiei" in Romanian means "Bridge of Iloaiei". He explains that the town took its name from the local bridge that crosses the Bahlui River. According to tradition, the bridge was built by a Jewish women named Iloaia (meaning wife of Ilie), who lived in the area in the early 1800s. She supposedly built the bridge to connect the inn with the postal station on the other side of the Bahlui River. Presumably the picture depicts Ilie and his wife Iloaia in front of the inn beside the river. [B-2].

---

[2] [KME] This legend is fascinating to me in particular because there is a tradition in our family, the Ilies, that our ancestors were innkeepers in Podu Iloaiei. Perhaps we are descended from this Ilie and his wife Iloaia.

1.1.2 The First Page

HRONIC (1818-1968)

Toponimicul Podu Lelioaei, forma veche a actualului Podu Iloaiei, este mult mai vechi decît tîrgul, întemeiat în al doilea deceniu al veacului trecut. S-a stabilit chiar că o așezare fortificată a existat pe aici încă în sec. IX—XIV [1]. Al. Graur presupune că numele locului ar proveni, în forma Podul Lelioaei, de la „soția unui Lalu, dar a fost înțeles ca Iloaia, soția unui Ile sau Ilie" [2].

Tradiția locală, încă vie la începutul veacului nostru, este reprodusă de C. Chiriță în 1888 [3]: „Și-a luat numirea, se zice, de la podul făcut peste Bahlui de către o femeie evreică numită Iloaia, care, la începutul veacului trecut, viețuia în această localitate, unde nu se afla decît un han, construit la drumul mare, iar pe cealaltă parte, de-a stînga Bahluiului, erau cîteva bordeie pe locul unde staționa poșta veche. În interesul de a se putea lega mai bine comunicația între poștă și han, evreica Iloaia a construit un pod statornic peste apa Bahluiului, care și azi poartă numele ei...".

Podul exista însă cu mult înainte de veacul al XIX-lea. Un călător polonez relata la 1700: „Poduleloi, pe rîul Bahlui, peste care este aici un pod mic de zid. Sînt numai colibe mici" [4]. Nu este exclus ca podul să se fi stricat între timp. În 1653 „Vasilie Vodă încă ce au putut strînge oști, degrabă le-au luat și au ieșit înainte la Podul Lelioaei. Acolo lovindu-se oștile au biruit Gheorghe logofătul și au fugit Vasilie Vodă la cuscrul său Hmil, hatmanul cazac... [5]. (E vorba de Bogdan Hmelnițki).

La începutul acestui veac era încă vie tradiția locală despre această luptă. Se afirma că soldații uciși ar fi fost îngropați pe dealul din fața bisericii. De copil căutam pe acolo comori rămase de la Vasile Lupu, dar fără prea

1.2 *In Memory of Itzik Schwartz-Kara (1906-2001)*

The following pictures were provided by Mr. Kara's sister, Chana Gelber.

Itzic Svartz-Kara and Family 1938
Clockwise: Itzic, Sister Basia, Golda, Ana, Brother Yosi, Sister Miriam, Mother Ester, and First Wife Anna

Itzic Svartz-Kara 1975.
Wife Tzila on the left and,
Sister Golda on the right.

1.3 *In Memory of Nathan P. Abramowitz (1917-2002)*

Nathan, son of Max and Minna Abramowitz, was born and educated in N.Y. and later settled in Cherry Hill, N.J. He was an electrical engineer whose career included consulting, manufacturing and management services in United States as well as Europe.

Upon his retirement his endless curiosity and wanderlust, as well as his intelligence and good humor, led him to pursue his interest in genealogy. His interest in his grandfather's and father's hometown of Podu Iloaiei introduced him to Itzik Schwartz-Kara's book, "The Jewish Community in Podu Iloaiei".

Nathan had this book translated from Romanian to English to make it available to people interested in their Romanian-Jewish heritage and acquaint them with the detailed town history, community life, education, synagogues and rabbinate of Podu Iloaiei.

He is survived by his wife, Lucille, and two sons.

2 About the Aug/2006 Edition

A number of additions and changes are being introduced with this new edition of Kara's book.

2.1 *Organization of Chapters*

The arrangement of chapters has changed and new chapters have been added.

	Chapter	Old Chapter#	Comment
1	Preface by KM Elias, 2006		New
2	Modifications Appearing in this Edition, 2006		New
3	Preface by N. Abramowitz, 2002		New
4	Obituary for Itic-Svart Kara, 2001		New
5	Foreword by Dr. S. Caufman, 1990	15	Formerly called "Afterword"
6	Introduction by I.Kara, 1990	1	
7	Chronicle (1818-1968)	2	
8	Economic Life	3	
9	Communal Life	4	
10	Private and Public Education	5	
11	Synagogues	6	
12	Rabbinate	7	
13	Hasidism	8	
14	Folklore and Ethnography	9	
15	Podu Iloaiei as Depicted in Literary Works	10	
16	Documentary Appendices	11	This edition does not include Appendix P, the 1898 census. Appendix P appears separately as a database in the JRI section of JewishGen. ???
17	At the Turn of the Century. Several Cumpulsory Additions	13	
18	I. Kara: History Studies. Selected Bibliography	14	
19	References	12	Formerly called "Notes" Now arranged by chapter.
20	Glossary of Terms		New
21	Glossary of Places		New
22	Glossary of People		New
23	Pictures	16	

2.2 *Footnotes*

In the Romanian edition of the book there's a chapter titled "Notes", which we are now calling "References". In this English edition the pointers in the body of the book appear in the format [A-1], [A-2], [A-3].

We've also added our own footnotes, indicated by the following prefixes:

- [Ed-Com] – these deal with words or concepts used in the book
- [KME] – these deal with the process of producing this book

In this English edition the pointers in the body of the book appear in the format [B-1], [B-2], [B-3].

2.3 *Glossaries*

During the course of editing this book, I've had a number of inquires from people with Podu Iloiaie ancestry looking for information about their families. In a number of cases I've been able to find them pertainent information by doing keyword searches throughout the Word document.

As a result I came to realize the need for a glossary of people and places mentioned in the book. This will be very helpful for genealogists searching for specific names.

2.4 *Printing this Document*

This document was originally written as an MS Word Doc file and later converted to PDF format. It was also converted to HTML format for hosting at www.JewishGen.org .

Some people however may prefer reading a document of this size (over 100 pages) from a printed hardcopy rather than from the computer monitor. The PDF version is ideal for this purpose as it is more printer-friendly than HTML. To obtain a copy in PDF format, contact KM Elias.

3 Preface by Nathan Abramowitz, June/2002

Podu Iloaiei was the shtetl of my father and my ancestors. While doing family research, I came across and was able to obtain a copy of a book called The Jewish Community in…Podu Iloaiei by Itzik-Schwartz Kara. Originally published in Iasi in 1925, the book was republished in 1990 in Bucharest by Hasefer Publishing House. I received permission from Hasefer to publish an English language translation of the book.

The initial translation was done by Eugene Hriscu of Iasi, Romania. Although English is not his first language, I was amazed at the quality of his English translation from the original Romanian text. KM Elias of Toronto clarified the Hebrew and Yiddish expressions, and, with the assistance of Dana Melnic of Toronto, resolved some of the idiomatic questions that arose as the work progressed. Catherine Richter, a professional editor, did an excellent job of editing and preparing the translation for publication. It was truly an outstanding group of people, and I gratefully thank all involved – including my wife Lucile whose patience and understanding allowed me to devote a great deal of time to this project.

A note about Dr. Kara: I was directly in touch with him via Mr. Hriscu. He expressed delight about having the book translated into English and requested several copies to distribute among institutions and his colleagues. Unfortunately, Dr. Kara passed away in May 2001 at the age of 94. His obituary, as presented by Dr. Silviu Sanie, is reproduced at the end of the book[B-3].

[3] [KME] In this edition the obituary is printed at the beginning of the book on page 15.

4 Obituary for Itic-Svart Kara, May/2001

The following obituary was delivered by Prof. Dr. Silviu Sanie

The passing of Mr. Kara marks our separation from the representative of an elite generation that had among its last gone to join their ancestors from the Iasi community Dr. S. Kaufman and Prof. S. Friedenthal. It was a *heder* generation for which Yiddish was truly a maternal language. A generation for which life had prepared a road full of obstacles they were the actors and the witnesses of some great catastrophes for the Jewish community.

Itic Svart was born almost 95 years ago in Podu Iloaiei, in a large family where faith and customs were highly respected.

The Svart family gave three personalities to the Jewish culture – Simha, Iulian and Itic – a sculptor, a writer – actor and one who was to manifest interest in many fields.

I.Svart graduated from The Faculty of French Language, but has also been a professor of Yiddish language and he followed this second calling for a longer time and it brought him great satisfactions.

These are some of the Yiddishist's accomplishments:

In 1948, he published a Yiddish language grammar. Within the short period of time when Salom Alechem's language was allowed to affirm itself in schools, his work proved to be most useful.

As the literary secretary of the Jewish State Theatre of Iasi, he translated from several languages into Yiddish and worked hard to improve the quality of the Yiddish language spoken by the actors. He loved the theatre and this is maybe the only area where his brother Iulian had an advantage – he was also an actor.

However, Yiddish is the language of many of Mr. Kara's writings. Certainly, he could have said as Mircea Eliade did about the Romanian language that it is "the language of his dreams". In Cernauti, he found himself in the proximity of several poets like Itic Manger (who later came to Iasi) and Eliezer Steinberg, in the very core of the cultural life of the "small Vienna", in the period between the two WW. The writer brought to the public facts and events that he wrote about in the Yiddish papers in Vilna, Warsaw, New York, etc. He coordinated some volumes of the paper "Bucarester Shriftn". The prose writer wrote many stories, some of them with autobiographic content. He later gathered them in the 1976 printed volume "A Moldavis Ingl" ("A Boy from Moldavia") and, in 1987, "Iurn fon Hofmung" ("Hope Years").

The man who traveled the world all the way to the Soviet Far East where Svart became Kara, the French professor who also spoke Russian and English continued to be the same "Moldavis ingl", but accomplishing many. He received awards from the Israeli Yiddish specialists and FCER's "J. Pineles" award.

The man who started his journey from a *stetl* has also been a folklorist, carefully recording some of the things he felt would disappear together with the world that gave them birth. Proverbs, sayings, children's holiday wishings and many more.

He had a call for history. Like Iacob Psantir in the XIX-th century, I. Kara knew that he had to save for the history the documents and moments of the communities' lives; he also published different testimonies that some considered of minor importance, but he understood their significance. He permanently improved the method, the style as well as the critical apparatus of his works. His writings touched issues from the cultural and socio – economical life. Historiography will remember him as the author of the monographs on Bacau, Podu Iloaiei, that was also published in German by the great humanist E. R. Wiehn, and "Contributions to the History of the Jewish Community of Iasi". He published in museum and academic institutes' magazines.

He published, together with Dr. Stela Cheptea, "Medieval Hebrew Inscriptions (aprox. 300) in Iasi" which was awarded by the Romanian Academy. He was a bibliophile. A scholar.

An unostentatious believer, but possessing extensive knowledge from his childhood and adolescence years (as described in his books), Mr. Kara was one of the main counselors of the Iasi community. He discretely guided the cultural activities, he possessed the skill, the patience and the understanding needed to be a *malomad* and to prepare those who trained to put *tefilim*, he conducted the Seder on Pesach, etc.

He was at the same time one of the main men who attended the *sil*.

He could talk to people of all ages and professions. He also knew, together with the missed Mss. Tili, how to be a pleasant host.

He was a man with an ever strong will to gather knowledge, quickly to adapt to all kinds of situations and places – from Podu Iloaiei. Iasi and Cernauti to the Soviet Far East and Berlin, as a soldier, professor, literary secretary, librarian, community activist and, above all, a writer and a historian. A full life that spread over almost an entire century.

The man we are saying good – bye now to was a complex and important personality, a representative symbol of the Iasi community.

5 Foreword by Dr. S. Caufman, 1990

In the 1990 version of the book this section appeared at the back of the book as an "afterword"

As a good Moldavian Jew, and as the president of the Jewish community of Iasi, I have a special interest in the past, present, and future of the community of Iasi, without neglecting the other communities in the district and even those in the neighboring districts.

Since I was born and spent my childhood in a Moldavian "shtetl," I am familiar with the way things used to be in those days of yore, in the Jewish borough, and I feel a part of the place, with its milieu, the concerns, the suffering and the joys, the strain and the victories of tens of thousands of Jews who lived in the towns and boroughs of Moldavia, its becoming a traditional, inextricable part of the Moldavian world, of the historic Moldavia.

As a matter of fact, the traditional culture in which I grew up and with which I have identified myself all through my life, and my interest for the life and culture of the Jewish population of Romania, make me totally capable of understanding and experiencing all that is depicted in I. Kara's writings dedicated to his native borough, Podu Iloaiei, which is located only 21 kilometers from Iasi and in whose cemetery, unfortunately, many of the victims of the "death train" are buried.

Finally, the person who is writing these lines has one more advantage: He knows the author I. Kara, alias Itic Svart, very well, Ithac ben Avi who for more than two decades was a member of the community's committee. Our relationship is not limited only to a long-lasting and close cooperation on the cultural and educational field. We are also familiar with his hard work and the results of his research in the field of the Jews' history in Romania, studies that have been carried on for more than half a century. We also know about his permanent co-working with the Federation of the Jewish Communities of Romania. This is one more reason to expect the most from the present monograph, a one of a kind piece of work in the field of monographs on the small Jewish communities of Moldavia, written by a qualified historian, the author of more than a hundred works published since 1939 both in the country and in prestigious international magazines.

I first read I. Kara's study as it was eight years ago, and I read it again with sympathy, curiosity, and exigency in its final form, and so I dare to make some observations.

The first chapter of this work is an incursion into the history of events of the Jewish community of Podu Iloaiei. The author has an open attitude when approaching the facts, placing them in the wider framework of the borough's development, the life of all of its inhabitants, and the activity of the entire commune. Thus, it provides a clearer image of the reality in its diverse aspects, with all of its contradictions and concords.

Regarding the tragic events of the years 1941 to 1944, some of my own personal experiences confirm the author's depictions.

The detailed presentation of the borough's economic life, based on novel, Hebrew sources, makes a chronological and synchronous analysis of the data at hand, confirming the general impression, that is not only mine, regarding the paramount role played by the Jewish population in the development of the town and the boroughs and even in the foundation of some of them.

In the chapter dedicated to the community life, the author resorted to considerable autobiographical data as well. This chapter is written more colorfully and sympathetically, with more emotional involvement, a style that the undersigned prefers to the author's sober tone that characterizes the other chapters. Reading the chapter on education, I felt a justified nostalgia. Fundamentally, many of the elements of the life and history of the Jewish community of Podu Iloaiei are common to most of the Moldavian towns in the 19th century and even in our century too, at least until 1940.

The chapter on folklore and ethnography was also quite meaningful to me. The author used to collect Yiddish folklore, ever since his high-school years, and has published it since 1933. He has pursued this "sin of the youth" until now. You do not have to be a historian to realize that the author has not used up all the available data in his monograph and that there is still money to be made in this field by future researchers.

I am particularly satisfied with the anthology of literary works dedicated to this town. The author offers translations of some Yiddish literary works. "The Rabbi of Podu Iloaiei" appeared in the volume *A Moldevish Inghl* (*A Boy from Moldavia*) by I. Kara, published in 1976 by Kriterion Publishing House in Bucharest. The great poet Itic Manger dedicated a wonderful ballad to this noble rabbinical figure. The anthology also includes a translation of the short story *Podu Iloaiei* by Simcha Schwartz (1900-1974), the author's older brother and a great playwright and famous sculptor recognized as such in France and Argentina. He is also the author of the delightful *Hotchpotch* and *Podeloier Times*, dated 1920. The funny character Dudl Consul was also portrayed in *A Boy from Moldova.*

I am sure that researchers will be very glad to find the numerous and substantial documentary appendices that include novel material gathered with much effort, meticulousness, and skill from archives and libraries. Qualified historians have made this last appreciation. How could I dare contradict them? Actually, this chapter is also written in a lively, fluent, convincing, and accessible style, without losing any of its strictly scientific value.

The Federation of the Jewish Communities should be praised for publishing this unique and highly valuable work. It can, of course, be improved upon and new material added, but it will surely set an example for others to write such valuable monographs for some of the country's other communities.

They will undoubtedly have the support of the communities and the Federation, which has published so many excellent historic works in the last years.

6 Introduction by I.Kara, 1990

While working on the essay "The History of the Jews in Romania until 1917" that was completed in 1976 and recently revised, I felt the need for such an incursion in the history of the Jewish community in my native borough. The first part, following the events until the year 1848, appeared in a short version in the Yiddish-written anthology "Bukarester sriftn", volumes I-VI (1978- 1983). The writing of a history of the Jewish population of Romania proved to be a difficult task considering the relatively limited amount of information that survived in the community archives, the insufficient material in the public and private archives, the small number of monographs dedicated to some communities and institutions, and the difficulties in consulting information, sources and studies.

Still, the historian Dr. M.A. Halevy has published in 1931 the monograph "The Jewish Communities of Iasi and Bucharest", volume I, (up to the year 1821), while "Iuliu Barasch History Society" supported (during 1886 - 1889) the elaboration of monographs of the Romanian Jewish communities. "The History the Ploiesti community "by Israel Sapira (1889) was the only one to be published; the monograph on the Bacau community by A.D. Birnberg remained in a draft form and I revised it in 1947; the monograph of the Botosani community by H. Ghinter could not be found.

In our century, there have been only several modest attempts to write monographs regarding our communities or some of their institutions. I mention here Nisim M. Derera's monograph (1906) and S. Semilian's (1931) regarding the Jews in Braila. The community in Craiova has been described in the works of Leon de Askenazi and M. Staureanu; short monographs were dedicated to the community in Roman by E. Schwarzfeld and I. Kaufman. Iosef Kaufman is the author of a two-volume work, "The Chronicle of The Jewish Communities of the Neamt District" (1928-1929), which includes a lot of valuable data and materials, but much insignificant detail as well. There are several incomplete monographs on the communities in Transylvania: Alba Iulia, Oradea, Timisoara signed by Dr. M. Eisler, E. Fleischer, Dr. I. Singer.

The articles that were once published by the press and even some of the articles that appeared in "The Magazine of the Mosaic Cult" have mainly a popularizing character; the original material that they sometimes bring can not replace the necessary scientifically-based monographs. The lack of information cannot be compensated even by the work of monumental proportions "Pinkas Hakehilot Romania", volume I (1970), volume II (1980) published by "Yad Vashem" Institute in Jerusalem or by the anthologies of occasional articles, memoirs, and memorial articles that appear in Israel and the U.S.A., in Hebrew, Yiddish, Romanian, English, German, Hungarian.

Putting together the comprehensive monographs regarding the Jewish communities that exist or existed in Romania between the two WWs remains an objective for historical research. For now, there are still to be collected materials and information from the people who spent their childhood in the towns and boroughs of the beginning of the century, as well as trying to find papers, documents, photos, objects that can prove useful for the study of our history. The importance of these monographs has been repeatedly emphasized by a great personality as His Eminence Dr. Moses Rosen, Chief Rabbi of the Mosaic cult and the president of' the Federation of' the Romanian Jewish Communities.

It has been pointed out that the monograph of a certain community, no matter how small it is, clarifies some aspects of the life of other similar communities. In fact, most of the events, situations, structures, activities, and mentalities were almost the same within the small communities in Moldova. The study of one community could end up in the drawing of conclusions that remain valid for other communities as well.

Several annexes were added to the present text, presenting in extenso original sources, many of them unpublished before, together with an anthology of the literary works that depict the life of this modest Moldavian borough. Several photos and illustrations have also been added.

I express my gratitude to the Iasi and Bucharest State Archives, The Library of the Romanian Academy, The Library of the "Al. I. Cuza" University, Iasi, the library and the archives of the Federation of the Romanian Jewish Communities (FRJC) as well as to all the people who supplied me with materials and information, thus contributing to the writing of this monograph.

I want to thank especially the FRJC and His Eminence Dr. Moses Rosen who showed a special interest in the publishing of this work.

The Author

7 Chronicle (1818-1968)

The place-name Podu Lelioaiei—the old form of today's Podu Iloaiei—is much older than the borough itself, which was founded in the second decade of the 19th century. In fact, a fortified settlement existed there from the 9th to 14th century.[A-1] According to Alexandru Graur, the name Podu Lelioaiei is probably derived from the "name of the wife of someone called Lalu, who was known as Iloaia, the wife of someone called Ile or Ilie."[A-2]

In 1883, C. Chirita depicted the local tradition that was still alive at the beginning of the 20th century: "It is said that [Podu Lelioaiei] took its name from the bridge that crosses the Bahlui River. The bridge was built by a Jewish woman named Iloaia, who lived in Podu Lelioaiei at the beginning of the 19th century. There was an inn, and on the other side of the river, the left side, there were several cottages where the old post-carriage station had been. Wanting to link the inn with the postal route, the Jewish woman Iloaia built a permanent bridge over the waters of the Bahlui River. The bridge still bears her name today."[A-3]

Actually, a bridge existed there long before the 19th century. In 1700, a Polish traveler related: "In Poduleloi, on the shore of the Bahlui River over which there is a small brick bridge, there are only small cottages."[A-4] It is possible that the old bridge was destroyed in the meantime. In 1653, "Ruler Vasilie and his army, which he had gathered in a hurry, camped at Podul Lelioaiei. The battle was fought there, and Gheorghe the chancellor won. Vasilie then fled to his father-in-law Hmil, the Cossack ruler."[A-5] (Hmil is Bogdan Chmelnitzki [1593-1657])

At the beginning of the 20th century, this battle was still mentioned in the local stories. It was told that the dead soldiers had been buried under the hill in front of the church. I remember myself as a child searching for buried treasures from the time of Vasile Lupu, but without much success. Some used to say that they found helmets, weapons, mail, skeletons, and other objects, while digging.

On June 10, 1655, Gheorghe Stefan, the ruler of Moldova, sent a letter from Podu Iloaiei to Gheorghe Rakoczi II, the ruler of Transylvania. Miron Costin related that Gheorghe Stefan's carts were robbed at Podu Iloaiei in 1655.[A-6]

In 1664, 1665, and 1673, the village of Podu Lelioae was mentioned.[A-7] A Dowry Act from January 15, 1664 stated: "my part of land from Podul-ii-leloe, which will be taken from that shared with my brothers … and a neighbor Ilia and his sons, who live in Podul-ii-leloe."[A-8]

Neculce's chronicle mentioned that under the rule of Constantin Cantemir (1685-1692) "troops of mercenaries were camped at Podu Iloae."[A-9] [A-10] In 1700, a Polish traveler found here "only a few cottages and a shortage of food and fodder. We spent the night outside in the cold."[A-11] After 1703, Mihai Racovita kept guards in Podu Iloaiei.[A-12]

The Swedish officer Weissmantel (1709-1714) mentioned the stone bridge in Podu Iloaiei.[A-13] The settlement was also mentioned in 1715.[A-14] Manuscript No. 1846 of the Iasi State Archives contains calculations for the income of the bar in Podu Iloaiei for the years 1800 to 1806.

As mentioned in the *Great Geographic Dictionary*, in 1810 "a certain number of Jews requested permission from the owner of the Totoesti estate to settle here and raise a borough. In 1818, as stipulated in ruler Calimah's document, the borough was founded near the bridge, taking the name Podul Iloaiei. Because the borough was located where the borders of several estates intersected, each owner granted permission for the foundation of a town on their property."[A-15]

This favorable geographic position — on the route from Iasi to Targu Frumos — explains why the founders of the town chose it, of course, at the invitation of the owner of the Totoesti estate. But how did some Polish Jews learn about the intentions of the Moldavian landlord? The borough was established at the confluence of the rivers Bahlui and Bahluiet.[A-16-A]

The founding of the borough of Podu Iloaiei was not an isolated event, but rather a part of a larger process of establishing new settlements. At the end of the 18th century and during the first half of the 19th century, 61 such settlements were established in Moldova, which at that time was of significant economic and social importance. "These small, semi-urban settlements promoted the most dynamic forms of socioeconomic life. Each settlement developed and enhanced the connection between the village and the city, their presence reviving the entire region. Economically, they were centers where raw materials were collected, and products were manufactured from these regional materials. They were also markets for products produced in the cities and abroad."[A-16-B]

The updated chronicle of the borough of Vladeni (later named Mihaileni) from November 16, 1826 stated in paragraph six that "the tax for selling spirits will be cashed by the owner of the estate as decided by the 1816 act issued for the borough of Podu Lelioaia and the 1823 act issued for the borough located on the Scobalteni estate."[A-17] If no mistake was made by the clerk, the preceding statement refers to the agreement between the future inhabitants of the borough and the owner of the estate, since the oldest document known to refer to our town is the one from 1816 (see Appendix A). In a letter to C. Palade, the owner of the estate, it was mentioned that the inn at Podu Iloaiei must be rebuilt.[A-18]

The act issued in 1818 by Scarlat Callimachi to the landlord C. Palade, regarding the establishment of the borough of Podu Iloaiei on the Totoesti estate that was owned by the latter, was not upheld. However in 1823, Stefan Roset, the guardian of Palade's estates after his death, managed to obtain from Ionita Sandu Sturza the renewal of the first act. It seemed that, owing to the current events, the settlement developed very slowly since it was not mentioned in the 1820 census. However, because the census was of a fiscal nature regarding taxes, the "absence" of the inhabitants of the new settlement could be explained by the tax exemption that was applied for several years, as was the case for other new settlements.[A-19] On May 25, 1823, the former first court official, Serban Negel who had been loyal to Ionita Sandu Sturza during the difficult first years of his rule, also obtained an act for the founding of a borough near Podu Iloaiei. Subsequently, the two settlements formed a single administrative entity.

On March 21, 1821, the villagers of Scobalteni were worried about the "carts and chariots that passed by Podu Iloaiei and up hill."[A-20] In fact, Beldiman wrote in *Tragodia*: "The road to Podul Iloaiei going up the hill / For the woods were close and the town defended still."

The activities of the Eterists[B-4] diminished the population of the developing borough of Podu Iloaiei. In 1822, Gheorghe Sion came to the Moldavian districts to appoint new chiefs of the administration. "All of the remaining inhabitants of Podu Iloaiei came to greet us here, where at that time there was only a post office, a tavern, and General Constantin Palade's great inn, then unplastered. And from among all the townspeople we met, we have chosen Constantin Drosul, who has little knowledge of reading and writing, and Neculai Mantu, the administrator of the Braesti estate, to administrate the Carligatura district."[A-21] The 1818 act that was renewed on July 25, 1823 and issued for "Podul-Leloea" on the estate of the deceased general C. Palade reestablished the 16 paragraphs of the agreement between the landlord and the future townspeople:

1) The tax on the sale of spirits "in all the town's streets and suburbs" will be 40 parale per measure [B-5]. Any smuggled alcohol will be confiscated and a fee will be paid.
2) The tax for wine is 30 parale. The wine will be measured on the outskirts of the borough by the administrator of the estate. The same rules apply for smuggling as above.
3) The tax for fuel oil and axle ointment is 10 parale per measure. The same rules as above apply for smuggling.
4) Jews who own a butchery will pay the landlord 2 parale per lamb, 4 parale per sheep, 6 parale per calf, 10 parale per weanling or young bull, 20 parale per cow, and 30 parale per ox.
5) Jews are allowed to bake their own bread and pretzels for home use only.
6) Candles made for personal use are tax-free. A tax will be paid for selling them.
7) Each person may keep up to three cows in the grazing field tax-free.
8) The sale of hay and barley is tax-free.
9) An annual tax for place of residence or shop will be paid: 2 lei per length measure [B-6]; the depth will be 18 measures long; with the agreement of the owner who has the first right to buy if the house should be for sale.
10) Homemade beer and hydromel can be sold tax-free; industrial production requires the owner's accord.
11) Two synagogues, two slaughter houses [B-7] "near the school" and the cemetery are exempt from taxation.

---

[4] [Ed-Com] The Eteria movement fought for the independence of Greece.
[5] [Ed-Com] A measure is 10 liters.
[6] [Ed-Com] A length measure is between 1.96 and 2.23 meters.
[7] [Ed-Com] ??? The word "hahami" is used here for ritual slaughter. It's from the Hebrew word "chachma". The "shochet", Hebrew for ritual slaughterer, is usually a rabbi or one who is well versed in the laws of ritual slaughter.

12) The day of the fair or the marketplace will be established on the developing main street that passes by the inn all the way to the main road.
13) Anyone may display his merchandise in front of his house; if done at the corner of the street or in the center of town, a tax must be paid to the owner.
14) A tax is also paid for an orchard, garden, or vineyard.
15) The owner's agreement is necessary for the construction of a factory.
16) If one does not build a home within a year of signing this contract, one loses the right to build one.[A-22]

The conditions imposed by Serban Negel for the founding of a borough on his estate Scobalteni were tougher and did not stimulate the borough's development. He asked 24 bani for each adult cattle slaughtered. The landlord had the right to build houses and stores without paying the tax, which was 10% of the rent for the rest of the townspeople. The right to sell spirits, fuel oil, bread, and meat, and the tax for weighing was cashed by the landlord exclusively. He also had a right for tax exemption for 30 men, whom he would bring from abroad "to maintain the security of the town."

The landlord also appointed the mayor of the town and the masters of the trade and manufacturing associations. The tradesmen from abroad were tax exempt for five years. Monday was fair day, and there would be eight more annual fairs. The inhabitants of Scobalteni and Podu Iloaiei could freely visit each other on the fair days.[A-23] But success did not come as expected, and Negel gave the Jews of Podu Iloaiei a lot of trouble.[A-24] Not until June 17, 1824, did 10 Jews manage to sign a more favorable settlement contract with Negel, although it contained "architectural" terms.[A-25] They had to pay a 4 lei tax per length measure for a 10 measure house. The houses had to be built one next to the other with board or shingle roofs, and with a space between them for the street. The selling of the houses had to have the accord of the landlord, and he had the right to make the first offer. The stores could not sell bread or wine to the Christians. Kosher meat could only be sold with the landlord's agreement. Jewish taverns could only host Jewish patrons. The 10 Jews could not resort to their rights as Sudits if they had a conflict with the landlord. Anyone who did not build a house within a year lost the right to settle. Each inhabitant of the borough had the right to free grazing for up to four cattle; a tax was collected for more cattle. The cemetery (50 square measures), the synagogue (25 square measures), and the public bath (15 square measures) were tax-free.[A-26]

The population was made up of Moldavians, Jews, Lippovans, Armenians, Greeks, and Gypsies. The 1824 census mentioned 4 Jewish Sudits (See Appendix B). The Sudits were "foreign citizens or natives who enjoyed foreign protection while living on Romanian territory, as stipulated by the terms of the treaties signed by the Western powers and the Turkish Empire."[A-27] Sura Herscovici was born in this town in 1826; she died in January 1935 at the age of 109.[A-28] On March 24, 1826, Iaakov, son of Smuel, sold a piece of land to the Lippovan Iacov, for which he had "a property document issued at the establishment of the borough" (see Appendix C). A receipt, issued in Scobalteni and dated April 18, 1828, was given to a small nobleman for 172 lei of merchandise that he purchased here from Haim and Itic.[A-29] The year 1827 was a dry one, and the occupation armies ate the few cereals that were left.[A-30]

According to information that I received in 1935 from the shochet Burah Svart, in 1828 there was a Chevra Kadisha, a burial society that was also functioning as a social assistance service for the poor. The register was lost during World War I.

In 1839, the foreign affairs minister Neculai Canta bought the estate and borough of Scobalteni for 200,000 lei from the guardians of the property of the deceased village chief Negel.[A-31]

In 1982, the Jewish cemetery in Podu Iloaiei still had some gravestones from 1829 and 1830. One of them was for Haim sin Meer, who died on 1 Adar 5589 (Wednesday February 18, 1829); another one belonged to Avram sin Moise, and was dated June 1829; a third certified that Iehuda ben Iaakov died on July 28, 1829. The gravestones of Efraim — son of Iehuda Leib from Tismenita — and Haim Moise sin Hers are dated 1830.[A-32]

A contract from 1830 offers information about the income of the owner of the borough. It stipulated an agreement for leasing the borough to Moise Juster and Herscu a Mendeloaie for 12,000 lei per year.[A-33] The inn had to be properly maintained and returned in good condition. The landlord, at the recommendation of the tenants, appointed the captain of the borough. The military were allowed to keep their "feeding lands," but had to pay tax on them. The landlord's Gypsies also had to pay "the tax of the land." The borough's cattle could graze for free on the grazing field. The tenants received ten measures of land [B-8],a place for a garden, and the right to use the waters from the Bahlui Mill upstream. They were also granted tax-free milling of 10 measures of wheat and corn. The garbage from the inn had to be deposited outside of the borough. All the buildings that were to be built remained in the possession of the landlord for three years after the termination of the contract. In 1831, Palade demanded the cancellation of the contract because Jews were not allowed to have "possessions." Herscu refused to return the advance payment of 6,000 lei. In fact, both the Jewish and Christian inhabitants of the borough were against Herscu, who was a dishonest tenant (see Appendix D).[A-34]

During the first years, the founders of the town were also the leaders of the Jewish community. Aspects of the modest day-to-day life are depicted in *The Official Paper of the Moldavian Principality*. In 1832, there was a lawsuit between Leiba "Rozil" and the townspeople "for refusing to pay the required taxes." Rozil was, of course, the tenant of the borough's income. That same year, another lawsuit was recorded between the Jews Richter and Barbalata, who had a dispute over "an iron hoop." A beautifully trimmed "matseva" in the style of the Jewish stone carvers was found at the grave of a Dov ben Samuel, who died in 1831.

It is noteworthy that the administration system of the town involved clerks, who were appointed by the owner of the estate, and thus defended the owner's interests. The first "captain of the borough of Poduleloaiei" was Manolache, who issued a register for the alcohol trade on May 11, 1828.[A-35] Another captain, Tudorache Popovici, was dismissed by the tenant Herscu Juster, who then took over as captain. The divan, however, reinstated Tudorache in his former function.[A-36] The activity and abuses committed by the town's captain will be discussed in more detail later on.

[8] [Ed-Com] Measure refers to a falca which equals 14,322 square miles.

The Organic Rule mentioned the cancellation of the tax system that had been applied to the Jewish population based on the tax on kosher meat. This tax served primarily to pay the rabbi, the shochet, and the rest of the community's clerks, as well as to cover the needs of the school, Talmud Torah, the asylum, hekdesh, etc. In the 18th century, the treasury noticed that its weak tax collecting system was not efficient with the Jews and decided to impose a common tax on the community. The leaders of the "Jewish guild" arranged the total amount of the tax with the treasury, and included the tax in the community's budget.[A-37] In 1831, the treasury tried to collect the taxes directly from each Jew, as stipulated by the Organic Rule, but "the trial proved that only the old system could efficiently collect the taxes from the Jews"[A-38] (see Appendix F).

The system of foreign protection for Sudits offered an advantage against abusive clerks. Here is a typical case from 1833: Iosef Coter, Moise Barbalata, Grinbaum, and Iancu Amoki, who would lease from the landowner the town's income in 1836, were arrested, beaten, and taken to Targu Frumos under the suspicion of insulting the subprefect of Carligatura County. The Prussian consul explained to the Russian general Mitcovici, who was president of Moldova's divan, that these men were Prussian subjects and asked for their release. On December 23, 1833, the French consul intervened in favor of the French subject Iosef Coter. The State's Secretary showed that the arrested men were born in this country and had their homes in Podu Iloaiei.

The tombstone of Slomo Iosef Leib - son of David, who died in Iasi in 1834, still exists today. The year 1835 was inscribed on the tombstone of Manili, the daughter of Mose Mirkis from Iasi, who was buried in Podu Iloaiei.[A-39] On February 12, 1853, "the assembly of the Jewish community from the boroughs of Podulelioaia and Scobalteni in Carligatura county" complained to the treasury that "not only had they endured poverty and lack of bread," but they also could not pay the Sudits' taxes. So they made up a common tax, which they offered for leasing. Some of the leaders who were Sudits railed against this tax. After voting, 32 Jews were for the tax and 36 Sudits and tenants were against it.

In 1835, 134 new households were built in Podu Iloaiei.[A-40] In 1835 and 1836, Moscul Barlacu and Iancu Mikioaia leased the town's income. Subsequently, they had disputes with Tudorache Radovici, the owner's head man. The conflict ended in 1846.[A-41]

The inhabitants of the town complained about the Jewish land administrator and obtained his dismissal on the grounds that he had no right to lease.[A-42]

We do not know the nature of the transaction that led to a lawsuit between Grigore Peris and several townspeople from Podu Iloaiei.[A-43] A conflict between Gavrilas, the administrator of the royal vineyards, and Froim seemed to build between 1835 and 1836. The same Gavrilas, no doubt the captain of the town, ordered his men to beat up a certain Jew named Solomon. Iancu Belcester, likely the chief of the local Jewish community, went with several tradesmen to demand an explanation from Gavrilas. Gavrilas accused them of coming to beat him up (see Appendix C).[A-44] It is possible that the conflict with

Herscu a Mendeloaie[B-9], the administrator of the town's income, caused the disputes.[A-45]

Because of the town's position on the main road, the central authorities were particularly concerned about its status. Thus in 1837, the bridge "on the road of the stagecoach" was repaired; its maintenance cost 3,279 lei.[A-46] In 1836, "all the Jews, locals, and Sudits" from the borough of Podu Iloaiei gathered to argue that some of those registered in the census were here only for short periods of time, had fled elsewhere or died, or had paid 4 galbeni as tax and the town pays for them. Some of those who did not pay the taxes were beaten and carried barefoot through the town. They asked for lower taxes and the right to implement their own taxes. The proposal was signed by Moise Berlescu, Solomon sin Herscu, Iosef Coter, Iancu from Targu Frumos, David Casap, Marcu Leizer Casap, Simha from Targu Frumos, and Solomon Richter. A three-year contract was signed with the collective tax collector for 5,200 lei per year.

The economic development of the borough was hindered by the 1823 act that was issued for the Scobalteni estate. On November 28, 1838, a new contract was signed with the new owner, Neculai Canta. Taxes for the sale of spirits and fuel oil were established. The tax was increased to 3 lei and 72 parale for each stanjen of a household 10 stanjeni long. The houses were to be built one next to the other and covered with board or shingle. The sale of meat, bread, and candles, the barbershop, kitchen, and scales were to remain the property of the owner. The church, cemetery, school, and public bath were tax exempt. A free grazing place was given for 90 cattle. According to the agreement, Toma Gavrilovici, Izrail sin Isar, and Avram Leiba had to pay the owner 37,350 lei (see Appendix H). The reinforcement act was dated May 2, 1839. On July 5, 1839, the captain of the town sent the list with those who were guarantors for the Jews: the community chief Moscu Berl and the Christian Gheorghe sin Vasile Velciul. The Armenian and Lippovan guilds also asked to have the right to appoint a community chief and to have an overall community tax as stipulated in a document found at the Iasi branch of the State Archives [B-10].

The economic life of the town followed its "usual" course. In 1839, Herscu called I. Ponici to trial for a debt of 100 galbeni.[A-47] [A-48] The year 1840 was marked on the beautifully carved tombstone of the elder Eliahu ben Dov Ber. That same year, the poet Costache Conachi bought from the fair several Gypsy workers: carvers, shoe and boot makers, and beer makers.[A-49] The Austrian agency appointed a guardian to manage the estate of Iosup sin Lupu Casapu, an Austrian subject.[A-50]

The value of all the shops in the borough in 1841 was 80 galbeni, 4,000 lei.[A-51] A property document for one of the town's buildings was dated the same year (see Appendix I).

The conflicts with the tenant of the town's income seemed never-ending. In 1841, 19 of the townspeople complained about Herscu Lesner, who had lent them money and grain in 1832 but was now being accused of forging the accounts.[A-52] To prove his innocence, the tenant obtained testimony from several other inhabitants that the leasing of the town's

[9] [Ed-Com] Herscu a Mendeloaie = Herscu son of Mendel's sister.
[10] [Ed-Com] 1759, opis 2008, file 30, f. 30, 35

income had been done correctly.[A-53] But the leasing partners were in conflict once again in 1842. Moise from Berlesti and Iancu Macioaiei argued that Tudorache, their partner, erected buildings using the employees and materials of the association. Owing to his carelessness, the wheat harvest was ruined. They also brought Christian witnesses.[A-54]

The leasing act was published in *Bulletin, Official Paper* and in *The Rural Paper*. In 1841, the townspeople regained the right to appoint the town's captain and to organize three seven-day fairs each year. The act was reconfirmed in 1848. A list of tradesmen from 1842 included 91 Christians, living mostly in the suburbs, and 66 Jews (see Appendix J). Here is an anecdote that is representative of the town's customs: Reiza Iosupovici, the wife of the runaway Samsa who had unpaid debts, asked the Justice for her dowry list to be given first priority.[A-55]

The town's food supply was leased in 1844, and the following prices were established: 16 parale for an oca of bread, 26 parale for beef, 24 parale for lamb, and 3 lei, 16 parale for an oca of candles.[A-56]

The trade papers, house selling acts, and other transactions that were done among the Jews had to be confirmed by the rabbi and then in court. In 1845, the rabbi Mose from Podu Iloaiei confirmed an act for the sale of a house for 1,676 lei (see Appendix K).

The privileges of the Sudits were decreasing. Many of them gave up their allegiance to the foreign power, as was the case for Leib Ihil and his wife Susie Hatul (Etl?) from Podu Iloaiei.[A-57] The Austrian agency dealt with the sale of the properties of the deceased Elias Berkenthal. Rabbi Mose confirmed that act in 1845. As guardians of Iosup's orphans, the same rabbi and Marcu sin Pascal sold an inn in town to the shochet Herscu Strulovici for 6,000 lei.[A-58]

In the beginning, a captain appointed by the landlord administered the town. Later on, the captain was appointed by the Treasury and was paid from the town's taxes. In 1841, the landlord-appointed captain received 100 lei per month, while the captain in Mihaileni was paid 200 lei and the captains in Stefanesti and Lespezi were paid 150 lei each.[A-59] The captain often abused his authority. In 1843, the Christian inhabitants of the town complained about the captain, "the man of the police," because he was enforcing hard punishments for small offences. Therefore, they asked for an inquiry.[A-60] Another request to appoint someone to replace this Tudorache Radovici was made on May 24, 1844 by "the community of Christians and Jews in the borough of Podu Lelioaiei." Several Christians and Jews signed the petition (see Appendix O). They brought testimonies from four Lippovans, three Romanians, and five Jews, who maintained that Tudorache was persecuting the bartender Toader Bamaruca, an honest man.[A-61]

The new administrative code stipulated for Podu Iloaiei one captain and two foot soldiers paid by the State.[A-62] The position of captain lasted until 1864, when a radical change took place in the administration system of small towns. But in 1846, the captain supervised the sale of bread and candles in the town. [A-63] In the same year, the tax collectors complained that they were not given enough kosher meat, and asked for the tax to be raised to 6 parale per oca like in Targu Frumos. [A-64] This complaint was repeated in 1847, but since the administration felt that there were not enough Christians living in town to buy the non-kosher meat, the town was not granted the right to have more cattle. [A-65] At this time, the leader of the Jews was Alter sin Strule.

An act of "everlasting property" was issued by N. Cantacuzino, the owner of the town, to Moise Itic for a place of 6 x 20 stanjeni on which Moise amongst others had shops and for which he paid tax and other contributions. [A-66] A similar act was issued to the Lippovan Stefan for a place of 2 x 16 stanjeni, on which he had shops. At that time the economic life of the borough was very much dependent on the days of the weekly fair.

We have no information on how the revolution of 1848 influenced the life of the town; however, we learned about the many victims of the cholera epidemic, most of who were poor.

In 1851, the tax that covered the needs of the community was 20 parale for each oca of beef.

The value of the buildings in town increased as the town developed. In 1852, Mendel Cat received 4,000 lei from Zamvel sin Bercu for a 2 x 15 stanjeni street shop located close to the bridge. .

The Cernauti-Botosani-Iasi road passed through Podu Iloaiei, while the salt road passed through Scheia and Targu Frumos. The work on the Iasi-Podu Iloaiei road was still in progress in 1854, and in 1860. Podu Iloaiei was mentioned in a list of towns inhabited by more than 100 families. In 1855, the price of regular bread was 24 parale for an oca. In 1856, an oca of good bread was 1 lei, an oca of meat was 1 lei and 8 parale, and an oca of candles was 4 lei, 12 parale. The semi-urban character of the town was becoming more and more apparent.

During the Russian occupation, grain was requisitioned from the population. Strul Avram Ringhelescu asked that the requisitioned goods be paid back. During that year, the consular privileges were still in place. The Austrian subject Samson sin Naftule obtained, with the support of the consulate, full rights over the property of his deceased brother Moise Itic, a Moldavian subject.

The tax was leased in 1858 to Aga Vasile Bosie. In 1859, the tenant was Copil Dulberger, who paid 27,500 lei per year. That year, several places in the proximity of the church and close to the grazing place were sold. In 1858, Haim sin Herscu, the delegate of the Great Synagogue, sold for 100 galbeni several houses that had been donated by Huda, the daughter of Hers.

In 1862, the community appeared to be well established. For example, "the representatives of the Jewish community" Herscu sin Moisa, Iancu Popescu (from Popesti), and Alter Strul confirmed the death of David sin Lupu, a third-degree tradesman; the death certificate was made official with an oval stamp that read: "The United Principalities. The Commission of the Borough Podul Iloaiei, 1859."

On the front of the Great Synagogue (which was seriously damaged between 1941 and 1945, and demolished in 1967) was inscribed the date of its inauguration: 5622[B-11],

---

[11] [Ed-Com] 5622 on the Jewish calendar which starts from Creation

corresponding to 1862. In 1865, they were still working on the road that passed through the town. During the same year, Mihail Kuhirsky opened a pharmacy. [A-67] Several letters published by K. Lippe in the Jewish magazine *Libanon* (April 1, 1868, No. 205) from Paris described the good relations between the Jews and the Christians living in the town, but also mentioned that the new policeman persecuted the Jews, shutting down their shops and forbidding them to wear their traditional clothing.

When civil status documents were introduced, the Jews began to register their newborn children at the town hall. One birth certificate from 1869 was signed by Lupu sin Herscu, a 36-year-old fiddler, and by Avram Marcusor, a tradesman. Vasile Petrovici, president of the ad-interim commission, was in charge of the "Civil Status Office." In 1870, the town hall leased to Isac Vecsler the right to collect taxes from the butcher shops in town. [A-68]

The Topographical Dictionary by Frunzescu (Bucharest, 1872) mentioned that 2,715 people were living in the borough of Podu Iloaiei, where the offices of the subprefecture, a telegraph, and a railway station were located. It also noted that the place was famous for "its huge, delicious melons." In 1873, the Jewish physician Ancel Hart, a 30-year-old Moldavian subject, settled in the town. He was still practicing there in 1898. His daughters were Sofia, Tereza, and Iuliana. In 1873, a huge fire destroyed all the houses made of wood. Only the church and 20 brick houses were saved. The losses amounted to 100,000 galbeni, but the insurance only covered 80,000 galbeni. The insurance companies were quick to cover the losses and as suchon October 16, 1874, Nuhem sin Mendel, S. B. Morgenstern, Ilie Marcu, Marcu Ghetel, Elie Itic sin Bercu, Ghersin Margulies, Faivel Candel, Moise sin Iosef, Francisca Botez, Moise Iacob Hahane, and Baruch Smilovici expressed their gratitude. [A-69]

One shochet, a long-time resident of the town, slaughtered chickens without following the rules, wanted to eliminate the tax, and didn't listen to anyone. He was dismissed in 1877 by Rabbi Taubes from Iasi[A-70], thus putting an end to this type of abuse, which was quite frequent in some Moldavian communities at the time.

We have no clear information on the participation of the Jewish population of Podu Iloaiei in the independence war. It is known, however, that at the beginning of the 20th century, seven "righteous" Jews lived in the town, most of whom were descendents of veterans of the 1877-1878 war. They owned bars or tax collection offices, and had the right to vote in the elections for the town's counsel and parliament. There is a Yiddish saying about this war: "mit im vesti nisht annemen Plevne." It means "you won't conquer Plevna with his support" and refers to a man who is not too smart or too diligent. There is also a Yiddish anecdote: A mother was saying good-bye to her son, who was leaving to join the army. She advises him not to wear himself out: "fis a terk in ri dich up," which means "if you shoot a Turkish soldier then you rest a bit." The son asks: "What if the Turk shoots me?" The mother laments: "Oh my, what possibly could the Turk have against my boy?"

Fires were quite frequent, just like in other Moldavian settlements. At the initiative of mayor Gheorghiu, fire extinguishers were purchased, and proved to be of great help in fighting the fire of 1880. The mayor, together with Xenofon Vlaste and Moise Wecsler, collected money on the day of the fire to help the victims. [A-71]

The legal status of the Jews who were born and brought up in this country and who enjoyed no foreign protection was quite precarious. In 1881, eight Jews, who were living in town and had four years of army service, were declared "foreigners." [A-72] Jews were still unjustly banished from their villages. In November 1881, Volf Avram was driven away from Obrojeni to Podu Iloaiei. He left behind a household, 20 cows, cornstalks, and other belongings. [A-73]

Particularly important was the campaign to obtain the title of urban commune for the settlement, which was the wish of most of the inhabitants. In 1881, the communal counsel, which had no Jews among its members, declared that "the interest of a small town is to be inhabited by various craftsmen and tradesmen no matter what their religion or ethnicity." They then emphasized that the townspeople had ancient rights and that restrictive laws (against Jews) would only hinder the development of the town, which if it became an urban commune would have a secondary school, a better hospital and pharmacy, a veterinarian, etc. It was also pointed out that the town was an important grain export center, which needs warehouses, better communication systems, etc. The prefecture was asked to intervene to the Minister of Internal Affairs in favor of ranking Podu Iloaiei as an urban commune. The request was rejected on January 20, 1882 following a demand from 14 non-Jewish tradesmen, who claimed that the borough should remain a rural commune so that they could protect themselves from Jewish competition. In fact the commune's counsel insisted on their request, but the Parliament rejected it. [A-74] Also in 1882, the state issued laws encouraging Jewish emigration, but no one from town emigrated that year. [A-75]

The November 26, 1882 issue of the magazine *The Brotherhood* published on page 7 information about the community of Podu Iloaiei, which was made up of approximately 150 families. The community taxes covered the needs of the rabbi and the two shochets, as well as the sponsorship of the Talmud Torah. There was a Hasidic court[B-12], and the tzadik enjoyed a good reputation in the town and in other communities. The Great Synagogue had been restored in 1876. Several confessional asylums[B-13] were in operation. There was a "heder" and a private tutor. Social assistance was provided on Pesach for "maot chittim". The community bath collected 100 galbeni annually. There was a "brotherhood fund" for helping the sick. Thirty students attended Talmud Torah.

Beginning in 1885, the town hall no longer leased the town's income. A relevant, unusual incident: the mayor - Nicolae Gheorghiu- a baptized Jew, was killed by a Greek named Procopie Dimitriu on August 18, 1888, even though another Jew had tried to stop the killer. [A-76] The victim had founded the town's church.

---

[12] [Ed-Com] Hasidic court is the Hasidic rabbi, his synagogue and his followers.

[13] [Ed-Com] Confessional asylums: probably religious institutions such as schools, charities, hospitals, etc.

Numerous attempts to support the town's development by having it ranked as an urban commune were all rejected by Parliament in 1892. In 1894, the tenant S. Schwartz sponsored the rural hospital. Emil Florescu and then H. Grigoriu were the practicing physicians; there were also a subsurgeon and 10 assistants. In 1895, Leopold Ferderber managed the pharmacy, and later became a communal counselor. That same year, a police station was founded, some of the sidewalks were repaired, [A-77] and the new building of the State school was opened; at this time, the mayor was D. Lupu. [A-78] Several fountains were also restored. In 1896, there was an attempt to close down the slaughterhouse that had been found to be unsanitary and the brick factory that had been managed for 25 years by Avram Cahane. The space for the marketplace was reduced by the shacks constructed by some people. [A-79]

The townspeople read newspapers. In 1897, L. Fruchtman was selling *The Opinion*, which was edited in Iasi. The Yiddish and Hebrew press were distributed by subscription. In the same year, 1,200 pieces of clothing were collected for the victims in Stefanesti. The community budget, managed by Zeida Rotenberg, was insufficient. Besides paying the rabbi, four shochets and three synagogue janitors, the wages of 10 day-time guards also had to be paid. [A-80] However, thieves continued to attack unhindered.

The economic crisis of 1898-1899 and the leaving of the Jews on foot from the country had a serious impact on Podu Iloaiei (see the chapter "The Economic Life"). In 1902, the commune's budget was insufficient again. The anti-Semitic mayor Lupu and the tax collector Ghedale Haimovici raised the tax on kosher meat. A committee of seven people was elected to ensure support for the community's primary school. [A-81] The community could not pay Dr. Hart.

In the communal elections of 1902, seven of the 156 voters were Jews. The commune (including two villages) was inhabited by 2,883 people. The above mentioned D. Lupu, an office attendant with five years of high school training, was reelected mayor. Of the eight counselors, only three knew how to sign their name. [A-82] From 1902 to 1903, and again in 1916, the monthly magazine *The Public Notary* was edited in Podu Iloaiei by D. Cassian, the commune's notary.

Marcu Ghetel, a wealthy estate tenant moneylender, and tradesman plays an important role in the life of the borough. In 1903, he brought laborers from Bucovina to work the land on his estate.

During the same year, a public garden was opened and visited by Minister Spiru Haret. In 1904, the new slaughterhouse was ready to be opened and a new Romanian popular bank called "Good News" was opened. From 1903 to 1908, the town's police proved ineffective against the large number of burglaries and attacks. One serious event was the fire at Vlaste's mill on June 10, 1904 that resulted in 200,000 lei in losses. The same year, Gheorghe Botez, who was later elected mayor a number of times, was appointed communal inspector of the Podu Iloaiei region. In 1905, the iron bridge over the Bahlui River was opened. In 1906, I. Sneer became the principal of the community's school, replacing Iancu Horodniceanu, who continued to work for several decades at the school. I, myself, studied at this school between 1914 and 1918, and later taught along with my former teachers during the school year of 1928/1929. At the beginning of 1907, the town hall requested that the town be supplied with water from the Timisesti River — the same source of water used by Iasi—based on a project that was later completed. [A-83]

During the violent spring of 1907, the peasant uprisings affected Podu Iloaiei to the same degree that they affected the rest of the country.

It is known, that from the beginning, there was an attempt to direct the focus of the North Moldavian villagers' complaints towards the Jews. Approximately 300 peasants came to Podu Iloaiei; the army was unable to stop the revolt. Tenant Druckman's house, among others, was destroyed, in addition to the shops in town (almost 50); merchandise was thrown in the mud. On the second day, the military squads from Harlau arrived and fired shots into the air. Twenty people were arrested. The March 3rd, 1907 edition of *The Opinion* of Iasi reported that the initiators of the revolt included the institutor Brudariu, Tita Pavelescu, and the gardener Ionescu.

According to *The Universe* (March 3, 1907; vol. 25, no. 60), "on March 1, 1907, almost 800 peasants came to town and committed indescribable acts of violence, devastating most of the houses and shops of the Jewish inhabitants, throwing merchandise into the street, and shattering and destroying everything that stood in their way. The following tradesmen were seriously injured: Zeida Schwartz, Itic Moscovici, Aba Blumenfeld, Iancu Merovici, and many others whose names are unknown. The windows of all synagogues and Jewish schools were broken as were the windows of the 'miracle-maker' rabbi's house, and those of the other rabbis."

In Iasi, a committee was established to help those whose households had been destroyed. On March 14, 1907, 3,000 lei were sent to Podu Iloaiei and distributed by A. Magder and M. Solomon. On March 17, Marcu Ghetel, Elias Solomon, and Saia Sternberg launched a campaign to help the poor who were living in the town.

One of the consequences of the uprising was the emigration of Jews to the United States. In June 1907, some families left. The devastation and the anti-Jewish regulations issued after the uprising led to a decay of the economic situation of the town, which was already precarious at that time. On April 1, 1908, the communal counsel was dissolved and in August was replaced with another one. The new counsel was led by Pavel Botez who contributed to the development of the commune and ensured a supply of drinkable water. One of the counselors was Xenofon Vlaste, the owner of the mechanic mill.

In 1909, there was a dispute regarding the issue of buying back from its two owners the land on which the town was situated. Matei Gane's heirs were asking for 150,000 lei; it was unknown how much Lucia Cantacuzino-Pascanu was asking for her part. An agreement was never reached. In 1909 a flood caused great losses to the town's Jews. However, a deal was signed with the engineer B. Diamant from Iasi regarding the use of the Timisesti source for the town's water supply. The town hall was to pay 43,000 lei.

The physician in the rural hospital was Carol Vitner, one of the few Jewish doctors paid by the State. As proof of his especially good reputation stands the fact that he was sent to Germany to specialize in bacteriology.

In 1910, a general economic crisis struck, affecting mostly the small tradesmen and craftsmen in the town. The epidemics of cholera and typhoid fever brought great concern, considering the poor hygienic conditions in town. In 1911, the floods from the Bahlui River caused serious damages.

As was the case in other towns, various forms of community assistance were established for those in need. As reported by the May 27, 1911 edition of *The Equality*, at the initiative of Aron Rosenthal, a society called Mata-Baseiter was founded to help the poor in case they became sick. The directing committee was made up of Moses Bucmann, president; Moses Schneier, vice president; Herscu Schwartz, cashier; and others.

New communal elections took place in Podu Iloaiei at the end of 1912. Const. Benuce was elected mayor.

The opening of the railway line between Podu Iloaiei and Harlau increased the importance of the local station, which became a railway junction. An advertisement that was printed in the newspaper by the person who restored the station, M. Vasilescu, described the restaurant as "first and second class" and promised to bring delicatessen and pates "from abroad." A few years later, M. Vasilescu declared bankruptcy after borrowing embezzled money from the station's cashier.

The outbreak of the 1913 war brought new examples of Jewish patriotism. In February and March, Jews gave money to the National Navy and Air Force. Jews from Podu Iloaiei were drafted for the campaign in Bulgaria; one of them died in service. The committee that was established to help the families of those fighting in the war consisted of the mayor, the priest, the postmaster, the chief of the station, the principal of the primary school, as well as three representatives of the Jews. The Jews also gave money to the Red Cross, in sums ranging from 1 to 20 lei. The victory of the Romanian troops raised hope that the problem of the Jews' citizenship would be resolved. In September, the families of those who were killed in the war, including the Jewish families, received help from the prefect.

Let's end the chronicle for the year 1913 by relating a dramatic event. Alexandru Ferderber, the son of a pharmacist and probably a baptized Jew, fell in love with a Jewish girl. The parents opposed the marriage, and the young couple attempted to commit suicide in the Jewish cemetery. They were taken to the hospital, from which they escaped. Several years later, the young man killed himself; it was his third attempt. In the meantime, the cholera epidemic that had ravaged the region during that year's campaign ceased.

The year 1914 brought to this modest town too the signs of the outbreak of a global war. Food was more expensive. Reservists were mobilized, and this raised the popular concern. A committee was formed in Podu Iloaiei to help those in need. The crisis resulted in bankruptcies. Several families immigrated to America with the help of the I.C.A. organization in Iasi. After the outbreak of World War I, living costs increased .

Between August 1914 and August 1916, the people of the town experienced worry and hope, joy and grief, and concern and cheer. Periodically, men under 40 years of age were drafted, making everyone think that there was going to be a war. On the other hand,

Romania's neutrality enabled Germany to make large acquisitions of food and raw material from Romania, and some tradesmen, noblemen, and wealthy peasants made good deals. Thus passed the years 1914, 1915, and the first half of 1916.

The Jewish population of the town realized with fear that the cataclysm was nearing, but there was still hope that those who had the right to citizenship would finally receive it. To avoid further confusions, The Native Jews' Union organized civil marriage services for the Jewish couples who had been married only religiously. My father Hers Svart was especially involved in this project. On March 23, 1916, the Jewish community in Podu Iloaiei organized a banquet in honor of the mayor Teodor Cazacu and the notary D. Cassian, who had attended the civil marriage ceremonies of more than 100 Jewish couples, giving legal support to the couples' family life, their right to succession, and the possibility that their children would receive citizenship.

In August 1916, Romania entered the war that, for the price of extreme sacrifices and suffering, was to bring territorial completion, a goal that had the full support of the Jewish population, particularly those living in Moldova. "Wives, sons, brothers, relatives, and friends are called under arms. Wives and children, mothers, sisters, fiancées, and relatives cry their heart out, while fathers discretely wipe off their tears." [A-84]

On August 21, 1916, a decree was issued, forbidding the use of any language other than Romanian. The ladies of the Romanian elite continued to "chirp out" in French, while strict regulations were enforced against Yiddish. The September 23, 1916 issues of *The Opinion* clearly stated that the issue at stake was the use of Yiddish: "In Podu Iloaiei, Jewish men and women are beaten on a legal basis [the famous 25 strikes to the ...] for using their native language."

Despite all the hardships, no Jew from Podu Iloaiei took advantage of the November 1916 decree that was issued for the Jews who wanted to emigrate. The democratic press was outraged, and pointed out that Jews should be given citizenship and not driven away.

After the first rough months of war, Podu Iloaiei became an important military and medical center. Many refugees settled here, coming from the occupied territories. The Jewish school and the synagogues were transformed into hospitals. Most of the Jewish families who had members, who had been called to fight in the war, were poor and did not get enough out of the modest help offered by the authorities. Jews were accused of racketeering, espionage, and many other sins. Nobody was spared the brutality of the police (major Schipor), not even women. However, the vast majority of the Jewish population endured the same sufferings as the rest of the population, lacking food, fuel, and soap and confronting a raging epidemic of typhus. Several military doctors died in duty. Among them was Siegfried Rosenthal, a young physician from Iasi, who died while taking care of the ill in the hospitals of Podu Iloaiei. In April, shacks were built outside of the town for the patients with typhus. The communal counsel was dissolved on May 12, 1917.

To prevent a shortage of vegetables, special areas were designated and students worked the land. On September 22, 1917, the general secretary of the Internal Affairs Ministry visited Podu Iloaiei and the vegetable garden of the Jewish school, which was supervised by Adolf Magder, the principal of the school. In October, the State school and the Jewish school began operating by taking turns in the building of the Jewish-Romanian primary school.

The war was still going on. The Bucharest peace treaty, the recommencing of the military maneuvers until the defeat of Wilhelmian Germany and its allies, was reflected in the town's life. In January 1919, the town became the center of one of eight areas used for the repatriation of the Russian troops. [A-85]

Jews, who were promised during the war that their sacrifices would earn them citizenship, were disappointed by the decree-law that granted naturalization based on complicated formalities. These formalities were even harder to fulfill because of the wickedness of the clerks. In September 1919, The Native Jews' Union opened a legal assistance office for the local Jews who were requesting naturalization. But public opinion was drawn to more pressing issues in the years 1918-1920: assistance for war orphans, social integration of the veterans, and rehabilitation of the invalids. Thus, the Native Jews' Union closed its offices, waiting for more just and efficient laws.

The reverberations of the Russian revolution raised hopes for a more democratic political life in the reunified Romania, including a solution to the Jewish demands. Meanwhile, the townspeople lacked food for their animals so the prefecture allowed the acquisition of a two months stock.

The new naturalization decree brought less complicated formalities, and thus the political parties became interested in the Jews' votes. The Jews joined Averescu's party ("di avereskeiner"), the party of the liberals and the peasants. Even N. Iorga published electoral leaflets in Yiddish. Beginning in 1921, the mayor's assistant was a Jew (Michel Sor and then Lupu Buchman).

The community elections also aroused disputes. On April 27, 1919, the old leaders (the traditionalists) lost the elections to the Zionist wing. The voting took place in the presence of the region's administrator D. Cassian and the mayor Popovici. Moise Buchman, Volf Fisler, Haim Orenstein, Moise Haim Anciu, Aron Ianculovici, M. Schor, V. Iosupovici, D. H. Hahamovici, Lipsa Maizner, and T. Herscoviciare were elected. The majority of the population, however, remained faithful to the old customs. A subscription list for the yeshiva in Buhusi was signed by 125 people, who donated various sums of money ranging from 1 to 20 lei. A bond with the past may have explained the new community elections in 1920 that were supervised by Adolf Magder. Some of the resigning members of the former committee were reelected. After only one year, new elections brought success to the Zionists. Michel Sor obtained for the commune a grant for the Jewish-Romanian primary school; he had argued that the enrollment of Jewish pupils in the communal school would cost much more (classrooms, teaching staff). In 1922, new community elections were held.

Personal ambitions and interests caused a climate of instability that also reflected the confusion created by the complex post-war circumstances. Indeed, the development of the economy in the unified country and the social-political unrest caused by the increase in anti-Semitism were the new issues that the Jewish towns in Moldova had to face. The more active Jews joined political parties and became assistants to mayors like Michel Sor and Sanielevici. Others in the community continued the old "machloket," disputes and conflicts on unimportant issues that had obvious negative consequences. For example, a group led by Simcha the tinker, who owned an oil deposit and a soda factory, hired one more shochet in 1923 and 1924, thus overcharging the community's budget. A candidate for the position of rabbi was brought in from Maramures [B-14]. The commission asserted that, although he was a good Talmudist, he could not speak modern Hebrew and thus could not be a rabbi here. After the death of Elie Rosental, Burah Svart remained as dayan.

The rising prices, the monetary crisis, and other economic hardships caused serious concern among the local people. The new law regarding the organization of cults stipulated the establishment of a community leadership. The new project, made up of 32 articles, was voted on by the general assembly on May 3, 1925 and published in a booklet (see Appendix R). The committee had 16 members. The community's moral and legal status became official on Oct 12, 1925.

The year 1926 was marked by political unrest and anti-Semitism. The united opposition won the communal elections with 603 votes in April 1926, but the newly elected communal counsel was dissolved. Rota, the principal of the public primary school, chaired the ad-interim commission, although he was accused of opportunism for joining in turn the liberal party, Cuza's party, and now Averescu's. The monument dedicated to the 1916-1918 war, which was built over several years from public donations, was inaugurated in September 1926.

The chronicle for 1927 opened with the community banquet organized by I. Rotental, an old Hebrew institutor. In February, the Zionist organization elected a new committee. The craftsmen protested against the increase in taxes that was imposed by the corporation.

The cultural society Iavne was renamed Achad Ha'am, while the Shalom Aleichem society celebrated two years of existence. In March, the Ceres mill was destroyed by a fire; the losses amounted to 8 million lei. The Jewish school obtained good results on the exam at the end of the school year. In September, The United Society presented the play *Manasse* by Ronetti-Roman.

The year 1928 was marked by economic difficulties. A banquet was organized to raise funds for the kindergarden that had begun functioning in October of the previous year. On Purim, the children presented a play in Yiddish that was prepared by their teacher Haia Derbandiner. A. A. Policman was the community leader and Rubin Epstein was the school principal. The community was confronted with the financial demands of the landowner Lucia Cantacuzino-Pascanu who owned the land on which the new school was built. The committee resigned on May 30.

The ad-interim commission, made up of six people, was not able to finish the restoration of the public bath because of a lack of money in the impoverished population. [A-86] Heroes' day was celebrated at the Great Synagogue.

[14] [Ed-Com] Maramures: the Western region of the country.

A large amount of money (800,000 lei) was discovered missing from the town hall. On August 2, 1928, a storm followed by heavy rain caused great damage to the town. In December, an ad-interim commission was established at the town hall with Moise Solomon as vice president. Insufficient drinking water became a problem. The traditional annual banquet organized by the community was held on February 7 and R. Epstein gave a speech. In 1929, the banquet was held in November.

The years 1929 and 1930 were marked by escalating crisis and anti-Semitism. It is true though that Maccabi and the charity society continued their activities. The ad-interim commission of the commune could not be legally established, since three of its members were not present at the oath-taking ceremony. These members were later accused of being against King Carol.

This was the community budget for 1930:

> REVENUES: Tax on kosher meat 528,456 lei; subventions 78,909 lei; school taxes 46,740 lei; public bath 13,800 lei; other revenues 27,444 lei; and burials 12,890 lei.
>
> EXPENSES: Overall expenses 141,892 lei; salaries 505,120 lei; 1929 deficit 137,318 lei; and 1930 deficit 77,091 lei. The total sum was quite impressive for a modest community, but the deficits represented a serious warning of the economic situation of the Jews living in the small town. [A-87]

Economic crisis and political unrest also marked the following year, 1931. In May, the communal counsel was dissolved and Pavel Botez and the former gendarmes' lieutenant Doroftei chaired the ad-interim commission. Here is an example of a political event that occurred that year: The eight sergeants in town, who were members of the Peasants' party, were replaced with members of the ruling party. In July, the bakers in town, who were waiting for an increase in the price of bread, went on strike causing a shortage of bread. A trial began against the cashiers who embezzled 800,000 lei that belonged to the town hall; so did a trial against the former mayor Tudorache, who probably was the chief of the "sergeants of the town" before the war.

On October 11, 1931, the three-year term of the community's committee came to an end. An ad-interim commission prepared the elections. The only list included M.H. Schor, Litman Vigder, Z. Anciu, Solomon Marcovici, Dr. S. Iancu, Herman Barat, Aron Aronovici, Iosef Blumenfeld, and Sender Cojocaru. A small Hebrew play was presented at the Hanukkah celebration. The teachers Etla Marcovici, Eti Credinciosu, and Fani Buium were honored.

The years 1932 and 1933 were dominated by the country's economic and political crisis. Yet even under these harsh conditions, solidarity among the people remained strong. A list of the donations for the Jewish hospital in Iasi included 30 Jews from Podu Iloaiei, who annually donated sums up to 300 lei. [A-88] In the same year, 65,080 lei of equipment belonging to the Jewish-Romanian primary school in town was deposited in the safe at the Iasi hospital.

The creation of the Romanian-Jewish party by Dr. Th. Pischer did not have much of an impact. On the other hand, the local Jews, as well as the rest of their coreligionists, reacted promptly to the news of the racist measures adopted against the Jews in Hitler's Germany. On April 27, 1933, a meeting was held at the Great Synagogue to protest Hitler's excessive measures. It was, in fact, an anti-fascist meeting.

But let us not anticipate, and instead follow the events of 1932 in their chronological order. On February 25, Maccabi celebrated 10 years of existence, and the short play *Der Geht* by Shalom Aleichem was performed. On March 26, a local group of pilgrims left for Eretz Yisrael. At the farewell party, the play *The Way to The Inner Self*, written by a local militant A. A. Policman, was performed in Yiddish.

The local police proved to be ineffective; four smoke shops were robbed in three weeks.

The community's committee had resigned in December 1931, but it was not until May 24, 1932 that an electoral bureau was formed to monitor the elections on June 5. The only list to be voted on had Dr. S. Iancu in the first position.

Changes were also taking place at the town hall. An ad-interim commission chaired by Tudose was appointed. With the elections coming, Goga's followers won the support of the lawyer G. Fisler, while the Peasants' party requested and obtained the support of the Jewish population. After their victory in the elections, they donated 200,000 lei to help the town's victims. In August there were debated issues such as the installment of electricity in the town and the building of a dyke in the Bahlui River to prevent floods and damage. In December, Maccabi performed *The Jackpot* by Shalom Aleichem in Yiddish, of course.

The assassination of I. G. Duca was considered to be a bad sign by the local Jews. The democratic parties were asking for the Jewish votes. Avram Orenstein was nominated for the position of mayor's assistant. In January 1934, the town was damaged by a terrible snowstorm, but it did not suffer any consequences from the earthquake in March 1934. In the communal elections, the government obtained seven counselor seats, while the national-peasants' opposition obtained only three.

The society of the Jewish craftsmen elected a new committee on May 16, 1934. Due to rising difficulties, the community's committee resigned in October 1934; some of its members were accused of embezzlement. Also in October, the issue of installing electricity was discussed again. The poor economic situation led Mayor Dr. Popescu to request and to obtain a cancellation of the tax on the household's value that had been established by the Peasants' Party.

The crisis and the ever-rising prices were still an issue in 1935. However, thanks to several millers from Iasi, however, the price of bread was reduced by 1 leu per kilo and as such Podu Iloaiei is exemplified by the press media. With respect to cultural activities, nothing of particular interest occurred in 1935.

The chronicle for 1935 mentioned a robbery attempt at the Ceres mill that was owned by two Jews. The bakers raised the price of bread, but Lupu Buchman, the mayor's assistant, negotiated with them and a compromise was reached. In February, the 25th anniversary of the Jewish school was celebrated. The committee included Moise Iancu Sor, president; Michel Sor, president of the school's committee; and Solomon Elias, the elder of the town. In April, one year later, Dr. Tenenbaum's death was commemorated, since everyone in town loved him, regardless of their religion. The town hall named a street after this popular physician. In July 1935, the grain market opened, causing serious problems for the small tradesmen in the grain business. A second pharmacy also opened.

On September 27, 1935, Moise Buchman died at the age of 73. He had been one of the community's leaders, and his sons, Ghetel the engineer and Lupu Buchman, played an important role in the community's life. Lupu Buchman was still alive in 1981.

In March 1937, the town hall reduced the tax paid by the bar tenants, thus reducing by 80,000 leithe State schools' income, which were subsidized from this fund. In fact, the entire communal budget was insufficient.

Dictatorial behavior could also be found among the Jews. The mayor's assistant appointed the community's leaders without calling elections, a decision that displeased a segment of the Jewish population. A new shochet was brought in without the committee's approval. The shochet was arrested on September 10. At the shochet's request, some Jews came to give him a "minyn" in his prison cell. He was released and then arrested again.

The year 1938 began with the sinister and tragic farce of the Goga-Cuza government that deeply affected the life of the town. How could the Jews not to be affected by the revision of their citizenship that conditioned their presence in economic life and by the various offensive measures that had been taken? This episode was a warning sign to the Jews, a prelude to the racist laws that were to come.

It is true, that by April 1938, the mayor P. Rusovici had accomplished a series of improvements: paving the main road; increasing threefold the revenues from the fairs; ensuring that the town was clean; and hiring eight street sergeants instead of the two "guards." The reopening of the grain market, controlled by I. Daderlat who forbade any deal of more than 100 kilos of grain, still threatened the existence of the small grain tradesmen. In only a few months, more than 4,300,000 kilos of grain were sold in this market.

In the spring of 1938 (13 Nisan 5698), Volf Fisler died. He was an erudite, enlightened bartender with a sarcastic personality, a specialist in Hebrew, and a former friend of the well-known Velvl Zbarjer. He had been a constant presence in the community's life eversince 1897. His sons proved to be just as active; they were interested in culture, as well as serving in the bar.

The community life continued. On December 3, 1938, the new leaders of the community took an oath in the presence of the rabbi Burah Svart, who was actually a dayan. The new leaders were Simon Lupu, B. Mayer, S. Friedman, Haim Spiegler, Iekel Blumenfeld, M. H. Goldenberg, Leizer User, M. Eintraub, Bercu Ioina, A. Aronovici, Ghedele Rabinovici, A. Mendelovici, and David H. Nusen.

In 1940, the process of forced integration into Romanian society began, along with the reexamination of the rights to Romanian citizenship (which had serious economic consequences for those who were denied citizenship), the drafting of Jewish reservists to serve in work battalions, and the restrictions imposed on cultural freedom. All of these caused tension and concern among the townspeople. The community carried on its activities despite the most difficult circumstances.

In 1940 and 1941, the situation of the Jews became noticeably worse. Yet the traditions were generally maintained in Podu Iloaiei: The shops were closed on Saturdays and the ritual laws were fulfilled according to the circumstances.

After Romania joined the war in 1941, the situation became even worse. The Jews were forced to do "community work" in conditions that are well known. Many families with missing men lived in poor conditions. The pogrom that took place in Iasi in June 1941 had a terrible ending in Podu Iloaiei.

The "death train" stopped at the station. More than 1,200 bodies were taken out of the wagons and buried in a common grave in the Jewish cemetery. After the war, the Federation of the Jewish Communities in Romania erected a monument at the martyrs' common tomb with an inscription in both Yiddish and Romanian: "Here are buried the victims of the savage massacres against the Jewish population."

The 800 survivors were led off the train. They were first hosted in the synagogues and then in the houses of the local Jews who took care of them the best that they could, thus showing a brotherly solidarity. [A-89]

Actually, the Jewish population in Podu Iloaiei knew that they could be evacuated from the town. This was to happen in 1941, but a postponement was obtained.

The late Moise Sor told me about an interesting event: When the order arrived to evacuate all the local Jews to Iasi, the communal council held a special meeting. The mayor was Dr. Ionescu, who was the physician at the local hospital and a good-hearted man. Both he and the chief of the police, as well as the teacher D. Dumitriu from Erbiceni, objected to the evacuation of the Jews, which would economically ruin the commune. The mayor interceded in the Jews' favor at the prefecture, but the prefect Adam, a member of Cuza's party, ordered the evacuation to be completed within 48 hours. A two-week postponement of the order was obtained with many sacrifices, and so the Jews were able to sell their belongings under less pressing conditions.

S. Cristian related on April 14, 1942: "This Saturday almost a thousand Jews from Podu Iloaiei arrived in Iasi, leaving behind their belongings and their shops, which had been temporarily closed. The evacuated Jews were left in the yard of the community building with no roof over their heads. Another 400 Jews were waiting to be evacuated from Podu Iloaiei. The evacuation order had been suspended last fall because of a lack of houses and the high cost of living. A landslide had just occurred in Ticau, and the Christian population there also had to be evacuated. The Jewish community in Iasi did not have the means to help the Jews in Podu Iloaiei. Dr. Gingold made no attempt to stop the evacuation." [A-90]

According to other sources, the community of Podu Iloaiei maintained a certain amount of autonomy in Iasi, having Lebel Ionas as its president. All that was necessary for living in this city had been purchased, and the community was still active.

After August 23, 1944, some of the local Jews, whose houses had not been affected by the fight that had taken place here, and some small grain tradesmen returned to the town, but they could never go back to living the same community life they had before.. There was even a shochet, Iosef Rosental, who had been a teacher of Hebrew at the community's school for many decades. The Census Statistics for 1947 estimated that the Jewish population of Podu Iloaiei was 300.

However, these individuals also moved soon to other cities and countries, such that in 1965, only a few old men were still living in the town. One of them, the smith Avram, used to go every Saturday to say the prayers all alone in the synagogue, which had been destroyed by bombs during the war. The community in Iasi sent a shochet each week to slaughter a bird for him. Soon these elders died, the last Mohicans of a community that had existed for 150 years.

Epilogue: I started to gather material for this monograph in May 1946. I came back to the town to find it seriously damaged by the war. The few Jews that remained did not realize that they were the last representatives of a many centuries old way of living in Eastern Europe—a world that was soon to end—and that new economic, political, and social life forms were being established in these realms. The borough, "dus shtetl," was passing from the harsh light of reality to an aura of legends and poetry. However, the borough left deep marks not only in people's souls, but also in the historical development of all Jews and the countries they lived in.

I have tried to depict here the history of a Jewish community in Moldova as seen through the eyes of a son of the community. I have tried to be objective and to exclude passion and bias from my writing. I have tried to present the events and the way of living, thinking, and feeling as a fragment of Eastern European Judaism in the context of the Romanian society.

This monograph remains, however, a Kaddish, a requiem for a disappeared way of life that has not been spared history's hardships. We have only love and understanding for the values that were created by the shtetl; this means a lot more than nostalgia and idealization.

8 Economic Life

The 1831 census offers the first comprehensive information about the population of the borough of Podu Iloaiei. Some of the data come from an act issued in April 1830. According to this source, the town consisted of 131 households with 13 Christian tradesmen who were tax-exempt and 85 Jews, locals, and Sudits; among them were three who were tax-exempt, three who were paying tax, 13 who were servants and were tax exempt, 15 who were bachelors and widows, and nine who were Gypsies. Assuming that there were five people in each family that would make a total of 905 people, which is an overestimate since another contemporary source indicated only 420 individuals.

The censuses, especially the ones done in 1831, 1838, and 1845 that are kept in the archives in Iasi and Bucharest, are considered to be of documentary importance. The Jewish population —"Judaeus" or "Ebrews" — had a special status in the census, and the references contain valuable information on different aspects of the community life. Although there have been many differences in the making of the questionnaire or the census, with many unjustified omissions and additions, in general the censuses offer a true image of reality.

The work on the first census began in 1831 and was completed the following year. In the book *Roumanie et les Juifs*, Verax (Radu D. Rosetti) compared the data from the 1831 census with the partial data from 1803 (the register of the peasants) and 1820 to emphasize the Jewish "invasion." This malicious interpretation of the data revealed his judeophobia and his "ardent" comments diminished the value of his work. [A-91] Referring to the 1831 census, Verax wrote that in Podu Iloaiei there were 281 local Jewish natives, 281 Christians, and 8 Sudits; a total of 570 people in 164 families. On page 44, he mentioned only 284 Jews. In a 1970 report, the researcher E. Negruzzi mentioned 109 Jewish children, estimating the total population at 560 people of whom 281 are Jews (see Appendix E).

Particularly important for the economic life of the town were the weekly fair days and the annual markets. Although the 1818 act allowed seven fair days per year, the owner of the estate neglected their organization, which led to a financial loss for him and the townspeople. The loss became more obvious after 1829, when the Adrianopol treaty stipulated the freedom of foreign trade for the Romanian Principalities. Meanwhile, the price of agricultural products had increased, as well as the demand for these products. An important grain trade was done at the fairs. The peasants used the money they obtained from selling their products to buy necessary items. The peasants, tradesmen, and craftsmen were making profits, though the profits were far greater for the owners or the tenants of the estates or towns, since they were collecting the taxes from the fairs.

That is why the inhabitants sent a note of complaint to the heirs of C. Palade, arguing that if the fair was cancelled they "would have no food" and be forced to "go back where each of them had come from." On October 20, the owner requested that the treasury renew the right to seven annual fairs, which it did, and then he made the usual announcements in the village papers and in *The Official Bulletin.* [A-92]

In 1842, these fairs were neglected once again by the owner of the town or by its tenant.

Industry began to develop in the town. On October 10, 1832, the brothers Boan from Bucovina, who owned a "plate factory" for 10 years, complained that taxes were demanded from them even though they were Sudits and the law also exempted them from paying tax because they were "manufacturers." [A-93] Referring to the pottery made in Podu Iloaiei, an industry that continued to exist in the 20th century, Dr. Slatineanu wrote that the ornaments were "made with a horn-like instrument or brush. The motifs are geometric or floral, pale or dark green, but rarely blue on a white background." The style of the local manufacturers seemed to have been influenced by that of the pottery makers living in the villages around Roman. (Could this have been the influence of the popular art of Csango?)

In 1836, there was a rudimentary spirit distiller with a six-bucket capacity that was valued at 1,490 lei. It belonged to the Jew Iancu from Carazeni.

The treasury inspector Ion Teodoru considered the numbers in 1831 census to be too small. On June 30, 1834, he found 23 "profit-makers," who he included among the taxpayers or patent payers. Ten of them had their own shops. The "profit-makers" practiced the following professions: one peddler, one grocer, one shoemaker, two butchers, two bar tenants, three teachers, four tailors, and five alcoholic beverage makers. The townspeople argued that not all of the "profit makers" were able to pay tax. A reexamination was done. Declarations were taken in the presence of the town's captain Colonel Constandin, the representatives of the Jewish community, and the former captain Tudorache. The result was that only seven "were worthy to pay tax." Of the others, two were Sudits, two were new arrivals to the town, two were underage, two were "free of settlement obligations," six "in all were poor and weak," and two family heads could take up a third-grade patent. The thorough observations revealed the poverty and low social position of the Jewish population that resulted from the repressive measures taken against the Jews as stipulated in The Organic Regulation (see Appendix L).

Jews were not included in the 1838 census. Using data from a taxpayer register from 1839, Verax estimated that there were 120 Jewish taxpaying family heads, to which he added 20% invalids, poor, and widows, for a total of 480 Jews. [A-94]

A complaint signed by the Jews in Podu Iloaiei and dated September 1845 indicated that there were 102 peasants in 1838. The old table referred to only 97 peasants, 68 of whom lived on Lascarache Cantacuzino's part of the estate and 29 on Nicolae Cantacuzino's part. [A-95]

The inauspicious economic status of the town was reflected in a request to the treasury, pointing out that "the Jewish ethnicity from the villages of Stefanesti, Hirlau, Burdujeni, Podul Lelioarei, and other similar boroughs" could not pay the annual tax of 60 lei, which was to be paid by each family head, because "commerce and their trades in these boroughs could not be compared to that practiced in the bigger towns." The commissions enforced taxes on shochets, some invalids, and some people who were underage. Some were registered twice and Sudits were also included. In the small towns, commerce was limited to trade. They asked that the tax be reduced to 40 lei for each head of family. [A-96]

Some of the relatives of the townspeople lived abroad. In 1842, Strule Moscovici and a servant Solomon, both native Moldavian Jews, passed through Galati on their way from Constantinople to visit the shop Strule had left in Podul Iloaiei. [A-97] The structure of the Jewish population in town in 1842 is best reflected by a "tax-money list" that was included in the "possession" register. At the "main road," there were 43 houses inhabited by Christians (Romanians, Lippovans, Bulgarians, Serbs and one Armenian) and 58 houses inhabited by Jews. In the suburbs, there were 40 houses inhabited by Christians and 15 by Jews (see Appendix M).

In 1845, the census showed the following structure of the Christian population [A-98]: On Lascar Cantacuzino's part of the estate, there were two tradesmen of second state, 14 of third state, and three apprentices, consisting of five Moldavians, one Serb, one baptized Armenian, one former German, five Lippovans, and six individuals with no mentioned nationality but who, no doubt, were Moldavian shepherds or cheese makers. On Neculai Cantacuzino's part, there were four third-state tradesmen, all Moldavians. The Christian craftsmen on Lascar's part consisted of nine third-state masters and nine apprentices, six of whom were Moldavians. On Neculai's part, there were four masters and two apprentices, all Christians. In terms of the practiced professions, there were one furrier, one cook, seven shoemakers, three fur coat makers, four tailors, two stone hewers, one rope maker, one woodcutter, one Polish wood carver, one joiner/adzer, and one carpenter. The structure of the Jews' professions was as follows: one small merchandise seller, one silversmith, three grocers, five intermediary tradesmen, one cotton dealer, one pail maker, one wagoner, four butchers, one synagogue janitor, one shoemaker, one sieve maker, two barkeepers, seven tailors, one grain dealer, one fur cap maker, two teachers, one torch carrier, one flour dealer, one horse merchant, one shochet, one carter, eight tradesmen at Lipsca, three bar tenants, two bakers, two merchants, 74 alcoholic beverage makers, two glaziers, two carpenters, one soles maker, one tax collector, one tobacco seller, two wine sellers, seven with no profession indicated, and three with no occupation.

The large number of alcoholic beverage makers can be explained by the fact that many Jews had been driven away from the villages and had settled in town. Indeed, the census mentioned 35 Jews who came from the villages, among whom only four were craftsmen. Some of them owned a house in town, while others lived in rented houses. Sixty-three Jews had their own houses, even the old rabbi Moise who, forced by poverty, rented a part of his house. One cannot be wrong in assuming that all the others lived in rented houses, as was the case for 61 tax-paying Jews and 23 newly married couples, elders, or poor who did not own a house.

The economic situation of the town was made difficult by the large number of Jews who had been driven away from their villages and had settled in small towns without the possibility of quickly finding an occupation, because of the limited range of economic activities that the modest settlement could offer. This economic-social process was not restricted to Podul Iloaiei. It could be generalized to all of Moldova, and had serious repercussions on the country's budget. Actually, in a letter dated December 20, 1845, "the entire community of Jewish tradesmen from Podu Iloaiei" complained that now they had to pay the tax for 181 people, compared to 102 in 1838. The document also mentioned that since "the first writing," that is since the drawing of the census, six taxpayers had died and 10 had moved "no one knows where" and could not be found "because our little town is surrounded by woods." At the end of "the table" indicating the part of the town on N. Canta's estate, it was mentioned that 27 people "have come from somewhere else." This explains the sudden growth of the Jewish population in town.

A comparison of the data regarding the situation of the town's population is of interest: 20 tradesmen with two apprentices, 13 craftsmen with 11 apprentices, Moldavians, Lippovans, Serbs, Armenians, one German, and one Pole. The rest of the Christian population lived in the suburbs and were engaged in agricultural activities. Professor Gh. Platon estimated that in 1845 there were 240 Jewish taxpayers and 143 Christian taxpayers, for a total of 1,815 people. Among the Christians were 21 tradesmen, 23 craftsmen, 63 taxpayers, 13 widows, and 23 elderly and invalids. Among the Jews, there were 129 tradesmen, 40 craftsmen, two apprentices, six of other professions, 18 with no specified profession, 31 elderly and invalids, and 14 widows. [A-99]

A complaint dated December 20, 1845 was signed by the following individuals: Simha from Targu Frumos, Moise from Berlesti, Iancu from Popesti, Moise sin Iancu Leib from Targu Frumos, Zisu Tvi son of Iosef, Tvi son of Iaakov, another Iaakov from Targu Frumos, David Casap, and Iaakov Leib. [A-100]

Appendix N includes a complete list of the Jews in Podu Iloaiei as stipulated in the 1845 census. Of interest are the specifications regarding the name days, places of origin, professions, and social status.

Around 1848, the fair and market days had a considerable impact on the economic life of the settlement. In 1847, Palade's heirs tried to forcefully bring "the people" to the fair, which was held each Sunday in Podu Iloaiei. Nicolae Cantacuzino complained on June 3, 1847 that for 20 years the fair had been held each Sunday in Scobalteni and asked that "the townspeople and tradesmen be allowed to make their trade on both sides of the Bahlui River." [A-101] On June 14, 1847, the State's Secretariat demanded from the Finance Department that the days of the fair be Sunday in Podu Iloaiei and Monday in Scobalteni. [A-102] During that year, a French mission found the population of the town to be 1,250 people. [A-103]

In 1848, cholera ravaged the town. An incomplete official report indicated that 39 Jewish and 6 Christian heads of family had died. However, professor Gh. Platon showed that 237 Jews and Christians died of cholera in Podu Iloaiei. [A-104] The French mission ranked the town as a village because of its rural style of life. The mission pointed out that the poor condition of the roads hindered economic activity, particularly cattle breeding. Podu Iloaiei and Targu Frumos were becoming profitable cattle markets. To obtain a better deal for his products, V. Bosie the owner of the Sarca estate formed a partnership with a Jew from Podu Iloaiei.

Of special significance was an address from July 27, 1853 that ordered Dumitru Buliu from Targu Frumos to come to Podu Iloaiei and make 15,000 bricks, for which he had already received money from Moise Lozneanu; the same was true for Constandin, also from Targu Frumos, who had received money two months before to make 8,000 bricks. The administrator of the Iasi district asked the police in Targu Frumos to comply with Moise Lozneanu's complaint.

Of special importance to the economic development of the town was the notification in 1854 that there were 20 steam mills in the Bahlui region; at least one of them was in Podu Iloaiei, of course. [A-105]

The statistics for 1859 indicated 996 Jewish and 881 Christian inhabitants in Podu Iloaiei, with no mention of their occupation. [A-106] The statistics for Moldova in 1859 showed for Podu Iloaiei: heads of family - 216 men and 39 women, with 473 men and 516 women, for a total of 989 Jews, to which are added 888 Christians.

In town, there was a factory that made vinegar from water and alcohol with the help of a machine. In 1859, Moise Rat, the owner of the factory, had a stock of 100 vedre of vinegar and another amount already in the process of being made. [A-107]

Wc havc no statistics or spccial data on the economic development of the town in the following decades. Its progress was hindered by its status as a rural settlement, which placed it under ever-increasing restrictions—legal or not—regarding the Jewish population. However, the building of the Great Synagogue, the hiring of a physician, the increasing number of inhabitants, the development of the grain trade, and the rising of the cultural level indicate the efforts made by the Jewish population to build a proper community in the vicinity of Iasi. A document issued at the end of the 19th century fully reflects the structure, situation, and dynamics of the Jewish population (see Appendix P).

The list of "the foreigners" drawn up in 1898 reflects the abnormal situation of the Jews in Romania during those years. The overwhelming majority of the Jews in town, who were born and brought up in this country (as were most of their parents) with no foreign protection and who had performed their military service, had no political rights and were forbidden many civil rights as well. Due to administrative stipulations, they were the victims of the arbitrariness of the police and of all the local authorities in general. The maintenance of the status of the boroughs as communes had negative repercussions on the national economy, although it satisfied the egotistical interests of those who wanted to restrain possible competition by making use of extra economic measures.

Summing up the data in the table, we obtained the following results: heads of family- 490 men and 53 widows; family members (under age 21) - 536 males and 829 females; of these 17 were not Jews with 11 children. Only 25 of the Jews were subjects of other states. There were also several "righteous" Jews, former combatants in the 1877/1878 Independence War or their descendents, or coming from Dobrogea.

The professions of the Jews in Podu Iloaiei were as follows: four barbers who also applied leeches; eight cabmen who were transporting people to and from the railway station and also to Iasi and Targu Frumos; six waggoners who transported goods inside and outside the town; three substitute teachers who were hired to help the four "melamdim," the heder teachers officially named the "the confessional asylum." The only furrier in town competed with 13 other fur coat makers who made thick coats, fur coats, and fur caps. The peasants who wanted their wool dyed solicited the help of three dyers. No receipts were used, but inscriptions were made on a wooden tally that was "attached" to the hank of wool to be dyed. The only braga maker in town was assisted by two confectioners; all three were Turks. Three Jewish bakers, assisted by two pretzel makers, were baking according to the Mosaic rules[B-15]. The coopers made keys, bathtubs, and vats. There was also a coffee shop, a brick factory, two kosher butchers, four synagogue janitors, two shoe makers, 12 boot makers who - like the fur coat makers - were also working for the surrounding villages, and 28 tailors and 8 dressmakers who worked only for the townspeople with modest incomes, since the dresses for the wealthy women were ordered in Iasi or a deluxe dressmaker was brought from Iasi. The only accountant in town worked for the rich man Marcu Ghetel, whose fortune was said to be worth 1 million gold francs.

To the 203 tradesmen of all kinds, we have to add the 30 merchants and the four "fisherman," who traded fish caught predominantly from the pond in Scobalteni. Eleven

[15] [Ed-Com] Mosaic rules: Jewish laws as outlined in the Torah (Moses).

Jewish blacksmiths and smiths and two wheelwrights also worked in the town. The presence of three teachers at the primary school, which was founded in 1892, was a sign of the modernization of the Jewish educational system. The four shochets, the rabbi, and the Hasidic court are discussed in another chapter. The only innkeeper in town took care of the inn. The three "business men" were probably wholesale tradesmen or private clerks. In addition to the Romanian physician who worked at the regional hospital, there was a Jewish physician who owned aprivate practice but also paid visits to the members of the mutual assistance association and the poor in the community. The presence of five midwives, one of whom was over 90 years old, indicates that the birth rate was high. Seventy-five Jewish workers helped to load and unload grain and other agricultural products, and worked at the oil press, at the wood warehouse, and as assistants in shops.

In the construction business, there were three masons, six carpenters, and a tinker. There were also a saddle maker, a carpet maker, and three water carriers. Only 12 people were listed as servants. I believe that some of those who were mentioned as "workers" did chores in other men's households. There was also an "animal doctor," who was famous in the neighboring villages. It is possible that the family men who were listed as "having no profession" were intermediaries or craftsmen without a shop or workshop of their own, and thus were not included in the fiscal records. In fact, the unmarried young people, who were listed as having "no profession," usually worked in their parents' workshop or shop.

Several observations: all unmarried young people over age 21 are considered heads of family, even though they continued to live and work in their parents' house (32 men and 60 women). Women who only had a religious marriage ceremony were considered heads of family, just like their husbands. There was a great number of old people and widows (85 widows, 14 elders between age 60 and 70, and nine elders between age 70 and 90). Actually, only 21 heads of family had no profession (see Appendix P).

The poor harvest and the economic crisis at the beginning of the 20th century had repercussions on the town's economy. In August and September 1897, three bankruptcies took place. The consequences of the crisis became more serious in 1899-1900 and later, especially for the craftsmen, leading to the famous mass emigration on foot that took place in 1900-1901 under dramatic conditions. On May 31, 1900, 100 people from Podu Iloaiei were about to emigrate. On July 16, 400 of the town's Jews left for America. Sraier, the representative of the local Jews, asked Auerbach, the ICA's delegate, to facilitate the emigration of the craftsmen, particularly the women whose husbands had emigrated the year before. [A-108] Auerbach promised to help. In July 1902, another 25 families of Jewish craftsmen from Podu Iloaiei prepared to emigrate. They had a 4,000 lei fund and asked for help from the committee in Iasi. The emigration continued over the next years, although at a slower rate. On July 20, 1907, more families from Podu Iloaiei left for America.

In 1910, 1,895 Jews lived in Podu Iloaiei, comprising approximately 68% of the town's total population. The decline in the Jewish population—there had been 1,962 Jews in 1899—was due to the emigration that took place during the years 1900-1901 and 1905-1906. Considering the occupations of those who had left, there were now 187 tradesmen, 15 tailors, 20 boot makers, eight smiths, three carpenters, and 175 people with other occupations such as coopers, tinkers, cabmen, wagoners, haircutters, bakers, coffee sellers, dyers, clerks, porters, day laborers, and intermediaries. In 1914, more families in town emigrated.

The years 1923-1924 were marked by price increases, especially for food, and by an acute monetary crisis.

The fair in Podu Iloaiei was no longer held after 1924. One time, the producers returned from the fair in Targu Frumos with all their merchandise unsold because the merchants did not have money to buy the merchandise. As usual, there were brutal, irresponsible, anti-Semitic forces that seized the popular discontent. In March 1924, the organization of the Sunday fair and the market day in Podu Iloaiei was terminated. An increase in taxes followed, and the tradesmen became worried. A committee called The Tradesmen's Council was elected; it was made up of nine Jews and one Christian (C. Ioan).

In 1925, the Small Credit Bank opened with the help of the Joint [B-16]. The short-term loans offered by the bank helped the small tradesmen and craftsmen to maintain their businesses and confront the various forms of discrimination. After a short period of stabilization, we were informed that, in 1928, the peasants and merchants in Podu Iloaiei had become impoverished. In the past, the town had exported 3,000 to 4,000 wagons of grain; however in 1928, nothing was exported and the local needs could not be satisfied. The cattle starved because of a lack of fodder. Some peasants left to find work elsewhere. Excessive taxes and bankruptcies hindered commerce. The new harvest was better, and on August 1, the grain market was opened. [A-109]

In 1926, The Commerce Bank opened, managed by Haim Orensteim. For several years, the Jewish craftsmen had been organized in a mutual assistance society that remained active until the Jews were evacuated in 1942. In 1929, and for many years thereafter, the president of the society was Avram Herman. At the general assembly held on May 1928 at the Tailors synagogue, the project of an independent office was launched.

The Ceres mill, estimated to be worth 8 million lei, was destroyed by a fire. It was rebuilt, and opened on February 22, 1928. On July 28, 1928, the grain market opened; one of the managers was Iancu Sneier. The Small Credit Bank expanded. In June, Israel Fisler, Strul Moscovici, and Litman Vigder were elected auditors.

The setting up of the grain market, on which taxes were imposed, brought losses to the small tradesmen. Due to a policy that stipulated an imposed compulsory price, the peasants preferred to go to other markets. A commission of 10 tradesmen presented their case to the Commerce Chamber in Iasi and offered a sum equal to that brought in by the taxes in exchange for the closing of the market.

The 1930 census indicated 1,601 Jewish inhabitants in Podu Iloaiei, who made up 40.4% of the total population. The decline in the population since 1910 was, of course, due in part to the exodus of the Jews to the larger cities. To a smaller degree, it was also due to emigration and the death rate during the war, which was particularly high because of the epidemics.

---

[16] [Ed-Com] The Joint refers to the American Jewish Joint Distribution Committee.

The various anti-Jewish actions in the 1930s deeply affected the economic situation of the local Jews. The process of impoverishment, Proletarian-ization, and social differentiation increased, and many intellectuals and qualified workers left the town. Thus, it was no surprise in 1941 that the Jewish community consisted of only 1,454 individuals, 37% of the total population.

After World War II, the economic role played by the Jewish borough was a thing of the past. The history of the Jewish community in Podu Iloaiei thus came to an end, one and a half centuries after its founding. It was a closed chapter.

9 Communal Life

The oldest Jewish community organization in Podu Iloaiei was Chevra Chedosha, the burial brotherhood that took care of the burials, the cemetery, and sometimes the poor who fell ill. The organization was established soon after the founding of the borough, but its records were lost during World War I. There were also other organizations such as Chevra Tehillim, which was set up for reading the psalms together, and other groups for the study of the Mishna or the entire Talmud. Their records were not saved, however.

The oldest documented society is the branch of the Israelite Alliance, which was founded at the initiative of the head office in Paris for the purpose of defending at least the civil rights of Jews in Romania. The committee in Podu Iloaiei was made up of Aron Goldental, president; Abraham Dov Katz, vice president; Solomon ben Haim, cashier; Dov ben Itchak, secretary; and Moise Gang and Ghedalie Horenstein, members.

In 1882, the existence of a brotherhood mutual assistance society was announced, providing a physician and free medication. [A-110] In 1889, Tomhei Ani'im was a well-established society that provided clothes for poor children. It was chaired by I. Lazar and Saie Steinberg, the latter was involved in community life until after World War I. [A-111] In 1894, Achim, a youth organization, was established to help the poor. The committee included Leon Landman, Herman Wechsler, H. Spirt, and Isidor Lazar. In 1895, Achim donated several items of furniture to the community's school. The traditional ladies' charity activities were formally organized some years later.

The Zionist organization played an important role in the community life of the Jewish population in Podu Iloaiei. The first section of Hovevei Zion[B-17] was set up in 1891 and was still active in 1894, when it sent its delegate Saie Steinberg to the congress in Galati. [A-112] Subsequently, its activities diminished, and, at the end of 1901, the society Carmel was reopened at the initiative of Ghersen Cohn. [A-113] Carmel had 35 members. In April 1902, the Maccabea branch was established, and was chaired by Iosef Solomon. The medical student Albert Spirt lectured. Sometime later, the Zionist society Dr. Herzl's Youngsters was established. It had 40 members, a reading group, and a committee led by Elias Reisch. At the congress in Bucharest in 1903, the young men Michel Sor and Iosef Rosental were delegated. The societies Carmel and Dr. Herzl sent delegates from other

[17] [Ed-Com] Hovevei Zion: The original modern Zionist organization established in the late 19th century.

towns to the congress in Basel. Dr. Herzl was still active in 1912 with a reading group and a library containing books in Romanian, Yiddish, Hebrew, and German. The president was the teacher I. Rosental. Literary meetings were organized quite frequently with readings in Yiddish and lectures on Jewish history. There are some data from 1914 on this society's activities. In 1915, the Zionist society Bnai Zion, Dr. Theodor Herzl merged with the group "The Light" in order to form a 150-member society. The leader was the future engineer Ghetel Buchman. The committee also included Vigder Iosupovici who later became president of the community; Adolf Kern who died during the war in 1917; Iancu Elias; the bookseller Jean Meirovici, Moise Solomon who later became the mayor's assistant; David Hers Hahamovici the self-educated tinker; Leon Sor who was still alive in 1978; Lupu Buchman who also was still alive in 1978; and Samuel Wechsler. In 1916, a Hebrew course was taught by Rubin Epstain, who was active in town until 1942 and lived to be 80 years old.

Between 1916 and 1918, any Jewish cultural activity was forbidden, and the library was closed. It was not until 1919, when the old Zionist section was reopened with six members, that the traditional celebration of Hanukkah was held, and a Hebrew course was attended by 30 students. I too, attended this course, which was held by I. Rosental. Literary meetings were also arranged at which Lupu Buchman and Simha Schwartz performed readings. The influence of the Zionists was also increasing in the community's committee. In 1922, a new committee of the organization was elected. The collection of funds and the Hebrew transformation of the school intensified. A kindergarten was set up and a sustained Zionist propaganda was carried on until the outbreak of World War II.

After a sports society was established, another one called Maccabi was founded in 1922 and remained more or less active for many years, organizing literary-artistic festivals, among other events. Moise Sor took part in the national leading committee of the Maccabi society. In 1924, Bention Nahman initiated and led a Mizrah[B-18] youth organization that presented the play *Tzezeit in Tzeshpreit* by Shalom Aleichem. In 1933, there was also a Gordonia society.

The socialist movement had followers in Podu Iloaiei, where Petre Taranu - an activist in this movement, died during the war, together with a Jewish socialist, under mysterious circumstances. In 1919, there was a socialist society in town. Two Jewish delegates, who were born in town, took part in the congress in 1921. Moise Elias remained with the Social Democrats, while Itic Mendelovici (later known as Jack Podoleanu) voted for the "Third International" party.

The followers of the leftist movement, who had Yiddish inclinations, founded in 1924 the cultural society Shalom Aleichem. They performed in Yiddish *The Siege of Tulcin* and plays by P. Hirsbein. Their tutors were Gedale Westler (1906-1978) and Itic Svart (later known as I. Kara). The committee also included Moise Sor (1908-1968), Ioel and Sulim Finchelstein, Bianca Lozner, Ana Zaharovici, and Ghizela Solomon. The society also had a library and organized literary meetings. In 1927, after two years of existence, Shalom Aleichem merged with the society Achad Ha'am and prepared a show with the play *Manasse* by Ronetti-Roman.

---

[18] [Ed-Com] Mizrahi: A religious Zionist organization established in the early 20th century.

In August 1926, the club Iavne opened, led by L. Buchman. There was also a chess club there. In March, the club took the name Achad Ha'am, and a new committee was elected.

There also existed in town several charity societies such as Ida Strauss, a society for the assistance of poor lying-in (confined) women. It was founded in 1912 and chaired by Ghizela Langberg. In 1919, Lupu Buchman established a philanthropic society called Baroness Clara de Hirsch for mature and young ladies. Between the two World Wars, a mutual assistance society of Jewish craftsmen, called "The Brotherhood" was also active.

The Native Jews' Union had existed in town ever since 1910. It intensified its activities around 1914, but especially after 1917, when the issue of granting citizenship to the Jews was at stake. The first decree legislating citizenship requested complicated formalities, which led the Native Jews' Union to organize a juridical office. After 1922, the importance of the Native Jews' Union diminished significantly because the Zionists supported the National Jewish Party and many Jews were registered in different political parties and thus their votes were dispersed. The elections for the leadership of the community were also an occasion for different political views and personal interests to be revealed.

Information on the various economic and professional associations is presented in other chapters.

In general, the community life of the town was never stagnant, even though there had been times—apart from the periods of maximum activity—when the activity was less intense. The fact that several local Jews asserted themselves in community, literary, or artistic life offered proof of the intense cultural and community climate.

We present biographical data on some of the most noteworthy representatives of the Jewish community in Podu Iloaiei:

GHETEL BUCHMAN: son of the leader Moise Buchman, an engineer, played an important role in the community life in Iasi.

LUPU BUCHMAN: brother of Ghetel Buchman, very influential, the author of many initiatives but only in his native town, has lived in Israel since 1981.

GHERSEN COHN: born in 1868, in his youth he was active in the press as the editor of *Di Yiddisher Tzukunft* (1899).

ELIEZER FRENKEL: born in 1920, made an early debut. His published work: *Naie Yiddisher Dichtung* (1935; co-author with I. Paner); *The Jewish Problem* (1946); *Dus Yiddisher Vort* (1947); and essays and literary criticisms.

BENTION ISCOVICI: see the chapter "The Hasidism."

I. KARA: born in 1906, historian, literary and theater critic, writer of prose. His published work: *Naie Yiddisher Dichtung* (1935; anthology); *Centuries Old Testimonies* (1947); *O Iur Yiddisher Literatur* (1947); *Yiddisher Gramatik* (1948); *A Moldevisher Yingle* (1976); and *Inghe Iurn* (1980).

IRA LANDMAN: see the chapter "The Rabbinate."

ADOLF MAGDER: principal of the community's school, URA activist. His published work since 1903: *Alia* (1913); *Great Errors* (1923); and *Wonder of Wonders* (1924).

SOLOMON PODOLEANU: publicist and historian. His published work: *The History of the Jewish Press in Romania* (1935); *Sixty Romanian Writers of Jewish Origin* (1935); and others.

ELIE ROSENTAL: see the chapter "The Rabbinate."

IULIAN SCHWARTZ (1910-1977): actor, cultural activist, and writer. His published work: *Der farkishefter shraiber* (1947); *10 Yiddisher folk sliden* (1947); *Literarishe dermonungen* (1975); and *Portret in eseien* (1979).

SIMCHA SCHWARTZ (1890-1974): actor, writer, and sculptor. His published work: *Baudelaire, Verlaine*. The artistic group Cameleon (Cernauti 1931-1934). Plays: The Theater *Hakl Bakl* (Paris 1945-1956).

ITIC SVART: see I. Kara.

LITMAN VIGDER (1901-1972): community activist and writer. His published work: Translations of Arghezi's poems in Yiddish (1965).

GHEDALE WESTLER (1906-1978): cultural activist, reciter, and man of the theater.

10 Private and Public Education

One of the first concerns of the Jews who founded the borough was to ensure their children's education and religious training. "Melamdim" teachers were brought to town. In 1834, there were three of them—Avram, Aron, and Moise. In 1845, there were six—Meer sin Fisel, Itic sin Bercu from Iasi, Strule from Todireni, Simon sin Lupu (who owned a house), Hoisie sin Liebu, Itic sin Moise, and Moise sin Mendel (who was old and ill). In 1882, the magazine *The Brotherhood* (page 361) noted that a Talmud Torah course was taught in town for the children of the poor. Although there were several confessional schools and a modern private teacher, some of the Jewish children attended the public primary school. The 1898 statistics indicated that there were four teachers and four assistants (belfer) living in town. There were also two private teachers who taught Romanian, Yiddish, German or French, and a little Hebrew, in addition to calligraphy and arithmetic. These teachers were Ihil Glanter and Leon Cramer. The latter was qualified to work as a teacher at the newly opened primary school. The traditional education system continued to function well after the opening of the Jewish-Romanian primary school, where at least two hours a day were spent on Jewish-related topics. In 1904, there were five confessional asylums (see Appendix S).

In the commune, public education began in 1862 for boys and in 1865 for girls; but it started to function properly only after 1867. Jewish students were also accepted. However, the boys had to have their head uncovered and attend the school on Saturdays, although they did not have to write. Most of the Jews in town had difficulty accepting these rules. Despite this, in 1884, the public primary school in Podu Iloaiei had 33 boys enrolled in the first grade, 17 of whom were Jews. There were 8 Jews and 5 Christians in the second grade, and 9 Jews and 5 Christians in the third grade. For the girls, there were 13 Jews and 13 Christians in the first grade, 12 Jews and 1 Christian in the second grade, 7 Jews and 6 Christians in the third grade, and 9 Jews and 1 Christian in the fourth grade. A school report showed that 15 of the 58 girls attending the primary school were Christian. The Jewish girls did not speak Romanian well, and they did not attend school on Saturdays and Jewish holidays. [A-114] In the fourth grade, there were no Christian students. The girls were not taught how to sew at school, and instead of the traditional national costume, they wore "long dresses that swept the street." The female teachers were paid poorly.

The number of Jewish students — especially the girls — remained high over the next years. In fact, in the girls' schools the Jewish students formed the majority. The Christian girls rarely graduated from the fourth grade. Here is the situation for the boys in 1886[15]: first grade, 27 Christians and 6 Jews; second grade, 9 Christians and 9 Jews; third grade, 8 Christians and 6 Jews; and fourth grade, 8 Christians and 4 Jews. The situation for the girls: first grade, 12 Christians and 11 Jews; second grade, 8 Christians and 7 Jews; third grade, 2 Christians and 10 Jews; fourth grade, 1 Christian and 5 Jews. In 1891, the winners of the scholar prizes were [A-116]: first grade, Dumitru Draganescu and Nathan Schonhaus; second grade, Haim Rotenberg and Dumitru Dumitras; third grade, Avram Zalman and Itic Leibel; and fourth grade, Vasiliu Haralamb and Gh. Cretulescu.

Alarmed by the poor attendance of the Christian students, the government came up with "the miraculous solution": the extreme limitation of the number of Jewish students! The 1883 law for public education, which was revised in 1896, stipulated that "the foreigners [of whom 99% were Jews — author's note] who enjoy no foreign protection will be accepted according to the school vacancies and will pay school taxes." Actually, the increase in anti-Semitism could be felt in the schools as well. The Jews decided to open their own primary school, following the example of the school set up in Iasi. In 1898, a year marked by a serious economic crisis, and two years before the mass emigration "on foot" in 1900, the teacher Pincu Svart founded the mixed Jewish-Romanian primary school. The school continued to function without him, in its own building on Garii (Railway) Street from 1902. I also attended primary classes at this school. When the school became too small for the increasing number of students, a new building was opened in 1914, where it continues to function today. The institution was supported financially by a committee. . The funds came from school taxes, the revenues of the annual banquet, and donations. A letter published in *The Israelite Courier* (November 1, 1903, page 3) noted that "the Jewish-Romanian school in our little town functions very well. The teaching staff is made up of: A. Magder, principal; I. Horodniceanu, teacher of Romanian language; I. Rosental, I Doroscanu, and S. Finchelman, teacher of Hebrew. For the excellent situation of the school, we have to thank the gentlemen in the school's committee and especially Mr. Z. Schor. A special thanks is owed to Mr. M. Ghetel, a rich man who donates a 1,200 lei subvention to the school each year. The committee decided to organize a banquet on October 7 in the school's benefit."

In August 1906, a new committee was elected, chaired by Saie Steinberg. The school functioned independently from the community, which was insufficiently organized and dealt only with cultural issues. *The Israelite Chronicle* from July 27, 1907 announced that the school needed a principal, who could teach Romanian; it also needed a Hebrew teacher. The president of the school's committee was the engineer Leon Brill. The frequent changes in the structure of the teaching staff were due to both poor pay for teachers and the committee's ambitions. In the beginning, Barad was appointed principal, then Adolf Magder in 1903, and Grinberg in 1906/1907. In June 1909, the school's committee and the school, chaired by the popular Dr. Margosches, were looking for a teacher of Romanian and German for the first and second grades, as well as a teacher of Hebrew for the third and fourth grades. A source of funds was the traditional banquet (held on January 25, 1909). At the banquet on January 20, 1912, the students presented a show in which they recited in Romanian and Hebrew.

Even after the opening of the Jewish-Romanian primary school, some Jewish children continued to attend the courses at the public school in the hopes of avoiding the difficult graduation exam at the end of the primary cycle. The exam took place in the public school with teachers, some of whom manifested chauvinistic beliefs. However, the Jewish children studied hard. As a result, they were better trained than most of the other students. During the school year of 1911/1912, the Jewish-Romanian primary school in Podu Iloaiei had 91 boys and 56 girls.

In 1913, a committee was formed to resolve the problem of erecting a new school building. Its representative, I. Astruc promised substantial help from the I.C.A. in Paris. The central hall was planned to be large enough to serve as a place where students could spend their free time during cold and rainy days and as a room for wedding ceremonies or banquets. The school's principal, the lawyer Adolf Magder who had been the author of some much appreciated initiatives, played a special role. In 1913, he wrote about the visit paid to the school by the minister Spiru Haret who, among others, had been extremely impressed by the students' work in the vegetable garden of the Jewish-Romanian primary school. [A-117]

A 30-page booklet, entitled *A Celebration*: *The Festivity of Laying the Foundation Stone of the New Building of the Jewish-Romanian Primary School in Podu Iloaiei,* was printed in Iasi on *May 11, 1914*. The booklet mentioned the choir that was conducted by the Hebrew teacher Iosef Rosental. After the religious ceremony performed by the old rabbi Ira Landman, the following people spoke: S. Steinberg, Rabbi Thenen from Iasi, Moritz Wachtel, Petre Constatinescu (a member of The Students' Center in Iasi who later became an academician; he died in November 1978), Aron Rosenthal, Moses Duff, Dr. Carol Vittner, Ghizela Wechsler, H. Gerner (a lawyer who was killed in the 1941 pogrom), Ioan P. Dumitriu (a school teacher from Iasi), Adolf Magder (the school's principal and initiator of the new building), and N. Ionescu (the school inspector). Funds had been collected since 1911. The vice president of the community was Iosef Svart, my grandfather. The author of the booklet was Flodam (Adolf Magder).

The inauguration took place on January 25, 1915. *The Israelite Courier* reported on February 7: "The administrative authorities were present, as were many guests from Iasi. The festivity opened with the royal anthem and Hebrew songs performed by the school's choir. A religious ceremony followed. The following people gave speeches: Schaia Steinberg (the president of the community), Rabbi Dr. Mayer Thenen from Iasi, Mrs. Ghizela Vexler (president of the former committee for the school's building), Ghetel

Buchman (on behalf of the Zionist section), Zalman Simon (a student), Dimitri (principal of the Medie school), Gerner, Dr. Vitner (the physician at the local hospital), Ms. Clara Herscovici (principal of the Steaua - Star school), Mrs. Roza Sufrin, Dr. Fany Brandman, and Adolf Magder (the founder of the building). D. Ionescu, the delegate from the Education Ministry, concluded the series of speeches. The schoolgirls from the professional school Steaua (The Star) in Iasi and the pupils from the school Dr. Adolf Stern performed brilliantly in a play. Then, the schoolgirls from Junimea (The Youth) No. 2, The Union of the Israelite Women, and the primary school Steaua, as well as the schoolboys from the local school, recited poetry. The festivity closed with a violin concerto played by Cerbu Solomon, Wiess Vainstein, and Osias Branchfeld, the delegates from the Lyra society in Iasi. At nine o'clock that night, a banquet in the school's benefit was held in the large hall of the new building. Owing to the work of Ms. Debora Aron and Mr. Lupu Buchman, the elegant bazaar, which was tastefully arranged, surpassed all expectations. The profit, which amounted to about 1,600 lei, was mostly owing to Mr. Steinberg and Mr. Magder's contributions. Many others donated money during the banquet."

During the war years (1916-1918), the school building was used as a military hospital; the courses were held in the old building. The students participated in the work in the vegetable garden, which was located on a lot that was given to the school outside the town. After the war, the Hebrew education system was modernized; even post-school courses were taught. Following Barad, Grinberg, and Magder, the next principal was Iancu Horodniceanu. He was followed by Abis Mendelovici in 1927-1928 and then by the excellent Hebrew specialist R. Epstein. In 1921, Michel Sor, as the mayor's assistant, obtained a subvention for the school from the mayoralty. He had argued that if the Jewish children enrolled in the public school—a right they were entitled to as Romanian citizens—another school would have to be built with an enlarged teaching staff. In 1933, the school prepared 110 students for the exam. At that time, the principal was Rubin Epstein and the teachers were Etla Marcovici and Tania Rotenstein.

In 1936, the 25th anniversary of the laying of the foundation stone for the school building was celebrated. M. I. Schor was the president of the community, Michel Schor was the president of the school's committee, and Lupu Buchman was the mayor's assistant. Solomon Elias, the veteran of the committee, was also present. The school operated until 1942 when the Jews in town were evacuated to Iasi for racist reasons. The last secretary of the school was Velvl Candel, who still possessed a portion of the community's archives in the 1950s.

11 Synagogues

The documents legislating the foundation of the borough in 1823 granted tax-free land for the construction of three synagogues: two on Palade's estate, which became the center of the town of Podu Iloaiei, and one on the Scobalteni estate. These synagogues must have been made of wood, just like in most of the other new boroughs, where the owner of the estate sometimes offered free of charge wood for construction of the synagogues.

At the beginning of the 20th century, the Jewish funeral processions that passed through the town stopped at a certain place on the road to the cemetery to say an "El mulei rachamin," because at this place a synagogue had once stood. The synagogue was probably the first one to be built after the founding of the borough. Not far from this place, but closer to the Iasi-Targu Frumos highway, there was Aziels Beth Midrash, the second oldest house of prayer. You could get there by following a narrow street that emerged from the highway at one end of the main road (a kind of Moldavian "Main Street"). It is known that a synagogue's floor must fall below the level of the street to respect psalm 130: "From deepening have I called on thee, my Lord." But this establishment was even deeper below the ground level, so that you had to descend several stairs. According to oral tradition, this was the oldest synagogue in town. All kinds of terrifying stories were told based on the belief that at midnight, the dead left their tombs and came to pray at the synagogue. In the past, diligent students stayed at the synagogue from dawn till dark to study the Talmud. During the summer, when the synagogue's windows were open, the students' thoughts were sometimes diverted from their study by the voices of the young dressmakers in the neighborhood who were singing and working hard for the women in the town and the villages. Love stories were sometimes born — silent, barely recognizable, and not exactly part of the study schedule.

There was also a story about a practical joke that ended tragically: one winter night, a young Talmudist had fallen asleep over his book. Two of his colleagues, practical jokers, blocked both doors and dressed themselves in sheets. They then knocked at the window, grievously singsonging. The young man woke up and tried the front door and then the back door, but everywhere he confronted "the ghosts." He suffered a nervous breakdown which marked him for the rest of his life.

The synagogue was destroyed during World War II.

A beautiful synagogue—named Scobalteni Sill till 1917, later renamed Iavne — was built on the place where the first synagogue in this part of the town had existed before. It was also probably made of wood and then rebuilt with bricks. Among its congregation were some of the town's important figures, such as Moise Buchman who could read beautifully from the Torah and David Leib Davidovici.

On the same street as the Great Synagogue, was the Hahnusas Orhim synagogue, that in the beginning probably belonged to a brotherhood with the same name. Some members of its congregation were also important personalities, for example Zelman Schor. On the same street, parallel with the main street, was the Tailors' Synagogue where the congregation consisted mainly of the craftsmen in town. There was also another house of prayer in the house of the Hasidic Rabbi Bention Iscovici.

But the most impressive synagogue both in terms of architecture and interior decoration was the Great Synagogue, which was built in 1876. An 1892 report of the Prefecture of the county of Iasi mentioned the existence in town of this synagogue and of five other houses of prayer. The Great Synagogue impressed its visitors with the quality of its traditional motifs: The Zodiac, the twelve tribes, the wailing wall, Rachel's tomb, the illustration of the psalm "By the river of Babylon, there I sat and wept," as well as some images of the Holy Land painted by a popular master. The wood sculpturing around the ark and the shrine were also remarkable, rich in floral elements but also zoomorphic, symbolic, and allegorical. There were griffins, two-headed eagles, lions, and stags. The items of the creed, which were made of silver or silver-plated, were the works of the Jewish master brass smiths, silversmiths, and lace makers who were renowned in the country for their skill and talent.

The synagogue was associated with many legends, such as: the deceased members of the congregation came to pray at midnight; the synagogue being dug up already built from under the clay hill that towered over it. The latter legend was identical to that of the Great Synagogue in Iasi, which I wrote about in 1938 in Vilna in the volume *Yiddisher Folklor* (number 34, page 151; published by YIVO[B-19]). During World War I, the synagogues in town were transformed into military hospitals. The Great Synagogue was damaged during the years of persecution and had to be demolished in 1973. The last Jewish inhabitant of Podu Iloaiei, Avram - the smith, used to go to the Great Synagogue each Friday and pray by himself.

After the demolishment of the synagogues, the holy scrolls and objects of the creed were brought to Iasi. Let's not forget that during their existence the synagogues were not only "Bait Tefilah," houses of prayer, but also "Bait Medrash," houses of study. Here the Talmud and the commentaries were studied, the Bible was popularized for the adults who had not studied it thoroughly in childhood, and the children were given elements of religious training and education at the heder, the confessional school. The synagogue was also a place of gathering for debating community issues, a "Bait Knesset."

The end of the synagogues' activity in Podu Iloaiei was also due to the rapid outflow of the Jewish population. Thus, the existence of the synagogues became useless. Their remembrance will not die within the souls of those who attended them, and will continue to live perhaps in some literary depictions (see the chapter "Podu Iloaiei as Reflected in Literature").

12 Rabbinate

The creation of the rabbinate of Podu Iloaiei seemed to correspond chronologically with the founding of the borough. The 1823 document exempted two shochet houses from paying tax. One of these houses, no doubt, belonged to the rabbi, since some time during that decade the town's rabbi was invited to a wedding by the famous rabbi of Iasi named Apter Rav. [A-118]

I believe that this was Rabbi Moise sin Leizer, who was registered in Podu Iloaiei in the 1831 census. He was also mentioned in a Hebrew act from 1834, and the 1835 census included him at No. 63 as "Moise the rabbi, the weak old man," meaning that he was ill. We do not know how long he led his community or who followed him, but between 1868 and 1878, the position was occupied by a famous rabbinical personality: Ghedalia Aharaon, son of Itahak Zoil from Lint, son-in-law of the rabbi Smuel Aba Sapira from the well-known Hasidic and typographical center of Slavuta, and nephew of the famous

[19] [Ed-Com] YIVO: A organization established in Vilna which documented European life.

Hasidic leader Pinchas from Korzec. He was born in 1814 and died in Podu Iloaiei on 15 Tevet 5638 (1878). His biblical exegesis *Chen Aharon* was printed and published by Elie Rosental in 1910 in Iasi (Progress Typography, 60 pages). The editor remembered that as a young man he had had the wonderful opportunity to listen to this appreciated rabbi's lectures and to take notes. Four decades later, he looked over the notes and published them. Elie Rosental was the author of the work *Sefer Iore Dea* (Seini 1925, 52 pages).

Uri Landman (1838-1916; also see the chapter "Podu Iloaiei as Reflected in Literature") followed in Rabbi Ghedalia's chair. He was the son of Rabbi Tvi Hirs from Strelitk and Kuty, and the nephew of Rabbi Ithak from Vijnita. According to some documents from 1892 and 1898, Uri Landman was born in Mihaileni and confirmed as rabbi by the rabbinical authorities from Lvov and Brody. He was a noble, erudite, and wise man. He also studied and wrote a lot. The writer Litman Vigder (1901-1972), who had been Landman's neighbor, told me that the common attic of their home was filled with the rabbi's manuscripts. Only one work from Landman's youth was published, a triple obituary, *Dismet Shlish* (Cernauti, 1885), dedicated to the memory of the rabbis Avraham Iaakov Fridman from Sadagura, Chanoch Henich from Alesk, and Mendel from Vijnita.

After Landman's death, no other rabbi was hired. Instead, the shochet Elie Rosental became dayan. In 1923, a group of faithful people tried to bring in a rabbi from Maramures. The candidate was an erudite Talmudist, but was less trained in the study of the Bible and modern Hebrew, and could not be accepted by the scholars in town. After Elie Rosental's death, the shochet Burah Svart became dayan. He was the last shepherd of the Jewish community in Podu Iloaiei.

The evacuation of the Jewish population from the town in 1942, and the events that followed, greatly diminished the Jewish presence in the area. The creed was being served by a shochet from Iasi, who also served Targu Frumos.

But let us return to the history of the shochets in Podu Iloaiei. The censuses from the 19th century mentioned some of their names. Let's not forget that they were the teachers of the Talmud and also the readers in the synagogue. A source from 1834 mentioned the name of Herscu the shochet, who was probably the shochet mentioned in the 1823 act. The 1845 census mentioned the shochets Marcus and Haim sin Iosup; the latter died of cholera in 1848. The 1898 foreigner's list mentioned the shochets Iosub, Elie, Haim, and Burah; Beiris was mentioned as a teacher.

During the first decade of the 20th century, several shochets, who I met as a child, worked in Podu Iloaiei. For example, Reb Beiris, a feeble and sickly old man, lived on a hill behind the Great Synagogue. He was appreciated for his devoutness, as well as his gentleness.

Elie Rosental was a tall, intelligent, ambitious, and erudite man, who was also very active and was eager to play a leading role in the community's life. He was a good Talmud and Hebrew specialist, and he also knew algebra. His sons were scholars: Iosub was, for several decades, an excellent Hebrew teacher at the Jewish school in the town, while his brother, Aron, worked in Hebrew journalism; Itoc Ioil, the third son was a tradesman, who also had good knowledge of the traditional culture. Elie Rosental dreamed of becoming a rabbi after he was elected dayan.

Moise Sor (1901-1977), a fine intellectual and a friend of mine since childhood, told me about an event that occurred around 1923-1924 when a classic machloket (conflict) began on a minor issue, but had serious implications. As a rival of Michel Sor, who was the former mayor's assistant and president of the community, Elie Rosental declared "treif" a bird that Michel had cut on a Thursday without thorough examination. My friend's father took notice and sent the chicken to the shochet Burah, who examined it carefully and declared it kosher without knowing the previous verdict. For his dishonest act, Elie was about to be dismissed. He maintained his position, however, by giving up the issue of the mikvah (the ritual bath) on which, until then, he had had an excessively strict position.

Burah Svart a very pious and good Talmudist (my brother Simcha studied with him) was a small, sickly man with a house full of children. He was appreciated for his honesty, gentleness, skill, and kindness. He became the dayan of the community after Elie Rosental's death. The shochet Heim was renowned for his intransigence on ritual issues. He would pray for a long time and was always busy with the study of the Talmud.

The youngest shochet, Moise, was a handsome man with a nice voice and a house full of children. His wife used to wear a hat over her wig (a concession to modern times), but it did not suit her for she was not that beautiful.

The evolution of the social life between the two World Wars raised many difficult problems for the religious leaders in town. Some merchants would keep their shops open on Saturdays and others would eat pork sausages in public. In general, the numerous and severe rules of the Mosaic ritual were no longer strictly respected.

Among the young people as well, controversies on acute issues were beginning to take shape. In the end, the mizrahist (religious) orientation did not prevail.

13 Hasidism

Within the general framework of traditional Jewish life in Podu Iloaiei, the Hasidism occupied an important place. In town, there were followers of different Hasidic rabbis (tzadikim), but they did not get into serious conflicts, as happened in other places. It was known that the famous tzadik David Toluer visited the town several times. [A-119] The rabbi Ghedalia Aharaon was considered a Hasidic. Later, Rabbi Alter Aharov Arie settled in Podu Iloaiei. He was the son of the rabbi in Sulita and the nephew of the rabbi from Zloczow and the famous tzadik reb Meirl Premislaner. According to data in a report from 1892, [A-120] the rabbi Alter Iscovici was born in 1840 in Galicia and "inherited the title of rabbi from his father."

The magazine *The Brotherhood* published a letter by Moses Schwarzfeld in 1882 (page 361) that told of a "ghiter id" in town who was visited by followers from other towns. In 1958, Heim Strulovici, the old leader of the community who settled in Podu Iloaiei in 1897, told me that primarily poor women and simple men consulted reb Alter. The rich people were the followers of the rabbis in Stefanesti, Pascani, or Buhusi.

In 1964, I obtained some information from Ruhel Klinger, an 86-year-old woman living in town. She remembered that her father had been a passionate follower of the rabbi

Ghedalia Aharov, who had died without leaving any descendents. Rabbi Alter came from Suceava around 1800. It was known that establishing a Hasidic court in a town could have favorable economic consequences; there would be followers who would come into town and who had to be hosted; businesses and marriages would be arranged, and the prestige of the place would increase. A typical example was the town of Sadagura.

After the death of the founder of the rabbinical dynasty on 7 Elul 5670 (August 1910), his son Bention, who was born in 1878, took his place. He was a strong and handsome man, but he lacked charisma. He and his entire family were killed during a bomb attack in Iasi in August 1944. They were buried in the cemetery in Pacurari (Iasi). Thus, the destiny of the Hasidic court in Podu Iloaiei tragically ended.

The rabbi's secretary was a red-bearded Jew. He was a smart man but was rather cynical and skeptical of his boss and, just like many other gabaim de tzadikim. It was known that the butlers and secretaries of important people tended to notice more the flaws than the qualities of their masters.

Itikl, the son and successor of the rabbi Bention, was 38 years old when he was killed by a bomb. As children, we had been colleagues in the study of the Talmud. We had been taught by a melamed from Lithuania, a severe but good teacher who lived at the rabbinical court. Unfortunately, his teaching qualities could not change the insufficient zeal that I had as a scholar. This was by no means a deficiency of the Hasidism in Podu Iloaiei.

To render complete the image of the religious life in Podu Iloaiei, we need to mention those erudite Talmudist merchants who contributed to the shaping of the cultural profile of the town at the beginning of the 20th century. Their presence promoted the subsequent development, even though it did so in a different way than expected and took another direction.

14 Folklore and Ethnography

The Jewish folklore in Podu Iloaiei was, of course, of Yiddish expression, although naturally, forms and influences of the Romanian local folklore can be seen.

When a child was born, the mother and the baby were defended against the evil spirits by a knife placed under the lying-in woman's pillow and by "kimpeturnbrivl," sheets of paper containing magic formulas that were pinned to the curtains, the door and the sheets that made up the canopy above the lying-in women's bed. If the newborn was a boy, on the seventh evening after his birth, just before the circumcision, the melamed came with his students to say the prayer "Shma Yisrael" [B-20] at the lying-in woman's bed. While entering, they sang in unison "Ghitn uvnt, mozl tov" (Good evening, mazel tov) and continued with the prayer. As they left, each child received a piece of "leicheh," rhombic-shaped gingerbread. Some of the children would ask for one more piece for a small brother at home. And so would end the ceremony of "Krismeleinen."

[20] [Ed-Com] Shma Yisrael: A prayer recited in times of great personal danger

The child was growing, and if he fell ill, he would be treated with "upshprehn," an exorcism, with embers extinguished in water, melted lead poured in water, and other Jewish and Romanian medicines and exorcisms. When the child was healthy, the mother would put him to sleep singing: "Inter deim kinds veighola / shteit a goldn tzighiola / Dus tzighiola iz ghefurn hondlen / rojinkes mit mondlen." (Under the child's carriage / Stands a golden goat / The goat is selling / Raisins and almonds / The child will learn / This is the best merchandise.) or "Dus kind vet lernen / Dus iz di beste shoire / Toire vesti lernen / Sfurim vesti shrabn / A ghiter, frimer id vesti, mirtzeshem, blabn." (Torah he will learn / Books he will write / A good, religious Jew he will / God willing remain.)

Every pious mother's dream was to have her boy become a rabbi. "Toire zolsti lernen / zan mit oel males / in noch tzi der chaene / vesti posken shales." (You shall learn Torah / It should be with all good character traits / And then with the countenance / You will render legal decisions.)

There was a different song for the girls, just as their lives would be different. The mother put her baby girl to sleep singing: "Di vest lernen biholeh / Di vest shtrikn tiholeh / In groisn zal / vet zan a bal / Mit di kleidoleh vesti mahn a vint / Sluf man kind, gezind / Sluf shion in dan ri / Mah di eighioleh tzi / Mah zei tzi in ofn / Ver ghezinterheit antshlufn." (You will learn books / You will knit kerchiefs / In a big hall / You will have a husband / With the dresses you will make a breeze / Sleep my child, healthy / Sleep restfully / Close your eyes / Close them, then open them / Go to sleep in health.)

If the child did not fall asleep, the mother would tell the story of the grandmother: "Amul, amul iz ghevein a bobitze, hot zi ghehat asa, asah kinderleh." (Once upon a time there was a grandmother, who had many, many children.) It is a story similar to that of "The Goat with Three Kids," a common motif in Slavic folklore. The grandmother leaves for town, ordering the children not to open the door for anyone. The children hide under the bed, under the table, behind the oven, under the trough, and in the closet. The bear comes and asks to be let in. The children refuse. The bear breaks down the door, enters, and eats the children, except for the one who hid behind the oven. When the grandmother comes back and finds out what has happened she goes into the woods and invites the bear, promising him a bath. The bear refuses twice, but cannot resist the third invitation. He comes and agrees to be given a bath. The grandmother strikes him with an ax, cuts open his belly, and saves her unharmed children, whom she bathes, changes their clothes, feeds them milk-boiled semolina, and puts them on a shovel and says: "Hait, in heider aran" (Hurry up to school).

When the child was three to four years old, he was taken to school for the first time, wrapped in a "tales," a prayer shawl and carried in his parents' arms. The teacher showed him the ancient Hebrew letters, hiding gingerbread letters between the pages.

The child grew and played in the field while singing an absurd little song: "Pantofl, pantofl / Der himl iz ofn / panti, panti / der himl is tzi / Der goisher got zitzt ofn feld / Eir hot a make, nisht kein ghelt." (Pantofl, pantofl / The heaven is open / Panti, panti / The heaven is shut / The Goishe god sits in the field [cemetery] / He has a sore [blemish] / No money.) The song is perhaps an irony to the spirits of the field. As a matter of fact, many children's songs in many languages contain expressions that mean nothing to us today.

This was the case for the counting game, which was a century old in Podu Iloaiei: "Endza, denza, dicha-dacha, pona knicha, shirl-pirl, tirl troosk / Eih hob deih arusghelozt." (The second line means I let you out.) When the last word was said, the indicated child had to run while the rest tried to catch him.

As the child grew even older, he would play "serjont-ganuv," meaning "the thieves and the cops." He would listen to and shiver when ghost stories were told. He would also cheer up with this absurd song: "A zin mit a reighn / Di kole iz gheleighn / Vus hot zi ghehat? / A inghiole / Vi hot eir gheheian? / Mendole / Hot men im bagrubn in a kendole." (A sun with a rain / The bride is having a baby / What did she have? / A little boy / What was he called? / Mendele / Who was buried in a pail.) Because of rhyming necessities, "a coffin" was replaced with "a pail" so that it would rhyme with "Mendole." Actually, there were happy songs for almost every name, for example: Moisole, koisole lompampir / Tontzn di vontzn hinter der tir … Kimt di bobe, leigt a lobe / Kimt der zeide, leigt er beide," (Moishe … / Insects are dancing under the door / Comes the grandmother and smacks them with a big hand / Comes the grandfather and smacks them both.) or "Itzik, spitzik nudleteshl …" (Yitschak, pointy one, bag of noodles …)

The girls played with dolls, usually made of rags. Their ears were pierced and they would wear a red wool thread until they got their first pair of earrings. Most of them did not go to heder, which was a type of crèche. At the Jewish-Romanian primary school, they studied in the same rooms with the boys but at separate desks. They learned to read Hebrew prayers and gained some knowledge of Hebrew. During break, the boys played "sheli sheloh, sheloh sheli." In this game, two rows of boys face each other. One of them runs quickly toward the opposite row trying to break the chain. If the boy succeeds, he can bring back with him a "prisoner" to strengthen his team. If he does not succeed in breaking the chain, he becomes a "prisoner" himself. Then someone from the other team makes his attempt, and the game goes on until the bell rings that it is time for classes. The girls played a game with Romanian words and an anti-monarchy message! One girl sits on a stone, while the others make a circle around her and sing: "Maria sits on a stone (ter) and brushes her fair hair. Suddenly her brother Carol appears (ter)." Carol makes a rude gesture, and the girls conclude: "Maria's a sweet angel, while Carol is a cheat."

The children, as well as the adults, looked forward to the Jewish holidays as major events in the monotonous life of the town. The month of Tishri, the month of the autumn festivities, kept everybody in a special tension and emotion. Rosh Hashana, the confession of the sins, the penitence, and the promise to respect during the next year all 613 godly commandments and all the interdictions, prepared everybody for the day of Yom Kippur.The fast, the tears, the prayers, and the whole apocalyptic atmosphere that lasted for 24 hours marked everybody for the rest of their lives. They were relieved when the nine days of "Sikes" (Sukkot) were coming, when they could sit in the "sike" (sukka), or the "cages" as the other co inhabitants called them. But they especially looked forward to the children's games with nuts, "hakafot", the procession with the rolls of the Torah, the calling to the Torah of all the boys on Simchat Torah, the nuts, the apples, the grape juice, and the little flags with an apple and a candle on top that symbolized the abundance of autumn.

The game with nuts was played in three ways: "in the pit," "ciccecode," and "in breitl." In the first scenario, you are supposed to throw from a distance a handful of eight nuts into a hole. Those that fall outside of the hole are taken by your game partner who throws next, and you wait to take the nuts that do not end up in the hole. In the second scenario, several nuts are placed on the ground at a distance, just like the skittles. The players try to hit them with a nut, and pick up those that they hit. For the third version called "on the board," a board is propped up against a wall and a nut is left to slide along the board. The nuts that are hit become the possession of the thrower. Nuts were much appreciated by the children, who made up this riddle: "What is taller than a house, smaller than a mouse, sweet as sugar, and bitter as gall?" Answer: The nut tree, the nut, its core, and finally the green skin of the nut.

A fierce rivalry took place among the owners of the small flags that were made of cut, colored paper with an apple and a candle at the top of the pole. Shalom Aleichem immortalized this tradition in his story *The Little Flag.*

Hanukkah was impatiently awaited not only for the story of the Maccabei's heroism, the cheering little candles, and the tasty food, but also for the Hanukkah gelt, the money offered as a present to the children by their parents, relatives, neighbors, and friends. The children would then buy pictures, marbles, toys, or even a small sleigh.

It would be futile to try to describe the cheer during Purim—the groups of masked people going from house to house sometimes accompanied by fiddlers performing folkloric plays on biblical subjects.

"Purim-shpiler," the amateur artists of Purim, were not only boys but also poor adults for whom the money they obtained from performing on Purim made up an important "capital." Among them "Ieruel the barefooted," nicknamed "the little horse," was outstanding. His nickname came from his Purim activities. In his Purim-shpil band, he played the part of Haman riding a horse that was symbolized by a broomstick. The "company" was made up of family members: sons, nephews, and sons-in-law. Locally, the tradition was maintained until the outbreak of World War II.

Also in honor of Purim there was a one-man show. The "artist" was Haim "parah," the bald, who was helped by his protean hat. As a "civilian," he was a poor, silent, and sad man, but on Purim he would juggle with his old, overworn, floppy hat. He would call it a cap, parodying a Jew from the country, or he would imagine it to be a straw hat and introduce us to a knave. At the end of his show, he would pretend it was an officer's cap and recite: Bin ich mir ghevorn a maiur / zei ech mer us vi a Shvartz iur." (Poor me, I became a major / and I look like hell). Also on Purim, Gypsy music bands and fiddlers stopped by the houses playing the fiddle, the flute, and the kobza. At each house, the Gypsies would receive some money, sweets, or a glass of wine. The Christians in town named the day of Purim "Haman," and took great pleasure in tasting the delicious "hamantashen", and exchanging the recipe for that of the famous Easter cakes.

Pesach was preceded by "Shabbat Hagadol," which was related to a most peculiar tradition (see the short story *Dudl Consul* in the annexed anthology).

The most anticipated segment of the Seder on Pesach was that with the "afikoimen," the piece of unleavened bread hidden at the beginning of the ceremony. Whoever found it received a present.

The trips on "Leckboimer" (Lag BaOmer) to the Holmului hill—the arch target shooting, the fights in the grass, and the meal served in common—were a joy. On Shavuot (Shvies), the children were charmed by "Akdumes," the festive recitation, the milk-based foods, and the permission to take a bath in the Bahlui River.

On Tisha be Av, the boys felt obligated to throw thistles in the girls' hair and the men's beards. It would bring tears to your eyes if you tried to pull out the thistles—real vegetal hatch hogs.

As the children grew up, they started singing love songs: "A libe, a libe iz ghit tzi shpiln / Mit a mentshn, nisht mit dir." (A love, a love is good to play / With a good person, not with you.) Others would sing more serious songs: "Mu adabru, mu asapru, oidchu, oidchu, tam-ta-ra-dei-ram / Ver ken zugn in dersheiln, vus der eins batat." (What can we say, what can we tell, more, more / Who can tell and retell what means one.) They also sang a version of "Ehad mi iodea?" from the night of Pesach. It goes like this: One is the only God; two - the tables of the laws; three - the patriarchs; four - their wives; five - the Pentateuch; six - the sections of the Talmud; seven - the days of the week; eight - the circumcision term; nine - the pregnancy; 10 - the Decalogue; 11 - the stars in Iosef's dream; and 12 - the zodiac.

Popular creativity also cultivated humor and satire, especially against the injustices, abuses, and lack of knowledge. The bar tenants were satirized because they did not have much in common with the knowledge of books. For example, a bar tenant says before Yom Kippur that he does not remember whether the prayer starts with "kol" or "bol", but is sure that the second word is "ghidre." The bar tender is referring to "Kol nidre," but he cannot tell the difference between two letters that look similar in Hebrew: K and B, and G and N. Another anecdote tells of a lecture held on Yom Kippur by a rich bar tenant in front of the minian he has organized at his house together with the bar tenants from the neigbouring villages: "Brothers! Hant iz aza groiser tug, bold vi <<ziua crucii (the day of the Cross)>>; vet ir zan evlavios, vet dumnezeu zan bucuros, az nishte, tu-va-n dumnezeii mamii voastre [B-21] … in zugts <<Lamnateiah>>. A rival shouts: "There is no need of <<Lamnateiah>>.

From among the proverbs and sayings, I have mentioned: "Eine baklugt zic, az dus steirtichl iz ir shiter, di andere-az di momelighe iz ir biter" (One woman complains / That the kerchief is not woven thick / The other that her cornmeal is bitter.) or "Veir'shot pares, deir tontzt zares" or the complaint of the daughter-in-law to her mother-in-law: "Ghei ech pavole / Zugt zi az ich-bin moale, ghei ich gich / ras ich di shich." (When I walk slowly / She says I am small / When I walk fast / I tear the shoes.)

Here are several examples of the local Yiddish folklore as it was before World War I. The choreographic folklore included "nohbe-tontz," "vulehl," "serbl," and broighes-tontz," while the musical folklore had "nigunim", especially the Hasidic one. The

[21] [Ed-Com] Romanian for I obscenity in your mother's gods

ethnographic "arsenal" included the "dreidl," the Hanukkah spinning top made of lead; the beautiful "Tfilin-zekl" and "Tales-zekl," the bags for carrying the phylacteries and the prayer shawl that a fiancée would embroider just before marriage; as well as other ritual embroideries for the Sabbath, Pesach, and other holidays. We have to mention the calligraphers, who made the ritual "graphics" (such as mizrah and kevisi), the stone and wood carvers, the lace makers, the silversmiths and others, all of whom were masters of the Jewish popular art. The musical art practiced by the choristers was much appreciated as it carried on a many centuries old tradition.

Let us not forget about the "badhen," the popular troubadour who, at weddings and family parties sang satirical or moralizing songs, made up flattering verse, and at the beginning of the 20th century, was the one to order the quadrille paces: "avansei, balansei, aine dame for …"

The specific culinary art included the cakes for the Sabbath and other holidays (especially Purim), hamantashen, kiholeh, petzea, ciulnt, all kinds of cornflower pastries, leventze, gingerbread, and other traditional cakes, which were representative of the ethnographic nature of the Jews in Podu Iloaiei.

A sociological curiosity was the way in which the children addressed their parents. The most frequent names were "Tote" and "Mome," that is Granpa and Granma. In more modern families, the names were "Fater" and "Muter," that is Papa and Mama. The native language was Yiddish, which was spoken even by the Christian employees. All Jews spoke Romanian, and often used the Moldavian dialect. Most of them read newspapers and wrote in Romanian. Only the "up-town" fiancés would write a short letter to their fiancées (and vice versa) in a sui generis German or French, which was often the creation of the teacher who tutored these young men and women. Anyhow, we were connected to the European cultural trends. … The public library that was endowed with books in Yiddish, Romanian, Hebrew, and later German and French existed in Podu Iloaiei from the beginning of the 20th century. This being told, I feel that I have digressed from the theme of this chapter, which was dedicated to folklore and ethnography.

15 Podu Iloaiei as Depicted in Literary Works

The small town of Podu Iloaiei has not often been described in the Romanian literature, and its image is far from complete. Sometime around 1840, C. Negruzzi described a rather negative image of the place.

For M. Kogalniceanu (*The Physiology of the Provincial*) in 1844, "women between the ages of 15 and 40 should live at least in Sulitoae or Odobesti, in Herta or Agiud, in Memornita or Podul Eloaie (Pont d'Aloia as it was said in an inspired or transpired translation). It's like they are born in Iasi, which means they are just as good to be loved." Vasile Alecsandri visited in 1846: "Millo's house in Podul Iloaiei …"

At the beginning of the 20th century, the humorist Gh. Braescu wrote in his story *The Lucky Man* (*Selected Works*, volume 1, Bucharest, 1967, pages 103-107): "The new cabinet minister for tolerance visited his native town, Podul Iloaiei (the Moldavians call it Podliloaci), and asked the people 'What are your concerns? What do you need?' He was asked for nails, an iron plate, a secondary school, glass, and the Jewish glass seller kept on insisting on windows."

Beno Solomon published a story *The Raoaiei Town* in 1934 in the magazine *Adam* (No. 67, 68, and 69) about his childhood memories of the small town of "Podeloi" (the Yiddish name for Podu Iloaiei).

Naturally, the Yiddish literature has been more generous with this particular shtetl, which was mentioned by Adolf Magder in his work *Alia*, published in Romanian in 1912.

The dramatist Isac Abramovici wrote *The Cheated Father-In-Law*, a Yiddish comedy inspired by A. Goldfaden's *The Two Kune-Leml*. The plot and characters are set in Podu Iloaiei, but nothing specifically links the comedy with this place. The manuscript was kept in the archive of the writer Iulian Schwartz, who mentioned the manuscript on page 22 of his book *Literarishe dermonungen* (Bucharest, 1975).

An accomplished satirical description of day-to-day life in the town in 1919 was given in a revue show conceived by Ghetel Buchman (who was killed in 1941 during the pogrom in Iasi), Lupu Buchman, and the engineer I. Kern. Simcha Schwartz (1900-1974), who was well known in the theater world and was also a writer and sculptor, published several excerpts of the novel *Podeloi* in Yiddish papers. The famous poet Itic Manger wrote *The Ballad of the Rabbi of Podu Iloaiei*. I. Kara depicted the life of the town in his works *A Moldevisher Yingle* (*A Boy From Moldova*; Bucharest, Kriterion Publishing House, 1976) and *Inghe Iurn In ... Veiniker Inghe* (*Young Years and Older Years*; Bucharest, Kriterion Publishing House, 1980). We mention the following stories: *A Boy From Moldova*, *Calman the Medicine Man*, *Dudl Consul*, along with an excerpt from the novel *The Spring of 1917* which was published by Iulian Schwartz (1910-1977) in the anthology *Bukareshter Shriftn*, I, 1978, pages 76-82.

Interesting memories about Podu Iloaiei and Hirlau were published in Israel by M. Landau (1894-1976). More recently, the musician Iehosua Gurevici published *Steitleh Mit Idn* in Yiddish (Tel Aviv, 1975), and later a shorter Romanian version under the title *From Podul Iloaie to Vacaresti Street* [B-22].

The image of the town is completed by the local folklore discovered and published by I. Kara in *Czernowitzer Bleter*, *Oifgang*, and *Yivo-Sriftn*, and by Iulian Schwartz in *Bucharest Writings* in Yiddish (volume IV, 1981).

For a comparison of Podu Iloaiei with other small towns in Moldova, Maramures, and Bukovina [B-23], we recommend the works of the poets Iacob Groper (1890-1966), Leon Bertis (1900-1980), and Samsn Ferst (1886-1968), and the works of the writers Luta Enghelberg (1878-1948), David Rubin (1893-1977), I. Vaidenfeld (1884-1966), H. Goldenstein, M. Held, D. Ionas, and V. Tamburu.

---

[22] [Ed-Com] Vacaresti: a famous street in Bucharest.
[23] [Ed-Com] Moldova, Maramures, and Bukovina are some of the historical provinces of Romania.

There are, of course, other works to be mentioned that were written either in Romanian or Yiddish and were published in Israel but were not available to us. It is possible that other works concerning Podu Iloaiei may still come up.

15.1 *The Ballad of the Rabbi of Podu Iloaiei*

By Itic Manger

The old rabbi from the town of Lelioaiei
His forehead wrinkled with worry, says promptly:
"The night has covered every lawn
What have I done since it was dawn?"
    His silent hands light a candle
    His tired face reflects a light that's even greater
    Weak, his fingers move attentively to all
    The shadows quiver strangely on the wall:
    "I've prayed, I've saddened, and I've wept
    Comfort to me the psalms forever kept"
    He murmurs, his heart throbs with pain:
    "On this week's day, my sadness brought shame"
He puts on the clothes he keeps for days of joy
And slowly walks along the way.
He sees the stars above as embers smoldering
To him, small silver flowers flickering:
"A miracle beyond compare, that has never been;
Praised be, my Lord, for this day and night have not
Been tainted with the shame my sadness brought!"
But look, the street lamp trembles in the night
Playing with shadows of whispers hiding from the light,
And see the servant take to the black well
A horse. When suddenly a distant trill
Comes in his ears, listens carefully,
A rustle of wings, an endless tune may be.
    The old rabbi from the town of Lelioaiei
    His forehead wrinkled with worry, says promptly:
    "It feels so good to walk on ground
    Each step is a pray, each move is a sound"
He walks and his beard is waving in the wind
… Of grief, drained has become his eyes' light spring
The old man is blind; but his heart bold
And light finds ways across the world,
Blue paths, from ancient, sacred times.
    The woods enclose him; the springs call out high,
    His steps are each a prayer to the skies.
    Watching, the trees stand up as magic swords
    To the beautiful paths, they're humble guards.

The woods enclose him even more and stronger
The old man feels weak and death can wait no longer
He lies as grass cut in the glades
As golden wheat is devoured by hungry sickles' blades.
The thoughtful midnight now comes down
Over the old man who has fallen on the ground:
- What whisper thee, old man? - I sing as once.
- Thy face is pale. - My heart is light.
- You're shivering with cold. - I do not feel,
Sweet, holy spirit soothes all my pain.
- Confess thee, brother. - I cannot, poor me
My past is grief and tears. I sit here silently.
For tears taint the face of earth
And the grace of this day's light diminishes.
The old rabbi from Lelioaiei town
To the night responds in a wise voice.
So dies the old man; the moon grows paler,
And with a smile, whispers in secret:
"Only the right and kind are worthy
of such a death, oh heavenly father!"

—Translated from Yiddish to Romanian by I. Kara

15.2 *The Rabbi of Podu Iloaiei*

by I. Kara

An old man of medium height, broad-shouldered, with a snow-white beard, a sharp, intelligent look underneath his long, silvery, rich eyebrows, and a strong, pleasant voice, dressed in modest, clean clothes, as is proper for a learned man. This is how I saw him 60 years ago.

On the eve of Yom Kippur, The Day of Atonement, just before the Kol Nidre prayer, said for the absolution of the faithful from punishment for their disregarded oaths, he was standing humbly in front of the altar in the large synagogue. He was dressed in white from head to heels, his tales for prayer embroidered with silver thread though stained yellow because of long time use, murmuring passionately "Tefilah zaka," the introduction prayer that shakes the souls of the faithful with emotion. Silently, in his inner self with tears and prayers and a high sense of responsibility for the mission he chose to assume, he was defending his flock on the terrible day of the final judgement.

Rabbi Ira (Uri) Landman, grandson of the tzadik of Strelite, was born in that Galician town on 24 Iyar 5598, meaning the spring of 1838. Having a sharp mind and inclined to study, he devoted himself to knowledge since his early youth. His ingenious commentaries were written in a capricious handwriting on long sheets of paper, which, to the end of his life, amassed in huge piles in the attic of his modest home. A small part of his works, written when he was young, was published in Cernauti in 1885 under the title *Salom's Tears*, a three-part necrology of some famous Hasidic rabbis. In town, where several other learned men were living, the rumor went that he could conceive a thousand interpretations concerning only the first word in the Bible, "Bereshit".

Although he led quite a secluded life, the world was no stranger to him. Since he was known to be a peace lover, he was often called on to mediate when delicate issues were at stake. In his older years, he was no longer an adept of the Hasidic law; though the rabbis from Pascani and Buhusi appealed to him on a dispute concerning a possible in-law relation between them.

His opposition to the Hasidic law was discrete but constant. The tzadiks from Pascani and Stefanesti had many adepts in town. Actually, a real Hasidic dynasty descending from Rabbi Meir from Premislean was established here. After 1860, Reb Alter founded this Hasidic center. He was followed by his son Ben Zion, who was killed with his entire family during the 1944 bombing.

At nightfall, on the Saturday of "sales-sides," the learned of the town would come to see Rabbi Ira and discuss his commentaries at that week's pericopa. He was also known for his intelligent, subtle humor, as well as for his morality. Even in his youth, he was greatly appreciated: "The Moldavian Jews recognize but three rabbi figures - Moshe Rabenu, Sifsei Hahamim (also known as Sabetai Bas from Prague who was a famous popularizer), and Reb Meir Premislaner." As an elder, he was asked to see a stubborn man who refused to divorce his wife with whom he no longer lived. The wise, old man answered by adapting an old popular saying: "Er heirt mich vi dem ruv" (meaning he follows my advice as the rabbi's, which could also be interpreted as he follows my advice as the cat's). Mocking his poor living conditions, he once said: "If you want to say that a house is in good wealth with plenty of food and clothes, you may say 'There is some extra for the rabbi, but it will probably never get to the rabbi.'"

Talking about a local moneylender, Avram from the huts, he used to say: "Now, his money keeps on multiplying even when he sleeps; in exchange, at the final judgement, he will sleep and above him the grass will keep on growing" (meaning he will not reach eternal life). His satirical remarks remained in the memory of the local people. Thus, in town, the story went about one time when the rabbi had to go to Iasi. He had agreed with the wagoner not to take along the women who were going to sell chickens to the market in Iasi. The wagoner did not keep his word. In the morning when the wagon stopped in front of the rabbi's house, it was crowded, which upset the rabbi. Then, a bold woman asked him: "Why don't you like to travel with us, Mr. Rabbi? Is it that you hate us so much?" "On the contrary," the rabbi sharply said and got up in the wagon. Another time, a woman came to him to complain that the boiling milk had spilled and got into the meat pot. The rabbi answered with a play on words in Yiddish: "If you had not hurried to the neighbors, the milk would not have spilled, either."

One more of his quips: The prefect of Iasi heard that a wise rabbi lives in Podu Iloaiei. One time, when he was inspecting the town, he called on the president of the community and asked him to arrange a meeting with the rabbi. The president chose the Hasidic rabbi who owned a better house. The discussion with this rabbi did not impress the prefect who expressed his disappointment on his way back. The president of the community told him that there is one more rabbi in town, and they went to the Rabbi Ira. The discussion, which was led by a translator, impressed the prefect who expressed his consternation that the first rabbi, whom he thought wasn't too great, lives so comfortably while the wise Rabbi Ira does not enjoy the same conditions. Rabbi Ira Landman answered: "The other rabbi makes his living from the Jews' troubles, while my life depends on their joys." The prefect was delighted with the answer.

Rabbi Ira used to say: "A community rabbi is like a headache, a Hasidic rabbi is like a stomachache; if your stomach aches, you don't know exactly what it is, while with the headache you know exactly what and where it hurts."

During the last years of his life, Rabbi Ira was sick for long periods of time. He became blind and someone had to take him by the hand to the synagogue, but he did not lose his sense of humor. Once, a child who did not enjoy studying was brought to him, and, as proof, the child could not answer even the most elementary questions about the Bible. So the rabbi exclaimed: "The rabbi of Podu Iloaiei cannot leave his congregation at this time, for this boy is not able to replace him." The first months of the 1916 war brought many troubles to Rabbi Ira. When his end was near, his son-in-law Iosl Schapira, the great grandson of the famous Rabbi Levi Itzac of Berdicev, was standing next to him. Iosl asked his father-in-law to give him his blessing. The old man answered: "You should give me your blessing, for our Heavenly Father listens to you more." Then, he took his son-in-law's hand, kissed it, and then passed away. A biblical expression could describe this as "death through a kiss."

15.3 *Podu Iloaiei*

by Simcha Schwartz

In town, nobody knows how many years old Zeida a Babii is. Since they can remember, he has had a white, curly beard and rosy, skinny cheeks almost like a baby's. Still, Marcu Ghetel is the only one who knows Zeida from his youth, from the time when they were partners in taking care of the town's taxes—a job they took over from the old Greek—and collecting the tax for passage on the bridge over the Bahlui river.

How many years ago did this happen? Mr. Marcu pretends not to remember. And the mystery of their old age haunts the imagination of the townspeople. Mr. Zeida has no idea how old Marcu is, and Mr. Marcu takes his revenge by saying: "I don't remember well."

But Kiva, the janitor of the synagogue, tells a story from which it becomes clear that "the old rotter," meaning Zeida, is almost 90. He heard the story from his grandfather, blessed be his name: It was sometime in the year 1859, when King Cuza took the throne. One day, the king passed through the town. It was the fast day of Tisha B'Av. It was incredibly hot, and the Jews, with their beards all tangled and wearing long coats and striped cloaks, were standing idly around the market tables and talking endlessly, so that the fast day would pass easily. Suddenly a beautiful carriage stopped right in the middle of the marketplace, and a young nobleman stepped down, wearing polished boots, a long mantle, and a small, black beard, as the French fashion dictated. He said in a loud voice: Who's the boss in this town?" The people didn't realize what was really happening, and the "nobleman" continued angrily: "Why, masters, do you still use forged weights?[xx] (text mentions Turkish Oka, which is a measurement tool that was adopted from the Turkish people, but which later was forged, in the sense that it was lighter than it indicated, being carved in its interior, thus fooling people into thinking they were getting more product than they actually were).Why do you sit here, around the tables, doing nothing instead of working your lazy bones? I shall give you land, as to the peasants. I shall see that you will be given land to work, you lazy ones!" While saying this, he took a small notebook from his pocket, wrote something in it, said goodbye, and went back to Iasi.

At first, they all thought he was some unknown, local nobleman, and they were merely surprised. But when they finally realized that it was the new king, the whole town started to worry: "My Lord, what a misfortune, what a calamity." They all ran to Mr. Zeida who, as a "friend" of the Greek who had much influence in the royal court, could give them advice.

Back then, Zeida was a man passed the age of 40, and his oldest son, Duvid Leib, was already married. Kiva makes all sorts of calculations, and he is very close to finding out Zeida's exact age. Just then, Dudl Consul opposes, contesting Kiva's calculations. The dispute is ready to begin. Dudl argues that 1869 is the year that Cuza [B-24] took the throne. This infuriates Kiva who looks straight at Dudl, plays nervously with his beard, and tells his opponent that "his head is full of manure" and that all he says is rubbish. "How could Cuza become king in '69, when he was forced to abdicate by Bratianu in 1960 and King Carol was brought to the throne in '66."

Dudl would have had something to say against the year '66, with which Kiva would have contradicted him in front of the other people. But he felt that they would not agree with him. Kiva was right, since 40 years of King Carol's rule was being celebrated right then.

So Kiva should be attacked from his weak side. Dudl attacks: " Let's leave the calculations. Anyway, Zeida remains the most honorable man in town." This time, Dudl didn't fail. Kiva's large beard moves with indignation: "Why? Maybe because, since I've known him, he has never given a nickel to the synagogue? Or to the poor?" Dudl answers back: "The town would not be the same without Zeida. Who managed to save the old public bath from demolition? I believe it was Zeida! Who talked the prefect into granting us a new place for the cemetery? He resolved many of our problems with his tears. Who brought forgiveness from King Cuza for giving us land? Wasn't it Zeida? He went to the palace in Iasi. He threw himself at the king's feet, he cried, ripped his beard, he persuaded the king to leave our town in peace."

"Really! Big deal! And now that the Jews from Bivolari have land, is their life worse than ours is? Stupid cows! You think that fighting for a bargain with the peasants, for a weight of salt or a box of fuel oil is a better thing than working the land?"

So the fight went on, and the people forgot about calculating Zeida's age, which remained an unsearched, blessed treasure.

—Translated from Yiddish to Romanian by I. Kara

Yiddish Translator's Note

I bring here some extra information about the real heroes of this story. The writer Litman Vigder (1901-1972) told me about some episodes characteristic of Zeida a Babii. The news of Theodor Herzl's death was much discussed by the townspeople. Surprised, the old Zeida asked: "Was he an important man? How much money did he leave?"

Zeida's wife was deaf and even stingier than he was. If someone entered their home and asked her for a loan (she was also a moneylender), she would think that the person is a beggar and yell to Zeida from the kitchen: "Zeida, don't give away a thing!"

After World War I, the old man deteriorated. It was a sad thing to see the physical and psychic degradation of a man whom, hardhearted as he was, used to be one of the community's leaders.

---

[24] [Ed-Com] Cuza – Alexandru Ioan Cuza was the first Romanian king to rule the newly united counties of "The Romanian County" and Moldova, known since 1862 as Romania. He ruled from 1859 until 1866, when he was was forced to abdicate.

Regarding the millionaire (in gold lei) Marcu Ghetel's spirit of economy, I remember the following story from 1919. To increase the number of riders on the railroads, fourth-class carriages were introduced on local routes; the carriages were actually trucks with wooden banks barely holding, and it was hard to climb in. Marcu Ghetel, almost 100 years old, had some business in Iasi. Following his eagerness to save money, he bought himself a fourth class ticket. When asked why, he answered: "Because there's no fifth class." It's true! Still, he donated a considerable sum of money to the primary Jewish-Romanian school in town that now bears his name.

When the news of Herzl's death was heard, Jan Meirovici, book seller and "printer" of the town (he printed "business cards"), member of the committee, and candidate to the position of community leader, displayed in his shop window a large portrait of this great personality draped in black. An employee of the town hall saw the portrait and discretely asked whom it represented. Meirovici informed him: "There used to be one Theodor who died, and this is his photo." This Meirovici was the first to publish illustrated postal cards depicting the primary Jewish school and the main streets of the town.

15.4 *"Podeloier Times" ("Podu Iloaiei Hotchpotch")*

World War I and the great changes it brought in Europe, especially the reunification of Romania, had among its consequences a remarkable increase in the Jewish population — both in quantity and quality — which strongly influenced the "local" Jews' cultural life, including the amateur theater. The amateur theater troupes, who had been performing since the end of the 19th century, were no longer satisfied with the old repertoire. They were looking for modern plays dealing with that time's reality — plays written in a more alert style, taking as a model the Romanian revue shows or, after 1919, the shows performed by the couple I.Sternberg-I.Botosanski who came from the other side of the Prut River [B-25] in 1914 and led a remarkable cultural activity.

Young intellectuals from small towns like Podu Iloaiei, Buhusi, Moinesti, and later Falticeni, Botosani, and other places, imagined revue shows on themes of local interest and with a marked satirical-social message. Several young people from Podu Iloaiei — the student Ghetel Buchman who was murdered in 1941 during the Iasi pogrom, the engineer Iancu Kern who died in the United States at an old age, and Simcha Schwartz (1900-1974) who later became a famous sculptor — wrote together the text and music, did the scene painting (with the help of Hamburger, the excellent makeup specialist from Iasi), found "actors" like A. Mendelovici (now a retired physician in Iasi), Levi Leibovici, Aron Iosupovici, and Velvl Buchman, and performed in the revue show "Podu Iloaiei Hotchpotch," twice in Podu Iloaiei and once in Tirgu Frumos.

It was the winter of 1919/1920, and the public impatiently awaited the premiere of the show to be presented in the local Yiddish dialect. The literary value of Sim Schwartz's prologue was higher than that of the parts written by the other two co-authors who used

---

[25] [Ed-Com] The other side of the Prut River means the part of Moldavia which was taken by the Russians in 1878, reunited with Romania in 1918, but taken once more in 1940 – old Basarabia – presently, the Republic of Moldova.

the pseudonyms Leteg and Bokai (Ghetel and Iakob, respectively). The author himself performed the prologue, and the text became known in Bucharest and Cernauti, and then in Paris, Buenos Aires, Holland, Eretz Israel, and elsewhere. None of the co-authors—nor their relatives or friends—was spared from the satire's sting. The following is the Romanian version of this prologue, which was sung on the motif from the "Hakdumot" prayers recited on Shavuot:

"Akdumois milin"
Before I start babbling, my beloved brothers,
Insistently I ask you, don't become upset.
We shall start right now with a serious matter
And later end with a lunch prayer
Here, we shall serve dishes that are special
By choice or fix menu, all at reduced prices.
The hotchpotch is boiled in butter and honey
Still, we couldn't leave apart just a bit of venom
The cooks put in lots and lots of salt
They do not know much; it is not their fault.
When one cook is deaf, the other is blind
And one who knows music cries out "Ghevalt"
The first one wants profit, but loses it all
With empty words, another fills the whole world,
The first one studies the undead and ghosts
The other, from the Bible all the verses quotes.
The first one, when sees something
Falls to its feet, declaring his love
The other likes old papers, I say,
And reads them all as the calf eats hay.
They cooked this hotchpotch, since
It's said in the book "with raw beans."
Reb Eli served us with ritual water
Mr. Hers Swars—some boiled gizzard.
Zeilig Moser gave us kosher meat
As the saying goes "like Usar's girl" [B-26]
Moise Buchman readily sold us wood for fire
While Arn Rosental put some gas on fire [B-27]
Iancu Leibovici rings the bell if danger
Ianculovici, Iosupovici bring a fire engine
David Leib Davidovici has good intentions.
The hotchpotch is ready thanks to all this help
So the good old tradition requires

---

[26] [Ed-Com] This is a play on words. Kosher in Romanian is spelled cusar and the Hebrew name Asher is spelled Usar. (The Romanian S is pronounced as an English SH). In Hebrew, Kasher can be read as K-Asher, meaning "Like Asher".

[27] [Ed-Com] Putting gas on fire means to be lazy.

And, please, don't give up just now.
Do not frown, come one, we're even
And the hotchpotch will be served in just a minute.

It would be too much to translate the whole text, which is composed of innuendoes that were familiar only to the local audience. It made a list of the small, local habits. Most of the people mentioned in the text were actually flattered to be at the center of "public attention." The rest showed "bonne mine au mauvais jeu," meaning good face for nasty jokes, while those who threatened to sue for defamation only increased the humor, success, and efficiency of the show, beyond its theatrical scope.

Dr. A. Mendelovici (1902-1980) who helped me reconstitute some of the verses, told me how much enthusiasm was put into the rehearsal and performance of this show, which, as a fact, had a short life on stage. The young artists went their separate ways and chose more "serious" careers. Still, the taste of the "Hotchpotch" remains on the lips of those who tasted it, back in those days.

15.5 *A Boy from Moldova*

by I. Kara

If the angel of life had forgot to hit a fillip under my nose, so I forgot everything that happened up in the heavens before I was born, I could have told you all about my genealogy. I could have told you about my father's grandpa, his father's father, Nuham sin Hers, also known as the "cheese man," since he traded "products" like fresh and processed cheese, lambs, wool, and skins. I stumbled upon his name in the 1849 census for Podu Iloaiei, my native town. The town was founded around 1816 in the Iasi district, in the vicinity of a small inn and bridge that were in the custody of a woman named Leia or Lelioaia, and so the name of the town became Podu Lelioaiei. The bridge over the Bahlui River is still standing, although it has been rebuilt.

Maybe I could have mentioned my father's grandma, his mother's mother, Motl, a short, agile old lady who would not let our parents spank us, telling them "don't hit the child" in Romanian so we would not understand. And they would listen to her. I was only three years old when she passed away, and I can only see her image as in a hazy dream.

I remember my great grandmother Basie much better—a tall, clever lady but moody and fastidious. If she were offered a seat among the older ladies at a wedding, she would be upset that they had put her among the "hags," and if her place was with the younger women, she would complain that they had placed her with the "teenagers". Yes, it was hard to satisfy great grandma.

I shall spare you my nostalgic memories about all my uncles, aunts, cousins, and other relatives from several generations. I won't go and describe my little town—all hidden among the hills, covered by forests, and close to the swamps of the Bahlui riverbed. The mosquitoes, malaria, and frog concerts are no source of inspiration.

I don't really remember any particular event before my fifth birthday. When I passed thirteen and, since I did not show a great deal of enthusiasm for my morning prayers, old Hana, the cook, would reproach me about my indifference and recall the time when I was less than three years old and would wear a towel instead of a "tales" and go visit the neighbors singing the Friday night prayer "Lecha N'Ranana" to everbody's amusement. "But now....- she used to say, and then let the sentence unfinished....."Now it's different; my mind should no longer be as a three-year-old's," I would answer her silently in my thoughts.

From the time of "heder," our modest confessional school, I shall evoke only several moments. Iosl "belfer," the teacher's substitute, would come home in the morning, recite the prayer together with the kids, and then take them to school. He carried a basket with the children's lunch on his back. During the rainy and muddy days in autumn, he would carry us on his back too. Each period with its own means of transportation.....

The "restrooms" at the heder were "natural." During the breaks, the kids would line up on the bank of the Bahlui River, and relieve nature with the open sky above their heads. If one considered that he was too close to the kid next to him, he would remember a local tradition and start shouting: "Your mother will give birth to cats!" And, since no one would have liked his mother to give birth to kittens, the person would move away without paying attention to what he trampled on. After the break, the air in the class didn't exactly smell like roses.

Strul melamed, my first teacher, was a good-looking man, broad-shouldered with a black beard and brown eyes. He had a good heart and, as a teacher, fulfilled his duties quite well. Soon, we moved to a more modern confessional school, with desks in rows and a blackboard, just like in the primary school. Here we studied the Pentateuch and even modern Hebrew using S. A. Gold's schoolbook printed by Samitca at Craiova. I still have one of those schoolbooks from 1912; I don't remember which edition. Even before I registered in the primary "Jewish-Romanian" school in town, our mother had taught us to read in Romanian and "a bit of French." During the Balkan war in 1913, I was able to read the headlines in the papers. The first grade of the primary school was no problem for me. Our mother, Ester, was an intelligent and beautiful woman, and she could adapt to all sorts of changes in life. She was born in Tirgu Ocna, in a family where the father was a ritual chicken slaughterer. She was the youngest among four brothers; she became an orphan at a very young age and married young. I don't know when or how she managed to learn French satisfactorily, in the company of the rich girls educated by Mademoiselle Petavain, or when she "picked up" German from the illuminist Professor Feldbau. She even learned the Bible in Hebrew and some of the Talmud, simply by listening. If needed, she could give some help to a less smart student of the Talmud. She helped her children with their first, most difficult steps in school. Mother learned Romanian at random, but she gained solid knowledge of the language and even learned Russian, around 1940, in Cernauti. She showed much understanding for her children's advanced ideas. Since she became a widow in 1928, she had to face heroically a harsh fate. Those close to her used to say as a joke that her children address her as "miss mamma!"

Our father, Hersl, dedicated his childhood and teenage years to the traditional study of the Bible, the commentaries, and the Talmud. He married at age 20 and quickly wasted the dowry money. Quite early, he showed the real side of his personality: energetic, persevering, driven to initiative and exploration, and displaying an optimism that wasn't always justified. He died at age 51, "a victim of the commercial honesty," consumed by disease in several days.

A curious thing: A social hierarchy was established by the way in which children addressed their parents. In modest families, "father" and "mother" were used. Other children more linked to the rural way of life used "granpa" and "grandma." In the "enlightened" families, children called their parents "vater" and "mutter" (German); in other houses, including our own, "papa" and "mam" (French) were used. Everywhere in town, the language to be heard was a Moldavian Yiddish, but you could also hear Romanian. An old nanny, Aunt Maria, could repeat the Hebrew prayers with the children and was familiar with the complicated Jewish ritual, even though she was a good Christian Orthodox.

When the 1913 war was over, and tens of Jewish soldiers returned, the only one missing was a poor widow's only son who had died in battle. This was a prelude to the world war that was drawing near. Between July 1914 and August 1916, the period when Romania maintained its neutrality, commercial life flourished. The Germans bought massive amounts of raw materials, cereals and food, and paid good money for them. Some merchants even made some fortune and started dreaming about extending their business to a larger city.

The mobilization on August 15, 1916 opened a page of crucial importance in history. A world was fading and with it the first years of the childhood of a boy from Moldova.

15.6 *Calman the Medicine Man*

by I. Kara

On Friday afternoon, Vasile the bath-house attendant hasn't even finished walking through town, ringing the bell and calling "Idara budara!" (To the bath, fellows!), when there they are, rushing to the community's bath with basin, oak broom, and clean clothes in their hands. Three of them were regular customers of the bath; they open and close the "party" of the weekly bath. After spending the first "session" of steam on the highest step in the room, they descend and solemnly take their seats on the large benches covered with mats in the room where they left their clothes before the bath. They talk about the quality of that day's steam and forecast the taste of the traditional goulash with hot corn flour, their Friday lunch.

The oldest of the three "musketeers" is Meir Kolomeier, an old man of long, lanky stature. He is a sales agent, a man trusted by the landlords who has seen many villages and towns. The second is Calman, the medicine man for cows. He is of medium stature, a little overweight with a rare, pointed, goat-like beard just like Meir's. The youngest is David, the sieve maker, who walks around the villages carrying his huge sieve on his back. He works for both landlords and peasants, winnowing their wheat. All three men wear rustic shirts and broad, red girdles over their thick cloth pants. Their entire life is linked more to the villages than to their little town. The bath is the place where they rest and recall the old times.

In their youth, the poor Jews of the town used to wear tight trousers, peasant shirt, girdles, and fur caps. You could distinguish them from the other peasants only by their mantle and their beard and side whiskers. They complain that the prices are high (it is 1912!) and remember the prices of the times before: three nickels for a measure of good wine[B-28], ten for a quarter kilo of smoked meat, and bread cost almost nothing. They mention with a sigh the buxom, hardworking, and daring bartender woman and many other things from their past youth, which they now see through pink glasses.

In the meantime, the people of the town rush to take their bath and return quickly to their homes. The three old men are lost in times of yore and are preoccupied with their repeated steam baths and cold baths; they do not realize that the time passes. They keep on talking and do not go home until the bath attendant comes in to tell them that the women have come to take their bath.

***

On the main street of the town, all of the houses' rooms that face the street are dedicated to some kind of business: stores, manufacturing, warehouse, bureau, butcher store, café, or candy store. This is the "commercial street." In the yard, there are warehouses, barns, stables, chicken coops, the summer kitchen, and sometimes a small garden. At Calman's house, everything takes place in the part of the house that faces the yard; in summertime, on the porch, and in winter, in the kitchen. He doesn't stay much at home. He lives his life mostly in the country, where there are stables, grasslands, sheepfolds, and winter camps. If someone needs him for some sick animal, he enters through the back door.

It's Saturday morning, on a day in September. At the open windows, the devoted Jews slowly recite that week's pericope from the Bible. Since dawn, Calman has sat on the porch bench, watching the people. On his head, he has his black fur cap, which he always wears; on his back, his old vest that he never leaves without. The red girdle is at its place as always, "keeping him in health." Suddenly, at the door, appears old Gheorghe, who is the shepherd at the sheepfold that belongs to Miss Pascanita, the owner of the Scobalteni estate. After saying "Good morning!" to each other, Gheorghe readily announces to Calman that there's no need to worry. There's no case of disease. He came to town with an "interest" at the local Court of Justice, and stopped by to visit his friend. Calman moves over so that the man can sit next to him, and together they go on recalling the old times. On their lips, the same sweet, soft, calm, and mild Moldavian dialect blooms.

"Do you remember, Calman, that summer night when you saved Ion Cutan's red cow and its calf from death?" And there go the praises to the unique breeding cow, nice and of good breed just like a maiden, even if the cow and generations of its cubs had passed away into eternity long ago with the butcher's kind help.

Calman rests his eyes on his six-blade pocketknife, with which he has saved so many cows from death. They remember a snow-stormed, moonless winter night when they

---

[28] [Ed-Com] a measure is about three pints.

rushed in a sleigh to a sheepfold, where the wolves had massacred sheep and lambs. Only Gheorghe's skill and cold-bloodedness in handling the horses saved them from being eaten by the wolves, for the pack was chasing them and roaring terribly. They also remember the village parties at which Calman never ate meat. But he was as skillful a dancer as anyone else in his large boots. As well, he was anyone's equal in drinking wine.

In town, Calman is considered too much of a "peasant," but they all respect him for his skill and hard work. He has saved many animals from disease or death: someone's cow or goat that provides food for the family, someone else's horse that is used to make a living. He even cured, with his herbs and medicines, the town's breeding ox that had an injured leg from jumping over a fence. Lost in memories, Calman doesn't realize that by now the people have filled the synagogue he also attends, and that the sermon has already begun. Fortunately, old Gheorghe remembers his "interest" that brought him to town. The old man drinks to the bottom his glass of strong brandy, takes a bite of the white bread that the lady of the house brought, says goodbye, and heads toward the Courthouse. Calman quickly grabs his Saturday "tales" and goes to the Aziel synagogue, the oldest in town, in which his father, grandfather, and great grandfather, one of the founders of the town, prayed.

***

The entire town is discussing the news that the postman has brought Calman a letter, together with two boat tickets for him and his wife, from his only son who immigrated to America many years ago. Calman is overwhelmed. It's true that the Balkan war and the Great War of 1914-1918, and the events that followed, produced radical changes in Calman's old world. His two friends died, many things changed in the village and in town, and nothing is as it used to be. "My, world, world ..."

Calman understands that he will have to leave behind all that has made up his life until now. He wishes to know where he is going, and he finds out. New York is a big city with as many inhabitants as Romania's entire population before the war; the houses have many floors ("They surpass the clouds," Calman says to himself) and people of different origins live there. Calman cannot imagine a city larger than Iasi. He was there several times, and the crowds of people, the tramway, the houses with two or three floors, the noise, and the motion left him perplexed. He came home and felt sick for a couple of days. And America is so far away. You go by train and by boat, and the journey never ends.

Calman is walking through the rooms of his home, feeling like a stranger since his wife sold or gave away everything and packed their bags. He only took his "tales" for prayer, his stamp collection, his coat, cap, and boots. His friends in town and from the villages accompanied him to the station. Calman looked like an oak tree that has been uprooted from its land in the woods of Arama (Cooper) and taken to be transplanted in America.

In New York, Calman lived for one more year, a plentiful life but a lonely one. Then the news came that the old man had died. His longing for his town, the field, the woods, the shepherds and the sheep, and the places that had made up his life for over 70 years had consumed him quietly.

Good people, the end of my story is sad. But this world's wheel never stops spinning, and it is in vain to cry over past times. The times are changing and so are we.

15.7 *Dudl Consul*

by I. Kara

In the small towns of Moldavia, "Shabbat Hagadol"—the Saturday before the celebration of Pesach—was considered the day of those who were bald or had some kind of scars on their heads, "kareches" the bald men. This was of course in memory of one of the ten plagues, with which Iehova struck the Egyptians. It was said that on that day, these people were supposed to go to Mitzraim. The practical jokers had already made up the list of all those with "bare heads," and they would display the list in front of the synagogue. Above the list, a bowl with cabbage juice was hung, supposedly a cure against baldness, as well as a damaged comb as a hint to those who, as children, would not bathe. In time, the "kareches" would receive some kind of citation order at their home, indicating the exact date and place to embark for Mitzraim. The town had fun on this subject, except of course those implicated, and the joke would last until the day of Pesach as a prolongation of the carnival-like Purim.

In my native town, the "shiny heads" had a diplomatic representative nicknamed "Dudl Consul." Otherwise, he was an interesting, picturesque character. He was descended from a notoriously poor family and had many jobs but little progress. Mainly he worked as a "stone hewer," a mason, but since few people built brick houses, he wasn't too busy. An incredible thirst for knowledge and science devoured this poor workman—the craving to become better and do extraordinary things, impulsive dreams about traveling to exotic countries. He was the double version of "Benjamin the third," Moldavian version, model 1900.

I don't believe Dudl ever attended the primary school, but he could read Romanian quite well, and he was one of the few in town who subscribed to the magazine *Sanatatea*. He read and carefully studied the articles in the magazine and tried to cure the sick ones in his large family by following the advice and prescriptions given in the pages. He was always ready to discuss medical subjects, and for him *Sanatatea* was almost a Bible.

One time, someone took him seriously and asked for the magazine to verify the arguments brought up in a discussion. The joker pretended to look over the articles. Seeing an ad for a medicine against hair loss, he showed it to Dudl who couldn't give an answer, for this was his weak spot.

Dudl passionately read *Popular Science and Travels Paper*. When the number of "students" in town (meaning high school boys) increased, Dudl tried to engage in discussions with them on physics and technique. During the students' vacation, he used to borrow their schoolbooks, and, in time, he became a passionate searcher for the much sought after "perpetuum mobile."

He lived in the basement of a miserable building, at one of our neighbors. Each year, the rivers Bahlui and Bahluiet "took pride in their waters" and flooded the field along with the suburbs of the town, the camps and huts of the Gypsies and poor Jews, and sometimes even the yards of the up-town houses. One spring, Dudl's yard became a pool. His imagination grew wild: He was feeling the call to navigate. He took an old bathtub from the cellar. For a mast, he used a no-longer-used shovel that he took from the neighboring bakery. He tied to the shovel the all-patched and only sheet in his home and proudly set out to explore the world. Fortunately, the "ship" stumbled upon the yard's fence, and our hero took only a cold bath in the muddy waters of the over flown Bahlui River. If he had somehow managed to leave the "harbor," the town would have counted one more poor widow and a household of orphans.

Dudl survived "the flood" and then tried to grow a coffee tree right in his backyard. The soil was just clay, covered with bricks, ash, and pieces of glass, among which weeds and thistles were growing. He remembered a picture from *Popular Science and Travels Paper*. With his family's last savings, he bought coffee beans and planted them in the clay that the flood had left behind. While waiting for the harvest, he and his family had at breakfast a cup of chicory [B-29] without milk and a slice of black bread with jam. The dream of a cup of genuine coffee with milk and cream and some fresh rolls was still far from reality. Such is life.....

After World War I—which for Dudl meant starvation, disease, and all kinds of miseries—new houses were built in town. Dudl could not "keep up" with the developments of science that reached the level of Einstein's works, but instead he had plenty of work as a bricklayer. He even had enough money to build a bakery oven on which he put the following message in capital letters: "Raised by David Pietraru in the year 1918."

Now he could peacefully pass away.

And he didn't have to wait for long.

(*A Boy from Moldova* by I. Kara, Bucharest, Kriterion Publishing House, 1976, p. 44-46)

---

[29] [Ed-Com] Chicory is a substance extracted from the flower of the chicory plant; it is used to make a drink that resembles coffee.

“Not far from the famous city of Iasi, there is the well-known, little town of Podu Iloaiei that became famous through the Svart family, which included four art creators; and not far away from the town there is a village very much the same as all the other nearby villages with good-looking houses covered with iron plate and poor people’s huts covered with straw.” (p. 75)

“And this is the story of the Velvl clan. His background was in Podu Iloaiei. Here, his great-great-grandfather Iancu Moise found a place to settle and founded a “dynasty” of shoemakers. He “ruled” for 30 years and had three sons, all shoemakers, of whom two had no offspring. The second son, Velvl’s great-grandfather, had two sons and three daughters. He was able to earn the first place in the family, but not the money to make a living. One must be extremely clever to see his three daughters married, especially in Podu Iloaiei. Velvl’s grandfather also proved to be a “clever” man. He married his daughters to his apprentices.” (p. 49)

(Haim Goldenstein: *A Century of Silence*, a novel written in Yiddish, Bucharest, Kriterion, 1979). Translated by I. Kara.

16 Documentary Appendices

16.1 *Appendix A: The Right to Sell Liquor, 1826*

Iasi State Archives (ISA)[B-30], letter M, 509, f. 289-292

The council of the town of Vladeni or Tirgu Nou from November 16, 1826 addresses to the King a report establishing that the right to sell liquors is given "… only to those who will receive the acceptance from the landlord as was communicated in the act issued in 1816 by King Scarlat Calimah VV, blessed be his name, and concerning the town of Podu Leloaia as part of the Scobalteni estate to which Your Majesty issued the 1823 act … "

16.2 *Appendix B: Census of 1824*

ISA, transport 166, op.184, no. 23
Sudits' census of 1824, Podu Iloaiei

1. Russian Sudit, Moscu Iticovici: born in Berdicev, settled for 20 years, 45 years old, Jewish clothes, married to a native. He has a shop of his own in the borough Podul Leloaiei in Carligatura county …

2. K. K. Sudit (Austrian – original note), Berl Leizer: born in Cernauti, settled for 22 years, Jewish clothes, married to a native. House of his own in Podul Lelioaiei, where he lives. Trades horses and rents bars. He is 26 years old.

3. K. K. Sudit, Moise Maer: born in Cernauti, settled for 12 years, 25 years old, Jewish clothes. House and shop of his own in Iasi. Rented shop in Podul Lelioaiei where he sells things of small value. Married in Cernauti.

16.3 *Appendix C: Sale of Land, 1826*

ISA Fond I. Kara. Agreement Act

I, undersigning in Hebrew, give my written agreement to Mr. Iacov Lipovean[B-31] that I know to have sold him a piece of land, which I have lawfully owned since the foundation of this town. The place has the following size: From the wall of Lipovean Marin's shop to the bridge over the Bahlui River owned by Serban Negel, mayor, including the piers that stand on this land. The land was sold for 60 lei and I received the total sum. He

30 [KME] Iasi State Archives… In the Romanian edition it is refered to as Arh. St. Iasi (ASI)

31 [Ed-Com] Lipoveans – Orignally refered to people of Russian origin, who settled in the region of the Danube River and the Black Sea. Later it was used to describe all those coming from Russia.

should hold this place as his own forever, and whatever he wishes to do with it he should do, since the land is rightfully his. I engage to obtain for this written agreement the approval of His Excellency General Constantin Palade, the forever owner of the estate to which this town belongs, so that the agreement should be recognized and the owner can use the land without anyone bothering him. And for these, I alone signed in Hebrew. March 24, 1826. I, Iaakov, son of Smuel.

This sale agreement, which I also received, validates the act.

General Constantin Palade

16.4 *Appendix D: Income Sharing Agreement, 1830*

ISA, letter P, 811, f. 23-24/1830, December 22, Iasi

The income made by the borough Podu Leloaiei, including the inn and the landlord's wine cellar which is rightfully owned by His Excellency General Constantin Palade, through the power given by the contract signed with General Palade, I sell the income to Mr. Moise Iuster and Mr. Herscu a Mendiloaiei for a three-year term starting on October 26, 1831, under the following terms:

1) Each year, I have to give him 12,000 lei, meaning exactly 12,000 lei to be paid in the following manner: 6,000 lei now at the conclusion of the deal and 6,000 lei on April 1, 1832 at the end of the first-year debt, and again 6,000 lei on October 1, 1832 and 6,000 lei on April 1, 1833, and so on without delay until all the agreed money is paid.

2) I am entitled to a share of the town's income from all sources as the contract stipulates, but not a penny more.

3) They are to keep the inn in the best state during this time, hiring a Moldavian innkeeper and trusting him to be capable of satisfying all the clients who may stay at the inn, no matter what their status. At the end of the period for this contract, they should give back the inn in clean, good condition, just as they received it.

4) All the townspeople, inhabitants, and visitors, no matter what business they are in, are to help them as much as possible, preventing any mistreatment from anyone. If a situation cannot be resolved, they are to let me know.

5) The captain of the town is to be nominated by the landlord's authority. Whoever they find fit for the job is to look after the merchants, both those living in town and those visiting. If the opposite happens, the captain will be dismissed at the proprietor's order. No one should claim anything from me, but only if one can arrange to have acceptance … [B-32]

6) All soldiers living in town who are under the military rule are not to be bothered in any way about working their land for their food as they have done until now,

---

[32] [Ed-Com] Probably unfinished text.

but they only have to pay the usual tithe in products or in any other way they find fit.

7) The Gypsies, who live in town and are owned by His Excellency the General, will be allowed to pay the tax wherever they are taken, except one man whose duty will be to guard the road and the bridge from which they are not to take any tax.

8) The cattle belonging to the town's merchants and soldiers may graze on the field that has been used until now, but their number is limited as stipulated in the contract.

9) Apart from the tithe on the town, I also have to pay with 20 measures [B-33] of grass field and ten measures of land from the Popesti estate, the part in the vicinity of Sirca, and land for a garden at the entry in Totoesti, which belonged to Andrei the gardener.

10) As until now, they are allowed to use the waters from the Bahluiet mill upwards.

11) They will be given permission to grind at the Podu Lelioaiei mill 40 measures of wheat or corn per year tax-free.

12) As in the former contract, regarding the land given to Iancu the carpenter, no one should give him any trouble in raising his building.

13) The trash resulting from the inn is to be taken out of the town and in no way to be deposited close to the inn, not even for a short time.

14) Any kind of building or annex raised on the estate or any kind of trade that does not have the acceptance of the forever owner will become part of the estate at the end of these years with no payment in exchange.

15) If they do not pay at the agreed upon time, I shall be free to sell the town's income and all the rest to any merchant I can find, and I shall be entitled to recover my debt from them without any opposition.

In the above-mentioned terms, I sold the income of the borough Podu Lelioaiei. If all terms are complied with they should have no trouble collecting the town's income until the end of the mentioned period of time. For this purpose, two similar contracts were made for each part and given legal power by my signature. December 22, 1830. Signed: Costache Pelin, moneylender.

On page 38, there is an added request from "the guardians of the deceased General C. Palade" dated November 9, 1831. It is agreed in the contract that the guardians may appoint the captain of the town who becomes the administrator. Tudorache Popovici who was appointed on April 15, 1830 was rejected by Herscu, who then took possession of the Totoesti estate. And it is known that the vice-president of the Divan made a decision

[33] [Ed-Com] a measure equals 14, 322 square meters

forbidding the Jews to lease land. The reconfirmation of the captain's appointment is requested.

On page 11 and 12, it is added the decision of the Divan that Herscu should get his money back and restitute the contract. C. Pelin offered the money, but Herscu refuses to accept it.

16.5 *Appendix E: Statistics*

In *La Roumanie et les Juifs* (Bucharest 1903, p. 14), Verax estimated the population of Podu Iloaiei in 1831 to be: 281 local Jews; 281 Christians; and eight Sudits of whom three are Jews (I.K.). In all, 570 people in 164 families. In a report from 1970, Dr. Ecaterina Negruzzi offered the following estimates: 281 Jews, of whom 109 are children, and 560 people in the whole population. The official census indicates that on Palade's estate there were 49 tribute-paying persons, each paying 30 lei per year, and five nontribute-payers. Among the tribute payers, we find the Jews Leiba sin Simon (baker), Moisa sin Iosap (undertaker), Iosap sin Leiba, Moise sin Leizer (brandy maker or seller), Itic sin Strul, Herscu sin Froim, Meier sin Leiba (janitor of the synagogue), Iosap sin Avram (undertaker), Smil sin Leiba (undertaker), and Herscu sin Fisel (undertaker). Living on Neculai Cantacuzino's estate, there were 15 Christian tribute-payers and the Jew Iancu sin Mendel, a ritual chicken slaughterer.

The final documents mention 57 tribute-payers on Palade's estate of whom 14 were Jews: Rabbi Moise sin Leizer, five undertakers, five with no profession mentioned, one butcher, one bath-house attendant, and one wagoner. On N. Canta's estate, there were 12 Christian tribute-payers, four tribute-exempted, and one Jew. The names of six Jewish Sudits were kept: Iosef Leibovici, Moise Ensiberg, Iancu Smil, David Kaufman, Haim Bekir (baker), and Laiba Margulies who did not appear in any of the previous lists (I.S.A., Moldova's State Secretariate, no. 68, 1832, f. 13). The other Jews not mentioned here by name were probably tribute-payers, widows, old, or handicapped. Actually, material published in the magazine *Albina Romaneasca* [B-34] in the supplement to issue no. 117 on February 23, 1831 lists the shops in Podu Iloaiei: 25 first class, 23 second class, and 14 third class. Another source points out that 70 Jews and eight Christians died from cholera in Podu Iloaiei in 1831.

16.6 *Appendix F: Taxes, 1833*

***Albina Romaneasca*, no. 28, April 20, 1833. Taxes**

The Treasury of the Principality of Moldova. No. 2649. The law for ensuring the collection of the taxes from the Jewish ethnicity.

Although article 47 from annex Z of chapter 3 of the Organic Regulation establishes the taxes paid by the Jewish ethnicity to be patents equally applied to all, as is the case for the other inhabitants, it has been found that it would be best to collect the taxes from the

[34] [Ed-Com] Albina Romaneasca means Romanian Bee

Jews in another way. Since the Jewish ethnicity from Esi [B-35] found this other way to be the only easy means of collecting the taxes to be paid by the Jews, it is established and brought to the public's knowledge the tax to be paid by the Jewish ethnics from both Esi and the other towns of the Principality, wherever the Jews will solicit, estimating the prices according to the tax for the meat to be sold and for chicken slaughtering in such a way that the taxes for the Jews will always be collected together with what is still to be paid as past debts. The payment of the tax should be done in the Jewish synagogue in the presence of a representative of the local administration and of the elders from all Jewish professions.

The law concerning the taxes to be paid by the fraternities of merchants and craftsmen through their leaders is published in *Albina Romaneasca* no. 34.

16.7 *Appendix G: Deposition, 1836*

I.S.A., Letter P., 646, No. 41, Podu Lelioaiei, February 16, 1836.

Deposition.

I, who shall afterward sign Jewishly, trust this deposition of mine in the hands of the merchants who are in judicial conflict with Mr. Gavrilas, administrator of the royal vineyards, maintaining that I know about their case, since at that time I happened to be on the street and saw the policemen pulling the man, Solomon, by his whiskers and beating him. So, I went to the house of the administrator Grigoras and asked him why Solomon was being beaten by the police. Other merchants had already arrived at the administrator's house. Grigoras rose immediately and shouted to the merchants: "Why have you come to beat me up?" The merchants said: "We have come to ask you why the policemen do such a thing, beating merchants in the streets?" This is what I have seen happening in my presence, for the merchants said nothing else to the administrator.

This is what I also stated in front of the commission, and I testify the same now in fear of God. And I signed in faith, February 16, 1836, Iancu Leib from Belcesti.

(Round stamp: Podul Iloaiei administration)

16.8 *Appendix H: Agreement with Owner of Estate, 1838*

I.S.A., Moldova State Secretariate, no. 552, f. 2, 1838.

Copy of the agreement signed between the inhabitants of Podu Iloaiei and the owner of the Scobalteni estate.

We the townsmen, Christians, Jews, and those in the suburbs of the borough of Podu Iloaiei on the Scobalteni estate owned by His Excellency Chancellor Neculai Canta, since we are forbidden to sell any alcoholic beverages as stipulated in the settlement contract,

---

35 [Ed-Com] Esi = Iasi

this being the exclusive right of the owner of the estate, made a request to the forever master, agreeing to the following:

1. Whoever intends to sell beverages should pay 1 lei and 42 bani for every 12 liters of brandy, 108 bani for 12 liters of rum, 81 bani for 10 liters of wine, and 54 bani for 15 liters of fuel oil or petroleum, following this payment arrangement for the entire time he keeps his business.
2. For each measure of land [B-36] that is given to us for our shops and is situated on the side of the street, we should pay a long-term rent that is established forever at 3 lei and 72 bani per year, no more or no less, during the time that we maintain our business. We shall be given ten more measures of land rent-free for the yard of each shop, no matter the breadth of the building. But the buildings that are to be built should have no space between them, not even the size of a palm, unless a street is planned to pass across. The roof of all the buildings will not be of any other material than board or shingle.
3. Butchery, bakery, candle making, barbershops, cooking, (balance) weighing, *mortasapie* [B-37] remain in the custody of the owner and we, the townsmen, shall have nothing to do with these, with the condition that the butcher is obligated to always have kosher meat and sell it at the price established on the other side of the town, on the estate of the deceased general Costaki Paladi; the same condition holds for candle selling.
4. If any of us, the merchants, is proven to have dared to bring alcohol in secretly, without the knowledge of the owner and without paying as agreed, all the alchool will be confiscated, and the merchant will be banished from the town and his shop will remain in the possession of the owner of the estate, without any possibility of forgiveness, for this is what we agreed upon.
5. We shall be allowed to build a church on the place of the cemetery at no cost to us. We will also be given land for the school and the public bath at no cost.
6. Any building built from now on will respect the plan of the town, without narrowing the space between shops.
7. Besides the conditions mentioned above, any merchant is allowed to run a business in his house or shop without any payment to the forever owner.
8. We, all townsmen present today and all those who settle in the future, are allowed to bring a herd of 60 cattle to graze in the field of the Scobalteni village at no cost. If there are more cattle, we shall buy a new place from His Excellency if he agrees to sell it to us.
9. His Excellency sold this agreement for the exact price of 37,350 lei, thirty seven thousand, three hundred, and fifty lei, to us who sign below: Toma Gavrilovici, Izrail sin Isar, and Avram Leiba. We are to pay in four rates of eight months each, paying the first rate on January 1 of the next year (1839) and the other three rates every eight month until the end of the two years.

---

[36] [Ed-Com] this measure varies from 1.96 to 2.23 meters.

[37] [KME] Mortasapie: This word was not translated. Nothing was found by searching with Google. I thought it may mean funeral undertaker or mortician (from Latin "mort", death). After consulting with a number of our Romanian friends, I was eventually told that "a sapa" means to dig. So mortasapie probably means a grave digger.

10. We shall keep this agreement, and those who settle in this town in the future will respect the old rules. So, until the completion of the formalities, we give to the forever owner for his assurance the contract that we signed and receive in exchange his copy.

November 28, 1838

(Two Jews and one Christian are signing.) (Similar to the original: Iordache Gavrilovici, baker.)

16.9 *Appendix I: Rental Agreement, 1841*

I.S.A., I. Kara fun d. November 25, 1841. Podu Iloaiei

Document to the peace-loving administration

For the piece of land of six measures in breadth and twenty measures in length that the merchant Moisa Itic possesses in the borough Podu Iloaiei, property of the undersigned, and on which he has his shops, he will pay rent and other taxes as established in the property contract, and I shall give him no trouble in using the land. This document addressed to the peace-loving administration was given to him with my signature and seal. In accord with the property contract, November 25, 1841, Ghika Ceacuz (?).

(The act comes from the I. Klingher family from Podu Iloaiei who gave it to me in 1966).

16.10 *Appendix J: Occupations, 1842*

I.S.A., package 10, no. 41.

Podu Iloaiei rent-payers list for 1842, from which I established the occupations of the Jewish rent-payers: 1 baker, 1 barrel maker, 5 butchers, 10 tailors, 2 lengths-measuring men, 2 shoemakers, 2 synagogue janitors, 1 fur cap maker, 3 teachers, 1 wheat flour seller, 1 candle carrier, 1 shochet, 1 stone mason, 2 brandy makers, 1 glass seller, 1 joiner, 1 tax collector, and 1 money lender.

16.11 *Appendix K: Sale of House, 1845*

I. Kara collection (Podu Iloaiei, January 8, 1845)

Certificate (translated from Hebrew)

Intended to be proof in the hands of Mr. Slomo, son of Avraham, and Mr. Mose Itchak, son of Naftali, who bought the house that was left here by the deceased Eliahu from his uncle Iaakov with the acceptance of the rabbi who assisted and Mr. Iaakov who assisted, as they received a letter from the rabbi of Sneatin. The mentioned house was sold for 1,676 lei, one thousand, six hundred, and seventy six lei, with the condition that the money be paid at the moment of delivering the papers to the authority, both the papers from the rabbi and the Court on our expanse. The above-mentioned associates will give Mr. Iaakov 1,000 lei and for the remaining 676 lei write a note to be paid on the day of Saint George (1845) at the latest. Mr. Iaakov took 20 galbeni in advance with the condition that, once the associates arrive in Iasi, no one should give them any trouble with the papers (signed) at the rabbi of Sneatin or at the Chancellor's office, though they must pay the whole sum they owe.

It also has been stipulated that we shall leave the things that are in the house, the windows, the barn, as well as the debt from the builders of the house who pawned their tools until the termination. Thus, we sign today, Wednesday the 29th of Tevet 5605, here, Podu Iloaiei, Iaakov, son of Zeiev (Lupu) Segal.

(Signed: Moise, the rabbi of this place.)

16.12 *Appendix L: List of Taxpayers, 1834*

I.S.A., tr. 644, op. 708, no. 502, f. 22-25.

Regarding the proposals made by the treasury's inspector Ion Teodoru on June 30, 1834 concerning "the good tax-payers," the representatives of the community and the former chief policeman of the town, Todorachi, made a statement in front of the actual captain of the town, Colonel Constandin. The commission establishes the following individuals:

1) Smil sin Itic, orphan of father, 17 years old, works as a porter, poor.
2) Avram, brother of Iosip the lengths measurer, 20 years old, poor, works for his brother.
3) Moisa the tailor, old, ran away from the town.
4) Itic the tailor, old, lives from charity.
5) Itic, brat David, 17 years old, orphan, poor.
6) Sloim, his brother, 20 years old, same situation as Itic.
7) Ghidale, son of Iancu Belcescu, 17 years old, married, helps his father in the trade business.
8) Sulim, butcher, pays the tax in Iasi.
9) Lupu, old, lived in the villages, poor.
10) Avram, teacher, came for six months from Iasi.
11) Moisa, teacher, same situation as Avram.
12) Avram, teacher, old, his wife owns a hut, poor.
13) Avram, tailor, 18 years old, from Tirgu Frumos, settled temporarily
14) Froim, bar owner, from Vaslui, rented a bar in Scobalteni for six months, Austrian subject, left Podu Iloaiei four years ago.
15) Solomon Herscu, business in Negresti, pays tax.
16) Leiba Meilich, opened a shop in town, not registered as a taxpayer.
17) Moisa Leiba, married for one year, a Sudit's son.
18) Saim, furrier, came from Suceava, taxpayer.
19) Moisa, bar owner, married, wants to rent a bar in the country.
20) Smil, bar owner, shoemaker in the suburbs, can pay tax.
21) Calman Ber, married, shop, can pay tax.

The conclusion of the administrator of Carligatura county (page 32): seven can pay tax, two are Sudits, two are new arrivals, two are not of age, two are not restricted by the settlement agreement, six are poor and helpless in all ways, and two can pay the third class tax.

16.13 *Appendix M: List of Rent Payers, 1842*

I.S.A., Manuscripts, no. 1842

A report on the money collected from the rent payers of Podu Iloaiei in 1842, following the official possession catalog. At the street, there are 43 houses inhabited by Christians (Romanians, Russians, Serbs, Armenians, and Bulgarians) and 58 houses inhabited by 54 Jews. In the suburbs of the town, there are 40 houses inhabited by Christians and 17 houses inhabited by 16 working Jews. Below are the names of the Jewish inhabitants in the order that they appear in the list: 1) Leiba Doroscanu; 2) Iosap Crestinu; 3) Smule from Tirgu Frumos; 4) Izrail sin Iosap; 4a) Tij Izrail; 5) Herscu Hahamul from Tirgu Frumos; 5a) Izrail sin Iosap; 6) David Casap; 7) Marcu Casap; 8) Smile Chioru; 9) Haim Croitoriul [B-38] ; 10) Munas; 11) Smil sin Ilie; 12) Sruli Popa; 13) Ilie Croitoriul; 14) Nusam sin Avram; 15) Marcu sin Avram; 16) Herscu Dascalu; 17) Avram sin Leibis; 18) Iosup Cotariul (deceased) [B-39] ; 19) Ghiza Seinova; 20) David sin Avram; 21) Smil sin Haim; 22) Zeilic sin Haim; 23) Marcu Berlescu; 24) Leiba Chitar; 25) Leiba from Totoesti; 26) Mahal Bujor; 27) Altar Rabinovici; 28) Lazar Barbalata; 29) Iancu sin Ghedale; 30) Froim Barbalata; 31) Moisa Barbalata; 32) Iancu Steclaritii; 33) Iancu Belcescu; 34) Leiba Zaraf; 35) Solomon Taxieru; 36) Lupu Fainariu; 37) David sin Iosup; 38) David Cotar, (deceased); 39) Sulim sin Marcu; 40) Zisu Faclier; 41) Marcu Osap; 42) Filal Rachieriu; 43) Sender Croitoriu; 44) barren place of Leiba Zaraf; 45) barren place of Haim Ber; 46) Iancu Mochioaiei; 47) Leiba sin Iancu; 48) Izrail Casap's sister; 49) Lupu Volf; 50) Haim from Popesti; 51) Meer Croitor; 52) Iancu Stoleriu; 53) Marcu Croitoriu; and 54) Moisa Ciobotariu.

In the suburbs: 1) Meer Ceaus; 2) Cos Butnar; 3) Smile Dascal [B-40] ; 4) Smile Croitor; 5) Herscu Pagu; 6) Altar Croitoru; 7) Avram Croitoriu; 8) Nusan Croitoriu; 9) David Croitoriu; 10) Smil Leib Ceaus; 11) Avram Rachieriu [B-41]; 12) Marcu Berlescu; 12) Marcu of Barbalata; 13) Herscu from the bar of Neculachi; 14) Golda Jidauca; 15) Iuchel Ciobotar [B-42]; 16) Iosap Chetrar; and 17) Idel Dascalu

The list contains the rent payers from one part of the town, which had two owners. I think it is Neculai Cantacuzino's part.

---

[38] [Ed-Com] Croitoru means tailor. In the 19th century it was common for people to use their trade as their last name.

[39] [Ed-Com] Cotariul means evaluator.

[40] [Ed-Com] Dascal means teacher.

[41] [Ed-Com] Rachieriu means a person who makes "rachiu" – an alcoholic drink made by distilling fruit or natural juices, sometimes adding some water and sugar, similar to brandy.

[42] [Ed-Com] Ciobotar means shoe, boot maker.

16.14 *Appendix N: List of Renters, Year??* [B-43]

I.S.A., tr. 1423, op. 1619, dossier 1025, Report.

The Jews from the Borough Podul Iloae Living on His Excellency Mayor Lascaras Cantacuzino's Estate. [B-44]

Columns (only those filled in): 1) Number of houses and shops; 2) Name and nickname; 3) Professions; 4) Authority; 5) Sudits; 5b) Helpless old people; 6) Widows; and 7) Notes.

No. 3. Herscu sin Iancu, bar owner, subject of the High Porte[B-45] from Glodurile village, lives with rent at a Christian's house.

No. 5. Moisa sin Herscu, tax collector, subject of the High Porte from Madarjaca Fetii, lives with rent at Herscu Croitor

No. 6. Pascal sin David, also a subject of the High Porte, old taxpayer, lives with rent at Herscu Avram sin Strule.

No. 7. Avram sin Strul, also a subject of the High Porte, old taxpayer, his own house.

No. 8. Mois sin Itic Lozneanu, also a subject of the High Porte, from Poenile Oancii, his own house.

No. 9. Itic sin Herscu, lime maker, subject of the High Porte, from Borseni in Neamt district, lives with rent at Moise Itic.

No. 10. Herscu Badiu, brandy maker, subject of the High Porte, from Stornesti, lives with rent at Ioan Rosan.

No. 11. Mihail sin Aizic, also a subject of the High Porte, from Drancea in Iasi district, lives in the same house.

No. 13. Ioina sin Pascal, also a subject of the High Porte, from Esi, lives with rent at Avram sin Strule.

No. 14. Nisal sin Avram, also a subject of the High Porte, old taxpayer, lives in the house of Solomon sin Iancu, no business, helpless old man.

No. 15. Marcu Esanu, brandy maker, subject of the High Porte, his own house, unregistered in the previous census.

---

43 [KME] Kara's book does not give a date for this list.

44 [KME] In Kara's book the entries go from 1 to 229, however for some unknown reason there are a lot of gaps. Perhaps they were missing from the source documents or they could not be deciphered. The following entries are missing: 1-2, 4, 12, 21-24, 29, 39-40, 42-43, 48, 79-81, 91-94, 97, 100, 102, 105, 118-119, 121, 143-144, 146, 151-162, 164-171, 173-179, 181-189, 191-194, 197-227

45 [KME] A subject of the "High Porte" means a subject of the Ottoman Empire. See glossary of terms.

Herscu sin Lupu, also a subject of the High Porte, lives in the same house, just married, Esanu's partner.

No. 16. Moisa sin Aron, also a subject of the High Porte, from Malaesti village in this district, lives with rent at widow Bruha's own house.

No. 17. Avram sin Leibu, wagoner, helpless old man, poor eyesight, lives from charity.

No. 18. Nuta sin Lupu, trades things of small value, subject of the High Porte, lives with rent in Avram sin Leiba's house.

No. 19. Gaina sin Froim, also named Herscu Gaina [B-46] no business, helpless old man, poor and in all vicious.
Iancu sin Haim, moneylender, subject of the High Porte, lives with rent at Munis from Tirgu Frumos.

No. 20. Haim sin Croitoru, tailor, subject of the High Porte, his own house.
Falic sin Herscu, butcher, subject of the High Porte, in that house in Tirgu Frumos.
Leiba Cazacu, cattle trading, helpless old man, also living in that house.

No. 25. Strule sin Itic, also named bartender, brandy maker, helpless old man.

No. 26. Marcu sin Pascal, also a subject of the High Porte, his own house.

No. 27. Bercu sin Strule, also a subject of the High Porte, lives with rent at David Grosul.

No. 28. David sin Ancel, butcher, subject of the High Porte, his own house.

No. 30. Herscu sin Smil, brandy maker, from Tirgu Frumos, lives in his inn.

No. 31. Zelic Caldarariu brandy maker[B-47], subject of the High Porte, also lives in this inn and also is from Tirgu Frumos.

No. 32. Izdrail sin Iosap, also a subject of the High Porte, his own house.

No. 33. Smil Baetul, also named Burlacu [B-48], also a subject of the High Porte, rented house.

No. 34. Avram Leiba sin Aron, also a subject of the High Porte, his own house.

No. 35. Iosap sin Bercu, also named Ursul [B-49], also a subject of the High Porte, his own house.

No. 36. Avram, son of Haim Lungu, also a subject of the High Porte, from Cristesti.

No. 37. Avram sin Lupu.

No. 37. Leiba Hanovici, also a subject of the High Porte, from Doroscani, his own house.

---

46 [Ed-Com] Gaina means hen and is used as a nickname for old people.
47 [Ed-Com] Caldarariu is a name derived form caldare, meaning bucket used for making brandy.
48 [Ed-Com] Burlacu: Romanian for bachelor
49 [Ed-Com] Ursul: Romanian for bear.

Alter, his son, no business, subject of the High Porte, lives in Hanovici's house.

No. 41. Aron sin Herscu, tailor, subject of the High Porte, from Esi, his own house. David sin Aron, horse trading, subject of the High Porte, from Botosani.

No. 44. Meer sin Faibis, brandy maker and grocer, subject of the High Porte, from Sirca, lives with rent at Danila sin Iosif Cotar.

No. 45. Danila sin Iosap Cotar, huckster, subject of the High Porte, lives in his own house.

No. 46. Ghita(l) Saina, widow.

No. 47. Solomon sin Avram, brandy maker, subject of the High Porte, from Cosateni, his own house.

No. 49. Solomon sin Haim, also a subject of the High Porte, his own house.

No. 50. Zelic sin Haim, also a subject of the High Porte, his own house.

No. 51. Avram Bercu, grocer, subject of the High Porte, lives with rent in Zeilic's house.

No. 52. Nuham sin Pascal, brandy maker, subject of the High Porte, lives with rent in Moise Barlic's house.

No. 53. Marcu, shochet, subject of the High Porte.

No. 54. Moscu Barlic or Moise sin David, brandy maker, subject of the High Porte, his own house

No. 55. Marcu, shochet, subject of the High Porte.

No. 56. Leiba sin Simon Chitariul, baker, subject of the High Porte, his own house.

No. 57. Ancel sin Strule, brandy maker, lives with rent in Moise sin Leiba's house.

No. 58. Moise sin Leiba, subject of the High Porte, from Totoesti, his own house.

No. 59. Iancu Leibu Teodorescu, subject of the High Porte, bar owner, has his house in Catesti.

No. 60. Haim Nuham sin Avram, wagoner, subject of the High Porte, lives with rent at Leibu.

No. 61. Mehal sin Pascal Bujor named Pisahovici, grocer and glass seller, lives with rent at Neculai Codrescu.

No. 62. Marcu sin Avram, brandy maker and grocer, lives with rent at the rabbi's.

No. 63. Moise Rabinu, rabbi, helpless old man.

No. 64. Mazar sin Moise Barbalata, brandy maker, subject of the High Porte, old.

No. 65. Faibis sin Herscu, brandy maker, subject of the High Porte, from Sirca.

No. 66. Ghidale sin Iancu Belcescu, brandy maker, subject of the High Porte, old.

No. 67. Froim sin Moise Barbalata, brandy maker, subject of the High Porte, old.

No. 68. Moise sin Herscu Barbalata, no business, helpless old man.

No. 69. Iancu sin David, brandy maker, subject of the High Porte, his own house.

No. 70. Moise sin Iancu Belcescu, brandy maker, subject of the High Porte, lives with rent in his father's house.

No. 71. Iancu sin Nisim Belcescu, brandy maker, subject of the High Porte, his own house.

No. 72. Avram sin Calman, no business, helpless old man, disabled.

No. 73. Solomon Tacsieru, brandy maker and grocer, subject of the High Porte, his own house.

No. 74. Froim sin Marcu, brandy maker, subject of the High Porte, lives with rent at widow from Roman.

No. 75. Mendel sin Avram, brandy maker, subject of the High Porte, from Sinesti, lives in the same place.

No. 76. Sulim sin …, brandy maker, subject of the High Porte, lives with rent at Itic from Roman.

No. 77. Calman Ber sin Moisa, brandy maker, subject of the High Porte, from Sinesti, his own house.

No. 78. Itic sin Leiba Moscu, brandy maker, subject of the High Porte, his own house.

No. 82. Marcu sin Leiba, brandy maker, subject of the High Porte, lives with rent at Trofin.

No. 83. Itic sin Moisa, brandy maker, subject of the High Porte, his own house.

No. 84. Zamvel sin Bercu, also a subject of the High Porte.

No. 85. Itic sin Haim Fisel, the same, from Sulita, lives with rent at butcher Marcu.

No. 86. Iancu sin Calman, joiner, subject of the High Porte, from Popesti, his own house.

No. 87. Moisa sin Iancu Calman, brandy maker, subject of the High Porte, his own house.

No. 88. Fisel sin Iancu, no business, helpless old man.

No. 89. Aba Labu named Zeilic, cattle trading, subject of the High Porte, from Zahorna, lives with rent at Fisel's daughter.

No. 90. Lupu sin Strule, also named Padurariul [B-50], flour seller, subject of the High Porte, has his own house.

No. 95. Zeilic sin Iancu, sells wine and brandy, subject of the High Porte, from Harpagesti, lives with rent.

No. 96. Avram sin Aizic, no business, subject of the High Porte, lives with rent at Luca Barnovi.
Solomon sin Leiba, no business, subject of the High Porte, lives with rent at Stefan the widow's son.

No. 98. Isac sin Avram, no business, helpless old man, lives in Balcani.

No. 99. Meer sin Fisil, teacher, subject of the High Porte, from Iasi, has his own house.

No. 101. Ili sin Avram, … and cotton seller, subject of the High Porte, from Iasi.

No. 103. Zisu sin Iosap, procession candle carrier, subject of the High Porte, from Erghiceni village.

No. 104. Danila sin Avram, … and things of small value, subject of the High Porte, lives with rent at Izdrail.

No. 106. Leiba Zaraf, brandy maker, subject of the High Porte, his own shop.

No. 107. Strul Avram sin Iosup, also a subject of the High Porte, from Sulita, lives with rent in the house of the widow from Piatra.

No. 108. Herscu sin Moisa Barbalata, also a subject of the High Porte, from Darajeni.

No. 109. Romascanita the widow.

No. 110. Mendel Surdu, no business, helpless old man, from Malaesti, has one crippled arm and is deaf.

No. 111. Haim Herscu sin Moisa, brandy maker, subject of the High Porte, his own shop.

No. 112. Iancu sin Leibu, silver lines metallic objects, subject of the High Porte, from Esi, lives with rent at widow Haita.
Widow Haita, husband left her.

No. 113. Iancu a Muchioaiei sin Marcu, brandy maker, subject of the High Porte, has his own house.

No. 114. Haniel sin Aron, Iancu's nephew, also a subject of the High Porte, lives with rent.

No. 115. Aron David sin Haim, also a subject of the High Porte, from Bulbucani, lives with rent in Lipova.

---

[50] [Ed-Com] Padurariul: Romanian for forester.

No. 116. Pascal sin Bentin, cattle trading business, subject of the High Porte, from Esi, lives with rent at the Russian.

No. 117. Moscu sin Mendel, brandy and wine maker, subject of the High Porte.

No. 120. Sender sin Irimia Croitoriu, tailor, subject of the High Porte, has his own house.
Smerl sin Rivel, fur cap maker, subject of the High Porte, lives with his father-in-law.

No. 122. Marcu sin Iancu, tailor, subject of the High Porte, his own house.
Aron sin Mendel, also a subject of the High Porte, lives in the house of Marcu sin Iancu.

No. 123. Moisa sin Pascal, shoemaker, subject of the High Porte, his own house, from Esi.

No. 124. Smil Leiba, janitor of the synagogue, janitor of the school, subject of the High Porte, from Esi.

No. 125. Avram sin Nisim, tailor, subject of the High Porte, from Esi.

No. 126. Avram sin Itic, no business, helpless old man, his right arm is crippled.

No. 127. Altar sin Strule, leader of the Jews, subject of the High Porte, has his own house.

No. 128. Malca the widow.

No. 129. Avram sin Copil, butcher, subject of the High Porte, from Esi, lives with rent.

No. 130. Iosap sin Leiba, barber, subject of the High Porte, his own house.

No. 131. Itic sin Bercu, teacher, subject of the High Porte, from Esi.

No. 132. Strule sin Iosap Chetrariu, tailor, subject of the High Porte, his own house.

No. 133. Strule sin Toderos, teacher, subject of the High Porte.

No. 134. Altar sin Meer, owns an alcohol-making machine, subject of the High Porte, lives with rent at Sruli.

No. 135. Simon sin Lupu, teacher, subject of the High Porte, his own house.

No. 136. Itic Zamvel sin Solomon, tailor, subject of the High Porte.

No. 137. Ilie's widow Haia.

No. 138. Avram sin Dascal, no business, subject of the High Porte, infirm and deaf old man.

No. 139. David sin Solomon, tailor, subject of the High Porte, his own house.

No. 140. Hoisie sin Leiba Dascal, teacher, subject of the High Porte.

No. 141. Buium sin Simon, water carrier, subject of the High Porte.

No. 142. Smil sin Iodos, no profession, old and blind.

No. 145. Osap Chetrariu, the same, old.

No. 147. Bercu sin Avram, bald and vicious old man, so nobody hires him.

No. 148. Iosap sin Iosap, shoemaker, subject of the High Porte.

No. 149. Ilie Croitoriu's widow Golda.

No. 150. Strule sin Mihailovici, wagoner, subject of the High Porte, lives in Tanase's house.
Leiba sin Simon, no business, old and insane.

No. 163. Lupu sin Haim, also old, infirm.

No. 172. Herscu sin Bercu, old tailor, insane.
Leiba a Iarmuchioaiei, trades things of small value, subject of the High Porte, his own little house.

No. 180. Meer sin Iancu, brandy maker, subject of the High Porte, from Albesti, lives with rent.

No. 190. Usar Iancu sin Smil, tailor, subject of the High Porte, lives with rent at Vornic Ioan.

No. 195. Rafail sin Usar, bar owner, subject of the High Porte, from Mircesti, lives with rent.

No. 196. Herscu sin Iancu, tailor, subject of the High Porte, has his own house.

No. 228. Moisa sin David, no business, old and sick.

No. 229. Lupu sin Smil Herscu, wagoner, has his own house.
Solomon sin Smil, brandy maker, subject of the High Porte, from Romanesti.
Aron Iancu, brandy maker, subject of the High Porte, from Bogoila, no house.
A. Ilie, bar owner, also a subject of the High Porte, from Basceaus, no house.
Strule sin David, no business, old.
Strule sin Iancu, no business, old, crippled leg.

In all, 121 inhabitants are subjects of the High Porte, 23 are elders, and seven are widows. (Jewish signatures: Lazar from Iasi, Zelic sin Haim, Simha from Tirgu Frumos, tax collector, Moisa Birlescu, Iancu Leib, Leib Ghitman.)

(After this, there is a sum of those who figured in the census): 68 tax-paying Jews were mentioned in the settlement act, of whom 47 were third-class merchants, six were third-class craftsmen, and 15 were elders. Four were dead, four moved to Jerusalem, Codresti, Bucharest, or Focsani, eight went nobody knows where, and 10 are listed as helpless.

The Jews from the Borough Podu Iloaiei Living On His Excellency Mayor Neculai Cantacuzino's Estate (61816). (All locals except those indicated as Sudits.) [B-51]

1) Herscu sin Iancu, horse seller, his own house.
   Meer from Larga, brandy maker, came from Larga.
2) Zambel sin Nuhim, soles maker, his own shop.
3) Lupu Lipscanu.
4) Altar sin Strule, brandy maker.
5) Mendel sin Strule, brandy maker.
6) Leiba sin Ida, tobacco seller, lives at Alter.
7) Smil Raizic, merchant, his own house.
8) Moisa sin Aron, merchant, lives with rent.
9) Ghersin sin Nuham, merchant, lives with rent.
10) Heilek sin Naftule, merchant, his own house.
11) Solomon sin Marcu, merchant, his own house.
12) Malca Reiza, widow.
13) Aron sin Lupu, brandy maker, came from Esi, his own house.
14) Leiba Grosul, also named Godal, brandy maker, his own house.
15) Heim sin Oizer, brandy maker, came from Zahorna.
16) Smil Itic sin Lupu, brandy maker.
17) Pinhas sin Iancu, brandy maker.
18) Moisa Haim sin David, brandy maker.
19) Leiba Sfart, brandy maker, from Boidinesti, his own house.
    Haim sin Itic, soles maker, lives with Sfart.
20) Itic sin Danila, brandy maker, from Tirgu Frumos, lives with rent.
21) Nuham sin Gersin, brandy maker, his own house.
22) Froim sin Ioise, brandy maker, rented house.
23) Leiba sin Herscu, brandy maker; he also lives with rent at Moise Bercescu.
24) Zamvel sin Marcu, brandy maker, his own house.
25) Strule sin Sulin, glass seller.
26) Ilie sin Nusam, merchant, trades cattle.
27) Faibis sin Marcu Froim, no business, old.
28) Iancu sin Smil, huckster, from Esi, lives with rent.
30) Itic sin Moisa, teacher, his own house.
31) Haim sin Iosap, shochet, lives with rent.
32) Simon Casap, butcher, his own house.
34) Mendel sin Leiba, brandy maker, lives with rent.
51) Leizer sin Solomon, brandy maker, his own house.
52) Mehal Obrejan, brandy maker, from Obresti, his own house.
53) Zeilic zet Faibis[B-52], brandy maker, lives with rent.
54) Iosap sin Herscu, brandy maker, from Lungani.
55) Avram sin Leiba, …, lives with rent.

---

[51] [KME] In Kara's book the entries go from 1 to 98, however for some unknown reason there are a lot of gaps. Perhaps they were missing from the source documents or they could not be deciphered. The following entries are missing: 29, 33, 35-50, 57-59, 64-65, 69-72, 86-88, 91-94

[52] [Ed-Com] Zet is the letter "Z" in Romanian. Its meaning in entries 53 and 56 is unknown.

56) Saia Leiba sin Iosap, no business, old, both legs crippled.
Herscu sin Strule, zet Iosap, brandy maker, his own house.
60) Moisa Iancu, brandy maker, lives with rent.
61) Iosap sin Itic, the same, from ?iganesti, lives with rent.
62) Herscu sin Avram, brandy maker, came from Hoisesti.
63) Leibu Itic sin Bercu, brandy maker, from Butuliac.
66) Mihail sin Iosap, sieve man, from Esi.
67) Marcu sin David, fur cap maker, from Lazareni.
68) David sin Mer, brandy maker, from Hanaseni, his own house.
73) Haim Sulim sin Iosap, brandy maker, lives with rent at Timofte, the winter coat maker.
74) Haim sin Marcu, brandy maker, from Popesti, his own house.
75) Iosap sin Smil, fur cap maker, his own house.
76) Strule sin Marcu Iosap, wagoner, lives with rent at Avram Leiba.
77) Ester the widow.
78) Herscu Croitoriu, tailor, lives with rent.
79) Izdrail sin Moisa, trades cattle, from Zahorna.
80) Mendel sin Solomon, huckster, from Sculeni.
81) Huna sin Rubin, butcher, from Tirgu Frumos.
82) Ilie Cusmariu, fur cap maker, from Tirgu Frumos.
83) Avram sin Iosap, joiner, bachelor, lives with rent at Leiba Zaraf.
84) Hescu sin Itic Saper, trades cattle, his own house.
85) Malca, widow.
89) Solomon Aparu, no business, old, sick, poor.
90) Moisa sin Mendel, teacher, old, poor, likes his condition.
95) Haim sin Herscu Lupu, brandy maker, lives with rent.
96) Leiba sin Itic, brandy maker, his own house.
97) Itic sin Haimovici, baker, from Esi.
98) Sosia Vadana.
Rahmil Leibu, horse seller, lives where he can.

(Total: 63 locals, five helpless elders, and four widows. Signed by the same persons: Leib Ghitman, Eliezer from Esi, Zeilic sin Haim, Simcha from Tirgu Frumos, tax collector, Iaakov from Tirgu Frumos, Moisa Barlescu, and Iaacov Leib). "29 Jews were mentioned in the settlement act: seven merchants of the third category, three craftsmen of the third category, one apprentice, and six tribute-payers. Subtract: three deceased, two moved to Esi and Tirgu Frumos, and three left for nobody knows where. Add: 12 married people, 27 who came from other places, and the inhabitants who were listed in the census for 1838" (A total of 70 Jews).

16.15 *Appendix O: A Complaint by the Community, 1844*

I.S.A., tr. 1772, op. 2020, dos. 3705, f. 15, May 24, 1844.

To the honorable Department of Internal Affairs, the community of Christian and Jewish inhabitants of the borough Podu Iloaiei complains.

It has been brought to the attention of the Honorable Department the unbearable consequences of Captain Tudorache Radovici's acts, who, living in this town, has so many times as a commissar brought us much misery. So now, in secret … so as the named commissar was appointed. As in all humble subjects, we pray for mercy and for getting rid of this pest, so that another one can be appointed, whoever may be found appropriate, except for the one mentioned above. For we are confident that one will find enough information by consulting the archives with the former commissars who brought us much trouble and misery.

(Signed: Tanase baker, Constandin Munteanu, Gligore community leader, Toma Popa, Timofte Cojocaru, Ion Svat…, Vasile Bucur, Vasile Velciu, Lazar sin Sasului, Constantin Bodescu, Gheorghe sin Nedelcu, Ion Ungurianul, Nica Ceausul, Gheorghe al lui [B-53] Iacob, Ion Bejanu, Ion Recleanu, Andrei Morariul, Costachi a Mosneagului, Ion a lui Iacob, Toader Raileanu, Lazar Micu, Vasile Carlateanu, Vasile d… Ion Cosiganul, Petre a Stalei, Gheorghe's nephew from Toma, Vartolomeu Costache, street lighting attendent, Axinte Ciobanu, Grigore Muntianu, Toma a… Gheorghe Ciubotar, Gheorghe Melencus, Vasile Tincu.

(Jewish signatures: Mose Sfarlester, Iaacov from Tirgu Frumos, Iehuda Leib, Faibis ben m… Pesach Barad, David Coda…, Israel ben Ancel, Mordechai…, Simcha from Tirgu Frumos, David ben Avraham, Ancel Iehuda ben Israel, Haim Tvi ben Mose, Tvi from Botosani, Daniel ben Iosef, Avraham ben Iehuda, Nachum ben Pesach, Eliezer Efraim, Mose Itchac, Mordechai Itchac, Mordehai ben Avraham, Dob ben Israel, Efraim from Tirgu Frumos, Itchac Leib ben Mose, Alter ben Meir, Salom Iaacov from Tirgu Frumos, Henich ben Froim Itchac, Zisu Hellir, Azriel ben Iosif from Tirgu Frumos, Iosif ben Dov from Roman, Menase from Totoesti, Tvi ben Iaacov, Lectel ben Iaacov, Iaacov Leib, Rachmiel Leib, Iechiel Michel ben Pesach Nisan, Dov ben Israel, Natan Avraham ben Israel).

[53] [Ed-Com] Al lui: Romanian for "son of".

16.16 ***Appendix P: Census, 1898***

I.S.A., Fond Iasi District Administration, No. 71, 1898

1898 Census of the Jewish Population Living in Podu Iloaiei

Note from KME ... The census appearing in Kara's book is a list of 722 Jewish households, showing the following information: Record#, Head of Family, Age, Occupation, How long in Podu Iloaiei, Spouse's Name & Age, and #of Children. It is not being reproduced in this edition because it is already available as part of the JewishGen Romania Database at

http://www.jewishgen.org/databases/Romania/PoduIloaieiCensus1898.htm.

Here is the first page as it appears in the book.

120

TABLOU

de străinii stabiliți definitiv în comuna tîrg Podu Iloaiei, plasa Bahlui, județul Iași

Nr. crt.	Capul de familie	Etatea sa	Meseria	De cînd este în comună	Numele soției	Etatea ei	Copiii	Observații
1	2	3	4	5	6	7	8	9
1	Mendel Ilie	34 ani	muncitor	6 ani	Toba Ilie	33 ani	5 copii	văduvă
2	Sura Ilie	56 ani	—	6 ani	—	—	—	
3	Bercu Solomon	49 ani	muncitor	20 ani	Dvoira S.	46 ani	4 copii	văduvă
4	Beila Şmil Lupu	41 ani	—	5 ani	—	—	7 copii	—
5	Avram Moscovici	38 ani	comerciant	15 ani	Rica	33 ani	1 copil	—
6	Vigder Goldinştain	39 ani	fierar	16 ani	Haia	33 ani	5 copii	—
7	Simon Iţic	31 ani	fierar	născut P.I.	—	—	—	—
8	Seindle Solomon	28 ani	—	născut P.I.	—	—	2 copii	—
9	Toba Litman	54 ani	moaşă	5 ani	—	—	—	—
10	Haiasîn Nuhăm	38 ani	croitoreasă	născut P.I.	—	—	—	—
11	Solomon sîn Moise	67 ani	precupeţ	născut P.I.	—	47 ani	5 copii	necăsătorit
12	Moise sîn M. Solomon	23 ani	muncitor	născut P.I.	—	—	—	necăsătorit
13	Michel Solomon	21 ani	muncitor	—	—	—	—	—
14	Chitla Altăr	31 ani	—	—	—	—	1 copil	—
15	Copel sîn Moise	48 ani	comerciant	5 ani	Haia Chitla	45 ani	3 copii	necăsătorit
16	Bercu sîn Moise	23 ani	precupeţ	5 ani	—	—	—	necăsătorită
17	Estera sîn Moise	21 ani	—	5 ani	—	—	—	—
18	Şmil M. Roşu	38 ani	comerciant	născut P.I.	Haia Roiza	36 ani	3 copii	necăsătorit
19	Marcu Strulovici	24 ani	comerciant	6 ani	—	—	—	—
20	Iosub M. Totoescu	46 ani	comerciant	născut P.I.	Tipra	41 ani	8 copii	văduv,
21	Herşcu Şor	68 ani	comerciant	născut P.I.	—	—	—	supus rus
22	Rifca sîn Avram	56 ani	—	2 ani	—			necăsătorită
23	Frima sîn Avram	56 ani	—	născută P.I.	—	—	—	necăsătorită
24	Alter Herşcu	58 ani	comerciant	—	Şura	54 ani	—	—

16.17 *Appendix R: The Statute of Podu Iloae, 1925*

Romania. The Jewish community of Podul Iloae.

The STATUTE of the Jewish community of Podul Iloae voted on by the General Assembly on May 3, 1925. Iasi, A. Grinberg Publishing House, 9 Unirei Street, 1925.

By the record no. 33037 from October 16, 1925, released by the court clerk's office at the Iasi Court of Justice, s. I, this community is granted the status of legal entity (no. 62/1925). The report of the General Assembly, which had Mr. Virgil Popovici, administrator of the Bahlui district, and Mr. C. Balan, president of the ad-interim commission of the commune, as its honorary presidents, and Mr. Michel Sanielevici as its full president and Mr. Iancu Horodniceanu as its secretary, describes the discussions and the voting of the statute.

Chapter I. The Community's Goals.

Article 1. All Jews living in Podul Iloae make up the Community of the Jewish Cult of Podul Iloae. The existence of this community dates from before the year 1823, and this statute reorganizes this community as modern times demand it.

Article 2. The name of the Community of the Jewish Cult of Podul Iloae can never and under no circumstances be changed.

Article 3. The missions of the Community are:

A. To take care of its clergy and to supervise through its commissions the practice of the Mosaic cult;
B. To take care of the institutions that are designed to educate the masses: the boys and girls primary schools, the professional schools, the kindergardens, the courses for adults, etc;
C. The maintenance and administration of the social assistance institutions, the public bath, the school's cafeteria, the asylum for the aged and disabled, the medical unit, and any other charitable institutions that are eventually established;
D. To administrate the holy establishments and the maintenance of the cemeteries.

Chapter II. The Organization of the Community.

Article 4. The community will be presided over and administered by a committee named the Guardianship of the Community and made up of 13 members elected by universal, equal, and direct vote. This committee will have four sections: a) the administrative section; b) the section for religion; c) the cultural section; and d) the section for public assistance and the holy establishments. Each section will have its own special set of regulations, according to the present statute.

Article 5. Three gentlemen will be in charge of each section. All sections put together form the Guardianship of the Community. The president of the administrative section is also the president of the guardianship, while the presidents of the other sections will be the vice presidents of the guardianship. The guardianship will have a cashier, a supervisor, and a secretary who will also be enrolled in the administrative section. The secretary accountant of the guardianship, as well as any other clerks to be employed when the circumstances demand it will be hired and paid only by the guardianship.

Article 6. The sections work autonomously, but in exceptional cases as well as at the times stipulated by the statute, when the reports will be presented, the general assembly of the guardianship would be called upon.

Article 7. The specific tasks of each section will be established by special regulations.

Chapter III. Revenues.

Article 8. Every member of the community, meaning every Jew who lives in Podul-Iloaei, has the duty to contribute either directly or indirectly in the form of the tax on kosher meat or the tax on the slaughtering of poultry. Those members of the community who do not subscribe to the paying of the tax will have to bring their direct contribution depending on the number of the members of their families and on their wealth. The taxpayers will be registered in a special record, will receive a community member card, and will enjoy all the rights conferred to them by this status.

Article 9. The community also has the following alternate sources of income: a) the statistics taxes on births, weddings, and deaths, other certificates, etc. The members of the community have the duty to inform the statistics section of any change that has occurred in their families; b) taxes on burials and gravestones, which will be differentiated into several classes according to the special regulation of the section that administers the holy establishments; c) the money from the making of the Passover matzoh, from the public bath, the school, the tax money on the kosher meat (a special regulation will establish the way of imposing this tax); d) the proceeds of money deposited in banks or other institutions for the benefit of the community, as well as the revenues from donated properties or from properties that will be donated to the community and from the personal or real estate purchased by the community; e) donations or voluntary gifts, as well as profits from the charity balls and from theatrical performances or cinema shows; f) in case the revenues do not cover the expenses required for the community's basic needs, the members of the community will have to accept a temporary tax that will depend on the needs at that time. In case of a surplus, the taxes on kosher meat and poultry slaughtering can be reduced.

Chapter IV. The Election of the Community's Guardians.

Article 10. All the Jewish inhabitants of Podul-Iloaiei, who are also contributors to the community's budget and own the membership card stipulated in Article 8, have the right and the duty to take part in the election of the community's guardians by direct, equal, and secret vote.

Article 11. In order for someone to be elected it is requested, besides the conditions that make him an elector, that he not have been blamed with a discreditable punishment and that he must have his payments to the community up to date.

Article 12. The elections will be based on lists containing the names of 13 candidates. Any Jewish organization, synagogue, or other ad-hoc formed group with at least 25 members is allowed to present its own list of candidates. The payment for the publishing of the list will also be presented. One candidate may appear on more than one list, but the endorsers of one list cannot guarantee a different one.

Article 13. The Guardianship of the Community is elected for a three-year term.

Article 14. The announcement for the gathering of the community for the new elections will be made 30 days before the term of the previous committee expires. During these 30 days, a special bureau will be in charge and will release the elector's cards free of charge. During this period of time, new electors will be included in the electors' record from among the persons who haven't been included by then, if, of course, they fulfill the conditions stipulated by Article 10. Also, this bureau will register the candidates' lists. These lists will each bear a distinctive sign, the candidates' names will be written both in Romanian and Hebrew and each will have a number. All the lists will be put on a single list in the order of their presentation at the bureau. Five days before the elections, the candidates' lists will be considered irrevocable and will be made public.

Article 15. The voting is done by applying the stamp "VOTED" on the distinctive sign, which means that the whole list was voted for as such. Candidates from several lists can be voted for by erasing with a pencil the names of those not voted for. Under no circumstances can more than 13 gentlemen be voted for.

Article 16. The voting is valid no matter the number of voters who show up to vote between eight in the morning and six in the evening during one day.

Article 17. The electoral bureau, which will be formed by two representatives from each synagogue and by one delegate from the commune who will be invited in due time by the previous committee, will manage the elections. The elections require a relative majority.

Article 18. The results of the election will be mentioned in a report signed by the delegate and the electoral bureau. This result will be communicated to the honorable mayor and to the public the next day. If, after five days, no legal appeal is made, the elected guardians are considered in function and the previous committee has the obligation to hand in the financial administration and the community's wealth during the next eight days.

Article 19. The cash belonging to the community, which is at the time kept by the former cashier or by other persons, has to be handed in to the new committee's cashier, unless it was deposited in a bank within 60 days of the elections. The newly elected guardians will take a vow before receiving their prerogatives in the presence of the community's rabbi and the delegate of the communal authority.

Chapter V. Sanctions.

Article 20. Any Jew who has lived in Podul Iloaiei for at least one year and refuses to obey the present statute, either not willing to contribute materially or commits infringements like refusing to hand in possessions or documents belonging to the community to its guardianship or encourages certain persons who do not have the necessary authorization or to whom this authorization has been declined to enroll in certain Jewish community functions, will be erased from the record of the community's members and will not be able to make use of, not even for a fee, any of the community's institutions, any assistance from the community's sections being denied until the issue is resolved.

Article 21. In those cases where the property or the documents of the community are being retained, the possibility remains to appeal to the enforcement of the penal code.

Article 22. The bureau of the administrative section will keep a special record of the persons who refuse to contribute to the community's budget, and their names will be made public at the end of each month.

Chapter VI. General Dispositions.

Article 23. Any contracts signed by the guardianship of the community remain valid and have to be considered by the next guardianship.

Article 24. The places that may become vacant in the guardianship, following death, resignation, or expulsion, will be given to those candidates who won the largest number of votes.

Article 25. In case the guardianship is dissolved or its majority is incomplete without the possibility of restoration as stipulated by Article 24, then, in order to avoid disturbances within the community, the remaining guardians have the duty to form an ad-interim commission made up of members of the Jewish community who will organize the election of the guardians in no more than 60 days.

Article 26. All the financial documents, receipts, confirmation of receipts, and money orders will have the president's signature or by special appointment the signature of the vice president of the administrative section.

Article 27. The community, as the rightful owner of all community properties, even if they apparently belong to private persons, will do all that is necessary and fulfill all the legal forms to obtain the full right of property over them.

Article 28. No religious function that requires a special qualification like a wedding service, religious divorce, religious assistance in the pursuit of justice if needed, the religious service, the ritual slaughtering of animals, the making of circumcisions, or the funeral service will be held in the area of this community by persons other than those employed by the guardianship of the community in accord with the contract they will agree upon. Any service that this article refers to that is performed by employees of the guardianship of the community whose contract has expired or by foreigners will be considered usurpation and they will be prosecuted in accordance with the country's laws. The guardianship has the right to temporarily authorize other persons who are not the employees of the guardianship, from other towns or from this commune, to perform the religious services mentioned above, in which case a written authorization from the guardianship is absolutely necessary. The guardianship reserves the right to revoke a given authorization. Any disputes on payments for the religious services that may arise between the parishioners and our employees will be resolved by the guardianship of the community.

Article 29. The regulations for each of the sections will be drawn up by the sections themselves and voted on by the guardianship of the community.

Article 30. Any statute or regulation previous to the present statute is and remains annulled.

Article 31. Changes to this statute or its entire modification cannot be done unless there is a motivated request from two thirds of the members of the community.

Article 32. The present leading committee that was functioning when the work on this statute began will continue to exercise its functions until the termination of the two-year term for which it has been elected; then it will proceed according to the dispositions stipulated by articles 10, 11, 12, and 13, and the following ones.

This statute was voted unanimously and the leading committee, especially Mr. President Michel Sanilovici and Secretary I. Horodniceanu, were given full authority to obtain the legalization of the statute and the recognition of the quality of legal and moral entity for our community. Thus, we have signed it.

Leading committee: President M. Sanilovici, Vice-president M. I. Schor, Cashier I. Schneer, and Secretary I. Horodniceanu. Members: Avram Solomon, Moise Solomon, Anciu S. Anciu, Moise Goldenberg, Haim sin Haim, Lupu Leibovici, Marcu Iosipovici, Lipa D. Maizner, Iechil Blumenfeld, and Moise Hachman.

(A booklet of 16 pages, format 32)

16.18 *Appendix S: Schools, 1904*

The Newspaper Evenimentul (The Event), Iasi, November 17, 1904, page 3.

The school under-inspector I. Petrov found several (Jewish) confessional schools in Podu Iloaiei that had no authorization. He wants them closed. They are located at Strul Veinberg's (Srul der poliser) on Lapusneanu St., Beris Dascalu's on Vanatorilor St., Iaic Dascalu's on Naaionala St., and Sami Frenkel's on Scob'laeni St.

16.19 *Appendix T: Schools, 1914*

The Newspaper *Egalitatea (The Equality)*, Year XXV, No. 30, May 23, 1914.

"The Laying of the Foundation Stone for the Jewish-Romanian school in Podul Iloaiei"

On May 11, 1914, this ceremony took place in the presence of a large audience. The following persons gave speeches: Sch. Steinberg, president of the community; Rabbi Dr. Thenen; Moritz Wachtel who praised the initiative and condemned the path of hatred; Petre Comarnescu, student and member of the Student's Society of Iasi, criticized the poor condition of the Jews living in the country; Aron Rosenthal, speaking in Hebrew on behalf of the local Zionist group, demanded a greater development of the Hebrew language; Ghizela Wechsler, former president of the committee that managed the building of the school, thanked all the donors; Adolf Magder related the hardships they had struggled with to obtain the necessary funds for the building of the school. Among the other people who spoke were Dr. Vittner, the physician at the communal hospital, institutor Dumitru from Iasi, Mozes Duff, and school inspector Ionescu who held the closing speech, praised the teaching staff and expressed his wish for a closer cooperation between the country's elements for its own well-being. Afterward, the founding document of the school was signed and built in the foundation of the school).

17 At The Turn of the Century. Several Compulsory Additions.

After completing the final draft of this monograph, I came across some sources that offer additional perspectives on the life of the Jewish community of Podu Iloaiei at the turn of the 19th century and into the 20th.

The peasants' uprisings in 1888 and those in the following years, as well as the economic crisis at the end of the 19th century, had even worse effects on the Jewish population due to a series of laws and administrative dispositions that were applied abusively and excessively. This was the case in 1897 when the mayor of the commune of Podu Iloaiei forced the community to pay from its budget the wages of 10 "daytime guardians" who were supposed to protect the interests of all the town's inhabitants. A sum of 450 lei was to be paid from the money collected from the taxes on kosher meat. This affected especially the population with modest revenues—the craftsmen, the workers, and the small merchants. The president of the community, Zeida Rosenberg, resigned because he could no longer pay the rabbi, the four shochets, some of the teachers, and the physician, and it was the same with the payments for social assistance and for his office. On the other hand, the guards, although paid, could not stop the frequent thefts that were taking place in the commune (see the newspaper *Opinia* of Iasi from July 27, 1897).

The abuses of the communal counsel continued in the following years. The Jews protested, though they did not ask for the dissolution of this local institution (see the newspaper *Evenimentul* of Iasi from July 18, 1900 "The Event of Iasi").

Despite the precarious economic situation, which worsened during the years 1898 to 1900, charitable acts were initiated by the Jews who felt united with their coreligionists who were in great need, as happened with the calamity victims in Stefanesti in the Botosani district (see *Opinia*, July 6, 1897).

One of the mayor's abuses was the order to close down the 25-year-old brick factory owned by the Jew Avram, while allowing others nearby to continue to function (see Iasi State Archives, the Prefecture's fund, record 87, 1896, page 13).

The situation caused some of the town's Jews to take part in the well known "on-foot emigration" in 1900. *Evenimentul* on April 30, 1900 writes that 100 of the townspeople are preparing to immigrate to America. After some time, we learn that their number grew to 400. This emigration trend continued during the following years. The paper *Evenimentul* on July 25, 1901 writes on page 3: "A delegate of the Jews named Sraier living in Podu Iloae arrived in town yesterday and pleaded to Mr. Auerbach (the representative of the I.C.A. in Paris—I.K.) the cause of a certain number of craftsmen from this small town who want to emigrate, especially the women who were left alone after last year's wave of emigrations. Mr. Auerbach promised to visit Podu Iloae in the weeks to come."

New hardships appeared after the promulgation of the Public Education Law in 1893, according to which the children of "aliens" will be received in limited numbers at schools, having to pay taxes, which was one more burden on most of the Jews' already slim budget. Striving to know the country's language better and become familiar with the elements of modern culture, the Jews had to build their own school. The initiative was taken in 1899 and became a reality in 1902.

In the meantime, the borough was developing. A public park was opened and town-planning projects were designed with the hope of obtaining the title of town (1903). The townspeople read Romanian papers; the distributor was L. Fruchtman in 1897. From among the hundreds of Jewish families, only six were considered "rightful," having civil and some political rights. They voted in the communal elections in 1902.

At the end of the century, the community's life becomes more diverse, moving beyond the strict framework of synagogues and, rarely, some charity society. The interest generated by the movement "Hoveve Sion" that started in the 1880s led to the opening of a local branch in 1881 that sent Saie Steinberg as its delegate to the congress in Galati in 1894. There, he presented an activity report. Upon his return, the society's activity was reorganized (see the supplement to the Yiddish paper *Folksblat* from January 12, 1895, page 2).

The society's activity continued with interruptions probably caused by internal rivalries. In 1901, the society Carmel reopened, led by Ghersen Cohn, who previously had edited a temporary Yiddish newspaper in Iasi with I. Finchelman and the student M. Sraier (see *Evenimentul*, May 5, 1902, page 3). In the same year, at the Zionist congress, the delegates were Michel Sor (who became the mayor's helper in 1923) and Iosef Rosental (who later became a Hebrew teacher). Also that year, the Zionist society Macabei was established, led by Iosef Solomon and Asbert Spaier (see *Evenimentul*, April 30, 1902). In the same year, the society Dr. Herzl's Youth opened, led by Elias Reisch and Vigder Iosupovici; it included a reading group with 40 members. Delegates from other towns represented this society and the Carmel society at the congress.

The following people gave a speech at that year's Hanukkah holiday: H. Meirovici, Spirt the medical undergraduate, and the teacher I. Rosental. The children recited and sang in Hebrew as well. More or less, these societies were active until 1916, owning a library of 1,000 books written in Romanian and Yiddish. Actually, between 1900 and 1916, there was a marked process of modernization of the community's life. A notable fact: The attention paid by the newspapers in Iasi, *Evenimentul* and later *Opinia*, to the events that concerned the Jewish community shows that these papers had an important number of Jewish readers and subscribers who had to be taken into consideration. Subsequently, around 1907, both papers not only stopped publishing any news about Jewish life, but also adopted an anti-Semitic attitude. The Jewish readers changed their preferences to the democratic papers *Dimineata* (The Morning) and *Adevarul* (The Truth). These papers had many readers before the Balkan war. The paper *Infratirea* (The Brotherhood) of the Local Jews Union also had many readers and, of course, so did other Jewish magazines and papers that appeared in Romanian or Yiddish. Some subscribed to the Hebrew press from abroad and read Modern Hebrew literature. Yiddish books, some written by second-hand authors and others by famous authors like Shalom Aleichem, I. L. Perea, Morris Rosenfeld, were much appreciated. Romanian books that appeared in the collections *Everybody's Library*, *Minerva*, and *Astra* were very popular since, due to the existence of the Jewish-Romanian primary school, all the young people were able to read and write in the country's language, although Yiddish was mostly resorted to in private.

Public lectures were held both in Romanian and Yiddish.

Overall, the social and cultural life of the town was very tumultuous and fruitful, much more than would be expected from an "insignificant Moldavian shtetl."

18 I. Kara: History Studies. Selected Bibliography.

Since 1938, I. Kara (Itic Svart) published over 100 studies and history papers of variable value and extent written in Yiddish (Y), Romanian (R), English (E), Ivrit (Iv), Spanish (S), and German (G).

This bibliography includes the most important of them in regard to their conception, synthetic structuring, and the new data they reveal. All of the following titles are listed in English.

Volume or Brochure Studies

1. Itic Svart. *Centuries Old Testimonies*. Bacau, 1947. (R)
2. Itic Svart. *30 Years of Yiddish Literature in Romania*. Iasi, 1947. (Y)
3. I.Kara et al. *From the Principalities' Union to the Romanian Independence War*. Iasi, 1977. (R)
4. I.Kara. *A Boy from Moldova*. Bucharest: Kriterion, 1976. (Y)
5. I.Kara. *The Young and ... the Less Young Years*. Bucharest: Kriterion, 1980. (Y)

Published in Magazines and Anthologies

1. Itic Svart. "The Record of the Funeral Fraternity of Vijnita." 1768. In *Yivo-Bleter*, Vilna, vol. 14, no. 5, September 1938, p. 125-135. (Y)
2. A.Steinhard (pseudonym). "Contributions to the History and Literature of the On Foot Emigrants of Romania. 1900." In *Yivo-Bleter*, New York, vol. 30, 1951, p. 294-298. (Y)
3. A.Lachover (pseudonym). "The Jews and the 1848 Romanian Revolution." Idem, vol. 51, 1951, p. 363-364. (Y)
4. A.Lachover. "Funeral Fraternities in 18th and 19th Century Moldova." In *Yive-Annual*, vol. 10, 1955, p. 300-319. (E)
5. I.Kara (Itic Svart). "New Data Regarding the History of the Yiddish Theater in Romania." In *Bleter far geszichte*, Warsaw, vol. 10, no. 1-2, 1957, p. 93-107. (Y)
6. I.Kara. "Feudal Institutions of the Jewish Population of Romania." Idem, vol. 12, 1960, p. 153-168. (Y)
7. I.Kara. "Jewish Manufacturers' Guilds in Romania." Idem. vol. 4, 1961, p. 138-145. (Y)
   Since 1957, all his works were signed with the pseudonym I. Kara.
8. "Hassidism, Rabbinism, Illuminism in Romania." In *Yiddische Kultur*, New York, no. 7 (p. 17-22), no. 8 (p. 44-50), no. 9 (p. 49-52), 1964. (Y)
9. "The Jewish Guild and its Masters." In *The Mosaic Cult Review*, no. 19, 1965. (R)

10. "25 Years of Yiddish Culture in Romania." In *Ykuf Almanach*, New York, 1961, p. 164-177 (Y)
11. "Pages from the History of the Denominational Education in Romania." In *MCR*, no. 165 (1967) and no. 288 (1971). (R)
12. "Fragments from Gh. Asachi's Publishing Activity." In *The Metropolitan of Moldova*, no. 3-4, 1968, p. 229-231. (R)
13. "An Unknown Portrait of Mihai the Brave" In *The Chronicle*, Iasi, February 18, 1967, p. 10. (R)
14. "Pages from the History of Jewish Publishing in Romania." In *RCM*, no. 195 (1968), no. 199 (1969), no. 209 (1969). (R)
15. "New Information on Hontaruse's Printing Machine." In *Karpaten Rundschau*, Brasov, January 3, 1969, p. 7. (G)
16. "The Jewish Print in Romania." In *Kiriyat Sepher*, Jerusalem, vol. 45, 1970, p. 287-298. (E)
17. "Hebrew Inscriptions in Piatra Neamt." In *Memoria Antiquitatis*, Piatra Neamt, vol. 1, 1969, p. 369-373. (R)
18. "Liber Amicorum." In *The Chronicle*, Iasi, no. 1, 1971, p. 10. (R)
19. "Fragments from the History of the Rabbinism in Moldova." In *RCM*, no. 262, 1971. (R)
20. "Rabbis and Scholars in Moldova." In *RCM*, no. 266 (1971), no. 269 (1972), no. 273 (1972). (R)
21. "Little Known Data on Prince Mihai the Brave." In *Acta Valachica*, T'rgoviste, p. 171-175. (R)
22. "The Record of the Cap Makers Guild of Iasi. 1878." In *RCM*, no. 275 (1972), no. 277 (1972). (R)
23. "Hebrew Funerary Inscriptions in the Botosani District." In *Memoria Antiquitatis*, Piatra Neamt, vol. 11, 1970, p. 523-531. (R)
24. "The Heirs of Barbu the Fiddler." In *The Chronicle*, Iasi, no. 36, 1972. (R)
25. "An Unprecedented Commercial Correspondence." In *The Yearbook of the A. D. Xenopol History Institute*, Iasi, vol. 9, 1972, p. 475-494. (R)
26. The same paper, in an augmented version, also appeared in *Yivo-Bleter*, New York, vol. 44, 1972, p. 78-107. (Y)
27. "Jewish Fiddlers in Moldova." In *RCM*, no. 320, 1974. (R and Y)
28. "Several Rare Manuscripts in Moldavian Libraries" In *T'rgoviste, a Citadel for the Romanian Culture*, 1974, p. 257-259. (R)
29. "Jewish Guilds in XVIIIth to Middle XIXth Century Moldova." In *Yivo-Bleter*, New York, vol. 45, 1978, p. 84-97. (Y)
30. "Rabbis and Scholarship in the Romanian Principality." In *RCM*, April 1, 1975. (R and Y)
31. "The Internal Organization of the Jewish Communities of Romania in the Past." In *Toladot*, Jerusalem, 1977, no. 15, p. 11-16. (R and Iv)
32. "The Beginning of the Jewish Settlements in Romania." In *Bukarester sriftn*, Bucharest, vol. I, 1979, p. 121-135. (Y)
33. "120 years of Yiddish Literature in Romania." In *Folks-sztime*, Warsaw, October 1978. (Y)

34. "Ninqua geta de la bellaza se perde." In *Nueva Presencia*, Buenos Aires, August 24, 1979, p. 8-9. (S)
35. "The Jews' Economic Life until the XVIIIth Century." In *Bukarester sriftn*, Bucharest, vol. 3, 1980, p. 97-104. (Y)
36. "The Jewish Population of Romania and its Organization in the Past." Idem, vol. 4, 1981, p. 160-172. (Y)
37. "An Unknown Commercial Stamp." In *The Yearbook of the Vaslui District History Museum*. vol. 2, 1980, p. 509-510. (R)
38. "120 Years of Jewish Printing in Romania." In *Folks-Sztime*, Warsaw, March 1981. (Y)
39. "The Economic Life of the Jews Living in Romania until 1848." In *Bukarester sriftn*, vol. 5, 1982. (Y)

19 References

Note from KME

- *The following numerically-sequenced notes by Kara, appeared at the back of his Romanian edition with the title "Notes". In this English edition the pointers in the body of the book appear in the format [A-1], [A-2], [A-3].*
- *In the Romanian edition the notes were not arranged by chapter.*
- *A.S.I. is cited many times in Kara's notes. It stands for "Arh. St. Iasi". In the English edition we are referring to it as Iasi State Archives (ISA).*

Chapter 6: Chronicle

1. Stefan Olteanu. "*The Evolutionary Process of State Organization in the south and east of the Carpathian Mountains, throughout IX – XV centuries*" as reflected in: "Studies, historical magazine", nr. 4/1974, map p.774.
2. Al. Graur. "*Name of Places*", Bucharest (quoted further as Buc.), 1972, p.85.
3. C. Chirita. "*Geographical Dictionary of the Iasi County*", Buc. 1888.
4. 4. P.P. Panaitescu. "*Foreign Travelers in the Romanian Counties*", Buc. 1930, p.94-95.
5. "*Chronicles…*", edition M. Kogalniceanu, T. I., second edition, p.358
6. "*Chronicles…*", edition M. Kogalniceanu, T. I., second edition, p.358
7. "*State Central Historical Archive Catalogue of Romanian documents*", vol. 3, buc. 1978, nr. 1087, 1159, 2322.
8. Z. Furnica. "*The History of Commerce in Romania*", Buc., 1908, p. XIII.
9. "*Towns and Boroughs. Moldavia*", vol. II, Buc., 1960, p.122.
10. "*Towns and Boroughs. Moldavia*", vol. II, Buc., 1960, p. 234.
11. P.P. Panaitescu, "*The Literary Works of*", quote, p.100
12. "*Chronicles…*", vol. II, p.353
13. "*Historical Magazine*", nr. 1/3, 1930, p.5.
14. "*Uricarul*" (Estate documents writer), vol. 17, p.25-26.
15. "*The Great Geographical Dictionary of Romania*", vol. V, article I, p. 14.
16. **a** "*The Great Geographical Dictionary of Romania*", vol. V, article I, p. 14.
    b Ecat.Negruti, from "*Historical Magazine*", nr. 8/1975, p. 1189-1190.
17. The Archives of the State of Iasi (quoted further as A.S.I.), letter M, 509, I, p.289-292. According to the 1774 Census, in Scobilteni, there used to live a Jew, Rahmin, tradesman. (I.M.E.R., II/2. Buc., 1990, document. 84).
18. A.S.I., packet 345, nr. 88.
19. E. Schwarzfeld. "*From the History of Jews. Populating, Repopulating and Founding of the Boroughs in Moldavia*". (quoted further as *Populating…*). Buc., 1914, p.47.
20. Constantin Erbiceanu. "*The History of Metropolitan Churches of Moldavia and Suceava*", Buc., 1888, p. 108-109.
21. Constantin Sion. "*The History of the Nobility in Moldavia*", Edition Hibanescu, Iasi, 1892, p.91.
22. "*Towns and Boroughs. Moldavia*", vol. II, Buc., 1960, p.96-98.

23. E. Schwarzfeld. "*Populating...*", p.103-106.
24. The Growing Collections of the Romanian Academy in the years 1920-1923, p.232
25. A.S.I. doc.548/16.
26. A.S.I. doc.548/16.
27. Stela Maries, in "*The Year Book of the Institute of History <<A.D. Xenopol>>*" Iasi, 1969, vol. 6, p.185.
28. "*The Opinion*", Iasi, January 16, 1935, p.2.
29. A.S.I. packet 591, nr. 63.
30. A.S.I. packet 591, nr. 63.
31. A.S.I. packet 344, nr. 254.
32. The dates of the mosaic calendar have been transposed in the current calendar format by using comparative tables, published by rabbi Solomon W. Freud, Wien, 1885. (Vienna)
33. A.S.I. packet 119, nr. 50.
34. A.S.I. packet 119, nr. 50., letter P/811, file 23-24; letter V, nr. 65, file 138 v.
35. Verax. "*La Roumanie et les Juifs" (Romania and Jews)*, Paris, 1903, p.14.
36. A.S.I., letter P/811; file 11-12.
37. I. Kara, in "*Bleter far gezichte*", Warsaw, vol. 12, 1959
38. A.S.I., tr. 875, work 997, file 371, p.22 from 1833
39. Col. I. Kara, Iasi.
40. C.C. Giurescu. "*The Romanian Principalities in the Nineteenth Century*", p.53-57.
41. A.S.I. packet 10, nr. 35-42.
42. "*The Administrative Manual of Moldavia*", I, p.525, appeal from May 14, 1835.
43. "*The Official Bulletin*", nr. 63/1835, p.239.
44. A.S.I. packet 646, nr. 41.
45. "*Bulletin*", official document, 1836, p.82.
46. "*Parliamentary Annals*", XIII, second part, p.643.
47. "*Towns and Boroughs...*", p. 241-243.
48. "*Bulletin*", official document, 1839, p.127.
49. A.S.I. packet 245, nr. 26, April 6, 1840.
50. "*Village Paper*", 1841, p.251-252.
51. "*Village Paper*", 1841, p.322, 407.
52. A.S.I., Secret Documents, nr. 798.
53. A.S.I., doc. 776, nr. 56.
54. A.S.I., packet 10, nr. 38-40.
55. "*Village Paper*", 1843, p.294.
56. A.S.I., Secret Documents, nr. 1228, file 26.
57. "*Bulletin*", official document, 1845, p.210.
58. A.S.I. fund I. Kara.
59. A.S.I., Secret Documents, nr. 340, file 105.
60. "*Towns and Boroughs...*", p. 280.
61. A.S.I., tr. 1772, work 2020, file 3705, p.30
62. "*Bulletin*", official document, 1845, p.478.
63. "*Village Paper*", 1846, p.127.

64. A.S.I., Secret Documents, nr. 1624, file 23.
65. A.S.I., Secret Documents, nr. 1624, file 17.
66. A.S.I. fund I. Kara.
67. A.S.I., packet 125, nr. 79.
68. A.S.I., packet 649, nr. 207.
69. "*The Iasi Newspaper*", September 18, 1874.
70. "*Uri Veisi*", nr. 65.
71. "*The Brotherhood*" (Newspaper), April 27, 1880, p.2.
72. "*The Brotherhood*", September 25, 1881, p.2.
73. "*The Brotherhood*", November 28, 1881, p.3.
74. A.S.I. the fund of the Iasi County Prefecture, 1881, nr. 69.
75. A.S.I. the fund of the Iasi County Prefecture, 1882, nr. 32.
76. "*The Jewish Magazine*", 1888, nr. 16, p. 437.
77. A.S.I., 1896, nr. 5.
78. A.S.I. the fund of the Iasi County Prefecture, 1895, nr. 5, file 5.
79. A.S.I. the fund of the Iasi County Prefecture, 1896, nr. 87.
80. "*The Opinion*", Iasi, July 6, 1897.
81. "*The Event*" (Newspaper), Iasi, July 14, 1904, p. 1.
82. A.S.I. the fund of the Iasi County Prefecture, 1902, nr. 35.
83. Most of the information regarding years 1903-1908 are extracted from the Iasi newspaper "*The Event*", while for the years 1909-1940, information is taken from the newspaper "*The Opinion*". The mentioned event can be found in an issue of this newspaper, published around this date. Other more important sources are described more explicitly in notes.
84. Constantin Kiritescu. "*The History of War. 1916-1918*", vol. 3, p.31.
85. A.S.I. the fund of the Iasi County Prefecture, 1918, nr. 27.
86. "*The Bulletin of the Jewish Community Union from the Old Kingdom*", year I, nr. 2, 1928, p.15.
87. "*The Bulletin of the Jewish Community Union from the Old Kingdom*", year I, nr. 12-14, October 1931, p.27.
88. The Report of the Jewish Hospital Guardianship from Iasi of 1932-1934, Iasi, 1935, p.20, 26, 60.
89. M. Carp. "*The Black Book*", vol. 2, p.33.
90. S. Cris-Christian. "*Four Years of Wrath*", Buc. 1945, p.114.

Chapter 7: Economic Life

91. Cf. Verax, "*Literary Works of*"
92. A.S.I., letter IA from 144, file 1 and 8.
93. A.S.I., tr. 875, works 997, file 407, p.1, 2.
94. Verax, "*Literary Works of*", p.14
95. A.S.I., tr. 1423, works 1619, register 1025, p.3.
96. A.S.I., Secret Documents, nr. 554, file 34, 35, February 28, 1839.
97. "*The Official Bulletin of Moldavia*", 1842, p.339.
98. A.S.I., County of Iasi, 1845, tr. 1619, register 1024.
99. "*Carpica*", Bacau, III, 1970, appendix III.
100. A.S.I., tr. 1423, works 1619, register 1025, p.3.

101. A.S.I., tr. 1768, works I/2017, file 422, p. 18, 21.
102. A.S.I., tr. 1768, works I/2017, file 422, p. 7.
103. "*The Magazine of Archives*", XII, nr. 1/1969, p.89.
104. "*The Scientific Annals of Alexandru Iaon Cuza University - IASI*", s.III, T. XIII, 1967, p.84.
105. "*The Magazine of Archives*", XII, nr. 1/1969, p.92, 94.
106. Verax, "*Literary Works of*", p.44.
107. "*The Development of the Moldavian Economy*", 1848/1864. Buc., 1963, p.221.
108. A.S.I. the fund of the Iasi County Prefecture, 1895, nr. 5.
109. Article written by M. Arcu in "*The Opinon*", Iasi, August 1, 1928, p.2.

Chapter 8: Communal Life

110. "*The Brotherhood*", Buc., 1882, p.361.
111. "*The Brotherhood*", September 22, 1889, p.1.
112. "*Folksblat*", Buc., January 12, 1895, p.3.
113. "*The Event*", Iasi, November 7, 1901, p. 3.

Chapter 9: Private and Public Education

114. A.S.I. the fund of the Iasi County Prefecture, nr. 86/1884.
115. A.S.I. the fund of the Iasi County Prefecture, file 117/1886.
116. A.S.I. the fund of the Iasi County Prefecture, nr. 1081/1891, file 7.
117. "*The Jewish Newspaper*", January 18, 1913, p.1.

Chapter 11: Rabbinate

118. "*The Jewish Magazine*", 1887, p.579.

Chapter 12: Hasidism

119. "Meain hachasidut", year 2, nr. 2, 1965, p.10-11.
120. A.S.I. the fund of the Iasi County Prefecture, nr. 89/1892.

20 Glossary of Terms

The following glossary was not part of Kara's work. It's an added feature of this English edition.

Legend: Heb=Hebrew, Rom=Romanian, Yid=Yiddish

Term	Language	Definition
a	Rom	Son of…
a lui	Rom	Son of…
Bani	Rom	Currency, plural of ban. 100 bani equals 1 leu.
Belfer	Yid	Teacher's assistant
Bereshit	Heb	"In the beginning". The book of Genesis.
Braga	Rom	Fermented soft drink.
Bucuros	Rom	Happily
Dayan	Heb	Judge in a religious court
Divan	Rom	An assembly of the nobles of the country
Dumnezeu	Rom	G-d
Ebrews	Rom	Hebrews
El mulei rachamin	Heb	Prayer said for the deceased
Eretz Yisrael	Heb	The Land of Israel
Gabaim de Tzadikim	Heb	Treasurers of the righteous ones. Refers to chief assistants of Hasidic rabbis.
Galbeni	Rom	An old currency. Literally coins made of gold
Ghiter id	Yid	Literally a good Jew, i.e. a good person
Ghitn uvnt	Yid	Good evening
Hahami	Heb	A ritual slaughter. It's from the Hebrew word "chachma", wisdom. (It may actually be a word used in old Romanian that came through Turkish???). Also called "shochet".
Hakafot	Heb	The ritual of dancing around the Torah.
Hamantashen	Yid	Special pastries eaten on Purim, formed in the shape of Haman's hat.
Hasidic	Heb	Religious Jewish sect which emphasized spiritual values
Heder	Yid	Literally a room in Heb but in Yid used for elementary school.
Hekdesh	Heb	Sanctified property – i.e. communal property, charity, etc.
Hidromel	Rom	A light alcoholic beverage made from honey
High Porte	Eng	The High Porte is a synonym of the government of the Ottoman Empire. Ottoman Porte, Sublime Porte, and High Porte are similar terms for the Turkish Babı Ali, the court of the sultan. When translated into English, the Turkish term Babi Ali means, literally, "High Gate". Porte is

Term	Language	Definition
		French for "Gate", therefore, the term High Porte is a bilingual combination of English High and French Porte that is equivalent to Babi Ali. (http://en.wikipedia.org/wiki/Sublime_Porte)
Judaeus	Rom	Jews
Kaddish	Heb	Prayer said for the deceased
Kobza	Rom	Type of lute.
Leu	Rom	The national currency of Romania (plural lei) One leu is subdivided into 100 bani (singular ban).
Lipoveans	Rom	Orignally refered to people of Russian origin, who settled in the region of the Danube River and the Black Sea. Later it was used to describe all those coming from Russia.
Machlokes	Heb	Long standing argument
Maot Chittim	Heb	Hebrew for "wheat money". This is money given to the poor for their Passover matzah.
Matseva	Heb	Tombstone.
Melamed	Heb	An itinerant teacher (plural melamdim)
Minyan	Heb	A quorum of 10 Jews for prayer.
Mishna	Heb	A codified collection of Jewish Oral Law compiled circa 200 CE. Together with the Gemara it forms part of the Talmud.
Mitzraim	Heb	Egypt
Moale	Rom	Soft
Mozl tov	Heb	Congratulations, literally lucky constellation (mazel tov)
Nigunim	Heb	Tunes
Oca	Rom	Measure of volume, equals 1.5 liters
Parale	Rom	Currency until 1968
Pericope	Latin/ Greek	An extract or selection from a book, especially a reading from a Scripture that forms part of a religious service. In a Jewish context it is the weekly Torah reading (Parsha).
Podu	Rom	Bridge
Sales-sides	Heb	Literally third meal, used in reference to a meal eaten on Sabbath afternoon (Shalosh Seudos)
Sanatatea	Rom	Health
Sheli sheloh, sheloh sheli	Heb	Literally his, mine, mine, his. A children's game
Shochet	Heb	A ritual slaughter.
Stetl	Yid	A Jewish market town in Eastern Europe
Sin	Rom	Son
Stanjen	Rom	Measure of length equal to 6 feet
Sudit	Rom	A foreign citizen or native who enjoyed foreign protection while living on Romanian territory, as stipulated by the terms of the treaties signed by the Western powers and the Turkish Empire.

Term	Language	Definition
Tales	Heb	A fringed prayer shawl worn by men during religious services
Talmud	Heb	Compilation of the Jewish oral law, consists of the Mishna and Gemara
Talmud Torah	Heb	Study of Torah. Also refers to religious school.
Talmudist		One who is knowledgeable in the Talmud
Treif	Heb	Non kosher food
Tzadik	Heb	Righteous one, a moniker used for Hasidic leaders.
Vedre	Rom	Measurement tool used in Moldova in the past, equaling approximately 15.2 litres.
Yeshiva	Heb	A Talmudic academy

21 Glossary of Places

The following glossary was not part of Kara's work. It's an added feature of this English edition. It appears in both PDF version available from KME and in HTML format at the JewishGen website.

Place	Chapter
Agiud	15
Albesti	16.14
Alesk	12
America	7, 8, 15.6, 17
Arama	15.6
Babylon	11
Bahlui	16.17
Bahlui region	8
Bahlui River	7, 8, 14, 15.3, 15.5, 15.7, 16.3
Bahluiet River	7, 15.7
Balcani	16.14
Barbalata	16.13
Basarabia, Old	15.4
Basceaus	16.14
Basel	9
Belcesti	16.7
Berdicev	15.2
Berlesti	8
Bivolari	15.3
Bogoila	16.14
Boidinesti	16.14
Borseni in Neamt	16.14
Botosani	15.4, 16.14, 16.15
Botosani district	7, 17
Braesti estate	7
Brody	12
Bucharest	7, 8, 15, 15.4, 15.7
Bucovina	7
Buenos Aires	15.4
Buhusi	7, 13, 15.2, 15.4
Bukovina	15
Bulbucani	16.14
Bulgaria	7
Burdujeni	8
Burlacu	16.14
Butuliac	16.14

22 Glossary of People

The Glossary of People was not part of Kara's work. It's an added feature of this English edition. It does not appear in the PDF version; however it is available in HTML format at the JewishGen website or in Excel format from KME.

22.1 *Overview*

There are hundreds of names mentioned throughout the book, making it a treasure trove for Jewish genealogists. We hope this glossary will aid them in finding the names they are researching.

In its native form in MS Word, names of interest can be found in this document quite simply by doing a global search for the name. There is one drawback with this approach however. We may not be using the same spelling that appears in the book. For example, if we are looking for Cohen, we are not going to find "Cohn", the way it is spelled in Romanian.

The search process becomes even more difficult when the document is hosted on JewishGen, with each of the 21 different chapters in a separate HTML file. That means if we are searching for Cohen we will have to do 21 searches. Using the glossary will make the job much simplier.

The glossary contains the following information:

Field	Description
Surname	The family name, as best we can ascertain from the Name.
Name	Can contain first name, surname, occupation, place of origin or combination of the above.
Date	
Desc	
Chapter	Chapter in the book where the person can be found.
Sequence#	Sequence number of the entry in the book. Two people with similar names, in close proximaty in the book, may be the same person or related persons. If the entry comes from the 1898 Census (Chapter 16.6) then the sequence number is the record number as it appears in the census plus 2000. For example, the 1898 census record# 246 appears in the glossary as sequence# 2246.

By default the glossary is sorted by Surname, Name and Sequence#. However other sort orders are possible.

In the description field we have captured only small pieces of information. It's usually worthwhile to go back to the appropriate chapter/s, in which the names of interest are found, to get the full information.

The glossary contains virtually all the people mentioned in the book, including the censuses in Chapter 16.

Please note that the Census of 1898 (Ch 16.16) is being hosted, in its entirety, at JewishGen as a separate entity with different search capabilities. Nevertheless some of the information is being included in the Glossary of People to allow for unified searches. If you do find names of interest in the glossary it's recommended that you go to the 1898 Census to get the additional information.

It should also be noted that some of the people listed in the glossary were not Jewish (eg. city officials, landowners, etc). Furthermore, the glossary is not restricted to Podu Iloiaiei residents. Some of the people listed had nothing to do with this town (eg. famous rabbis, writers, etc).

Some people appear to have multiple listings in the glossary. For example:

Name	Date	Description	Chapter
Moise Berlescu	1836, 1842	From Berlesti; proposal for taxes; litigation	7
Moisa Birlescu	n/d	Renters list; tax collector, signatore	16.14
Iekel Blumenfeld	1938	Community leader	7
Iechil Blumenfeld	1925	Jewish Community Constitution; committee member	16.17
Moise Iuster	1830	Municipal income	16.4
Moise Juster	1830	Business transaction	7

Notice the variations in spelling from one entry to the next.

22.2 *Challenges in Finding Names in this Book*

Some JewishGen/PoduIloaiei researchers have been disappointed not finding their ancestors in the various censuses in the book. I must caution that these censuses in their current form may not be complete. The material went through several different processes:

- Kara transcribing from the source documents (which themselves may have been incomplete)
- Printing of Kara's book
- Translation into English

But I wouldn't rush to any conclusions. I was also perplexed why the siblings of my great-grandparents were missing from the 1898 census, until I found other civic records showing them residing in some of the surrounding communities.

Another major obstacle in identifying ancestors is the fact that a large number of entries appear without surnames. Apparently the adoption of surnames was a rather late innovation in Podu Iloiaiei. Nat Abramowitz couldn't find his father on the census because he didn't adopt the name Abramowitz until he left Podu Iloiaiei for America.

Others were more successful in finding their ancestors amongst the non-surnamed entries such as Avram sin Moise. So look closely at all the entries.

Another issue is the fact that the letters in the Romanian alphabet do not always sound phonetically the same as they do in English. Consequently the Hebrew and Yiddish origins of many given names listed in the census may not be readily apparent. In a separate document titled "Introduction to the 1898 Podu Iloaiei Census" we have a table showing the Hebrew and Yiddish origins of many given names.

22.3 *Dates*

Code	Meaning	Example
C	circa	c 1857
B	birth	1843 b
D	death	1895 d
b&d	birth & death	1843-1895 bd
n/d	no date	n/d
+	after	1843+

22.4 *Surnames*

Surnames are generally derived from one of four sources:

1. the name of the person's father (patronymic) - eg. Abramovici, Nathansohn
2. the person's locality - eg. Berliner
3. the person's occupation [B-54] - eg. Tischler (carpenter)
4. a descriptive nickname for the person - eg. Klein (small)

Many of the people listed in the census show only one name. They usually apear to be first names; however some may be surnames. And even with surnames, we can never indeed be certain that they are surnames.

Except for the 1898 census, most people in the censuses are listed by one name only and with many of these it is difficult to determine whether the name is a first name or surname. This is illustrated by the following examples.

[54] [KME] In a separate document titled "Introduction to the 1898 Podu Iloaiei Census" we have a list of occupations mentioned in that census, translated from Romanian into English.

The name David followed by one of the following:

1. Abram
2. Abramovici
3. a lui Abram
4. ben Abram
5. sin Abram
6. son of Abram [B-55]

In the first example, the name Abram may be a surname, however it may just be another given name for David (ie a middle name). With regards the other five examples, the question is whether they are patronymic surnames, derived from one of David's ancestors named Abram, or was Abram simply the father of David? [B-56]

The same question applies, if the name David is followed by names such as these: Berliner, Tischler, Klein. Are they surnames, derived from one of David's ancestors who was from Berlin or was a carpenter or was small? Or were these attributes of David himself?

Wherever a surname was in question, we considered it a surname. If there was no surname we put "ZZZ" in the surname field, so that it would appear at the end of the list.

⍰ ⍰ ⍰ ⍰ ⍰ ⍰ ⍰ ⍰

To see the Glossary of People in HTML format, visit www.JewishGen.org .
To obtain a copy in Excel format, contact KM Elias.

---

[55] [KME] Our translators usually left the words “sin” and “lui” as-is in the censuses, however in the narrative parts of the book they often translated them as “son”.

[56] [KME] My great-grandfather is listed in the 1898 Census as “Mendel Ilie” while his brother is listed in the civic records of 1883 as “Faval sin Ilie”. We know from their tombstones, that their father was Yehuda, not Ilie. So perhaps the family was originally known by the surname “sin Ilie”, derived from an earlier ancestor named Ilie; however by 1898 the name had been shortened to “Ilie”.

23 Pictures

I. Kara (right) in Podu Iloaiei, 1975

National Street, in Podu Iloaiei

Author's family - June 28, 1898
Ita Ruhla & Iosif Svart (grandparents)
Ghitla & Hers Svart (parents)

Rabbi Elie Rosental (deceased 1927)

Chanuka Menora (approx. 1920)
Belonged to Rabbi Itcovici of Podu Iloaiei.

Jewish-Romanian school, Podu Iloaiei, 1913.
Teachers: Horodniceanu Iancu, Rosental Aron

Jewish-Romanian school, Podu Iloaiei, 1929.

A group of soldiers T.R.,
from Podu Iloaiei (1916)

Shalom Aleichem Cultural Assembly, Podu Iloaiei – June 23, 1927
Front, R-L: Herman Elias, Bianca Lozner, Ghizela Solomon, Itic Svart;
Top, R-L: Milu Horodniceanu, Ioel Finchelstein, Ghedale Westler, Moise Sor

[Ed-Com] Shalom Aleichem Cultural Assembly. The caption in the book says the names are listed right-to-left, putting Itic Svart Kara at front-left. However we know from other pictures that Kara is the man at front-right.

Zionist Organization, Podu Iloaiei, 1920

R O M Â N I A

COMUNITATEA CULTULUI EVREESC
DIN
— PODUL-ILOAE —

STATUTUL

Comunității Evreești din Podul-Iloae
Votat în Adunare Generală din 3 Mai 1925.

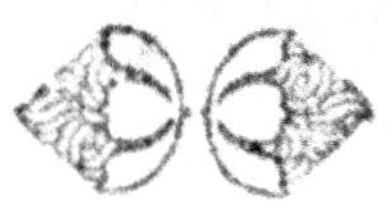

— IAŞI —
TIP. A. GRÜNBERG STR. UNIREI 9
— 1925 —

The Jewish Cult Community of Podu Iloaiei
The Statute of the Jewish Community of Podu Iloaiei
Voted in the General Assembly of May 3rd, 1925
Published by A. Grunberg, Unirii Street #9
Iasi, 1925

The Great Synagogue of Iasi

Great Synagogue of Iasi, Romania. Exterior restoration complete.
Photo: Dan Trandafir 2015, courtesy The Federation of Jewish Communities of Romania.

Iasi is the capital of Moldova and as such is one of the major cultural centers of Romania. For centuries the city was an important center of Jewish culture and religion for Northern Moldova and Bucovina. The city once supported a large Jewish population, though the community was devastated during the Romanian Fascist period and the Holocaust. Before World War II, the Jewish community of the city probably was half of the total city population. During the Iasi Pogrom of June 29-July 6, 1941, and its aftermath, about 14,00 Jews were killed or deported, about half the Jewish population of Iasi.

In 2015, the Jewish community in Romania is very small and poor, with limited political and cultural influence. Despite the relatively large Jewish population of Romanian origin in the United States and Israel, the plight of Jewish heritage sites in Romania had not received the attention and support given to Germany, Poland, Lithuania and some other countries. The Romanian Jewish Community carried responsibility for a very large number of extant synagogues and other sites, but has had very limited resources and staff to monitor, maintain and restore them. Only the Great Synagogue of Iasi survives and it is there that the history of Jewish Iasi, its destroyed synagogues and its devastated and dispersed Jewish population resides.

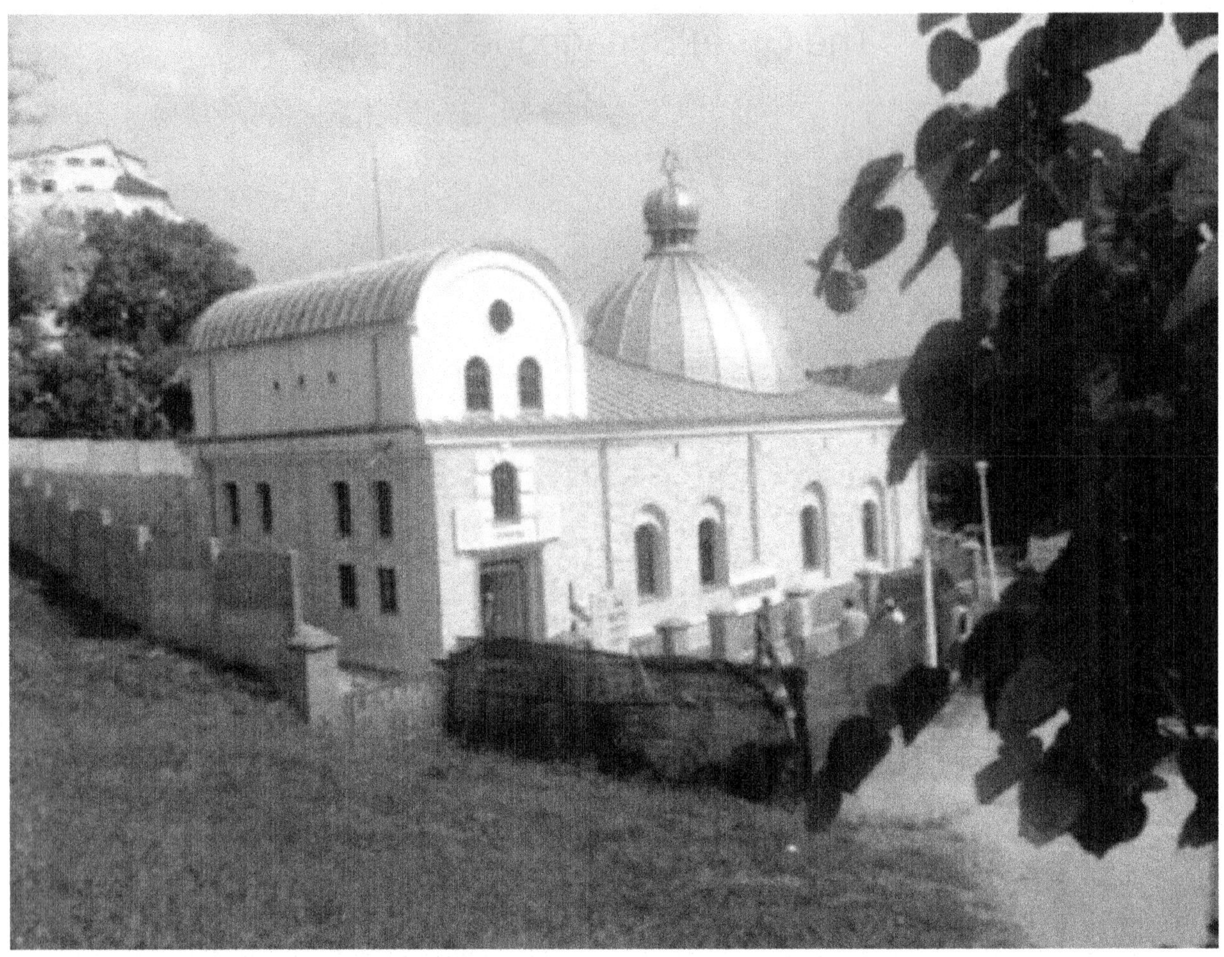

Great Synagogue of Iasi, Romania. Exterior restoration complete.
Photo: Dan Trandafir 2015, courtesy The Federation of Jewish Communities of Romania.

The Great Synagogue is the oldest in Romania and one of only two synagogues still standing in a city that before World War II had more than 100. It was built in 1670-71, for a small Jewish community, and subsequently rebuilt or restored in 1761,1822, and 1863.

In 2006, attempts to restore and preserve the Iasi synagogue began anew and has continued intermittently to the present, 2015. Architect Lucia Apostol of the Federation of the Romanian Jewish Communities, has been leading the restoration. Currently (2015) there are efforts to restore the Aron ha-kodesh, the Holy Ark. The Great Synagogue is recognized as a Romanian National Historic Monument. In 2013, The World Monuments Fund (WMF) placed the Iasi synagogue on its 2014 Watch List of endangered cultural heritage sites, one of 67 sites worldwide so designated.

Iasi, Romania. Great Synagogue. Exterior restoration complete.
Photo: Dan Trandafir 2015, courtesy The Federation of Jewish Communities of Romania.

Iasi, Romania. Synagogue. Photo: ISJM files, photographer and date unknown

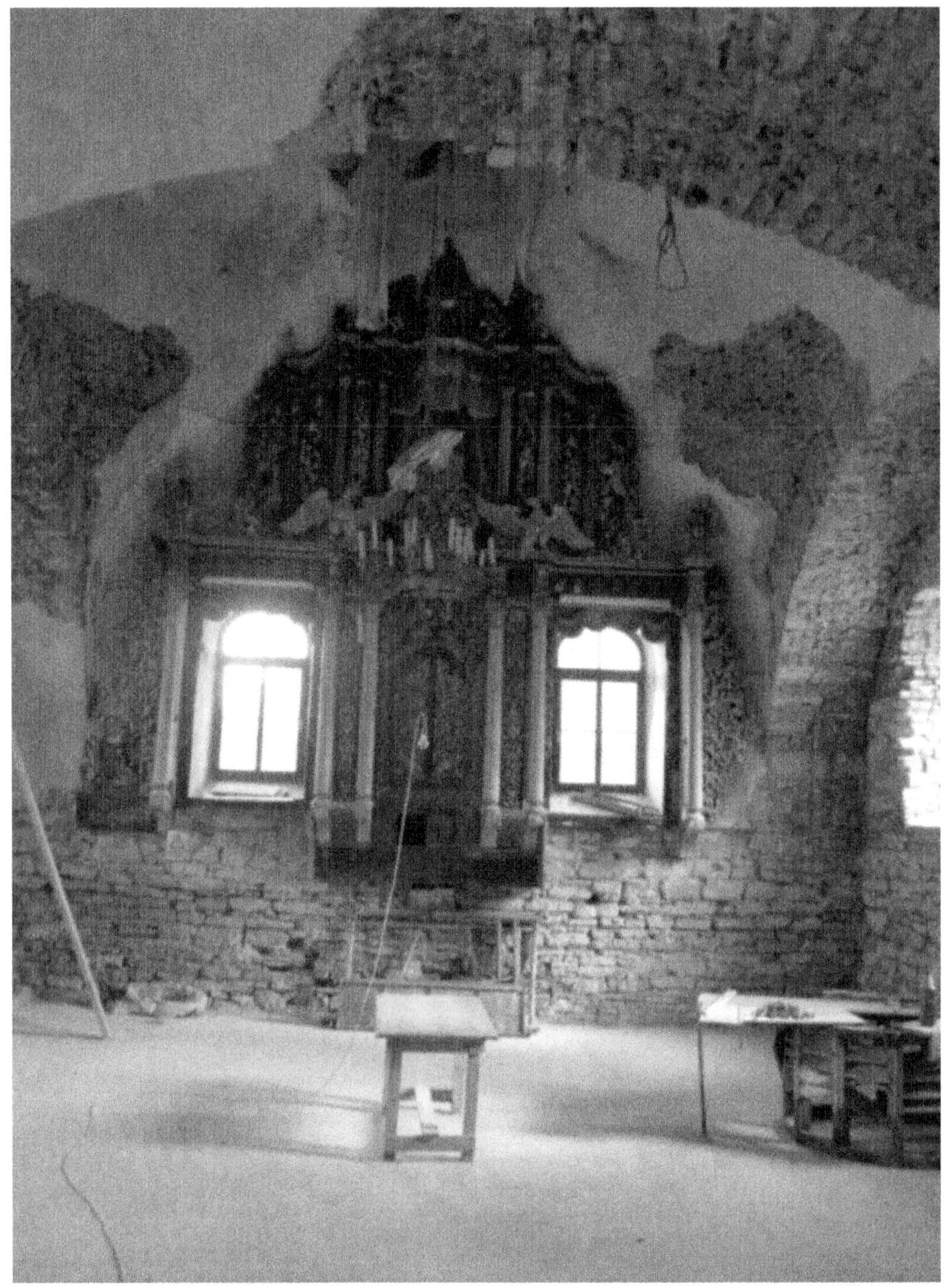

Iaşi, Romania. Great Synagogue, interior with striped walls; Ark still in situ.
Photo: FedRom (2013) The Federation of Jewish Communities of Romania.

Based on and excerpted from the blogs of Dr. Samuel Gruber